# The Philosopher Li Zehou

SUNY series in Chinese Philosophy and Culture
―――――――
Roger T. Ames, editor

# The Philosopher Li Zehou
## His Thought and His Legacy

Edited by

JANA S. ROŠKER and ROGER T. AMES

**SUNY PRESS**

**FF** | UNIVERSITY OF LJUBLJANA
Faculty of Arts

Published by State University of New York Press, Albany

© 2025 State University of New York

All rights reserved

Printed in the United States of America

No part of this book may be used or reproduced in any manner whatsoever without written permission. No part of this book may be stored in a retrieval system or transmitted in any form or by any means including electronic, electrostatic, magnetic tape, mechanical, photocopying, recording, or otherwise without the prior permission in writing of the publisher.

Links to third-party websites are provided as a convenience and for informational purposes only. They do not constitute an endorsement or an approval of any of the products, services, or opinions of the organization, companies, or individuals. SUNY Press bears no responsibility for the accuracy, legality, or content of a URL, the external website, or for that of subsequent websites.

**EU GPSR Authorised Representative:**
**Logos Europe,** 9 rue Nicolas Poussin, 17000, La Rochelle, France
contact@logoseurope.eu

For information, contact State University of New York Press, Albany, NY
www.sunypress.edu

This publication was supported by the University of Ljubljana, Faculty of Arts

### Library of Congress Cataloging-in-Publication Data

Names: Rošker, Jana, 1960– editor. | Ames, Roger T., 1947– editor.
Title: The philosopher Li Zehou : his thought and his legacy / edited by
　　Jana S. Rošker and Roger T. Ames.
Description: Albany : State University of New York Press, [2025] | Series:
　　SUNY series in Chinese philosophy and culture | Includes bibliographical
　　references and index.
Identifiers: LCCN 2024039348 | ISBN 9798855801705 (hardcover : alk. paper) |
　　ISBN 9798855801729 (ebook)
Subjects: LCSH: Li, Zehou.
Classification: LCC B5234.L4874 P45 2025 | DDC 181/.11—dc23/eng/20241202
LC record available at https://lccn.loc.gov/2024039348

# Contents

Introduction     1
    *Jana S. Rošker and Roger T. Ames*

## Part 1.
## Li Zehou, the Philosopher

1. Li Zehou, Wily Provocateur     15
    *Michael Nylan*

2. Li Zehou in the Tradition of Masters and Commentators     59
    *Paul J. D'Ambrosio*

3. A New Alternative to the How-to-Live Concern     79
    *Wang Keping*

## Part 2.
## Culture in the Mirror of History

4. Sedimentation and Gene-Culture Coevolution     107
    *Jordan B. Martin*

5. Situated Cognition and Historical Perspective: Li Zehou and Contemporary Aesthetics     143
    *Rafal Banka*

## Part 3.
## Freedom, Autonomy, and Justice

6. Autonomy and the Nature of Ruist Morality: Li Zehou and Mou Zongsan    163
   *David Elstein*

7. Justice, Harmony, and the Good Life of *Guanxi*: Li Zehou's Response to Liberalism    189
   *Andrew Lambert*

8. A Deep Harmony Account of Justice    219
   *Chenyang Li*

## Part 4.
## Humanist Harmony and Limitless Equilibrium

9. Emotion as Substance: A Concrete Humanist Moral Framework    241
   *Robert A. Carleo III*

10. Measure Without and Beyond Measure: Brief Notes on the Primary Category of Li Zehou's *Anthropologico-Historical Ontology*    263
    *Wu Xiaoming*

11. A Post-Marxian Dialogue on the Subject–Object Relation: Li Zehou and Adorno on the Dialectics of Aesthetic Subjectivity    295
    *Jana S. Rošker*

## Part 5.
## From Aesthetics to Ethics

12. Li Zehou on the Distinction and Interaction between Ethics and Morality    327
    *Jinhua Jia*

13. The Philosophy of Beauty as an Ethics of Freedom:
    From Kant to Li Zehou; Perspectives of an Attractive Line
    of Thought                                                              355
    *Gregor Paul*

14. Li Zehou's Major Works on Chinese Aesthetics: *The Path of
    Beauty* and *The Chinese Aesthetic Tradition*                           385
    *Karl-Heinz Pohl*

# Part 6.
# Discursive Dialogues

15. The Origins of Chinese Culture and the Question of
    Shamanism: Li Zehou and Xu Fuguan                                       407
    *Maja Maria Kosec*

16. Fruits of Practice: A Comparative Analysis of Li Zehou's
    Concept of Sedimentation and the Buddhist Idea of the
    Transformations of Storehouse Consciousness (*Ālaya*)                   431
    *Dawid Rogacz*

17. Number and Mathematics in Li Zehou's *Critique of
    Critical Philosophy*                                                    447
    *Sydney Morrow*

Li Zehou's Key Works: A Comprehensive Chronological
Bibliography of His Most Significant Publications                           463

Contributors                                                                473

Index                                                                       481

# Introduction

Jana S. Rošker and Roger T. Ames

In his lifetime, Li Zehou was one of China's most prominent philosophers, transforming Confucian philosophy into a resource for positive change. He reinterpreted the tradition from earliest times down to the present day, from a critical rereading of the *Analects* to formulating his own aesthetic theory. In this effort, he was inspired by Marx and Kant, but he was not a Marxist or a Kantian. And he was not a Confucian either. Li Zehou was, and remains, an original. He was the philosopher Li Zehou.

For readers interested in exploring his biography, Chapter 2.2 of Jana Rošker's *Following his Own Path: Li Zehou and Contemporary Chinese Philosophy* (State University of New York Press, 2019) is highly recommended. Additionally, Chinese-speaking readers should not miss the first part of Yang Bin's 杨斌 exceptional study, *Li Zehou xueshu nianpu* 李泽厚学术年谱 (*A Chronicle of Li Zehou's Academic Work*), published by Fudan University Press in 2015.

On November 2, 2021, Li Zehou passed away, and China and the world were deeply saddened by the loss of one of the most important and distinctive scholars of our generation. To pay tribute to his legacy and to make his philosophical ideas more accessible to a wider group of young scholars of philosophy in Europe, a PhD and postdoctoral summer school dedicated to his theories was organized and held at the University of Ljubljana in Slovenia in June of the following year.

And thus precisely one year after Li Zehou's passing, on November 2, 2022, a remarkable tribute was held in his honor. Despite the ongoing COVID-19 pandemic and the travel restrictions that ensued, a large number of scholars, researchers, and students from Asia, Europe, and the USA came together in a fourteen-hour online conference. The event transcended seven different time zones and attracted several dozens of individuals who specialize or are deeply interested in Li Zehou's philosophy, demonstrating the extent of his impact across the globe. The commemoration served as a testament to the lasting legacy of Li Zehou and his profound influence on the philosophical landscape.

The online conference, organized by the editors of this volume with the dependable help of PhD student Maja Kosec from the University of Ljubljana, proved to be a captivating and enriching experience. It was characterized by lively discussions, fruitful dialogues, and constructive debates that left an indelible impression on all the participants. Without a doubt, the conference was a valuable opportunity for us to expand our knowledge and deepen our understanding of Li's intriguing theories. We can confidently say that each one of us learned a great deal from this process.

The present volume is witness to the collaborative efforts of numerous scholars participating in this interesting event. The essays contained within were first presented during the commemorative conference and then subsequently enriched through fruitful debates among the participants. As such, this volume represents a passionate and dedicated endeavor to ensure that Li Zehou's philosophy endures and continues to inspire scholars, particularly the younger generation of academics, both in China and around the world. It is our hope that this collection will serve as a catalyst for ongoing scholarship and discourse, contributing to the legacy of Li Zehou.

The organizing and editorial work invested in the summer school, the digital conference, and the present volume was supported by the Slovenian Research and Innovation Agency (ARRS) as part of the research core funding for Asian Languages and Cultures (P6-0243).

This book is organized into six distinct sections, each of which examines a different facet of Li Zehou's work. The scope of the sections is extensive, not only covering Li's general contributions to Chinese and global philosophy but also delving into his ideas on history, culture, and politics, as well as his theories on methodology and aesthetics. By providing a comprehensive analysis of Li's multifaceted philosophy, we hope to have created a valuable resource for scholars and enthusiasts alike who seek a deeper understanding of this remarkable philosopher's intellectual legacy.

The volume begins with a section, "Li Zehou, the Philosopher," that introduces Li Zehou as a unique philosopher and a deep but unconventional thinker. The section opens with Michael Nylan's essay "Li Zehou, Wily Provocateur." Nylan describes the basic foundations of Li's thinking and shows how and why it represents a unique and innovative approach to Chinese philosophy, ethics, and political thought. By combining elements of Marxism, liberal democracy, and the Chinese Enlightenment, Li developed a comprehensive worldview and a complex theoretical system that is both forward-looking and deeply rooted in tradition. His ideas offer a positive vision for the future of China and the world, and they deserve careful consideration by anyone interested in the intersection of philosophy, politics, and culture.

The second chapter, "Li Zehou in the Tradition of Masters and Commentators," is by Paul D'Ambrosio, who problematizes the traditional notion of philosophy through the lens of Li Zehou's work. By examining Li's ideas, D'Ambrosio challenges the typical understanding of philosophy and offers a new perspective on the subject. The author points out that sometimes Li Zehou's work can be difficult to translate or understand due to both style and content. When viewed from a Western perspective, Li's analysis of Western philosophy can be confusing or contain inaccuracies, and his explanations of Chinese thought may sometimes seem one-dimensional. However, it is important to note that Li's work was strongly influenced by his own cultural background and philosophical tradition, a fact that should be taken into consideration when evaluating his ideas. Seen from this perspective, Li's work can be appreciated for its broad and deep theories that serve as responses to numerous deep philosophical questions and as starting points for further discussion. Despite not always adhering to strict logical arguments, strict scholarly conventions, or principles of formal analyses, Li is acknowledged to be a phenomenal thinker.

In the third essay of this section, "A New Alternative to the How-to-Live Concern," Wang Keping discusses Li Zehou's practical philosophy of subjectality, which, among other issues, addresses the concern of how to live a good life by emphasizing the development of human capacity as the singularly most important factor in becoming fully human. Wang also highlights the significance of the aesthetic dimension of Li Zehou's work and sheds light on its practical implications, asserting that in Li's theory, aesthetic engagement is integral to achieving human subjectality and fulfilling human potential.

The second section is composed of two chapters that delve into Li Zehou's ideas related to the theme expressed in its title, "Culture in the Mirror of History." These chapters offer in-depth analyses and critical commentaries on two key aspects of Li Zehou's thought, which are closely tied to the central theme of this section. Each chapter provides unique insights and perspectives, making valuable contributions to our understanding of Li's ideas.

The first is Jordan B. Martin's "Sedimentation and Gene-Culture Coevolution." This chapter discusses the ideas of Li Zehou regarding his sedimentation theory, which proposes that culture influences the evolution of the human brain. This prediction has been confirmed by empirical science, and the chapter explores the evidence supporting this claim, with the concept of gene-culture coevolution introduced as a way to explain this influence. The essay also discusses the relationship between sedimentation theory and GCC and finds a significant degree of consonance between the two, which helps clarify some apparent contradictions in Li's view of biological evolution.

The second chapter of this section, Rafal Banka's essay "Situated Cognition and Historical Perspective: Li Zehou and Contemporary Aesthetics," explores the compatibility of Li Zehou's aesthetic and the contemporary research into experience-based aesthetics. Experience-based aesthetics is a distinct aesthetic discipline that moves beyond the traditional focus on the philosophy of art and aesthetic values to a broader perspective situating the aesthetic within the context of sensuous experiences that extend beyond art and art appreciation. By adopting this approach, experience-based aesthetics enables us to examine the aesthetic as an integral component of our perceptual and cognitive processes. This expanded view of aesthetics also creates exciting opportunities for interdisciplinary research. In his discussion, Banka demonstrates that one of the main contributions of Li's theory is its historical and phylogenetic perspective, which elevates it to a meta-aesthetic level.

The next section, "Freedom, Autonomy, and Justice," explores Li Zehou's political philosophy in three chapters. The first, by David Elstein, is titled "Autonomy and the Nature of Ruist Morality: Li Zehou and Mou Zongsan," and deals with some ethical and moral foundations of Li's political theories. First, Elstein explains why Mou Zongsan's interpretation of Ruist (Confucian) morality was strongly criticized by Li Zehou. But he also reveals that both philosophers share some common ground in their understanding of morality, particularly in their acceptance of a Kantian view that morality is known a priori. His essay examines Li Zehou's analysis of Ruist morality as presented in his *History of Classical Chinese Thought*. While there are indications that Li did not fully comprehend Mou's ideas, his critiques certainly highlight some of the challenges in Mou's interpretation. However, Li's own understanding of Ruist morality reveals certain conflicts and inconsistencies, largely stemming from his adoption of Kant's moral framework. In Elstein's view, this is particularly puzzling, given Li's emphasis on the role of emotional experience in Ruist ethics. While Kant argues that moral principles must be known a priori and must not be influenced by feelings, Li suggests that morality is both empirical and a priori—that is, it is learned through experience, yet is also universal and inherent to human nature. This attempt to reconcile empirical and a priori elements of morality fails to resolve the tension between the two. Indeed, the author concludes that Li could better explain the universality of morality by focusing on emotional experience rather than by invoking the idea of a priori knowledge.

This chapter is followed by Andrew Lambert's contribution, which points to a different aspect of Li's ethical and political ideas, as can be seen from its title, "Justice, Harmony and the Good Life of *Guanxi*: Li Zehou's Response to Liberalism." Lambert proceeds from Li Zehou's famous, and often misunderstood, statement that "harmony is higher than justice," which has sparked numerous debates and discussions. This essay aims to investigate this assertion and delve deeper into Li's concept of harmony by exploring two key themes in his work: *guanxi* 關係 or relational attachment, which he elevates to the level of a guiding doctrine, and of the value of aesthetic experience. Lambert explores the interplay between *guanxi* networks, practical reason, and the good life in response to Li's criticisms of Michael Sandel's work. By placing relationality at the forefront, this perspective highlights the potential for generating aesthetic goods in everyday social interactions, thus adding to Li's interest in *guanxi*. This alternative conception of the good life presents a compelling argument for the integration of *guanxi* networks into discussions of morality and aesthetics. Lambert posits that Li's diverse interests provide enough room for interpretation, specifically regarding how his aesthetics and moral philosophy intersect. As a result, the perspective presented in this essay is a legitimate, albeit imaginative, effort to broaden Li's intellectual inheritance.

Chenyang Li, the next author in this section, also deals with Li's theory of the relation between justice and harmony, in an essay titled

"A Deep Harmony Account of Justice." In this chapter, the crucial question of the relationship between the fundamental human values of harmony and justice is explored through a conception of deep harmony. The argument put forth is that on a fundamental level, harmony grounds justice, while justice serves the purpose of harmony. Chenyang Li's paper is divided into four parts. First, Li Zehou's perspective that "harmony is higher than justice" is presented and criticized from some different points of view. Second, alternative views are examined to provide context for the author's own argument. Third, the notion of deep harmony is explained, drawing on the Confucian tradition. Finally, the author proposes that, based on the perspective of Confucian deep harmony, harmony serves as both the metaphysical foundation and the ultimate goal of justice. In other words, deep harmony accounts for the existential context in which justice is to be established, and justice, in the form of norms and rules, ultimately serves the purpose of social harmony.

At this juncture, the reader may be curious as to Li Zehou's stance on the correlation between his understanding of harmony, the role of humans, and the natural equilibrium that is an integral aspect of classical Chinese, particularly Confucian philosophy. The fourth section, titled "Humanist Harmony and Limitless Equilibrium," endeavors to shed light on this matter through three distinct perspectives.

The first article is connected with Li's emotion-based ontology. In his chapter "Emotion as Substance: A Concrete Humanist Moral Framework," Robert A. Carleo III offers some valuable reinterpretations and new explanations of Li's concept of "emotion as substance" (*qing benti* 情本體), which has often been misunderstood. Carleo explains that these misunderstandings are due to Li's unconventional ideas about emotion and substance. This chapter aims to clarify the meaning of *qing* by explaining its various connotations and highlighting its connection to the tangible, contextual, and sensory aspects of our environment, feelings, and facts. Li proposes that we view *qing* as a "substance," *benti*, to acknowledge that our relationships with the world, reality, and other people are fundamentally situated and inherent. However, this does not imply that feelings are metaphysically essential or foundational. Instead, *qing benti* emphasizes the importance of concrete human experience in shaping our ethical and moral values, with our interdependence forming the basis of human reason and human values. In Carleo's view, Li's theory of "emotion as substance" is a form of moral rationalism and Confucian relationism that also supports liberal individualism, offering a distinctive and comprehensive approach to humanism. In contrast to Confucian cosmic idealism, which Li criticizes for neglecting history and cultural sedimentation, Li's ethics emphasizes the role of history in shaping metaphysics and culture as a confluence of influences. The author concludes that Li Zehou's framework of "emotion as substance" offers valuable insights and a strong foundation for contemporary moral thinking.

The next chapter is Wu Xiaoming's "Measure Without and Beyond Measure: Brief Notes on the Primary Category of Li Zehou's Anthropologico-Historical Ontology," which primarily deals with the important notion of *du* (度, "grasping the proper measure"). The author delves into Confucius's perspective on *du*, which he defines as rules and regulations. He then points out that this interpretation bears a striking resemblance to Li Zehou's philosophical concept of *du*, as demonstrated by a fictional story of Confucius visiting Laozi. This correlation between historical and contemporary ideas may not be coincidental, and yet has been largely ignored in modern thought. However, investigating these potential connections can reveal new insights and generate novel ideas. By examining the overlooked aspects of Li's philosophy, the author demonstrates that his thesis on *du* represents a new direction and points to a profound mystery in Chinese thought. In fact, Li's thesis on *du* transcends his ontology, even though he frequently brings it back into his ontology. This study thus represents an initial attempt to "explain and liberate" the latent power of the omnipresent and enigmatic concept of *du* in Li Zehou's philosophy.

Jana S. Rošker's chapter also deals with Li's concept of *du*, albeit from a different perspective. In her contribution, "A Post-Marxian Dialogue on the Subject-Object Relation: Li Zehou and Adorno on the Dialectics of Aesthetic Subjectivity," she examines the neo-Marxist paradigms of Li Zehou and Theodor W. Adorno in their views on the connection between the subject and object of perception and cognition. First, she examines the key components and advances of Marxist epistemology that serve as the foundation for their aesthetic theories and perceptions. Next, she illustrates how Li Zehou's aesthetic theories and epistemology, particularly with regard to his interpretation of the subject-object relationship, align with the Marxist framework. Following this, she establishes a constructive relationship between Li's ideas and Adorno's concept of the "primacy of the object" and his criticism of "identitarian philosophy." During this discussion, she highlights certain contradictions in Adorno's idea of breaking away from an identitarian theoretical model. Finally, she proposes an alternative solution grounded in Li Zehou's notion of "subjectality," with a focus on the dialectical nature of the subject-object relationship and the vital role of the concept of *du* in this context.

In the next section, we explore the distinctive nuances of Li Zehou's profound and noteworthy correlation between aesthetics and ethics. Titled "From Aesthetics to Ethics," this section encompasses three chapters that approach this crucial relationship from diverse angles and vantage points.

It opens with Jia Jinhua's chapter "Li Zehou on the Distinction and Interaction between Ethics and Morality," which focuses on Li's specific use of the terms *ethics* and *morality*. The author regards this differentiation as immensely important for the understanding of Li Zehou's philosophy, because it belongs to the three major distinctions on which it is constructed. She explains that in Li's system *ethics* refers to social customs and norms, whereas *morality* refers to innate individual psychology. While this distinction is not entirely original, it aligns with the views of some philosophers, including Schelling and Hegel. However, what sets Li's understanding apart is his description of how the two categories interact and influence each other. This unique perspective is distinct from the ideas put forth by other philosophers and better reflects the historical reality of human experience. Jia Jinhua's chapter provides a lucid explanation of Li's theory by delving into concrete instances of the interplay and synergistic relationship between the socio-ethical norms embodied in early Chinese rituality and the inherent moral tenets of classical Confucianism.

This chapter is followed by Gregor Paul's essay dealing with "The Philosophy of Beauty as an Ethics of Freedom: From Kant to Li Zehou: Perspectives of an Attractive Line of Thought." Paul's text explores the concept of reconciling personal desires with moral and social obligations through the idea of harmonious freedom. He discusses the theories of Kant and Schiller, which focus on the free play of the human faculties of mind and perception of beauty, and he explains Li's agreement with them. However, Li believes that these theories are abstract and cannot be put into general practice without correction and supplementation by Marxism. Li emphasizes the importance of the historical development of humankind and the invention and spread of tools in the possibility of intersubjective human experience. Li uses the Chinese aesthetic tradition as an example of how individuals can bring together individual desires and social obligations by following aesthetically appreciative conventions resulting from the development of rites, music, arts, and literature.

The next chapter, "Li Zehou's Major Works on Chinese Aesthetics: The Path of Beauty and The Chinese Aesthetic Tradition," is by Karl-Heinz Pohl, who is widely known as the first translator of one of Li's most significant books, The Path of Beauty, into German. Pohl provides an overview of the history of aesthetics in China, comparing and contrasting Li Zehou's two major books on the subject: The Path of Beauty and The Chinese Aesthetic Tradition. He discusses key concepts in Li's thought, including anthropological concepts from Marx, as well as ideas such as sedimentation, significant form, cultural-psychological formation, and the unity of Heaven and humankind. The chapter concludes by examining how Li's thought was influenced by both Marx and Confucius, but ultimately returning to Confucian thought while incorporating some upgraded Marxist ideas.

From what we have seen so far, Li Zehou was intellectually an extremely receptive philosopher who consistently incorporated other theories and thought streams into his own philosophy. He skillfully merged these ideas with his own to enrich and develop them, resulting in numerous novel perspectives on reality.

The final section of this volume, "Discursive Dialogues," focuses on the interactions Li Zehou had through philosophical dialogues with other scholars and currents of thought. It presents three different examples of such interactions, and in the first chapter of this section, Maja Kosec explores Li Zehou's views on the origins of Chinese culture. In this context, Kosec delves into Li's particular interpretation of shamanism, and thus her chapter is aptly titled "The Origins of Chinese Culture and the Question of Shamanism: Li Zehou and Xu Fuguan." As the title suggests, Kosec contrastively analyzes Li's theory of the origins of Chinese culture by comparing it with Xu Fuguan's theories on the same subject.

In the next chapter, "Fruits of Practice: A Comparative Analysis of Li Zehou's Concept of Sedimentation and the Buddhist Idea of the Transformations of Storehouse Consciousness (Ālaya)," Dawid Rogacz explores the parallels between Li Zehou's concept of sedimentation (*jidian* 积淀) and the idea of the transformations of storehouse consciousness (*ālaya vijñāna*) in Yogācāra Buddhism. The chapter provides a comparison between these two approaches and concludes that both view individual subjectivity and its cognitive faculties as a long-term result of the coagulation (sedimentation) of human action, which is collectively stored and transmitted through generations. Rogacz proposes that Li Zehou's perspective can be seen as a materialist, historicist, collectivist, and anti-utopian "philosophical nephew" of Yogācāra thought, with both belonging to a larger philosophical family of conceptions of subjectivity and the structuring of human consciousness.

The third chapter, "Number and Mathematics in Li Zehou's Critique of Critical Philosophy," marks the end of the section and of this volume. In it, Sydney Morrow elaborates on the effects of Li Zehou's transfiguration of Kant's philosophy, through which the unknowable darkness of the human origin is being replaced by the anthropo-sociological basis of human material evolution. She analyzes this transformation in the context of mathematics, starting with an exposition of its importance for Kant's theoretical system, particularly regarding the schema of number. In the next step, she contrasts Kant's schema with Li Zehou's view of number and the mathematical sublime. After illuminating Li's critique of Kant's theory of number, including its weaknesses and insufficiencies, she explains his own view through a cogent interpretation of his discussion of the subjective formation of aesthetic and axiological judgments. Despite the apparent differences between Li Zehou's view on the mathematical sublime and Kant's theory, Morrow shows that they ultimately arrive at a similar conclusion. Furthermore, she highlights the fact that Li offers a fresh perspective on the issues of number and the mathematical sublime, by pointing toward the possibility of the Kantian sublime without a mathematical, and thus a priori, foundation. This provides us with a new pathway to approach these problems and broaden our understanding of the concept. Measured with the criteria of conventional and formally irreproachable methodology, this path is surprising, intriguing, and illuminating all at the same time.

And so is Li Zehou's philosophy in general. We thus hope this volume will serve as a fitting tribute to his remarkable contributions to Chinese philosophy and culture, and as a vision for future generations of scholars and thinkers. The chapters in this volume honor Li Zehou's enduring legacy not merely as a repository of precious knowledge. Beyond the analysis and interpretation of his profound contributions, Li Zehou's thought emerges as a vibrant source of inspiration, propelling us toward new philosophical insights into the nature of reality and the complex web of relations that define our shared humanity. By engaging with his work, we aim to broaden the scope of transcultural philosophical exploration and enrich our comprehension of the world and our interconnectedness within it.

The insights contained within these essays can doubtless deepen our understanding of Li Zehou's philosophy and its significance, and we believe they will ignite further discussions and debates that push the boundaries of our knowledge and understanding. Let this volume stand as a testimony to the enduring impact of Li Zehou's ideas and a celebration of the intellectual diversity and richness of Chinese philosophical thought.

# Part 1
# Li Zehou, the Philosopher

# 1

# Li Zehou, Wily Provocateur

MICHAEL NYLAN[1]

Li Zehou's thinking rests securely upon three legs, to adopt the early metaphor of the stable tripod: a firm commitment to early Marxism, to democracy, and to a type of Chinese enlightenment, through art and philosophy, "with Chinese characteristics." With equal justice, one could style these as three broad layers of sedimentation contributing to Li's psycho-social formation, adopting Li's vocabulary. My essay originally aimed to explore each of these three areas of Li's activities in turn, but many essays in this volume ably discuss Li's lifelong commitment to Marxism, so further exploration of that topic in this essay seems unwarranted. Suffice it to say that Li held to the belief that Marx's rather unsystematic writings on humanity's future envisioned a thrilling new potential for at least the most enlightened human beings who would be propelled by their aesthetic drives to be "self-created" and "creating."[2] With that firmly in mind, this essay focuses first on Tiananmen and its aftermath, the time when Li's preoccupation with democracy was most evident, and second on Li's exploration of flourishing with "Chinese characteristics," a theme Li explored repeatedly in his later years, while in exile.[3] Inevitably it touches a cluster of key problems with which Li Zehou wrestled throughout his lifetime: (1) How to Sinify Marxism? (2) How to deploy aesthetics to maximize the power of the CCP line? (3) How to create a Maoist and then post-Maoist aesthetics? (4) What should the role of the vanguard of the proletariat be, and who may play that role?

Unfortunately, Marx left Li to his own devices to try to figure out why a vanguard would, sooner or later, come to assess its own situation accurately, and be motivated by its clear-eyed assessments to revolt *collectively* against the status quo on behalf of the cooperative use and control of economic resources.[4] Moreover, Marx's remarks on the Asiatic mode of production are predictably sketchy, verging on incoherent. Consequently, theories by Marx or attributed to him were but complicating factors when the urban intelligentsia in China sought to claim a leading role in democratic revolutions, as was true at Tiananmen, I will contend. As Li wrote,

> In the historical context of China in the 1970s, I raised the question "What is the original meaning of 'practice' in Marxism?" . . . [G]oing "back to classical Marxism," for me, means not just a return to the old theory of productive forces, but also answering the call to create a new theory of subjectivity—a theory concerned with developing the idea of a human "cultural-psychological formation" or "sedimentation"—that is, an internal *"humanized nature" that is relatively independent of the material world*. This would be a genuine Marxist theory of psychology, and definitely not just a mixture of Marxism and Freudian psychology.[5]

As always, the devil is in the details, but how much independence did Marx ascribe to culture, human nature, or aesthetic creations in his writings? Very little or none, so far as I can see, and this is where Li—to my mind, but plainly not to his—diverged sharply in his understanding of the world from Marx, as he tried, over and over again, to align his actual and theoretical worlds, often invoking a distinctive radical variation on "cultural conservatism" that owed something to the Enlightenment and something to Chinese tradition.

Before plunging into the biographical, however, it seems wisest to state the obvious: that in the People's Republic of China (hereafter PRC), as in modern Euro-America, not all self-styled "liberals" or "neoliberals" have been pro-democratic, whether one conceives "democracy" to mean "representative democracy" or greater egalitarianism.[6] Specifically, the leadership of the Leninist-style Chinese Communist Party (hereafter CCP), despite its own claims to being both democratic and Marxist (and thus "scientific" and "historical"), has tended to see its primary task as paternalistic; it styles itself as the vanguard of the progressive forces in the nation-state, even if a paternalistic vision can in no way reasonably be traced to Marx.[7] As the Party's neat narratives go, an embrace of paternalistic values offers better odds than democracy for a brilliant revolutionary future that simultaneously reestablishes an immensely valuable link (without it, irreparably broken) to a unitary pre-1911 "tradition" (to be valued on ethnic grounds). To make its case, the CCP must distort some basic aspects of Chinese history after 1921 (the date of the founding of the CCP in China), and likewise of Chinese history prior to 1911. As a trained historian, I am no stranger to the idea that modern nation-states engage in myth-making, in aid of forging a more unified imagined community and providing the rationale for keeping the current powerholders firmly in control. So the CCP's propensity to cherry-pick the past does not come as a shock, and yet an awareness of the deadly consequences of this propensity pervaded Li's thinking and that of his compatriots who had lived through the Great Leap Forward (1958–1962) and the Cultural Revolution (1966–1976).[8]

## Vital Ghosts: Tiananmen (1989)

Jean-Luc Godard's comedy *Masculin/Feminin*, released in 1966, sports the subtitle "The Children of Marx and Coca-Cola," and critics deemed the movie "naive and knowing, irritating and engaging."[9] The next year, Godard made *La Chinoise*,[10] whose plot centered on a group of pampered Parisian youths forming a Maoist collective—though physical labor was in markedly shorter supply than Little Red Books—debating in lofty style the merits of revolutionary violence, with results by turns hilarious or sobering. That movie's epigram solemnly intones, "We should replace vague ideas with clear images!" Somehow for me, an ardent moviegoer since my undergraduate days, Godard captured a whiff of the spirit that would hover twenty-some years later over the Tiananmen protests, not to mention the anti-humanist poststructuralism and rampant consumer culture that swept the land after the "first timid step in the long march."[11] At Tiananmen, too, the frenzied bouts of collective activity by the children of Marx were hopelessly jumbled, at once naive and knowing, supremely wily and utterly half-baked. As readers likely know, Li Zehou was one of the guiding forces encouraging the young to gather at the Tiananmen protests. Yet a Chinese friend who was born around that time remarked in a recent email, "Li Zehou I know had a huge influence in China in the 1980s, especially among the youngsters." To her, in her late twenties, Li was already an old ghost inhabiting a shadowy past. How thin our present sense of culture and history is becoming.

By way of review for newcomers to the China field, this section summarizes a few dramatic events that occurred during the last three weeks leading up to June 4, 1989, events in which Li Zehou played a major role.[12] One could, of course, begin a Tiananmen narrative a year earlier with another powerful cinematic piece, the six-part TV series *River Elegy* (*He shang* 河殤), which aired twice in 1988 on China Central TV and became "perhaps the most influential TV series of all time."[13] By *He shang*'s distinctly skewed perspective on Chinese history, a strong alliance between Chinese-style administration and Confucian tradition had forged an essentially unchanging "ultra-stable" China spanning the premodern and modern eras that had proven to be impervious to science and democracy, despite the critical importance of these new modes of thinking to civilizational advance.[14] Many consider the prelude to the spring of 1989 to be this set of gloomy ideological propositions bandied about a year earlier, if they do not trace events even further back, to the failures of the "Democracy Wall" movement of the winter of 1979 to 1980.[15]

Still, the backdrop for events in 1989 was celebratory. First, 1989 was the fortieth anniversary of the founding of the People's Republic of China, and the success of the economic reforms that swiftly followed Mao's death in 1976 was to be a core theme of the festivities. Second, the PRC was looking forward to the upcoming visit scheduled for May 15 to 18 by Mikhail Gorbachev, then President of the Soviet Union, as the summit signaled the likelihood of "normalized" Sino-Soviet relations[16] and the general recognition of China's rapid rise to world-power status.[17] (While some CCP leaders were predictably fearful of what Gorbachev's "opening up" reforms might mean for China, the dissolution of the Soviet Union would not come to pass for two more years.) For the first time since its founding in 1949, then, the PRC was operating in a relatively peaceful international environment deemed conducive to its domestic economic goals. Then, just as all news agencies were converging in Beijing in mid-May to cover Gorbachev's visit, Beijing students, teachers, and workers seized the moment to pressure the CCP to consider a list of demands devised to usher in a more democratic government,[18] after which negotiations quickly soured.

Even with a clear memory of these events, I have been shocked to see how compressed the timetable was, and how quickly the different actors, official and unofficial, responded to the unfolding drama before them. Events that would shape the lives of several generations turned on a dime. Reading between the lines, Li Zehou and many leading intellectuals—fellow signers of the open letters addressed to the CCP in 1989[19]—had come to feel that China was sufficiently industrialized to leapfrog some of the most deplorable aspects of Marx's historical stage of capitalism, by introducing a more free and equal society in the here and now. After all, by 1989, the PRC had been liberated from semi-colonial and semi-occupied status for a full forty years, and was therefore in a position to substitute a more nuanced pride in Chinese accomplishments for crude hyper-nationalistic appeals and a personality cult.[20] But well-read Chinese intellectuals were canny enough to see that a flawed economic analysis of the previous century no longer sufficed for a comprehensive explanation of past, present, and future societies or individuals, in line withMarx's exhortation to study real people, in their needy and sociable conditions. Yet any fair reading of Marx, not to mention Marxism, assigned a very marginal role in human history to any factors beyond material production, and thus barely considered such superstructural features as status or culture.

Up to then, Marxian thought had been influential in China in three incommensurate ways:

1. as a source of ideas for students of society, including academics in certain disciplines (e.g., sociology and history);

2. as a creed or "orthodoxy" to which organized bodies, including political parties and nation-states, deliberately or ostensibly subscribed;

3. as a broader philosophy asking people to consider values and ends, public and private.[21]

Most of those who gathered at Tiananmen (not all) were perfectly willing to see Marxism continue in China as a source of ideas or a value system, so long as it did not remain the only source or set of values on offer in the PRC. Above all, Marx (and Engels) wrote "to attract disaffected workers, to discourage utopian schemes, and to push the middle classes beyond constitutionalism into *economic* revolution."[22] And while some came to Tiananmen with utopian schemes, most came fired up by such bread-and-butter issues as worsening job prospects, rampant inflation, and pervasive corruption within the ranks of the CCP.

Li and other senior backers of the second democracy movement at Tiananmen had had ample time to ruminate on contradictions within Chinese society. They understood that local definitions of the terms used for "democracy" (either *minben* 民本 or *minzhu* 民主) did not necessarily mean "electoral" or "representative democracy" to most citizens of the PRC, but they reckoned, quite correctly, on the broad popular appeal among many constituencies of "benevolent rule" in the name of the "common good" (i.e., less inequality and corruption).[23] They felt that while Deng Xiaoping had undertaken to begin an economic revolution under the banner of the "Four Modernizations," the "unfinished" work of revolution would need a very different kind of cultural advance than had been envisioned either by Mao or by the CCP Standing Committee, one led by a "vanguard of the proletariat," by which they meant principally themselves.

It was Lenin who had coined the term "vanguard of the proletariat" in his eagerness to proclaim a unique status for the party he led, but in China after Liberation it was far from clear who was the proletariat and who could become its vanguard. Consulting Marx's *The German Ideology* clarified little, for Marx merely stated, "The class which has the means of material production at its disposal has control at the same time over the means of mental production."[24] The identity of the dramatis personae who were to lead the revolutionary action was never specified. Broadly speaking, intellectuals, as "knowledge producers," could evade membership in the bourgeoisie, since they typically lacked substantial control over the means of their production;[25] even when comparatively well remunerated, they did not own the schools that hired them or the publishing houses they relied upon for the dissemination of their output. And the intellectuals were, by and large, very poor, at least by comparison with high-level cadres in the CCP, and so ready to forge strong alliances with other propertyless urbanites.[26] Then, too, in 1989, in the decade after China's universities reopened in late 1979, only the "luck of the draw" separated China's intellectuals from workers in general, especially those working in urban factories.[27] For all the foregoing reasons, intellectuals saw themselves as members of the proletariat, along with the urban factory workers, and they were primed to play the role of vanguard, despite Mao's suspicion that the group was a breeding ground for potential rightists.[28]

Perhaps because senior intellectuals, students, and workers had shared so many common experiences (including hard labor), public intellectuals still played an outsized role in the PRC imaginary in the post–Cultural Revolution climate, after being shunted to the side or even persecuted for a decade. Historically, of course, elite "intellectuals" in China had long claimed a much "thicker" identity in the production of ideological discourse than in many other places, either as uniquely qualified "bearers" or "witnesses" to "historical memories" relating to Chineseness or as the only citizens qualified to engage in "patriotic worrying" on behalf of the nation, thanks to their higher education or richer experiences, in China and abroad.[29] For cogent reasons, many senior intellectuals who converged on Tiananmen, hoping to change the course of Chinese history or advise those who would change it, did not want to hear any more denigration of Chinese tradition of the sort that many leading intellectuals had become accustomed to since the "New Culture" movement of the early twentieth century.[30] Nor did they welcome the reduction of hallowed "traditions" to whatever latest ideological claptrap the CCP was pushing.[31] In this they were emboldened, since even Deng Xiaoping had admitted that the party often had talked a "lot of bluster."[32]

These facts and perceptions formed the backdrop for the events of late spring, 1989, which can be summarized as follows.

By *May 13*, by the *Washington Post*'s account, "More than 1,000 university students began a hunger strike in the center of Beijing . . . pressing their demand for a dialogue with the government."[33] Pronouncing their love for democracy "over rice," the hunger strikers noted, "We've already demonstrated and boycotted classes. This is our last resort." On the morning of May 13, Yan Mingfu, then head of the Communist Party's United Front, called an emergency meeting of student leaders and intellectuals, including Liu Xiaobo with Chen Ziming and Wang Juntao (both in the Beijing Social and Economic Sciences Research Institute).[34] Yan delivered two important announcements at the meeting: first, Gorbachev's planned visit to Tiananmen Square had been canceled, nullifying most of the leverage the students had hoped to exert in their talks with government and CCP officials; and second, "the government" was prepared to begin immediate dialogue with the student leaders. (As became clear, the PRC leaders in command after June 4 were far angrier about worker participation in the Tiananmen protests, feeling that the proletariat protesters had betrayed the very hand that had fed them.)[35]

On May 14, twelve intellectuals issued "Our Urgent Appeal for the Current Situation." That group included Yan Jiaqi (political scientist), Bao Zunxin (philosopher), Li Honglin (liberal CCP theorist), Dai Qing (reporter with the *Guangming Daily*), Yu Haocheng (former director of the Mass Publishing House), Li Zehou (then research fellow at the Philosophy Institute of the Chinese Academy of Social Sciences, or CASS), Su Xiaokang (one of two scriptwriters for *River Elegy* and lecturer at the Beijing Broadcasting Institute), Wen Yuankai (professor at the China University of Science and Technology), and Liu Zaifu (director of the Literature Institute, under CASS).[36] Thanks largely to the good connections of the signatories, this appeal was published in the *Guangming Daily* and broadcast on China Central Television (CCTV).

Very much like Yan Mingfu, the group of "concerned intellectuals" published a nuanced rhetorical appeal carefully crafted to calm tempers. On the one hand, the senior intellectuals asked that the turmoil be declared a "patriotic democracy movement" and the illegal student organization be declared legal. On the other hand, the intellectuals asked the students to show enough faith in their institutions to leave the square to deescalate the conflict. Additionally, in this appeal the intellectuals offered to join the hunger strike themselves if the Tiananmen demands were not met by the CCP, and they followed up the public appeal with group and individual visits to the square to address those gathered there. As the official statement on Tiananmen by the China News Agency later reported unsympathetically, "*These people* also went to Tiananmen Square many times to make speeches and agitate . . . . They slandered our government as 'an incompetent government,' saying that, through the fasting students, 'China's bright future can be envisioned.'" On May 14 and 15, many of the students came to question the motives of the signers of the Appeal, alleging that they, as moderates, were being manipulated by the government.

Meanwhile, on the evening of May 14, Yan Mingfu kept his promise of the previous day and met with two student leaders. In his meeting with them, he declared the student meeting "patriotic," i.e., legal, but he also pleaded with the students, through their representatives, to leave the square. Despite Yan's major concession, the planned meeting grew increasingly chaotic as it went on. Ultimately the students decided to refuse Yan's requests/demands, for many of them were mightily displeased once they learned that the meeting was not being broadcast on TV and radio, as they had hoped. This returned the situation to a stalemate, even after Yan went to the square himself, where he offered to be held "hostage" by the students, as testimony to his own good faith in negotiating. Yan then conveyed the student demands to the hard-liner Li Peng and pleaded with him to recognize the movement as "legal and patriotic," but Li refused. That competing student factions expressed different views did not help the situation, nor were the competing factions within the CCP in one accord.

By May 16, a small group had formed the "Beijing Union of Intellectuals," asserting the group's right to style itself as working class and oppressed. The same day, members of the union circulated the "16 May Declaration"[37] warning that "a promising China might be led into the abyss of real turmoil" if the government did not accept the political demands made by the people brave or foolhardy enough to join the Union. Nominally headed by Yan Jiaqi and Wu'erkaixi, the Union was promptly pronounced illegal by the CCP, which did not take kindly to threats. Apparently in response to the declaration, Zhao Ziyang used the occasion of his meeting with Gorbachev on May 16 to leak the information that much of the CCP was still under Deng Xiaoping's direction, although Deng officially by then had relinquished all power.[38] (Zhao would later pay dearly for this indiscretion.) And while some professional "China watchers" from the United States pronounced Tiananmen to be "more like a fairground than . . . a site of insurrection,"[39] within four days, Li Peng had imposed martial law in Beijing, with the blessings of Deng Xiaoping and Yang Shangkun.

Over the next two weeks, *from May 20 to June 4*, halfhearted attempts at dialogue collapsed repeatedly, with some of the young now suspicious of any compromise whatsoever, so that many came to expect that there would likely be bloodshed in the streets sooner, rather than later. One may consult Chai Ling's tearful interview on this. What had gone so wrong so quickly? It was quite simple: "Through the highly contagious symbolic act of taking to the streets, Chinese had declared that their days of waiting compliantly for the party to reform itself democratically from the top were over."[40] A great many of the CCP leaders were outraged, including Li Peng and Deng Xiaoping. Such hardliners, "in the face of a mounting challenge against the regime," persuaded colleagues that nothing lay ahead except "chaos, disorder, and the impending defeat" of the status quo, if they did not act swiftly and decisively to suppress the movement.

Thankfully, the literature on authoritarian regimes increasingly distinguishes Leninist-style authoritarian regimes from non-Leninist-style regimes, with the latter seeking to co-opt elections and legislatures to credibly distribute spoils while neutralizing rivals.[41] By contrast, Leninist-style regimes often tend to sustain themselves by creating entirely new governmental units to supplant the previous system's units when distributing portfolios, so they may appear to be super-stable—that is, until they do not, and ideological splits, purges, and coups ensue. Mindful of the CCP's propensity for violence, Li Zehou responded to the unfolding events of Tiananmen, as did many older intellectuals, by urging the groups jostling for attention at Tiananmen to disperse and choose quiet steady "reform" over attention-grabbing heroics. Having witnessed the fury of the CCP in earlier eras, his group wanted to avoid bloodshed at all costs, especially among the ranks of the future leaders for the country, and they were also fearful lest the economic reforms be scaled back, if the conservatives came into sole control of the CCP. Looking back, it seems they were right to be frightened for and by some of the younger leaders at the square, since some of the leaders, Chai Ling and Wu'erkaixi in particular, welcomed the spilling of revolutionary blood, just so long as it was not theirs.

In the immediate aftermath of Tiananmen, Li Zehou was put on house arrest for three years, until 1992, although he was never formally arraigned on one or more charges. During that time, Li was subjected to much "heavier self-criticism" than most others, as everyone at his work unit knew. Because his "crimes" were purely his own influential ideas, Li was forbidden to publish new works or to have his previous work sold in the PRC and he was denied access to overseas travel and to "dangerous" Hong Kong publications. Eventually, as his prolonged confinement became an embarrassment to the government and an impediment in international fora, Li was granted permission to see some foreign visitors, when a very few others accused of amorphous crimes against the state (e.g., Wang Shuren and Zhang Xianyang) were not.[42] In 1992, Li asked for and secured a visa to work in the United States. During the 1990s, he mainly lived in Boulder, Colorado, where he was invited to teach at Colorado College.[43] In 1994, he and Liu Zaifu repeated their earlier injunctions to "say farewell to revolution," to the mingled outrage and approbation of their readers in the Sinosphere.[44] Evincing outrage, for instance, were members of the party faithful, including Fang Keli then director of the Graduate Program of the Academy of Social Sciences.

Fang questioned the "ideological intent" behind Li's argument against revolution, accusing it (quite illogically) of subverting Marxist ideology and the regime ruling in its name.[45]

"The ghost of Tiananmen stubbornly refuses to leave the mansion of Chinese politics," said Timothy Brook, an assertion that is both true and untrue, depending on one's perspective and one's age.[46] The 1990s in China witnessed an outpouring of secondary scholarship, whose chief aim was to rewrite or whitewash the facts. Leadership by public intellectuals, workers, or students in any movement (especially Tiananmen) constituted the gravest of threats to the present social order, it was alleged; only leadership by the CCP could be trusted to steer the economy to benefit the PRC, domestically or internationally. As one commentator wrote (safely outside the PRC, it must be noted),[47]

> In contrast to this [reinforced] memory of the Cultural Revolution, no collective memory has been formed about the crackdown of the 1989 pro-democracy movement because of the absence of a public forum for such a memory. The general silence about and lack of memory of the 1989 Tian'anmen incident [in the PRC] is symptomatic of the plight in which Chinese intellectuals find themselves [as self-designated memory-keepers].
>
> For many Chinese intellectuals, these new historical factors are compounded by their particular sense of marginalization and disillusion. Chinese intellectuals in the 1980s played an important role in social enlightenment, not because of a strong institutional base, but because of their symbolic role as victims and cultural and moral standard-bearers in an unfree society. Cultural pluralism in the nineties has undermined this role of intellectuals [as has t]he rise of popular culture and the commercializing and commodifying forces behind it.[48]

Understandably confused and humiliated, surprising numbers of the well-educated began to flirt with, profess, or repeat vast conspiracy theories that just happened to dovetail neatly with the official CCP position alleging a vast Western conspiracy to contain China, led by the United States. (I hesitate to dub members of this group "intellectuals" on the basis of their college degrees, since that term implies more confrontational stances to the nation-state.)[49] Post-Tiananmen, not a few of the well-educated preferred to think of themselves as cultural "philosophers" and "advisers" to CCP technocrats, whom they deigned to serve while ever so tentatively broaching Enlightenment ideas at planning sessions.[50] "Enlightening" unwashed peasants struck many would-be and actual advisers as too daunting a task.[51] Li Zehou had a different history, as some may recall: he was born a poor peasant, and he had made it, against the odds, to university. This may go some way to explaining why he dreamed of more thoroughgoing reforms, which he came to realize, post-Tiananmen, could only be achieved by better and more broad-ranging humanistic education in the PRC.

As it turned out, then, the 1990s acquired just as pronounced a character as the 1980s, with the New Cultural Conservatism of the '90s priding itself on spurring "a rational rejection" of the alleged radicalism, utopianism, and political romanticism of the 1980s' sociocultural critiques. Presenting itself as a sane return to "realistic thinking" after "pointless intellectual turmoil" and ceaseless bickering, the New Neocons reserved their most severe hostilities for the May Fourth movement and the 1980s, because both disturbed acceptable neoliberal norms of a homogenized, consumer-driven, and legitimized political "reality" wherein "Chinese tradition" could be saved for posterity.[52] Two logically separable rhetorical aims therefore drove the 1990s' proposals to "rehabilitate" Chinese tradition: (1) the contention that Chinese cultural traditions and innovations have all along been just as impressive as those ascribed to Euro-America, despite dismissive remarks by unthinking racists; and (2) a willingness to pave the way for greater shows of loyalty to be rendered to the CCP and its helmsmen, on the grounds that members of this group—and they alone—could advance a leadership style with "Chinese characteristics."

Feeding this rhetoric since the 1990s have been diverse protean arguments for Chinese exceptionalism, many of which pit what they called "localism" against what they construe to be Western-style "universalism."[53] As understood by the Chinese themselves, such exceptionalism, being a nationalistic or "patriotic" discourse, can safely navigate the tricky sociopolitical contours of Chinese identity by stressing what is "good" and "great" about China, while castigating the Western Other as "barbarian" and "bent on destruction."[54] Like white supremacy in the United States, Chinese exceptionalism in the PRC is a powerful drug that dulls the heart and brain, and as an opiate manifesting social Darwinist and Romantic conceits, it is the very opposite, to my mind, of what Marx and Li Zehou wished for humanity: that large parts of it would manage to wriggle out from under the institutional props designed to foster sundry addictions to irreality.[55]

So, Li Zehou played starring roles in several successive "culture fevers" speaking to real conditions "in the world of men," even if he was never much of a joiner.[56] In a country full of intellectuals boasting in media events of how much they "worried about China," Li never portrayed himself as a worrier, yet he never quit worrying about unnecessary, even counterproductive bloodletting involving real people.[57] In fact, Li portrayed himself as a mild-mannered eccentric, a kind of happy-go-lucky guy content to live alone, so long as he was fortunate enough to be left alone by the powers-that-be.[58] But Li was mindful of the conditions of his release. By my tentative reading, Li struggled throughout his work to establish a "possibilist" or "in-between" position for Chinese tradition, one that took account of constraint and creativity in each and every era of Chinese history, not just his own.[59] Woei Lien Chong's appraisal captured Li's distrust of extremists well: "Li's own life work is a consistent attempt to define the role of human agency in such a way that the extremes of determinism and voluntarism can be avoided."[60] Small wonder that Li's own comments on nearly every topic that touched on the political—and *everything* was political for Li—are nearly always downright difficult-to-parse, in that being, not coincidentally, like many passages in Marx that conjure humanity's inchoate yearnings to live on and to live well.

Let us consider one of Li's most artful yet provocative moves: "On the issue of social order, in some sense, I am for authoritarianism."[61] Li certainly figured that *for the moment, in some sense*, authoritarianism would and possibly *should* be practiced, so as to speed modernization. Given the swift and brutal crackdown at Tiananmen, chances were that the CCP's leadership would prove to be invincible in the near future and perhaps for a very long time. In formulating a new intellectual *strategy*, Li evidently trusted that those who "appreciated his tone" would find the latest iteration of his positions to be continuous with the radical social and political criticism he had uttered in the 1980s.[62] Tactically, the overall message conveyed by Li's optimistic symposium speech "Where the Enlightenment is Heading" (delivered in the spring of 1989) seems not too dissimilar from the central exhortation outlined in *Farewell to Revolution*,[63] or in numerous publications after the 1990s.

Li was subtly undercutting the polemics launched by the "Asian values" crowd and the "patriotic" faction of the CCP, who insisted that China's own distinctive political culture *was* unabashedly "autocratic" and that to be authentically Chinese therefore entailed unwavering obedience to one's superiors.[64] For practiced readers schooled in political rhetoric, it is hard to miss Li's quiet disgust in his concurrent statement that he sincerely hoped authoritarian rule would not be *openly* defended in China, lest it be "regulated, legitimized, and turned into an obstacle to progress."[65] In this crucial respect, then, Li differed from so many other public intellectuals of the 1990s who reversed course and came to hail authoritarianism as the ideal or only guarantor for rapid modernization.

Surely the context of his remarks in the first half of the 1990s should be considered when assessing his limited approval of the center's policies. When Li uttered that statement, most analysts, East or West, confidently predicted that a further decentralization of power away from the CCP was bound to accompany further economic reforms, and not the rapid recentralization of power that has taken place under Xi Jinping since March 2013, which has only accelerated since March 2018.[66] The notion that rising GNP would inevitably promote a push for democratic reforms has proven to be disastrously wrong in every country where liberals relied on this scenario; in nation after nation, demagogues have appeared. Evidently, in the PRC, many, if not most, citizens have deemed rapid gains in GDP and GNP ample justification to give their allegiance to the sovereign leadership of the CCP, for China's economic ascent and superpower status made Chinese citizens both richer and proud.[67]

I would argue, with Ci Jiwei, that the Chinese elite's wholehearted embrace of neoliberal doctrines and mentality, before but especially after Tiananmen[68]—a version of "trickle-down" Voodoo Reaganomics larded with references to "self-made men," massive consumption, and an elite "meritocracy"—has promoted a widening chasm between the ideals espoused by many "civilized" Chinese and the stark realities of the "nasty and brutish" competition within Chinese society.[69] At a minimum, we can now say this with confidence: within ten years after Tiananmen, a number of surveys showed that citizens in the PRC were in sharp disagreement about the best path forward to take for themselves or their country, but nonetheless tended to agree on matters more closely tied to culture.[70] My hunch is that this pattern would be even more pronounced today in the PRC, were it possible to conduct social scientific surveys there, but Sino-American antagonisms preclude that.[71]

## Chinese Culture as a Unique Form of "Humanized Nature"

Marx wrote, somewhat confusingly, "Labour is man's coming to be for himself."[72] This apparently means that all kinds of disciplined and purposeful labor, including material production and self-reflective thinking, shape the life form that each individual person evolves within society over time. From the Marxian perspective, any mode of production represents two things at a minimum: a system of behavior and the effect(s) of earlier behaviors (what people had been doing before the specific product came into being).[73] Yet labor is far more than a means and an end, a type of in input and end product, insofar as it contains the potential to become a dynamic medium of "self-expression" and hence "self-affirmation."[74] Because human beings feel the need to play a part in the ordered environments in which they find themselves and to have others regard them with approbation, how a person envisions herself is inevitably a function of what the person has done, what others have done in the person's proximate social and cultural environment, and how those activities in the aggregate are viewed during her lifetime and afterward. Every personal experience, then—even that of the confirmed maverick or eccentric—concurrently reflects, to a greater or lesser degree, a cultural and sociopolitical inheritance, with labor quite possibly the most significant of all personal experiences. Still, when others own the means of production, the worker does not tend to feel that her labor is essentially or substantially *voluntary*. Furthermore, in capitalist societies—and all of us, East or West, global south or global north, now live in such societies—what matters most is the ability and opportunity to earn a living wage, with the result that the laborer easily becomes little more than a mere commodity to herself, to the employer, and to society-at-large. Alienation ensues.

Inspired by Marx, Li Zehou tried to conceive a world where two desiderata might be achieved: first, productive work would remain self-expressive and so in some imaginary ledger the "possession" of the person working, without having its value calculated in monetary terms extrinsic to the work; and second, the form taken by the self-expression need not diminish, let alone usurp the dignity of others. In the more "free and equal" future world Marx gestured toward, workers would ideally be able to perceive their own contributions in both their historical and contemporary contexts and workers would thereby gain a much deeper appreciation of their own intrinsic worth. If the most hopeful visions came true, the safe enclaves promised the bourgeoisie in "civil society" would become more accessible to all.[75] Equipped with a more fine-grained sense of their own predicaments as well as their predecessors' contributions, and operating from a place of relative safety, knowledge production could then accelerate, even as the very process helped producers learn to exert some degree of control over themselves, their own time, and their own bodies.

Perhaps the greatest obstacle to this sunny future can be traced to one fact: in real time, equality and freedom, so often conflated—as during the Tiananmen protests, and in multiple manifestos, past and present—are "opposed to each other in their presupposition, content, and effect"; as one political theorist put it, "only equality can be considered a democratic principle within politics"; by contrast, "freedom as an internal political matter is the principle of the [anti-government] bourgeois legal state."[76] Over the last century or so, so-called "populist" leaders have availed themselves of the disjointedness to curtail personal freedoms sharply in the name of some supposed future greater equality, even in defiance of the majority will. This observation must be kept in mind when we see how unhelpful are the labels "conservative" and "radical," particularly when the phrase "with Chinese characteristics" is applied to "society," "culture," "politics," or Li Zehou himself.

In today's increasingly globalized and tribalized world, more and more Chinese (with Li among them until his death) have been asking how they can best contribute to a better (i.e., more constructive) globalized future. Yes, they want to "save China" not only from external foes, but also from the domestic groups who they believe will deter it from achieving its age-old ideals. But in the internationalist spirit enjoined by Marx and other revolutionary leaders, they want additionally to help "save the world," by contributing their own perspectives to enrich the overly simplistic pictures that Western modernity (especially of the neoliberal sort) devises, popularizes, and imposes.[77] Wittgenstein once framed humanity's problem nicely when he remarked, "Man is a creature who makes pictures of himself and then comes to resemble the picture."[78] For Wittgenstein, this farcical aspect of human endeavors represented a grave rebuke of his early work on language as play, but for Li Zehou, as for Xunzi before him, the labor entailed by this endless picturing and re-picturing by the thinking person was *the* quintessential human capacity most deserving of honor. And since Li was convinced that no formative contributions could result from abstractions, Li preoccupied himself with sketching the varieties of human expression that people speaking and writing Chinese have most admired over time. Such authentic insights into Chinese history were more likely to provide a firmer foundation for PRC citizens' true "self-expression" and "self-affirmation," if only because they resonated with past experiences, he said.[79] (Needless to say, his was a very different project from the one that the CCP has espoused throughout its seventy-year history: to impose a highly selective version of national "traditions" on Chinese citizens as "fates" handed down from on high.)[80]

Enter, stage right, Li Zehou's culturalism "with Chinese characteristics," which enraged scolds (some living safely outside the PRC) who accused Li of becoming an "essentialist" or an accommodationist sellout. One might profitably compare the substance of Li's arguments with those of Hannah Arendt, stage left. For Arendt never assumed in *The Human Condition* that there could be a single, fixed "human condition" that determines how we can, do, and should act politically, since the human condition for each of us is "historically specific and profoundly variable," with new features of our modern predicaments quite unprecedented.[81]

So what, when all is said and done, is this culturalist understanding of "Chinese tradition" in Li's formulations, and how does Li frame it as a fund of resources that can stimulate modern Chinese to further refine their current modes of thinking and enliven their styles of living?[82] For long decades, Li was certainly arguing against philosophers who would measure the worth of Chinese traditions by the standard of "universality . . . grounded in the very nature of human experience."[83] For Li (as for every other Chinese master I know of), all experience is highly situated, at once profoundly subjective and comprehensively shaped by the daily rituals the national and local cultures urge or impose, plus the institutions and practices they valorize.[84] Cultural immersion is achieved by displaying at least the characteristic airs (*fengdu* 風度) of a given time and place, as by mulling over its prevailing perspectives and provocations. Thus style in Chinese tradition *is* content, not some superfluous refinement; the impressive bearing, decorum, and clothing marks the *junzi* 君子[85] as much as any course of objectively observable action he or she embarks upon in this "one world."[86] For Li, one's daily practice, in consequence, is to consist largely of conscious, pleasurable conformity to and instantiation of the "actual emotions and situation as roots" (*qing benti* 情本體),[87] in the serene belief that such engender activities enrich the experiences of all subscribers to the community, not least the *junzi* as a person of cultivated patterns (*wen ren* 文人).[88] These are the "essentials" (*yao* 要) we have to work with as human beings, and they suffice for our flourishing.[89]

None of Li's writing makes much sense, unless one accepts on faith his firm belief in salvific sedimentation, in the redeeming qualities of special aesthetic experiences. It was Freud, of course, who persuaded us that our unconscious was sedimented, not in the sense of fixed and immoveable layers weighing us down, but in the manner of a Roman cityscape, wherein a single structure could conceivably incorporate parts of walls from the eighth and early fourth centuries BCE, the third and the eighteenth centuries CE.[90] By Freud's powerful account, in mental life nothing that has once been formed can truly perish; everything is preserved miraculously in eminently suitable circumstances, with no part occluded. The result is that all parts of the Roman cityscape, in their several parts and in their interconnections, impress themselves favorably on the spirit of the person traveling through the streets of Rome. It was not for nothing that Li always claimed that he was introducing psychology into philosophy, even if he was also one to seriously entertain the main message of the *River Elegy* series: that wholesale Westernization was badly needed if China was ever to stride confidently into the larger world. In this connection, it is crucial, I think, that Li always pushed for an integrative view of past, present, and future, rather than a reductive view, believing endeavors that support and transmit rich human experiences in all their stunning diversity to be, by definition, more realistic, less false, and thus more likely to conduce to a form of liberation and joy. A contrast may illuminate this: unlike Gao Xinjian, the Nobel Prizewinner, Li never traffics in either "total wisdom" or "total detachment." Instead, he argues for layered complexities, for Kant and for Confucius, for Tao Yuanming and for Du Fu, for peasants and for intellectuals—virtually anything that ties people to *this world of humanity's making*.[91]

Let me relate my own experience: when I first stumbled upon *Reading the Analects Today* (*Lunyu jindu* 論語今讀), I was in awe of the pains Li had taken to lay out the successive phases of commentarial readings for every line in the *Analects*, from the Han to the Song to Ming-Qing and the Republican era, before interjecting his own analysis, which occasionally admitted to puzzlement or boredom. And I was thrilled by the indisputable proof attesting how discrete those layers of commentarial traditions actually were, as it allowed me to quickly home in on the conceptual gaps between the Han and Song interpretive layers. That initial reaction, I now see, was rather superficial, as Li's larger project was to demonstrate just *how many* Chinese pasts are available to readers of Chinese today, and indeed to anyone who cares to contemplate China and its modern fate.[92] China is ample beauty incarnate, by this view, which hardly precludes the claims of other ethnic or national groups to locate beauty elsewhere.[93] To be heartened by humanity does not require genius, thank god, only a love of beauty.

In aesthetics, Li kept insisting that he did not agree with Nietzsche's vision of aesthetics, which was "to study the creation of art from the perspective of the will to power," i.e., from a male point of view, rather than from the female "appreciation of art," which Nietzsche characterized as passive.[94] Li wanted to understand "beauty itself" and to set aside Nietzsche's ugly binary to focus on humanity's basic need to create or appreciate great art when making things, an idea he got from Hegel's *Lectures on the Philosophy of Fine Art*. From Kant, Li got the argument that a sense of beauty (and aesthetic judgments, in contrast to other human faculties) inevitably takes into account other people's judgments (past and present). Accordingly, for Li, a sense of beauty is neither a pure reflection of one's own consciousness or of social conventions. Li's preoccupation with needy humanity compelled him to denounce any idea that beauty and a sense of beauty are somehow "mechanical reflections" of the material conditions, rather than a human compulsion to a specific mode of thinking and practice (in Li's memorable phrasing, the self-creative and co-creative will to humanize nature) that is both prior to the material conditions of artists and viewers and shaped by those material conditions.

## Several Radical Moves

Feuerbach and Marx had agreed that man's "peculiar capacities are developed only in intercourse with his fellow human beings" and "a belief in God is nothing but the belief in human dignity."[95] This Li felt, too, and strongly. To facilitate his own project, Li upended three features of hallowed Chinese tradition. In his first radical reversal, the classical *tiyong* 體用 dichotomy proposed by the "Self-strengtheners" of late Qing, and specifically Zhang Zhidong (d. 1909), turned into "Western learning for the substance, and Chinese for the application." Li knew his world history well enough to be little bothered by the fact that the historical origins of science and democracy are claimed by Euro-American boosters; all Li wanted was to have today's Chinese hasten to avail themselves of the benefits of science and democracy,[96] as he believed them to be prime concerns contributing to the development of the PRC as a modern nation-state. He knew meanwhile that those claims look ever more laughable under close examination, and so may "wither away" like the old-time religions, with a little luck; and that each Euro-American country that came to embrace science and democracy did so in its own unique way. Ostensibly Li's slogan echoed Deng's famous formula "socialism with Chinese characteristics," but in fact Li aimed to complicate or undercut Deng's slogan by arguing that modernization, technocratic and cultural, will only prosper in China when the old autocratic powerholders with their anti-scientific and anti-democratic policies are removed from office.[97] So while there are passages in which Li sounds as if he belongs firmly in the camp of the *guocui* 國粹/*guoxue* 國學 figures, it is simply that Li felt, deep in his gut, that if China had survived the depredations by the Japanese and Great Powers, the polity would surely survive its own autocrats, though Chinese culture might collapse if confronted by a second Cultural Revolution. In sum, he saw no real reason why China could not develop its own distinctive style of Enlightenment science and democracy without incurring the taint of "spiritual pollution." However, Li cautions, in the China Century the world's second largest economy will need to reframe its task going forward: its present urgent task is no longer to "save" the country from extinction or dismemberment by enemy powers, despite CCP propaganda. The country and its leaders now need to consider how best to satisfy the citizenry in enlivening ways.

To that end, Li Zehou happily upends an article of faith first articulated by Marx but greatly elaborated by vulgar Marxists: that all local culture (including local religion) is but the superstructure (i.e., a pale reflection generated by the economic conditions), whereas the dominant form of material production determines the precise structural forms taken by all human activities. Li finds this structure/superstructure dichotomy unhelpful, since for Li subjective and objective conditions coexist in dynamic interplay, propelled by a "foundational" human compulsion: to humanize nature and imbue ordinary life with beauty. In Li's accounts, beauty thrills us because it instantiates, conveys, and satisfies a need equally felt by the creator of a piece of art and by whoever appreciates the creation; creator and connoisseur are then bound inextricably together by invisible ties. As humanity itself, plus its drive for beauty, has primacy for Li, any particular form that material production assumes in any given era becomes secondary. Li's ambition was boundless: he wanted to give humanity the tools to create and enjoy beauty, with history itself one of those tools.[98] This was no arid "academic argument" for Li. To advance his ideas, he had to go against the two reigning experts in the field of aesthetics in the PRC, Zhu Guangqian (1897–1986) and Cai Yi (1906–1992), at an early age.

Li Zehou was also one of the most prominent theorists to insist that nationalist agendas and Enlightenment values were diametrically opposed, even if he conceded that the latter sometimes had to yield to the former during indisputable crises over individual or national survival. At the same time, Li resolutely opposed those postmodernists who decried the many entanglements of the Enlightenment ideals with colonial hegemonic projects. To commemorate the seventieth anniversary of the May Fourth Incident in 1989, Peking University organized a symposium, and many people gave speeches, which was the occasion for Li's analysis of "Where the Enlightenment is Heading." (Note that this symposium took place as the occupation of Tiananmen Square by students and workers was building force.) In his rousing talk, Li began by optimistically proclaiming national salvation and enlightenment to be "mutually reinforcing" goals, but Li then had the temerity to decouple "national salvation" from "leadership by the CCP," even as he refused to equate all May Fourth–type struggles for greater personal autonomy with "the best interests" of "the people." (He had discerned the split between freedom and equality, it seems.) A man of passion himself, Li said he preferred rational to passionate changes, and above all, he condemned violence (as very likely to beget more violence), to the intense irritation of a great many people in the audience that day.[99] Plainly, for a long time, Li was intent upon constructing a "third way" forward as a vanguard of a more profound change than Liberation had sought.[100]

Equally plainly, while no one can predict when the country will move from "developing" to "developed" nation-state status, intellectuals who once sympathized with protests against authoritarian leadership have grown increasingly comfortable moving in neo-authoritarian circles,[101] particularly when Confucian learning is reduced to a managerial technique for industrial firms on the Singaporean model, supplemented by a method for conflict resolution aiming to "avoid the problems afflicting the West."[102] With this limited "management" Confucianism, the teachings of Confucius, the social critic and reformer, have been repackaged for political purposes so that they boil down to "obedience to one's superiors in the hierarchy (chiefly parents and bosses), devotion to the nation-state, here equated with the CCP, and protection of the family by the family, rather than by work units or the state."[103]

I imagine Li countering this validation of unthinking deference by something like the statement Hannah Arendt made in *The Human Condition*: "What I propose . . . is a reconsideration of the human condition from the vantage point of our newest experiences and our most recent fears. . . . What I propose, therefore, is very simple: it is nothing more than to think about what we are doing."[104] Surely, the most compelling aspects of Li's vast output are his wide-ranging erudition, his willingness to query long-standing commonplaces, and his propensity to juxtapose categories that others box themselves in with.[105] We would be falsifying our sense of the man if we tried to apply the usual labels to Li Zehou in the conventional academic fashion, casting him as cultural conservative or as anti-radical,[106] and unwise to "read into" Li's own psycho-social formation any one set of enthusiasms. By my reading, Li's intention was always to probe the current consensus understanding (parts of which he shared and parts of which he queried) in ways calculated to engage his Chinese audiences especially.[107] In stark contrast to Liu Xiaobo, the *enfant* terrible, Li did not adhere closely to any one thinker or any one line (and especially not to Nietzsche's nihilist superman).

There is no higher complement a historian can pay another person than to say that he made the past come alive, thanks to his profound interest in dynamism and vitality (both ineffably beautiful for Li). I often disagreed with the specifics in Li's analyses, for example, in the generalizations that appear in his sweeping *Path of Beauty*, but on fairly nitpicking grounds. To date, I have not read in Li's work an explicit exhortation to "Let a Hundred Flowers Bloom," but I feel confident that this is where Li wanted all of us (with or without Chinese characteristics) to get to, before we press ourselves to ask, early and often, "What Is to Be Done?" As Lin Min remarks, Li's books "are [all] meant strictly for the present social reality."[108]

To raise any question of "what is to be done" about the "present social reality" is to ponder the likely early Russian roots of Li's theories. Li, after all, was steeped in the Russians, especially the three Russian literary critics of the mid- to late nineteenth century who were hailed in translations into Chinese as "proto-Marxists" or even "quasi-Marxists": Vissarion Belinsky (1811–1848), Nikolay Dobrolyubov (1836–1861), and Nikolay Chernyshevsky (1828–1889).[109] These three "revolutionary democrats" had had the benefit of seeing either the collapse of revolutionary efforts in 1848 or the unholy alliances forged between the bourgeoisie and autocrats after the short-lived Paris Commune in 1871, or both. In their lifetimes, Dobrolyubov and Cherynshevsky had moreover witnessed the formation of the Utopian Socialists and early anarchists, but these groups repelled them, as they did Marx and Li.[110] What Li shared with the Russians was a strong "sense of social responsibility, political commitment, and moral vision": a "compelling sense of urgency," a "concern for the lives of human beings, whose miseries could not be explained away or assuaged by any philosophical system or human necessity," and the firm conviction that "art is lifeless . . . if it is not a question, or an answer to a question."[111] As György Lukács put it, the three insisted on this single principle: "Our ideal should be not a castrated, disembodied, denuded creature; our ideal should be a whole, real, many-sided, complete, fully developed man [i.e., human]."[112] As a Chinese counterpart to these three literary critics, Li's writings echoed Dobrolyubov's sentiments: "The poet creates a whole, finds a vital link, fuses and transforms the diverse aspects of living reality," after which the age-old story of human struggles can be made to illuminate "an instinctive consciousness of . . . [the] inalienable right to love, happiness, and life."[113] One wonders, too, whether Li did not learn lessons in agile evasion from these three Russians, who managed to circumvent heavy-handed censors, just as Li intended to do.[114] Not that Li's own tradition did not supply a wealth of comparably subtle thinkers (e.g., Zhuangzi, Xunzi, and Yang Xiong) for whom "borrowing" concepts and approaches to life became a self-conscious art form, but one cannot have too many models of good lives lived with pleasure in mind. So we should not be surprised to find Li Zehou, a latter-day wily revolutionary democrat himself, deploying literary criticism to critique autocrats in power. He realized that politics itself is a kind of theater, an aesthetic exercise. The only surprise, perhaps, was how well he wielded his knife, but then he had a friend in Butcher Ding.

## Conclusion

Right now, elite intellectuals in the PRC, within and outside the party, are divided over questions about tactics, theories, fallback positions, and the precise nature of actual, ever-shifting political realities, questions unresolved since before Tiananmen:

1. the degree to which property should be privatized and regulated (the two being different);

2. the degree to which the "dictatorship" that supposedly will transition to perfect or near-perfect socialism should be led by elites claiming to represent a meritocracy; by "the people" (an amorphous term, which occasionally includes virtual illiterates); or by the CCP as "stewards" of the people's "fate";

3. the degree to which some form of "constitutionalism" (meaning rule by law at a minimum, plus freedom of speech, of association, and of the press, and seldom any form of representative democracy at a maximum) should be instituted in the near future as a stabilizing mechanism;[115] and

4. whether the highest form of patriotism is exhibited by infinite "patience" with current CCP policies or by "loyal opposition" to the CCP, publicly expressed, or by something in between these two poles.

Evidently, these issues bedevil conversations in China just as much as they do in Euro-America.

Of the various mainstream positions on these contentious issues, Li Zehou's positions post-Tiananmen edged at points close to those articulated by the "New Left" writers (as represented by such figures as Han Yuhai), since Li never abjured Marxism or quit taking it seriously. And yet other passages in Li's post-Tiananmen writing have him sounding a great deal more like the sunny "democratic socialists" who push Kant and the neo-Kantian Rawls, investing human beings with near-godlike capacities.[116] None of this should astonish, since Li had no choice but to study Marx in his early years, and, as a young academic, during his "sent down" stint in the countryside, he availed himself of the opportunity to write a major study of Kant, which gave him some of the language he needed to articulate many of his own ideas.[117] Once we circumvent the labels, not so much separates the well-read Marxist from the liberal democrat, it seems, aside from the latter's insistence on the individual's sovereign legal rights *against* the state, since both agree on the basic requirements and opportunities needed to ensure human dignity for all citizens in this one world.[118]

Still, it's a reminder of how pervasive modern academic silos are that many China watchers who self-identify as leftists, including the formidably learned David Ownby, were not well acquainted with Li's corpus before Li was forced upon their attention by events. Here is Ownby writing shortly after Li died: "I was struck by the fact that certain expressions, concepts, and turns of phrase that are widely used in the Chinese intellectual world, and that had heretofore struck me as simply idiosyncratic, were in fact Li Zehou's inventions, and thus stand as monuments to the impact he has had over several generations of Chinese thinkers."[119]

Nonetheless, for nearly the whole time I've been reading Li, by fits and turns, I confess to having felt sometimes a smidgeon of condescension for the "incoherence" of his positions. After embarking on this more focused study trying to integrate several of Li's writings, to bring to light more to the man, I readily admit that it is I who failed to understand. For it is abundantly clear that Li was always defying gravity by keeping any number of balls up in the air, the better to arrest our gaze. Consistency and coherence were likely very far down on his "to do" list.[120] Li was only consistent in his insistence on the richness and diversity of the human experience; he never stopped opposing the "homogenous, monotonous, and boring."[121]

I have been struck by Li's remark in an interview, "There is an old Chinese saying: 'There are no good people at a struggle session (批判会), and no bad people at a memorial service.'"[122] So rather than intoning the predictable encomiums, let us honor Li's restless inventiveness by being more open to the supreme artfulness of the rhetoric he wielded in his more outrageous formulas, as in his exquisite in-between positions, with due acknowledgments to Zhuangzi. Li demonstrated the sedimented layers of multiple Chinese traditions and, by implication, every other world tradition now threatened with ossification or obliteration by preening powerholders with their polished Newspeak.[123] He, like Marx, was in effect urging us to transcend our petty identity politics and self-important academic defenses, these being dangerous distractions from the more pressing human tasks at hand. That there may still be time to do this, East and West, is amazing enough.

As readers should know, a conference in Li's honor was to be held when Li was alive and doubtless plotting his next moves. The conference was much delayed because of the pandemic, and now Li is gone. I have often wondered where Li's priorities would have been traveling, were he alive today, given the spectacular acceleration in inequality in the PRC in recent years and the degree of environmental collapse there.[124] Li's adult life, as suggested earlier, was preoccupied, in one way or another, with two political questions: How much should the "dictatorship of the proletariat" be guided by a small vanguard group of intellectuals, and how rapidly should democratic tools be expanded to larger groups of students, workers, and farmers? Both questions, it need hardly be said, presumed that power should not be as concentrated in CCP hands as it was in 1989, let alone today.[125]

I am very grateful to have had the opportunity to put down on paper these preliminary thoughts. I am not sufficiently well-versed in Marx or in Li Zehou's entire body of writing, so I welcome comments and criticisms from those who got to know him better, particularly as I was left with more puzzles than ever when I sat down to write.

## Notes

1. I would here like to express my deep thanks to three fine scholars: Roy Chan (University of Oregon), Thomas Hahn (independent scholar, Berkeley), and Jana Rošker (University of Ljubljana). Each contributed constructive comments that allowed me to refine my thinking, for which I am very grateful. Needless to say, all mistakes are my own.

2. This reading is also to be found in China Miéville, who insists that Marx's various claims in *The Manifesto* are to be read as a "fervent recruitment drive . . . the opposite of that supposed certainty of a desire outcome." See China Miéville's *A Spectre, Haunting: On the "Communist Manifesto"* (Chicago: Haymarket Books, 2022), 104.

3. This essay presumes that serious students of Li Zehou will have reviewed such foundational works as Lin Min's "The Search for Modernity: Chinese Intellectual Discourse and Society, 1978–1988: The Case of Li Zehou," *China Quarterly* 132 (1992): 969–98.

4. Of course, in an irony of ironies, most places that adopted the Marxist-Leninist model were agrarian societies deemed "backward" at the time. As John Plamenatz, *Karl Marx's Philosophy of Man* (Oxford: Oxford University Press, 1973), 180–82, notes, no revolution has yet occurred in the way Marx predicted. Engels, looking back, said that he and Marx had wildly overestimated the chances for a proletarian revolution in the near future. For the distinction

between Marx's thought and Marxism, see Gareth Stedman Jones, *Karl Marx: Greatness and Illusion* (Cambridge, MA: Harvard University Press, 2016). Readers only learn that Marx's "end of history" (i.e., the end of the capitalist relations in society) will witness two triumphs: maximal self-realization for each individual and maximal expansion of the productive forces, with large surpluses required to fund the leisure activities allowed the much larger class of future workers, not just the members of the bourgeoisie.

5. Li Zehou, "Subjectivity and 'Subjectality': A Response," *Philosophy East and West* 49, no. 2 (1999): 174–83.

6. The profound contradictions that undergird today's liberal-democratic thinking have led many intellectuals, inside and outside the Party, to prefer a more robust and sustained political authoritarianism invoking paternalistic political values. See Ci Jiwei, *Democracy in China: The Coming Crisis* (Cambridge, MA: Harvard University Press, 2019). Only recently the CCP has claimed that China was historically "democratic," and the CCP was returning China to its original path. See "China: Democracy that Works," a propaganda paper generated by the State Council Information Office of the PRC on December 4, 2021, english.scio.gov.cn/whitepapers/2021-12/04/content_77908921.htm?bsh_bid=5657987748.

7. Our two sightings of Marx—Marx's own writings and Marx and Engels collaborations—must never be conflated with the curious amalgamations of nationalism and peasant revolution that have invoked Marx posthumously, in quite selective ways, under slogans espousing a hyphenated "Marxism-Leninism" or "Marxism-Leninism-Stalinism," in one-party dictatorships that took control leading "unfinished revolutions" in multiple countries, starting with the Soviet Union and proceeding to countries influenced by the Soviet model, including the People's Republic of China and North Korea under the Kims.

8. Note that other experts on early Marx who have been ignorant of Chinese traditions also have discerned in Marx this interest in a superior vision of humanity that could accommodate the finest of the local characteristics.

9. Pierre Billard, ed., *Masculine Feminine: A Film by Jean-Luc Godard* (New York: Grove Press, 1969), 270.

10. The title already spoofed Maoist slogans: "La Chinoise, ou plutôt à la Chinoise: un film en train de se faire" (The Chinese, or, rather, in the Chinese manner: a film in the making), which emphasized "becoming" (not "being") with special Chinese characteristics. The students, thinking themselves to be committed revolutionaries determined to bring on major social change, see radical politics as a fashionable distraction from the serious business of making a living.

11. *La Chinoise*.

12. Events had been heating up long before mid-May. For example, on February 26, an "open letter" emphasized the importance to modernization of democracy and science to national development, while expressing concerns "raised out of sincere patriotic feelings," which identified corruption, bureaucratic

speculation, and inflation as immediate concerns. That February 26 open letter, signed by Li, suggested concrete reforms: (1) political structural reform (i.e., political democratization), resulting in the rule of law and the reduction in corruption; (2) freedom of speech and freedom of press as basic to structural reform; and (3) release of political prisoners, including Wei Jingsheng. It warned that Party leaders after Mao had focused too much on short-term economic benefits, and had paid insufficient attention to the country's long-term future. On March 15, a second "Open Letter to the Party and Government from Thirty-three Famous Chinese Intellectuals" reiterated the content of the physicist Fang Lizhi's earlier letter, saying that both science and democracy were vital to China's future development. The March Letter was signed mainly by writers and artists (e.g., Bei Dao), and researchers or professors of philosophy (including Li Zehou).

13. Melvyn Bragg et al., "The May Fourth Movement," in *In Our Time*, produced by Simon Tillotson, radio series, December 9, 2021, BBC Radio 4, 53:00, www.bbc.co.uk/programmes/m001282c. *He shang* was not a "documentary," as it is usually billed. Perhaps the best account of the series appears in the *Bulletin of the Concerned Asian Scholars* (1991): 3–33, which features work by Mark Selden and Edward Gunn. Wang Jing (in the same issue, 23–32) gives us the backstory: the CCP, having let the documentary air on CCTV beginning on June 12, 1988, had grave doubts about its "cultural nihilism" within a month, and so it banned the series temporarily in July. Nonetheless, probably due to a personal intervention by Zhao Ziyang, the series was rebroadcast in mid-August, and re-banned by September.

14. Jin Guantao, an expert "advisor" to the script writers who also makes cameo appearances in *River Elegy*, exerted great influence on the film's writers, who came to accept his idea that while dynasties may come and go in China, their basic form remains the same and they always revert to their super-stable type. Trained as scientists (not as historians), Jin and Liu Qingfeng co-authored an essay entitled "Traditional Society in China: An Ultrastable Structure," *China Heritage* (1980). That website speaks of "China's resilient dynastic system—and its reconfiguration under the . . . hegemony of the Chinese Communist Party."

15. See also note 19.

16. For the first time since the Cold War began after World War II, China was on good terms with both the Soviet Union and with the US, and was not trying to play one superpower against the other. Gorbachev's visit was preceded by three months by the visit of President Bush.

17. The percentage of the urban population working in factories had grown, as had the scope of mechanized agriculture. That said, China accounted in 1989–1990 for only 2 percent of the world's total trade, and directed over 70 percent of her trade to the Asia-Pacific region (where the China trade accounted for only 5 percent of the total). For a hilarious reminder that foreign policy decisions typically reflect the realm of perceptions, see *The Americans* TV series,

wherein the protagonists (Russian spies embedded in a Washington, DC, suburb) struggle mightily to "make sense" of US politics, so that they can report back to their Kremlin masters.

18. How "democracy" was to be construed was never entirely clear. Chai Ling's behavior (recorded in an ABC interview) and two appearances by Wu'erkaixi (May 18 appearance on CCTV in his pajamas and his subsequent June 3 interview with FBIS), as one of two leaders of the outlawed Beijing Union of Intellectuals, suggest that some student leaders simply intended to replace the senior CCP officials with their own leadership. Liu Xiaobo on May 27, seven days after the imposition of martial law in Beijing, remarked that Wu'erkaixi already spoke just like some self-important bureaucrat, but Liu felt that swagger could prove useful, so long as Wu'erkaixi took the trouble to become a true leader, i.e., one who could benefit from his direction and advice.

19. I have looked for a copy in Chinese or English of the May 14, 1989, declaration by the twelve Beijing intellectuals, including Li Zehou. So far, no luck. A rough translation is found in *Beijing Spring, 1989: Confrontation and Conflict, The Basic Documents*, edited by Michel Oksenberg et al. (Armonk, NY: M. E. Sharpe, 1990).

20. As Gao Mobo wrote, "To their understanding, the Chinese May Fourth Movement that was meant to enlighten the Chinese was *hijacked* by nationalism/communism that was perceived as necessary to save China from oblivion. To their shock they 'discovered' that there was nothing revolutionary about the 1949 Revolution, that there was nothing modern about the CCP and that the system dictated by Mao was feudal . . . Li Zehou . . . developed the idea that there was tension between the narratives of Chinese nationalism and the Enlightenment and that the tragedy for China was that the Enlightenment had to give way to nationalism amid foreign invasion." Gao Mobo, *Constructing China: Clashing Views of the People's Republic* (London: Pluto Press, 2018), 87–88; italics added.

21. Cf. Plamenatz, *Karl Marx's Philosophy*, 20. Plamenatz presumed that Marxism as a creed was dying out, but I see a resurgence of interest (some definitely self-interested) in Marx in a wide range of writings in China insisting on socialism as the patriotic "roots" of contemporary Chinese. See, for example, Nicola Spakowski, "Gender Trouble: Feminism in China under the Impact of Western Theory and the Spatialization of Identity," in *Feminisms with Chinese Characteristics*, ed. Ping Zhu and Hui Faye Xiao (Syracuse: Syracuse University Press, 2021), 37–64.

22. Terrell Carver, "Reading Marx: Life and Works," in *Cambridge Companion to Marx*, ed. Terrell Carver (Cambridge: Cambridge University press, 1991), 10.

23. These are old slogans in classical Chinese, as my work on the *Documents* classic and *Xunzi* have shown me. Most of the people on the street took "democracy" to mean "anti-corruption," rather than electoral representation, though the latter goal was announced by some students, and advertised as

the goal when the Goddess of Liberty was erected at the Square. Yali Peng, "Democracy and Chinese Political Discourses," *Modern China* 24, no. 4 (1998): 433, describes *minben* as "to rule benevolently without necessarily asking the consent of the ruled."

24. *The German Ideology*, cited in Richard Miller, "Social and Political Theory: Class, State, Revolution," in *Cambridge Companion to Marx*, ed. Terrel Carver (Cambridge: Cambridge University Press, 19919), 56. Lorenz Lüthi, *The Sino-Soviet Split: Cold War in the Communist World* (Princeton: Princeton University Press, 2008), 8, defines ideology as "a set of beliefs and dogmas that both construct general outlines—rather than a detailed blueprint—of a future political order, and define specific methods—*though no explicit pathways*—to achieve it" (italics mine).

25. Miller, "Social and Political Theory," 62.

26. Guo Moruo was, of course, an exception as first President of the Chinese Academy of Sciences from 1949 until his death in 1978.

27. Reviewing old footage from Tiananmen, one cannot help but be struck by how articulate, well-read, and sophisticated, politically and culturally speaking, were the Beijing residents who worked in the city's many industries.

28. Of course, Mao himself was an intellectual, given his training and employment at university. But the CCP's need to assign blame led some to read Wang Ruoshui's 王若水 "Wei rendaozhuyi bianhu" 為人道主義辯護 (In Defense of Humanism), *Wenhuibao,* January 17, 1983, as the impetus for the train of events that led to Tiananmen. Wang was stripped of his post at the head of *People's Daily* during Deng's "anti–spiritual pollution" campaign in the summer of 1983, and the fall of his patron Zhou Yang followed. See Merle Goldman, "Citizens' Struggles in China's Post-Mao Era," *International Journal of China Studies* 3, no. 3 (2012): 271–83.

29. Gloria Davies, *Worrying about China: The Language of Chinese Critical Inquiry* (Cambridge, MA: Harvard University Press, 2009). This "worrying" has not diminished much in today's era when some hold that globalization threatens China's "unique" identity.

30. "New Culture" was usually enfolded into the May Fourth Movement of 1919, though it began earlier and ended later. Over time, Li Zehou would lavish praise on Lu Xun, to the puzzlement of some of his devotees.

31. Cf. the Confucius Institutes, begun in 2004, where the worst-run of the units (totaling roughly 530–550 in number, in 146 countries) reduce Chinese culture to food and calligraphy.

32. Also relevant was the CCP's own "resolution on Certain Questions in the History of Our Party (June 1981)," which pronounced Mao "70% correct and 30% wrong."

33. Daniel Southerland, "1,000 Students Begin Hunger Strike in Beijing's Main Square," *Washington Post,* May 14, 1989.

34. Both of these "black hands," as unrepentant supporters of the Tiananmen Square activities, were rounded up and sentenced to thirteen years of hard labor. Basically, these two became the "fall guys" accused of conspiracy against the state, as the CCP could hardly claim that it, a revolutionary party, had suppressed a popular revolt. Both men were quietly released in the spring of 1994 on the grounds of "medical parole," apparently in a deal to secure a trade treaty with the US. But Chen, who did not leave the country, remained on strict house arrest until 2002. In August 2005, a journal with which the two men's former Institute unit was associated was shut down less than two hours after it published the essay "A Strong Nation Cannot Eat Its Own Children."

35. The sentences for students were comparatively lenient.

36. Cf. Frederic E. Wakeman Jr., "The June Fourth Movement in China," *Items* 43, no. 3 (1989), issuu.com/ssrcitemsissues/docs/items_vol43_no3_1989. See also Oksenberg, Sullivan, and Lambert, *Beijing Spring*.

37. See Stephen Field, "*He shang* and the Plateau of Ultrastability," *Bulletin of Concerned Asian Scholars* 23 (1991): 4–13. For the Beijing Union, see Asia Watch, "Update on Arrests in China," *News from Asian Watch*, January 30, 1991, 12, www.hrw.org/reports/pdfs/c/china/china911.pdf.

38. For this summary of events derived from the state-sponsored PRC media accounts, see Robert F. Ash, "Quarterly Chronicle and Documentation (July–September 1990)," *China Quarterly* 124 (1990): 760–81. Right at the beginning of the meeting, Zhao supposedly said, "Comrade Deng Xiaoping's helmsmanship is still needed for the most important issues. Since the 13th National Party Congress, we have always reported to Comrade Deng Xiaoping and asked for his advice while dealing with the most important issues." He also said that this was "the first time" that this "decision" by the Party of China had been disclosed to the public.

39. Orville Schell, cited in Sanjib Baruah, "Considerations on Democratic Resurgence," *Economic and Political Weekly* 24, no. 49 (1989): 2726.

40. See Richard Gordon and Carma Hinton, producers, *The Gate of Heavenly Peace* (Boston: Long Bow Group, 1995), documentary, 180 min.

41. See, for example, the entire March 2016 issue of the *Journal of East Asian Studies*.

42. However, in the January 1994 issue of *Yuandao*, a chastened Wang Shuren joined Han Demin to discuss the "cultural nihilism" and the thoroughgoing anti-traditionalism that had characterized China since the May Fourth movement. See Li's co-authored "Wenhua de weiji, ronghe yu chongjian" 文化的危机, 融和与重建 (The Crisis of Culture, Reconciliation, and Reconstruction), *Yuandao* 1 (1994): 95–114; and Han Demin 韩德民, "Chuantong wenhua de weiji yu ershi shiji fanwenhua sichao" 传统文化的危机与二十世纪反文化思潮 (The Crisis of Traditional Culture and Twentieth-Century Anti-culture Trends), *Yuandao* 1 (1994): 311–40.

43. See David Kelly and Anthony Reid, "Weathering a Political Winter: The Chinese Academy of Social Sciences 1990," *Australian Journal of Chinese Affairs* 24 (1990): 347–55, esp. 352.

44. Marx himself wrote, after the suppression of the Paris Commune, that "in these circumstances . . . any attempt to upset the new [French] government . . . would be a desperate folly." See David McLellan, *Karl Marx: A Biography* (Basingstoke: Palgrave Macmillan, 2006), 365, for details.

45. Summary by Ben Xu, "Contesting Memory for Intellectual Self-Positioning: The 1990s' New Cultural Conservatism in China," *Modern Chinese Literature and Culture* 11, no. 1 (1999): 184, writing of Fang Keli, *The Developing Course of the Neo-Confucianism, the Preface of The Schools of the Modern Neo-Confucianism* (Beijing: Zhongguo shehui kexue chuban she, 1995), 62. Fang, a New Confucian philosopher and a member of the CCP, is best known for theories that attempt to fuse Marxism and Confucian theories. Fang has been quick to attack anyone who expressed different views of the role of Marxist or Confucian theories, including Jiang Qing. See Ming-huei Lee, "A Critique of Jiang Qing's 'Political Confucianism,'" in *Confucianism: Its Roots and Global Significance*, ed. David Jones (Honolulu: University of Hawai'i Press, 2017), 102–12.

46. Timothy Brook, "Review of Dingxin Zhao, *The Power of Tiananmen: State Society Relations and the 1989 Student Movement* (Chicago: University of Chicago Press, 2001)," *China Quarterly* 180 (2004): 1100–1.

47. Ben Xu is Professor of English, Saint Mary's College of California (Moraga).

48. Xu, "Contesting Memory," 166, 159. The bracketed material has been added by me, as I believe it is implied.

49. Early modern European intellectuals during the Enlightenment opposed absolute monarchy and fixed dogmas and thus expressed a "disenchantment" with the worlds they knew. Many Russian theorists sharply distinguished the "intelligentsia" (dissidents seeking substantial socioeconomic changes) from the "intellectuals" (proponents of great accommodation with the status quo). One may consider the growth of Orientalism and self-Orientalism from this lens.

50. The parallels with the Trump White House enablers should be obvious to Americans.

51. An astute comment is registered by Gao Mobo in *Constructing China*, 87: he notes that while individuals who belong to the Chinese political or intellectual elite may be unaware of their class interests, the elite group *as a collective* is aware, when it conceptualizes China and the world. Early in the post-Mao era, members of this group realized they were "backward," and they blamed their own backwardness on the semi-colonial status of China and the short-circuiting of the May Fourth reform proposals by the warlords and Japanese; May Fourth reformers and their disciples then turned to nationalism to "save China" from invasions. This did not prevent them from condemning those less fortunate than

them as unwashed slobs. That said, Gao's reasoning is occasionally flawed, in casting Noam Chomsky as a "dissident," instead of a highly prominent public intellectual who was allowed to speak and travel freely. (I know this because my mentor Henry Rosemont Jr. was Chomsky's lifelong friend.)

52. Zhang Yiwu, a leading postmodern-postcolonial theorist in China, positions new cultural conservatism as an audacious protest against many fallacies shared by Chinese intellectuals in the 1980s. He, like Ben Xu, equates "realistic" thinking with support of the status quo.

53. "Laozi never changed world history" is how one dismissive colleague at UC-Berkeley put it, to my utter astonishment, in a faculty meeting on curricular policy. On unthinking Eurocentrism, see Jack Goody, *The Theft of History* (Cambridge: Cambridge University Press, 2006).

54. Here one cannot but think of Carl Schmitt's odious but powerful theory of friend-enemy.

55. Benjamin Ho, "Understanding Chinese Exceptionalism: China's Rise, Its Goodness, and Greatness," *Alternatives: Local, Global, Political* 39, no. 3 (2014): 164–76. Originally, Chinese exceptionalism was billed as a way to provide Chinese policymakers maximum traction and legitimacy when China confronts the outside world; it has now become far more multi-purpose and pervasive. "Addiction to irreality" is the phrase used by James Baldwin in his 1965 debate with William F. Buckley at the Cambridge Union, to describe white Southerners, who felt the need to portray all "Negroes" as shiftless and undeserving of the vote.

56. For example, nearly everyone in China among Li's contemporaries was getting his ideas from Hegel, but Li Zehou got very few ideas from Hegel and many more from Kant. (That said, the problem of beauty is associated most closely with Hegel's phenomenology and his *Philosophy of the Right* (1821).) In another famous move, Li refused a gift from Jin Yong, the novelist, not wanting to be beholden to Jin, whose writings and generosity he admired, believing Jin Yong to be far more than a "martial arts novelist," as he was a fine historian as well. The phrase "in the world of men" comes from the title of a *Zhuangzi* chapter.

57. See notes 12 and 29 above. This was the principal reason that Li co-authored *Farewell to Revolution*.

58. This careful self-styling is on view in Li Zehou, "Interview with Li Zehou, *Southern People Weekly*, 'Li Zehou Thanks His Readers in His Final Interview,'" trans. David Ownby, *Reading the China Dream*, n.d., www.readingthechinadream.com/interview-with-li-zehou.html.

59. See note 20, above, for Gao Mobo's observation regarding the hijacking that was perceived as necessary to save China.

60. Li, "Interview," and Woei Lien Chong, "Combining Marx with Kant: The Philosophical Anthropology of Li Zehou," *Philosophy East and West* 49, no. 2 (1999): 120–49.

61. Li Zehou 李泽厚 and Wang Desheng 王德胜, "Guanyu wenhua xianzhuang, daode chongjian de duihua" 关于文化现状道德重建的对话 (Dialogue on the Current Cultural Situation and Moral Reconstruction), *Dongfang* 5 (1974): 69–73, esp. 70–71; 6 (1974): 85–87 (hereafter cited as "Dialogue").

62. "Dialogue."

63. In 1999, Li Zehou co-authored with Liu Zaifu a book entitled *Gaobie geming—ershi shiji Zhongguo duitan lu* 告別革命——二十世紀中國對談錄 (*Farewell to Revolution—A Critical Dialogue on Twentieth-Century China*) (Taibei: Maitan chuban, 1999), which argued that China's twentieth-century history of revolutions had brought few positive results and much bloodshed. An unscientific poll of several friends who lived through Tiananmen in China found them agreeing that Li had remained radical-left in his thinking after he left the PRC, despite being labelled a "cultural conservative."

64. Li denied, for example, that "obedience" to superiors was China's "destiny" or "fate." On the culture of obedience in the 1990s, see John Phillippe Béja, "The Rise of National-Confucianism," *China Perspectives* 2 (1995): 8.

65. See "Dialogue." Although Li Zehou tries to keep a distance from open defenders of neo-authoritarianism, he shares with them the same logic of sociopolitical development in China, says Xu, "Contesting Memory," 181n10.

66. Xi has skillfully eliminated many major rivals through targeted "anti-corruption" campaigns, campaigns that accomplish a second end as well, in co-opting the "corruption" theme advanced at Tiananmen for different ends.

67. Shen Tong, "Will China Be Democratic?" *Journal of World Affairs* 154, no. 4 (1992): 139–54.

68. Wang Hui argued that the Tiananmen events made the embrace of Reaganomics all the more fervent, for the CCP desperately sought to divert attention from political matters by deploying rampant consumer capitalism. Readers should recall that Ci shows similarly painful contradictions within US society.

69. The phrase "nasty and brutish" comes from Hobbes.

70. Peng, "Democracy," esp. 433.

71. See above, for Peng Yali's definition of *minben* as benevolent rule, without the consult of those ruled.

72. Karl Marx, *Karl Marx: Early Writings*, trans. and ed. T. B. Bottomore (New York: McGraw-Hill, 1964), 203.

73. A good example of this insight: A worker works all day long with her time clocked on a piece of machinery invented and produced by others before her.

74. Here I follow Plamenatz, *Karl Marx's Philosophy*, 118–19.

75. Joseph Cropsey, "Karl Marx," in *History of Political Philosophy*, ed. Leo Strauss, and Joseph Cropsey (Chicago: University of Chicago, 1987), 807: "Civil society represented for Marx an individualistic enclave in society, a realm of privacy" secured by bourgeois exploitation; thus civil society is "given its essential

character by the self-assertiveness of men, one against the other, in the name of their inalienable, irreducible rights."

76. Carl Schmitt, *Constitutional Theory*, trans. and ed. Jeffrey Seitzer (Durham, NC: Duke University Press, 2008), continues in §17-1: "As to the word 'freedom' one has to say that freedom in the sense of an individual freedom which is owed by nature to each particular human being is a liberal principle." "The conflict that cannot be overcome is that between the consciousness of the liberal individual and democratic homogeneity." See Carl Schmitt, *The Crisis of Parliamentary Democracy*, trans. Ellen Kennedy (Cambridge, MA: MIT Press, 1988), 8, 17.

77. See Jack Goody in note 93, below.

78. Wittgenstein's idea, in *Philosophical Investigations*, trans. G. E. Anscombe (New York: Macmillan, 1953), 309, was "a picture held us captive."

79. As Paul D'Ambrosio has noted in his paper, even when Li was writing ostensibly about a Western thinker (e.g., Kant), he was using Kant as a prompt or provocation to elaborate his own ideas.

80. Here I think of the so-called "Asian Values" discourse, which tells citizens that one-party rule and dictatorship constitute the inalterable destiny of the "Asian Way." To be fair, the CCP invented remarkably few of these invented traditions; most appeared first in Republican-era textbooks by Liang Qichao, Qian Mu, or others (i.e., in the very textbooks that the early CCP leaders had been trained in).

81. Hans Sluga, "Hannah Arendt as a Diagnostic Political Thinker," *On Philosophy* (blog), August 30, 2022, www.truthandpower.com/blog/?p=1642. As Sluga's blog notes, Arendt avoided talk of "human nature," as that catchphrase was usually taken to identify "a determinate human essence from which we can deduce both how humans act and how they should act. For Arendt, there is, in fact, no human nature, in this precise sense. There are only the varied conditions in which we find ourselves."

82. Li's concept of "sedimentation" (*jidian* 積澱) is very rich, and not unlike the historian's emphasis on "path dependence" in history. At the same time, one wonders about the degree to which most contemporary Chinese are actually steeped in the specifics of Chinese tradition, given the many ruptures that have occurred over the past century (e.g., the occupation of territory by the Japanese, the adoption of pinyin, the swing to neoliberal Reaganomics).

83. Edward Slingerland, "Virtue Ethics, the *Analects*, and the Problem of Commensurability," *Journal of Religious Ethics* 29, no. 1 (2001): 118. Three years' mourning makes a poor "proof" for Slingerland's claim, since this is hardly a universal custom to honor their dead.

84. In this, he reminds me of several feminist philosophers, including Simone Weil and Elizabeth Anscombe.

85. Robert Cummings Neville seems relevant, for he describes the importance of "orienting" the body when performing certain deeds in ritualized settings; see Robert Cummings Neville, "Orientation, Self, and Ecological Posture," in *Confucianism and Ecology: The Interrelation of Heaven, Earth, Human*, ed. Mary Evelyn Tucker and John Berthrong (Cambridge, MA: Harvard University Press, 1988), 265–73.

86. "One world" refers to Li's insistence that there is no reality "out there" for us to strive to model; this is the world of which we are part and to which we respond.

87. Li Zehou, "A Response to Michael Sandel and Other Matters," trans. Paul J. D'Ambrosio and Robert A. Carleo III, *Philosophy East and West* 66, no. 4 (2016): 1082. Like all of Li's neologisms, this one has troubled many a translator. I do my best here, and prefer this to Li's own rendering of the phrase as either "emotion-as-substance" or "substance, root, body, final reality." By adding "situation" I seek to capture Li's emphasis on the interplay between *jing* 經 and *quan* 權, the constants and the contingencies, elaborated early on in the Classics and masterworks. Li and his translators often disagreed about the messages that would or would not be sent to Chinese vs. Western readers, with some of these disagreements on view in Li Zehou and Jane Cauvel, *Four Essays on Aesthetics: Toward a Global View* (Lanham, MD: Lexington Books, 2006). Certainly, humanity has the capacity to expand the Dao (or is it *dao*?), by *Analects* 15/29.

88. In rereading several interviews with Li, I was struck how much he admits this form of belief is his own version of a religious faith (e.g., in Li and Cauvel, *Four Essays on Aesthetics*, 180). That there are no certainties, only potentials for pleasure, is a classical belief, to be found in the *Analects* and *Fayan* 法言, and elsewhere. Again and again, Li returned to the idea that we must come to trust the "dynamic, constantly shifting relationships" between emotion and reason to shape our individual and collective endeavors, as a good swimmer works with the currents.

89. Cf. Richard Sennett's trilogy devoted to *homo faber*, particularly his *Together: The Rituals, Pleasures, and Politics of Cooperation* (Harmondsworth: Penguin, 2012).

90. See *Civilization and its Discontents*, for example. Freud thought he knew this story (much of it now discredited): The oldest Rome was the Roma Quadrata, a fenced settlement on the Palatine; next came the Septimontium phase, a federation of the settlements on the different hills; next, the city bounded by the Servian wall; and later still, the city that the Emperor Aurelian surrounded with his walls, which bore witness to all the transformations during the periods of the republic and the early Caesars. See the *The Hellenistic Monarchies and the Rise of Rome*, edited by S. A. Cook, F. E. Adcock, and M. P Charlesworth, vol. 7 in *Cambridge Ancient History* (Cambridge: Cambridge University Press, 1928), 7.

91. For this reason, I am unconvinced by part of his friend Liu Zaifu's account of "Li Zehou's Aesthetics: Moving On after Kant, Marx, and Confucianism," in *Li Zehou and Confucian Philosophy*, ed. Roger T. Ames and Jinhua Jia (Honolulu: University of Hawai'i Press, 2018), as Liu seems to merge his own self with that of Li Zehou in dubious ways.

92. I have never been sure China is "Confucian China" but I am certain that thinking about the questions raised by Confucius, among others, never stopped.

93. To my mind, Li Zehou's sense of China recalls Sima Qian's sense of China, as both approach the "spiritual" or "sacred" character of the human. See Michael Nylan, "Sima Qian: A True Historian?" *Early China* 24 (2000): 1–44.

94. Liu, "Li Zehou's Aesthetics," 255, citing Li on Nietzsche.

95. Ludwig Feuerbach, *The Essence of Christianity*, trans. Marian Evans (London: Kegan Paul, 1893), 32.

96. Here Li in his pragmatism could not differ more from the anthropologist Jack Goody, *Theft of History*, who tried to counter every clever move made in the shell game arranged by Euro-Americans, to no avail, so far as I can see. The official summary of the book begins this way: "The 'theft of history' . . . refers to the take-over of history by the west. That is, the past is conceptualized and presented according to what happened on the provincial scale of Europe, often western Europe, and then imposed upon the rest of the world."

97. There is some indication that Xi Jinping wants to follow Mao in "guiding" the scientific and technology sectors through administrative command; much remains to be seen, however. See Li Yuan, writing in *The New York Times*, August 28, 2022, "Xi Jinping's Vision for Tech Self-Reliance in China Runs into Reality": "Since 2019, the phrase 'new whole nation system' has also started appearing in Mr. Xi's speeches and party documents in the context of conquering key tech challenges."

98. Marx and Li emphasized tools a great deal more than rationality: Marx says, in *The Poverty of Philosophy* (Marx/Engels Internet Archive, 1999), www.marxists.org/archive/marx/works/1847/poverty-philosophy/, that "The hand-mill gives you society with the feudal lord; the steam-mill, society with the industrial capitalist." The manmade environment is the expression of the society, and its institutions demonstrate that people are capable of independence and intelligence.

99. This is reported in Li, "Interview."

100. The lesson of the Paris Commune that Marx ingested was summarized in a statement that he and Engels wrote: "The working class cannot simply lay hold of the ready-made State machinery, and wield it for its own purposes." See Monty Johnstone, "The Paris Commune and Marx's Conception of the Dictatorship of the Proletariat," *Massachusetts Review* 12, no. 3 (1971): 447–62. This is an assertion found in the preface in *Arkhiv Marksa i Engelsa* (Moscow, 1934), vol. 3 (8). Cf. the Preface to the 1872 German edition of "Manifesto of the

Communist Party," in Karl Marx and Friedrich Engels, *Karl Marx and Friedrich Engels: Selected Works* (London: Lawrence and Wishart, 1950), vol. 1, 22. Lenin took this statement to mean that "Marx's idea is that the working class must break up, smash the 'readymade state machinery,' and not confine itself merely to laying hold of it." But this is hardly the only plausible reconstruction of the statement; others invite a reimagining of a future world in which power relations will be redefined, thanks to the help of the vanguard.

101. Rong Jian is one example.

102. Incidentally, this model didn't work so well when it tried to introduce Confucian learning as a religion in Singapore. See Béja, "Rise of National-Confucianism."

103. Michael Nylan, "Li Zehou, the Voracious Pupil and Radical Conservative," in *Philosopher Li Zehou—Proceedings from the Online Conference in Memory of Li Zehou Held on November 2, 2022, the First Anniversary of his Passing*, ed. Maja Maria Kosec (Ljubljana: Znanstvena založba Filozofske fakultete, 2022), 202.

104. Nylan "Li Zehou, the Voracious Pupil," 202.

105. His treatment of Chinese classical thought keeps taking thinkers out of their assigned boxes and showing them off for our delectation.

106. As Ben Xu did in an intemperate essay, written from the safety of the United States. See Xu's "Contesting Memory."

107. Lin Tongqi and Li Minghua, "Subjectivity: Marxism and 'The Spiritual' in China Since Mao," *Philosophy East and West* 44, no. 4 (1994): 609–46, esp. 633, for example, read an awful lot into Li's enthusiasm for Lu Xun, while tying this to Heidegger. I call this overreading. No older citizen of the PRC cannot sometimes be thinking of Lu Xun. More relevant, perhaps: Li never discounted the possibility that a non-Chinese person might come to appreciate *some* of the insights offered by Chinese tradition, but equally he never assumed that all aspects of Chinese tradition would resonate equally well with those whose "sedimented selves" had not been schooled by a "sedimented culture" that stressed emotion, harmony, and aesthetics to the same degree or in the same way as the Chinese of whom he wrote.

108. Lin Min, "Search for Modernity," 974.

109. See Ralph E. Matlaw, ed. *Belinsky, Chernyshevsky and Dubrolyubov: Selected Criticism* (New York: E. P. Dutton, 1962). I do not read Russian, but those who do praise the quality of these translations and Matlaw's editorial comments. In Chinese, a total of two essays exist in Chinese on the three critics: Zhuang Kuicheng 庄桂成, "Bie, Che, Du yu Zhongguo 20 shiji wenlun," "别、车、杜与中国20世纪文论 (Belinsky, Chernyshevsky, and Dubrolyubov and Twentieth-Century Chinese Literature), *Tansuo yu zhengming* 探索与争鸣 2 (2011): 133–36; Dai Xun 代讯 and Chen Yi 陈谊, "Bielinsiji de Zhongguo miankong" 别林斯基的中国面孔 (The Face in China of Belinsky), *Beijing Shifan daxue xuebao (Shehui kexue ban)* 北京师范大学学报 (社会科学版) 274 (December 2019): 55–68. On the Russian scientists' influence on the PRC during Li's formative years, see

Thomas H. Hahn, "'Ecological Civilization' and 'Beautiful China,'" (lecture, University of California, Berkeley, History Department, November 17, 2022) (copies upon request from th.hahn@gmail.com).

110. Unlike the utopians, they refused to indulge themselves with ideas of withdrawals from society and, unlike the anarchists, they refused to believe that state power in any era, past, present, or future, must always be centralized, monopolistic, and coercive, and hence illegitimate. Bakunin's 1873 statement exemplifies the political anarchist's position: "If there is a State, there must be domination of one class by another and, as a result, slavery; the State without slavery is unthinkable—and this is why we are the enemies of the State." See Mikhail Bakunin, *Statism and Anarchy*, trans. and ed. Sam Dolgoff (Mikhail Bakunin Reference Archive, 1971 [1973]), www.marxists.org/reference/archive/bakunin/works/1873/statism-anarchy.htm.

111. See Matlaw, *Belinsky, Chernyshevsky and Dubrolyubov*, xi.

112. See György Lukács, *Studies in European Realism* (New York: Howard Fertig, 1950), 105 (On "Russian Democratic Literary Criticism").

113. See Matlaw, *Belinsky, Chernyshevsky and Dubrolyubov*, xvi.

114. Lukács notes that all three Russians had to be wily writers, intent upon using their theoretical statements to persuade members of the liberal bourgeoisie to think more critically about the powers-that-be. Consistency was never their main goal; to persuade people in shifting circumstances was the goal. (Political realists such as Stuart Hampshire, Raymond Geuss, and Hans Sluga would agree that diagnosis followed by prescription is the only way to effect real change in a real world.)

115. Nearly every group highlights the "stabilizing role" their policy proposals will have on Chinese society as a whole. Needless to say, not all these contradictory claims can be true.

116. For example, in Li and Cauvel, *Four Essays*, Li calls humanity "divine."

117. Andreas Møller Mulvad, "China's Ideological Spectrum: A Two-Dimensional Model of Elite Intellectuals' Visions," *Theory and Society* 47, no. 5 (2018): 635–61, outlines four positions, one of which (the "stalwart statist" from the "commanding heights") would plainly not be favored by Li Zehou, in 1989 or afterwards.

118. The key dispute is about how Marxist "parties and groups claiming to speak for the proletariat" should behave in practice.

119. Li, "Interview."

120. He repeatedly said as much in his several interviews.

121. Li, "Interview."

122. Li, "Interview."

123. Geremie R. Barmé, "New China Newspeak 新华文体," *China Heritage*, n.d. [2012], chinaheritage.net/archive/academician-archive/geremie-barme/grb-essays/china-story/new-china-newspeak-%E6%96%B0%E5%8D%8E%E6%96%87%E4%BD%93/.

124. On this, see Richard Smith, "*Guanxi* and the Game of Thrones: Wealth, Property, and Insecurity in a Lawless System," in *China's Engine of Environmental Collapse* (London: Pluto Press, 2020), 126–53.

125. Recall that the educational levels among factory workers and students were far closer in 1989 than today, given the vagaries of the Cultural Revolution policies on education (basic and advanced).

# Bibliography

Ash, Robert F. "Quarterly Chronicle and Documentation (July–September 1990)." *China Quarterly* 124 (December 1990): 760–81.

Asia Watch. "Update on Arrests in China." *News from Asia Watch*, January 30, 1991. www.hrw.org/reports/pdfs/c/china/china911.pdf.

Bakunin, Mikhail. *Statism and Anarchy*. Translated end edited by Sam Dolgoff (Mikhail Bakunin Reference Archive, 1971 [1973]). www.marxists.org/reference/archive/bakunin/works/1873/statism-anarchy.htm.

Barmé, Geremie R. "New China Newspeak 新华文体." *China Heritage*, n.d. [2012], chinaheritage.net/archive/academician-archive/geremie-barme/grb-essays/china-story/new-china-newspeak-%E6%96%B0%E5%8D%8E%E6%96%87%E4%BD%93/.

Baruah, Sanjib. "Considerations on Democratic Resurgence." *Economic and Political Weekly* 24, no. 49 (1989): 2725–27.

Béja, John Phillippe. "The Rise of National-Confucianism." *China Perspectives* 2 (1995): 6–11.

Billard, Pierre, ed. *Masculine Feminine: A Film by Jean-Luc Godard*. New York: Grove Press, 1969.

Bragg, Melvyn, Rana Mitter, Elisabeth Forster, and Song-Chuan Chen. "The May Fourth Movement." Produced by Simon Tillotson. *In Our Time*, BBC Radio 4, December 9, 2021. Radio series, 53:00. www.bbc.co.uk/programmes/m001282c.

Brook, Timothy. "Review of Dingxin Zhao, *The Power of Tiananmen: State Society Relations and the 1989 Student Movement* (Chicago: University of Chicago Press, 2001)." *China Quarterly* 180 (2004): 1100–1.

Carver, Terrell. "Reading Marx: Life and Works." In *Cambridge Companion to Marx*, edited by Terrell Carver, 1–22. Cambridge: Cambridge University Press, 1991.

Chong, Woei Lien. "Combining Marx with Kant: The Philosophical Anthropology of Li Zehou." *Philosophy East and West* 49, no. 2 (1999): 120–49.

Ci, Jiwei. *Democracy in China: The Coming Crisis*. Cambridge, MA: Harvard University Press, 2019.

Confucius. *Analects*. Cited according to the standard paragraphs and verses, as per Ruan Yuan, 阮元, Shisan jing zhushu, fu jiaokanji 十三經注疏附校勘記 (preface 1815); reprint, Beijing: Zhonghua shuju, 1980.
Cook, S. A., F. E. Adcock, and M. P. Charlesworth, eds. *Cambridge Ancient History*, vol. 7, *The Hellenistic Monarchies and the Rise of Rome*. Cambridge: Cambridge University Press, 1928.
Cropsey, Joseph. "Karl Marx." In *History of Political Philosophy*, edited by Leo Strauss and Joseph Cropsey, 802–28. Chicago: University of Chicago Press, 1987 [1963].
Cummings Neville, Robert. "Orientation, Self, and Ecological Posture." In *Confucianism and Ecology: The Interrelation of Heaven, Earth, Human*, ed. Mary Evelyn Tucker and John Berthrong, 265–73. Cambridge, MA: Harvard University Press, 1988.
Dai Xun 代讯 and Chen Yi 陈谊. "Bielinsiji de Zhongguo miankong" 别林斯基的中国面孔 (The Face in China of Belinsky). *Beijing Shifan daxue xuebao (Shehui kexue ban)* 北京师范大学学报 (社会科学版) 274 (2019): 55–68.
Davies, Gloria. *Worrying about China: The Language of Chinese Critical Inquiry*. Cambridge, MA: Harvard University Press, 2009.
Fang Keli. *The Developing Course of the Neo-Confucianism, the Preface of the Schools of the Modern Neo-Confucianism*. Beijing: Zhongguo shehui kexue chuban she, 1995.
Feuerbach, Ludwig. *The Essence of Christianity*. Translated from the 2nd edition by Marian Evans. London: Kegan Paul, 1893.
Field, Stephen. "*He shang* and the Plateau of Ultrastability." *Bulletin of Concerned Asian Scholars* 23 (1991): 4–13.
Gao, Mobo. *Constructing China: Clashing Views of the People's Republic*. London: Pluto Press, 2018.
Geuss, Raymond. *History and Illusion in Politics*. Cambridge: Cambridge University Press, 2001.
Goldman, Merle. "Citizens' Struggles in China's Post-Mao Era." *International Journal of China Studies* 3, no. 3 (2012): 271–83.
Goody, Jack. *The Theft of History*. Cambridge: Cambridge University Press, 2006.
Gordon, Richard, and Carma Hinton, producers. *The Gate of Heavenly Peace*. Documentary, 180 minutes. Boston: Long Bow Group, 1995.
Gunn, Edward. "The Rhetoric of *He Shang*: From Cultural Criticism to Social Act." *Bulletin of Concerned Asian Scholars* 23 (1991): 14–22.
Hahn, Thomas H. "'Ecological Civilization' and 'Beautiful China.'" Lecture given at University of California, Berkeley, History Department, November 17, 2022.
Han, Demin 韩德民. "Chuantong wenhua de weiji yu ershi shiji fanwenhua sichao" 传统文化的危机与二十世纪反文化思潮 (The Crisis of Traditional Culture and Twentieth-century Anti-culture Trends). *Yuandao* 原道 1 (1994): 311–40.

Ho, Benjamin. "Understanding Chinese Exceptionalism: China's Rise, Its Goodness, and Greatness." *Alternatives: Local, Global, Political* 39, no. 3 (2014): 164–76.

Jin Guantao, and Liu Qingfeng. "Traditional Society in China: An Ultrastable Structure." *China Heritage* (1980).

Johnstone, Monty. "The Paris Commune and Marx's Conception of the Dictatorship of the Proletariat." *Massachusetts Review* 12, no. 3 (1971): 447–62.

Kelly, David, and Anthony Reid. "Weathering a Political Winter: The Chinese Academy of Social Sciences 1990." *Australian Journal of Chinese Affairs* 24 (July 1990): 347–55.

Lee, Ming-huei. "A Critique of Jiang Qing's 'Political Confucianism.'" In *Confucianism: Its Roots and Global Significance*, edited by David Jones, 102–12. Honolulu: University of Hawai'i Press, 2017.

Li Yuan. "Xi Jinping's Vision for Tech Self-Reliance in China Runs into Reality." *New York Times*, August 28, 2022.

Li Zehou. "Interview with Li Zehou, *Southern People Weekly*, 'Li Zehou Thanks His Readers in His Final Interview.'" *Reading the China Dream*, n.d. Introduction and translation by David Ownby. www.readingthechinadream.com/interview-with-li-zehou.html.

Li Zehou. "A Response to Michael Sandel and Other Matters." Translated by Paul J. D'Ambrosio and Robert A. Carleo III. *Philosophy East and West* 66, no. 4 (2016): 1068–1147.

Li Zehou. "Subjectivity and 'Subjectality': A Response." *Philosophy East and West* 49, no. 2 (1999): 174–83.

Li Zehou and Jane Cauvel. *Four Essays on Aesthetics: Toward a Global View*. Lanham, MD: Lexington Books, 2006.

Li Zehou 李澤厚 and Liu Zaifu 劉再復. *Gaobie geming—ershi shiji Zhongguo duitan lu* 告別革命—二十世紀中國對談錄 (*Farewell to Revolution—A Critical Dialogue on Twentieth-Century China*). Taibei: Maitan chuban, 1999.

Li Zehou 李泽厚 and Wang Desheng 王德胜. "Guanyu wenhua xianzhuang, daode chongjian de duihua" 关于文化现状道德重建的对话 (Dialogue on the Current Cultural Situation and Moral Reconstruction). *Dongfang* 东方 5 (1974): 69–73; 6 (1974): 85–87.

Li Zehou 李澤厚 and Wang Shuren 王树人. "Wenhua de weiji, ronghe yu chongjian" 文化的危机, 融和与重建 (The Crisis of Culture, Reconciliation, and Reconstruction). *Yuandao* 原道 1 (1994): 95–114.

Lin Min. "The Search for Modernity: Chinese Intellectual Discourse and Society, 1978–1988: The Case of Li Zehou." *China Quarterly* 132 (December 1992): 969–98.

Lin Tongqi, and Li Minghua. "Subjectivity: Marxism and 'The Spiritual' in China Since Mao." *Philosophy East and West* 44, no. 4 (1994): 609–46.

Liu Zaifu. "Li Zehou's Aesthetics: Moving On after Kant, Marx, and Confucianism." In *Li Zehou and Confucian Philosophy*, edited by Roger T. Ames and Jinhua Jia, 255–77. Honolulu: University of Hawai'i Press, 2018.

Lukács, György. *Studies in European Realism*. New York: Howard Fertig, 1950.

Lüthi, Lorenz. *The Sino-Soviet Split: Cold War in the Communist World*. Princeton, NJ: Princeton University Press, 2008.

Marx, Karl. *Karl Marx: Early Writings*. Translated and edited by T. B. Bottomore. New York: McGraw-Hill, 1964.

Marx, Karl. *Poverty of Philosophy*. Marx/Engels Internet Archive, 1999. www.marxists.org/archive/marx/works/1847/poverty-philosophy/.

Marx, Karl, and Friedrich Engels. *Karl Marx and Friedrich Engels: Selected Works*. 2 vols. London: Lawrence and Wishart, 1950.

Matlaw, Ralph E., ed. *Belinsky, Chernyshevsky and Dubrolyubov: Selected Criticism*. New York: E. P. Dutton, 1962.

McLellan, David. *Karl Marx: A Biography*. Basingstoke: Palgrave Macmillan, 2006.

Miévelle, China. *A Spectre, Haunting: On the "Communist Manifesto."* Chicago: Haymarket Books, 2022.

Miller, Richard W. "Social and Political Theory: Class, State, Revolution." In *Cambridge Companion to Marx*, edited by Terrel Carver, 55–105. Cambridge: Cambridge University Press, 1991.

Mulvad, Andreas Møller. "China's Ideological Spectrum: A Two-Dimensional Model of Elite Intellectuals' Visions." *Theory and Society* 47, no. 5 (2018): 635–61.

Nylan, Michael. "Li Zehou, the Voracious Pupil and Radical Conservative." In *Philosopher Li Zehou—Proceedings from the Online Conference in Memory of Li Zehou Held on November 2, 2022, the First Anniversary of his Passing*, ed. Maja Maria Kosec, 136–206. Ljubljana: Znanstvena založba Filozofske fakultete, 2022. as.ff.uni-lj.si/sites/default/files/documents/proceedings%20JRMK%204.pdf.Nylan, Michael. "Sima Qian: A True Historian?" *Early China* 24 (2000): 1–44.

Oksenberg, Michel, Lawrence R. Sullivan, and Marc Lambert, eds. *Beijing Spring, 1989: Confrontation and Conflict, The Basic Documents*. Introduction by Melanie Manion. Armonk, NY: M. E. Sharpe, 1990.

Peng, Yali. "Democracy and Chinese Political Discourses." *Modern China* 24, no. 4 (1998): 408–44.

Plamenatz, John. *Karl Marx's Philosophy of Man*. Oxford: Oxford University Press, 1973.

Schmitt, Carl. *Constitutional Theory*. Translated and edited by Jeffrey Seitzer. Durham, NC: Duke University Press, 2008.

Schmitt, Carl. *The Crisis of Parliamentary Democracy*. Translated by Ellen Kennedy. Cambridge, MA: MIT Press, 1988.

Selden, Mark. "Introduction." *Bulletin of Concerned Asian Scholars* 23 (1991): 3–5.
Sennett, Richard. *Together: The Rituals, Pleasures, and Politics of Cooperation.* Harmondsworth: Penguin, 2012.
Shen, Tong. "Will China Be Democratic?" *Journal of World Affairs* 154, no. 4 (1992): 139–54.
Slingerland, Edward. "Virtue Ethics, the *Analects*, and the Problem of Commensurability." *Journal of Religious Ethics* 29, no. 1 (2001): 97–125.
Sluga, Hans. "Hannah Arendt as a Diagnostic Political Thinker." *On Philosophy* (blog). August 30, 2022. www.truthandpower.com/blog/?p=1642.
Smith, Richard. "*Guanxi* and the Game of Thrones: Wealth, Property, and Insecurity in a Lawless System." In *China's Engine of Environmental Collapse*, 126–53. London: Pluto Press, 2020.
Southerland, Daniel. "1,000 Students Begin Hunger Strike in Beijing's Main Square." *The Washington Post*, May 14.
Spakowski, Nicola. "Gender Trouble: Feminism in China under the Impact of Western Theory and the Spatialization of Identity." In *Feminisms with Chinese Characteristics*, edited by Ping Zhu, and Hui Faye Xiao, 37–64. Syracuse, NY: Syracuse University Press, 2021.Stedman Jones, Gareth. *Karl Marx: Greatness and Illusion.* Cambridge, MA: Harvard University Press, 2016.
The State Council Information Office, the People's Republic of China. "China: Democracy that Works." White paper. December 4, 2021. english.scio.gov.cn/whitepapers/2021-12/04/content_77908921.htm?bsh_bid=5657987748.
Wakeman, Frederic E. Jr. "The June Fourth Movement in China." *Items* 43, no. 3 (1989). issuu.com/ssrcitemsissues/docs/items_vol43_no3_1989.
Wang Jing. "*He shang* and the Paradoxes of Chinese Enlightenment." *Bulletin of Concerned Asian Scholars* 23 (1991): 23–32.
Wang Ruoshui 王若水. "Wei rendaozhuyi bianhu" 為人道主義辯護 (In Defense of Humanism). *Wenhuibao*, January 17, 1983, 3. A partial translation appears in *Inside China Mainland*, June 1983, Supplement 7–8.
Wittgenstein, Ludwig. *Philosophical Investigations.* Translated by G. E. Anscombe. New York: Macmillan, 1953.
Xu, Ben. "Contesting Memory for Intellectual Self-Positioning: The 1990s' New Cultural Conservatism in China." *Modern Chinese Literature and Culture* 11, no. 1 (1999): 157–92.
Zhuang Kuicheng 庄桂成. "Bie, Che, Du yu Zhongguo 20 shiji wenlun" 别、车、杜与中国 20 世纪文论 (Belinsky, Chernyshevsky, and Dubrolyubov and Twentieth-Century Chinese Literature). *Tansuo yu zhengming* 探索与争鸣 2 (2011): 133–36.

2

# Li Zehou in the Tradition of Masters and Commentators

Paul J. D'Ambrosio

Li Zehou can be extremely frustrating. In translating his works or writing on his thought, one encounters a host of difficulties with both the style and content. Li's analysis of Western philosophy, from the Greeks through Kant, Nietzsche, Heidegger, and up to Sandel, is often puzzling, misleading, or just plain inaccurate. Explanations of Chinese thought, including his detailed work on the *Lunyu*, are often unapologetically subjective and one-sided. From the perspective of contemporary Western philosophical discourse, these difficulties are highly problematic. We might even go so far as to say that Li is hardly a decent scholar, much less a "philosopher."

However, in the context of his own philosophical tradition, Li Zehou comes off much differently. In this paper I will locate Li Zehou in that tradition, one that can be understood, at least in part, as revolving around a philosophy of masters and commentators. Viewed in this intellectual tradition, we can gain a fuller appreciation of Li's work. As a sometimes master and sometimes commentator himself, Li Zehou is—as he is coming to be increasingly recognized—a phenomenal thinker with theories both broad and deep. Like a commentator, Li unabashedly presents particular readings that can elucidate difficult passages, but these are always in service of the development of his own philosophical theories.

Like a master, Li does not provide narrow responses to narrow problems or strictly logical arguments, and he sometimes does not provide arguments at all—his ideas function best when they are taken as starting points for further discussion, and as outlines for responding to various issues.

In this way, he is not just an outstanding representative of a "masters and commentators" tradition, but also a philosopher in a truer, more old-fashioned sense. Today "philosophy" often connotes "academic philosophy." For those outside of the discipline, and especially those outside of academia, this study lives largely in an ivory tower. For all the celebrations of "philosophy as a way of life," the common criticism of philosophy as being confined to this tower is, for the most part, accurate. Academic books on philosophy are read by and written for academics; academic conferences are attended by academics. This is in contrast to the texts by philosophical masters, both Chinese and Western, that today's philosophers study. Plato, Nietzsche, Confucius, and Zhuangzi were not writing for a small field of two dozen academics, and it is because they did not that their works had such power.

The most inspiring works in philosophy reflect on the world writ large, making the familiar strange and broadening our understanding of the world. By contrast, academic treatments of such works tend to do the opposite, examining a small number of minute details so as to shrink and familiarize the object of study.

In this connection, Li Zehou appears more as a philosopher of old than a scholar of today. He has a number of academic "bad habits" that I will discuss, including taking liberties with style, misreading and misquoting his interlocutors, and offering questionable translations of terms, but contextualized in the greater Chinese tradition and alongside the magnetism of his ideas, these idiosyncrasies end up placing him closer to the philosophers he works with than the contemporary scholars he might be compared to. In this article I will celebrate Li Zehou for being a first-rate philosopher while also, or perhaps because of this, a less-than-impressive academic.

## Philosophical Interests and Style

Li Zehou first gained wide recognition in China for his works on aesthetics. According to Li, aesthetics are foundational to Chinese culture. Even separating aesthetics from other subjects, such as ethics or politics, is somewhat inaccurate when trying to fully comprehend the Middle Kingdom. Yet, a few years later, as he slowly became more exposed to and interested in Western academia, the titles of Li's works begin to include "ethics," and he increasingly shifted his focus to questions of morals and ethics.

Karl-Heinz Pohl, a friend and translator of Li Zehou, has suggested that the move toward ethics might have been due to Li's realization that aesthetics is not broadly interesting to Western academic audiences. Whereas in China a large number of scholars were intrigued by Li's work on Chinese aesthetics, the same could not be said in the West. Li thereby began to research ethics and morality to appeal to Westerners.[1] However, Pohl agrees with Robert Carleo and others that, rather than a "pivot," we might understand this as a shifting of emphasis—for Li, aesthetics and ethics have never been anything but fully intermingled.[2] So while the titles of his works and many of the theories he deals with were progressively related to "ethics," this is perhaps an organic development from his earlier focus on aesthetics—albeit one with a definite nod to the interests of Western philosophy professors.

Li's understanding of aesthetics and ethics as fundamentally integrated (or perhaps even "unified") is probably best described in more familiar Chinese terminology as "aesthetics and ethics have the same root (ben 本)." Already, this treatment of philosophical schools violates the trajectory of contemporary academic studies, which are often about narrow treatments, particular and fixed descriptions, and dissection. Bringing ideas together, appreciating their interconnections or shared root, and developing understanding further—looking for how we can move ahead in studies—marks Li's works.

Even in his historical accounts of the development of thought in the Chinese tradition, Li could not help but advance wildly unique perspectives. Rather than claiming to provide a precise analysis, for example, of the intellectual movement of the Wei-Jin period, he classifies it as a Zhuangzi-based attitude or *feng du* 风度. In less than twenty pages, he provides a fascinating discussion of the *Zhuangzi* and the general movement of scholars such as He Yan, Wang Bi, Guo Xiang, and the Seven Worthies of the Bamboo Grove. For those looking for an account of whence this movement came about, a detailed philosophical investigation of how Confucian and Daoist themes were reimagined, or how we might trace major ideas in Wei-Jin thought to the fall of the Han, Li's work is disappointing.[3] It cannot serve to replace that of others like Tang Yongtong's 湯用彤 *Essays on Wei-Jin Period Xuanxue* 魏晉玄學論稿 (1957), or the primary sources themselves. Indeed, Li's discussion shares more with Lu Xun's 魯迅 *Wei-Jin Period Attitudes and Other Things* 魏晉風度及其他 (1927) than with Tang's work or other classical philosophical histories such as Feng Youlan's *A Short History of Chinese Philosophy* (1948).[4] And yet, for those well versed in Wei-Jin writings and the scholarship around them, Li offers an exciting perspective. One does not so much learn *about* this period from Li as one feels inspired to engage with it oneself. In the hands of Li, readers do not dissect Wei-Jin thought; they are opened to it, and by it.

This short discussion of the Wei-Jin period is contained in Li's book *A History of Classical Chinese Thought* 中國古代思想史論 (2008). "On" is a good way to translate *lun* 論 here, which can also mean "discussion," "analysis," "illuminate," "consider," or even "theory," and has been used as a standard format of philosophical discourse in China since at least the Wei-Jin period. Without this character, we would expect a history in the more traditional sense. But that is not what Li provides. Like Confucius, whose views are transmitted in the *lun-yu* 論語, Li is so much telling the reader the right way to think or to act as providing inspiring suggestions for reflection.

Later in his life, Li utilized yet another method in his works. Rather than the comparatively straightforward treatises—even if many of them were essays (*shuo* 說/*jiang* 講), "outlines" (*gangyao* 綱要), or "readings" (*du* 讀), which were written like the *lun* discussed above—Li wrote "interviews." These interviews were not actual interviews. No one was asking Li questions (although some interviews between scholars or journalists and Li do exist, as do discussions with professors).[5] These "interviews" represent Li's more relaxed writing style. As Deng Delong, a longtime friend and funder of English translations of Li's works describes, "Professor Li has turned to 'interviews' as a method of philosophical writing. He is tired of trying to 'prove' his ideas. It is easier to write this way for Professor Li. He is old and not so much interested in academia."[6] Works such as *A Response to Sandel and Other Matters* 回應桑德爾及其他 (2014) were written entirely in this format.

Reading these supposed interviews, it is quite clear that they are manufactured. The questions give it all away. They are too perfect, each exactly formulated to allow Li to continue his line of thinking, every one expressing an intimate knowledge of that thinking. None really push back on Li. And the "interviewer" never points out mistakes or inaccuracies, which, for example in *A Response to Sandel and Other Matters*, exist.

Deng has compared Li's choice to write interviews with Plato's dialogues. Both might have been inspired by actual discourse, but it does not matter if they were. The dialogue format allowed Plato to express his ideas in ways he saw fit, and the style and content are purposively matched. This intertwining of style and content is present in other masters as well. Nietzsche's aphorisms perfectly suit his pointed insights. Confucius's short sayings, or cutting discourses, are instructive in their brevity, and in their being targeted at specific students in particular contexts. And how could the philosophy of the Zhuangzi be expressed without "metaphorical language" (*yuyan* 寓言)?

Today philosophy professors do their best to write in clear, logical, and tightly argued structures. There is little variance in what is "acceptable" to academic standards. Few, if any, of our philosopher-heroes, those we all write about, would be even close to publishable today. As a result, when we seek to "explain" and "analyze" the thought of Plato, Nietzsche, Confucius, Zhuangzi, and others, we do so through a style they themselves would very likely reject if not severely criticize. However, Li's work is an exception to this. In his essays, outlines, readings, and interviews, Li's style, as well as the content of his works, often more closely resembles those we write about than the accepted standards of contemporary Western philosophical discourse.

## Li as a Bad Scholar

Besides these issues of style, there are other ways in which Li's work does not conform well to the expectations of contemporary discourse. In translating *A Response to Sandel and Other Matters* (2016), Robert Carleo and I often joked that the more appropriate title would simply be "And Other Matters."[7] Written in the interview style, it was quite clear that while the "interviewer" and Li were familiar with Sandel's work, they did not really study it. Michael Sandel, who read an early draft of the translation, was taken aback as to how Li was able to publish a manuscript so full of mischaracterizations of his work. While at first these glaring misunderstandings are quite troubling, it has since become clear that they are at best secondary, and in fact relatively unimportant when reviewing this contribution as a whole.[8]

In broad strokes, we can understand Li's "response" as in fact expressing similar points to Sandel's own position, despite Li often being critical and seeking to correct Sandel's partial appreciations of crucial philosophical issues, like the importance of harmony, the relationship between emotions and reason, and the conception of the person.[9] Sandel's general backboard is based on critical counters to John Rawls's theory of justice and others who hold similar views—he is especially negative on libertarian positions. In many places Li's "corrective" on Sandel's views is simply a misreading. Rather than responding to Sandel's alternative to a Rawls-like position, Li responds to that Rawls-like position himself and proffers something similar to or almost exactly the same as Sandel. In other words, Li is responding more to Rawls than to Sandel, and his response to Rawls often echoes Sandel's own.

There are also many details that Li gets wrong about Sandel. He misunderstands Sandel's discussion of the "trolley car problem," and generally fails to appreciate Sandel's dialogue style of philosophizing. He does not realize that Sandel presents various perspectives as part of his argument, thinking, instead, that "Sandel's evaluations are often uncertain and waver between approaches and standpoints," which Li finds problematic.[10] Additionally, Sandel's most fundamental philosophical approach, whereby the values of one's communities are recognized as meaningfully constituting the person and their own values, thoughts, and feelings, is lost on Li. The latter sees the former as relying heavily on "abstract principles" and constantly reproaches him accordingly. Those familiar with Sandel's work will find this absurd. Equally absurd is Li's reprimanding Sandel for not considering concrete particulars in his discussion of markets—when Sandel's entire point is about the constitutive role of communities in establishing conceptions of the person, values, and the like.

Many Kantian scholars have reservations about Li's work on Kant similar to those just outlined in regard to Sandel. However, when viewed not so much as a professor trying to elicit the true meaning of Kant, or narrowly define some particular part of his thought, Li's work becomes more meaningful. Truly, what Li says about Kant is far less interesting than what he says about his own thought. *A Response to Sandel and Other Matters* should be read the same way. The "response to Sandel" is not a very good piece of scholarship. What Li writes about his own understandings (the "and other matters")[11] is far more valuable. So rather than reading Li as responding to Sandel, it is best to take his text as comments about his own thought with reference (accurate or not) to Sandel and others. And really, what he says about Sandel does not matter. His own thought is more than enough.

Before discussing Li's own theories—the "magnificently inspirational" Li—there are two other idiosyncrasies that should be mentioned: misquotation and inaccurate translations of Chinese terms. Both issues are most apparent to translators, but they are still visible to any close reader of Li's works. The fact that these small grievances, significant by contemporary academic standards, are more or less ignored, and that Li's gravitational force does not suffer because of them, attests to the richness of his thought.

First, translators can have difficulty finding quotes (in Chinese) that Li references, or ideas he attributes to a variety of thinkers. For example, there are places where he quotes from Heidegger, Hegel, or Marx, yet no such quote can be found in their works. More significantly, he sometimes attributes ideas and understandings to thinkers that many deem completely inaccurate. Thinking of these issues in the same way as Li's readings of Sandel and Kant again demonstrates their relative unimportance. However, when we compare this with what is standard in Western academia, we quickly notice that Li is not a very good "philosophy professor."

Another issue that has been particularly bothersome for those who translate and work on Li's thought—and has brought about much contention in these circles—is his list of preferred translations for particular terms. There are basic Chinese vocabularies that Li insists should be translated in particular ways, and many of his translators—who have a better command of English than Li—disagree. For example, Jana Rošker, Robert Carleo, and Andrew Lambert have taken issue with Li's desired translations such as "culture of optimism" for *leguan wenhua* 樂觀文化 and "guanxi-ism" for *guanxi zhuyi* 關係主義.[12] But the most contested term, which appears in not less than six of Li's own neologisms, is *benti* 本體. The above-mentioned translators have each written a good deal on this term.[13] Li asked that it be translated as "substance, root, body, final reality" and often "ontology" when coupled with other terms. Translators and scholars have noted that while Li might want to call this "substance" or "ontology," his use differs sharply from the way those terms are understood in (much of) Western philosophy. (This issue is not limited to Li—many Chinese scholars face the same difficulties when borrowing heavily from Western philosophy, and of course the same happens the other way around.)

These issues—misunderstandings of his philosophical interlocutors, specious references, and confusing translation requests—have not dampened the gravity around Li, in the same way that the sometimes

## Li as a First-Rate Philosopher

In some sense it is slightly awkward to talk about Li Zehou's ideas as "theories." Certainly he has ideas that resemble theories, but the way he treats them, and how one should approach them as a reader, invites a different attitude than more familiar theories. Some of Li's most compelling theories include *guanxi*-ism (*guanxi zhuyi* 關係主義), emotion as substance (*qing benti* 情本體), emotio-rational structure (*qing-li jiegou* 情理結構), theory of two morals (*liang de lun* 兩德論), one-world theory (*yi ge shijie* 一個世界), sedimentation (*jidianlun* 積澱論 or *jidianshuo* 積澱說), and harmony as higher than justice (*hexie gaoyu zhengyi* 和諧高於正義).[14] In some sense it is slightly awkward to talk about Li Zehou's ideas as "theories." Certainly he has ideas that resemble theories, but the way he treats them, and how one should approach them as a reader, invites a different attitude than do more traditional theories. Here we look briefly at these theories before discussing how Li himself treats them, and how they might be approached.

*Guanxi*-ism, which some scholars think should be translated "relationism," is the idea that persons are constituted entirely by their relationships, or *guanxi*, with others. In sharp contrast to Western individualism, *guanxi*-ism vehemently rejects theories that posit a self, soul, or anything prior to relationships that endows meaning. *Guanxi*-ism also rejects conceptions such as Sandel's, which take a foundational power of reflection or agency as being pre-given. Even critical reflection is seen as being born from interpersonal interactions. Approaches to ethics and morals should echo this conception, and there are strong implications for thinking about emotions and the relationship between emotions and reason.

One of Li's keys for reading early Confucian thought and its traditional developments is "emotions as substance." This position argues that emotions are the foundation of individual psychology as well as of communities and interactions. Confucianism has always upheld this position, Li thinks, and it is instructive for understanding humanity the world over. Rather than basing a philosophy on the act of learning, which is so heavily grounded in reason and can be taken as pure and therefore unchanging in some sense, Confucianism bases much of our understanding on emotions. This gives an important place to emotional cultivation—emotions need to be cultivated (with reference to reason). Thus everything that relies on emotions (as substance) can be cultivated as well—persons, relationships/ethics and morality, emotions, tradition, and our humanity itself.

Cultivation happens mainly through the inter-instructive mingling of emotions and reason, occurring within the individual, through their interactions with others, and in communities more generally. Li writes, "The emotio-rational structure refers to the concrete intersection of emotion with reason and emphasizes that emotions and reason exist in dynamic, constantly changing relationships of different ratios and proportions with one another."[15] This is implied already in the abovementioned concepts and once again marks, for Li, a critical contribution that Chinese thought has to make to global philosophy. Western thought, Li says, lacks this type of appreciation.

The "theory of two morals" references "modern social morals" (*xiandai shehuixing daode* 現代社會性道德) and "religious morals" (*zongjiaoxing daode* 宗教性道德). Before modern times there was no real distinction between these two morals, but as reason came to dominate, individualistic conceptions of the person gained popularity, and abstract principles were developed. Modern social morals were gradually separated from religious ones. The latter are related to conceptions of the good, convictions, values, and beliefs held by individuals and communities. They are largely based in tradition and rely strongly on emotional elements. By contrast, modern social morals are almost the opposite. Here reason dominates, conceptions of the good are drowned by "rights," and the importance of beliefs and tradition are downplayed. The relationship between the two types of morals is balanced by "proper measure" (*du* 度).

All of Chinese thought is based on a "one-world theory"—which needs to be defined through contrast to Western (and other) "two-world theories." A two-world theory holds that there is another (typically more perfect, ideal, transcendent) world, which should serve as a model for this one. This concrete world is full of particulars that include messy details, accidents, contingencies, and other less-than-ideal, less-than-perfect, and very much not transcendent factors. In this world, achieving goodness, beauty, or justice will always be compromised by the very imperfections of concreteness.[16] Only in another, more perfect place can they fully exist; here we can only mirror them and at best realize just some small fraction. According to a one-world theory, ideals can be models, but we never imagine escaping concreteness, or idealize a world without imperfections. There will always be messy particulars to deal with, and all our understandings should appreciate them. So while a two-world theory might accuse emotions of being fickle and influencing people in undue ways, a one-world theory does not suppose we could somehow get rid of them, nor would it want to. A one-world theory takes "emotions as substance," that is, as the foundation of human existence. Relatedly, *guanxi*-ism, the importance of cultivation, and the interweaving of emotions and reason are all based on a one-world theory. A two-world theory might see a core soul or self as covered by particulars and thereby downplay the influence of others and cultivation. It could also prioritize reason and at least partially reject emotions. Li's ideas are thus all based on and grown from a one-world theory. This allows him to rethink historical progress as well as conceptions of human interactions.

One of Li's most versatile and intriguing ideas is "sedimentation." Like rocks that sediment over time, individuals, cultures, and humanity itself develop through the accumulation of experiences. Loose materials can be made stable and even become extremely solid, eventually serving as the basis for further layering. Li uses this to explain a host of different phenomena. In the aesthetic realm, humans transformed natural objects into expressions of beauty. From here a sense of beauty was developed and has grown. Again, this happens in individual persons, cultures, and humankind. Rituals, which Li sees as essential for many parts of humanity, were sedimented from shamanistic practices. Songs and dances slowly became rites and ceremonies. Today they still exist and are foundational—even if they are extremely thin or all but forgotten. Thinking about humans as a conglomerate of *guanxi*, framed through emotional-rational structures, and against the background of a one-word theory, we come to view agency and the power of reflection as gradually sedimented (again in the individual, culture, and humanity) through time. Moral principles too, including something "absolute" such as Kant's categorical imperative, are the result of sedimentation. As will be discussed below, Li's broad application notwithstanding, there can be many other areas where "sedimentation" might be usefully applied.

The final idea we will consider here is Li's proposal that "harmony is higher than justice." He takes "harmony" as broadly indicative of a Chinese approach to morality/life, and "justice" as a Western counterpart—which he characterizes, perhaps to an extreme, as overly rational, abstract, and principle based. But Li never really describes what "harmony" means, nor does he satisfyingly discuss "higher." He more or less throws these ideas out and sees what others make of them. When questioned in interviews, be they with others or written by himself, Li quickly turns the question to the interviewer, or else evades by carrying on a corollary discussion. For example, when directly asked (by himself in the interview style) to describe what he means by "harmony being higher than justice," Li responds, "That's impossible." He continues, "As I mentioned before, philosophical ethics can only provide certain main ideas. The development or unfolding of such details belongs to other areas such as political philosophy, psychology, and philosophy of religion. This requires the research of many more specialists. More importantly, the aspects falling under political philosophy require more complete empirical resources from which to draw on."[17] He similarly passes off detailed descriptions of sedimentation and other major ideas to so-called "specialists" even though he is the one who coined or proposed them.

Li's response to being asked to describe what "harmony is higher than justice" means wonderfully encapsulates his philosophical attitude. His ideas are not "theories" in the sense of being an explanation that can be proved and is consistent with observations or the results of scientific research. They are better understood as jumping-off points, as proposals that we can use to think about the world, to discuss. In sum, one should think *with* Li (as opposed to merely thinking *about* him)—he is not interested in his ideas being "tested" or in "proving" them in an academic sense.

Once again, Li is unconventional. Not merely disregarding academic standards, he seems actually unable to meet them. If he cannot show, or even explain, what "harmony is higher than justice" means, or provide adequate proof of sedimentation, the one-world theory, or his other major ideas, why should we listen? How can he say other specialists need to take him seriously and test his ideas?

The academic conventions surrounding philosophical theories, their explanations, proofs, and general attitudes taken toward them, are actually quite at odds with those great philosophers of the past we reference or theorize about. In this regard, Li's work functions like, and can be read in the same vein as, Confucius, Plato, Zhuangzi, or Nietzsche. They too discuss their ideas, but never seek to fully prove them. In many cases they simply "throw something out there" for others to think *with*. The reason we study and revere these thinkers is that their ideas really are worth reflection, not because they provide adequate explanations or proofs. They help us interpret the world, think about ourselves, and live together, even while not being even close to being acceptable by current academic standards. Only time will tell if Li is a giant of philosophy, but his ideas certainly seem, to many, up to snuff.

## A Tradition of Masters and Commentators

The Chinese tradition of thought that became labeled "philosophical" begins with masters (*zi* 子) texts. While this recognition is sometimes challenged by those who believe it might somehow degrade these texts in the eyes of Western philosophy professors, it is clear that "masters" texts form the foundation for what we call Chinese philosophy. In many ways, the records from or of the masters remind of the classical "philosophers" in Western thought. These works feature much less emphasis on analytical reasoning, logical rigidity, and reference to the discourse than do modern and contemporary works. The Chinese masters may be further differentiated from the mainstream Western philosophical tradition in that masters texts are often comparatively more obtuse. For example, the *Yijing*, *Analects*, *Laozi*, and *Zhuangzi*, and even more straightforward classics such as the *Mengzi*, *Xunzi*, *Sunzi*, or *Hanfeizi*, can rely on highly contextualized observations, difficult-to-parse comments, or simple sayings that are rich and broad enough to have become idioms. More often than not, these texts do not provide "reasons" for what they promote, and there is even less in the way of argument or proof—though there is no shortage of scholars looking for them. Whereas many classics of Western philosophy aim to convince readers through reasoning and argumentation, demonstrating, for instance, how other viewpoints are incorrect or incomplete,[18] Chinese masters texts, and the commentarial tradition that follows, rely on proffering ideas and then having readers check them against their own life experience.

The "truth" or efficacy of what masters texts advance is concrete and fully embedded in the nitty-gritty of contextualization, relationships, and emotions. Accordingly, relying on pure argumentation, theoretical discussion, or too much abstraction is not only counterproductive but not really possible. Western philosophical texts thrive on those methods because they are part and parcel of their philosophical positions and methodology. Strong reference to a two-world theory, notions such as "pure reason," and abstract visions of justice are well served by the dialogues of Plato or Aristotle's "writings." By contrast, Chinese philosophy needs to be realized by the reader because it is always contextual and decided within concrete situations. Like nearly all Chinese philosophers, Li Zehou emphasizes the importance of *du* 度, which he translates as "proper measure," and which is also referenced as the *jing* 經 and *quan* 權 dynamic—in other words, weighing (*quan*) doctrines, principles, or rules (all of which are *jing*) in particular situations. This is how masters texts function, and it is why "obscurity" is a valuable method.

The tradition that developed therefrom is predominately constructed through commentaries. These are widely misunderstood as being, and intended to be, mere exegeses of original (mostly "masters") texts. The two main forms of commentary, *shu* 疏 and *zhu* 注, which are both translated as "commentary" in English, can be broadly understood as "annotations" and "explanations," respectively. There are many commentaries that function mainly as annotative and explanatory, for example the *Lunyu Jijie* 論語集解 commentary to the *Analects* overseen by He Yan 何晏 (d. 249), without much philosophical originality. Other commentaries, such as Zhu Xi's 朱熹 (d. 1200) *Lunyu Jizhu* 論語集注 or Wang Bi's 王弼 (d. 249) *Lunyu Shiyi* 論語釋疑 to the *Analects* or his *Laozi Daodejing Zhu* 老子道德經注 commentary to the *Laozi* are philosophically rich but also include glaring "mistakes." Wang Bi famously "misreads" *chugou* 芻狗 "straw dogs" in chapter 5 of the *Laozi* as "straw and dogs," which has led many to proudly proclaim they have a better understanding of this section than the Xuanxue genius.[19]

The commentarial tradition is sometimes misunderstood because it functions according to the *jing-quan* model. Extracting the "truth" either of reality or what some master has said is uninteresting from this standpoint. Masters texts are masters texts because they provide excellent *jing*. The criterion for a good *jing* is applicability beyond some one time or certain situations, contoured by specific aspects yet still proving efficacious for promoting some general value. These *jing* are then *quan*ed according to *du* or proper measure. The goal of a commentator in this lineage is therefore to properly (*du*) weigh (*quan*) masters texts (*jing*) to fit well their times and situations. Exegesis and annotations are a necessary step in this process, but variance is encouraged, and rejection or re-readings are allowable as well. (The danger of this system is traditionalism or conformism, and it is on these grounds that the Chinese tradition is often criticized.)

The approach continues to this day. Some contemporary scholars, such as Yang Guorong 楊國榮 and Huang Yong 黃勇, sometimes treat Chinese classics the way Western classics are normally treated, that is, as containing propositions that are more or less true and can be assessed accordingly.[20] For example, they argue about types of "relativism" or "concerns with Being" in the *Zhuangzi*,[21] or look at Confucian texts in terms of "the Good" or "virtue ethics."[22] Terminology, method, and, it seems, the very way that they read these texts are forged with the adoption of foreign molds. Other scholars retain more of a "master-commentator" style, including Chen Guying 陳鼓應, Wang Bo 王博, and also Li Zehou. Chen and Wang are both poetic in their styles, draw seamlessly from various classics, and are not concerned with completing linear arguments formed though reading Chinese philosophy in a "propositionalized" fashion. We might further distinguish this latter method by saying that it philosophizes *with* texts as opposed to philosophizing *on* them. Philosophizing *on* as a method is important and informative, but it does not capture what Chen Yun 陳贇 refers to as the "spirit" or "essence" (*jing shen* 精神) of the texts.[23] In lieu of further elaborating on the difference between philosophizing *with* versus *on* a text, which overlap to a large degree, we can discuss Li's own style—which well illustrates the point.

Two of the most discussed and contested passages in the *Analects* have been 17.21 and 13.18. According to Li, 17.21 is one of the most "crucial" passages of the entire book. In the passage, Zai Wo asks if it would be okay to mourn for one year instead of three, and Confucius says that so long as his heart-mind would be "at ease" (*an* 安) then he should do it. After Zai Wo leaves, Confucius harshly criticizes him—clearly no one should feel "at ease" with mourning for only a year after the death of a parent.

Li writes that "Confucius's 'ritual' is established on a principle of psychological emotions."[24] In this way "subjective human emotions" are the "first principle" in Confucian thought. Whether it is "'three years' or 'one year' is not at all important." The three years is just a way of carrying on what was done in the past.[25] While some have argued that three years mourning is justified by the three years one is held by their parents after birth, and others go so far as to say there is "universality . . . grounded in the very nature of human experience,"[26] Li emphasizes the "subjective" and "emotional" aspects. Yes, we should look to our experience, but not as something "universal." Experience of emotions, institutions that promote them, and the rituals thereby developed tell us everything. Li is not interested in an ultimate justification, or really any "reason" in a contemporary philosophical sense of the word.[27]

In his comments on 13.18, as is true of Li's entire work on the *Analects*, we find again an appeal to emotions and a resistance to identifying a perfectly logical line of thought or universal reasoning behind what Confucius says. 13.18 is the famous "sheep stealing" passage where Confucius says that a father and son should cover for one another. Li's attitude here is characteristically light-hearted and "flowing." The world of Confucius and Mencius is based on clans; family is important, as are related virtues. The relation between these values and the law has constantly changed, but we can appreciate that emotions are important here and worth philosophical consideration. Indeed, this issue speaks also to sociology and psychology. So when we think about family-based considerations and their conflict with public good, we need to be broad in what we consider. Li concludes that when considering the "upright" and "justice" (*gongzheng* 公正) in the *Analects*, we need to recognize that they are always related to emotion.

Many others, both in the Chinese tradition and more recently, have explored all sorts of explanatory acrobatics to justify what Confucius says. It is reasonable, right, or an expression of "justice" for such and such reasons. Li differs. He invites readers to open their considerations to various aspects, look at methods in other disciplines, allow themselves to find emotional avenues, and think concretely about their own experiences when being instructed by Confucius. Li thus becomes both master and commentator in his own work.

## Conclusion

It would be interesting, though perhaps overly pedantic, to wax on about the virtues of incorporating more "master-commentator" thinking into philosophy today. Surely the pendulum is currently swinging hard in the other direction and at some point will rest before moving back in the opposite way. Along the reverse trajectory, the style of philosophy found in the works of masters, developed by commentators, and exemplified by people like Li Zehou will be invaluable—and not just for academic reasons, but for real-life ones as well. For now we can note the importance of Li's work on a smaller scale and hope that more thinkers come to emulate him.

Broadly speaking, Li—and the style of philosophy he represents—begins with some simple observations about the world: There are some things that simply cannot be described well in language and other things that *should* not be described in language (and yet others that at least should not be described in detail). Realizing this, we sometimes reflect without claiming to know everything or explain everything. We philosophize in an open manner: open to the world, to others, and to future developments. Academic philosophy would do well to better appreciate, and not merely through talking about it, the efficacy of these points. They are, after all, surprisingly simple and mundane.

In our everyday life the efficacy of *not* explaining every detail is ever present. My thirteen-year-old nephew does not need to know everything, at least not yet. Sometimes the best way through an argument is to simply "move on" and not go into the finer points of everything said or all that led up to the disagreement. And if we cast our net further and are really honest about it, we find that many things in life either cannot or should not be discussed or thought about at all. To do so, and do so by employing systematic line-by-line propositional thinking, is often counterproductive at best. Logic is a great tool in math and physics, but what place does it have with family and friends? If it does benefit us in thinking about who to give ventilators to or what groups to vaccinate first, it still does not touch on the concrete or the human—not to speak of the emotional—aspects and results of these interactions.

Contemporary academic philosophy is unlikely to admit that there are perhaps more "truths," more insights into human interaction, and perhaps better reflections on living in Leo Tolstoy's *Anna Karenina* than in Plato's dialogues. For those who believe the possibility of literature outdoing "philosophy," or who sometimes favor a not speaking or hinting over explanation, Li Zehou is a true philosopher.

Like Confucius, Plato, Nietzsche, or Zhuangzi, if we apply current academic standards to Li he is certainly lacking. But when we contextualize him in a master and commentator tradition, reading him in a *jing-quan* style and appreciating the power of hinting and silence over thorough explanation, we can better appreciate the breadth and consequence of his manner of philosophizing *with* texts, rather than merely *on* them.

## Notes

1. This argument was made by Karl-Heinz Pohl in his talk "Chinese Aesthetics and Li Zehou's Major Contributions: *The Path of Beauty* (Meide licheng 美的历程) and *The Chinese Aesthetic Tradition* (Huaxia meixue 华夏美学)" at the Summer School on Li Zehou and Contemporary Chinese Thought hosted by the University of Ljubljana, June 16, 2022.

2. Carleo made this point in the question-and-answer portion of Pohl's talk (see footnote 1). In the subsequent discussion Pohl agreed.

3. Li Zehou 李澤厚, *Zhongguo gudai sixiang shilun* 中國古代思想史論 (*A History of Classical Chinese Thought*) (Beijing: SDX Joint Publishing, 2008).

4. Feng Youlan also wrote a long history of Chinese thought in Chinese and has several other works that discuss Xuanxue. It does not matter which one Li is thinking of, if any.

5. We have examples of both in Li's *Shenme shi daode* 什麼是道德 (*What Is Morality*) (Shanghai: ECNU Press, 2015).

6. Personal communication: I had this conversation with Deng Delong several times in 2014 and 2015.

7. This a reference to Lu Xun's title, mentioned above.

8. One example is "The International Conference on Michael Sandel and Chinese Philosophy" held at East China Normal University, Shanghai, March 8–10, 2016, and subsequent publication of Michael J. Sandel and Paul J. D'Ambrosio, ed., *Encountering China: Michael Sandel and Chinese Philosophy* (Cambridge, MA: Harvard University Press, 2018). These were direct results of research on Li's work.

9. For a detailed discussion of this, see Paul J. D'Ambrosio, "Approaches to Global Ethics: Michael Sandel's Justice and Li Zehou's Harmony," *Philosophy East and West* 66, no. 3 (2016): 720–38.

10. Li Zehou, "A Response to Michel Sandel and Other Matters," trans. Paul J. D'Ambrosio and Robert Carleo III, *Philosophy East and West* 66, no. 4 (2016): 1098.

11. By "Other Matters" Li actually means the appendixes; for example, there is one on Legalism and Confucianism. However, Robert Carleo and I like to appreciate it from a different perspective.

12. Jana S. Rošker, "Enriching the Chinese Intellectual Legacy: A Review of Li Zehou's *A History of Classical Chinese Thought*," *Social Epistemology Review and Reply Collective* 8, no. 12 (2019): 1–7; Jana S. Rošker, *Becoming Human. Li Zehou's Ethics* (Leiden: Brill, 2020); Robert Carleo, "The Moral Self and its Relations," in *Beyond Comparison*, eds. Dimitra Amarantidou and Geir Sigurðsson (Albany: State University of New York Press, 2023), 200–17; Li, *A History of Classical Chinese Thought*.

13. Jana S. Rošker, *Following His Own Path: Li Zehou and Contemporary Chinese Philosophy* (Albany: State University of New York Press, 2019); Carleo, "The Moral Self and its Relations"; Li Zehou, *A History of Classical Chinese Thought*.

14. For in-depth treatments of some of his basic terminology, see Rošker, *Following His Own Path*; Paul J. D'Ambrosio, Robert Carleo, and Andrew Lambert, "On Li Zehou's Philosophy: An Introduction by Three Translators," *Philosophy East and West* 66, no. 4 (2016): 1057–67.

15. Li, "A Response to Michel Sandel and Other Matters," 1082.

16. In a recent work titled *In Praise of Failure* (2022), Costica Bradatan defines "failure" as basically "concreteness." In other words, the inability to be perfect and live up to other-worldly standards is what constitutes "failure" in the eyes of many.

17. Li, "A Response to Michel Sandel and Other Matters," 1098.

18. Contemporary academic standards have instilled in me the need to apologize profusely for these being gross generalizations.

19. Wang Bi of course has a very good reason for reading the passage this way, which is part of his own philosophical understanding. He is not necessarily arguing this is how the passage should be read, but making his own point. (See Paul J. D'Ambrosio, "Wang Bi's 'Confucian' Laozi: Commensurable Ethical Understandings in 'Daoist' and 'Confucian' Thinking," *Religions* 13, no. 5 (2022): 417.)

20. This is to say that they often emphasize this type of treatment. In many ways Yang and Huang still treat masters texts and commentaries as masters texts and commentaries, and they never lose sight of a *jing-quan* dynamic. Other scholars, particularly in the analytic tradition, appreciate *jing-quan* on a superficial level, and do not allow it to significantly inform their methodology.

21. Yang Guorong 楊國榮, *Zhuangzi de sixiang shijie* 莊子的思想世界 (*Zhuangzi's World of Thought*) (Shanghai: Huadong Shifan Daxue chuban she, 2009).

22. Huang Yong 黃勇, *Dangdai meide lunli: Gudai Rujia de gongxian* 當代美德倫理: 古代儒家的貢獻 (*Contemporary Virtue Ethics: Contributions from Ancient Confucianism*) (Shanghai: Oriental Publications Center, 2019).

23. Chen Yun 陳贇, *Zhuangzi zhexue de jingshen* 莊子哲學的精神 (*The Essence of Zhuangzi's Philosophy*) (Shanghai renmin chuban she, 2016).

24. All translations are my own unless otherwise noted.

25. Li Zehou 李泽厚, *Lunyu jindu* 論語今讀 (*Reading the Analects Today*) (Beijing: SDX Joint Publishing, 2008), 523.

26. Edward Slingerland, "Virtue Ethics, the *Analects*, and the Problem of Commensurability," *Journal of Religious Ethics* 29, no. 1 (2001): 118.

27. Li's philosophical style and "masters"-like interaction are well exemplified in the next part of his explanation of 17.21. Here he mentions the works of A. C. Graham, David Hall, Roger Ames, and others before saying that he

differs mainly on seeing the Chinese society as largely born from "Shamanism rationalized." (Li, *Reading the Analects Today*, 524) He also says the work of Ames goes too far in emphasizing the differences between East and West, and then simply writes "In this book there is no way I can talk about this in a detailed way" (ibid.). After all, Li says, he's "discussed this all before." This is a great example of how he has poignant remarks that are well worth considering, but do not need to be fleshed out detail by detail. We will return to this in the conclusion.

# Bibliography

Bradatan, Costica. *In Praise of Failure: Four Lessons in Humility*. Cambridge, MA: Harvard University Press, 2022.

Carleo, Robert. "The Moral Self and its Relations." In *Four Exemplars of Ru* 儒 (*Confucianism*), edited by Paul J. D'Ambrosio, Dimitra Amarantidou, Geir Sigurðsson, and Hans-Georg Moeller 200–17. New York: Springer (forthcoming 2025).

Chen, Guying. *The Annotated Critical Laozi: With Contemporary Explication and Traditional Commentary*. Translated by Paul J. D'Ambrosio, Ouyang Xiao, et al. Boston: Brill, 2020.

Chen Yun 陳贇. *Zhuangzi zhexue de jingshen* 莊子哲學的精神 (*The Essence of Zhuangzi's Philosophy*). Shanghai: Shanghai renmin chuban she, 2016.

D'Ambrosio, Paul J. "Approaches to Global Ethics: Michael Sandel's Justice and Li Zehou's Harmony." *Philosophy East and West* 66, no. 3 (2016): 720–38.

D'Ambrosio, Paul J. "Wang Bi's 'Confucian' Laozi: Commensurable Ethical Understandings in 'Daoist' and 'Confucian' Thinking." *Religions* 13, no. 5 (2022): 417.

D'Ambrosio, Paul J., Robert A. Carleo III, and Andrew Lambert, "On Li Zehou's Philosophy: An Introduction by Three Translators." *Philosophy East and West* 66, no. 4 (2016): 1057–67.

Feng Youlan. *A Short History of Chinese Philosophy*. New York: The Free Press, 1948.

Huang Yong 黃勇. *Dangdai meide lunli: Gudai Rujia de gongxian* 當代美德倫理：古代儒家的貢獻 (*Contemporary Virtue Ethics: Contributions from Ancient Confucianism*). Shanghai: Oriental Publications Center, 2019.

Li Zehou. *A History of Classical Chinese Thought*. Translated by Andrew Lambert. New York: Routledge, 2020.

Li Zehou 李澤厚. *Huiying Sangde'er ji qita* 回應桑德爾及其他 (*A Response to Sandel and Other Matters*). Beijing: Sanlian Bookstore, 2014.

Li Zehou 李泽厚. *Lunyu jindu* 論語今讀 (*Reading the Analects Today*). Beijing: SDX Joint Publishing, 2008.

Li Zehou. "A Response to Michel Sandel and Other Matters." Translated by Paul J. D'Ambrosio and Robert A. Carleo III. *Philosophy East and West* 66, no. 4 (2016): 1068–1147.

Li Zehou 李澤厚. *Shenme shi daode* 什麼是道德 (*What Is Morality?*). Shanghai: ECNU Press, 2015.

Li Zehou 李澤厚. *Zhongguo gudai sixiang shilun* 中國古代思想史論 (*A History of Classical Chinese Thought*). Beijing: SDX Joint Publishing, 2008.

Lu Xun 魯迅. *Weijin fengdu ji qita* 魏晉風度及其他 (*Wei-Jin Period Attitudes and Other Things*). Shanghai: Shanghai Century Publishing Group, 2010.

Rošker, Jana S. *Becoming Human. Li Zehou's Ethics*. Leiden: Brill, 2020.

Rošker, Jana S. *Following His Own Path: Li Zehou and Contemporary Chinese Philosophy*. Albany: State University of New York Press, 2019.

Rošker, Jana S., "Enriching the Chinese Intellectual Legacy: A Review of Li Zehou's A History of Classical Chinese Thought." *Social Epistemology Review and Reply Collective* 8, no. 12 (2019): 1–7.

Sandel, Michael J., and Paul J. D'Ambrosio, ed. *Encountering China: Michael Sandel and Chinese Philosophy*. Cambridge, MA: Harvard University Press, 2018.

Slingerland, Edward, "Virtue Ethics, the *Analects*, and the Problem of Commensurability." *Journal of Religious Ethics* 29, no. 1 (2001): 97–125.

Tang Yongtong 湯用彤. *Weijin Xuanxue lungao* 魏晉玄學論稿 (*Essays on Wei-Jin Period Xuanxue*). Beijing: SDX Joint Publishing, 1957.

Wang Bo 王博. *Zhuangzi zhexue* 莊子哲學 (*The Philosophy of Zhuangzi*). Beijing: Peking University Press, 2004.

Yang Guorong 楊國榮. *Zhuangzi de sixiang shijie* 莊子的思想世界 (*Zhuangzi's World of Thought*). Shanghai: Huadong Shifan Daxue chuban she, 2009.

3

# A New Alternative to the How-to-Live Concern

## Wang Keping

In his last three decades, from the 1990s until his passing in 2021, Li Zehou claimed on many occasions that the key telos of philosophy lies in the consideration of human destiny per se. Such a destiny is assumed to have as its foundation stone human capacity coupled mainly with human living and human becoming. Accordingly, Li devotes much effort to explicate his anthropo-historical ontology or historical ontology of anthropology as one of the fundamental theories in his thought. On this account, he is preoccupied with the issue of how to live, and proposes the full development of human capacity as an alternative to address it. Such a development is a process of human becoming, during which human capacity is developed to its full extent in light of human subjectality[1] as the ultimate outcome of human fulfillment. This discussion commences with ontological reflections on what I will term "the how-to-live concern" with reference to Confucian, Kantian, and Marxist philosophy. It then proceeds to examine the structure of human capacity in terms of the cognitive, moral, and aesthetic dimensions. Along this line of thought, it moves on to look at a trifold aesthetic engagement in the dynamic interaction among the acts of illuminating the true, furnishing the good, and making life worth living through the beautiful. All this points to the Heaven-Earth realm of human living that is metaphysicized in Li's conception of aesthetics as the first philosophy.

## The How-to-Live Concern

The how-to-live concern is a pivotal one in Li Zehou's practical philosophy of subjectality in view of anthropo-historical ontology. This concern can be specified as "how the human being is to live." It is in fact a transfiguration of the Kantian question about "What is the human being?" or "What can the human beings make of themselves?" Simply put, it is a question about the possibility of human becoming per se. It is indirectly approached in the Three Critiques, and directly approached in the *Anthropology from a Pragmatic Point of View*. As Kant himself could not expound it any further because of his death, Li Zehou resumes the incomplete task and explores it from a practical instead of transcendental standpoint. In fact, Li deviates from Kant at this point by giving up the concept of universal necessity a priori, and goes ahead to ally with Marx by accepting the idea of social objectivity that comes from human practice or making-using tools in labor. Moreover, he returns to classical Confucianism and rediscovers relevant sources so as to develop his ontological method of human becoming and human living alike.

As noted in Li's exploration, what is prior to the how-to-live concern is the why-to-live question. The question is brought forth against the status quo of the human condition shrouded in diverse strictures, including such social and psychological ills as injustice, inequality, poverty, deprivation, frustration, depression, madness, loneliness, nothingness, cares, worries, anxieties, and so forth, not to speak of such destructive threats as civilizational clashes, international conflicts, regional wars, and terrorist attacks, among many others. Worse still, the biggest of all challenges comes from the hard fact that life is short, and death can befall all persons alike at any moment. In extreme cases, at the critical moment of death some may realize that they have never lived, because their life has been concealed in a so-called life that has been lived against their free will and natural rights. All this seems to revive the hidden echo of the old *skepsis* of "to be or not to be" in Hamlet's soliloquy. Nevertheless, an optimistic outlook can arise with a ray of hope that makes human life worthwhile by virtue of pragmatic wisdom, principally in the aesthetic and ethical domains.

In this context, a renowned stance advocated by Martin Heidegger is facing death in order to live, although this has some of the negative overtones of modern existentialism. In contrast, Confucius advocates a more positive attitude, advising people to live without bothering about death, because "unknown yet is life, much less is death."[2] This attitude implies three things at least: (1) The first priority is given to life instead of death, according to the logical inference that if life itself is not understood yet, how death can be? (2) Life is related to the human world and the living reality, while death is related to the underworld and odd fantasies of spirits, ghosts and deities, and Confucius focuses on the former but ignores the latter. (3) Life is this-worldly by nature, whereas death is focused on the afterlife in eschatology. What is to be cherished is the true value of life, and what is to be suspended is the natural term of death. For in Chinese convention, the span of life is often likened to the cycle of grass,[3] and the arrival of death comes to all things alike. Both of them are natural and unavoidable. But how to live a life, especially a worthwhile one, is open to many choices and possibilities.

To strengthen the argument given above, Confucius offers a number of relevant alternatives. One of them is "Having heard the Dao in the morning, one may die content in the evening."[4] This indicates that it is necessary to make the greatest efforts possible to attain real knowledge of the Dao in one's lifetime. Conceived as the paramount principle of reciprocal humaneness and universal love, the Dao purports to build up the moral character of a superior person, and to facilitate humane governance for the common good. This being the case, one may feel gratified and even have a happy death after having attained the Dao itself. Confucius expects people to make the most of life in order to find the Dao, because it embodies the greatest worth of living and the truest virtue of humaneness. In addition, Confucius claims that "a man with lofty ideals and humane virtue never gives up the virtue of humaneness to save his life, but sacrifices his own life to accomplish the virtue of humaneness."[5] As this states, a person of this type demonstrates a fine personality and noble spirit, and is morally obliged to tread upon the sure path of humaneness as the highest principle, similar to the categorical imperative in Kant's ethics or theoethics. In order to retain their moral character and fulfill their social commitments, those who follow the Confucian expectation are ready to put aside personal interest and sacrifice their lives for the common good, according to the required obligations of virtuous humaneness *par excellence*. Take Yan Hui, a disciple of Confucius, for example. It is claimed that to draw bitter joy from his persistent exercise of reciprocal humaneness, he did not retreat a single inch within three months when living a hard life with meager daily provisions. He was highly praised by his master because they both shared the same values and ideals.[6] All this leads to "the exemplary paradigm of Confucius-Yan's joy"[7] that has been promoted by Neo-Confucianism ever since the Song Dynasty (970–1279).

As observed from the foregoing exposition, the positive attitude toward life upheld among Confucians is coupled with moral obligation, social commitment, heroic spirit, an altruistic orientation, and so on, which can be traced back to the rites-music heritage. As read in the *Discourse on Music*,[8] for instance, the conception of *yue* as music indicates a historical continuity from antiquity. It is hereby identified with *le* as joy.[9] Such an identification not only reveals a defining property of music itself, but also has a strong impact upon the Chinese mentality. It enhances the musical sensibility in an aesthetic sense, remolds the joy-conscious character in an anthropological sense, and consolidates the optimistic spirit in an ontological sense. These three aspects are interwoven in the deep structure of Chinese cultural psychology and the philosophy of life at large.

In practice, the musical sensibility helps heighten the aesthetic awareness of the artistic, moral, and social functions of music; the joy-conscious character rejects no bitter joy and seeks delight from varied experiences, including miserable encounters; and more significantly, the optimistic spirit enables people to become what they are, never losing a ray of hope at confrontation with the gravest crises and hardships. Thus they are prone to perceive the interaction between the negative and positive sides of all matters, and prepare for the complex interplay between fortune and misfortune in changing and even delicate situations. This being true, they tend to be on guard against potential dangers, and live in high consciousness of crises and emergencies, from which they draw pragmatic wisdom, wary pleasure, and useful strategies to tackle any unexpected challenges or catastrophes. Knowing well the uncertainty of human existence sandwiched between Heaven and Earth, they have no other choice but to resort to self-reliance under all circumstances. In Li's elucidation, Chinese culture is one of optimism by nature, running parallel to the joy-conscious character and aesthetic sensibility. It is directed to a positive stance toward human life, and an active motivation of human becoming. All this is found relevant and helpful to sort out the why-to-live question and the how-to-live concern.

## The Structure of Human Capacity

Li revisits classical Confucianism with particular reference to Kantian moral anthropology and Marxian practical philosophy. To address the how-to-live concern, he proposes an anthropo-ontological approach, which is both material and formal in kind. It is material because of its instrumental function, and formal because of its conceptual guidance. It is recommended because it is said to meet the two determinants of human nature: the satisfaction of sensory needs and the fulfillment of conceptual demands. Judging from the anthropo-ontological standpoint, human nature is the outcome of human culture, a complicated and interwoven synthesis of two leading aspects: animality and sociality. One originates from the sensory needs that are required to preserve physical existence and reproduction of the species; the other is derived from human socialization and cultural education, hence rejecting brutal carnalism and beastlike behavior.[10] These two aspects are historically cultivated and sedimented into human capacity, the process of which is proclaimed to range from Marx's techno-social structure (the material dimension) to Kant's cultural-psychological formation (the mental dimension). It follows that human capacity as such underlies human nature, gratifies human needs, and secures human existence. Along this line of thought, its full development is seen as a working alternative to handle the how-to-live concern.

Being the most important component of human nature, human capacity arises out of the cultural-psychological formation comprising at least three dimensions—the cognitive, aesthetic, and moral—which in sequence, according to Kant, involve the faculty of correct understanding, the action upon moral laws, and the power of judgment.[11] Conspicuously, Li Zehou branches off here to his own historical ontology, and conceives of the human being as a historical being by nature. He thus proceeds to reflect on the constitution of human capacity in view of Marx's approach to techno-social substance, Kant's articulation of human mentality, and the Confucian notion of emotional substance. However, he strives to go beyond their respective limits, and opens up a new window on the development of human capacity. As he argues,

> Historical ontology comes from Marx, Kant, and Chinese tradition, but deviates from them to quite some extent. More specifically, it differs from Marx, who merely heeds the social

aspect of homo sapiens but ignores the psychic dimension of the individual. It differs from Kant, who ascribes the psychological form to the superhuman reason but neglects its origin of historical living in actuality. It differs from Chinese tradition, which lays an excessive stress on usefulness but makes light of the vital importance of abstract speculation. However, historical ontology as such absorbs and integrates them all. It generally brings forth its key arguments via the concepts of pragmatic reason and joy-conscious culture, and intends to deal with the issues of psychological constitution concerning an all-round realization of personal potentials in modern life.[12]

What does Li do then in accord with this argument? He moves on to endow the structure of human capacity with the three elements of "free intuition, free will, and free enjoyment."[13] In his explanation, "free intuition" is in contrast to "original intuition." It is surely human intuition as is derived from the power of imagination and the cognition of experience in Kant. It is hereby distinct in terminology, but identical to rational intuition as a cognitive faculty for logic, mathematics, and dialectic concepts. It is represented in the mode of "rational internalization," and traced back to human practice by using, making, innovating, and adjusting tools for diversified forms of labor in a long process. During this process, a variety of lawful models and forms are preserved and accumulated in the practical activities of humankind, which are then transformed into an informational system of languages, symbols, and cultures, and finally internalized, condensed, and sedimented into the human psychological formation. All this builds up the human capacity of appreciating and understanding the world at large. The capacity is cultural in essence. It contains an intellectual structure acquired through learning from infancy. As regards the ability of rational intuition, it is the same as the ability of free creation according to Albert Einstein, and is termed "free intuition" by Li himself.[14] Rationality is by and large the potential for the praxis of reason. Human rationality is a formal constitution internalized through the application of reason to both materially practical and symbolically rational activities. Such activities are associated not only with the development of the intellectual faculty for scientific knowledge, but also with the nourishment of the creative mentality for aesthetic sensibility, among other capabilities.

"Free will" is thus pointed to ethics and the reality of human existence. It brings out the scope of human subjectality that overrides utilitarian superficiality. In Kant, the will bears the capacity to act according to the principles as moral laws that are produced by practical reason. Such reason assumes freedom and action in order to let them function appropriately and effectively. Since Kant regards moral laws as categorical imperatives that unconditionally command everyone to comply by in the same way, the only way to act freely in the full sense of exercising moral autonomy is to act upon categorical imperatives to the fullest extent. In this case, a will to act freely and universally means a will to act morally and autonomously according to categorical imperatives, which in turn gives rise to free will and makes the agent become immediately conscious of moral laws. Hence in Kant's definition, if the determining ground of a will is none other than the universal lawgiving form of categorical imperatives, a will of this kind must be thought of as independent of the natural law of causality. Such independence suggests freedom in the strictest or transcendental sense. Therefore, a will for which the mere lawgiving form mentioned above can alone serve as a law is a free will.[15]

Undoubtedly, categorical imperatives are unconditional and universal requirements. They prescribe moral dignity, represent moral autonomy, and also encompass unmatchable force, and well reveal the ethos of Kant's moral sense, which is noble and idealistic. As discerned in his historical ontology of anthropology, Li asserts that individual practice is required to set up the structure of the subjective will, and individuals are expected to shoulder the obligation for the existence and development of humankind. Such moral sense and action make up the psychological mode of the human subject, and go beyond the specific interests of any era, society, and group. Naturally, they are conducive to the formation of willpower and moral psychology as a result of "rational coacervation."[16] Such coacervation comes out of human practice, action, emotion, desire and other sensibilities, just like the "rational internalization" that occurs in cognitive activities through sensory intuition. It then ends up in the true form of a free will in ethics, corresponding to free intuition in epistemology and so forth. Moreover, its moral worth coordinates the unity of humankind as a whole while upsetting the causal law and utilitarian effect. Bearing the features of the sublime, it arouses such moral feelings as "admiration and reverence."[17] These feelings are self-conscious and rational, characteristic of human beings alone.

As for "free enjoyment," it purports to enjoy the perception and experience of pleasure in the beautiful through sensory intuition and aesthetic judgment. It is free by nature, because the beautiful as a free form is not merely the union of lawfulness and purposefulness, but the product of humanized nature (the world). Corresponding to this free form is the aesthetic state of mind as a synthesis of sensation and rationality in one sense, and as an outcome of humanized internal nature (humankind) in the other.

More specifically, the aesthetic state of mind can be seen as the final attainment of human subjectality, and also the most explicit manifestation of human capacity. At this point, what is of humankind in its historical entirety is sedimented into what is of a human individual; what is rational is sedimented into what is sensible; and what is social is sedimented into what is natural. As a consequence, the nature of animal-like senses is humanized, and so is the nature of animal-like psychology. For example, *eros* becomes love; natural kinships become human relationships; natural senses become aesthetic faculties; and instinctive lust becomes aesthetic feeling. All this entails the true mode of free enjoyment and the ultimate aspect of human subjectality through historico-cultural sedimentation.[18] In other words, all this implies aesthetic capacity characterized by "rational melting" in accord with "aesthetic sedimentation."[19]

All in all, "free intuition" is coupled with "rational internalization," and "free will" with "rational coacervation." Both of them grow out of a sensation in which rationality is either internalized or coacervated. As for "free enjoyment," it is aligned with "rational melting," for it arises out of rationality sedimented in sensation. "Free intuition" and "free will" are expressed in the ability, action, and volition of rationality, whereas "free enjoyment" is expressed in the desire, feeling, and expectation of sensation. It is through the service of "free enjoyment" that human convergence with nature is rendered attainable. This convergence connotes the oneness between Heaven and humans. In Chinese tradition, it stands for both the aesthetic realm of human life and the ontological realm of super-moral being, thus facilitating the possibility of superseding the religious by the aesthetic. For the essence of beauty is, according to Li, the embodiment of human fulfillment. The philosophy of beauty is the summit of all humanities. And here what is explored relates to the possibility of human subjectality, and what is revealed relates to the formation of cultural psychology.[20]

## Beyond Aesthetic Engagement

According to a recent investigation, the notion of human subjectality is taken as a "new conception of the human self."[21] Because of its objective existential features, human subjectality is not constrained to the level of each human subject alone. It is assumed to include the ability to establish interactive relationships with others in the living environment that involve a variety of expressions of human community, such as society, nation, class, and organization. Hence Li Zehou intends to advocate two kinds of human subjectality: one is directed to each individual's identity, and the other to the human race as a whole. Both of them help humanity create a structure of human subjectality, a structure that is supra-biological and deeply rooted in a universal necessity. As a rule, the objective dimension of human subjectality can be found in the social realization of material reality through the process of production. It demonstrates itself not merely in the structural connection between technology and society, but also in the linkage between social existence and practice. Meanwhile, human subjectality accentuates the subjective level of social consciousness, which reveals itself in culturally conditioned mentalities or psychological formations. Following this paradigm, the constitutions of human subjectality are basically differing from the subjective awareness of human individuals. Instead, they are related to the products of human history that manifest themselves not only in the formations of spiritual and intellectual culture, but also in the structures of ethical and aesthetic consciousness.[22]

As Li himself observes, "Analytical philosophy, structuralism, and many other streams of the contemporary capitalist world (like for instance philosophical methodology or epistemology) are cold philosophies, which overlook the substance of subjectality. In addition, Sartre's existentialism, the philosophies of the Frankfurt School, and other fashionable currents (like for instance the philosophy of rebellion or the philosophy of emotion), on the other hand, are blindly propagating the individual subjectality. They have nothing to do with the practical philosophy of subjectality."[23] To my understanding, "cold philosophies" are presumed to be the philosophies that do not merely "overlook the substance of subjectality," but also neglect the emotional substance as the fundamental root of human becoming. They are most likely left under the overarching impact of conceptual abstraction or instrumental rationality. As regards the particular case of human individuals, when the development of human capacity is up to a full degree, it leads to the highest degree of human individuality, freedom, autonomy, and independence—in short, the highest achievement of which a human as human is capable. It is at this stage that the wholeness of human becoming is enhanced in light of human subjectality per se.

However, there arises some doubt about Li's critique of the so-called "cold philosophies," as it appears overgeneralized, if not overstated. Take "the philosophies of the Frankfurt School," for example. They are not that "cold" because they are characterized by a type of critical theory based on strong social, political, and human concern and commitment, although they have hardly championed any specific and real action to transform the social structures and political conventions they criticize. As discerned in the *Aesthetic Theory* by Adorno, what is persistently emphasized are the social and political functions of art associated with the truth-content and anti-world *tour de force* in need. On this account of art per se, sociality and autonomy, art and science, ideology and truth, political option and stance toward praxis (*Stellung zur Praxis*) and so forth are all put into due consideration and reflection. Moreover, when it comes to the discussion of artistic engagement, Adorno maintains it is intended to change the status quo from which the social ills are derived rather than to cure the social ills themselves. This in a way corresponds to the essential category of aesthetics proper. Interestingly, when he turns to the role of art and aesthetics as well, Adorno directs much attention to the impact, *Erlebnis*, and shudder (*Erschütterung*) of art in particular, which are connected not merely with the social and political aspects, but also with aesthetic and emotional values.[24] After all, Adorno's aesthetics leaves the reader under the impression that it focuses more on the truth-content of art, while it takes the emotionality of art for granted. Otherwise, Adorno himself would not redouble his efforts to revive and promote modern aesthetics in light of critical theory and negative dialectics at all. For what he strives to do is to raise public awareness of the social and real-world drawbacks in one sense, and in the other to inspire the public courage to improve the human condition in the living world as such.

Historically speaking, Li's notion of human subjectality was initially employed to highlight the rise of enlightenment in early 1980s soon after the disastrous period of the Cultural Revolution (1966–1976) in China. It was proposed to fill the ideological vacuum, and to spur a self-conscious pursuit of value selection and political freedom for self-development. Intellectually speaking, it was designed to alter the old-fashioned guardianship discourse in order to meet the growing political needs of the great majority, and the necessary theoretical needs of the emerging reforms in their initial development. At that time, the curtain of ideological manipulation was somewhat lifted because of its self-defeating effect on the one hand, and the pressing demand for a new space of thinking on the other. It was then replaced by a humanistic rediscovery of Marxism with reference to the Western heritage of humanism. Guardianship discourse was very dominant for a decade or so during the harsh years of the Cultural Revolution, and then reduced and changed considerably when the Open Door Policy was introduced to accelerate the process of reform. All this entailed a period of New Enlightenment in China throughout 1980s. Hence the promotion of human subjectality can be seen as one of the hammers used to break the ice of theoretical and ideological rigidity.

As to the key characteristics of human subjectality, they tend to cover individual uniqueness, practical sociality, historical sedimentation, cognitive initiative, moral autonomy, creative ability, aesthetic transcendence, and the like. Comparatively speaking, Li himself distinguishes his concept of subjectality from the Kantian notion of subjectivity, and formulates it in terms of anthropo-historical ontology as well as practical philosophy. He further develops it together with human capacity, but proposes it as the acme of human capacity and the ultimate outcome of human fulfillment. He attributes it to the possibility of aesthetic transcendence in association with disinterested satisfaction, purposefulness without a purpose, detachment from the immediate reality, and so forth. For this reason, Li puts much more stress on the aesthetic dimension of human capacity in general, and of human subjectality in particular.

He tries to do so for a number of reasons. First and foremost, the real meaning of human living is essentially aesthetic, for a relevant contemplation enables a person to find a way of living well in an artistic, purposeful, and disinterested manner in spite of the socio-psychic ills noted above. Such a manner applies not only to a moral will, but also to a world outlook. According to Li's articulation of aesthetics as the first philosophy, it encourages the individual to choose a worldview through creative imagination based on sensible preferences. As an aesthetic choice, such a worldview embodies a world picture of beautiful order. Even though the picture cannot be concluded as true or false, a worldview that is aesthetically imagined provides much food for thought. In this respect, the real theme of aesthetics is about the entire world and a human life of sensibility instead of art alone. Human life is to be eventually realized through the joy or pleasure experienced in landscapes underlying the Heaven–human convergence. Hence the "grand aesthetics" of the Chinese type is considered to be the truest when compared with its counterpart in other cultures. Such aesthetics is treated as the first philosophy, because it implies an intuitive assumption of the world (the cosmos) that exists in a mysterious mode and lies beyond the limit of human knowledge. Accordingly, the human worldview itself contains a mixture of "rational mystery" and "sensible mystery," which is inclined to provoke a profound feeling of admiration and a mystical experience of faith.[25]

Second, aesthetic experience is both sensuous and spiritual in effect. It is conducive to the growth of aesthetic sensibility that is both the bud and fruit of human capacity. It is more significant in that it entails spiritual sublimation in a range of "aesthetic transcendence."[26] At this point, it straddles two interrelated states: the initial state of human becoming and the supreme state of human fulfillment. According to Li, "Aesthetic experience is related to sensuous and animal-like desires. For this reason, pleasures drawn from music and sexuality have become prevailing in pop culture today. However, aesthetic experience attempts to go beyond such desires, and strives for 'transcendence' in a pure spiritual scope. It is therefore differentiated from mere entertainment and decoration, and intended to pursue a supra-biological state and living realm."[27] However, the "transcendence" mentioned above is not "pure" at all, for the human being can only hanker after it within the physical body from which the mind cannot be separated. It is therefore called "aesthetic transcendence" that relies on not merely the interaction between the mind and body, but also the interconnection between objective and subjective time. What is meant by "objective time" is to live in the stream of time with spatial occupation, which features the numbers of the date, month, and year due to social objectivity. It is accounted for by human birth, mortality, and the body that takes up the organic space. What is meant by "subjective time" is temporality without spatial occupation, which is symbolized by immortality or eternity with respect to the spiritual home of historical being and the infinite state of creative mind in particular. Give this, only the experience of the reality that all is nothing (no meaning, no causality, no utility) but still stays alive appears to be a mastery of temporality. As detected in Chinese tradition, such transcendence is usually obtained from the mystical experience of "Heaven–human oneness," and drawn from the concordance between the human cultivation and the cosmic rhythm hidden in both humanized nature and naturalized humanity. All this is linked with the "emotional substance" as the fundamental root of human becoming.[28] In order to facilitate the extension of subjective time, for example, it is of theoretical importance to bring "aesthetic transcendence" into the focus of human thinking, because it entails aesthetic self-consciousness and spiritual sublimation. As we humans cannot perceive any real thing except under the conditions of space and time, both objective and subjective time cannot grow out of space in a narrow sense. However, if a distinction between them is to be made, objective time is thought of as related to the space and time of sense experience in general, whereas subjective time is thought of as related to the space and time of psychic experience at large. A typical example is the conception of "the wind and moon turning out in a day" (momentary existence) as "the broad sky being of ten thousand years" (eternal existence). The former scene implies the space and time of sense experience on a specific occasion, and the latter scene implies the space and time of psychic experience merging into long history. The conception as such is achieved through sudden enlightenment and self-liberation as a consequence of human enculturation and cultivation, pertaining to transcending sense experience and securing spiritual freedom, which enables humans to shift from the finite sphere into the infinite one as is embodied in the boundless communion with the Heaven–human convergence as well as the range from the remote past to the current present and even the forward-looking future. This is fundamentally a different type of spatial and temporal experience on the part of human beings who are higher organisms with rational faculty and cultural mechanisms. A reference to Cassirer and Bruno in this context would shed light on this point.[29]

Third, aesthetic education is recommended to substitute for religion, not only because the former does not oppose the search for "perfect" experience of religious spirit, but also because human existence connects the physical body with the unconscious cosmic rhythm, which gives rise to the Heaven–human convergence in association with "aesthetic transcendence." By virtue of fostering fine taste, aesthetic education helps individuals to overcome the tragic sense of nothingness and hardship of human existence. As acknowledged in Chinese tradition, this tragic sense is twofold at least—say, "void and non-void"—in the meantime. It is void in terms of nothingness, and non-void in terms of immediate reality, both of which implicate the dual properties of the phenomenal world and the human condition. Under such circumstances, people are encouraged to face hard facts without any expectation of divine protection or redemption, and to approach an aesthetic realm of this-worldly living in pursuit of aesthetic rather than inward transcendence. Such a realm of living is sustained by "emotional substance" with a tendency to cherish life in the stream of time and make it worthwhile by all means. As a necessary and sufficient condition, the way of cherishing life awakens individuals to the extent that they will be ready to drop all illusions, and to tackle all changes, events, occasions, and contingencies encountered during the course of life.[30]

Last but not least, the aesthetic realm of this-worldly living in spiritual freedom is metaphysical and ontological in kind, for it is directed to the full development of human capacity, the self-realization of human subjectality, and the whole becoming of human as human. In this scope, aesthetics is taken as the first philosophy due to its embodiment of the beautiful order and the mystical vision of the cosmos in its entirety. Accordingly, the way of cherishing life becomes a true aesthetic experience of an ontological kind, even though it is akin to contemplating a sunset over the hills or scrutinizing a poem in landscapes. All this supposedly comes out of the following fact: "Man is self-awakening in his own way. He accepts his accidental and limited existence, and struggles to survive without blaming God or others. He tries to learn from the bottom and then moves up to the above, which means metaphorically to approach spiritual freedom through personal cultivation. . . . Therefore, the ideal of human becoming as the final end of nature will be realized . . . in the pursuit of aesthetic metaphysics through emotional substance."[31] Ostensibly, "the ideal of human becoming as the final end of nature" is none other than the full development of human capacity in light of human subjectality. Li thereby champions an aesthetic approach that means more than it seems. It is designed to cover three interrelated acts of illuminating the true, furnishing the good, and making life worthwhile through the beautiful.[32]

## The First Act

To begin with, the act of "illuminating the true through the beautiful" (*yi mei qi zhen* 以美啟真) is to make the most of aesthetic feeling and free imagination. It is underlined by the "aesthetic double helix" that may also lead to new findings in science and technology.[33] Herein the notion of "double helix" is borrowed from the discovery of DNA's molecular composition that encodes the information for making proteins. It is used metaphorically with an aesthetic tag to suggest that the secret of aesthetic feeling and judgment be decoded in the future development of brain and genetic sciences.

Clearly, both aesthetic feeling and free imagination are stressed due to their functions not simply in aesthetic experience and artistic creation, but also in scientific discovery and technological invention. The beautiful is at this point related to what is called the "thing in itself" (*Ding an sich*) in the Kantian saying. What can be known are the sensory objects that are conjectured as mere appearances stemmed from the "thing in itself." What is unknown is the "thing in itself" that affects human senses and faculties when it comes to thinking over this given noumenon. The cosmos as a whole exists according to its natural lawfulness, but remains largely unknown to human beings. Such lawfulness is "created" by exercising "the proper measure" (*du* 度). As a rule, it engages not only in logical and dialectical discursion, but also in human emotion and imagination. It thus signifies a key to "transcendental imagination" and the core of "illuminating the true through the beautiful."

Moreover, the act as such is also intended to inspire the cognitive power and gain real knowledge of a new type of "thing in itself," a type that is tallied with the "synergistic coexistence of humanity with the cosmos."[34] This is a metaphysical assumption without which aesthetic experience would have no origin, and sense of form would find nowhere. The cosmos presents the object a priori, whereas the cognitive power of a man-made symbolic system resembles the subject a priori. Both of them are unified through human praxis from the perspective of anthropo-historical ontology. With the help of "illuminating the true through the beautiful," a person manages to peer into the mysteries of the cosmos and to secure a position for humankind therein. It is via such an active life that the communion between humanity and the cosmos is made possible. It is therefore essential to have a metaphysical hypothesis of such a "thing in itself" in order to attain the synergistic concordance and coexistence of humanity with the cosmos (nature), because it will generate an indispensable premise, enabling humans to bring forth an order to the cosmos or the world in which they reside.

On this occasion, humans are apt to give a beautiful order to the cosmos or the world. The beautiful order is essentially cosmic and worldly, sensible and divine. It is by no means a by-product of pure subjective willfulness or wishful thinking. Instead, it is a manifestation of the crucial relationship between the beautiful and the true on the one hand, and between human emotion and rational truth on the other. Furthermore, it concerns not only the theory of knowledge, scientific discovery, and technological invention, but also the deep meaning and significance of anthropo-historical ontology. For example, Sir Michael F. Atiyah affirms that mathematics arises out of "invention" instead of "discovery." In this field, humans are characteristically able to make choices out of thousands of possibilities according to the law of beauty. This insight corresponds with Li's affirmation: the development of mathematics originated from the abstraction of sensible operations, which exemplifies a special case of "illuminating the true through the beautiful."[35] That is to say, the abstract and the sensible are interactive as much as the true and the beautiful. In all these cases, the law of beauty counts much more than expected.

## The Second Act

The act of "furnishing the good through the beautiful" (*yi mei chu shan* 以美儲善) is to draw aesthetic feeling from an underlying faith in emotional substance, and to find inspiration for a sound human interaction with the cosmos.[36] Such faith and inspiration help people to take up an affective view of the cosmos. This view in turn fosters a quasi-religious feeling for the cosmos, and facilitates an aesthetic awareness of the concordance between humanity and the cosmos, which will be conducive to establishing the Heaven-Earth realm of human living (*tian di jing jie* 天地境界).[37]

In principle, the Heaven-Earth realm is both moral and aesthetic in kind. It calls for emotional and faith-based support, thus resorting to the inner historicity of the human being, and cherishing the natural span of life within this world. That is to say, it is so worldly that it never bothers about how to pray God for a prerogative admission into so-called paradise. As a lifestyle, the realm is recommended as a Chinese way of dwelling poetically on the Earth. It may be perceived as a fantasy a priori from a quasi-religious or religious standpoint. However, it is pragmatically positive because it encourages people to exist in this world despite all the difficulties and hardships they face. It is schemed to work with an affective view of the cosmos, carrying out a kind of self-conscious affinity for the synergistic concordance between humanity and the cosmos.[38]

The cosmos is structurally tripartite, including Heaven, Earth, and humankind at large. As to the Heaven-Earth realm, it is twofold in essence, signifying a way of human living between Heaven and Earth in one sense, and a tri-unison of Heaven, Earth, and humankind in the other. It usually features inseparableness and harmoniousness among the three parties involved. According to Zhuangzi, an individual at this stage could go so far as to claim that "Heaven and Earth coexist with me, and the ten thousand things are one with me."[39] As Heaven and Earth are symbolic of the cosmos in the Chinese mentality, the Heaven-Earth realm can be also recognized as the cosmic realm, in which human beings have thus become cosmic beings and reached moral transcendence. They are then prone to embrace the cosmos (nature) as their spiritual home, and to shoulder a sense of mission to take care of it. They will commit themselves to eco-environmental protection, rethink their self-development in light of cosmic harmony, and hanker after their convergence with Heaven, Earth, and the myriad things. For in Chinese thought-way, the conception of the human self is assumed to accommodate the existence of external things. It is owing to this interlinkage that humans are expected to embrace the mission not only to facilitate the growth of things between Heaven and Earth, but also to converge with Heaven and Earth (the cosmos) in a trifold whole. All this conduces to Heaven-human oneness or cosmic harmony.

The cosmic harmony of this kind comes by and large from the synergistic concordance and coexistence between humanity and nature. It mainly depends on the two most crucial modes of social practice and human enculturation: "humanized nature" and "naturalized humanity." Judging from their developmental sequence and interactive connection, humanized nature contributes a precondition to naturalized humanity, and naturalized humanity in turn serves as a complementary counterpart to humanized nature. In brief, "naturalized humanity" involves at least four primary activities. The first is to perceive nature as a shelter and facilitate a harmonious relationship; the second is to return to nature for aesthetic contemplation of its beautiful landscapes; the third is to help the myriad things in nature grow properly through appropriate protection; and the fourth is to learn how to breathe naturally (e.g., through appropriate practice of *qigong* (氣功) as breathing exercise somewhat similar to yoga) in order to conciliate the rhythm of human body and heart with that of nature, which is most likely to entail Heaven–human oneness. All this is associated with a kind of aesthetic feeling or state of mind, in which the rational is fused with the emotional, the subject identified with the object, the social consciousness accompanied by individual freedom, and the sense of the finite coupled with the sense of the infinite. In short, by virtue of "naturalized humanity," human individuals will return to nature and dwell poetically so long as they are capable of freeing themselves from the control of instrumental rationality, from the alienation due to material fetishism, and from the enslavement by the systems of power, knowledge and language, among others.

As one of the activities mentioned above is aligned with aesthetic contemplation and appreciation, it thus operates through free enjoyment as part of human cultural-psychological formation. Compared with the service of the humanized faculties and emotions, the "naturalized humanity" exposes humans to free enjoyment in an aesthetic and spiritual sense. For this reason, Li asserts the superiority of the aesthetic dimension to the cognitive and ethical dimensions. The aesthetic dimension is neither the internalization of reason (the cognitive) nor the condensation of reason (the ethical), but the sedimentation of both reason and sense. Aesthetically speaking, it helps rectify the seven human emotions including joy, anger, sorrow, fear, love, hate, and desire (*qi qing zheng* 七情正) and arouse the delight in Heaven–human oneness (*tian ren le* 天人樂).

Interestingly, the idea of "furnishing the good through the beautiful" results from transformational creation. It purports to implicitly synthesize the Marxist conception of applying the law of beauty to human practice, the Kantian assumption of beauty as the symbol of morality, and the Confucian preoccupation with moral nourishment via emotional substance. The beautiful can be divided into two primary kinds, known as the pure and the dependent, whereas the good can be divided into the unconditional (absolute) and the conditional (utilitarian). Teleologically, these two categories are interwoven with each other despite the tendency that one is used as the means while the other taken as the end. Functionally, they are both underpinned by the pragmatic worth of aesthetic metaphysics in terms of the cultural-psychological formation through social practice and spiritual praxis, among others.

## The Third Act

What follows here is the third act of "making life worthwhile through the beautiful" (*yi mei li ming* 以美立命). It is aimed at emancipating individuals from all cares and worries concerning life and death, enabling them to live at ease and without fear.[40] It is widely perceived in the Chinese mentality that humans are mortals, and thus they will certainly die. Facing their natural term, they each live on resolutely disregarding the limited span of time they are given. Intellectually and emotionally, they learn from past experiences in order to find a way out, endeavor to have a better understanding of human existence under varied circumstances, and manage to appreciate the infinite and mysterious cosmos. Sentimentally if not sorrowfully, they retain their attachment to life and cherish it even though they are highly aware of their destined death. Still, they are prepared to confront whatever happens to them. They know the fact that they are bound to eventually vanish into the stream of time. However, they are mostly determined to uphold their will to live, and ready to die for such a reason: it is better to cherish life, and have no fear of death, as it is sheer folly to be haunted by life-and-death anxiety. Having reached this level of self-knowledge, they come closer to the Heaven-Earth realm of human living, and tend to have aesthetic feelings mixed with admiration and reverence.

Notably, human life has a natural term, and human living is a dynamic process, with both subjected to the hierarchy of human needs. When the basic needs (physical and material) are gratified, the higher needs (social, aesthetic and spiritual) come along. Judging from an aesthetic point of view, the sense of beauty occupies an important ranking. As noted in this regard, there arises a free play of such faculties as human perception, intuition, imagination, judgment, and understanding. They all work interactively and help people to sublimate their aesthetic sensibility, taste, and wisdom, which in turn leads them to contemplate and appreciate the beautiful. What is beautiful in nature and art is ubiquitous in varied forms, genres, styles, structures, and symbols. It waits for a mind's eye or a musical ear to find it out. In general, it can be divided into three broad types, encompassing what pleases the ear and the eye (*yue er yue mu* 悦耳悦目), what delights the mind and the wish (*yue xin yue yi* 悦心悦意), and what inspires the will and the spirit (*yue zhi yue shen* 悦志悦神).

Briefly, the first type particularly appeals to the senses of hearing and sight. It involves beautiful forms, images, appearances, shapes, colors, sounds, and rhythms, among other elements. These can be widely perceived and enjoyed due to their visual and aural features, inviting attractions, sensuous pleasures, and so forth. They are available in natural scenes, landscape paintings, pop songs, folk dances, country music, and the like.

The second type largely delights the mental state and the intentional wish of the contemplator. It comprises more significant forms, meaningful contents, grotesque images, magnificent proportions, sophisticated métier and artistic tour de force. These components can be apprehended and appreciated through an integrated working of such faculties as aesthetic sensibility, understanding, imagination, association, judgment, feeling, and so on. They are usually applied to works of art and landscapes blended with culturescapes in unique settings. The aesthetic experience at this stage is facilitated by means of deep apperception and percipience, thus touching the mental state, affecting the intentional wish and, above all, provoking more reflections and ponderings.

The third type inspires the will and the spirit, conducive to evoking a kind of cosmic spirit and mysterious feeling. It covers something great, sublime, symbolic, and even divine. It can be effectively perceived by means of serene contemplation and sudden enlightenment. It is therefore quasi-religious in that it spurs peak experience, transcending all kinds of sensuous pleasures and psychological delights. Such experience conforms with both the Heaven–human oneness and the cosmic realm of human living. On this account, what is void is also non-void for individuals of high aesthetic sensibility and wisdom, because they live poetically in freedom from cares, fears, worries and other tangible entanglements. Such a way of life is contemplative, detached, disinterested, harmonious, and peaceful. It appears as if it were this-worldly and other-worldly at the same time. It is expounded and metaphorically expressed in many classical Chinese poems and literary essays.

## Conclusion

As shown in the foregoing discussion, the how-to-live concern is linked with the human condition today. Li Zehou proposes the full development of human capacity as an alternative to address this concern. When human capacity reaches its greatest height, it gives rise to the accomplishment of human subjectality. Both of them are intimately interrelated because they share similar determinants. The ideal state of human subjectality is treated as the acme of human capacity and the ultimate outcome of human fulfillment, standing for the highest achievement of which a human is capable.

In order to obtain the final objective, much emphasis is placed on the aesthetic dimension of both human capacity and subjectality, as this dimension is both an emerging stage of human development and the final end of human fulfillment. Characteristically and teleologically distinguished from its Western counterpart, Chinese aesthetics is deployed as a foundation stone of Li's historical ontology, practical philosophy, and aesthetic metaphysics. It is closely allied with such notions as emotional substance, proper measure, emotio-rational structure, and pragmatic reason.[41] It is expected not only to enhance the development of human capacity, but also to address the how-to-live concern with aesthetic sensibility and wisdom. As such, it is intended to lead individuals to approach the ideal of human subjectality as a new conception of the human self, emancipate them from socio-psychic entanglements for the sake of spiritual freedom, and eventually enable them to live a worthwhile life in this world rather than the next.

Incidentally, when applied to creating the beautiful, the proper measure is commended by Li Zehou so as help individuals develop skill into art, transform creative freedom into spiritual freedom, and sublimate artistic appreciation to aesthetic transcendence. Moreover, its application is coupled with "illuminating the true through the beautiful," because they are both directed to the special role of practical aesthetics. Similarly, the conception of emotional substance as a fundamental root of human psychology is connected with the act of "furnishing the good through the beautiful," because they are both pointed to promoting the internal value of aesthetic metaphysics. All this is due to the conviction that the beautiful illuminates the true and symbolizes the good. Accordingly, the aesthetic sensibility of the beautiful serves as an enlightening energy that inspires the contemplator to gain insights into the epistemological worth of the true, and to cultivate the moral consciousness of the good.

Regarding the trifold engagement in the interactive acts stated above, it makes the most of the aesthetic dimension that straddles a number of provinces including the true, the good, the beautiful, and human living. It is aimed at the attainment of aesthetic transcendence mainly grounded on two paramount orientations: the Heaven–human oneness and the culture of optimism. They both represent the primary ethos of Chinese culture at large. The oneness of this kind is often treated as the supreme aesthetic realm in line with the Heaven-Earth realm of human living. The optimism as such originates from the Chinese music-rites heritage that features joy-consciousness and an aesthetic stance toward everyday life. Historically and practically, this has had a strong impact on the Chinese cultural tradition and national mentality. Naturally and effectively, it evokes an aesthetic sensibility in a metaphysical sense, remolds the joy-conscious temperament in an anthropological sense, and consolidates the optimistic spirit in an ontological sense. These three traits are interwoven in the deep structure of cultural psychology and life philosophy in China. Empirically and actually, the aesthetic sensibility pertains to the aesthetic appreciation of the beautiful in art and nature, the joy-conscious temperament makes the national mentality accustomed to granting bitter joy or drawing delight from sufferings and miseries, and the optimistic spirit, all the more instructive and significant, enables Chinese people to become what they are, never losing a ray of hope at confrontation with the gravest crises and hardships. They are thus ready to acknowledge the interaction between the negative and positive sides of all matters, and to prepare for the possible interplay between fortune and misfortune in varied situations.

This being true, they tend to prepare for the worst and hope for the best. They usually get accustomed to crisis-conscious thinking, and keep alert against potential dangers even in peacetime. Meanwhile, they manage to appreciate bitter joy while searching for possible alternatives to cope with unexpected problems and challenges. Knowing well the difficult condition of human existence as sandwiched between Heaven and Earth, they have no other choice but persevere in self-reliance under all circumstances. To the extent of their self-consciousness of human living as such, they are distinct from Christians, who have the good fortune to be exposed to divine grace and redemption. Hence in many cases the Chinese majority are liable to suffer more, and paradoxically enjoy more, because of their enculturated sense of bitter joy either in difficult situations or under harsh conditions. They are fond of human living with an optimistic spirit and matter-of-fact attitude. They tend to celebrate a joy-conscious and morality-based life in this world. In general, their way of life is like a boat moving against the current. It beats on, so persistently, no matter what difficulties it confronts, as has been repeatedly proven through the many ups and downs in the long course of Chinese history.

# Notes

1. This special concept in Chinese is *zhutixing* (主體性), coined by Li Zehou, and distinguished from subjectivity as *zhuguan xing* (主觀性) in certain cases, as explored in his philosophical discourse.

2. Confucius, "The Confucian Analects," in *The Four Books*, trans. James Legge (Changsha: Hunan Press, 1995), 11:12.

3. The old saying in Chinese is *ren sheng yi shi, cao mu yi qiu* (人生一世, 草木一秋).

4. Confucius, 4:8.

5. Confucius, 15:6.

6. Confucius, 6:11.

7. It is expressed in Chinese as *Kong Yan le chu* (孔顏樂處), which is recommended as a lifestyle in line with the classical Confucian ideal.

8. Xunzi, *The Xunzi*, trans. John Knoblock (Beijing: Foreign Languages Press, 2016), 648–9.

9. The Chinese notion of *yue* as music and that of *le* as joy are distinct in pronunciation but share the same Chinese character (樂).

10. Li Zehou, "Human Nature and Aesthetic Metaphysics," in *International Yearbook of Aesthetics: Diversity and Universality in Aesthetics*, vol. 14, ed. Wang Keping (Beijing: International Association for Aesthetics, 2010), 4.

11. Immanuel Kant, *Anthropology from a Pragmatic Point of View*, trans. Robert Louden (Cambridge: Cambridge University Press, 2006), 90–93.

12. Li Zehou 李澤厚, *Shiyong lixing yu legan wenhua* 實用理性與樂感文化 (*Pragmatic Reason and a Culture of Optimism*) (Beijing: Sanlian Bookstore, 2005), 108. All translations are my own unless otherwise noted.

13. These three concepts are termed in Chinese as *zi you zhi guan* (自由直觀), *zi you yi zhi* (自由意志), and *zi you xiang shou* (自由享受).

14. Li Zehou 李澤厚, *Pipan zhexue de pipan: Kangde Shuping* 批判哲學的批判: 康德述評 (*Critique of the Critical Philosophy: A Commentary on Kant*) (Beijing: Renmin Press, 1984), 425–26.

15. Immanuel Kant, *Critique of Practical Reason*, trans. Mary Gregor (Cambridge: Cambridge University Pres, 2015), 26.

16. In Chinese this term is *li xing ning ju* (理性凝聚).

17. According to Kant, "Two things fill the mind with ever new and increasing admiration and reverence, the more often and more steadily one reflects on them: the starry heavens above me and the moral law within me. I do not need to search for them and merely conjecture them as though they were veiled in obscurity or in the transcendent region beyond my horizon; I see them before me and connect them immediately with the consciousness of my existence." Cf. Kant, *Critique of Practical Reason*, 129.

18. Li, *Critique of the Critical Philosophy*, 434–35.

19. Li, "Human Nature and Aesthetic Metaphysics," 5.

20. Li, *Critique of the Critical Philosophy*, 436.

21. Jana S. Rošker, "Li Zehou's Notion of Subjectality as a New Conception of Human Self," *Philosophy Compass* 13, no. 5 (January 2018): 1.

22. Rošker, "Li Zehou's Notion of Subjectality," 3–4; Li Zehou, "The Philosophy of Kant and a Theory of Subjectivity," in *Analecta Husserliana—The Yearbook of Phenomenological Research* 21, ed. Anna-Teresa Tymieniecka (Dordrecht: D. Reidel, 1986), 136; Li Zehou 李澤厚, *Meixue si jiang* 美學四講 (*Four Lectures on Aesthetics*) (Guilin: Guangxi Normal University Press, 2001), 43.

23. Li Zehou 李澤厚, "Guanyu zhutixing de buchong shuo ming" 關於主體性的補充說明 (A Supplementary Explanation of Subjectality), *Journal of the Graduate School of Chinese Academy of Social Sciences* 1 (1985): 21.

24. Theodor W. Adorno, *Ästhetische Theorie* (Frankfurt: Suhrkamp, 2012), 334–80.

25. Liu Zaifu 刘再复, *Li Zehou meixue gailun* 李澤厚美學概論 (*A Conspectus of Li Zehou's Aesthetics*) (Beijing: Sanlian Bookstore, 2009), 218–19.

26. Li uses the term as *shen mei chao yue* (審美超越) because he rejects the term of inward transcendence (*nei zai chao yue* 内在超越).

27. Li, "Human Nature and Aesthetic Metaphysics," 8.

28. Li, "Human Nature and Aesthetic Metaphysics," 8.

29. According to Cassirer, "we must analyze the forms of human culture in order to discover the true character of space and time in our human world.... There are fundamentally different types of spatial and temporal experience. Not all the forms of this experience are on the same level. There are lower and higher strata arranged in a certain order." (Ernest Cassirer, *An Essay on Man* (New Haven and London: Yale University Press, 1975 [1944]), 42). According to Bruno, man's self-liberation leads to what follows. That is, "Man no longer lives in the world as a prisoner enclosed within the narrow walls of a finite physical universe. He can traverse the air and break through all the imaginary boundaries of the celestial spheres which have been erected by a false metaphysics and cosmology. The infinite universe sets no limits to human reason; on the contrary, it is the great incentive of human reason. The human intellect becomes aware of its own infinity through measuring its power by the infinite universe." Ibid., 15.

30. Li, "Human Nature and Aesthetic Metaphysics," 10–11; Liu, *A Conspectus of Li Zehou's Aesthetics*, 230.

31. Li, "Human Nature and Aesthetic Metaphysics," 13; Liu, *A Conspectus of Li Zehou's Aesthetics*, 218, 228–89.

32. Li, "Human Nature and Aesthetic Metaphysics," 7.

33. Li, "Human Nature and Aesthetic Metaphysics," 7.

34. In Chinese it is termed as *ren yu yu zhou gong zai* (人與宇宙共在).

35. Liu, *A Conspectus of Li Zehou's Aesthetics*, 222.

36. Li, "Human Nature and Aesthetic Metaphysics," 7.

37. This notion can be traced back to *Xin yuan ren* 新原人 (*The New Original Men*) by Fung Yu-lan (Feng Youlan, 1895–1990) in 1947. It is mainly concerned with an approach to freedom, moral transcendence, and self-awakening.

As regards moral transcendence, Fung examines four realms of human achievement as follows: the natural realm, which is characterized by simplicity based on naturalness; the utilitarian realm, which is characterized by self-interestedness based on sociality; the moral realm, which is characterized by righteousness guided by moral substance; and the Heaven-Earth realm, which is characterized by serving Heaven-Earth in pursuit of moral transcendence. Cf. Fung Yu-lan (Feng Youlan) 馮友蘭, *Ji gao ming er dao zhong yong* 極高明而道中庸 (*Reach the Greatest Height and Brilliancy and Follow the Path of the Mean*) (Beijing: China Guanbo Dianshi Press, 1995), 367–434.

38. Liu, *A Conspectus of Li Zehou's Aesthetics*, 228–30.

39. Zhuangzi, *The Complete Works of Zhuangzi*, trans. Burton Watson (New York: Columbia University Press, 2013), 71.

40. Li, "Human Nature and Aesthetic Metaphysics," 7.

41. Wang Keping, "Li Zehou's View of Pragmatic reason," in *Li Zehou and Confucian Philosophy*, ed. Roger T. Ames and Jinhua Jia (Honolulu: University of Hawai'i Press, 2018), 240–47.

# Bibliography

Adorno, Theodor W. *Ästhetische Theorie*. Frankfurt: Suhrkamp, 2012.

Adorno, Theodor W. *Meixue lilun* 美学理论 (*Aesthetic Theory*). Translated by Wang Keping from C. Lenhardt's English version. Shanghai: Shanghai Renmin Press, 2020.

Ames, Roger T., and Jia Jinhua, eds. *Li Zehou and Confucian Philosophy*. Honolulu: University of Hawai'i Press, 2018.

Cassirer, Ernest. *An Essay on Man*. New Haven and London: Yale University Press, 1975 [1944].

Confucius. "The Confucian Analects." In *The Four Books*. Translated by James Legge. Changsha: Hunan Press, 1995.

Fung, Yu-lan (Feng Youlan) 馮友蘭. *Ji gao ming er dao zhong yong* 極高明而道中庸 (*Reach the Greatest Height and Brilliancy and Follows the Path of the Mean*). Beijing: China Guanbo Dianshi Press, 1995.

Kant, Immanuel. *Anthropology from a Pragmatic Point of View*. Translated by Robert Louden. Cambridge: Cambridge University Press, 2006.

Kant, Immanuel. *Critique of Practical Reason*. Translated by Mary Gregor. Cambridge: Cambridge University Press, 2015.

Li Zehou 李泽厚. *Li Zehou mei xue gailun* 李澤厚美學概論 (*An Introduction to Li Zehou's Aesthetics*), edited by Liu Zaifu. Beijing: Sanlian Bookshop, 2009.

Li Zehou 李泽厚. "Guanyu zhutixing de buchong shuoming" 關於主體性的補充說明 (A Supplementary Explanation of Subjectality). *Zhongguo shehui kexue yuan yuanjiushengyuan xuebao* 1 (1985): 14–21.

Li Zehou. "Human Nature and Aesthetic Metaphysics." In *International Yearbook of Aesthetics: Diversity and Universality in Aesthetics*, vol. 14, edited by Wang Keping, 4. Beijing: International Association for Aesthetics, 2010.

Li Zehou 李澤厚. *Meixue si jiang* 美學四講 (*Four Lectures on Aesthetics*). Guilin: Guangxi Normal University Press, 2001.

Li Zehou. "The Philosophy of Kant and a Theory of Subjectivity." In *Analecta Husserliana—The Yearbook of Phenomenological Research 21, The Phenomenology of Man and of the Human Condition, II: The Meeting Point between Occidental and Oriental Philosophies*, edited by Anna-Teresa Tymieniecka, 135–49. Dordrecht: D. Reidel, 1986.

Li Zehou 李泽厚. *Pipan zhexue de pipan: Kangde Shuping* 批判哲學的批判: 康德述評 (*Critique of the Critical Philosophy: A Commentary on Kant*). Beijing: Renmin Press, 1984.

Li Zehou 李澤厚. *Shiyong lixing yu legan wenhua* 實用理性與樂感文化 (*Pragmatic Reason and a Culture of Optimism*). Beijing: Sanlian Bookstore, 2005.

Liu Zaifu 刘再复. *Li Zehou meixue gai lun* 李澤厚美學概論 (*A Conspectus of Li Zehou's Aesthetics*). Beijing: Sanlian Bookstore, 2009.

Rošker, Jana S. "Li Zehou's Notion of Subjectality as a New Conception of Human Self." *Philosophy Compass* 13, no. 5 (2018): e12484.

Wang Keping. "Li Zehou's View of Pragmatic Reason." In *Li Zehou and Confucian Philosophy*, edited by Roger T. Ames and Jinhua Jia, 225–52. Honolulu: University of Hawai'i Press, 2018.

Xunzi. *The Xunzi*. Translated by John Knoblock. Beijing: Foreign Languages Press, 2016.

Zhuangzi. *The Complete Works of Zhuangzi*. Translated by Burton Watson. New York: Columbia University Press, 2013.

# Part 2
# Culture in the Mirror of History

# 4

# Sedimentation and Gene-Culture Coevolution

Jordan B. Martin

In a collated work that he endorsed as a "veracious . . . academic biography,"[1] the nonagenarian Li Zehou placed great importance on the validation of his sedimentation theory generally, and specifically on the confirmation of the proposition that "culture influences the brain," even going so far as saying, "if [that proposition] were to be proven, I think it would be of greater significance than all of my books put together."[2] This was in fact a recapitulation of a hope he had expressed approximately a decade previously: "I want to confirm whether or not culture influences the brain, whether or not in a few hundred years vestiges of Chinese culture will be discoverable in [the brain], and used as proof of my sedimentation theory."[3]

Had Li merely been hoping that his sedimentation theory would be recognized by future scientists as an early formulation of a by-then widely accepted scientific truth about phylogenetic-level effects of culture on hominin brains in general, then it is to be sincerely hoped that before his passing he had occasion to feel bolstered by Marthe Chandler's recent (and to my mind quite correct) verdict that "sedimentation is consistent with much of anthropology and social psychology."[4] Indeed, Chandler's paper does a fairly comprehensive job of presenting the scientific evidence (although not necessarily the underlying theory) supportive of Li's ideas about "sedimentation of species" (*yuanshi jidian* 原始積澱),[5] in which social imitation in tool use and manufacture among our hominin ancestors led gradually to "theory of mind" and language. Apart from the phylogenetic-level effects of *yuanshi jidian*, however, it seems from the above passage that Li was also interested in effects at the level of ontogeny—do specific cultural traits and practices affect individual brains in a way that correlates with some physical observable? Again, we can answer in the affirmative. Given the great store Li explicitly placed in the question itself, it seems like an answer well worth giving in some detail.

Before I adduce all the supporting empirical evidence, however, it will be necessary to first outline the basics of both the sedimentation theory and of one of contemporary science's leading interdisciplinary research paradigms that probe and explain the causal factors underlying the influence of culture on the brain, namely gene-culture coevolution (GCC). To my knowledge, despite a documented familiarity with the evolutionary biologist Edward O. Wilson (whose passing came approximately a month after Li's),[6] Li doesn't seem to have been particularly aware of the development of GCC. Nonetheless, there are significant areas of agreement shared by GCC and sedimentation theory, and both GCC and sedimentation theory seem like useful cross-disciplinary bridges for those familiar with one but not the other. As we will see below under "Sedimentation and Gene-Culture Coevolution: Consonance," the introduction of GCC also helps resolve an apparent contradiction in Li's published views on biological evolution. Finally, however, some dissonance and ambiguity arises from the juxtaposition of sedimentation theory with GCC. The dissonance is instructive, and useful for sharpening our awareness of some of the internal tensions in Li Zehou's thought that have been pointed out previously. In my fifth section, "Sedimentation and Gene-Culture Coevolution: Dissonance and Ambiguity," I also clarify an ambiguity, albeit in a necessarily speculative manner.

## Sedimentation and Gene-Culture Coevolution: Two Theories in Outline

I will start with a brief outline of the two theories.[7] Let us begin with sedimentation theory. Li analogizes the formation of human nature to geological processes. In geology, some particular episodes of relatively short periodicity may bring about radical change in terrain features, while more ubiquitous features closer to the bedrock are the result of processes of longer periodicity. The high-variance superficial features are more malleable, but even the deeper and less malleable structures are nevertheless in constant flux. As for geology, so for human nature: nothing is absolutely fixed and invariant, and a range of different technological, cultural, social, and biological factors influence the constitution of one's human nature, but this doesn't mean we can't meaningfully speak of a common human nature if we drill down deep enough: "to repeat, the common human nature I'm talking about here, I don't think it's an endowment of Heaven, nor is it something had from the outset, but is rather the product of anthropo-historical [processes of] accumulation."[8] The core idea here is that what is "transcendental with respect to the individual, is still formed via accumulative (*jidian* 積澱) [processes] that are empirical with respect to humankind in the aggregate."[9] Different aspects of this core idea are reflected in a range of pet phrases Li employs: "the empirical becomes the transcendental,"[10] "culture influences the brain,"[11] "intelligence is produced via culture,"[12] "humankind created itself,"[13] and so forth.

For Li, experiential practice is the link between aesthetics and human nature, the link between *Four Essays on Aesthetics* and *A Theory of Anthropo-Historical Ontology*. One of the most important such practices (although far from the only relevant one) that influenced our common human nature was the manufacture of tools, an endeavor in which our Pleistocene (and arguably even late Pliocene) ancestors spent millennia engaged:

> Aesthetics (or a sense of beauty) originally didn't have anything to do with art, it showed up in the process of humankind's operations/labors in using/manufacturing tools . . . during the operations and activities of using/manufacturing tools, more types of the psychological functions we possessed were reinforced. Among these, the functions of imagination and comprehension particularly need to be mentioned. Together with the instinctual animal desires and perceptions, they produced a greater complexity of combinations, interweavings and infiltrations, upon which they gradually formed the chimerical and almost unfathomable changefulness of the cultural-psychological formation (*wenhua xinli jiegou* 文化心理結構).[14]

Some Chinese scholars have found the sedimentation theory's leap from aesthetics to paleoanthropology and/or philosophy to be overly theoretically difficult;[15] others have found its "content motley, indistinct, and difficult to grasp."[16] As to the former, for better or worse, similar such charges are frequently to be heard leveled at interdisciplinary projects; as to "indistinctness," it seems evident from title headings such as "the formation of the human hand needs to be taken seriously"[17] that Li was from quite early on unabashed in deriving empirical predictions from his theory. And "motley" is really just a pejorative term for "diverse." But we need not get into the weeds with a comprehensive analysis of the sedimentation theory's merits and defects. What we'll mainly be concerned with here is to facilitate the comparison with GCC, and also to ask whether the evidentiary landscape has changed with respect to the propositions "culture influences the brain," "the empirical becomes the transcendental," et cetera since the year 1994, a year in which Xu Mengqiu declared that "neither contemporary psychology and neurobiology, nor indeed anthropology, have thus far provided results or data sufficient to clarify this issue."[18] (Sneak preview: "they have.") Of course, these evaluations are mainly in respect of phylogenetic *yuanshi jidian*. Li's conception of sedimentation comes in three types, however: in addition to *yuanshi jidian*, the accumulative processes also occur both at the ontogenetic level of the individual and at the intermediate level of human cultures. When we come to review the influence of culture on the brain, we will make our analysis at all three such levels.

What is gene-culture coevolution? As a research paradigm, its nascent period began with the work of Luigi Cavalli-Sforza and Marcus Feldman in the early 1970s, and through the efforts of Robert Boyd, Peter Richerson, Joseph Henrich, and others in recent decades, has by now entered its mature period. The core idea of GCC is that *Homo sapiens* (and other hominid species prior to their extinction) reliably inherit(ed) not only a biological endowment but also a cultural endowment, and that these two sources of inheritance[19] influence(d) each other. Readers of Li Zehou would be familiar with one particular example of such influence in which the causal flow runs from biology to culture: cultural norms that accommodate rather than negate the kin-oriented partiality observed ubiquitously in the biological domain are more likely to be successful;[20] biology influences culture. For this exact reason, as Donald Munro initially argued[21] and Li Zehou with some qualification agreed,[22] the Ruist strategy of grounding human-hearted love (*ren'ai* 仁愛) in biologically supported partiality toward kin was a good one. But crucially, the causal flow can also run in the other direction, from culture to biology: inherited cultural practices and norms can bring about intergenerationally stable alterations in the selection pressures faced by genomes, and indeed these selection pressures can be quite strong. Cultural norms can thereby potentiate non-Lamarckian functional adaptation across shorter periodicities than would be possible in many cases via natural selection alone. This point perhaps merits an unambiguous recapitulation: GCC does not entail any type of scientifically illegitimate "Lamarckian" inheritance of acquired characteristics. We will return to this point in the next section.

The emergence of lactase persistence is the canonical "proof of concept" example of gene-culture coevolution. The reason the majority of the global adult population exhibit lactose intolerance at differing levels of severity is that intolerance to lactose is actually the default condition for physiologically mature individuals of the vast majority of mammalian species, *Homo sapiens* included. Unweaned mammalian infants secrete the enzyme lactase, which is necessary for uncomplicated digestion of the lactose in milk, but will cease the (usually unnecessary) production of lactase after weaning. *Homo sapiens* are one of the rare species of which some substantial subpopulations continue to rely on lactose as an energy source after weaning, generally obtaining it from domesticated ungulates. Prior to the domestication of these ungulate species and the development of a considerable body of cultural knowhow pertaining to dairying on the part of prehistoric human populations, the production of lactase in humans did not persist past weaning. Even for contemporary populations, those without a history of dairying—which is the greater half of humanity—generally do not have the mutated alleles that confer lactase persistence. The frequencies of incidence of lactase persistence alleles for various populations are strongly correlated with that population's history of dairying,[23] and this is an example of cultural traits changing the strength of selection pressures faced by genomes. That is to say, this is an example of causal flow from culture to biology. This example of GCC is admittedly unrelated to the brain, but it is the unambiguous proof of concept for GCC as a scientifically legitimate process by which the human brain (as proponents will further stipulate) has been powerfully sculpted during prehistory.

Lastly, before moving on to a further underscoring of the consonances between sedimentation theory and GCC, it would seem to be in the interests of fairness and thoroughness to point out that the story

Li tells about *yuanshi jidian* is also broadly compatible with other rival models of the development of intelligence in the *Homo* lineage, models such as, for instance, Steven Pinker's "cognitive niche" hypothesis. This model also emphasizes coevolution between genes and the various human cognitive innovations,[24] but GCC differs from this model crucially in GCC proponents' affirmation of cultural traits as themselves being the targets of Darwinian evolution (in addition to the genomes of their bearers). I mention this here as an important feature of GCC that it seems appropriate to background here in the outline, but under "Sedimentation and Gene-Culture Coevolution: Dissonance and Ambiguity," below, I will scour the available textual evidence and attempt on that basis to sketch out a projection of what Li might have thought of such an idea.

## Sedimentation and Gene-Culture Coevolution: Consonance

Let us return now to the apparent contradiction in Li's views on biological evolution, foreshadowed in the introduction. The deployment of GCC allows for a cogent resolution of this ambiguity, so this is a good place to start in discussing the consonance between GCC and sedimentation. Let us now describe this seeming contradiction: Li frequently makes assertions such as "that by which humans love each other . . . comes from an upgrade of natural biological emotions,"[25] and refers to human nature as being "mutable, evolutionary and molded by humans themselves from their animal biological base,"[26] quite evidently recognizing humans and their emotional dispositions as having evolved from an "animal biological base." Does Li, then, concur with the overwhelming consensus of the scientific community that biological evolution occurs via the operation of selection upon the variation provided by genetic mutation? This is actually a surprisingly difficult question to answer. His references to DNA are more often figurative than literal,[27] and his "Response to Paul Gauguin's Triple Question" contains the following prima facie confusing exchange (emphases mine):

> [Li Zehou]: First, let's talk about Gauguin's first question: Where do humans come from? There are generally two answers. The first is that God created humans. . . . Second, since Nietzsche declared that God is dead, [sociobiology] has

become rather popular in academia. This theory holds that *human beings come from animal gene mutation.* Consequently, human society is *merely* a continuation of the animal world.

[He Daolin]: That is to say, humankind is a sort of hairless ape, and we are no different from animals. Animals too have social organizations and ethics. They even have some sort of political machinery. You can find plenty of literature on this topic. Books such as Desmond Morris' Naked Ape and Frans de Waal's Chimpanzee Politics are well-known, popular, and very influential.

[Li Zehou]: Since the theme of the conference was Confucian philosophy, I remarked that Chinese Confucianism *agrees with neither of these two answers*. Rather, it regards civilization and culture as historical products with a historical progression of formation and development. To put it briefly, it can be said that the human race creates herself. I've been maintaining this view for decades.[28]

The assertion that human society is *merely* a continuation of the animal world is indeed very much at odds with the views of both Li and of Ruism more broadly if and when too great an emphasis is placed on the word "merely"—while it is evident that for both there is a processual and gradual development from the animal to the human, it is nonetheless equally evident that humans are something else important besides. So this seems unproblematic. But it seems very much implicit in Li's response that he (and Ruism more broadly) *also* disagree(s) with the idea "that human beings come from animal gene mutation." Was Li, for all his recognition of humans as beings evolved from an "animal biological base," nevertheless genuinely denying that evolution occurs via the operation of selection upon genetic mutation?

Despite the above exchange, I think we can answer this question with a confident "no"—he wasn't. Importantly, GCC helps fill in the details of how this could be so. Let's begin by examining a couple of pieces of countervailing textual evidence. In a chapter of *An Outline of Ethics* dating to 2006, Li asserts that "recently, it has become something of a fashionable stance in contemporary ethics to be . . . anti-evolution, anti-science, anti-history, and anti-individual."[29] Li shortly afterward confirms that he "opposes this trend or fashion."[30] This double-negative opposition to opposition to evolution and science is encouraging, but not quite conclusive—perhaps Li's understanding of evolutionary science could be quite different from that of the scientific community. Later, however, in another chapter of the same work, this time dating from 2012, he also states that "reason is that by which humans broke with the natural processes of evolution which arise via genetic mutation in animal genera,"[31] confirming that he does see evolution in non-human animals at least as driven by genetic mutation—that is to say, he accepts the basic premise of mutation-driven evolution.

How, then, should we understand Li's above-cited rejection of the idea that "human beings come from animal gene mutation"? In the context of the said rejection of sociobiology's (purported) description of humans as *mere* extensions of the animal world, and also in the broader context of the centrality of the notion of subjectality (*zhutixing* 主體性) qua "productive practice"[32] as opposed to "pure bestial physiological 'existence'"[33] in Li's thought, my abductive faculties suggest to me that in the above-cited dialogue Li isn't really espousing the (frankly preposterous) idea that mutation-driven evolution played no role in transforming australopithecines into *sapiens*, but is rather opposing the idea that our hominin ancestors were merely *passive* participants in the evolutionary process, merely that one blithely lucky primate species that just so happened to win the mutational lottery and retain the few serendipitous "silver bullet" mutations that would then propel us inevitably and unstoppably along the path to anatomical modernity. What Li rather wants to emphasize is that in the course of many hundreds of thousands of years of tool manufacture, our ancestors were *active* participants in techno-social practices from which eventually sprang forth full-blown subjectality, language, theory of mind, and rapid encephalization, and without which even a few advantageous genetic mutations would still have been insufficient for the human race to have "create[d] herself."

GCC provides the theoretical vocabulary to flesh out Li's ideas and resolve this ambiguity. The GCC model would agree with the gist of Li's ideas on *yuanshi jidian*,[34] but it has the additional merit of specifying in greater detail precisely the causal pathways by which "culture influences the brain," precisely how "the empirical becomes the transcendental": the reliable intergenerational presence of "empirical" techno-social practices such as tool use creates the sustained selection pressures that help sweep favorable mutations (whether favorable for encephalization, memory, fine motor control, impulse control, etc.) to fixity in a population, making improved performance of the techno-social practice "transcendental" for subsequent generations.[35] Such improved performance in turn strengthens the selection pressures to which further such favorable mutations are subject—such is the "ratcheting"[36] process of gene-culture coevolution. Importantly, without active participation in the techno-social practice, the ratcheting process cannot get started—it requires humans to "create themselves," otherwise the favorable mutations will be unable to sweep to fixity. Equally, without the mutation-driven genetic evolution, the ratcheting process cannot get started—without the strengthening influence of biological evolution, the techno-social practices will remain impotent, local, even more vulnerable to loss via adverse extrinsic shocks,[37] and fail to be amalgamated into mental structures. Such a picture validates Li's intuitions about the active participation of human subjects in the evolutionary process without placing Li's published views on *yuanshi jidian* at odds with the basic principles of evolution via genetic mutation. This is the first point of consonance we wish to highlight, although its generality means it applies to various subdomains of the sedimentation theory.

Before moving on to the current evidence for the influence of culture on the brain, let us dwell a little longer on the consonance evident in one of those subdomains in particular: the formation of a panhuman "cultural-psychological formation." Li's ideas on universal human nature as sketched in the previous section clearly bear a resemblance to those of Darwin in The Descent of Man, and especially to the following highly revealing scribble in his "Notebook M": "Plato . . . says in Phaedo that our 'necessary ideas' arise from the preexistence of the soul, are not derivable from experience—read monkeys for preexistence."[38] Li's notion of the "transcendental" as used heretofore in this paper differs from both Platonic necessary ideas and also Kantian antinomies—the constitution of the "cultural-psychological formation" is indeed much closer to what Darwin had in mind, with the aggregate of the experiences during the evolutionary history of our hominid, primate ("monkeys for preexistence"), and even mammalian ancestors substituting respectively for *anamnesis* and pure reason. Rošker clarifies Li's view as follows: "In the transformation of empirical into transcendental, reason can . . . only be constructed through the social and material objective nature of historical development, because it is derived from human experience. . . . In this model, in which no transcendental formations can exist completely detached from experiences because they are constituted and shaped through sedimentation of historical practice, reason is constructed through the historical activities of practice, which is then integrated into mental structures."[39] For Li, rather than being a necessary condition of reasoning or sensibility, the "transcendental" is an "empirical" part of universal human nature in that it derives from experiential evolutionary history and has been functionally integrated into mental structures, ready to be drawn out by experiences across the lifespan of the individual without being either reflexively innate or necessary.

An example may be useful here. On Li's account, such qualities as loyalty and trustworthiness are (in his sense) transcendental, and he is quite explicit that they are not just some "abstract inheritance," but through the process of sedimentation have actually been physiologically integrated with our "neurons and synapses."[40] Li also makes clear, however, that they are not reflexively innate or universally necessary—there are certain occasions, for instance, on which one may legitimately demur from "the famous 'do not lie' of Kantian ethics."[41] Even more telling, though, is Li's account of the reasons why loyalty and trustworthiness are neurophysiologically "baked in" (albeit still overrideably so): even admitting that there are significant regional, cultural, and religious differences revealed in the anthropological record, Li avers, "there are yet simultaneously many commonalities, which are precisely the shared requirements for supporting the continuation of humankind's common form of group[-living] existence (*qunti shengcun* 群體生存)."[42] As for Li here, group-functional explanations of both cultural adaptations and the biological adaptations that they facilitate via GCC are, for many GCC theorists, a critical part of the causal picture for the emergence of large-scale human cooperation and prosociality[43]—this is another point of consonance. We will come back to this issue of group-functional adaptation in Li's ideas about sedimentation just before my conclusion.

Finally, let us conclude by explicitly spelling out an important implication of reading Li's historicized process of sedimentation as a process of gene-culture coevolution (or vice versa). The implication is this: on the basis of this reading, and in the absence of some passage in Li's corpus that has not yet come to my attention, he is exculpated from any potential charge of having put forth an illegitimately Lamarckian theory of culture's influence on the brain—yes, culture changes the brain in ways both non-heritable and heritable, but for the latter it does so at the level of phylogenetic evolution rather than ontogenetic development, and it does so by stably altering the legitimate Darwinian selection pressures faced by genomes across relatively short spans of evolutionary time.

## Culture Influences the Brain

Having made the case for the consonance of sedimentation and GCC, we now turn to enumeration of the empirical evidence for the influence of culture on the brain, some (but not all) instances of which are unambiguous examples of gene-culture coevolution, the underlying causal machinery of which we have by now obtained a clearer understanding. As foreshadowed under "Sedimentation and Gene-Culture Coevolution: Two Theories in Outline," we will structure this attempt to validate the proposition (so highly valued by Li Zehou) that "culture influences the brain" by reference to all three of Li's types of sedimentation: *yuanshi jidian* at the phylogenetic level, individual sedimentation at the ontogenetic level, and also cultural sedimentation. Before commencing with the enumeration, it may pay to spend a few more sentences discussing individual and cultural sedimentation, given that the foregoing sections have mostly focused on *yuanshi jidian*.

"Cultural sedimentation" describes the process by which the non-universal traits of cultural phylogeny stably propagate intergenerationally through various populations, resulting in a "diversity [that] necessarily emerges among different cultures, producing different kinds of psychological sedimentation."[44] This is due to "substantial differences among social institutions, human relations, ideologies, religious beliefs, lifestyles, values, thinking patterns, and expressions of emotions."[45] For some such cultural traits (such as, for instance, knowhow associated with the dairying lifestyle), the genetic side of the gene-culture coevolution equation may have produced associated biological adaptations which are genetically heritable, whereas in other cases what is intergenerationally inherited will mostly be cultural—this will depend on the complexity of the biological adaptation, and the strength and duration of the selection pressure.

"Individual sedimentation" is the product of more or less idiosyncratic life experiences (many of them culturally mediated) across the course of the ontogenetic development of a given individual; according to Li it is "the first two levels of sedimentation . . . applied to the individual mind,"[46] and that whereby "each individual enjoys a multivalent and variant development . . . which makes the intricacy of individual differences incomparable with that of any other animal."[47] It seems quite feasible at this ontogenetic level of individual sedimentation that, should they be searched for either with present-day or future technology, physical signatures of the effects of a specifically isolable culture could show up in the brain, although, as we shall see, genetically heritable biological adaptations that evolved in the brain due to selection pressures imposed by specific cultural traits and corresponding to Li's notion of cultural sedimentation have also been demonstrated—no doubt these also would have been of interest to Professor Li. We will begin our survey of the current evidence with those results which correspond to individual sedimentation.

To begin with, culturally transmitted practices such as music, reading, counting, and so forth undoubtedly affect the "software" of the brain. For proficient abacus users, the regions of their brains responsible for visual working memory are often imprinted with a "mental abacus," the rapid and accurate deployment of which is often accompanied by unconscious movements of the fingers.[48] Whether there is[49] or is not[50] a meaningful distinction between software and wetware is a matter of some dispute, but what is not in dispute is that the influence of culture on the brain extends well past what we might folk-neurologically label "software upgrades" to the brain (as exemplified by the mental abacus), and in fact extends to physical changes to wetware, which are well within the capabilities of present-day technology to detect: the (cerebral hemisphere-linking) corpora callosa of readers and writers are thicker than those of illiterate individuals;[51] for musicians, not only are their corpora callosa thicker, but their cerebella are larger, and they have "brain areas of greater size or grey matter density in the medial portion of primary auditory cortex (Heschl's gyrus), inferior frontal gyrus and superior parietal cortex."[52] Causality flowing from the cultural practices to neurophysiological changes should not, of course, be inferred directly from such correlations, but it seems more likely than not to be a relationship at least partially of causality, given that longitudinal studies have also shown that, for instance, grey matter density in areas of the brain responsible for processing visual-motion information observably increases after beginner jugglers undertake a three-month intensive training program.[53] It seems quite reasonable to conclude, then, that the abovementioned are examples of cultural practices influencing the brain, corresponding to Li's notion of individual sedimentation at the ontogenetic level.

Let us move past ontogeny and "appli[cation] to the individual mind," and on to results corresponding to Li's notion of "cultural sedimentation." As for the lactase persistence case, so too for the two examples that we will discuss here: they can be interpreted as examples of specific cultural traits influencing heritable genetic features that affect the brain. Relative to panhuman *yuanshi jidian*, this level of sedimentation seems to tally more closely with the target of Li's expressed hope that "vestiges of Chinese culture" in his brain would be legible to scientific investigation. The first example concerns the negative correlation between tonal languages and derived haplogroups of the *ASPM* and *Microcephalin* genes. These two genes are both associated with development of the brain. In general, most correlations between linguistic types and genetic variants are spurious, non-causal correlations due to historical and environmental factors. One particular study, however, found that after statistically controlling for such factors, the negative correlation described above remained statistically significant, indicating a likely causal connection.[54]

Is this a case of culture affecting genes or vice versa? If, as the researchers conclude to be likely, this correlation is indeed non-spurious, then regardless of the direction of the causal flow, this would in either case be an instance of brain-affecting gene-culture coevolution. The researchers themselves conclude that this may be a case of small biases introduced by brain-affecting genetic variants gradually exerting an influence on cultural transmission at the population level ("the brain influences culture");[55] Harvard evolutionary biologist Joseph Henrich suggests that, on the contrary, it may have been linguistic variants that furnished the conditions enabling the derived haplogroups to propagate ("culture influences the brain").[56] Again, either scenario constitutes a valid instance of GCC, but the latter scenario is the one that matches Li's "culture influences the brain" proposition as an instance of cultural sedimentation.

There is less room for disagreement regarding the direction of the causal flow in the second of our examples: Joan Chiao and Katherine Blizinsky have found that occurrence frequencies of one of two allelic variants of 5-HTTLPR were strongly correlated with measured levels of collectivist (as opposed to individualist) values for subjects sampled from various nations.[57] 5-HTTLPR is a polymorphic region in a serotonin transporter gene, the concentration of serotonin in the brain's synaptic clefts being significantly determined by whether the individual in question has the so-called "long" (higher concentration) or "short" (lower concentration) version of the allele. This in turn has effects upon—although (obviously) does not entirely determine—a range of psychological characteristics, including one's affinity for collectivist/individualist values. In this case, the researchers hold not only that the correlation between collectivist/individualist values and allelic distribution is the result of GCC, but also that the causal flow is from culture to genes, with collectivist cultural values militating for the selection of the short allele.[58]

How could this be the case? There are three scenarios worth canvasing here, all of which are characterized by this causal flow from culture to genes. The first is the scenario to which Chiao and Blizinsky took their results to be complementary,[59] that is, the well-known hypothesis advanced by Corey Fincher and Randy Thornhill, wherein collectivist/individualist values are predicted by pathogen prevalence in the regions to which the populations are resident. According to this theory, supported by data analysis performed by Fincher and Thornhill, collectivist values play a functional role as cultural anti-pathogen mechanisms. In a second scenario advanced by Henrich and Daniel Hruschka, however, governmental efficacy is a better predictor of collectivist/individualist values, though they admit a potential role for pathogen stress at deeper (presumably prehistoric) time scales.[60] In a final scenario, researchers drawing specifically on data sampled from various regions inside China avoided the statistical confounding of pathogens with rice cultivation (due to heat), and argued that labor-intensive rice cultivation requiring highly coordinated irrigation systems (as against the much less interdependent and less labor-intensive cultivation of wheat) predicts collectivist/individualist values better than the pathogen prevalence theory does.[61]

The final two scenarios exhibit a more clear-cut causal flow from cultural factors (governmental efficacy and agriculture type) to collectivist cultural values to selection of the short allele of 5-HTTLPR being favored. In the absence of any causal role for pathogen prevalence, it would be highly implausible that, in the pre-agricultural period, short allele bearers just so happened to already predominate in the regions in which they would eventually come to be favored after the dawn of agriculture. However, even allowing for some small causal role to be played by pathogen prevalence in the pre-agricultural period just drives the *terminus post quem* for the emergence of collectivist values further back in time—in the end, it is the cultural values driving selection of the genetic variant, later to be further strengthened by agricultural developments. This is therefore an example of "culture influencing the brain" via cultural sedimentation, and via GCC.

Given these scientific findings showing that (to use Li's term) cultural sedimentation can shape heritable brain-affecting genetic variants, one may worry that such theories could give succor to racists, and such worries are perhaps best tackled directly. The main point to emphasize is that such heritable genetic predispositions are not incapable of being overridden. In discussing the Dediu and Ladd result, Joseph Henrich commonsensically writes, "to be clear, *any human child* raised anywhere can learn the local language, but natural selection may be tinkering with the genetics of just how easy or hard it is, which depends on the enduring features of local languages."[62] My own children represent good examples of an overridden genetic predisposition. Their patrilineal (Anglo-Saxon) ancestors spoke non-tonal languages, as did their matrilineal (Mongolian) ancestors, and yet they have easily acquired (tonal) Mandarin as a mother tongue. By the same token, children may be socialized to internalize collectivist or individualist values regardless of their 5-HTTLPR allele. As such, these culturally shaped genetic differences cannot (and should not) be regarded as a basis for racist discrimination, but neither can (or should) they be regarded as completely causally inert.

Finally, let us raise some specific examples of culture's influence on the brain corresponding to *yuanshi jidian* ("species sedimentation"). Just as the lactase persistence case is the canonical "proof of concept" for GCC, so the cases raised above in which we see causal flow from culture to genes can be taken as a "proof of concept" for the sedimentation theory at the two levels below *yuanshi jidian*. However, when dealing with *yuanshi jidian*, evidence pertaining to whether in particular it was culture or genes that *first* kicked off the ratcheting process has become irretrievable. Given that it is unclear which of culture and/or genes was the causal prime mover, let us first get some facts about human neurophysiological evolution on the table, and then we can interpret them (necessarily speculatively) as cases of "culture influencing the brain." What is not in dispute, however, is that as discussed in my previous section, causal flows in both directions will be required for further ratcheting, regardless of whether culture or genetics was in fact the prime mover.

*Australopithecus afarensis* had a mean brain mass of 442 grams, whereas several significant advances in brain mass have endowed modern male

*Homo sapiens* with a mean brain mass of 1450 grams; by way of comparison, modern male chimpanzees have a mean brain mass of 406 grams.[63] Of course, absolute brain mass is far from the only factor influencing functional performance—after all, elephant brains weigh two or three times as much as human brains do, and the brains of some cetaceans are heavier again[64]—but human brains do have a unique structural attribute in that their neocortices have "apparently evolved an unprecedented level of direct access to the motor neurons," and this "increased access of the neocortex to diverse lower motor neurons probably made humans more dextrous in a variety of realms, ranging from hand movements to vocalization."[65] Humans do indeed exert excellent motor control over the tongue, face, maxilla, mandible, vocal cords, and hands: we humans are far weaker in general than chimpanzees, but our evolutionary cousins cannot thread a needle,[66] let alone sing a song while doing so.

FOXP2 is a gene associated with brain development and possessed by many different vertebrate species, and the FOXP2 protein is highly conserved, having only undergone a single amino-acid change in the 130 million years of evolutionary history that separated the chimpanzee-human last common ancestor (CHLCA) from the mouse. In the mere 4.6 to 6.2 million years separating the CHLCA from modern humans, however, the FOXP2 protein has already undergone two fixed amino-acid changes.[67] After it was discovered that precisely those members of a four-generational family who have a mutation in this gene all demonstrate severe verbal dyspraxia,[68] FOXP2 became popularly known as "the language gene," but apart from being heavily implicated in orofacial and vocal control,[69] it is also expressed in many other parts of the body. One influential early study suggested that the derived alleles of FOXP2 in human populations rode a selective sweep to fixity within the past 200,000 years,[70] which is to say, very approximately around the time anatomically modern humans began their exoduses (yes, plural) from Africa. This 200,000-year timeframe has by now been widely rejected following the discovery by paleogeneticists of the fact that the derived FOXP2 allele was shared with Neanderthals,[71] indicating that the selective sweep had occurred before the split of humans from our common ancestor with the Neanderthals (approximately 600,000 years ago). Endocasts reveal ongoing development of the language-critical Broca's area from virtual absence in australopithecines to a reasonably well-developed level in *Homo ergaster* to highly developed in *Homo sapiens*; the language-critical low larynx position exhibits the same pattern of development, *Homo ergaster* being at an intermediate level of development between australopithecines and *Homo sapiens*.[72]

How would the above-summarized neurophysiological infrastructure facilitating both advanced motor facility and linguistic capacity have come about? Are the two connected? Li is one in a long line of thinkers beginning with Darwin and Engels to have thought that tool use and manufacture was the link between advanced motor control and language, and he emphasizes both the social-pedagogical and semantics-through-motor-activity aspects of a coevolutionary scenario driven by tool manufacture and use.[73] As it turns out, contemporary neuroimaging has indeed revealed significant functional and anatomical overlap of both language and manual practice centered on Broca's area and the inferior frontal gyrus, and this "provides support for a 'technological pedagogy' hypothesis, which proposes that intentional pedagogical demonstration could have provided an adequate scaffold for the evolution of intentional vocal communication."[74] The idea here is that cultural knowhow ensured a consistency of techno-social practice, which helped mature and solidify the relevant neurophysiological infrastructure through "behavioral co-optation of truly pluripotent (multifunctional) structures,"[75] which continued thereafter to be functionally and anatomically associated through to their present level of development. The motor control neuro-infrastructure required for early gestural communication may thereby have gotten a "free ride" due to selection for tool practice, or even vice versa.[76]

Is this still too hand-wavy? A certain amount of hand-waving is unavoidable in dealing with the entropy-tarnished record of events stretching back to the Pleistocene and even late Pliocene, but the greater resolution that Li supplied to the picture sketched by Engels has become yet clearer again: first, neuroimaging has confirmed Li's prediction of a connection between language and tool practice in the form of incontrovertible functional and anatomical overlap; second, GCC fills in an important gap existing between prehistoric cultural practice and contemporary functional neuro-infrastructure in Li's overall causal picture, a gap that was previously filled for better or worse by the sedimentation metaphor alone—as described in "Sedimentation and Gene-Culture Coevolution: Consonance," cultural practice acts on the brain by way of providing sustained selection pressure on the neuro-infrastructure, which then in turn makes the cultural practice "transcendental" (in Li's sense) for subsequent generations, thereby initiating a mutually reinforcing virtuous spiral, one in which "culture influences the brain" regardless of which of the two was in fact the prime mover. Does this, then, fulfill Li's prediction that "the neuroscience of the future will be able to give a fundamental explanation"[77] of the cultural-psychological formation as sedimented by *yuanshi jidian*? Future technology—whether operating on Li's brain or some other brain—may well give a higher resolution explanation with more empirical detail fleshed out, but what GCC has already provided is the "fundamental explanation," that is, the theoretical foundations upon which that explanation is constructed.

## Sedimentation and Gene-Culture Coevolution: Dissonance and Ambiguity

Having already shown how GCC is not only consonant with the sedimentation theory, but indeed can usefully strengthen its theoretical foundations in a way that (if our suppositions above in "Sedimentation and Gene-Culture Coevolution: Consonance" are correct) is faithful to Li's central commitments, we now finally turn to two points of dissonance or at least ambiguity that arise from the juxtaposition of GCC with Li's thought. The first concerns the role of Kant in Li's thought. The second—as foreshadowed at the end of "Sedimentation and Gene-Culture Coevolution: Two Theories in Outline"—concerns the notion of cultural evolution, which is a major point of difference from rival theories of the role of culture in hominid evolution. How would this aspect of the GCC paradigm fit with Li's thought?

Let us begin with Kant. There is good reason why the subtitle (康德述評) of Li's monograph *Critique of the Critical Philosophy*, as translated by Rošker, is "A New Approach to Kant"[78] and why the English title of the Sanlian edition is (rather airily) translated as "*Kant in a New Key*": despite the critiques, Li Zehou clearly also thought of himself as building upon Kant's philosophical enterprise in some way. Is this even a theoretically coherent way of conceiving of Li's ideas though? Both Andrew Lambert[79] and Jana Rošker have given good reasons for reservations on this point, the most compelling of which is possibly Kant's explicit prohibition on historicizing or empiricizing the rational, which, as Rošker avers, "would probably [have led Kant to] regard Li's approach as pure nonsense."[80] These are existing known tensions in Li's ideas, and Rošker has stated in private communication that she believes that Li has "resolve[d] this tension by connecting the [empirical and transcendental] realms in a dynamic process of change, which constitutes a paradigm of a historicized worldview." I agree with this, and wish to further show that GCC gives us a slightly more fine-grained view of precisely how this "dynamic process of change" occurs. But first let's go for a quick snorkel through the primary literature to get a better handle on Li's affinity for Kant.

Perhaps oddly, Li's view of Mencius is a good place to start this particular discussion. Li's ethics are self-professedly Xunzian in orientation,[81] and he is often to be found defending the rehabilitation of Xunzian thought.[82] Conversely, Li struggles to find anything particularly complimentary to say about Mencius. There is a chapter in his *Outline of Ethics* entitled "Mencius' Immense Contribution," but one immediately suspects this purported "immensity" is rhetorically compensatory for the degree to which Li damns Mencius with faint praise in the chapter.[83] Using very direct language, he repudiates the core Mencian ideas of innate knowledge (*liangzhi* 良知)[84] and four sprouts (*si duan shuo* 四端說),[85] and apart from a brief nod to Mencius's prioritization of populace over ruler (*min gui jun qing* 民貴君輕), the only other "contribution" by Mencius that Li cares to point out is his championing of a "character of individual autonomy" (*geti duli renge* 個體獨立人格), especially as reflected in the well-known Mencian aphorism "He cannot be led astray by riches and honor, moved by poverty and privation, or deflected by a power or force."[86] When further pressed as to whether that represents the entirety of Mencius's "contribution," Li replied simply that "that one single point [was] enough."[87] Why does Li single out this one particular point alone?

In short, it is because this autonomy and self-reliance in moral decision-making, this willpower (*yizhi liliang* 意志力量),[88] which is virtually the only thing of value Li can find in the *Mencius*, is precisely also the thing that he most values in Kant. As Li tirelessly recapitulates,[89] the morally commendable quality he praises in Mencius and labels "condensation of reason" (*lixing ningju* 理性凝聚)[90] is precisely the wherewithal to submit to the categorical imperative regardless of the cost to one's own interests, and it is also that which separates humans from the beasts. Elsewhere, Li explicitly links that same Mencian aphorism to the notion of "free will" (*ziyou yizhi* 自由意志), which allows humans to carry out the dictates of the categorical imperative.[91] The contemporary philosophical literature on free will is sufficiently copious to get a whole herd of oxen sweating, but Li never really engages with it, and the fundamentally un-Kantian empiricizing of free will becomes an acute issue again here: Li in fact has a historicized genealogical story to tell about the "condensation of reason," one which he expects to be validated someday by neuroscience.[92] Very well, so where is the dissonance here with GCC?

The dissonance, in fact, only arises if we take Li to be proposing some form of Kantian doctrine of free will. Kant's doctrine of free will springs forth from pure reason, but proponents of GCC will tend rather to agree with the verdict of mainstream evolutionary psychology that "from an evolutionary or biological standpoint, the capacity to override an initial response and substitute another response is an immense step forward and can be powerfully adaptive."[93] That is, proponents of GCC will agree with the evolutionary genealogical account, which Li does in fact support. Free will for Li is a GCC-compliant psychological attribute that is an evolutionary adaptation for hominid social life—this is not at all Kantian. Given that Li's notion of free will (and indeed his notion of the relationship between the empirical and the transcendental more broadly) is not at all Kantian, why do we see such frequent laudations of Kant and Kantian free will in his corpus?

I think Ryan Nichols has provided an excellent template for understanding Li's appeals to Kant. Building upon but also diverging quite markedly from the ideas of David Hall and Roger Ames, Nichols has advanced what he calls an "influence principle" as crucial to understanding the projects of some early Ruist figures:

> According to the influence principle, the primary aim of the early Confucian writers, editors, and redactors was to influence people so as to increase the probability that Chinese society would . . . achieve peace and stability. The aim of their recorded reflections about morality is neither to believe the true and disbelieve the false nor to construct a theoretical architecture of mutually supporting ethical commitments about right action. . . . Envisioning Confucius and Mencius as a pair of theory-makers with roughly the same goals as an Aristotle or a Kant unavoidably and unjustly diminishes their reputation.[94]

I think the same applies, mutatis mutandis, to understanding Li's scholarly project. He is not attempting to construct "a theoretical architecture of mutually supporting ethical commitments" that add up to a form of Ruicized Neo-Kantianism that could occupy an irreproachably coherent compatibilist position in the theoretical landscape of western philosophical discourse on free will. No, rather he is inventing and deploying catchy neologisms, telling a grand narrative beginning from human prehistory, augmenting it with a stupendously erudite range of anecdotes and intriguing marginalia, marshaling in authoritative names like Hume and Kant to bolster it all, weaving in his quasi-encyclopedic knowledge of the intellectual history of the East and West, and joyfully but not necessarily fastidiously deploying scientific results where they seem useful to the cause. GCC helps smooth the path leading to this understanding of Li as writing mainly under the aegis of the influence principle: once we start seeing "condensation of reason," "free will," etc. as functional social adaptations with a historical evolutionary history and stop seeing them as items of theoretical philosophical componentry, we can thereby obviate the "unjust[] dimin[ution of Li's] reputation" as a shoddy theory-maker and appreciate his suasive genius.[95]

Finally we turn back briefly to the idea, accepted by many proponents of GCC, that culture itself evolves under the influence of processes of Darwinian selection. Again, as for the core ideas of GCC, so too for cultural evolution: excellent summaries abound,[96] but we will supply a very brief one. In principle, Darwinian selection can operate upon any substrate that exhibits variance, differential fitness, and heritability of fitness. This includes not just the DNA molecule, but also information. Memes will therefore become adapted to their environment via a process of multigenerational selection, just as genes do—such is the core idea of memetics. Cultural evolution theory differs from classical memetics significantly in the emphasis it places on continuous (rather than discrete) cultural traits (rather than memes) tending in the long term to confer benefit on the groups who possess those traits. The removal of group-deleterious traits from the pool of cultural variants and optimization of the group-beneficial ones will be expedited by between-group competition (i.e., "cultural group selection"), such that in the long run cultural traits become well adapted to the cultural and physical environments of their possessors. They are blindly but intricately "designed" by an entropy-subverting and Designer-less process of multigenerational selection, the operations and even results of which are often causally opaque to the trait's possessors. Many proponents of GCC also hold that Darwinian selection operates upon cultural traits in this way.

Whether or not Li would have accepted such a notion is something of an ambiguity. As argued in the foregoing sections, there seem to be compelling reasons and plenty of textual evidence to indicate that Li would have been amenable to GCC, and in fact did have something quite similar in mind. Can the same be said of him with respect to the evolution of group-beneficial and prosociality-engendering traits by cultural group selection as described in the above paragraph? The textual evidence for such a view is much more thin on the ground. There is still a case to be made, but we must give less credence to conclusions drawn.

The first point is a little vacuous, but still worth making: as shown above, Li not only accepts but actually accords significant importance to biological evolution, indicating that he understood the explanatory power of Darwinian selection. This alone doesn't get us very far, though. However, Li also uses some very suggestive language and concepts in his discussions of the origins of ritual (*li* 禮). I have argued elsewhere that an incipient form of cultural evolution discoverable in the *Xunzi* provides a good answer to this question of the origins of ritual,[97] and Li—who is, non-coincidentally and as noted above, a self-professed Xunzian—gives a very similar type of answer to this question, using distinctly Darwin-tinged language to do so. Consider the following sentence, which is preceded in the previous paragraph by the assertion that "religious morality" (*zongjiaoxing daode* 宗教性道德) is just a type of "social morality" (*shehuixing daode* 社會性道德) prescribing the norms that allow human groups to sustain their way of life under given temporal and environmental constraints: "At its root, morality is the norms and criteria that sustain within-group interpersonal relations, it is the gradually forming and constantly evolving product of the constantly changing habitat [in which one] survives and to which [morality must make] constant and subtle adaptations, [thereby] becoming a type of long-enduring and non-artificially-designed custom."[98] It would be rather unsound to seize on the use of the word *evolution* here and triumphantly conclude this to be an unambiguous invocation of cultural evolution theory, *quod erat demonstrandum*. In Chinese as in English, the word *evolution* is often used in a manner quite free of any Darwinian connotations to mean simply "development." It seems pretty clearly Darwinian, however, in this context, accompanied as it is by talk of environmental conditions, non-artificial design of customs,[99] adapting to the habitat in which the group survives, and so forth. Both memeticists and cultural evolutionists could probably see silhouettes of their own theories in Li's assertions here.

Li goes on, however, to tip the scales in favor of cultural evolution over memetics. Recall that theorists of cultural evolution generally expect evolution to select for group-beneficial traits in the long run, whereas memeticists generally see memetic selection as favoring the propagation of only the meme itself, or at most the meme in tandem with the individual whose brain harbors it. Now consider the following statements made by Li:

> From apes down to humans, *Homo* from the beginning have been a type of group-living biological genus in which individual survival has been tightly linked together with group survival. To struggle for their own survival, individuals must also struggle for the survival of their group (the clan, the household, the organization, the nation, the class, the state). This type of struggle or even sacrifice became the final ethical reality which made humans human. Any group will need these types of ethical imperatives, and will turn them into a conscientious awareness which restrains and rules over the individual in order to sustain the continued survival of the group and the genus.[100]

Taking this passage together with the previous one, from which it is only separated by approximately a page, the following picture emerges: without having been artificially designed for the purpose, cultural traits pertaining to moral norms nevertheless evolve to adapt themselves to local conditions gradually and subtly over time, and in doing so they don't necessarily benefit the individual, but they do benefit the group and promote its survival. This doesn't quite pass muster as a rigorous formulation of cultural evolution theory, but it is sufficient to suggest that Li had some homologous idea in mind, and perhaps even (though much more speculatively) to suggest that he may have accepted the operation of Darwinian processes on prosociality-engendering cultural traits. With much more certainty, though, it also suggests that even if he would have rejected the idea of Darwinian processes operating on culture, he certainly tended toward group-functional explanations of culture rather than the meme-functional and individual-functional explanations of classical memetics.

## Conclusion

What have we shown in this essay? First, that a review of the present evidentiary state of play with respect to the proposition that "culture influences the brain"—a proposition the confirmation of which Li

Zehou regarded as "of greater significance than all of [his] books put together"—indicates strongly that this proposition is already confirmed for all three types of sedimentation described by Li: *yuanshi* sedimentation, cultural sedimentation, and individual sedimentation. Perhaps our focus on this evidentiary landscape will sharpen even further with the advance of investigative technologies, but Li's prescience on this particular point is already well established.

Second, that there are significant consonances between gene-culture coevolution and Li's sedimentation theory, and indeed, that GCC provides a theoretical model that can supplement and augment Li's causal picture of the evolution of the hominin cultural-psychological formation. Supplementing it in this way helps clarify the apparent contradiction in Li's view on hominin evolution whereby he appears to reject the scientific principle of evolution via selection acting upon mutational variants—in fact, what Li wishes to emphasize is the crucial role of our ancestors' *active* engagement in techno-social practices without which the *passive* acquisition of lucky mutational variants alone would have been insufficient to sustainably drive the neurophysiological changes evident in the course of evolution from australopithecines to *sapiens*. The core logic of GCC suggests that active engagement in techno-social practice changes the strength and duration of the selection pressures which sweep beneficial mutations to fixity. This core logic also provides a more scientifically explicit picture of just how "culture influences the brain," how "the empirical becomes the transcendental" in Li Zehou's sense.

Third, the introduction of GCC clarifies our understanding of one of the known tensions in Li's corpus, that is, the fact that his "empiricization" of Kantian rationality is illegitimate from a strictly Kantian point of view. GCC affirms and fleshes out the picture that Li evidently had in mind of "free will" as a sort of Mencian-flavored psychological adaptation to hominid social life, the ability to override initial responses and submit selflessly to ethical norms. In this connection, I have suggested that Li's scholarly project in general and his treatment of "free will" and the relationship between the empirical and the transcendental in particular is oriented by an "influence principle" whereby Li prioritizes suasive efficacy over absolute theoretical consistency.

Finally, we have discussed an ambiguity with respect to Li's potential views on cultural evolution, a thesis theoretically separable from GCC itself but nevertheless also upheld by many proponents of GCC. We have shown that Li prefers group-functional explanations for the sedimentation of the human cultural-psychological formation, which suggests (but does not conclusively prove) that Li may have accepted the notion that culture itself evolves via Darwinian processes. In our view, this in turn suggests that cultural-evolutionary and GCC models are respectively more consonant with Li's ideas on sedimentation than are memetic and cultural niche models.

## Notes

1. "[材料] 真實 . . . 的學術傳記" Unless otherwise noted, all translations are by me. Li Zehou, foreword to Ma Qunlin, 馬群林, *Rensheng xiao ji: Yu Li Zehou de xuni duihua* 人生小紀: 與李澤厚的虛擬對話 (*Chronicle of a Life: A Virtual Dialog with Li Zehou*) (Nanjing: Nanjing Daxue Chubanshe 南京大學出版社, 2022).

2. Ma Qunlin, *Chronicle*, 517–18.

3. "我是想證明文化是不是影響了大腦，幾百年後，是不是可以從 . . . [大腦裡] 發現中國文化的殘跡，證明我的積澱理論," "Li Zehou: Zhengzhi minzhu bushi feidei mashang shixian" 李澤厚: 政治民主不是非得馬上實現," (Li Zehou: Political Democracy Needn't be Realized Immediately), *Southern People Weekly*, June 11, 2010, news.sina.com.cn/c/sd/2010-06-11/162620459655_4.shtml.

4. Marthe Chandler, "Li Zehou, Kant, and Darwin: The Theory of Sedimentation," in *Li Zehou and Confucian Philosophy*, ed. Roger T. Ames and Jinhua Jia (Honolulu: University of Hawai'i Press, 2018), 279.

5. I have adopted this flexible rendering of *yuanshi jidian* from Jana Rošker as suited to context here. Other common alternatives are "elementary sedimentation" and "primitive sedimentation," but I have generally preferred to use the pinyin directly. See Jana S. Rošker, *Following His Own Path: Li Zehou and Contemporary Chinese Philosophy* (Albany, NY: State University of New York Press, 2019), 48. For other key terms and phrases I will generally (but not always) default to the glossary at the end of Jana S. Rošker, *Becoming Human: Li Zehou's Ethics* (Leiden: Brill, 2020), 320–32.

6. On the issue of E. O. Wilson's status as a proponent of GCC, despite his having coauthored a book entitled *Genes, Mind, and Culture: The Coevolutionary Process*, there have been those such as Feldman and Laland who have preferred to see him as representative of the sociobiological tradition, which is certainly also how Li Zehou saw him. Whatever one may think of how far *Genes, Mind, and Culture* and his later writings in *Consilience* distanced him from the stereotypical notion of sociobiology and how closely the results approximate to what we now recognize as GCC, it is nevertheless difficult to paint Wilson as having been on the theoretical forefront of GCC as it developed rapidly after the turn of the millennium. See Li Zehou 李澤厚, *Renleixue lishi bentilun* 人類學歷史本體

論 (*Anthropological Historical Ontology*) (Qingdao: Qingdao Chubanshe 青島出版社, 2016), 118–20; and Marc W. Feldman and Kevin N. Laland, "Gene-Culture Coevolutionary Theory," *Trends in Ecology and Evolution* 11, no. 11 (1996): 453.

7. For a fuller summary of sedimentation theory, the obvious jumping-off point in the secondary literature would be the treatment given in the second chapter of Rošker, *Following His Own Path*, 47–65. For GCC, apart from the by now somewhat dated review article authored by Feldman and Laland and cited in note 7 above, the entire sixth chapter of Richerson and Boyd's *Not by Genes Alone* provides a good general outline, but in particular pages 191–95. See Peter J. Richerson and Robert Boyd, *Not by Genes Alone: How Culture Transformed Human Evolution* (Chicago: University of Chicago Press, 2005), 191–236.

8. "我這裡講的共同人性，重複一下，是認為它並非天賜，也不是生來就有，而是人類歷史的積澱成果。" Li, *Theory*, 475. "Sedimentation" is the established rendition of Li's neologism 積澱 as referring to the theory itself, although I have translated it differently here to better fit the context.

9. "對個體來說是先驗的，對人類總體則仍由經驗積澱而成," Li, *Theory*, 88.

10. "經驗變先驗," Li, *Theory*, 109.

11. "文化影響大腦," Ma, *Chronicle*, 517.

12. "智力產生於文化," Li, *Theory*, 109.

13. "人類本身創造了自己," Li, *Theory*, 4.

14. "審美 (或美感) 本與藝術無干，它出現在人類使用—製造工具的操作—勞動過程中……在於使用—製造工具的操作活動所擁有更多種類的心理功能在這裡得到了確認。其中，要特別提到的是想象功能和理解功能，由於它們與動物本能性的情慾和感知覺產生了更為複雜的組合、交織、滲透，便逐漸形成了變化多端似乎難以窮盡的心理結構," Li, 490. As it is one of Li's technical terms, I once again follow Rošker in the translation of *wenhua xinli jiegou* (see the above-cited glossary).

15. Xue Fuxing, "Li Zehou houqi shijian meixue de neizai maodun" 李澤厚後期實踐美學的內在矛盾 (Intrinsic Contradictions in Li Zehou's Later Period Practical Aesthetics), *Qiu shi xuekan* 求是學刊 30, no. 2 (2003): 101–2.

16. "內涵駁雜、模糊、難於把握," Cao Junfeng 曹俊峰, "'Jidian shui' zhiyi" "積澱說" 質疑 (Interrogating this "Sedimentation" Idea), *Xueshu yuekan* 學術月刊 7 (1994): 103.

17. This was translated from a 1964 paper. See Li Zehou, "An Outline of the Origin of Humankind," *Contemporary Chinese Thought* 31, no. 2 (1999): 20.

18. "無論是當代心理學、神經生理學，還是人類學，都尚未提供足以說明這個問題 [的] 成果和材料," Xu Mengqiu 徐夢秋, "Jidian yu zhongjie" 積澱與中介 (Sedimentation and Intermediaries), *Xueshu yuekan* 學術月刊 7 (1994): 108.

19. GCC is also sometimes known as Dual Inheritance Theory.

20. This is not to say it is impossible for norms that push directly against this particular causal flow from biology to culture to achieve short-term fixity in a certain population. But stochastically speaking, in the long run, we would expect institutions such as the kibbutz that attempt to mandate such norms to fail to achieve widespread uptake—and this is in fact what we do see.

21. Donald Munro, *A Chinese Ethics for the New Century: The Ch'ien Mu Lectures in History and Culture, and Other Essays on Science and Confucian Ethics* (Hong Kong: The Chinese University Press, 2005), 49–51.

22. See Li Zehou 李澤厚, "Guanyu 'Youguan lunli xue de da wen' de buchong shuoming" 關於《有關倫理學的答問》的補充說明 (Explanatory Addendum to the "Questions and Answers Regarding Ethics"), *Zhexue Dongtai* 11 (2009): 30. See pages 26–27 for the qualifications. For a further discussion of Li's reception of Munro's ideas, see sections 3.3.1 and 3.3.2 of my doctoral dissertation: Jordan B. Martin 馬兆仁,"Yanhua lun shi yu xia de Meng Xun yitong" 演化論視域下的孟荀異同 (An Evolutionary Perspective on Divergence and Concordance in Mencius and Xunzi) (PhD diss., Hunan University, Yuelu Academy, 2022).

23. Ruth Mace, "Update to Holden and Mace's 'Phylogenetic Analysis of the Evolution of Lactose Digestion in Adults' (1997): Revising the Coevolution of Human Cultural and Biological Diversity," *Human Biology* 81, no. 5/6 (2010): 621–24. See also Andrew Szilagyi, "Adult Lactose Digestion Status and Effects on Disease," *Canadian Journal of Gastroenterology and Hepatology* 29, no. 3 (2015): 149–56. A reviewer has suggested, based on anecdotal observation, that within a generation or two many individuals from populations without a history of dairying seem to now be capable of digesting lactose without severe discomfort. This may be the result of microbial adaptation (see Szilagyi, "Adult Lactose Digestion," 149) across the course of ontogeny. Such adaptations generally result in trade-offs, however, and as such there is still strong selection pressure on alleles conferring lactase-persistence.

24. Steven Pinker, "The Cognitive Niche: Coevolution of Intelligence, Sociality and Language," *Proceedings of the National Academy of Science* 107, no. 2 (2010): 8995–96.

25. "人之所以愛人......是由生物性自然情感提升而來的," Li, *Theory*, 101.

26. Li Zehou, "Response to Paul Gauguin's Triple Question," in *Li Zehou and Confucian Philosophy*, ed. Roger T. Ames and Jia Jinhua (Honolulu: University of Hawai'i Press, 2018), 23.

27. See Li, *Theory*, 329–30; Li, "Response," 25. See also his early notion of an "aesthetic double helix," Li, *Theory*, 490.

28. Li, "Response," 19.

29. "今天，反進化論、反科學、反歷史和反個體......已經成了當代倫理學的時尚風景," Li, *Theory*, 107.

30. Li, *Theory*, 107.

31. "人以理性突破了動物族類基因突變引起進化的自然過程，開創了不同於其他動物的人的歷史," Li, *Theory*, 168.

32. See Li Zehou 李澤厚, "Guanyu zhutixing de buchong shuoming" 關於主體性的補充說明 (A Supplementary Explanation of Subjectality), *Zhongguo shehui kexueyuan yanjiushengyuan xuebao* 1 (1985): 15.

33. "純動物生理性的'存在,'" Li, *Theory*, 449.

34. Though the GCC story may have a slightly larger abundance of factor inputs to the "sedimentation" process: see, for instance, the chart on page 300 of Joseph Henrich, *The Secret of Our Success: How Culture is Driving Human Evolution, Domesticating Our Species, and Making Us Smarter* (Princeton, NJ: Princeton University Press, 2016).

35. Of course, such latent facility still requires practice and use over the course of ontogeny in order to realize, so we are speaking of the "transcendental" in a weaker sense than it is used in many philosophical contexts.

36. See the fifth chapter of Henrich, *Secret*, esp. 56–58.

37. See, for instance, Joseph Henrich, "Demography and Cultural Evolution: How Adaptive Cultural Processes Can Produce Maladaptive Losses—The Tasmanian Case," *American Antiquity* 69, no. 2 (2004): 197–214, esp. 198–200.

38. Charles Darwin, "Notebook M," in *Charles Darwin's Notebooks 1836–1844*, ed. Paul H. Barrett et al. (Cambridge: Cambridge University Press, 1987), 551.

39. Rošker, *Becoming Human*, 195–96.

40. Abstract inheritance (*chouxiang jicheng* 抽象繼承) was a concept and/or phrase due to Feng Youlan 馮友蘭. See Li Zehou 李澤厚, "Guanyu 'Lunli xue zonglan biao' de shuoming" 關於 "倫理學總覽表" 的說明 (An Explanation of the "Schematic Overview of Ethics Chart"), *Zhongguo wenhua* 1 (2018): 11.

41. Li, "Schematic Overview," 11.

42. "但同時又仍有許多的共同點, 即維持作為人類所共同擁有的群體生存延續的同樣要求," Li, 11.

43. See Peter Richerson et al., "Cultural Group Selection Plays an Essential Role in Explaining Human Cooperation: A Sketch of the Evidence," *Behavioral and Brain Sciences* 39 (2016): e30.

44. Li, "Response," 24.

45. Li, "Response," 24.

46. Li, "Response," 25.

47. Li, "Response," 25.

48. Michael C. Frank and David Barner, "Representing Exact Number Visually Using Mental Abacus," *Journal of Experimental Psychology: General* 141, no. 1 (2012): 134.

49. Daniel Dennett, "The Software/Wetware Distinction: Comment on 'Toward a Computational Framework for Cognitive Biology: Unifying Approaches from Cognitive Neuroscience and Comparative Cognition' by W. Tecumseh Fitch," *Physics of Life Reviews* 11, no. 3 (2014): 367–68.

50. W. Tecumseh Fitch, "Toward a Computational Framework for Cognitive Biology: Unifying Approaches from Cognitive Neuroscience and Comparative Cognition," *Physics of Life Reviews* 11, no. 3 (2014): 334.

51. Alexandre Castro-Caldas et al., "Influence of Learning to Read and Write on the Morphology of the Corpus Callosum," *European Journal of Neurology* 6, no. 1 (1999): 23.

52. Steven Mithen and Lawrence Parsons, "The Brain as a Cultural Artefact," *Cambridge Archaeological Journal* 18, no. 3 (2008): 417–18.

53. Mithen and Parsons, 418.

54. See Dan Dediu and D. Robert Ladd, "Linguistic Tone is Related to the Population Frequency of the Adaptive Haplogroups of two Brain Size Genes, ASPM and *Microcephalin*," *Proceedings of the National Academy of Sciences* 104, no. 26 (June 2007): 10944–49.

55. Dediu and Ladd, 10947.

56. Henrich, *Secret*, 255.

57. Joan Y. Chiao and Katherine D. Blizinsky, "Culture-Gene Coevolution of Individualism-Collectivism and the Serotonin Transporter Gene," *Proceedings of the Royal Society B: Biological Sciences* 277 (2010): 532.

58. Chiao and Blizinsky, 531.

59. Chiao and Blizinsky, 534.

60. Daniel J. Hruschka and Joseph Henrich, "Institutions, Parasites and the Persistence of In-group Preferences," *PLOS One* 8, no. 5 (2013): e63642.

61. Thomas Talhelm et al., "Large-Scale Psychological Differences Within China Explained by Rice Versus Wheat Agriculture," *Science* 344 (2014): 603–8.

62. Henrich, *Secret*, 256.

63. Alexandra A. De Sousa and B. Wood, "The Hominin Fossil Record and the Emergence of the Modern Human Central Nervous System," in *Evolution of Nervous Systems*, vol. 4, ed. Jon H. Kaas, and Todd M. Preuss (London: Academic Press, 2007), 327.

64. Suzana Herculano-Houzel, "The Remarkable, Yet not Extraordinary, Human Brain as a Scaled-up Primate Brain and its Associated Cost," *Proceedings of the National Academy of Sciences* 109, no. 1 (2012): 10661.

65. Georg F. Striedter, *Principles of Brain Evolution* (Sunderland, MA: Sinauer Associates Inc, 2005), 324–25.

66. Henrich, *Secret*, 282.

67. Wolfgang Enard et al., "Molecular Evolution of *FOXP2*, a Gene Involved in Speech and Language," *Nature* 418 (2002): 870.

68. Kay D. MacDermot et al., "Identification of FOXP2 Truncation as a Novel Cause of Developmental Speech and Language Deficits," *American Journal of Human Genetics* 76, no. 6 (2005): 1074.

69. Xu Shuqin et al., "Foxp2 Regulates Anatomical Features that May Be Relevant for Vocal Behaviors and Bipedal Locomotion," *Proceedings of the National Academy of Sciences* 115, no. 35 (2018): 8799.

70. Enard et al., "Molecular Evolution," 871.

71. Johannes Krause et al., "The Derived FOXP2 Variant of Modern Humans was Shared with Neandertals," *Current Biology* 17, no. 21 (2007): 1908.

72. Richard G. Klein, *The Human Career: Human Biological and Cultural Origins*, 3rd ed. (Chicago: University of Chicago Press, 2009), 411.

73. See Li, "Outline of the Origin," 22–24.

74. Dietrich Stout and Thierry Chaminade, "Stone Tools, Language and the Brain in Human Evolution," *Philosophical Transactions of the Royal Society B: Biological Sciences* 367 (2012): 82.

75. That is, the structures of the inferior frontal gyrus; Stout and Chaminade, 77.

76. Henrich, *Secret*, 251.

77. Li, *Theory*, 490.

78. Rošker, *Becoming Human*, 300.

79. Andrew Lambert, "Determinism and the Problem of Individual Freedom in Li Zehou's Thought," in *Li Zehou and Confucian Philosophy*, 94–114 passim.

80. Rošker, *Becoming Human*, 258.

81. Li, *Theory*, 177.

82. See most obviously Li Zehou 李澤厚, "Ju meng qi xing xun xue—Wei 'Lunli xue gangyao' yi bian" 舉孟旗 行荀學—為《倫理學綱要》一辯 (Raise the Mencian Banner, Practice Xunzian Philosophy: A Defense of the *Outline of Ethics*)," *Tansuo yu zhengming* 4 (October 2017): 58–62.

83. This chapter is in dialogue form, so it seems possible that Li himself was not responsible for the titling, although he does indeed use the phrase "immense contribution" in the dialogue. Li, *Theory*, 176–79.

84. Li, *Theory*, 177.

85. Li, *Theory*, 176. Interestingly, Li rejects the four sprouts idea on the supposition that, of the four, only the "mind of compassion" (*ceyin zhi xin* 惻隱之心) could plausibly be an "animal instinct" (*dongwu benneng* 動物本能). Kin selection is of course the basis for much of the "compassion" evident in the animal kingdom. I have elsewhere made a full analysis of the relationship between kin selection and the Mencian four sprouts idea; see Zhu Hanmin 朱漢民 and Jordan B. Martin 馬兆仁, "Qinyuan xuanze neng fou yinzheng Mengzi zhi si duan shuo?" 親緣選擇能否印證《孟子》之四端說? (Is Kin Selection Confirmatory of the Mencian "Four Sprouts" Idea?) *Zhongguo Zhexue* 中國哲學 10 (October 2021): 57–64.

86. "富貴不能淫, 貧賤不能移, 威武不能屈." Mencius, *Mencius*, trans. Irene Bloom (New York: Columbia University Press, 2009), 62. See Li, *Theory*, 176.

87. "這一點就足夠了," Li, *Theory*, 176.

88. Li, *Theory*, 177.

89. On these points, see Li, *Theory*, 131–33, 166, and 487–88.

90. Li, *Theory*, 177.

91. Li, *Theory*, 20.

92. Li, *Theory*, 90.

93. Roy F. Baumeister, Brandon J. Schmeichel, and Kathleen D. Vohs, "Self-Regulation and the Executive Function: The Self as Controlling Agent," in *Social Psychology: Handbook of Basic Principles*, eds. Arie W. Kruglanski and E. Tory Higgins (New York: Guilford Press, 2007), 519.

94. Ryan Nichols, "Early Confucianism is a System for Social-Functional Influence and Probably Does Not Represent a Normative Ethical Theory," *Dao: A Journal of Comparative Philosophy* 14, no. 4 (2015): 513.

95. As someone presently working in Chinese academia, I offer the following piece of completely unsupported personal anecdote: I believe I have seen Li's suasive genius at work in convincing some humanities scholars (particularly those with a primary interest in Chinese philosophy) of the value of stepping out of the confines of the disciplinary boundaries of "literature, history, and philosophy" (*wenshizhe* 文史哲) and making a little more frequent contact with consilient reality at its joints.

96. See, for example, Alex Mesoudi, "Cultural Evolution: A Review of Theory, Findings and Controversies," *Evolutionary Biology* 43 (2016): 481–97; Richerson and Boyd, *Not by Genes Alone*, 58–98; Tim Lewens, "Cultural Evolution," in *The Stanford Encyclopedia of Philosophy*, ed. Edward N. Zalta, Summer 2020 Edition, plato.stanford.edu/archives/sum2020/entries/evolution-cultural/.

97. Jordan B. Martin, "Incipient Cultural Evolution in the *Xunzi* as Solution to The *Liyi* Origin Problem," *Dao: A Journal of Comparative Philosophy* 22, no. 1 (2023): 63–87.

98. "道德本是維繫群體人際關係的原則、準繩，它是一種逐漸形成並不斷演化、微調以適應不斷變化著的生存環境的產物，成為一種非人為設計的長久習俗," Li, *Theory*, 33.

99. Elsewhere, Li talks about how shamanism and social rituals were crucial in shaping human nature, and in this connection quite specifically asserts that it was "not the individual creation of some sage, worthy or prophet" (非某個聖賢先知的個體創作). This seems very much like a rejection of the Xunzian "sagely creation" story (see *inter alia* the first few sentences of the "Discourse on Ritual" chapter of the *Xunzi*) in favor of a cultural evolution narrative. See Li, *Theory*, 474.

100. "從猿到人，人類一開始便是某種群居生物族類，其個體生存是與該群體生存緊密連接在一起的。個體為自己也就必須為群體（氏族、家庭、團體、民族、階級、國家）的生存而奮鬥。這種奮鬥甚至犧牲，成了人之所以為人的最後的倫理學的實在。任何群體都需要這種倫理要求，其將它變為自覺意識來約束、統治個體，以維護其群體與族類的生存延續。" Li, *Theory*, 34.

# Bibliography

Baumeister, Roy F., Brandon J. Schmeichel, and Kathleen D. Vohs. "Self-Regulation and the Executive Function: The Self as Controlling Agent." In *Social Psychology: Handbook of Basic Principles*, edited by Arie W. Kruglanski and E. Tory Higgins, 516–39. New York: Guilford Press, 2007.

Cao, Junfeng 曹俊峰. "'Jidian shui' zhiyi" "積澱說" 質疑 (Interrogating This "Sedimentation" Idea). *Xueshu yuekan* 7 (1994): 101–7.

Castro-Caldas, Alexandre, Miranda P. Cavaleiro, I. Carmo, A. Reis, F. Leote, C. Ribeiro, and E. Ducla-Soares. "Influence of Learning to Read and Write on the Morphology of the Corpus Callosum." *European Journal of Neurology* 6, no. 1 (1999): 23–28.

Chandler, Marthe. "Li Zehou, Kant, and Darwin: The Theory of Sedimentation." In *Li Zehou and Confucian Philosophy*, edited by Roger T. Ames and Jinhua Jia, 278–312. Honolulu: University of Hawai'i Press, 2018.

Chiao, Joan Y., and Katherine D. Blizinsky. "Culture-Gene Coevolution of Individualism-Collectivism and the Serotonin Transporter Gene." *Proceedings of the Royal Society B: Biological Sciences* 277 (2010): 529–37.

Darwin, Charles. "Notebook M." In *Charles Darwin's Notebooks 1836–1844*, edited by Paul H. Barrett, Peter J. Gautrey, Sandra Herbert, David Kohn, and Sydney Smith. Cambridge: Cambridge University Press, 1987.

De Sousa, Alexandra A., and B. Wood. "The Hominin Fossil Record and the Emergence of the Modern Human Central Nervous System." In *Evolution of Nervous Systems*, vol. 4, edited by Jon H. Kaas and Todd M. Preuss, 291–336. London: Academic Press, 2007.

Dediu, Dan, and D. Robert Ladd. "Linguistic Tone is Related to the Population Frequency of the Adaptive Haplogroups of Two Brain Size Genes, *ASPM* and *Microcephalin*." *Proceedings of the National Academy of Sciences* 104, no. 26 (2007): 10944–49.

Dennett, Daniel. "The Software/Wetware Distinction: Comment on 'Toward a Computational Framework for Cognitive Biology: Unifying Approaches from Cognitive Neuroscience and Comparative Cognition' by W. Tecumseh Fitch." *Physics of Life Reviews* 11, no. 3 (September 2014): 367–68.

Enard, Wolfgang, Molly Przeworski, Simon E. Fisher, Cecilia S. L. Lai, Victor Wiebe, Takashi Kitano, Anthony P. Monaco, and Svante Pääbo. "Molecular Evolution of *FOXP2*, a Gene Involved in Speech and Language." *Nature* 418 (2002): 869–72.

Feldman, Marc W., and Kevin N. Laland. "Gene-Culture Coevolutionary Theory." *Trends in Ecology and Evolution* 11, no. 11 (1996): 453–57.

Fitch, W. Tecumseh. "Toward a Computational Framework for Cognitive Biology: Unifying Approaches from Cognitive Neuroscience and Comparative Cognition." *Physics of Life Reviews* 11, no. 3 (2014): 329–64.

Frank, Michael C., and David Barner. "Representing Exact Number Visually Using Mental Abacus." *Journal of Experimental Psychology: General* 141, no. 1 (2012): 134–49.

Henrich, Joseph. "Demography and Cultural Evolution: How Adaptive Cultural Processes can Produce Maladaptive Losses—The Tasmanian Case." *American Antiquity* 69, no. 2 (2004): 197–214.

Henrich, Joseph. *The Secret of Our Success: How Culture is Driving Human Evolution, Domesticating Our Species, and Making Us Smarter*. Princeton, NJ: Princeton University Press, 2016.

Herculano-Houzel, Suzana. "The Remarkable, Yet not Extraordinary, Human Brain as a Scaled-up Primate Brain and its Associated Cost." *Proceedings of the National Academy of Sciences* 109, no. 1 (2012): 10661–68.

Hruschka, Daniel J., and Joseph Henrich. "Institutions, Parasites and the Persistence of In-group Preferences." *PLOS One* 8, no. 5 (2013): e63642.

Klein, Richard G. *The Human Career: Human Biological and Cultural Origins*, 3rd ed. Chicago: University of Chicago Press, 2009.

Krause, Johannes, Carles Lalueza-Fox, Ludovic Orlando, Wolfgang Enard, Richard E. Green, Hernán A. Burbano, Jean-Jacques Hublin, et al. "The Derived FOXP2 Variant of Modern Humans was Shared with Neandertals." *Current Biology* 17, no. 21 (November 2007): 1908–12.

Lambert, Andrew. "Determinism and the Problem of Individual Freedom in Li Zehou's Thought." In *Li Zehou and Confucian Philosophy*, edited by Roger T. Ames and Jinhua Jia, 94–117. Honolulu: University of Hawai'i Press, 2018.

Lewens, Tim. "Cultural Evolution." *The Stanford Encyclopedia of Philosophy*, edited by Edward N. Zalta. Summer 2020 Edition. plato.stanford.edu/archives/sum2020/entries/evolution-cultural/.

Li Zehou 李澤厚. "Guanyu 'Lunlixue zonglan biao' de shuoming" 關於 "倫理學總覽表" 的說明 (An Explanation of the "General Scheme of Ethics"). *Zhongguo Wenhua* 1 (2018): 1–15.

Li Zehou 李澤厚. "Guanyu 'Youguan lunlixue de da wen' de buchong shuoming" 關於《有關倫理學的答問》的補充說明 (Explanatory Addendum to "Some Questions and Answers Regarding Ethics"). *Zhexue Dongtai* 哲學動態 11 (2009): 26–33.

Li Zehou 李澤厚. "Guanyu zhutixing de buchong shuoming" 關於主體性的補充說明 (A Supplementary Explanation of Subjectality). *Zhongguo shehui kexueyuan yanjiushengyuan xuebao* 中國社會科學院研究生院學報 1 (1985): 14–21.

Li Zehou 李澤厚. "Ju Meng qi xing Xun xue—Wei 'Lunlixue gangyao' yi bian" 舉孟旗 行荀學—為《倫理學綱要》一辯 (Raise the Mencian Banner, Practice Xunzian Philosophy: A Defense of the *Outline of Ethics*). *Tansuo yu zhengming* 4 (October 2017): 58–62.

Li Zehou. "An Outline of the Origin of Humankind." *Contemporary Chinese Thought* 31, no. 2 (1999): 20–25.

Li Zehou 李澤厚. *Renleixue lishi bentilun* 人類學歷史本體論 (*Anthropological Historical Ontology*). Qingdao: Qingdao chuban she, 2016.

Li Zehou. "Response to Paul Gauguin's Triple Question." In *Li Zehou and Confucian Philosophy*, edited by Roger T. Ames and Jinhua Jia, 18–30. Honolulu: University of Hawai'i Press, 2018.

Ma Qunlin 馬群林. *Rensheng xiao ji: Yu Li Zehou de xuni duihua* 人生小紀: 與李澤厚的虛擬對話 (*Chronicle of a Life: A Virtual Dialog with Li Zehou*). Nanjing: Nanjing Daxue chuban she, 2022.

MacDermot, Kay D., Elena Bonora, Nuala Sykes, Anne-Marie Coupe, Cecilia S. L. Lai, Sonja C Vernes, Faraneh Vargha-Khadem, et al. "Identification of FOXP2 Truncation as a Novel Cause of Developmental Speech and Language Deficits." *American Journal of Human Genetics* 76, no. 6 (2005): 1074–80.

Mace, Ruth. "Update to Holden and Mace's 'Phylogenetic Analysis of the Evolution of Lactose Digestion in Adults' (1997): Revising the Coevolution of Human Cultural and Biological Diversity." *Human Biology* 81, no. 5/6 (2010): 621–24.

Martin, Jordan B. "Incipient Cultural Evolution in the *Xunzi* as Solution to the *Liyi* Origin Problem." *Dao: A Journal of Comparative Philosophy* 22, no. 1 (2023): 63–87.

Martin, Jordan B. 馬兆仁. "Yanhua lun shi yu xia de Meng Xun yitong" 演化論視域下的孟荀異同 (An Evolutionary Perspective on Divergence and Concordance in Mencius and Xunzi). PhD diss., Hunan University, Yuelu Academy, 2022.

Mencius. *Mencius*. Translated by Irene Bloom. New York: Columbia University Press, 2009.

Mesoudi, Alex. "Cultural Evolution: A Review of Theory, Findings and Controversies." *Evolutionary Biology* 43 (2016): 481–97.

Mithen, Steven, and Lawrence Parsons. "The Brain as a Cultural Artefact." *Cambridge Archaeological Journal* 18, no. 3 (2008): 415–22.

Munro, Donald. *A Chinese Ethics for the New Century: The Ch'ien Mu Lectures in History and Culture, and Other Essays on Science and Confucian Ethics*. Hong Kong: The Chinese University Press, 2005.

Nichols, Ryan. "Early Confucianism is a System for Social-Functional Influence and Probably Does Not Represent a Normative Ethical Theory." *Dao: A Journal of Comparative Philosophy* 14, no. 4 (2015): 499–520.

Pinker, Steven. "The Cognitive Niche: Coevolution of Intelligence, Sociality and Language." *Proceedings of the National Academy of Sciences* 107, no. 2 (2010): 8995–96.

Richerson, Peter J., and Robert Boyd. *Not By Genes Alone: How Culture Transformed Human Evolution*. Chicago: University of Chicago Press, 2005.

Richerson, Peter, Ryan Baldini, Adrian V. Bell, Kathryn Demps, Karl Frost, Vicken Hillis, Sarah Mathew, et al. "Cultural Group Selection Plays an Essential Role in Explaining Human Cooperation: A Sketch of the Evidence." *Behavioral and Brain Sciences* 39 (2016): e30.

Rošker, Jana S. *Becoming Human: Li Zehou's Ethics*. Leiden: Brill, 2020.

Rošker, Jana S. *Following His Own Path: Li Zehou and Contemporary Chinese Philosophy*. Albany: State University of New York Press, 2019.

*Southern People Weekly* 南方人物週刊. "Zhengzhi minzhu bushi feidei mashang shixian" 李澤厚: 政治民主不是非得馬上實現 (Li Zehou: Political Democracy Needn't be Realized Immediately). *Southern People Weekly*, June 11, 2010. news.sina.com.cn/c/sd/2010-06-11/162620459655_4.shtml.

Stout, Dietrich, and Thierry Chaminade. "Stone Tools, Language and the Brain in Human Evolution." *Philosophical Transactions of the Royal Society B: Biological Sciences* 367 (January 2012): 75–87.

Striedter, Georg F. *Principles of Brain Evolution*. Sunderland, MA: Sinauer Associates Inc., 2005.

Szilagyi, Andrew. "Adult Lactose Digestion Status and Effects on Disease." *Canadian Journal of Gastroenterology and Hepatology* 29, no. 3 (2015): 149–56.

Talhelm, Thomas, X. Zhang, S. Oishi, C. Shimin, D. Duan, X. Lan, and S. Kitayama. "Large-Scale Psychological Differences Within China Explained by Rice Versus Wheat Agriculture." *Science* 344 (2014): 603–8.

Xu, Mengqiu 徐夢秋. "Jidian yu zhongjie" 積澱與中介 (Sedimentation and Intermediaries). *Xueshu Yuekan* 學術月刊 7 (1994): 108–10.

Xu, Shuqin, Pei Liu, Yuanxing Chen, Yi Chen, Wei Zhang, Haixia Zhao, Yiwei Cao, et al. "Foxp2 Regulates Anatomical Features that May Be Relevant for Vocal Behaviors and Bipedal Locomotion." *Proceedings of the National Academy of Sciences* 115, no. 35 (2018): 8799–804.

Xue, Fuxing 薛富興. "Li Zehou houqi shijian meixue de neizai maodun" 李澤厚後期實踐美學的內在矛盾 (Intrinsic Contradictions in Li Zehou's Later Period Practical Aesthetics). *Qiu shi xuekan* 30, no. 2 (2003): 97–103.

Zhu Hanmin 朱漢民 and Jordan B. Martin 馬兆仁. "Qinyuan xuanze neng fou yinzheng Mengzi zhi si duan shuo?" 親緣選擇能否印證《孟子》之四端說? (Is Kin Selection Confirmatory of the Mencian "Four Sprouts" Idea?)." *Zhongguo zhexue* 10 (October 2021): 57–64.

5

# Situated Cognition and Historical Perspective
## Li Zehou and Contemporary Aesthetics

RAFAL BANKA

This chapter is concerned with how Li Zehou's aesthetic can contribute to contemporary aesthetics research. When Li's main achievements in aesthetics are discussed, they are mainly located where Li focuses on questions connected with art history and theory.[1] This approach can be largely illustrated by Li's two flagship works, *The Path of Beauty* (1994) and *The Chinese Aesthetic Tradition* (2010), which explore the distinct character of Chinese aesthetics, as manifested in artworks and artistic activity. Whereas these two publications undeniably instantiate and implement Li's conception of aesthetics, I argue that the salience of Li's aesthetic project gravitates toward more philosophically informed questions, and this is where it is most pertinent for contemporary aesthetics. This will be demonstrated in two stages. First, by turning to Li's philosophical motivations, I will show that his aesthetic project belongs to the family of theories that can be described as experience oriented, in contrast to the study of aesthetic values and philosophy of art. This will allow me to proceed to the second stage, in which I will demonstrate how Li's aesthetic contributes to research within the theories that focus on the experience and role of the aesthetic in widely construed cognitive processes.

I will show that Li's foundations of aesthetics, especially subjectality, invite interdisciplinary complementation regarding the cognitive processes in humans.[2] This, in turn, will allow me to demonstrate that, although there are aesthetic conceptions that consider the aesthetic as a material component of cognitive processes in humans, they are mostly concerned with how a given subject—an individual determined by their widely construed embeddedness in an environment—apprehends reality regardless of temporal location. What makes a significant difference in Li's theory is a phylogenetic perspective, which allows us to view the aesthetic in humans in anthropological and historical terms. I will also argue that in this sense Li's aesthetic concurrently functions as meta-aesthetics—a conception that provides a systematic insight into the nature of the development of the particular, relative to culture and historical location and aesthetic theories in the history of humankind.

The chapter has the following structure. First, I will sketch a map of research within philosophical aesthetics. Next, by discussing Li's philosophical inspirations, I will discuss the essential features of his aesthetic theory that place him among aestheticians concerned with the nature of aesthetic experience, or more precisely, that underscore the role of the aesthetic in experience and cognitive processes. This will be followed by referring to Li's concept of subjectality and beauty to situated cognition, where I will argue for autopoietic enactivism. Finally, I will demonstrate how Li's theory can contribute to contemporary aesthetics research, which I will map by referring to the representative theories of Bence Nanay and Wolfgang Welsch. I will argue that the contribution lies in the historical perspective of Li's theory.

## Defining Aesthetics

The concept of "aesthetics" covers a broad semantic field that goes far beyond philosophy. For instance, the term is not uncommon in art, or even literary theory, as well as in reference to some other areas of life, such as fashion or sport.[3] Since this chapter focuses on the philosophical contribution of Li's theory, I ignore the fuzziness of the term brought by the extra-philosophical context and confine my discussion to how aesthetics is understood as a philosophical discipline.

Unlike ethics or epistemology, aesthetics as a philosophical discipline is conceptualized in a considerably nonhomogeneous way. The distinction between these foundational conceptions can be attributed to the assumptions concerning the discipline of aesthetics;[4] this allows aesthetics to be conceived as referring to a diverse discipline or an umbrella term for considerably distinct philosophical enterprises.[5] I propose that on a general level a tripartite subdivision can be made.

The first area of research subscribes to a common intuition that aesthetics is essentially the study of beauty. In other words, aesthetics is a branch of value studies characterizable by the concentration on values labeled "aesthetic," such as beauty, ugliness, or the sublime. This study involves the problems concerning how aesthetic values are related to the properties of objects or events, as well as moral values.[6] Conceived in such a manner, aesthetics usually locates these relationships in nature and art, which is believed to be the natural habitat of aesthetic values.

The second area can be perceived as an analytical emancipation from the above axiological paradigm. It grows from an assumption that artworks and their reception do not necessarily involve aesthetic values. The center of gravity of the discipline is thus shifted toward art, which demarcates the territory of aesthetic investigations.[7] Consequently, this field of human activity is subject to a considerably diverse philosophical analysis that can but does not need to be axiologically informed. A representative discussion in this area is the ontology of artworks.[8] This conception of aesthetics is referred to as the *philosophy of art* and accounts for the majority of contemporary aesthetics research, especially in Anglo-American academia.

The third direction of studies in aesthetics differs significantly from the above. Unlike distinguishing a specific type of artifacts or layer of reality, this approach conceptualizes aesthetics in terms of a broadly construed human apprehension of reality. Within this conception, it assumes an anatomy of experience, in which the aesthetic is an indispensable component. Within the Western tradition, this concept of aesthetics can be traced back to Alexander Gottlieb Baumgarten, who coined the word *aesthetica* from the original Greek *aisthēsis* (αἴσθησις), which refers to sensuous perception.[9] This entails that the aesthetic relates to and is built into the senses and cognitive processes built on them. This intuition is brought to a mature shape in Kant's first and third *Critiques*, where aesthetics applies to sensibility and is concerned with sensations and how representations in sensibility are formed according to the principles already present in the mind.[10] This approach, which can be roughly described as experience oriented, allows us to conceptualize aesthetics beyond both beauty and art.[11] Among the three ways of conceptualizing aesthetics, the experience-oriented one seems to be most stand-alone and consolidated.

There are some important aspects of experience-oriented aesthetics that should be paid attention to. A central one is that the aesthetic is not a peripheral dimension of cognition that can be identified as an accidental feature or response that accompanies the apprehension of reality. Accordingly, the aesthetic makes sensuous apprehension possible, or at least determines the character of it—in other words, the aesthetic is of cognitive importance. What also requires note is that aesthetics so conceived does not aim at replacing epistemology. Whereas epistemology is concerned with conditions that determine mostly propositional knowledge, aesthetics is oriented at the very process or anatomy of experience rather than how it is valid or true. However, this difference in focus does not rule out plausible overlaps, especially when questions concerning the functioning of mind and human cognitive involvement in the world emerge.[12]

Focusing on various dimensions of cognition naturally exposes experience-oriented aesthetics to an interdisciplinary approach in two ways. First, within philosophy, aesthetics naturally overlaps with some aspects of the philosophy of mind and perception, which provide a fine-grained insight into the nature and processing of sense perception. Second, beyond philosophical disciplines, the sensuous, embedded conception of aesthetics invites a turn to experimental sciences that explore cognitive processes, such as psychology or neuroscience.

To briefly sum up, the above three different conceptualizations of aesthetics allow us to organize aesthetic theories with regard to their foundations and objectives. Although many aesthetic theories incorporate more than one approach, this tripartite subdivision reflects the dominant concern of a theory, which can be traced back to how the discipline is fundamentally conceptualized.

## Li's Aesthetic as a Form of Cognition

As already mentioned, although many important and influential writings by Li are devoted to art, they should be treated more as an illustration of his philosophical aesthetic, which is more fundamentally constructed and applies to a considerably wider range of human activity. From a general perspective, it can be argued that since beauty, next to aesthetic experience, is a central notion of Li's aesthetic, his theory is of an axiological character. The aim of this section is, among other things, to clearly rule out alternative classifications of Li's theory by showing the primacy of experience consisting of human perception and engagement in reality.

The experiential orientation of Li's theory can be clearly seen already at the stage of constructing his philosophical framework. It can be said that Li's theory has been informed to a considerable degree by Confucius, Karl Marx, and Immanuel Kant. For this reason, my discussion focuses on this.

With regard to aesthetics, Li's interest in Confucius' philosophy is concentrated on the role of emotions. The emotional dimension in humans is central in Confucian ethics, which as a variety of virtue ethics consists in developing one's *ren* 仁—the moral ideal that is realized as sensitivity forged in a practical way.[13] The emotional components of *ren* guide human agency by ensuring a morally proper interaction with others. This forging of the sensitivity guarantees, or, in fact, is tantamount to, Confucian moral traits achieved by practicing propriety (*li* 禮)—a prescribed behavioral repertoire. The function of propriety is twofold. In Confucian ethics, moral behavior should not be treated as a manifestation of a virtue, since *ren* is a psychological trait embedded in one's behavior. Therefore, in one sense, propriety constitutes the performative extension of *ren*.

What matters more for aesthetics is on a different front. It is believed that these forms of practice, namely propriety, work in another direction, which has the capacity of shaping human emotions in a way that is desired by Confucian morality. Thus, the Confucian moral project should be understood as blended, concurrent processes of performing propriety and molding human sensitivity. Otherwise, if these two functions of propriety were disjointed, Confucian ethics would be incorrectly understood as inclining toward deontology or being a more self-reflective rather than practical project.

It has to be underscored that being *ren* in Confucianism is not to be understood solely in ethical terms. In Confucianism, one's moral advancement is the measure of humanity, and, in this sense, the emotional substance that is shaped by recursive proper behavior functions as an ontological or generic dimension of the human being. Accordingly, emotionality provides an ontological standing. Equally importantly, being *ren* means being knowledgeable in terms of possessing practical knowledge of how to behave in human interactions. Since here behavior combines emotional and performative aspects, emotional substance is the measure not only of moral competences, but also of cognitive ones.

That human practice has the capacity of molding cognitive emotions is important for aesthetic reasons, because Confucians include artistic activity along with other forms of propriety.[14] This shows that activities in which one experiences the aesthetic are formative for human character traits and, as mentioned above, cognitive competences. In fact, the aesthetic is regarded by Confucius as the factor that brings *ren* cultivation to completion. In fragment 8.8 from the *Analects* Confucius says, "Find inspiration in the Odes [*shi* 詩], take your place through ritual [*li* 禮], and achieve perfection with music [*yue* 樂]."[15]

Confucius conveys that self-cultivation takes place in stages. Accordingly, the *Odes* provides good examples from the past;[16] this is followed by practice to be carried out in accordance with propriety, but the "final touch" is given by music. The molding of human emotional structures takes place at all three stages but, as Li remarks, the first two stages are entangled in discourse and social norms, respectively. Contrary to these stages, music comes in an unmediated form and therefore can forge emotions in the most direct way.[17] The role of an aesthetic component in self-cultivation is even more explicit in fragment 6.20: "One who knows [*zhi* 知] it is not the equal of one who loves [*hao* 好] it, and one who loves it is not the equal of one who takes joy [*le* 樂] in it."[18] The fragment draws attention to the fact that being intellectually aware of one's actions is less valuable than liking them and, finally, taking pleasure in them. This type of pleasurable state should be understood in aesthetic rather than ethical terms. The main reason for this consists in the fact that the pleasure is not connected with the outcomes of actions or expectations thereof.[19] Instead, the pleasure consists in focusing on how an action is performed.[20] This type of pleasure, by virtue of supervening on form rather than content, is usually associated with aesthetic rather than epistemic or moral contexts. It is, for instance, very similar to an understanding of aesthetic appreciation. According to Gary Iseminger, "Someone is appreciating a state of affairs just in case she or he is valuing for its own sake the experiencing that state of affairs."[21] Accordingly, the appreciation supervenes on the very qualitative dimension of experience, which is naturally associated with the form rather than purposiveness of an action.

As can be seen from the above, the aesthetic in Confucianism is inseparable from emotions, cognition, and practice. More specifically, the aesthetic matters most in constructing cognitive emotional structures, where not only can it instrumentally give the "final touch" to human sensitivity but it also puts human interaction in an aesthetic mode, which appears to go beyond what is usually labelled ethical.

Another important aesthetic element from Confucianism that matters for Li's theory is that human emotions are in practice shaped in collective activities. From this perspective, the "raw" emotionality of the human species is calibrated to assume a socialized, or humanized, form.[22] This entails that human emotionality with an aesthetic component is not only confined to an individual subject but is also extended to the experiences of collective and intersubjective character.

Marxism is the second philosophical formation that contributes to understanding Li's aesthetic in an experiential paradigm. Li's theory is specifically informed by early Marx, as formulated in *Economic and Philosophic Manuscripts* from 1844. This text underscores the role of labor—the material practice of transforming nature, thanks to which humans create themselves as humans and engage the world in a humanized relationship with them. Li's aesthetic project takes over labor in the strict sense of Marx, as a uniquely human practice of manufacturing and using tools. Li is informed by human practice in two respects. The first one is internal and consists of, among others, altering human senses, and subsequently perception, as well as its extension to consciousness and mental actions.[23] Thanks to this, humans have developed the ability to perceive and, what follows, actively transform the world beyond the original, physiological motivation, in a uniquely humanized fashion. In this sense, perception is not a transparent tool in cognitive processes. What matters for Li's project here is that the humanization of sense organs has developed aesthetic perception. This can be illustrated by musical hearing, which significantly informs the character of human engagement with the world, including the cognition of it. From this perspective, the aesthetic is deeply embedded in experience, which, in Marxism, integrates cognition and practice.

The second way Li is informed by human practice is the historical character of such practice. Marx locates humanization processes not in a singular lifetime existence but in the human species as a whole, which has been involved in labor throughout the history of humankind. This historical plasticity of human cognitive structures implies that the "aesthetic mode" of human practice also changes over time.

The above two traditions strongly inform Li's aesthetic construction in two fundamental ways. First, they connect the aesthetic with a uniquely human apprehension of reality. By this, Li naturally gravitates toward experience-oriented theories. But there is something equally important that cannot be overlooked here—that in both Confucianism and Marxism experience is not of a receptive character. Experience should be viewed as part of human active engagement with reality by way of propriety or labor—within the human strata or generally the whole material world.

Kantianism informs Li's aesthetics in a way that is very different from the above two philosophies. This difference can be attributed to the highly speculative character of Kant's philosophy. Accordingly, Kant's point of departure is the abstract subject and their cognitive faculties, where the importance of the aesthetic is discussed in a highly fastidious way. The most important aspect is that, in Kant's account of experience, the aesthetic does not simply make experiences aesthetic, but rather it makes any experience possible. Kant constructs aesthetics as a science of what takes place in sensibility—how representations are formed according to the principles already present in the mind.[24] This process is explained by figurative synthesis performed by the imagination, which adjusts what comes to sensibility in the way that it can be accommodated by the concepts of the understanding.[25] As such, the aesthetic is an indispensable stage in cognition.

Although Li overturns the Kantian project by reinterpreting the architecture of the a priori cognitive apparatus as a sediment of social practice,[26] he determines the subject as the departure point of his own aesthetic project. In this sense, his critique of Kant is also an inspiration for constructing an aesthetic that is oriented at experience.

To briefly sum up, Li's threefold inspiration informs his project in two major ways. First, it locates the aesthetic in experience. At the same time, it contrasts his understanding of aesthetics with philosophy or art and axiology, in that the aesthetic is not necessarily linked to values or art, but instead is an important factor in the human apprehension of reality. Second, especially due to Confucian and Marxist influences, the aesthetic is not a "readymade" and unchanging piece of human cognitive equipment, but rather is "in the making." The incessant molding of the aesthetic, both in individual and historical humans, is necessarily achieved by way of practice.

## Situating Subjectality and Beauty

These aspects intersect in Li's fundamental notion of subjectality—historically extended humanity that continuously changes through the practice of tool production and use. More precisely, it is conceptualized as two dynamic structures: technological (*gongjubenti* 工具本體) and psychological (*xinlibenti* 心理本體). The first one constitutes the human species, understood as unique animals involved in tool practice. Since the structures are generic features of humans, they are understood as an ontological substance of humankind.

The aesthetic is embedded in psychological structures, which are immediately connected with cognition. Among other things, psychological structures are constituted of emotional substance (*qingganbenti* 情感本體), which has been sedimented into humans through tool practice. This calibration of "raw" emotions, and disconnecting from the physiological level adaptive motivations, is referred to by Li as "new sensuousness" (*xin ganxing* 新感性).[27] Thanks to this process, humans enjoy an aesthetic perception that organizes their cognition of reality, and what follows determines the character of subjectality's engagement with reality by way of practice.[28]

Subjectality is not an abstract entity defined in terms of purely mental capacities; it is a living subject that is psychologically and biologically embedded, as well as being situated in the material environment. Hence the processes that constitute subjectality, especially those connected with practice and cognition, invite an interpretation in terms of situated cognition.

I believe that subjectality can be best accommodated within an autopoietic enactivist paradigm. Enactivism views cognition as intrinsic to embodiment, environment, and sensorimotor capacities in biological, psychological, and cultural contexts,[29] by which it provides a comprehensive insight into cognition on different levels. An equally important characteristic of this approach is how it conceptualizes cognition: "cognition is not the representation of a pregiven world by a pregiven mind but is rather the enactment of a world and a mind on the basis of a history of the variety of actions that a being in the world performs."[30] Cognitive processes, conceived in the above way, are highly compliant with subjectality, where sedimentation is an incessant process necessarily grounded on subjectality's engagement that transforms the material world. Enactivism offers a framework that allows us to encapsulate the dynamic character of cognition, especially with regard to the plasticity of cognitive structures. This aspect is further determined by autopoietic enactivism, where a living organism, embedded in an environment, is defined as an autopoietic system "that is organized as a self-producing network of processes that also constitute the system as a topological unity."[31] On this interpretation, subjectality is to be defined by its plastic cognitive structures.

Finally, enactivism does not separate cognition and action. Francisco J. Varela, Evan Thompson, and Eleanor Rosch describe perception as follows: "(1) Perception consists in perceptually guided action, and (2) cognitive structures emerge from the recurrent sensorimotor patterns that enable action to be perceptually guided."[32] The plasticity of cognitive structures (here perception) confirms abandoning the clear boundary between subject and object—it is necessarily constituted and incessantly remolded via recursive enactments.

Conceptualizing subjectality as an autopoietic system, whose psychological structures are reconfigured in a sensorimotor way, opens the field to explaining the function of the aesthetic in cognitive processes. For this reason, enactivism has to be complemented with appraisal theory, which focuses on the function and constitution of emotions. According to appraisal theory, humans "evaluate events in terms of the perceived relevance to their current needs or goals, including considerations of their ability to cope with the consequences and the compatibility of the underlying actions with social norms and self-ideals."[33] An appraisal, apart from being an impression of an emotional character, is an event of valuation with regard to how it is related to the temporally immediate and remote aims of an appraising agent. In this sense, emotion built into enactment is cognitive in that it informs an autopoietic system with regard to how to respond to an event. This can involve a reconsideration of perception and sensorimotor enactment.

The emotions that emerge in appraising processes are not atomic. They are viewed as temporally extended emotional episodes built of elementary appraisals. An aesthetically material one is the so-called "novelty appraisal," which results from contact with the environment and acknowledging a change therein. It is often followed by a short feeling of pleasantness or unpleasantness. Importantly, intrinsic pleasantness, apart from sensorimotor, also applies to more complex interaction levels, including the conceptual, and can be informed by preferences that are culturally sensitive, which can include aesthetic appraisals.[34] Aesthetic pleasure is believed to emerge in non-habituated, precarious conditions, which are triggered by "cognitively puzzling" changes in the environment and require the reconfiguration of the autopoietic system. This overlaps with Li's claim that aesthetic pleasure occurs in perceptually fresh situations, and it wanes by way of perceptual recursion.[35]

Considering the enactively situated subjectality, which includes the cognitively important aesthetic component, one can proceed to a central notion of Li's aesthetic: beauty. Contrary to multiple theories that identify beauty with a value, Li locates it in the engagement of subjectality with the world. Li writes that beauty emerges in "the interplay of subjective practice and objective reality, not of subjective consciousness and objective nature."[36]

Li, apart from expressing a view that beauty is not subjective but objective by virtue of emerging in practice that accords with objective laws, underscores that beauty does not emerge through an active engagement of the subject. The activity should be understood not as active perceptual processing but rather as a material practice. In enactivist terms, beauty is an enactment in which an autopoietic system adjusts itself to the environment (of which it is part) in a meaningful way.

Regarding the feeling of pleasure that emerges in such "aesthetic practice," Li explains it through the isomorphic structures of gestalt psychology. Accordingly, he claims that the brain produces representations (especially structurally), identical with perceived objects, and that the match so achieved is a harmonious state that produces pleasure.[37] In addition to the fact that this theory is highly unlikely,[38] resorting to isomorphic structures does not agree with Li's concept of subjectality in a consistent way for two reasons. First, the isomorphic structures presuppose a subject-object model. Second, it seems very unlikely that all aesthetic experiences involve representations, especially structural ones.[39] Li's account of beauty as the feeling of aesthetic pleasure can be more consistently explained by enactivism, which avoids these two problems. It explains the experience in terms of enactment, where the aesthetic feeling can be attributed to appraisals. Enactivism also naturally fits the theoretical framework as an autopoietic system that is part of an environment, and thus necessarily conforms to the laws thereof.

## Compatibility and Contribution

As has been shown, not only is Li's aesthetic experience oriented, but it can also be naturally complemented by a situated cognition conceptualization and cognitive theories from experimental sciences. In order to show how Li's theory is conversant with, and more importantly, can contribute to contemporary aesthetics research, I will briefly refer to Bence Nanay's and Wolfgang Welsch's concepts of aesthetics, which I believe to be representative for mapping the horizon of the field.

Nanay proposes that research into aesthetics can be largely encapsulated or problematized within the philosophy of perception. He construes perception in a broad way, by going beyond pure sensibility and complementing the discipline with, for instance, conceptualization or top-down processing.[40] Importantly, this approach is not confined to one specific direction of research into aesthetics. To illustrate this, Nanay refers to a fundamental debate concerning the nature of aesthetic experience. This problem can be theorized in three major ways, which aim at investigating the properties represented in aesthetic experience, the role of aesthetic experience in mental processing, and the intrinsic properties of aesthetic experiences.[41] Accordingly, the philosophy of perception can serve as a paradigm for aesthetic discussions.

Another benefit from employing the "perceptual paradigm" is that aesthetic problems constructed in this way can be further investigated with empirically informed methodologies,[42] and quite often this can result in reformulating theoretical claims with evidence delivered from experimental sciences.

Thus construed, aesthetics research locates the aesthetic in the sensuous apprehension of reality, which is largely seen through perception and processes that are interconnected with it.

It can be said that Welsch's conception of aesthetics is motivated by disconnecting the discipline from the confinements of art-related studies and embracing the whole scope of human activities, which entails multiple paradigms of aesthetics research.[43] This postulate is further supported by two reasons. The first one is a highly intense aestheticization of human life, which has comprehensively informed human practice. This results not only in the aestheticization of some areas of human life, but lifestyles and global processes largely formatted by an aesthetic component.[44] This can be illustrated by consumer culture, wherein an aesthetic conception of life has dominated economic or environmental concerns.

The second, more philosophically apt reason is a change in the human apprehension of reality. It underscores that human cognition is deeply embedded in the aesthetic processing of reality. On the epistemic level, this results in even organizing scientific knowledge according to aesthetic factors. Welsch believes that this has largely been caused by the prevalent electronic mediation of reality, which makes reality more plastic in terms of aesthetic processing.[45] Hence, the account of reality has largely become a narration of it. This, in turn, leads to an important cognitive shift, which downplays metaphysical foundations and stops at the level of appearances.[46]

Welsch's theory not only uncovers the complexity of human apprehension in terms of cognitive processing, but also underscores that these processes leave their mark on reality as the scope of human practice. This requires a new philosophical insight, where an experience-oriented aesthetics seems to be of special utility.

Li's theory is situated in this aesthetics research landscape not only due to his locating the aesthetic in cognitive processes; the theories also share an openness to complementation with methodologies and results from experimental cognitive sciences. By this, they can become part of naturalized aesthetics research.

Not only is Li's theory compatible with the objectives of experience-oriented aesthetics, subjectality-founded aesthetic can also offer an important contribution to this field. What reveals the greatest potential of Li's aesthetic to this research is the historical perspective of his project. This can be viewed in three main aspects. First, while most naturalized aesthetics provide accounts of how the aesthetic matters in cognitive processes, they usually concentrate on an ontogenetic perspective. In this respect, Li's theory provides a phylogenetic insight into the changes of human cognitive and aesthetic apprehension of reality.

How this perspective makes a difference can be illustrated by multimodal perception, which assumes an interrelation of sense modalities.[47] This perspective seems to be particularly relevant nowadays, when humanity is undergoing an unprecedented technological leap and operates sophisticated electronic tools, such as tablets and smartphones. These devices largely rely on visual modality and changes therein, and on the multimodal level can also be viewed as a different engagement with reality via different tool practices.

Second, Li's theory views different aesthetic theories as relative to the tool practices from their temporal locations. This approach underscores that aesthetics should be viewed as a dynamic process, whose transformations can be explained by changes in human practice and the sensuous apprehension integrated with it throughout historical time.[48]

Third, the above view entails a methodological observation that new theories do not falsify preceding ones, since all theories hold when viewed as relative to the tool practices from their temporal locations.

This, in turn, can lead to a perdurantist interpretation of aesthetics as a whole that is composed of temporal parts, which are aesthetic theories from all temporal locations. On this interpretation, Li's theory is of a twofold character. It is a "temporal aesthetic" growing from contemporary tool practice, but concurrently, it is also an aesthetics or meta-aesthetics, due to offering a holistic account of differences between the constituent theories.

## Notes

1. In fact, on the basis of Li's aesthetic theory, these can be to a great extent understood as synonymous.

2. Although Li himself does not engage his project with empirical sciences, he remarks that his claims are likely to be verified and further explored by psychology and brain sciences. Li Zehou, *A New Approach to Kant: A Confucian-Marxist's Viewpoint* (Singapore: Springer, 2018), vii.

3. It has to be noted that these areas of human activity can illustrate the philosophical aesthetic.

4. Apart from this subdivision, within specific conceptions of aesthetics discipline, one can also distinguish between different aesthetic schools, such as, for instance, Roman Ingarden's ontological approach within the philosophy of art. Roman Ingarden, *The Literary Work of Art*, trans. George G. Grabowicz (Evanston, IL: Northwestern University Press, 1973).

5. How differently aesthetics can be understood is reflected in Bence Nanay's proposal of viewing aesthetics through the prism of philosophy of perception, which redefines the discipline as belonging to the "metaphysics and epistemology, broadly construed," rather than "value theory" philosophy subdiscipline. Bence Nanay, "Philosophy of Perception as a Guide to Aesthetics," in *Aesthetics and the Sciences of Mind*, ed. Greg Currie et al. (New York: Oxford University Press, 2014), 115.

6. This can be illustrated by Plato's concept of objective beauty that belongs to the forms and the beauty of objects that participate in this very form. Rafal Banka, *Cognition and Practice: Li Zehou's Philosophical Aesthetics* (Albany: State University of New York Press, 2022), 113–14.

7. This shift of interests is described by Katherine Thomson-Jones and Kathleen Stock with reference to British philosophy in the early twentieth century. Katherine Thomson-Jones and Kathleen Stock, "Introduction," in *New Waves in Aesthetics*, ed. Katherine Thomson-Jones and Kathleen Stock (London: Palgrave Macmillan, 2008), xi.

8. An example of this research can be Ingarden's ontology of literature (1973) or Sherri Irvin's study of ontological difference in visual artworks. Sherri

Irvin, "The Ontological Diversity of Visual Artworks," in *New Waves in Aesthetics*, ed. Katherine Thomson-Jones and Kathleen Stock (London: Palgrave Macmillan, 2008), 1–19.

    9. Richard Shusterman, *Pragmatist Aesthetics: Living Beauty, Rethinking Art* (Lanham, MD: Rowman and Littlefield, 2000), 264.

    10. Immanuel Kant, *Critique of Pure Reason*, trans. Norman Kemp Smith (Basingstoke, UK: Palgrave Macmillan, 2007), A20/B34. It also has to be underscored that both Baumgarten and Kant did not downplay the role of art in their philosophical investigations. In fact, Baumgarten includes poetry and art in his definition of aesthetics, but what matters here is sensuous cognition. Banka, *Cognition and Practice*, 4. Apart from his intricate account of the role of aesthetics in sensibility, Kant also developed a philosophy of art that was associated with adherent, otherwise dependent beauty. Immanuel Kant, *Critique of the Power of Judgment*, trans. Paul Guyer (New York: Cambridge University Press, 2002), 5:356.

    11. One can place Gary Iseminger's concept of aesthetics within this family of theories. Iseminger operates with a concept of the aesthetic state of mind, which is the appreciation of a state of affairs "just in case she or he is valuing for its own sake the experiencing of that state of affairs." Gary Iseminger, "The Aesthetic State of Mind," in *Contemporary Debates in Aesthetics and the Philosophy of Art*, ed. Matthew Kieran (Oxford: Blackwell, 2006), 99. This understanding of aesthetics abandons the prerequisite of certain types of objects or events, whose experience evokes the aesthetic. Here, priority is given to the very nature of experience. This directs aesthetics as a discipline toward the "how" rather than "what" of experience.

    12. Such cases can be illustrated by Kant's discussion of the judgment of taste or relationship between the purposiveness of nature and pleasure. Kant, *Critique of the Power of Judgment*, 5:187, 5:256.

    13. For a detailed account of Confucian ethics as virtue ethics, see Rafal Banka, "Psychological Argumentation in Confucian Ethics as a Methodological Issue in Cross-Cultural Philosophy," *Dao: A Journal of Comparative Philosophy* 15, no. 4 (2016): 594; Banka, *Cognition and Practice*, 14–18.

    14. Evidence for this can be found, for instance, in fragments 3.3 and 8.8 of the *Analects*. Confucius, *Analects with Selections from Traditional Commentaries*, trans. Edward Slingerland (Indianapolis: Hackett, 2003), 17–18, 80.

    15. Confucius, *Analects*, 80.

    16. The fact that the *Odes* is poetry is not necessarily important here. As Li remarks, at the time of Confucius the work was treated as an educational source rather than a work of art. Li Zehou 李澤厚, *Zhongguo meixue shi* 中國美學史 (*History of Chinese Aesthetics*) (Hefei: Anhui wenyi chuban she, 1999), 112.

    17. Li Zehou, *The Chinese Aesthetic Tradition*, trans. Maija Bell Samei (Honolulu: University of Hawai'i Press, 2009), 49–50.

    18. Confucius, *Analects*, 59.

19. In this case, such pleasurable actions would be egoistically motivated.

20. That Confucians are focused on the formal aspect of propriety has been underscored in, for instance, *Analects* 3.12 and *Xunzi* 17.11 and 19.22. Confucius, *Analects*, 21–22; Xunzi, *Xunzi: A Translation and Study of the Complete Works*, trans. John Knoblock (Beijing: Foreign Languages Press, 1999), 547.

21. Iseminger, "The Aesthetic State of Mind," 99.

22. Li, *The Chinese Aesthetic Tradition*, 54–57.

23. Banka, *Cognition and Practice*, 27; Karl Marx, "Economic and Philosophic Manuscripts," in *The Marx-Engels Reader*, trans. Martin Milligan, ed. Robert E. Tucker (New York: Norton, 1978), 88.

24. Banka, *Cognition and Practice*, 42.

25. Kant, *Critique of Pure Reason*, B151.

26. Li, *A New Approach to Kant*, 128–29.

27. Li Zehou and Jane Cauvel, *Four Essays on Aesthetics: Toward a Global View* (Lanham, MD: Lexington Books, 2006), 87.

28. This can be illustrated by aesthetic preferences for facial features that are correlated with high estrogen and testosterone levels in females and males, respectively, and preferences for landscape that is associated with rich supplies of nutrition. Anjan Chatterjee, *The Aesthetic Brain: How We Evolved to Desire Beauty and Enjoy Art* (New York: Oxford University Press, 2013), 13, 14, 48–49.

29. Francisco J. Varela, Evan Thompson, and Eleanor Rosch, *The Embodied Mind: Cognitive Science and Human Experience* (Cambridge, MA: MIT Press, 1993), 172–73.

30. Varela, Thompson, and Rosch, *The Embodied Mind*, 9.

31. Evan Thompson, "Living Ways of Sense Making," *Philosophy Today* 55, suppl. (2011): 114–15.

32. Varela, Thompson, and Rosch, *The Embodied Mind*, 173.

33. Klaus R. Scherer, "Introduction: Cognitive Components of Emotion," in *Handbook of Affective Sciences*, ed. Richard J. Davidson, Klaus R. Scherer, and H. Hill Goldsmith (New York: Oxford University Press, 2003), 564.

34. For a more detailed account of appraisals, see Banka, *Cognition and Practice*, 107–9.

35. For more detailed account of aesthetic pleasure, see Banka, *Cognition and Practice*, 158. This role of the aesthetic also patterns with Kant's explanation of matching universal laws and the manifold, which is of contingent character. Kant believes that the "cognitive validation" of the match is marked by the feeling of pleasure, which disappears once habituated. Kant, *Critique of the Power of Judgement*, 5:187.

36. Li and Cauvel, *Four Essays on Aesthetics*, 54.

37. Li and Cauvel, *Four Essays on Aesthetics*, 51–52.

38. For details, see Tomasz Maruszewski, *Psychologia poznania* (*Cognitive Psychology*) (Gdańsk: Gdańskie Wydawnictwo Psychologiczne, 2002), 49.

39. For instance, in most performance arts, such as dance, the performer is unlikely to have a structural representation when experiencing aesthetic pleasure.
40. Bence Nanay, "Philosophy of Perception as a Guide to Aesthetics," 104.
41. Nanay, "Philosophy of Perception as a Guide to Aesthetics," 108.
42. Nanay, "Philosophy of Perception as a Guide to Aesthetics," 112.
43. Welch even coins a special term, "artistics," to denote the art-focused studies that are usually taken as aesthetics. Wolfgang Welsch, *Undoing Aesthetics*, trans. Andrew Inkpin (London, Sage 1997), 78.
44. Welsch, 81–82.
45. Welsch, 85.
46. Welsch, 15.
47. Bence Nanay, "Philosophy of Perception: A Road Map with Lots of Bypass Roads," in *Current Controversies in Philosophy of Perception*, ed. Bence Nanay (New York and Abington: Routledge, 2017), 15.
48. In fact, Li employs an analogous view to the dynamic of mathematical and scientific theories. For instance, he claims that ancient land surveying practices led to the conceptualization of space in Euclidean geometry and classical mechanics. Together with technological progress, these conceptualizations were supplanted with non-Euclidean geometry and quantum mechanics. Li, *A New Approach to Kant*, 56–58.

# Bibliography

Banka, Rafal. *Cognition and Practice: Li Zehou's Philosophical Aesthetics*. Albany: State University of New York Press, 2022.

Banka, Rafal. "Psychological Argumentation in Confucian Ethics as a Methodological Issue in Cross-Cultural Philosophy." *Dao: A Journal of Comparative Philosophy* 15, no. 4 (2016): 591–606.

Chatterjee, Anjan. *The Aesthetic Brain: How We Evolved to Desire Beauty and Enjoy Art*. New York: Oxford University Press, 2013.

Confucius. *Analects, with Selections from Traditional Commentaries*. Translated by Edward Slingerland. Indianapolis: Hackett, 2003.

Ingarden, Roman. *The Literary Work of Art*. Translated by George G. Grabowicz. Evanston, IL: Northwestern University Press, 1973.

Irvin, Sherri. "The Ontological Diversity of Visual Artworks." In *New Waves in Aesthetics*, edited by Katherine Thomson-Jones and Kathleen Stock, 1–19. London: Palgrave Macmillan, 2008.

Iseminger, Gary. "The Aesthetic State of Mind." In *Contemporary Debates in Aesthetics and the Philosophy of Art*, edited by Matthew Kieran, 98–112. Oxford: Blackwell, 2006.

Kant, Immanuel. *Critique of Pure Reason*. Translated by Norman Kemp Smith. Rev. 2nd ed. Basingstoke, UK: Palgrave Macmillan, 2007.

Kant, Immanuel. *Critique of the Power of Judgment*. Translated by Paul Guyer. New York: Cambridge University Press, 2002.

Li Zehou. *The Chinese Aesthetic Tradition*. Translated by Maija Bell Samei. Honolulu: University of Hawai'i Press, 2009.

Li Zehou. *A New Approach to Kant: A Confucian-Marxist's Viewpoint*. Translated by Jeanne Haizhen Allen and Christopher Ahn. Singapore: Springer, 2018.

Li Zehou. *The Path of Beauty: A Study of Chinese Aesthetics*. Translated by Gong Lizeng. Hong Kong: Oxford University Press, 1994.

Li Zehou and Jane Cauvel. *Four Essays on Aesthetics: Toward a Global View*. Lanham, MD: Lexington Books, 2006.

Li Zehou 李澤厚 and Liu Gangji 劉鋼紀. *Zhongguo meixue shi* 中國美學史 (*A History of Chinese Aesthetics*). Hefei: Anhui wenyi chuban she, 1999.

Maruszewski, Tomasz. *Psychologia poznania* (*Cognitive Psychology*). Gdańsk: Gdan´skie Wydawnictwo Psychologiczne, 2002.

Marx, Karl. "Economic and Philosophic Manuscripts." In *The Marx-Engels Reader*, translated by Martin Milligan, edited by Robert E. Tucker, 66–125. New York: W. W. Norton and Company, 1978.

Nanay, Bence. "Philosophy of Perception: A Road Map with Lots of Bypass Roads." In *Current Controversies in Philosophy of Perception*, edited by Bence Nanay, 1–19. New York: Routledge, 2017.

Nanay, Bence. "Philosophy of Perception as a Guide to Aesthetics." In *Aesthetics and the Sciences of Mind*, edited by Greg Currie, Matthew Kieran, Aaron Meskin, and Jon Robson, 101–20. New York: Oxford University Press, 2014.

Scherer, Klaus R. "Introduction: Cognitive Components of Emotion." In *Handbook of Affective Sciences*, edited by Richard J. Davidson, Klaus R. Scherer, and H. Hill Goldsmith, 563–71. New York: Oxford University Press, 2003.

Shusterman, Richard. *Pragmatist Aesthetics: Living Beauty, Rethinking Art*. Lanham, MD: Rowman and Littlefield, 2000.

Thompson, Evan. "Living Ways of Sense Making." *Philosophy Today* 55, suppl. (2011): 114–15.

Thomson-Jones, Katherine, and Kathleen Stock. "Introduction." In *New Waves in Aesthetics*, edited by Katherine Thomson-Jones and Kathleen Stock, xi–xix. London: Palgrave Macmillan, 2008.

Varela, Francisco J., Evan Thompson, and Eleanor Rosch. *The Embodied Mind: Cognitive Science and Human Experience*. Cambridge, MA: MIT Press, 1993.

Welsch, Wolfgang. *Undoing Aesthetics*. Translated by Andrew Inkpin. London: Sage, 1997.

Xunzi. *Xunzi: A Translation and Study of the Complete Works*. Translated by John Knoblock. Beijing: Foreign Languages Press, 1999.

# Part 3

# Freedom, Autonomy, and Justice

# 6

# Autonomy and the Nature of Ruist Morality

## Li Zehou and Mou Zongsan

### David Elstein

Li Zehou's wide-ranging work made him the most influential mainland Chinese philosopher of the latter part of the twentieth and into the twenty-first century. He is known for incorporating Marxism and Kantian thought along with traditional Chinese philosophy. Li stands out for several reasons. He took Marxism seriously without being dogmatic about it, he emphasized the need to take into account the historical and cultural conditions of thought, he developed his own philosophical views through deep engagement with many thinkers, and he constructed his own interpretation of the history of Chinese thought that did not adhere to the two main trends in Chinese scholarship of the time: doctrinaire Sinicized Marxist thought and the New Ruist[1] philosophies from Hong Kong and Taiwan that largely followed Mou Zongsan. Li knew of Mou's work and responded to him in some of his writings on the history of Ruism, but had some pointed criticisms of Mou's interpretation of Ruist philosophy. And yet, a closer look at Li's own analysis of Ruism reveals some deep tensions that do not get fully resolved.

The chief tension comes from something Li and Mou share: an understanding of morality that accepts a great deal of the Kantian picture of what it must look like. Although Li criticizes Mou for neglecting the empirical reality of feelings in morality, he appears not to notice the difficulties to his own interpretation caused by trying to meld empirical and a priori aspects. Li does misunderstand some aspects of Mou's thought, but his criticisms nevertheless get at some serious difficulties for Mou's interpretation. However, his own interpretation of Ruist ethics is not free from problems. In this essay, I will explore Li's criticism of Mou's interpretation of Ruism and examine his own understanding of Ruist ethics. I will argue that Li does not provide a satisfactory account of Ruist morality either and, like Mou, this is because he still accepts much of the Kantian description of what morality has to be that colors his interpretation of Ruist thought. Although I think Li's criticisms of Mou were not entirely justified, I will explore where he believed Mou went wrong, and how he tried to avoid the same problems in his own interpretation of Ruism. The argument I want to make is that Li can retain what he wants from Kant, while making his interpretation of Ruism more consistent by removing the appeal to the a priori and focusing on the role of feelings.

## Mou's Account of Ruist Morality

Before we look at Li's criticism of Mou, it will be useful to summarize briefly Mou's position to understand better where Li objects. Mou of course follows the Mengzi line, emphasizing the continuity between Mengzi and Song-Ming Ruism. Li mainly takes issue with Mou's characterization of Song-Ming Ruist morality, and so that is a reasonable place to begin. In his major work *Heart-Mind and Human Nature in Themselves* (*Xinti yu xingti* 心體與性體), Mou argued that Song-Ming Ruists were engaged in the same philosophical quest as Kant: establishing the a priori conditions of morality. For Kant, what defines morality is that its commands are necessary and unconditional. Necessity cannot be established based on any empirical knowledge, and so morality has to be known a priori. Mou agrees: "If the moral law cannot be established on an a priori, universal, and efficacious basis, then there can be no true, pure moral behavior to speak of."[2] The a priori basis of moral practice is the freedom and autonomy of the will.[3] Song-Ming Ruists did not use the terminology of autonomy or the free will, but rather talked about the heart-mind and human nature as fundamental realities in themselves, not as empirical appearances. Mou concludes that what Song-Ming Ruists were doing was examining the a priori basis of morality, with their own vocabulary.[4]

Autonomy for Mou requires independence from interests, inclinations, and external control. It must be independent from anything empirical. Morality has to be founded on a principle that the will gives to itself, not something that comes from outside it. Mou writes, "Any moral principle that is created by anything related to an object or an object's particular character that determines the will is an unreal and inconsistent moral principle. As far as the will is concerned, it is heteronomous." A will that is decided or controlled by anything external is not a free, autonomous will.[5] As he put it elsewhere, free will cannot be an effect brought about by something else; it can only be a cause.[6] In addition, he writes, "If it requires a lower interest from something external to stimulate it, then it is not the fundamental heart-mind; it is not the true, autonomous will that gives the law to itself."[7] Morality requires the will to determine itself, free from the influence, control, or stimulation of an external object. That is autonomy.

The key point is that morality requires an unconditional command to be real, which is a product of a free, autonomous will. Through moments of moral response to a situation in the world (such as Mengzi's example of seeing a child about to fall into a well), the fundamental heart-mind reflexively becomes aware of itself, a process in which this heart-mind grasps itself intellectually and not sensibly.[8] This fundamental heart-mind is the author of the autonomous command given to itself which makes morality possible. "Morality means action based on an unconditional categorical imperative. The issuer of this unconditional categorical imperative . . . in China is called the fundamental heart-mind, benevolence in itself, or innate moral awareness, and it is our nature in itself."[9] We see here the Kantian influence: morality must be unconditional, which means it cannot be based on anything sensible. It must therefore be autonomous, not depending on anything outside the self. This leads Mou to identify a faculty capable of issuing autonomous commands free from any external influence, the fundamental heart-mind. What he calls the orthodox line of Ruism emphasized autonomy, and went a step beyond Kant in showing that morality was a reality and not merely a postulate.

## Li Zehou's Criticisms of Mou

One of the most immediate differences between the two philosophers that leaps out when comparing them is very different understandings of what the task of philosophy is. Mou's concept of philosophy comes out in the passages quoted above: the task of moral philosophy is to provide a sure foundation for morality. Because morality has to command universally and unconditionally, it cannot be based on anything sensible. Experience can only provide contingent truth, not necessary truth. This means that empirical examination of morality can never provide the grounds for an unconditional moral principle, because empirical truth could always be otherwise. Morality has to be a priori, which led Mou to develop his moral metaphysics. Although some later New Ruists, notably Liu Shuxian, allowed room for some particular cultural expressions,[10] the fundamental moral principles have to be universal. Morality cannot be one thing in China and something else in Germany. The task of philosophy is to understand the universal.

Li plays much greater attention to history and culture and how thought intersects with these. He says that the reason for divergent understandings of Kongzi's thought is insufficient understanding of the historical and social circumstances in which Kongzi lived and which contributed to his thought. Kongzi's thought, according to Li, expressed some aspects of clan and aristocratic society at the time.[11] It then follows that grasping Kongzi's thought properly requires better understanding of those circumstances that influenced its development and expressions. Li is not suggesting some kind of materialism where social and economic conditions simply determine thought. Kongzi developed what Li calls a cultural-psychological formation (*wenhua xinli jiegou* 文化心理結構) that exercised major influence on the future development of Chinese culture and the way Chinese people think. In other words, thought influences cultural and social conditions while also being influenced by them. History, social norms, reason, and emotion interact in complex ways, shaping internal motivations as well as external rules.[12]

The upshot of this is that philosophy is not a form of pure thought entirely divorced from social, economic, and political conditions. Li does not claim that the truth of philosophical claims is an empirical matter. He does, however, have a different understanding of what philosophy is about. He did not agree with Mou that the point of philosophy is to discover a priori, universal truths, moral principles in particular. Li sees it differently: the cultural-psychological formation and wisdom of a nation are not unchanging things outside of space and time that can be understood a priori. The task of Chinese philosophy specifically is to understand the Chinese cultural-psychological formation, eradicate its errors, and transform it to meet the new century.[13] Philosophy is necessarily connected with the sensible world. This is the foundation of Li's criticisms of Mou's interpretation of Ruism: Mou was trying to eliminate anything sensible from Ruist ethics, but this is not how most Ruist scholars understood their work, and furthermore it cannot be done.

Sensibility in the form of psychological feeling is necessarily connected to Ruist ethics in Li's understanding. Mou followed Kant in strictly separating psychological feelings from true morality: anything contingent—anything belonging to the world of appearances—could not be the basis of morality. This led him to develop his moral metaphysics to understand the a priori conditions of morality. Mou therefore employed the autonomy/heteronomy distinction in his historical work on Ruism, insisting that the orthodox line of Ruism always emphasized the autonomy of morality. Free will still has a major role in Li's Ruism, but in a very different way than Mou.[14] Li's deepest dispute with Mou is about the place of emotions. Mengzi said the foundation of moral responsiveness is a heart that is not unfeeling to others, an illustration of which is the feeling of alarm and compassion that anyone would have when seeing a child about to fall into a well.[15] Li asks, what could a heart that is not unfeeling to others be, if not some kind of psychological feeling or response in the sensible world?[16] For this reason, the basis of morality cannot be found apart from the sensible world.

Morality is thus more multidimensional in Li's thought than it is in Mou's. Because it is not an a priori examination, it includes historical, cultural, technological, psychological, and biological factors (hardly an exhaustive list). All of these things shape human thought and contribute to the cultural-psychological formation of a nation and an individual, without determining it.[17] Li does not say that philosophy should be strictly naturalistic, but it certainly should not entirely ignore the sciences.[18] Philosophy cannot pretend that knowledge of the sensible world is utterly irrelevant for understanding morality.

The concern for sensible feelings manifests in one more way in Li's philosophy: the role of joy and satisfaction of desires. He does not advocate asceticism. Echoing Dai Zhen, Li is critical of Song-Ming Ruist philosophers for failing to recognize the importance of desires, which he believes had terrible effects.[19] Liu Zongzhou is held up as a model by Mou, but Li criticizes him for a near-religious asceticism that lost any significant objective content and "became unusually dry religious commands with no vitality."[20] In Mou as well, it is hard to find much room for or value in satisfying any desires or having joy in life. It is true that

Mou says the fully manifested free, autonomous will is holy and so feels no sense of conflict. It takes joy in the moral law it gives to itself.[21] And yet this is evidently very different from the joy of fulfilling desires or aesthetic experience generally. Mou says almost nothing about music, which for Li is critical to completing oneself as a person.[22] Joy occupies a much more central place for Li, defining Chinese culture.

## Li's Account of Ruist Morality

Although Li has a different conception of what philosophy is that leads him to the above criticisms of Mou's interpretation of Ruism, he retains significant Kantian influence in his own understanding of Mengzi especially. Li does not end up as far from Mou as he himself seems to think. The basis of the moral norms is different, but Li still ends up incorporating the fundamentals of the Kantian understanding of morality, and as a result introduces significant tensions in trying to make morality both transcendental and cultural, a priori and empirical. Because of this, Li ends up according more significance to Xunzi, who he argues does not have the transcendental aspect of Mengzi and most Song-Ming Ruists. This is an advantage for Li, while it renders Xunzi unacceptable heteronomy for Mou. And yet it does not entirely resolve the tension in Li's thought.

As described above, Li believes it is important to attend to historical and cultural factors when understanding a tradition of thought such as Ruism. This is not, however, the same as stating that the truth of its claims depends on contingent historical and cultural factors. However, there is a necessarily empirical element to morality for Li. He emphasizes both reason and emotions, what he calls the "emotio-rational structure" (*qing-li jiegou* 情理結構).[23] Crucially, emotions are essentially related to moral norms.

One of Li's clearest statements of this is found in his analysis of Mengzi. Mengzi "made psychological principles the foundation and starting point of his entire theoretical construction," and his political and economic framework was "entirely built on psychological feelings and principles."[24] The most fundamental of these is the heart-mind that is not unfeeling to others—a general feeling of empathy. Li is careful to call this a psychological feeling or sensation. It is worth pausing a moment to consider precisely how Mou and Li are different.

To do so, let us look at what both philosophers had to say about Mengzi's example of witnessing a child about to fall into a well. This is of course the example Mengzi himself offered to illustrate what he meant by a heart-mind that is not unfeeling to others, and further as an illustration of the feeling that is the basis of humaneness.[25] For Mou, seeing a child about to fall into a well is manifestly a perception that belongs to sensibility. However, the moral response, the feeling of alarm and compassion, is reflexive awareness of one's own mind that is intellectual, not sensible: "This awakening due to astonishment is like the red sun rising out of bottom of the sea; it is not at all sensible. Therefore, the reflective verification in question is the illuminating awareness of intellect itself reflecting its own light back onto itself and not a phenomenal mind different from itself sensibly and passively coming to cognize it, which could never reach it in itself. So this reflective understanding is purely intellectual and not the passivity of sensibility."[26] My purpose here is to understand Mou's claims, not to evaluate them, so I will pass over most possible objections.

We do need to raise one question: when this response is elicited by a sensible event (the sight of the child), how can Mou say it is purely intellectual and has nothing to do with sensibility? I believe the answer is to distinguish causal dependence and logical dependence. When Mou says this moral awareness is intellectual, that is another way of saying it is a priori. A paradigm of a priori knowledge is mathematical knowledge: one can calculate the angles of a thousand-sided figure independently of whether a thousand-sided figure has ever existed. Clearly, certain experiences will be causally necessary to have the concepts of a thousand-sided figure, angles, calculation, and so on. One will need to have a language and probably some exposure to fundamental mathematical concepts. This will be due to sensible experiences. However, once the concepts are acquired, one can use them to derive new knowledge that is not dependent on any particular sensible experience. Knowledge of the sum of the angles of a thousand-sided figure is causally dependent on the sensible experiences necessary to acquire the relevant concepts, but not logically dependent on any sensible experience of such a figure (or whether it exists at all). We can take Mou as saying something similar: the awareness of one's fundamental heart-mind is causally dependent on a sensible experience like seeing the child, but the nature of that awareness is not sensible but intellectual.

Li, by contrast, makes a much simpler point. The feeling of alarm and compassion elicited by seeing the child *is* a psychological feeling directly related to sensibility. Mou developed various terms for the moral feelings and the moral mind to show that these were not part of appearances or sensibility, but a different category of feeling entirely that was intellectual, such as "moral feelings of illuminating awareness" (*mingjue jueqing* 明覺覺情) or "ontological moral feelings" (*bentilun de jueqing* 本體論的覺情).[27] These feelings are empirical in the sense that they are something the agent experiences, but they come from the fundamental heart-mind and so Mou classifies them as something other than appearances. They are not ordinary emotions that belong to sensibility. Li sweeps all that aside and simply recognizes that these are psychological feelings, and furthermore asserts, "Since Kongzi, the key characteristic of Ruism has precisely been that it has been built on principles of psychological feeling."[28] He dispenses with a priori or intellectual feelings and categorizes the moral feelings as psychological responses, apparently on par with any other psychological feeling.

This would all be neat and tidy, except that after saying that Mengzi built his theory on psychological principles, Li immediately throws a wrench into this by also insisting that morality is a priori in Mengzi and Song-Ming Ruism as well (notably, not Xunzi). He follows up his analysis of the example of a child falling into a well with a discussion of ethical relativism and absolutism, stating that all philosophical ethics falls into these two types. Crucially, in relativism "human nature possesses no a priori moral character." Morality is necessarily linked to sensibility. By contrast, in ethical absolutism "morality is above the human realm and so its origin has nothing to do with sensibility. It is a supraempirical or a priori command that controls and dominates sensibility."[29] The deduction Li appears to make is this: all ethics is a form of relativism or absolutism; absolutism holds that morality commands universally; a universal command must originate in the a priori; Mengzi holds that morality commands universally and so is an ethical absolutist; and therefore the origin of moral norms must be a priori. Li himself then notes the connection to Kant, saying the unconditional nature of moral obligation is similar to Kant's categorical imperative.

As it turns out, in parallel to emphasizing the psychological basis of Ruist morality, Li also agrees that the universal and unconditional nature of morality means it also must be a priori. What Mengzi did, according to Li, was blend both emotions and the categorical imperative: "[Mengzi's theory] took the a priori universality of the categorical imperative and directly connected it to the human feelings of the empirical world (mainly 'the feeling of alarm and compassion,' which is in fact sympathy) and further made these (psychological feelings) the basis."[30] Morality is at the same time a priori and empirical. Li ends up returning to a Kant-influenced understanding of morality, reading this into not only Mengzi but Song-Ming Ruists as well.[31] Yet the element of feeling belonging to sensibility is also present as well, setting up an uneasy tension. We will return to this tension later. The point I wish to highlight now is how Li is critical of Mou Zongsan for ignoring the importance of sensible feelings while sharing the Kantian understanding that morality must be a priori in order to be unconditional.

Before moving on, let us take stock of where we are. Li criticized Mou for disregarding psychological feelings is his explanation of Ruist morality. In Li's view, Mengzi built his ethical theory by deriving moral norms from feelings and psychological responses. However, this is still a kind of ethical absolutism that makes universal and unconditional demands. There is an analogy with Kant's categorical imperative. Morality is both a priori and empirical, based on psychological feelings and also based on universal principles.

## Evaluating Li's Interpretation

We will begin with Li's objections to Mou before evaluating Li's own interpretation. Li's chief objection is that Mou neglected the emotions; Ruists did not strictly divide reason and emotion, but aimed at integrating both in the emotio-rational structure.[32] Their concern was not primarily metaphysical, but was about addressing the problems of real life, taking into account practical psychology.[33] When much of Mou's work was devoted to developing Ruist moral metaphysics, using morality to confirm the two-tier ontology of appearances and things in themselves, this criticism has some bite. Of course, Mou was hardly alone in this; modern Chinese philosophy rapidly professionalized, with most representatives spending their careers in academia. Liang Shuming is the noteworthy exception.

Nevertheless, it is a fair point that human psychology is incorporated in traditional Ruist morality, and Mou, out of concern to show that morality is a priori, dismissed anything psychological as merely empirical. One could reasonably question whether Song-Ming Ruists, when they used terms such as "fundamental heart-mind" (benxin 本心) or "heart-mind of the Way" (daoxin 道心), necessarily meant something apart from the world of appearances. Attention to emotions such as concern for one's parents, compassion for suffering, and sympathy for those in need is frequently found in Ruist texts. The psychological importance of a supportive community of family, friends, and teachers is likewise a common theme. Joy in following the Way as well is highlighted by Kongzi, Mengzi, and Xunzi, while joy is rarely found in Mou's works. Emotions do play a significant role in Ruist thought.

However, a supporter of Mou could respond that Li has misunderstood Mou's position. It is true that Mou dismisses anything empirical as a source for morality, but that does not entail dismissing all feelings or emotions. Li does not pay sufficient attention to Mou's category of intellectual or ontological feelings, which are not sensible in nature. Lee Ming-huei in particular develops this aspect of Mou's thought, expanding on Mou's category of ontological feelings that are a priori, and arguing that in Ruism reason and emotion are united, not mutually exclusive as in Kant.[34] This sounds very close to Li. Whether these feelings should be categorized as psychological (*xinli de* 心理的) is a difficult question. Li appears to think of psychology as necessarily belonging to sensibility. In that case Mou's moral feelings would not be psychological, since he denies that they are sensible in nature. Nor are they products of discursive, conceptual thinking.[35] And yet these feelings are some kind of mental state or awareness, and in that sense belong to psychology. It is not clear whether Li has fully appreciated the distinctiveness of Mou's position on the different categories of feelings, sensible and intellectual.

What this does not resolve is whether Mou's use of ontological feelings as a category and intellectual intuition is an accurate interpretation of Ruist philosophy. And there Li raises some serious questions, at the very least. Mou's interpretation gets some support from Mengzi's division of the greater and lesser within the person.[36] The greater—the moral feelings—maps neatly onto Mou's category of ontological feelings of the fundamental mind, and the lesser—sense perceptions and ordinary desires—maps onto feelings and desires that belong to appearances.[37] Yet we may wonder whether Mengzi meant "greater" and "lesser" to have any ontological significance, or simply to be a value claim about which feelings should be given priority. In favor of Li's interpretation, we notice that when Mengzi is discussing the moral responses (as in the examples of the child falling into a well or the king freeing the ox), he focuses on the experience of the feelings, with very little in the way of metaphysics. In fact, we might go step further and say that for Mengzi, what seems to be important is not any kind of theoretical belief about morality (even that human nature is good), but being disposed to have the right feelings in response to the right situations at the right times. I will not go further into how Mou could responds to this, because his response and further questions could occupy a book at least. I will merely say that there may be something to Li's claim that psychology is important, and we can learn something from how he approaches the issue of emotions.

The way Li resolves the tension between the a priori and empirical is to favor Xunzi over Mengzi. Although he does not make this so evident in his *History of Classical Chinese Thought,* in some other works he makes clear his opposition to founding morality on the a priori and the need for a historical approach to understanding morality based on sedimentation of certain cultural conditions, circumstances, and ways of thinking. For Li, this fits Xunzi's way of thinking more closely, and so he is inclined toward Xunzi. "Mengzi's thought is transcendental whereas Xunzi's is empirical. My own theory of sedimentation relies on the accumulation and solidification of experience to explain what is often 'innate' or 'transcendental' for the individual (what I refer to as 'the empirical for humankind becoming a priori for the individual' *jingyan bian xianyan* 經驗變先驗). Thus of course I lean toward Xunzi here."[38] As other scholars have observed, Li is critical of Western philosophy for overreliance on reason and abstraction.[39] His theories of the emotio-rational structure and cultural-psychological formation are correctives to this. Morality is not a priori, but rather "learning and education are morals' real source."[40] Learning, which includes ritual but goes beyond it, is of course a great point of emphasis in Xunzi precisely because morality must be learned. Li's favoring of Xunzi makes sense, and is one more major point of difference with Mou Zongsan.

All problems would be solved and my essay could end here, except for two more issues. First, recall Li's distinction between ethical relativism and absolutism. In ethical relativism, morality is rooted in human social life, depending on sensibility. Significantly, Li says Xunzi's philosophy falls in this category.[41] Xunzi was arguably not a relativist himself, but more importantly, Li is not: historicism is definitely not relativism in his view.[42] Yet if morality based on human social life *is* relativist, how can Li not accept relativism?

Second, it is doubtful whether Li can avoid attributing any innate moral capacities to human beings. Li claims that "no human capacities are a priori or innate, but rather belong to humans as a result of history and education."[43] Even supposing that is an overstatement and Li did not intend to rule out any biological capacities at all, he is right that there is a major difference between him and Kant in terms of seeing reason and moral norms as historical, not a priori.[44] And yet, can Li sustain this position? Is not the tendency toward sociality itself an innate capacity? The tendency toward forming groups and establishing moral rules to begin with? If not, could we learn and internalize morality at all? Here Li recognizes the difficulty for Xunzi: How do we learn to regulate ourselves with rituals in the first place? He admits that there must be some innate capacity to make that possible. "Xunzi also emphasizes that the heart-mind that has the function of rationality has a certain a priori quality."[45] It seems this must be true for Li as well. The emotional capacities themselves that he makes foundational for morality cannot be entirely learned (though particular forms and manifestations could be).

And hence Li's position still has its difficulties. He does not accept complete relativism, but agrees with Kant that universal morality must be based on a priori principles, which he rejects. He favors a historical account of morality, but will find it hard to explain how this is possible without positing any innate capacities. Let us consider how to address these tensions.

## Transforming the Transcendental into the Empirical

One approach, taken by Jana Rošker, is to argue that Li has overcome the opposition between the transcendental and the empirical that is embedded in European philosophy. There are capacities that are a priori from the individual perspective, but they are shaped through historical development. In Li's framework, "No transcendental form can exist independent of experience. The transcendental arises from the empirical, and reason is nothing mysterious but rather something constructed from the historical practices of humankind."[46] And Rošker is of course correct that Li regularly uses the phrase "the empirical for humankind becoming a priori for the individual."[47] Li's view is that what seems a priori or innate from the point of view of the individual is the result of the sedimentation of millions of years of human practice, in which making and using tools is the fundamental practice.[48] Reason itself is social and historical in this sense. This is true of the categorical imperative as well:

it is not a necessary product of pure reason, but comes about through sedimentation.[49] Sedimentation is the building up of human psychological forms[50] and, as the name implies, happens over very long time horizons. As individuals are not aware of this development and the results can feel innate to them, Li loosely speaks of the products of sedimentation as a priori for the individual.

The question is whether it is appropriate to say that forms of thought developed by sedimentation are a priori. Or, put slightly differently, is the characterization of Li as overcoming the opposition of empirical and a priori (transcendental) apt? I think not. As Rošker recognizes, "The psychological structures of thought are also products that come about through culture." There is an essential component that is formed through learning.[51] As quoted above, Li believes morals are learned. Ways of behaving can feel natural and necessary once they become part of one's character. One can learn to respond automatically and effortlessly, as with one's native language (and note that Li follows Wittgenstein in connecting language learning to acquiring a way of life).[52] But what Kant and Mou meant by a priori was not how something felt to the individual, but whether it truly is knowable in a way that is not logically dependent on some particular experience. If morals have a cultural and learned component, they are not independent from experience in this way.

Li is naturally free to stipulate a different meaning for *xianyan*, but then he is not dissolving the opposition between the empirical and a priori. He is simply using those words in a different way. The question of how learned structures can have universality does not go away. I believe we need to take a different approach.

## Resolving the Contradiction

I want to consider whether there are ways to resolve the tensions in Li's thought while preserving his fundamental insights. That means when Li says, "The key characteristic of Ruism has precisely been that it has been built on principles of psychological feeling," we read "psychological feeling" in a commonsense way, as the ordinary feelings of sensibility. We take seriously his claim that what distinguishes Ruism from Kant is that Ruist ethical principles "are intimately linked to sensible existence and psychological feelings. They are not purely formal, but appeal to a basis in the social and psychological."[53] In short, Li thought Ruists were doing something very different from Kant. Can we take this claim seriously and still maintain some level of universality in morality, such that moral progress is a sensible notion?

My answer is not quite, not in the way that Li tries to, but that there is a way to preserve the universality of morality that is a key concern of his. When we understand why Li (and Mou) accepted the Kantian concept of morality, we understand something important about their thought. We also find a way to resolve the above problems in Li. To understand this, we must go back to his distinction between relativism and absolutism. In relativism, there can be no universal ethical standards. Human nature is not inherently good. Morality, Li says, is based on human social life, by which I take him to mean that it depends on the values, standards, and goods of a particular society.[54] Absolutism is just the opposite. It is universal and unconditional. Due to the influence of Kant, both Li and Mou thought that any universal and unconditional principle had to be a priori, because empirical knowledge is always contingent and could turn out to be different.

The first thing to note is that "unconditional" is not a term that should be applied to any moral principles, even Kant's. Kant says the categorical imperative applies to all rational beings, so its application is conditional on rationality: it does not apply to nonrational beings. Li's Ruist morality has to be even narrower, because it has a basis in the social and psychological. We can make this even more specific: the psychological feeling that Li mentions most frequently, and the one that distinguishes Ruism from Kant, is humaneness or benevolence (*ren* 仁). Let us imagine an alien species of rational but not social beings. They reproduce in the manner of some snakes or sea turtles: the male and female have no lasting relationship, and once the female lays her eggs, her parental involvement is done. If either parent ever meets their children again, it is an accident and they treat each other as strangers. This species is self-sufficient and solitary, forming no social group with others of its kind (or any other species). It is perfectly capable of rational thought—maybe some of its members have deduced mathematical truths for fun. However, it has no social feelings, because it is not social. In particular, it lacks the sense of humaneness.

Kant's categorical imperative could still apply to this species, because they are rational in the necessary way.[55] But Li's Ruist morality could not apply here, because *ex hypothesi* this species lacks the social feelings that ground Ruist morality. They have a psychology, but it would be a psychology of a very different order. They do not feel compassion for others and have no concept of family (the basis of *ren* 仁 according to Mengzi). With no social groups, they have no feeling of what is socially right (*yi* 義) and no disposition to follow social rules (*li* 禮). When seeing a child of their own species about to fall into a well (or meet with some other bad end), they feel wholly indifferent. What is pathological in a human being is simply normal psychology to them. Ruist morality can have no meaning for them, because they lack the requisite feelings that are the source of Ruist moral principles. But I believe Li would say such a lack of morality is not possible for human beings.

My point with this admittedly far-fetched example is to get a better sense of what "universal and unconditional" mean for Li. I suggest that what they should mean are "universal and unconditional for all normal human beings," because as it happens normal human beings have the psychology that Ruism is based on. As Li says, Ruist ethics are not purely formal principles, but have a basis in the social and psychological (and these turn out to be connected). But it is a contingent fact about human beings that we are highly social: obviously not every species is. Because we are social, we have a psychology that is extremely sensitive to what people around us are thinking and feeling. If that is the basis of morality, then this is not known through a priori reason. Li is correct about that. It is not a necessary fact about human beings that we have the moral feelings that Mengzi identified, not in the same way that it is a necessary fact about triangles that their angles add up to 180 degrees. It is a logical contradiction to imagine a triangle with angles adding up to 360 degrees, but it is not logically contradictory to imagine human beings as more like the aliens I sketched above. That is not what we are, but we could have been.

Fortunately for Li's purposes, he can preserve some degree of universality in morality without giving it an a priori basis, which in fact it does not have according to him. This universality seems to be the critical point. Although he says that moral rules are formed through human social life, this itself sets boundaries on what is possible morally: it has to make human social life possible. This is in fact consistent with Li's view: "I see all of ethics and morals, including justice, as serving the continuous extension of human existence."[56] This will draw limits on what human morality can be. If human nature is universal (as Mengzi claimed), then that provides the requisite general moral principles. It is true that this will not be unconditional in a strict sense, but I argue that it does not matter. No moral principle, even the categorical imperative, is truly unconditional.

When we look at why one might be concerned with morality being conditional, we see that there is no cause for worry with making morality dependent on human psychology. One reason for concern might be that psychologically people fail to feel the pull of a moral principle, or feel it too weakly. It is simply a fact that people often are not motivated to do what we believe they should do. No philosophical argument will make that fact go away. Kant's position is not any better (and arguably worse) than Mengzi's or Wang Yangming's here.

A more significant reason to worry is that if morality is conditional, we in fact will have insufficient justification for insisting that some individuals or groups abide by the moral principles, because they do not satisfy the first part of the conditional. And then we will be back to some form of relativism, where the moral rules apply only to certain people and not to others. When the source of morality is universal human nature, this disappears because everyone who meets the criteria for being human will satisfy the conditional and morality will apply to them. Here it is worth observing that Mengzi defined humanity in moral terms, not biological: being human means having the requisite moral capacities, not being *Homo sapiens*. Even Song-Ming Ruists, who often attributed attenuated moral capacities to animals because they still had the Pattern even if it was not fully expressed, still thought only human nature could fully realize the Pattern and thus only humans were fully moral beings.[57] Modern New Ruists often assert that *every* biological human has the moral capacities. I think this is debatable at the least, but is ultimately not a pressing question. Even if we allow that some small percentage of the population are sociopaths who lack the capacity for morality, this is no obstacle to attributing moral responsibility to everyone else.

How common sociopaths are is itself an empirical question, but I do not think it is very important to have a definitive answer to it in order to recognize that moral responsibility applies to the overwhelming majority of people. We can admit right off that not every biological *Homo sapiens* is a moral agent or will become one; people with severe mental disabilities, for example, may be exceptions. The more difficult question is whether there are people who can function at a level that permits them to be independent and engaged in social life, exercising most of the rights and capacities of being a person, and yet lack the moral responses that Ruists believe define humanity. I suspect the answer is "yes." Yet they are clearly outliers and do not make it impossible to define a morality that applies to *almost* every human being. Notice that when he is faced with the question of whether someone is capable of being morally responsive, Mengzi's answer is not to defend theoretically the claim that every single human being is. It is to find an example where that person *was* morally responsive in something like the correct way, showing that *that* person has the requisite capacities.[58] The assumption seems to be that sociopathy is rare. If Ruists (and modern psychologists) are wrong about its rarity, it would cause problems for their moral theory, but the possibility of sociopathy does not make it incoherent.

To sum up, basing morality on human nature means Li can have the level of universality he requires from morality without trying to make it a priori, as in fact he believes it is not (under the conventional definition of *a priori* in English). It does mean sacrificing the unconditional nature of morality, but not much is lost by doing so. It was never entirely unconditional to begin with, and the conditions are so easy to satisfy that the demands of morality will still apply to almost every functioning human being. It will not turn into complete relativism. Li said that in Mengzi, morality is both a priori and based on the psychological feelings of human nature. Since there is a contradiction here, Li turns to Xunzi instead, but this created other problems. By giving up the a priori aspect in Mengzi, he can stay true to his interpretation of Ruist tradition, basing morality on psychological feelings particular to humanity, and still have what he wants in a moral theory, which is pluralism without falling into relativism. To do so, he simply has to give up on the Kantian conception of morality, in which universality must be a priori.

## Conclusion

Both Li Zehou and Mou Zongsan faced a difficult task: interpreting Ruist ethics in a way to preserve its essential insights while influenced by a Kantian definition of morality that required a priori moral principles in order to command necessarily and universally. There is debate about how Kantian Mou was and it is fair to say Kant was primarily a foil for him, a comparison that enabled him to bring out what was distinctive about Ruism and Chinese philosophy generally. Though he accepts a lot of Kant, the disagreements are also plain, and ultimately he wanted to show where Ruism surpassed Kant. The Prussian philosopher plays a similar role for Li. Li and Mou both disagree with aspects of Kant's thought, but one point I want to bring out here is how both were deeply influenced by his approach to morality, even when there is no question that Mou accepted more of it than Li did. The categorical nature of morality made a strong impression on the overseas New Ruists, and we see from Li that it influenced mainland Ruist philosophers as well. The *how* of Kant's introduction into Chinese thought is well known.[59] Why Kant made such an impact is a more difficult question, and this is not the place to explore it.

What I have tried to show here is that accepting Kant's definition of morality causes trouble for both Li and Mou. Ruist philosophers, whether Mengzi or Xunzi or Song-Ming thinkers like Zhu Xi or Wang Yangming,[60] do not derive purely formal moral principles from reason alone. Feelings play a strong role in justifying morality for them. This is what Li and Mou have to explain. I will not go further into whether Mou's solution is successful here, but I have argued that Li cannot have it both ways: if morality is based on ordinary psychological feelings (as Ruist morality is for him), it cannot be a priori in the common understanding of that term. If it is a priori, it cannot be based on psychological feelings. He has to choose. I have further suggested that he can preserve the role of feelings without losing what he wants from morality, which is to apply universally. He simply has to recognize that Kant was wrong: morality can be (sufficiently) universal without being a priori.

Two twentieth-century European philosophers might have proved useful to Li, allowing him to see that he did not have to accept Kant's definition of morality: Philippa Foot and Ludwig Wittgenstein. Foot takes aim at the supposed categorical nature of morality in her famous article "Morality as a System of Hypothetical Imperatives" (1972). She began to cleave apart the identity of hypothetical imperatives and self-interest, showing that there can be hypothetical imperatives that have nothing to do with self-interest. Then one can be committed to the goal of a particular hypothetical (say, the well-being of others) for moral reasons quite apart from one's own good (though these could overlap as well).

Li mentions Wittgenstein several times, but as far as I know does not reference his lecture on ethics, where Wittgenstein puzzled over the supposed categorical nature of morality. As he notes, if someone plays tennis badly, but says they do not want to play any better, then that is the end of the matter. Once the goal (playing tennis well) is rejected, it makes no sense to say that they should improve. But morality is different. If someone is behaving like a beast, but says they do not want to behave any better, that is not the end of the matter. They are not thus freed from any obligation.⁶¹ They cannot simply decide to reject the goal of behaving decently. But Wittgenstein cannot make any sense of this. "The *absolute good*, if it is a describable state of affairs would be one which everybody, independent of his tastes and inclinations, would, *necessarily*, bring about or feel guilty for not bringing about. And I want to say that such a state of affairs is a chimera. No state of affairs has in itself, what I would like to call, the coercive power of an absolute judge."⁶² He concludes that whatever we are doing with moral language, it is not describing some such state of affairs. Which is another way of saying that a categorical imperative is incoherent.

What I have suggested here is that when we think of morality in an alternative, less Kantian way, the problems Li faces diminish if not disappear. Morality does not have to be a priori. This would not show that Ruists' ethical theory is correct; the question here is definitional. If one accepts the Kantian definition of morality, then Ruism is not a true moral philosophy (as Hegel thought), at least not without considerable interpretive gymnastics. With a different definition of morality, Ruism is a moral theory and might be a good one. My argument boils down to saying that Ruists—Li and Mou included—need not accept Kant's conceptions of morality. It does not have to a priori or only based on reason, *if* there are hypothetical imperatives that are not self-interested (as Foot argued) and *if* (as I have argued) there are some hypothetical imperatives that one must accept in order to be fully human, or better, that every person (in the philosophical sense) does accept.

Then the answer to that hypothetical interlocutor who says "Yes, I'm behaving badly but I do not want to behave any better" is "You *do* want to behave better, and you show it through your actions and your feelings." And then we could do what Mengzi did, showing instances in which he did exhibit compassion (or honesty or fairness, and so on). Or what Wang Yangming did, pointing out that people have feelings of sympathy for living and non-living things that have been damaged or destroyed.⁶³ This effort might not always be successful. Perhaps in a few cases we find someone who has *no* history of moral actions at all (at best, actions motivated by self-interest that happened to conform with morality), and is able to persuade us that they feel no shame, no guilt, no compassion, no sense of fairness, or any other moral feeling. What then? "This person is simply lost. What difference is there between a person like this and an animal? What point is there in rebuking an animal?"[64] Since there have been accounts of human actions, there have been accounts of people behaving like beasts. Plato and Aristotle could not make that go away, and neither could Kant or Mill. It should not be a strike against Ruists that their moral theory cannot wholly preclude it either.

## Notes

1. I use "Ruist" and "Ruism" for greater fidelity to the Chinese designations for this philosophy, which are not derived from "Kongzi" (Confucius).

2. Mou Zongsan 牟宗三, *Xinti yu xingti 1 ce* 心體與性體 1 冊 (*Heart-Mind and Human Nature as Reality Book 1*), vol. 1, *Mou Zongsan quanji* 牟宗三先生全集 (*Collected Works of Mou Zongsan*) 5 (Taipei: Linking Books, 2003), 1:148. Translations are my own, except when another published translation is cited.

3. Mou, *Heart-Mind and Human Nature*, 1:11.

4. Mou, *Heart-Mind and Human Nature*, 1:10.

5. Mou, *Heart-Mind and Human Nature*, 1:136.

6. Mou Zongsan 牟宗三, *Zhi de zhijue yu Zhongguo zhexue* 智的直覺與中國哲學 (*Intellectual Intuition and Chinese Philosophy*), *Mou Zongsan quanji* 牟宗三先生全集 (*Collected Works of Mou Zongsan*) 20 (Taipei: Linking Books, 2003), 247.

7. Mou, *Heart-Mind and Human Nature*, 1:171.

8. Mou Zongsan 牟宗三, *Xianxiang yu wuzishen* 現象與物自身 (*Appearances and Things-in-Themselves*), *Mou Zongsan quanji* 牟宗三全集 (*Collected Works of Mou Zongsan*) 21 (Taipei: Linking Books, 2003), 105.

9. Mou, *Intellectual Intuition and Chinese Philosophy*, 245–46.

10. Liu Shu-hsien 劉述先, "'Li yi fen shu' de xiandai jieshi" 「理一分殊」的現代解釋 (The Contemporary Explanation of "Pattern Is One, Its Manifestations Are Many"), in *Lixiang yu xianshi de jiujie* 理想與現實的糾結 (*The Tension between Ideals and Reality*) (Taipei: Student Books, 1993), 157–88.

11. Li Zehou 李澤厚, *Zhongguo sixiangshi lun* 中國思想史論 (*History of Chinese Thought*), vol. 1 (Hefei, China: Anhui wenyi chubanshe, 1999), 1:11.

12. Li Zehou, "A Response to Michael Sandel and Other Matters," trans. Paul J. D'Ambrosio, and Robert A. Carleo III, *Philosophy East and West* 66, no. 4 (2016): 1079.

13. Li, *History of Chinese Thought*, 1:300–1.

14. Robert A. Carleo III, "Is Free Will Confucian? Li Zehou's Confucian Revision of the Kantian Will," *Philosophy East and West* 70, no. 1 (2020): 63–83.

15. Mengzi, *Mengzi*, trans. Bryan W. Van Norden (Indianapolis: Hackett, 2008), 2A6.

16. Li, *History of Chinese Thought*, 1:265.
17. Li, *History of Chinese Thought*, 1:258.
18. Li Zehou, *The Origins of Chinese Thought: From Shamanism to Ritual Regulations and Humaneness*, trans. Robert A. Carleo III (Leiden: Brill, 2018), 265.
19. Li, *History of Chinese Thought*, 1:256–57.
20. Li, *History of Chinese Thought*, 1:266.
21. Mou, *Appearances and Things-in-Themselves*, 80, 84.
22. Andrew Lambert, "Li Zehou: Synthesizing Kongzi, Kant, and Marx," in *Dao Companion to Contemporary Confucian Philosophy*, ed. David Elstein (Cham, Switzerland: Springer, 2021), 291–92.
23. For more on emotion in Li's thought, see Jia Jinhua, "Li Zehou's Reconception of Confucian Ethics as Emotion," in *Li Zehou and Confucian Philosophy*, ed. Roger T. Ames, and Jinhua Jia (Honolulu: University of Hawai'i Press, 2018), 155–86.
24. Li, *History of Chinese Thought*, 1:47.
25. *Mengzi*, 2A6.
26. Mou, *Appearances and Things-in-Themselves*, 105.
27. Lee Ming-huei, "Mou Zongsan: Between Confucianism and Kantianism," in *Dao Companion to Contemporary Confucian Philosophy*, ed. David Elstein (Cham, Switzerland: Springer, 2021), 259–60.
28. Li, *History of Chinese Thought*, 1:265.
29. Li, *History of Chinese Thought*, 1:50.
30. Li, *History of Chinese Thought*, 1:50.
31. Li, *History of Chinese Thought*, 1:237–38.
32. Li, *The Origins of Chinese Thought*, 239.
33. Li, *History of Chinese Thought*, 1:269. Li's position here is interestingly similar to Xu Fuguan's, but Li rarely mentions Xu in his historical work and seemed unaware of this convergence.
34. Lee Ming-huei, "The Debate on Ren between Zhu Xi and Huxiang Scholars," in *Confucianism: Its Roots and Global Significance*, ed. David Jones (Honolulu: University of Hawai'i Press, 2017), 41–53; Lee Ming-huei, "Confucianism, Kant, and Virtue Ethics," in *Confucianism: Its Roots and Global Significance*, ed. David Jones (Honolulu: University of Hawai'i Press, 2017) 92–101.
35. Mou Zongsan, *Appearances and Things-in-Themselves*, 105.
36. *Mengzi*, 6A14, 6A15.
37. Mou Zongsan 牟宗三, *Yuanshan lun* 圓善論 (*On the Perfect Good*), *Mou Zongsan quanji* 牟宗三全集 (*Collected Works of Mou Zongsan*) 22 (Taipei: Linking Books, 2003), 44–50.
38. Li, "A Response to Michael Sandel," 1094.
39. Paul J. D'Ambrosio, Robert A. Carleo III, and Andrew Lambert, "On Li Zehou's Philosophy: An Introduction by Three Translators," *Philosophy East and West* 66, no. 4 (2016): 1060.

40. Li, "A Response to Michael Sandel," 1112.
41. Li, *History of Chinese Thought*, 1:50.
42. Li, "A Response to Michael Sandel," 1109, 1120, 1135.
43. Li, "A Response to Michael Sandel," 1107.
44. Li, *The Origins of Chinese Thought*, 230–31.
45. Li, *History of Chinese Thought*, 1:122.
46. Jana S. Rošker, *Interpreting Chinese Philosophy: A New Methodology* (London: Bloomsbury Academic, 2021), 128–29.
47. There is some disagreement about translation. According to Rošker, in China *xianyan* 先验 is usually used to translate "transcendental" rather than "a priori," and so she renders this phrase as "transformation of empirical into the transcendental" (Jana S. Rošker, *Becoming Human: Li Zehou's Ethics* (Leiden: Brill, 2020), 191–92).

When I consulted with three translators of Li's works into English—Paul D'Ambrosio, Robert Carleo III, and Andrew Lambert—all told me that Li himself preferred "a priori" to translate his use of *xianyan*. However, he was not always precise about questions of terminology throughout his works. In any case, though "a priori" and "transcendental" are not the same, the differences do not affect the point here much.

48. Li Zehou, "Subjectivity and 'Subjectality': A Response," *Philosophy East and West* 49, no. 2 (1999): 175–76.
49. Rošker, *Becoming Human*, 12.
50. Li Zehou 李澤厚 and Liu Xuyuan 劉緒源, "Li Zehou tan xueshu sixiang san jieduan" 李泽厚谈学术思想三阶段 (Li Zehou Discusses the Three Phases of His Academic Thought), *Shanghai Literature* no. 1 (2011): 77.
51. Rošker, *Becoming Human*, 211.
52. Li, "A Response to Michael Sandel and Other Matters," 1112.
53. Li, *History of Chinese Thought*, 1:240.
54. Li, *History of Chinese Thought*, 1:49–50.
55. Whether they would apply it in the way that Kant did is another question. In particular, I suspect that they would analyze Kant's example concerning beneficence in the *Groundwork* very differently. However, this is not our concern here.
56. Li, "A Response to Michael Sandel and Other Matters," 1076. Note that this is by no means limited to biological existence. As the aesthetic is fundamental to humanity for Li, it would also have to include beauty.
57. An example is Zhu Xi in *Categorized Conversations of Master Zhu*, "Nature and Pattern 1," 41, ctext.org/zhuzi-yulei/4#n586443.
58. *Mengzi*, 1A7.
59. K'o-wu Huang, "Liang Qichao and Immanuel Kant," in *The Role of Japan in Liang Qichao's Introduction of Modern Western Civilization to China*, ed.

Joshua A. Fogel (Berkeley: Institute of East Asian Studies, University of California Berkeley, Center for Chinese Studies, 2004), 125–55; Martin Müller, "Aspects of the Chinese Reception of Kant," *Journal of Chinese Philosophy* 33, no. 1 (2006): 141–57.

60. Li and Mou agree that Xunzi was not a candidate for autonomous morality to begin with. They disagree about Zhu Xi, Mou considering him heteronomous while Li argues his ethics is autonomous.

61. Ludwig Wittgenstein at al., *Lecture on Ethics* (Chichester, UK: Wiley Blackwell, 2014), 44.

62. Wittgenstein at al., 46.

63. Wang Yangming, "Questions on the Great Learning," in *Readings in Later Chinese Philosophy: Han to the 20th Century*, ed. Justin Tiwald, and Bryan W. Van Norden, trans. Philip J. Ivanhoe (Indianapolis: Hackett, 2014), 242.

64. *Mengzi*, 4B28.

## Bibliography

Carleo, Robert A. III. "Is Free Will Confucian? Li Zehou's Confucian Revision of the Kantian Will." *Philosophy East and West* 70, no. 1 (2020): 63–83.

D'Ambrosio, Paul J., Robert A. Carleo III, and Andrew Lambert. "On Li Zehou's Philosophy: An Introduction by Three Translators." *Philosophy East and West* 66, no. 4 (2016): 1057–67.

Foot, Philippa. "Morality as a System of Hypothetical Imperatives." *Philosophical Review* 81, no. 3 (1972): 305–16.

Huang, K'o-wu. "Liang Qichao and Immanuel Kant." In *The Role of Japan in Liang Qichao's Introduction of Modern Western Civilization to China*, edited by Joshua A. Fogel, 125–55. Berkeley: Institute of East Asian Studies, University of California Berkeley, Center for Chinese Studies, 2004.

Jia, Jinhua. "Li Zehou's Reconception of Confucian Ethics as Emotion." In *Li Zehou and Confucian Philosophy*, edited by Roger T. Ames and Jinhua Jia, 155–86. Honolulu: University of Hawai'i Press, 2018.

Lambert, Andrew. "Li Zehou: Synthesizing Kongzi, Kant, and Marx." In *Dao Companion to Contemporary Confucian Philosophy*, edited by David Elstein, 277–98. Cham, Switzerland: Springer, 2021.

Lee, Ming-huei. "Confucianism, Kant, and Virtue Ethics." In *Confucianism: Its Roots and Global Significance*, edited by David Jones, 92–101. Honolulu: University of Hawai'i Press, 2017.

Lee, Ming-huei. "The Debate on Ren between Zhu Xi and Huxiang Scholars." In *Confucianism: Its Roots and Global Significance*, edited by David Jones, 41–53. Honolulu: University of Hawai'i Press, 2017.

Lee, Ming-huei. "Mou Zongsan: Between Confucianism and Kantianism." In *Dao Companion to Contemporary Confucian Philosophy*, edited by David Elstein, 255–75. Cham, Switzerland: Springer, 2021.

Li Zehou. *The Origins of Chinese Thought: From Shamanism to Ritual Regulations and Humaneness*. Translated by Robert A. Carleo III. Leiden: Brill, 2018.

Li Zehou. "A Response to Michael Sandel and Other Matters." Translated by Paul J. D'Ambrosio and Robert A. Carleo III. *Philosophy East and West* 66, no. 4 (2016): 1068–1147.

Li Zehou. "Subjectivity and 'Subjectality': A Response." *Philosophy East and West* 49, no. 2 (1999): 174–83.

Li Zehou 李澤厚. *Zhongguo sixiang shilun* 中國思想史論 (*A History of Chinese Thought*), vol. 1. Hefei: Anhui wenyi chuban she, 1999.

Li Zehou 李澤厚 and Liu Xuyuan 劉緒源. "Li Zehou tan xueshu sixiang san jieduan" 李澤厚談學術思想三階段 (Li Zehou Discusses the Three Phases of His Academic Thought). *Shanghai wenxue* 1 (2011): 72–77.

Liu Shu-hsien 劉述先. "'Li yi fen shu' de xiandai jieshi" 「理一分殊」的現代解釋 (The Contemporary Explanation of "Pattern Is One, Its Manifestations Are Many"). In *Lixiang yu xianshi de jiujie* 理想與現實的糾結 (*The Tension between Ideals and Reality*), 157–88. Taipei: Student Books, 1993.

Mengzi. *Mengzi*. Translated by Bryan W. Van Norden. Indianapolis: Hackett, 2008.

Mou Zongsan 牟宗三. *Xianxiang yu wuzishen* 現象與物自身 (*Appearances and Things-in-Themselves*). *Mou Zongsan quanji* 牟宗三全集 (*Collected Works of Mou Zongsan*) 21. Taipei: Linking Books, 2003.

Mou Zongsan 牟宗三. *Xinti yu xingti 1 ce* 心體與性體 1 冊 (*Heart-Mind and Human Nature as Reality Book 1*), vol. 1. *Mou Zongsan quanji* 牟宗三先生全集 (*Collected Works of Mou Zongsan*) 5. Taipei: Linking Books, 2003.

Mou Zongsan 牟宗三. *Yuanshan lun* 圓善論 (*On the Perfect Good*). *Mou Zongsan quanji* 牟宗三全集 (*Collected Works of Mou Zongsan*) 22. Taipei: Linking Books, 2003.

Mou Zongsan 牟宗三. *Zhi de zhijue yu Zhongguo zhexue* 智的直覺與中國哲學 (*Intellectual Intuition and Chinese Philosophy*). *Mou Zongsan quanji* 牟宗三先生全集 (*Collected Works of Mou Zongsan*) 20. Taipei: Linking Books, 2003.

Müller, Martin. "Aspects of the Chinese Reception of Kant." *Journal of Chinese Philosophy* 33, no. 1 (2006): 141–57.

Rošker, Jana S. *Becoming Human: Li Zehou's Ethics*. Leiden: Brill, 2020.

Rošker, Jana S. *Interpreting Chinese Philosophy: A New Methodology*. London: Bloomsbury Academic, 2021.

Wang Yangming. "Questions on the Great Learning." In *Readings in Later Chinese Philosophy: Han to the 20th Century*, edited by Justin Tiwald and Bryan W. Van Norden, translated by Philip J. Ivanhoe, 238–50. Indianapolis: Hackett, 2014.

Wittgenstein, Ludwig, Edoardo Zamuner, Ermelinda Valentina Di Lascio, and D. K. Levy. *Lecture on Ethics*. Chichester, UK: Wiley Blackwell, 2014.
*Zhuzi yu lei* 朱子語類 (*Categorized Conversations of Master Zhu*). Edited by Li Jingde 黎靖德. *Chinese Text Project*. ctext.org/zhuzi-yulei.

# 7

# Justice, Harmony, and the Good Life of *Guanxi*

## Li Zehou's Response to Liberalism

Andrew Lambert

Li Zehou's claim that "harmony is higher than justice" (和諧高於正義)[1] has aroused much discussion. This paper examines this claim and how Li's notion of harmony might be further developed by exploring two prominent themes in Li's work: *guanxi* 關係 or relational attachment, which Li elevates to the level of guiding doctrine or "ism" (*guanxi-zhuyi* 關係主義),[2] and aesthetic value and experience.

## Introduction: Understanding "Harmony Is Higher than Justice"

Li Zehou's claim that "harmony is higher than justice" appears in various places, but most prominently in his response to the work of Michael Sandel.[3] What does Li mean by "justice," by "harmony," and by the claim that the latter is "higher" than the former?

*Justice* is a term with multiple meanings, but a clarifying comment by Li is helpful: "Justice is primarily a rational principle (*li* 理), whereas harmony involves the integration of emotion and reason (*qing-li* 情理)."[4]

The relevant sense of "justice" here is not a singular virtue or ideal of justice, but rather the more general normative appeal to abstract principles of conduct—moral principles—that can be used to assess conduct and order a group or community. Thus, included under the broad rubric of "justice" are principles such as the categorical imperative, the greatest happiness of the greatest possible number, as well as John Rawls's account of justice as fairness.[5] Li's inquiry also concerns the origin of, and rationale for, the appeal to abstract normative principles ("Justice") to govern the "collective life of humankind."[6] This latter concern leads Li to consider how justice emerges within historical and cultural contexts, rather than existing as a universal feature of human communities and moral psychology that transcends time and place. This allows Li to make certain cross-cultural comparisons and develop a critique of justice as the foundational (moral) measure of conduct.

Li's critique of the justice that he associates with Sandel and with Western liberalism and individualism more generally might be summarized as twofold. First, these formal principles are too abstract to be relevant to the practical dilemmas that arise within everyday social life.[7] Second, general normative principles emerge "from the ground up," not from abstract reason; general principles emerge form concrete social practices. They are extensions of the practical norms that emerge within historically and culturally specific practices or ways of life. In Li's words, "rational principles or reason itself come from the living existence of humankind and are not a priori."[8] In the case of China, rituals, emerging first from shamanistic practices,[9] were instrumental in the generation of moral norms. Rituals were gradually institutionalized and the norms or principles integral to them were codified and became more general norms of conduct. This process had a psychological dimension. They internalized principles or standards implicit in rituals, which become part of their moral psychology, guiding evaluative judgments. Furthermore, according to Li, the rituals and their norms were partly a response to everyday emotions and feelings, which were incorporated into, and shaped, the rituals. As a result, both external historically established practices and shared affective reactions to circumstance informed the formation of guiding norms.

If general moral norms are, in fact, the product of particular histories and contexts, then the moral weight attributed to abstract general normative principles is questionable. Li's disquiet about "justice" is that "the direct application of abstract principles to specific situations is methodologically inappropriate."[10] Li is thus skeptical about attempts to solve social or moral problems without reference to the particulars of a situation. For example, he is skeptical about general pronouncements about the moral permissibility of raising prices in times of natural disaster.[11] In addition, implicit in Li's critique of justice are a series of challenges to liberalism and individualism more generally, to be discussed below. These include questions about the self, specifically as unencumbered and atomistic, its relation to market economics, and individualistic conceptions of the good life.

The "harmony" in Li's claim can be characterized in two ways. First, it refers to emotion and reason combining successfully to produce practical judgments; decisions aimed at justice are, problematically, solely matters of reason. This balance of the two practical forces is an ideal manifestation of the "emotio-rational structure" (*qingli jiegou* 情理結構): "The emotio-rational structure refers to the concrete intersection of emotion with reason and emphasizes that emotions and reason exist in dynamic, constantly changing relationships of different ratios and proportions with one another."[12] It is important to note that although the term *qing* 情 is frequently translated as "emotion," it has a wider range of meanings; these include "feeling" and "affect," and even experiences that might be classified as aesthetic.[13] *Qing* also refers to circumstance or context. The variegated nature of *qing*, within its role in guiding judgment, is important to later arguments.

A second dimension of Li's account of harmony is that the regulative emotions he emphasizes are bound up with everyday human relationships. This includes forms of relationship common in classical and later Confucian literature, including the five cardinal relationships (*wulun* 五倫).[14] Accordingly, Li speaks of the "emotional harmony within the family seen in the *Analects*."[15] To capture this aspect of Confucian life, Li emphasizes the Chinese social phenomenon of *guanxi*, variously translated as "social bonds," "relational attachments," or "particularistic ties." *Guanxi* are "warm" relationships that involve some form of familiarity, such as kinship and friendship.[16] Li's use of the neologism "Guanxi-ism" (*guanxi zhuyi* 關係主義) or "relationalism" "stresses the particular nature of interpersonal relationships as being fundamental to ethics."[17] Li directly contrasts the moral and conceptual framework of *guanxi* relationality with doctrines of individualism: "Here there is almost no conception of free, equal, independent individuals. There are only interactive *guanxi* or relations."[18]

*Guanxi* are crucial to the creation of harmony. According to Li, since moral norms and emotions were shaped by particular histories and social pratices, *guanxi*, too, must be subject to such conditioning. Specifically, people's affective or emotional responses coalesced or "solidified" around ordered and graded human relationships (*renlun* 人倫) (father and son, husband and wife, ruler and ruled, etc.), which acquired both normative weight (roles came with social obligations) and emotional force (natural emotions, such as father's affection for son or son's reverence for father, were a source of motivation). As a result, relationships became both sources of guiding principles and social obligation, and central features of people's psychology: "This socialized person is not rationally but also emotionally cultivated."[19] This beneficial integration is the foundation of harmony: "The permeation of emotion into these relationships of responsibility facilitates social harmony."[20] Li summarizes the contrast between justice and harmony as "a major difference in terms of ethics between the traditional Chinese ideal of harmony, in which ritual regulations are generated from emotionality, and the Western tradition's ideal of justice, in which absolute value is given to reason."[21]

Why is harmony to be considered "higher" than justice? The simplest answer is that practical judgments that result from emotions working in tandem with rationality are "higher" or more efficacious than purely rational judgments. Emotional responses partly determine which norms or principles become standards, and also regulate the application of these principles. The judgments that derive from emotional-rational harmony thus better secure the "continuous extension of human existence"[22]—the fundamental goal of human action. In addition, the emotional harmony found in social life constructed around ordered human relationships is key both to traditional Chinese notions of the good life and society and, Li implies, perhaps to any society;[23] this includes a "Western" society currently characterized by justice, in which is "justice is the first virtue of social institutions."[24] Finally, more generally, harmony is a regulative ideal relevant to many areas of human life, including harmony between people, mind and body, and humans and nature.[25]

## Assessing "Harmony Is Higher than Justice": Problems and Possibilities

Before evaluating the plausibility of this claim, we should consider what lies behind it: Why does Li seek to make this claim and what values does it express? As D'Ambrosio points out,[26] while Li is nominally critiquing Sandel's work, there is less disagreement than Li suggests. Nor is Li dismissing the need for justice, since harmony in some sense regulates rather than undermines it. Taking into account the full range of Li's response, it is better understood as Li's attempt to assess the worth of liberal individualism and to find within the Chinese tradition meaningful correctives to it. This explains why, for example, Li's claims about harmony and justice express a fundamental difference between Chinese culture and Western culture: "Chinese culture looks for harmony where the West strives for justice."[27] Implicit in this claim is the belief that different cultural traditions give rise to different conceptions of the good life and ethical conduct.

Implied in Li's appeal to harmony as an ethical ideal is a contrast between an ideal of equality, possessed by all humans, and an ethics that begins from complementary differences between people, particularly differences in social roles and relationships. Li writes, "The fundamental 'equality' of people is now stressed, as we see in Rawls. However, don't people still live within various relationships of inequality or at least non-equivalence of older and younger, senior and junior, upper and lower, right and left, near and far, close and distant?"[28] Li's account of harmony attempts to capture the everyday observation that human relationships are typically not understood via an appeal to an abstract notion of equality, which purportedly transcends the obvious differences that characterize many relationships. Grounding his general theory specifically in the Chinese tradition, and classical Confucian thought in particular, he notes, "They are composed of unequal relationships between superiors and inferiors, parents and children, husbands and wives, older and younger siblings, and friends (which include distinction between older and younger). Here there is almost no conception of independent, equal, free individuals."[29]

Differences in wealth, education, life experience, and many other dimensions could easily be added to this list. Each social relationship is understood to arise naturalistically, as a general feature of human life, and each particular relationship is characterized by distinctive emotional responses. Furthermore, the applicable emotion can vary within a dyadic bond, according to seniority and so on. So, fathers might be beneficent toward sons, while sons revere fathers.[30] These "biological emotions" then become felt "obligations" of various kinds, tailored to particular roles, which undergird social order: "Parents' affection, children's filiality, older brothers' care, younger brothers' respect, husbands' proper conduct, wives' obedience, elders' gratitude, juniors' obedience, rulers' humaneness, ministers' loyalty."[31] This internalization of biological or social relations, to create emotions that entail a sense of social or even moral obligation, is a further form of harmony: a harmony of complementary personal attitudes and obligations, with people "bound together by warm emotional ties."

This is an attempt to develop a conception of ethics that begins from human relatedness. As to what this relatedness consists in, and how it impacts upon and guides action, Li's answer draws on quite rigid notions of human relatedness and appeals to historically sedimented social norms to guide conduct thought and feeling within these relationships. In the next section, I attempt to develop a related but importantly different account of an ethics of relatedness that draws on other elements in Li's thought. This is because the account presented here faces various objections.

Li's work can be difficult to assess because it is often suggestive rather than explicit, consisting of a series of insights and bold claims, with arguments rarely fully articulated. He "offers space for readers to reflect,"[32] to reconsider their fundamental assumptions about ethics and the self, but rarely fully addresses objections. In addition, Li is usually writing for a Chinese audience. His generalizations about the West, and the difficulties such simplifications creates, are less important than Li's effectiveness in stimulating a rethink of traditional Confucian ideas and their place in modernity. Within the confines of this approach, Li's motives and goals in promoting harmony are clear. These include the conviction that universal foundational moral principles—the topic of much twentieth-century Anglophone moral theorizing—are too vague to guide practical judgments, which must respond to the confusing detail of everyday social life. Furthermore, Li's belief that both moral norms and patterns of emotional response are rooted in culture and history implies a rejection of arguments for ahistorical foundations to moral judgment.[33]

Li's promotion of harmony as an ideal also raises questions about popular conceptions of the self, specifically the kind of assumptions about the self relied upon by theorists of justice such as Rawls. Rawls assumes an egalitarian conception of a rational and self-interested subject, who is rationally compelled to engage in a form of social contract. But as several Western thinkers have pointed out these assumptions can be challenged. In particular, the developmental pathway of the self is overlooked, such as the role of the family in nurturing a self sensitive to rational considerations.[34] Li seeks a more realistic picture of the psychology of human action, one in which emotion is crucial to good practical judgment and naturalistic human bonds are integral to human flourishing.

There are, however, several problems with Li's claim that harmony is higher than justice. One concern is whether Li replaces one abstraction, to which he objects, with another abstract schema whose relation to practical decision-making is equally tenuous. Li objects to reliance on general moral principles, and offers an idealized notion of practical wisdom as "proper measure" (*du* 度), in which emotion and reason attain a dynamic balance. However, how such balance is achieved, or how a person or group can know when it has been achieved, remains unclear. Insisting that all moral judgments and governing principle be derived contextually does little to clarify this picture.

Another difficulty is possible inconsistency. In Li's work there is both the insistence that general moral norms should emerge from historically embedded social practices and an insistence that at least one general moral norm is universal. Li embraces Kant's categorial imperative, at least in some form;[35] yet his critique of Michael Sandel's approach to moral questions is partly based on the claim that "values, justice, politics, and education all must be concretely analyzed and evaluated within specific historical conditions."[36] Li has a partial explanation for this stance—notably that the categorical imperative is historical and empirical in origin, an early development of human cognition in response to social practice. Still, however, if one such general abstract normative principle is accepted, then it cannot be the case that abstract normative principles are not relevant to human conduct. This raises the question of whether there are other general moral principles that should be adopted.

The difficulty most relevant to the present paper, however, is the linking of harmony to the traditional social roles esteemed by the Confucian tradition. A society in which each knows their place in a larger order, and submits to the duties and demands of their station, might produce a harmony characterized by social order and lack of practical conflict. It is also plausible that patterns of emotional response structured by biological and social roles might help guide practical judgments toward resolutions of practical dilemmas, while also offering subjects some satisfaction in the fulfillment of their roles. However, the harmony thereby generated might be morally questionable. There are the familiar questions of whether hierarchical or patriarchal relationships are compatible with the aspiration to human freedom and respect for the individual, themes that also feature prominently in Li's thought.

In addition, Li also accepts the role of the market in modern economies, since free exchange increases the material well-being that Li considered important to Chinese modernity. But when the traditional notion of ordered human relationships, with its particular historical origins in Confucian thought, interacts with the productive and social forces created by modern democratic market economies, it is unclear whether the former can retain its effectiveness. New forms of human relatedness emerge, and might be characterized by new patterns of emotional and affective response. This is an instance where Li's attempts to both preserve traditional Confucian values and also advocate for greater freedom and individual expression raise puzzling questions. For example, how many of the practical or ethical dilemmas that arise in contemporary liberal democratic consumer society can be resolved via norms that are rooted in the five cardinal relationships of Confucian thought? Also, is the human subject conditioned by market forces and logic compatible with a subject oriented toward these relationships?

Defenses of this framework of ordered human relationships have been offered, such as a modified understanding of role.[37] This includes the argument that strong familial relations can nurture capacities or dispositions that can be extended to guide conduct in non-familial relations and situations. In what follows, I explore an alternative account of how relationships and the intersubjective emotions and feelings generated therein can generate and guide action. The account also suggests a conception of harmony, which can serve as an alternative to justice. This attempt is a response to Li's view of his own work: "Macro perspectives like mine do not directly resolve questions, but they attempt to illuminate philosophical issues for us."[38]

## Rethinking Relationality and Harmony

This alternative account builds on Li's account of harmony, while avoiding the criticisms noted. It retains Li's conviction that the Confucian tradition "combines psychology and ethics at its core,"[39] such that what counts as ethical partly depends on how human psychology is modeled. Li's view that the moral psychology of rationalist moral theory is impoverished, and that good practical judgment draws on affective experience, is increasingly common in Anglophone ethics.[40] While Li often naturalized biological emotions, connecting them to fixed patterns of feeling and normative response within relationships, his work hints at other models of psychology and practical deliberation grounded in emotion (*qing*). For Li, "psychology" is a variable, about which we gradually accumulate insight, often through scientific means. But Li's approach was to forge ahead, speculatively, in the belief that science would clarify his provisional accounts.[41] The reconstruction below honors that spirit of adventure.

In his critique of liberal individualism, Liang draws on two contrasting psychologies of action, which he attributes to Liang Shuming.[42] These are a psychology centered on desire and a psychology characterized by the motivating affections and emotions (*qing*) that arise in *guanxi*. Both desire and emotion are sources of practical motivation. While the distinction between desire and emotion is not clearcut and is only tentatively sketched by Li, we might summarize it as follows. Desire is an attraction toward certain objects or ends, material or non-material. For example, there are bodily desires (food and sex are classical Confucian examples), and desires triggered by the contact of the senses with the material world (seeing and then desiring chocolate).[43] An additional, more reflective and prudential, form of desire is central to liberal individualism's conception of the good life. Desire gives rise to personal goals. Such desire is at the heart of Mill's classic liberalism, in which individuals "grow and develop . . . according to the tendency of the inward forces which make it a living thing."[44] These forces can be understood as desires, and freedom to pursue them is fundamental. Under the influence of reason and prudence, motivating desires form a coherent set of future goals. Bernard Williams characterizes more sophisticated complexes of desires as "projects."[45] Such projects vary, from getting an education to learning chess or making money. Individuals orient their lives toward projects, to varying degrees, which also provide a primal motivation to proceed onward with life.[46] Furthermore, what sorts of desires or projects might appear is left open; their origins remain obscure, and imagination can generate innumerable desired ends.

Emotions or *qing* are distinct from desire. They are often characterized as a belief accompanied by a feeling, which can motivate action.[47] For Li, the achievement of the early Chinese tradition was to refocus emotions from religious superstition to realm that could yield reward: "human emotions . . . found expression and satisfaction in the practical psychology and ethics of social life."[48] Emotions arising within and directed toward personal relationships became central to ethical conduct. Crucially, emotion and desire provide two different sources of motivation, and emotions can sometimes overwhelm desire—such as self-sacrifice, against self-interest, out of feelings of loyalty.[49]

Li's distinction between desire and emotion reveals a problem with the understanding of the self and the good life within the liberal tradition, which follows from treating desire as the fundamental force of human conduct. One consequence is that emotions are a neglected topic with a minimal role in this account of the good life. More importantly, over-emphasizing the practical significance of desire can lead both to misunderstanding of the self and to an impoverished understanding of practical deliberation. Li writes, "Desires are directly linked to the sensory feelings (pleasure and pain) of the individual's body. Theoretically this means that they can be elevated to conceptions of absolute, transcendental 'selves' or atomic individuals that are independent of other people and other similar principles of pure reason. This is modern individualism. While desires often serve as the foundation of emotions, emotions can be better understood as the psychological reactions of interrelatedness with other people and things."[50] People identify with their desires and "projects," but this produces a sense of self whose connection to the surrounding social world is uncertain. Since desires are experienced privately, linked to the individual body and private conceptions of a worthwhile life, this self can appear as an independent or "transcendental" entity. This analysis also drives Li's critique of free market capitalism:[51] desires, incited by sensory experience, attach to various goods and lifestyles and are easily manipulated.

Emotions, in contrast, "cannot be purchased monetarily."[52] Emotions, structured around social relationships and social practices, keep the individual tethered to the local social world and to the relationships they engage in therein. Complex affective responses to concrete social practices and relationships make it difficult for individuals to conceive of themselves as atomic individuals whose connection to others is merely voluntary or a matter of consent. Awareness of relationally oriented emotions strengthens understanding of the self as relational.

The contrast between emotions and desires is ethically important. If ethics requires overcoming selfishness, commonly understood as selfish desires, then the emotions aroused when dealing with others provides motivations that counteract such desire.[53] Li identifies many such social emotions,[54] including shame. Aroused when faced by others in a community, shame is a powerful force that can regulate social life, and in place of legalistic procedural ideals of justice.[55]

Understood in this way, it is clear why Li insists that emotions (*qing*) are integral to practical judgment. Not only do they moderate the effects of rational principles, but relation-oriented emotions also keep the individual connected to the local social world in which they must live. Of course, the advocate of individualism might question whether the individual *should* be bound to others in the local social world. The task, then, is to show how, for those attracted by the classic liberal conception of the good life and concerned about social bondage and a possible lack of freedom, a relationally oriented life can generate worthwhile forms of the good life. Here, this means exploring how the affective experiences of a relationally oriented life (*guanxi*) can yield valuable forms of harmony.

A first step is to reconsider the term *qing* 情, hitherto translated as "emotion." As noted, *qing* encompasses not only emotion but also a broad range of affective states such as feelings and aesthetic experiences. The capaciousness of *qing* permits additional ways of understanding its role in practical judgment and the good life. I am interested in what might be called *aesthetic experience*, although no sharp distinction will be made between this and emotion. For example, pleasure and delight can be aesthetic experiences but can also be classified as emotions. Still, there are ways in which valuable aesthetic experiences can shape practical deliberation in distinctive ways.

This approach is one way to bring Li's interest in aesthetics into dialogue with his ethics and deepen his defense of harmony; moreover, the cultivation of an aesthetic sensibility has long been regarded as integral to Confucian notions of good character. This examination of the role of aesthetic experience in practical deliberation will, following Li's analysis of emotion, focus on *guanxi* and relationality (*guanxi zhuyi*). These remain the locus or context for the emergence of harmony. However, some differences from Li's response to Sandel should be noted.

Most importantly, the affective experiences to be discussed are not defined by or confined to the emotions traditionally associated with Confucian bonds and social roles. Similarly, they are not primarily understood as being structured around received social norms or as particular emotional responses to specific categories of relationships (father and son, etc.).[56] These contribute instrumentally to the conception of harmony to be presented, since shared social history often is a valuable resource to draw on in social interactions. However, they are not as crucial to this alternative conception as they appear to be in Li's account of *guanxi*'s value. As a result, it is possible to retain the central importance of concrete relationships of familiarity and value of harmony, as identified by Li and in a manner broadly consistent with classical Confucian thought, but without assuming those relationships conform to a tradition and are fixed in nature. This allows us to revisit Li's claim that harmony is higher than justice, using a revised notion of harmony that is rooted in aesthetic experience within relationships.

## An Alternative Harmony: Aesthetic Goods Generated through Relationality

What is this alternative conception of harmony? In some respects, it is expressed by the familiar Confucian metaphors of harmony, the blending of soup and the creation of musical harmony. It is the skillful bringing together of different elements to produce an overall effect. Note how implicit in such harmony is a particular practical judgment: that the relevant parts have been brought together optimally or at least sufficiently well, confirmed by a feeling or experience, which might be characterized as an aesthetic experience, of fittingness or aptness. Indeed, this experience of fittingness or aptness is one feature of this alternative account of harmony.

However, consistent with Li's approach, this harmony is located within a defined context: everyday social life and the human relationships that constitute much of that daily life (*guanxi*). Accordingly, harmony is thus harmonious interaction. This is the task of bringing together relevant constitutive elements of a social interaction in order to create valued experiences or feelings; in fact, the experiences or feelings generated are the goal of the interaction (in contrast to realizing desires and projects). This account of harmony generated through social interaction in everyday day life addresses Li's question of "how to reestablish an emotional harmony of diverse relationality"[57] while retaining his convictions that *guanxi*, ritual, and *qing* (emotion/aesthetic experience) are fundamentally constitutive (*benti* 本体) of human life.

This ideal of human conduct, the generation of affective experiences in social interaction, is common in the Chinese tradition. The paradigm of people participating in shared social events and successfully integrating various elements to produce felt or emotional effects is ritual. Li's work on ritual and shamanistic practice places ritual at the heart of communal life: "totemic shamanistic song and dance centered on sacrificial ritual, consolidated, organized, and reinforced primitive communities, arousing and unifying human consciousness, intention, and will."[58] Ritual provided an early conception of normativity, imparting in participants norms that govern communal life. But ritual also reinforced communal and social bonds by providing an occasion that aroused a collective focus and interest, which we might describe as moving or memorable social events and spectacles. Li gives an example from the *Zhouli* or *Rites of Zhou*:

> The sons of the state are instructed in music and dance; they are taught to dance the Yunmen, Daquan, Daxian, Daqing, Daxia, Dahu, and Dawu. With the six pitch standards, six bronze pitchpipes, five pitches, eight kinds of instruments, and six kinds of dance, a great concert is held to summon the spirits; to bring harmony to the states, concord to the people, calm to the sojourner; to appease distant tribes, and to set into motion the things of the phenomenal world.[59]

Michael Nylan characterizes early China as a culture of "edifying public or semi-public spectacle."[60] Rulers organized elaborate public rituals with broad participation. Such rituals or events yield various forms of aesthetic goods, such as excitement, awe, and feelings of loyalty, which bound the people to the ruler and created a sense of solidarity within the group. Similarly, shamanistic practices generated collective ecstatic experiences, as part of a communion with spirits and the departed.[61] Such events reinforced people's roles and relationships to each other, with each playing their role in the creation of a consummatory event. Presumably, even those of low social status, who might "participate" in ceremonies only as attendees, still contributed to the overall effect by, for example, swelling the size of the gathering and imbuing it with a certain atmosphere or sense of occasion. Aesthetic goods were created by both vivid spectacle and more abstract social meaning and symbolism. The latter, like literature, yields aesthetic goods by stimulating imagination, while the former offers sensory pleasures.

Work in other disciplines confirms the importance of shared social experience to communal bonds. In anthropology, there has long been an interest in communally experienced higher states or making certain experiences special, on account of their effects on relations within the group. This is seen in the distinction between sacred and profane,[62] and is discussed in cross-cultural contexts by Ellen Dissanayake[63] and Edith

Turner.[64] In his study of ritual, anthropologist Victor Turner developed the notion of *communitas* to describe events that prompted collective unity and purpose.[65] Edith Turner further developed this notion, stating that "Communitas is a group's pleasure in sharing common experiences with one's fellows" and "communitas may be found when people engage in a collective task with full attention—often a matter of ordinary work."[66] These various studies differ in how they develop the idea of a collective social event that grounds communal life, and it is not possible to discuss their differences here. But this aspect of human social life has received little attention from philosophers, and even less regarding how it can form the basis for an ethics. Such studies reinforce Li's conviction that communal order and ethical life begins not with legislative wills or social contracts but in ritual interaction.

Engaging in a ritual does not necessarily require a personal bond with other participants. That said, it does often create bonds of familiarity and good will. More importantly, one social function of ritual, especially larger and more elaborate ritual, does influence more personal social interactions: namely, given their power and effect, organized social events looms large in people's consciousnesses, providing satisfying memories or rousing anticipation for future participation. Their appeal means that these social events anchor commitments to communal life. In order to secure a repeat of cherished experiences, people are more willing to accommodate others—fellow participants—in daily life, adjusting other ends and ambitions so as to facilitate repetition of the rituals. This model of human interaction—participatory social interaction that generates valued emotions and aesthetic experiences that in turn guide relations within the group—can serve as a paradigm for other forms of human interaction. We now turn to the question of how such affective and aesthetic goods can be realized in more personal and less scripted interactions: everyday life conducted around *guanxi*.

Li's discussion of *guanxi* makes clear the importance of human relationships to the good life. He writes, "Life's significance emerges only in the context of interpersonal relationships within real world society,"[67] and that what mattered most in Confucius's intellectual milieu were "considerations of time-bound interpersonal relationships and human emotion."[68] Similarly, reflecting on *Analects* 11.11 ("Not knowing about life how can we know about death; not knowing how to deal with human affairs how can we know about the affairs of ghosts?") and *Analects* 18.6 ("If I don't associate with the followers of men then with whom am I to associate?"), he writes, "The significance of life and death were entirely contained within human relations and the relationships among 'you,' 'I,' and 'others.' These relationships are fundamental; they are reality; they are truth."[69]

Li sometimes talks of the value realized within such everyday human relations and interactions in terms of aesthetic value. He writes of "the Chinese philosophy and aesthetics he [Confucius] and his disciples inaugurated, in which aesthetic appreciation takes the place of religion and in which transcendence is placed squarely within the realm of human relations and the perceptual world."[70] He also notes, "Ultimately, then, the philosophy of existence is not found in speculation, faith, or divine grace, but in the fluid and changing emotions themselves, humanized, as it were, and carrying with them the accumulated achievements. These emotions themselves become a fundamental power that stimulates interpersonal becoming."[71]

In elevating the importance of the aesthetic in human life, Li belongs to that line of Chinese intellectuals who grant aesthetic experience the importance traditionally attributed to religion in the Abrahamic tradition.[72] For Li, it is in the experience of certain "humanized" emotions that transcendence is experienced, understood as an exalted form of experience. This suggests one of the highest practical or ethical tasks then is to generate such affective or emotional experiences, and to do so "within the realm of human relations." But how exactly is this achieved?

Li's account of *legan wenhua* 樂感文化, or a culture characterized by a sensitivity to delight provides one answer.[73] In it, delight or pleasure (*le* 樂) is fundamental to what he claims as a Chinese attitude toward life (in contrast to cultures characterized by guilt or shame). Confucian cultivation is connected with mastery of the traditional Six Arts[74] and emotional and affective experience are central to good judgment, yielding, "a rationality grounded in the historical (the experiential) and the affective (human relations)."[75] Li explains this approach to life by analyzing each phrase of *Analects* 8.8, "Be awakened by poetry, be established by ritual, be perfected in music." Aesthetic goods are realized along with ever more elevated states of self-cultivation. (Poetic) language arouses the individual, mastery of ritual both internalizes social norms and cultivates practical skills, while music increases the capacity for emotional response. I have discussed the meaning and significance of delight (*le*) and *legan wenhua*,[76] and will not repeat those details here.

Instead, returning to Li's analysis of practical reasoning, and the dialectic of harmony and justice, I focus on what forms of practical deliberation best realize affective experiences within human relationships and shared social interaction. Stated another way, what does moral psychology look like when it is governed by a concern to realize aesthetic value in interpersonal interaction?

## Practical Judgment and Relational Harmony

Practical deliberation can take many forms.[77] Here, however, we focus on two contrasting accounts, which roughly follow the distinction between justice and harmony as ideals governing practical deliberation. The first is integral to the liberal good life discussed above, constituted by the realization of desires and projects. It is characterized as instrumental reasoning toward defined goals and projects. Desired projects prompt a chain of instrumental reasoning about necessary means, and give rise to additional, subordinate desires pertaining to those means.

Justice is integral to this kind of deliberation. Autonomous individuals follow their own personal projects, which can be mutually incommensurable, with no ranking of relative worth possible. Within this picture of desire-based action, justice, as the appeal to rational moral principle, is needed because ends conflict and their incommensurability requires an impartial perspective from which to adjudicate. Justice represents the search for impartial principles that fairly govern all individuals—the abstract moral principles that Li criticizes. Li's resistance to justice, however, arises not merely because it appeals only to abstract rational principles and neglects emotion. His source of his concern lies much deeper. As his reply to Sandel makes clear, he is also concerned about recognizing differing conceptions of the self and finding value in traditional Chinese conceptions of the good life.

Li's account of practical and moral judgment—the balance of reason and emotion and reliance on the emotions of *guanxi*-centered life—serves as an alternative conception of the good life. But, given the problems noted with that account, we can further explore what the psychology of action looks like when it is oriented around realizing affective or aesthetic goods (*qing*) in the realm of everyday human relations. This account honors and extends many of Li's philosophical and ethical commitments. Furthermore, it might even appeal to those attracted or habituated into the liberal individualist outlook, by directing attention to an overlooked account of the good life.

We have already introduced the ingredients structuring this second account of practical and moral judgment: the sustaining of human relationships, and emotions or feelings that, even in the absence of explicit justification or rational argument, are trusted to determine judgment. Added to these is the practical ideal of conduct oriented towards the generation of shared aesthetic or emotional goods through social and personal interaction.

This second approach is characterized by the muted appeal of personal projects or ends that are conceived of independently of others (independently of social interactions); such projects register less in deliberation than goods realized though shared social events. This account does not mean diminished autonomy, however, such as a failure to exercise practical judgment; it is simply that non-project goods are valued more highly. These are goods realized through social interactions, in which the practical ends aimed at can vary from interaction to interaction, since it is the interaction itself that generates what is valued. Accordingly, the relevant goods cannot be thought of as personal projects that transcend everyday social interactions.[78] To better understand what forms of practical deliberation better secure aesthetic goods realized through social interaction, consider another famous account of practical deliberation, provided by John Dewey.[79]

Dewey was also concerned with how aesthetic value can be realized in experience and through action. Specifically, Dewey distinguished two different approaches to practical deliberation: practical deliberation guided by "ends-in-themselves" and practical deliberation guided by "ends-in-view."[80] "Ends-in-themselves" refer to "some fixed end beyond activity at which we should aim."[81] Dewey's distinction is partly a response to the traditional view, often associated with Aristotle, that humans have an intrinsic purpose or nature that it is good to fulfill. This furnishes humans with ends at which their activity should aim. Ends-in-themselves also refer to special moral aims or ideals, which function as governing principles that transcend the subject's present activity. This includes, for example, the utilitarian principle of maximizing the best overall consequences. In Dewey's words, "the doctrine of fixed ends-in-themselves at which human acts are—or should be—directed . . . was made the cornerstone of orthodox moral theory."[82]

Echoing Li's rejection of justice, Dewey rejects the idea that practical moral judgment should be governed by general moral principles that transcend the actual problem under consideration; such an account does not accurately reflect how human psychology—i.e., practical deliberation—can or should function. Stated more broadly, Dewey resists the idea that practical deliberation should be unnecessarily constrained by intransigent or fixed ends or considerations, as this "puts the center of moral gravity outside the concrete processes of living."[83]

In place of fixed ends and transcendent principles, Dewey suggests that human practical reasoning be oriented around "ends-in-view." These are ends or "foreseen consequences" that "arise in the course of activity and which are employed to give activity added meaning and to direct its further course."[84] Ends, correctly understood, are not something fixed, which condition and constrain imagination and action, but rather are ideas or consequences that appear during the course of activity itself. In deliberation during dynamic activity, a person's focus moves from end to end.

Dewey's distinction between ends within practical deliberation offers two insights into the kind of practical deliberation that best realizes aesthetic value within human interactions. First, Dewey is concerned that fixed or intransigent ends unduly restrict practical deliberation. We might extend this concern, and question the value of being bound to substantial personal ends and projects, which are kept psychologically detached from the many personal and social interactions in everyday social life. This coheres with Li's questioning of individualism and of views of the self that emphasize separateness. Pursuing complex personal projects and ends is an appealing notion of the good life, but commitment to it can obscure other worthwhile ends that offer qualitatively different goods. Holding to fixed projects, to be fulfilled over time or in the future, might desensitize a person to more immediate possibilities and goods. A key insight of Dewey is that worthwhile ends often appear during the course of practical activity, rather than preceding it and determining in advance what deliberation should achieve, and also thereby constraining what feelings or emotions might arise. An argument can be made for allowing ends to be more malleable, more contingent on how an activity or interaction unfolds. This allows for the realization of value within an interaction, which might be missed when pre-existing concerns direct the course of that interaction. The question is then "Can a social interaction in itself be valuable so as to make this more malleable notion of ends worthwhile—and make up for what is lost by not structuring a life around individualistic projects and goals?" This leads us to the second insight.

Dewey's account of pursuing ends-in-view describes the reasoning often needed in dynamic everyday social interaction. Within the daily rolling series of personal and social interactions that make up everyday life, many interactions involve responding by developing new, unanticipated, and immediate ends of action not apparent prior to the interaction. Arguably, these episodes of human interaction that occur throughout the day are sources of novelty and sites of creativity rarely matched by other quotidian activities (explicitly creative pursuits excepted). Furthermore, the goods that can be realized through those interactions make worthwhile an openness to pursuing those ends as they appear. This openness enables participants in a social interaction to harmonize their ends. Harmonizing does not necessarily mean the same ends; they need only be compatible or, preferably, complementary within the interaction. Simple examples of this might be the unforeseen flow of an engaging conversation, as various ideas come to mind, or how tone or conduct toward a person can quickly change as perceptions of their situation alter. Dewey's account thus gives some insight into the psychology associated with conduct based on *guanxi* and social interactions that derive from them. In summary, Dewey helps to clarify the connection between *guanxi* and the affective goods of *qing*. Simply put, Dewey's account relativizes ends to particular contexts. Ends are relativized to the social interaction that is unfolding, and to which a person is responding. Within the Confucian tradition, as Li sometimes presents it, the ends that come into view are aesthetic goods.

Dewey's approach to practical reasoning is also informed by an appreciation of aesthetic experience.[85] In Dewey's account, aesthetic experience arises when phenomenal or sensory experience takes a certain form or exhibits a certain quality, such that it becomes "an experience."[86] "An experience" is generated from the "raw material" of everyday experience or "everyday events, doings and sufferings that are universally recognized to constitute experience."[87] Simple examples are a wonderful meal or an awe-inspiring and memorable storm. Such elevated experiences are not present when experience is merely mundane, and consciousness or attention drifts. Aesthetic experiences are characterized by certain formal features of experience. These experiences form a unified whole, such that there is a "single quality that pervades the entire experience in spite of the variation of its constituent parts."[88] Such experiences are also distinguished by a movement toward completion or consumption. This enables Dewey to talk of "art in human experience."[89]

Dewey outlines how everyday experience can be distinguished by aesthetic qualities. We can transfer this insight to Li's account of relationality and everyday social life. Specifically, we can examine how the interactions between people in everyday social life yield various aesthetic goods. What form do these goods take? Instead of equating aesthetic value or goods with formal features of experience, as Dewey does, we can consider how everyday social interactions between those with some basis of familiarity (*guanxi*) can yield other forms of aesthetic value. These aesthetic goods are collectively sufficient to constitute a conception of the good life, and collectively instantiate the ideal of "harmony."

There are several ways in which aesthetic goods might arise through interpersonal interactions. We have already discussed ritualized interaction and the goods derived therein. Here I outline a few other forms these aesthetic goods might take.

At the most basic level of social interaction, aesthetic goods arise from "hitting the mark in the everyday," or "focusing the familiar" to use Ames and Hall's translation[90] of *zhongyong* (中庸)—a term that Li also employs in his analysis of social life.[91] This involves moderating desires, finding sufficiency (*zhizu* 知足),[92] and attempting to secure this-worldly joys and satisfactions, while meeting "the needs of everyday life and maintaining a harmonious and stable organic system in the here-and-now," which "valued human relationships and other connections."[93] As Li notes, "All schools of Chinese philosophy, including the Confucians, Mohists, Laozi, Zhuangzi, and even Chan Buddhism, highly value a sensuous consciousness and life as it naturally arises."[94] The Confucian tradition, in particular, emphasizes how this consciousness can be attained through relational attachments. As for the aesthetic goods thereby realized, various experiences are associated with well-conducted simple social interactions. For example, borrowing from Dewey,[95] such interactions can provoke an arousal of interest and a sense of absorption and focus, while the successful completion of episodes of interaction throughout the day, both structured and practical as well as unscripted and leisurely, can yield feelings of satisfaction at what has been accomplished, or feelings of usefulness or self-esteem at being able to navigate the social world. Earlier, we noted the experience of "fittingness," and this value is also relevant to social interactions, as the satisfying sense that the various elements of an interaction have been brought together appropriately. Other forms of aesthetic goods could be explored, but this brief account shows how simple human social interaction can yield goods that make the experience of those interactions ends in themselves.

Next, aesthetic goods of interaction can also be described in terms of music and musicality more generally. Both allow for "idealized diversity while providing happiness and satisfaction,"[96] and this explains why, in early China, music is associated with coordination of human conduct on a grand scale, as government: "Classical Confucianism . . . proposed the connection between music and governance (as 'yue yu zheng tong' 乐与政通)."[97] As noted, delight or pleasure is a prominent aesthetic good generated by social interaction, and its connection to music is made explicit by the dual meaning of le (樂/乐)—as "music" and "delight."[98] I have elsewhere discussed how skilled social interaction that generates delight can be understood by comparison with musical interaction, and the aesthetic goods thereby realized,[99] and will not go into detail here. To summarize, attention to others, improvisation, deference, and timing of actions and speech so as to make appropriate contributions at the right moment are all cultivated skills that create delight-like states in social interaction.

Finally, another category of aesthetic goods might be described as religious feelings. These, however, are aesthetic in nature rather than based on theological commitments, and are drawn from traditional Confucian ideas. Perhaps the simplest such feeling is reverence (*jing* 敬). Confucius provides a paradigmatic example of being visibly affected by a social engagement, such that "his countenance would change visibly and his legs would bend" (*Analects* 10.3). Similarly, reverence appears to be an outcome of relationships with parents or elders.

More diffuse religious feelings can also characterize well-conducted relationships and interactions. The first concerns "ceaseless generation" (*shengsheng buyi* 生生不已) or the experience or sense of a process of ceaseless generation. This includes both the satisfying experience of the flow of events in the world before one—the endless series of rolling social interactions that make up the day—and a more explicitly relational sense: a sense of being part of a chain of beings that stretch from the past into the future. This awareness partly explains the importance of familial reverence (*xiao* 孝), and this awareness is also expressed as reverence toward ancestors.

Other similar feelings include that all things are complete within oneself (*wanwu jie bei yu wo yi* 萬物皆備於我矣, *Mencius* 7A4) and a feeling of possessing flood-like qi (*haoranzhiqi* 浩然之氣, *Mencius* 2A1). These are nominally claims steeped in metaphysical commitments. But, perhaps building on such metaphysical beliefs, they are also expressions of feeling that arise when the various relationships or *guanxi* go well, or when feeling "complete" or energized through such engagements. Finally, and perhaps most diffuse, is the feeling of unity that emerges from successfully completed interactions, and which instantiates the guiding ideal of "the unity of cosmos and the human" (*tian ren he yi* 天人合一) within the realm of everyday interpersonal relationships. In summary, all of these ideas can be understood as expressing valued feelings that partly arise from well-conducted social interactions.

To summarize, these various feelings and experiences are practically significant. They confirm the value of the ends pursued as these arise within dynamic social interactions. The feelings and emotions are thus markers of successful interaction, and when produced daily and over time comprise a substantive conception of the good. This is a clear illustration of how *qing* or affective experience can shape practical judgment, working alongside judgments based on rational principle and calculation. This account is intended to further illustrate the kind of harmony Li has in mind when he speaks of a balance between reason and emotion (*qing*). *Qing* can be" higher," because it is more fundamental to the good life outlined above. The feelings and aesthetic experiences indicated constitute their own reward, they are the "fruits" (*shi* 實, Mencius 4A27) of the right kind of conduct within relationships. Thus, they justify that approach to life in which relationality is made central, and the psychology of individualistic pursuits secondary. This is a meaningful extension of Li's claim that "harmony is higher than justice."

## Concluding Remarks

Some difficulties with this account should be noted, since it does not accommodate all of Li's varied claims and arguments about emotion, *guanxi*, and harmony. Li's account of harmony typically emphasizes external moral norms and social obligations and their role in shaping emotion, and this leaves less scope for relativizing good action to whatever generates aesthetic goods within social interactions. Similarly, Li often implies that emotional responses are sedimented from historical social practices, such that the most practically important emotions felt within *guanxi* frameworks are relatively static. In contrast, this account seeks to broaden the scope of relevant feelings and also the range of relationships of familiarity that matter, beyond those typically governed by social roles.

The account presented here, however, can accommodate Li's account of the external and historical rootedness of social norms. Generating aesthetic goods often involves building on shared understandings of historical practices and norms. Personal greetings, for example, rely on established social norms to create felt, aesthetic rewards. Quirky or malcoordinated greetings can fail to generate such goods. More importantly, I believe there is sufficient openness within Li's wide-ranging concerns, particularly on the question of how his aesthetics relates to his moral philosophy, that the account presented here is a valid, if creative, attempt to extend Li's legacy.

This paper, responding to issues raised by Li's response to Sandel, explored how placing *guanxi* networks at the center of practical reason and the good life can generate aesthetic goods in everyday social interaction, and how these collectively constitute a plausible conception of the good life. This extends Li's interest in *guanxi* or relationality, and offers another way to substantiate the ideal of harmony through them, one which can be placed alongside individualism and its requisite justice. Whether or not harmony is higher than justice then depends on whether this alternative conception of the good life is more convincing. This question can be left open, however. In the spirit of Li's pluralistic historicist approach, it is enough to recognize that people can be culturally conditioned toward one approach rather than another. Nor should we assume only these two conceptions of the good life, or that a single life cannot adopt different conceptions at different times. What matters is that approaches that foreground *guanxi* relationality need not rely on fixed and possibly restrictive notions of relationships. In this alternative conception of the good life, there is still room for imagination, creativity, and the pursuit of ends-in-view, all of which express autonomy while reaping aesthetic rewards.

# Notes

1. Li Zehou, "A Response to Michael Sandel and Other Matters," *Philosophy East and West* 66, no. 4 (2016): 1093.

2. Li Zehou 李泽厚, *Huiying Sangde'er ji qita* 回應桑德爾及其他 (*A Response to Sandel and Other Matters*) (Beijing: Sanlian Bookstore, 2014), 24; Li, "A Response," 1080.

3. See also Li, A *Response*, 25. Li makes a similar claim in his *Outline of a Philosophy* (*Zhexue Gangyao*): "Confucius said, 'In hearing court cases I am like others, but the important thing is to prevent them in the first place' (Analects 12.13). Here 'court cases,' which concern decisions about what is just, are secondary. Harmony (harmony in human relationships, between humans and nature, and the mind and body) is the higher standard." Li Zeihou 李泽厚, *Zhexue gangyao* 哲学纲要 (*Outline of a Philosophy*) (Beijing: Peking University Press 2011), 114; translation from Paul J. D'Ambrosio, "The Confucian Philosophy of Harmony, Li Zehou, and Michael Sandel's Suggested Collaborative Approach to Philosophy," *Comparative and Continental Philosophy* 11, no. 1 (2019): 78.

4. Li, "A Response," 1069.

5. Li, A *Response*, 8; John Rawls, *A Theory of Justice* (Cambridge, MA: Harvard University Press, 1971).

6. Li, A *Response*, 8.

7. Li, "A Response," 1083, 1090, and passim.

8. Li, "A Response," 1077.

9. Li Zehou, *The Origins of Chinese Thought: From Shamanism to Ritual Regulations*, trans. Robert Carleo III (Leiden: Brill, 2018).

10. Li, "A Response," 1078.

11. Li, "A Response," 1078.

12. Li, A *Response*, 38; translation from D'Ambrosio, "The Confucian Philosophy of Harmony," 133.

13. For a discussion of the differences between emotion, feeling, mood and belief, see Saam Trivedi, *Imagination, Music, and the Emotions: A Philosophical Study* (Albany: State University of New York Press, 2017).

14. Li, "A Response," 1097.

15. Li, "A Response," 1098.

16. For discussions of *guanxi*, see Andrew Kipnis, *Producing Guanxi: Sentiment, Self, and Subculture in a North China Village* (Durham, NC: Duke University Press, 1997); Mayfair Mei-hui Yang, *Gifts, Favors, and Banquets: The Art of Social Relationships in China* (Ithaca, NY: Cornell University Press, 1994); Thomas B. Gold, Doug Guthrie, and David Wank, eds., *Social Connections in China: Institutions, Culture, and the Changing Nature of Guanxi* (New York: Cambridge University Press, 2002).

17. Paul J. D'Ambrosio, Robert Carleo III, and Andrew Lambert, "On Li Zehou's Philosophy: An Introduction by Three Translators," *Philosophy East and West* 66, no. 4 (2016): 1057–67.

18. Li, "A Response," 1097.

19. Li, "A Response," 1095.

20. Li, "A Response," 1092.

21. Li, "A Response," 1079.

22. Li, "A Response," 1093.

23. Li, "A Response," 1093.
24. Rawls, *A Theory of Justice*, 3.
25. Li, "A Response," 1093.
26. Paul J. D'Ambrosio, "Approaches to Global Ethics: Michael Sandel's Justice and Li Zehou's Harmony," *Philosophy East and West* 66, no. 3 (2016): 730.
27. Li, "A Response," 1093.
28. Li, "A Response," 1099.
29. Li, "A Response," 1097.
30. This is not always the case, however; friends are not characterized by differing emotional responses. Also, the relation between gender and emotional response is a challenge for Li's account of harmony, given possible patriarchal implications, but cannot be addressed here.
31. *Liji*, quoted by Li, "A Response," 1097.
32. Paul J. D'Ambrosio, "Li Zehou's 'Harmony is Higher than Justice': Context and a Collaborative Future," *Asian Studies* 8, no. 1 (2020): 141.
33. Li's embrace of Kant's categorical imperative should be understood as part of his historicist approach and not as an acceptance of an ahistorical moral foundation.
34. Annette Baier, "The Need for More Than Justice," *Canadian Journal of Philosophy* 17, no. 1 (1987): 41–56.
35. Li, "A Response," 1104.
36. Li, "A Response," 1078.
37. Roger T. Ames, *Confucian Role Ethics: A Vocabulary* (Hong Kong: Chinese University Press, 2011).
38. Li, "A Response," 1074.
39. Li Zehou, *The Path of Beauty: A Study of Chinese Aesthetics* (New York: Oxford University Press, 1994), 46.
40. For example, Michael Stocker, "The Schizophrenia of Modern Ethical Theories," *Journal of Philosophy* 73, no. 1 (1976): 453–66; Michael Stocker, *Valuing Emotions* (Cambridge: Cambridge University Press, 1996).
41. Li, "A Response," 1113.
42. Li, "A Response," 1075; Liang Shuming 梁漱溟, *Zhongguo wenhua yaoyi* 中國文化要義 (*Fundamentals of Chinese Culture*) (Shanghai: Shanghai People's Press, 2005), 80.
43. Li, "A Response," 1080.
44. John Stuart Mill, *On Liberty* (London: Batoche Books, 2001), 55.
45. Bernard Williams, "Persons, Character, and Morality," in *Moral Luck: Philosophical Papers 1973–1980*, ed. James Rachels (Cambridge: Cambridge University Press, 1981), 5.
46. Mill writes, "It is only the cultivation of individuality which produces, or can produce, well-developed human beings." Mill, *On Liberty*, 59.
47. Trivedi, *Imagination, Music, and the Emotions*.

48. Li, *The Path of Beauty*, 46.
49. Li, "A Response," 1107.
50. Li, "A Response," 1080.
51. Li, "A Response," 1075.
52. Li, "A Response," 1075.
53. Liang writes "所謂'因情而有義'之義,正從對方關係演來,不從自己立場出發" (Liang, *Fundamentals of Chinese Culture*, 90)—roughly, "the obligation attaching to emotion (*qing*) comes from relations with others, and does not begin from one's own perspective."
54. Li, "A Response," 1113.
55. Li, 1090.
56. Strictly speaking, this attempt to put the affective experiences of relationality at the heart of ethics is indifferent to the question of whether single emotions characterize particular bonds or relationships (e.g., reverence of child for parents). Such singular emotions might be constitutive of harmony, but they need not be; other affective experiences can also sustain and direct relationships and social interaction.
57. Li, "A Response," 1102.
58. Li Zehou, *The Chinese Aesthetic Tradition*, trans. Maija Bell Samei (Honolulu: University of Hawai'i Press, 2009), 3.
59. "Chunguan Zongbo" 春官宗伯 chapter, in Li, *The Chinese Aesthetic Tradition*, 5.
60. Michael Nylan, "The Politics of Pleasure," *Asia Major* 14, no. 1 (2001): 84.
61. Thomas Michael, "Shamanism, Eroticism, and Death: The Ritual Structures of the Nine Songs in Comparative Context," *Religions* 10, no. 1 (2018): 17.
62. Emile Durkheim, *The Elementary Forms of the Religious Life: A Study in Religious Sociology* (Oxford: Macmillan, 1915).
63. Ellen Dissanayake, *Homo Aestheticus: Where Art Comes from and Why* (Seattle: University of Washington Press, 1995).
64. Edith Turner, *Communitas: The Anthropology of Collective Joy* (New York: Palgrave MacMillan, 2012).
65. Victor Turner, *The Ritual Process: Structure and Anti-Structure* (Chicago: Aldine, 1969).
66. Edith Turner, *Communitas*, 2–3.
67. Li, *The Chinese Aesthetic Tradition*, 55.
68. Li, *The Chinese Aesthetic Tradition*, 54.
69. Li Zehou, *A History of Classical Chinese Thought*, trans. Andrew Lambert (New York: Taylor and Francis, 2020), 319.
70. Li, *The Chinese Aesthetic Tradition*, 57.
71. Li, *The Chinese Aesthetic Tradition*, 56–57, translation modified.

72. Cai Yuanpei provides perhaps the best-known modern articulation of this view in "Replacing Religion with Aesthetic Education," trans. Julia Andrews, in *Modern Chinese Literary Thought: Writings on Literature, 1893–1945*, ed. Kirk Denton (Stanford, CA: Stanford University Press, 1996). See also Xu Fuguan 徐復觀, *Zhongguo yishu jingshen* 中國藝術精神 (*The Spirit of Chinese Arts*) (Taihung: Tunghai University, 1966), 150–57; Tu Weiming, "Embodied Knowledge: Body, Heart/Mind, and Spirit in Confucian Aesthetics," *Asian and Asian-American Philosophers and Philosophies Newsletter* 5, no. 2 (2006); and Li Zehou and Jane Cauvel, *Four Essays on Aesthetics: Toward a Global View* (Lanham, MD: Lexington Books, 2006).

73. Li Zehou 李泽厚, *Shiyong lixing yu legan wenhua* 實用理性與樂感文化 (*Pragmatic Reason and a Culture of Optimism*) (Beijing: Sanlian Publishing, 2005); Li, *A History of Classical Chinese Thought*, 317–25.

74. Li, *The Chinese Aesthetic Tradition*, 49.

75. Li, *A History of Classical Chinese Thought*, 317.

76. Andrew Lambert, "Determinism and the Problem of Individual Freedom in Li Zehou's Thought," in *Li Zehou and Confucian Philosophy*, ed. Roger T. Ames and Jinhua Jia (Honolulu: University of Hawai'i Press, 2018), 94–117; Andrew Lambert, "From Aesthetics to Ethics: The Place of Delight in Confucian Ethics," *Journal of Chinese Philosophy* 47, no. 3-4 (2020): 154–73.

77. Approaches range from analytic dissection of the cognitive structures of practical reason and moral judgment (Robert Audi, *Practical Reasoning and Ethical Decision* (London: Routledge, 2006)) to the appeal to broad heuristics internal to a culture to guide judgment (Thomas Kasulis, *Intimacy or Integrity: Philosophy and Cultural Difference* (Honolulu: University of Hawai'i Press, 2002)).

78. One personal project might be participation in social interaction, seemingly collapsing the distinction between the two conceptions of the good life. But in such cases, the ends pursued would still not transcend the interactions. See the discussion below on two types of deliberative ends.

79. For another attempt to bring Li's and Dewey's thought into dialogue, see Catherine Lynch, "Li Zehou and Pragmatism," *Philosophy East and West* 66, no. 3 (2016): 704–19.

80. John Dewey, *Human Nature and Conduct* (Mineola, NY: Dover, 2002), 223–25.

81. Dewey, *Human Nature and Conduct*, 223.

82. Dewey, *Human Nature and Conduct*, 224.

83. John Dewey, *Ethics* (New York, NY: Henry Holt, 1909), 329.

84. Dewey, *Human Nature and Conduct*, 225.

85. John Dewey, *Art as Experience* (New York, NY: Perigee, 1934).

86. Dewey, *Art as Experience*, 35.

87. Dewey, *Art as Experience*, 3.

88. Dewey, *Art as Experience*, 37.
89. Dewey, *Art as Experience*, 5.
90. Roger T. Ames and David Hall, *Focusing the Familiar: A Translation and Philosophical Interpretation of the Zhongyong* (Honolulu: University of Hawai'i Press, 2001).
91. Li, *A History of Classical Chinese Thought*, 349.
92. The folk phrase *zhizu chang le* 知足常樂, roughly appreciating sufficiency and thereby finding enduring delight, is commonly traced back to chapter 44 of the *Daodejing*, where the phrase *zhizu* appears.
93. Li, *A History of Classical Chinese Thought*, 317.
94. Li, *A History of Classical Chinese Thought*, 320.
95. Dewey, *Art as Experience*, 4–5.
96. Li, "A Response," 1097–98.
97. Li, "A Response," 1098.
98. For an extensive study of the role of pleasure or delight (*le*) in Chinese thought, see Michael Nylan, *The Chinese Pleasure Book* (Princeton NJ: Princeton University Press, 2021). On the emotional effects of music, see David Konstan, "Being Moved: Motion and Emotion in Classical Antiquity and Today," *Emotion Review* 13, no. 4 (2021): 282–88; Trivedi, *Imagination, Music, and the Emotions*; on music's social and political ramifications, see Erica Brindley, *Music, Cosmology, and the Politics of Harmony in Early China* (Albany: State University of New York Press, 2012).
99. Lambert, "From Aesthetics to Ethics."

# Bibliography

Ames, Roger T. *Confucian Role Ethics: A Vocabulary*. Hong Kong: Chinese University Press, 2011.
Ames, Roger T., and David Hall. *Focusing the Familiar: A Translation and Philosophical Interpretation of the Zhongyong*. Honolulu: University of Hawai'i Press, 2001.
Audi, Robert. *Practical Reasoning and Ethical Decision*. London: Routledge, 2006.
Baier, Annette. "The Need for More Than Justice." *Canadian Journal of Philosophy* 17, no. 1 (1987): 41–56.
Brindley, Erica. *Music, Cosmology, and the Politics of Harmony in Early China*. Albany: State University of New York Press, 2012.
Cai Yuanpei. "Replacing Religion with Aesthetic Education." Translated by Julia Andrews. In *Modern Chinese Literary Thought: Writings on Literature, 1893–1945*, edited by Kirk Denton, 182–89. Stanford, CA: Stanford University Press, 1996.

D'Ambrosio, Paul J. "Approaches to Global Ethics: Michael Sandel's Justice and Li Zehou's Harmony." *Philosophy East and West* 66, no. 3 (2016): 720–38.
D'Ambrosio, Paul J. "The Confucian Philosophy of Harmony, Li Zehou, and Michael Sandel's Suggested Collaborative Approach to Philosophy." *Comparative and Continental Philosophy* 11, no. 1 (2019): 68–83.
D'Ambrosio, Paul J. "Li Zehou's 'Harmony is Higher than Justice': Context and a Collaborative Future." *Asian Studies* 8, no. 1 (2020): 127–46.
D'Ambrosio, Paul J., Robert A. Carleo III, and Andrew Lambert. "On Li Zehou's Philosophy: An Introduction by Three Translators." *Philosophy East and West* 66, no. 4 (2016): 1057–67.
Dewey, John. *Art as Experience*. New York: Perigee, 1934.
Dewey, John. *Ethics*. New York: Henry Holt, 1909.
Dewey, John. *Human Nature and Conduct*. Mineola, NY: Dover, 2002.
Dissanayake, Ellen. *Homo Aestheticus: Where Art Comes from and Why*. Seattle: University of Washington Press, 1995.
Durkheim, Emile. *The Elementary Forms of the Religious Life: A Study in Religious Sociology*. Oxford: Macmillan, 1915.
Gold, Thomas, Doug Guthrie, and David Wank. *Social Connections in China: Institutions, Culture, and the Changing Nature of* Guanxi. New York: Cambridge University Press, 2002.
Kasulis, Thomas. *Intimacy or Integrity: Philosophy and Cultural Difference*. Honolulu: University of Hawai'i Press, 2002.
Kipnis, Andrew. *Producing Guanxi: Sentiment, Self, and Subculture in a North China Village*. Durham, NC: Duke University Press, 1997.
Konstan, David. "Being Moved: Motion and Emotion in Classical Antiquity and Today." *Emotion Review* 13, no. 4 (2021): 282–88.
Lambert, Andrew. "Determinism and the Problem of Individual Freedom in Li Zehou's Thought." In *Li Zehou and Confucian Philosophy*, edited by Roger T. Ames and Jinhua Jia, 94–117. Honolulu: University of Hawai'i Press, 2018.
Lambert, Andrew. "From Aesthetics to Ethics: The Place of Delight in Confucian Ethics." *Journal of Chinese Philosophy* 47, no. 3–4 (2020): 154–73.
Li Zehou. *The Chinese Aesthetic Tradition*. Translated by Maija Bell Samei. Honolulu: University of Hawai'i Press, 2009.
Li Zehou. *A History of Classical Chinese Thought*. Translated by Andrew Lambert. New York: Routledge, 2020.
Li Zehou 李泽厚. *Huiying Sangde'er ji qita* 回應桑德爾及其他 (*A Response to Sandel and Other Matters*). Beijing: Sanlian Bookstore, 2014.
Li Zehou. *The Origins of Chinese Thought: From Shamanism to Ritual Regulations and Humaneness*. Translated by Robert A. Carleo III. Leiden: Brill, 2018.
Li Zehou. *The Path of Beauty: A Study of Chinese Aesthetics*. Translated by Gong Lizeng. New York: Oxford University Press, 1994.

Li Zehou. "A Response to Michael Sandel and Other Matters." Translated by Paul D'Ambrosio and Robert A. Carleo III. *Philosophy East and West* 66, no. 4 (2016): 1068–1147.

Li Zehou 李泽厚. *Shiyong lixing yu legan wenhua* 實用理性與樂感文化 (*Pragmatic Reason and a Culture of Optimism*). Beijing: Sanlian Bookstore, 2005.

Li Zehou 李泽厚. *Zhexue gangyao* 哲学纲要 (*Outline of a Philosophy*). Beijing: Peking University Press, 2011.

Li Zehou and Jane Cauvel. *Four Essays on Aesthetics: Toward a Global View*. Lanham, MD: Lexington Books, 2006.

Liang Shuming 梁漱溟. *Zhongguo wenhua yaoyi* 中國文化要義 (*Fundamentals of Chinese Culture*). Shanghai: Shanghai People's Press, 2005.

Lynch, Catherine. "Li Zehou and Pragmatism." *Philosophy East and West* 66, no. 3 (2016): 704–19.

Michael, Thomas. "Shamanism, Eroticism, and Death: The Ritual Structures of the Nine Songs in Comparative Context." *Religions* 10, no. 1 (2018): 17.

Mill, John Stuart. *On Liberty*. London: Batoche Books, 2001.

Nylan, Michael. *The Chinese Pleasure Book*. Princeton, NJ: Princeton University Press, 2021.

Nylan, Michael. "The Politics of Pleasure." *Asia Major* 14, no. 1 (2001): 73–124.

Rawls, John. *A Theory of Justice*. Cambridge, MA: Harvard University Press, 1971.

Stocker, Michael. "The Schizophrenia of Modern Ethical Theories." *Journal of Philosophy* 73, no. 1 (1976): 453–66.

Stocker, Michael. *Valuing Emotions*. Cambridge: Cambridge University Press, 1996.

Trivedi, Saam. *Imagination, Music, and the Emotions: A Philosophical Study*. Albany: State University of New York Press, 2017.

Tu Weiming. "Embodied Knowledge: Body, Heart/Mind, and Spirit in Confucian Aesthetics." *Asian and Asian-American Philosophers and Philosophies Newsletter* 5, no. 2 (2006).

Turner, Edith. *Communitas: The Anthropology of Collective Joy*. New York: Palgrave MacMillan, 2012.

Turner, Victor. *The Ritual Process: Structure and Anti-Structure*. Chicago: Aldine, 1969.

Williams, Bernard. "Persons, Character, and Morality." In *Moral Luck: Philosophical Papers 1973–1980*, edited by James Rachels, 1–19. Cambridge: Cambridge University Press, 1981.

Xu Fuguan 徐復觀. *Zhongguo yishu jingshen* 中國藝術精神 (*The Spirit of Chinese Arts*). Taihung: Tunghai University, 1966.

Yang, Mayfair Mei-hui. *Gifts, Favors, and Banquets: The Art of Social Relationships in China*. Ithaca, NY: Cornell University Press, 1994.

8

# A Deep Harmony Account of Justice

CHENYANG LI

Li Zehou has been one of the most original philosophers of our times. Honoring his legacy requires us to take seriously his identity as a philosopher, rather than merely as an accomplished historian of ideas. That is, we should not only learn from his scholarly findings and interpret his views, but also engage him earnestly in philosophical discourse to advance our common cause of philosophical exploration. In this paper, I draw inspiration from Li Zehou's work and develop a view on an issue in which he has been deeply interested: the relation of harmony and justice.

Harmony and justice are two primary human values, and their relation is an important metaethical question.[1] While John Rawls regarded justice as "the first virtue of social institutions,"[2] Li Zehou famously asserted that "harmony is higher than justice." There are also thinkers who hold that harmony and justice are equally important, as will be discussed below. In this paper, I utilize a conception of deep harmony to develop a view that, on the fundamental level, harmony grounds justice and justice serves the purpose of harmony. This paper has four parts. The first part, "Harmony Higher than Justice," presents and problematizes Li Zehou's view. Next, "Tension Between Justice and Harmony" examines alternative views to set the stage for my own argument. The third part, "The Notion of Deep Harmony," articulates the notion of deep harmony, drawing from the Confucian tradition. In the last part, "A Deep Harmony Account of Justice," I advance a view that, from the perspective of Confucian deep harmony, harmony serves both as the metaphysical foundation and as the ultimate goal of justice. That is, ontologically, deep harmony accounts for the existential context in which justice is to be established; metaethically, justice as instituted in the form of norms and rules ultimately serves the purpose of social harmony. Thus, this paper provides further justifications for my previous claim that "a harmonious society is a just society."[3]

## Harmony Higher than Justice

Unlike those Chinese thinkers who gravitated toward harmony in philosophical reconstructions, the contemporary thinker Li Zehou held both harmony and justice as important concepts.[4] These two concepts perform different functions in Li's grand philosophical system. The concept of harmony belongs to the category of "transforming people through morals," whereas justice belongs to the category of "rule by law."[5] However, Li did not see harmony and justice as on equal footing, and maintained that "harmony is higher than justice." As he wrote, "There are interpersonal harmony, harmony between the mind and body, and *tian-ren* harmony (harmony between humanity and nature). As the guiding principles for and proper constructions of modern social morality on the basis of the 'emotio-rational structure' and relationism (*guanxi*-ism), these are the highest and the most fundamental form of 'the common good' and 'the good life' that sustain the continuity of humanity. These are what the ultimate goal consists in."[6]

Li's claim that "harmony is higher than justice," however, does not imply a rivalry between these two ideals, nor that one should trump the other. As Paul D'Ambrosio has aptly observed, "Li Zehou proposes the idea that 'harmony is higher than justice' as a way towards thinking about a more collaborative interaction between the two notions."[7] Furthermore, as Jana Rošker has correctly reminded readers, here we should not confuse Li Zehou's reference to harmony with a frequent misconstrual of the notion in terms of conformity. For Li, harmony is "harmony in diversity."[8] In Li Zehou's view, Chinese culture heavily values the role of emotions in human society, in comparison with the Western emphasis on rationality. The importance of the role of emotion is manifested in the Chinese way of life, where social relations or *guanxi* are central. In this way of life, harmony plays a leading role. However, the rational is not missing in Chinese culture. As Rošker explains, "While the Western concept of justice is linked to rational approaches, Li's harmony does not only pertain to emotion, but rather to the complementary relation between reason and emotion."[9]

In Li Zehou's words, Chinese culture has maintained an "emotio-rational structure," which enables Chinese people to incorporate both harmony and justice in their lives. However, justice itself is not the ultimate goal of society—harmony is. Harmony reflects the "emotio-rational structure" and relationism (*guanxi*-ism), which Li held to be the backbone of Chinese culture. He further clarified, "Harmony is higher than justice that clearly discriminates between right and wrong and maintains fairness and reasonability. But harmony cannot replace justice. Rather, harmony is to be achieved on the basis of justice. Hence, harmony can only channel and properly construct justice; it cannot determine or control justice."[10] Bearing this in mind, we can accept Wang Keping's description of Li's view of harmony and justice as "hierarchical."[11] That is, harmony is placed as a higher achievement than justice even though it also dependent on justice. Because harmony has to be achieved on the basis of justice, it presupposes justice. In Li's words, "there must be justice first before we can seek harmony."[12]

Li's view on justice and harmony gives us much to reflect on issues of social and political philosophy. What remains unclear, however, is whether Li Zehou's system can accommodate a robust concept of justice. For Li Zehou, the "emotio-rational structure" in Chinese culture maintains the consistency of the emotional and the rational. It accommodates both justice and harmony. In such a structure, Li emphasized, the emotional is the "root," the "substance."[13] In Li's view, that ideal combination of justice and harmony leads to a social order. In his example of criminal punishment, criminals of capital offenses are executed on the grounds both of the law and of the emotional responses of the people when public outrage cannot be extinguished without carrying out an execution.[14] However, it is also a fact that justice sometimes contradicts harmony, at least under certain circumstances. It may be argued that an orderly society needs a robust justice system, which may at times operate against strong public opinions; a capital punishment can thus be circumvented in accordance with justice regardless of strong public opinion to the contrary. In stressing the consistency between the emotional and the rational (*heqing heli* 合情合理, literally, "in accord with both emotion and reason"), between harmony and justice, Li Zehou has left many questions unanswered.

## Tension between Justice and Harmony

*Prima facie*, there is a tension between justice and harmony. Justice is to be carried out on the basis of principles and rules; harmony calls for compromises and flexibility. As such, justice and harmony seem to point in different directions. In her nuanced study of the sense of justice in Confucianism, Erin Cline calls readers' attention to the Confucian idea of justice, which had been previously neglected in the academic literature, while highlighting its importance. In her discussion, Cline raises questions regarding the consistency between harmony and justice. Confucius said, "When the multitude hate a person, you must examine them and judge them for yourself. The same holds true for someone whom the multitude love."[15] Cline interprets this as suggesting that Confucius holds that a good society requires its members to judge situations in a fair and balanced way, even when their judgment goes against the majority.[16] Cline sees this as raising questions for the goal of harmony in society. As Cline comments: "The problem, however, is that it simply does not seem to be the case that judging situations in a fair and balanced manner and defending one's judgments against the objections of others always is a means to harmony, unless one thinks of harmony as a long-term goal that can be achieved only by challenging norms and standards and encouraging certain virtues in members of society despite their resistance to it."[17] Here Cline refers to harmony in the sense of social harmony, which people usually have in mind when discussing the term. She does not elaborate on the possibility that harmony as a long-term goal is to be obtained only by challenging social norms, and if so, under what conditions such challenges can be justified for the sake of harmony. She reads the passage as suggesting that Confucius values fairness and good judgment even when they do not help to preserve harmony. Cline elaborates, "Indeed, harmony could be attained fairly easily in some cases simply by going along with the judgment of the majority. But what Kongzi [Confucius] indicates in these passages is that he thinks it is wrong to sacrifice one person for the sake of harmony. Or, perhaps more accurately, if one person's well-being is sacrificed in the name of preserving harmony among the majority, then the state of affairs is not really harmonious at all."[18] The question raised here is important for understanding the relation between harmony and justice. If justice sometimes requires us to go against harmony, how can these two fundamental notions be reconciled? Li Zehou did not address such a question, even though it is unavoidable as we examine how justice relates to harmony. However, Cline's question requires an answer from anyone who takes the connection between harmony and justice seriously.

Various efforts have been made to balance harmony with justice. In an article entitled "Connecting Harmony and Justice: Lessons from Feminist Philosophy," Dascha Düring problematizes a tension between the two concepts. She argues that the idea of justice may have to be comprehensibly revised if it is to be compatible with harmony. In her view, harmony and justice can be compatible in two ways. First, we may consider harmony and justice as offering complementary hermeneutic and normative frameworks in the sense that these are taken to apply to different domains of human life. For instance, it may be the case that harmony pertains to such realms of human life as personal virtues and emotional attitudes, interpersonal relationships, and social institutions insofar as these concern informal rites, practices, and roles, whereas justice may provide a framework for interpretation and normative reasoning concerning the basic structure of society or its major social institutions. The second way to make harmony and justice compatible is to revise the way we understand justice and related concepts. On such a reading, Düring writes, "Confucian harmony and Rawlsian justice are thus not held to be compatible (let alone mutually enhancing) as it stands, but are thought to possibly be made compatible when the conceptual framework of justice is reinterpreted and integrated within the larger hermeneutic and normative model of harmony."[19] Düring argues for tackling the issue from both sides. On the one hand, justice needs to be reconceptualized without a rigid separation of the public and private spheres, as usually assumed in Rawlsian justice. On the other hand, Confucian harmony (in its traditional form) needs to adequately and effectively address issues of social inequalities, including gender inequality. Thus, by making adjustments on both sides, justice and harmony can be made compatible. Düring holds that feminist philosophy has an important role to play in this process,[20] but her position does not imply that there is no difference between the public and private. The target of her criticism is a clear "distinction" between, or a rigid separation of, the two spheres. According to her view, for instance, legislation against domestic violence as a form of justice is legitimate even though it reaches into the private sphere of individual homes. Such rules of justice can enhance harmony, both in the public and private spheres. In this regard Li Zehou would agree with Düring, because justice establishes the ground rule of a precondition for striving toward harmony in the family. I will return to this idea of enhancing harmony through justice in the next section.

Along a similar line of pursuing compatibility, but in a much broader scope, Joshua Mason argues for a sweeping reconceptualization of justice and harmony. In his recent book *Justice and Harmony: Cross-Cultural Ideals in Conflict and Cooperation*—to my knowledge the first book specifically on the relation between justice and harmony—Mason argues that justice and harmony are to be made complementary, and maintains that they are two of the greatest human ideals. It would be too much a loss of our cultural heritage if we let justice be limited to merely a procedural mechanism, or if we allowed harmony to be taken as excessive censorship (or even suppression for the sake of conformity, one may add), as found in some parts of the world today. Mason writes, "My considered conviction is that these are beautiful ideals that should continue to shine forth as inspirational forces. I hope we can find ways of thinking about and working toward cross-cultural conceptions of justice and harmony that honor the breadth and the depth of these ideals."[21] While taking harmony as the fundamental "root" of human value, which stands prior to all other moral notions, Mason conceptualizes justice in terms of harmonic justice, and harmony as just harmony. For him, root harmony is the ideal that expresses the felt goodness of one's interpenetrating embeddedness in tradition and community; harmonic justice is justice conceived in view of the human condition situated in human history; just harmony is adjusted harmony that has taken up the demands of justice. Mason places root harmony at a more fundamental level than harmonic justice and just harmony. This seems to be consistent with Li Zehou's view that harmony is higher than justice. Mason's harmony is to be completed in just harmony, a harmony of a "higher quality." In order words, for Mason, the Confucian idea of harmony needs to be transformed by incorporating justice. This also seems to resonate with Li Zehou's view that harmony has to be realized on the basis of justice.

Both Düring and Mason attempt to reconceptualize justice and harmony in order to reconcile the tension between the two. However, while their ideas are useful for us to think through related issues, they do not directly address the kind of question raised by Cline. If we confront the tension between justice and harmony squarely, as Cline has, how should an approach be developed? In the rest of this paper, I attempt to utilize the concept of deep harmony to formulate a view that both faces up to the tension between justice and harmony in practical levels and reconcile the two concepts theoretically. I call such an approach "a deep harmony account of justice." I will first explore the notion of deep harmony as developed from the Confucian tradition, and then construct an account of justice from such a perspective.

## The Notion of Deep Harmony

In principle, I agree with Li Zehou that harmony is higher than justice. I take this to mean that, on the level of social practice, even though justice is a precondition for harmony, our ultimate goal should not terminate with justice—we should strive further, for harmony. The good life is realized through intrapersonal harmony between the mind and body, interpersonal harmony in society, and harmony between humanity and nature.[22] I also agree with Dascha Düring and Joshua Mason that, one way or another, harmony and justice can be compatible. To put it a more straightforward way, "a harmonious society is a just society."[23] Beyond the practical level, however, I hold that, ontologically, harmony is more fundamental than justice. That is to say, harmony is higher than justice not only in the sense Li Zehou has advocated, as a higher goal of human pursuit, but also higher on a conceptual level, as any current form of social justice has to be built on the concept of harmony as its ultimate grounding. To account for harmony and justice at both the practical and ontological levels, we need a concept of "deep harmony."

The Confucian conception of harmony (*he* 和), as I advocate here, represents the process of the bringing-together of different elements to generate a coexistence through mutual enhancement, mutual accommodation, mutual adjustment, and mutual transformation.[24] I have identified the following characteristics of Confucian harmony:

1. Heterogeneity. Harmony presupposes two or more coexisting parties. These parties are not uniform and they possess varied dispositions.

2. Tension. Various parties interact with one another. Tension between various levels arises naturally from difference.

3. Coordination and Cooperation. While tension may result in conflict, it also places constraints on parties in interaction and generates energy to advance coordination. In coordination, the involved parties make allowances for one another and preserve their soundness.

4. Transformation and Growth. Through coordination, tension is transformed and conflict is reconciled into a favorable environment for each party to flourish. In this process, the involved parties undergo mutual transformation and form harmonious relationships.

5. Renewal. Harmony is achieved not as a final state, but as stages in an ongoing process. It admits of degrees. A harmonious relationship is maintained through continuous renewal.[25]

Through such processes, each party realizes its own potential while contributing to the larger collective whole in which each is a participant, or, as Roger Ames has put it, harmony is "the art of optimal contextualizing within one's roles and relations."[26] Unlike the way in which "harmony" has been commonly understood in the West,[27] such a notion of harmony is both dynamic and deep. On the one hand, it is dynamic because it points to an active process rather than a static state.[28] On the other, it is deep harmony because it stands for the idea that harmony is the driving force for the formation, transformation, and the operation of things in the world at all levels.[29] In this view, harmony accounts for all forms of existence. At each subsequent level, harmony takes place in generating new forms of existence and in sustaining the present forms of existence in the context of previously generated conditions that have also been products of prior processes of harmonization. As such, deep harmony penetrates all spheres of existence in the world.

The idea of deep harmony is traceable to a view from ancient Chinese cosmogony that the world emerged from the primordial chaos (*hundun* 混沌) through processes of harmony, or more accurately, of harmonization (*he* 和). The Jing: Guan 經:觀 article of the Mawangdui Silk Texts, for instance, quotes the Yellow Emperor speaking of the state of the original chaos (*hundun*) and the beginning of the world: "There was neither darkness nor brightness, neither *yin* nor *yang*. With *yin* and *yang* not being set, I have nothing to name for. Then it started to be divided into two, as *yin* or *yang*, and further divided into the four seasons."[30]

The original chaos is characterized as *qi* 氣, or energy-matter. It began as formless. *Yin* and *yang* are not entities in themselves. Instead, they stand for different formations of *qi* in correlated states. On this cosmogenic account, the original chaos self-differentiates into the two types of *qi* in the forms of *yin* and *yang*; the interactive processes of these two forms of *qi* lead to the generation of all subsequent things in the world.

The Daoyuan 道原 article of the Mawangdui Silk Texts similarly describes the original state as the undifferentiated primordial Oneness: "In the very beginning, all things were undifferentiated and unsubstantiated. The undifferentiated and unsubstantiated is the One; the One perseveres. . . . Its name is One, its home is non-substantiation, its nature is effortless action, and its function is harmony."[31] This "One" is the original whole of the chaos. The author of the text explicitly designates the working of the One as *he* 和. In this view, the "One" does not have a pre-given form. The subsequently formed world is generated through a process of harmonization. The contemporary philosopher Ding Sixin 丁四新 writes, "In the Daoyuan text, the idea of 'harmony' is not about harmonious relations among formed things. Rather it is the necessary and sufficient condition for generating the myriad things. Fundamentally speaking, without harmony there cannot be the generation of concrete things."[32] Such a cosmogenic view of harmony presents the idea on an ontological level. The harmony of the original One is prior to the harmony between or among formed things on the practical or ontic level.

According to such a view, each subsequent level of formed things is cosmologically nested on a prior level and process of harmony, so on so forth, traceable all way to the very beginning of the world, the One. This kind of harmony is deep harmony. Taking into consideration such a view, harmony takes place among existing conditions (e.g., people and things) for their optimal coexistence and further regeneration; in the meantime, it also accounts for the existence of these conditions themselves as they are the products of prior processes of harmony. Such a concept, I maintain, provides a new angle for us to account for the relation between justice and harmony.

## A Deep Harmony Account of Justice

On the issue of whether we can come up with a uniform and universal scheme of justice merely by thinking rationally, as John Rawls has attempted, Rawls's critics offered different views. Michael Sandel has argued that the answer to the question of justice has to do with "the circumstances of justice." The circumstances of justice refer to a society's background conditions that necessitate certain mechanisms in order for the society to function properly.[33] For example, in a more or less familial setting, where people are closely bonded with affections, justice is less relevant.[34] Even though Li Zehou disagreed with Sandel in many ways, he nevertheless shared such an insight with Sandel but went a step further. Li said, "Justice is not a contract between individuals; it comes from the historical situation or context of people's collective existence."[35] For Li Zehou, schemes of justice may change not only because social circumstances in the same society vary, as Sandel has argued, but also because each historical phase of society may be different. As a qualified Marxist and historicist, Li Zehou held that the purpose of morality is to enable the continuation of human existence, and he took today's human society as an outcome of its historical evolution. For Li, the historical context of justice includes not only the different social settings of today, as Sandel has alluded to, but also different types of societies throughout history. Thus, in comparison with Sandel, who launched a sociological argument against Rawls, Li Zehou presents and argument that is anthropological and historicist. Or, to borrow from Jana Rošker, Li's approach is based on his "anthropo-historical ontology."[36] In Li's account of justice, history and culture play important roles. I believe, however, we can go yet another step further in supporting Li Zehou's view. We can go on to the ontological not only in the anthropo-historical sense, but also in the deeply metaphysical and cosmological senses. For that, we need to appeal to the concept of deep harmony.

From the perspective of deep harmony, justice has to be defined in the context of the human condition and the overall environment in which human beings find themselves situated. From this view, the present set of the human condition and its overall environment is not an eternal given, but is rather the outcome of prior processes of harmonization in the world. Had the prior processes of harmonization been different, our present situation would also be different. And thus justice would be different. In primitive societies, polluting the air was simply not a problem because people had not developed such capacities back then. But now, polluting the air has become an issue of justice. Furthermore, on the deep harmony account, the operating mechanism of the atmosphere of the Earth today is an outcome of prior processes of harmony in the cosmological sense; had it been able to absorb pollution instantly and without limits, we would still have no issue of justice with regard to pollution, even if we were to possess the same capacities as today to produce it.

One may wonder, in the context of our discussion of Rawls, Sandel, and Li Zehou, what is the point of appealing to the concept of deep harmony for contextualizing justice? In the direction that Sandel and Li Zehou have worked, the perspective of deep harmony further broadens our horizon and enables us to further see why Rawls's approach falls short in figuring out what justice is. If humanity and indeed the entire world could have been different, our conception of justice would also be different. Merely thinking from the unitary rational mind presently possessed by humanity does not give us a uniform and universal scheme of justice. The view of deep harmony may not directly affect how people pursue justice in society, but it does offer a different philosophical perspective and let us see that harmony is more fundamental than justice and is higher than justice on a conceptual and ontological level.

Now I turn to the issue raised by Erin Cline. Cline detects a tension between justice and harmony. At least in some circumstances, pursuing justice does not promote harmony.[37] In fact, at times justice requires us to breach harmony. How can we account for such a divergence of justice from harmony? Does it mean that justice and harmony are not compatible after all?

I would like to resolve this problem by developing an account of justice along the lines of rule utilitarianism, but on the basis of deep harmony. Utilitarians hold that moral actions are those that maximize utility. If every action maximizes utility, then the totality of all actions will also maximize the overall utility in the world. However, sometimes an action that immediately maximizes utility goes against justice. For instance, sacrificing an innocent person by using his organs to save the lives of five others may maximize utility in the world, but it clearly violates our sense of justice. One way to get around this kind of problem without giving up entirely on the meta-ethic notion of utility is to adopt a different way of counting utility. Therefore, there is rule utilitarianism. Rule utilitarians hold that the overall utility can be maximized when society sets up moral rules for people to follow. The appropriateness of moral rules is determined by whether, in following them, people will act to maximize utility. Once these rules are determined, society can judge the right and wrong of particular actions by seeing whether they conform to them. Even if a particular action does not maximize utility in itself, it is nevertheless moral as long as it conforms to a moral rule, the function of which tends to maximize utility. Take for example the case of sacrificing one healthy individual's life by taking his organs to save the lives of five others. Rule utilitarians do not necessarily deny that such an action in itself may maximize utility. However, they will maintain that such a practice as a rule will not maximize social utility. Instead, a rule that prohibits such a practice will maximize social utility, and therefore such a rule is nevertheless justified on the basis of the principle of utility maximization. On such an account, the principle of utility is used to evaluate moral rules instead of particular actions. Compliance with these rules, therefore, provides the standard for evaluating particular actions. There is a vast amount of literature on rule utilitarianism, both for and against, but it is not my aim to assess rule utilitarianism as an effective moral theory. Here I only tap into its strategy to make an analogous move for my argument of justice in view of deep harmony.

Justice, from the perspective of deep harmony, is manifested in a set of rules that society devises to regulate human behavior for the purpose of overall harmony and harmony in the long run. Under a social system of justice, an action is just if it complies with rules of justice. This is the case even if a particular action that is in compliance with the rules of justice disrupts harmony in a particular situation and context. Take the example from Erin Cline on *Analects* 15.28 again.[38] In Confucius's view, virtuous persons should make a judgment on actions in accordance with the actual situation, even if that goes against the majority and may cause disharmony in the immediate context. Cline's challenge may be addressed in two ways. First, from a Confucian perspective, judging things differently from the majority may not necessarily cause disharmony. Confucius advocated harmony in terms of "harmonizing without homogenizing" (*he er butong* 和而不同).[39] A healthy society should maintain adequate space for people to disagree without causing disharmony. Difference, or "heterogeneity" as quoted earlier, is a necessary component for harmony. Second, even when disagreements may cause disharmony at times, as Cline has rightly observed, as a rule allowing people to disagree will contribute to social harmony in the long run and on a larger scale. Just as in rule utilitarianism, a particular action may not maximize utility in itself, but it is nevertheless a right action as long as it complies with a moral rule that tends to maximize utility.

Ancient Chinese thinkers repeatedly advocated instituting social rules for the sake of harmony, even though they did not directly address the issue in terms of the relation between harmony and justice. For example, the philosopher Shi Bo referred to various efforts by ancient kings to promote harmony, including their "establishment of the nine social rules to uphold pure virtues, and putting together the ten offices to regulate the multitudes." Shi Bo claimed that by doing so the ancient kings "achieved harmony at the highest level."[40]

In ancient China, social rules were mostly in the form of the rules of ritual propriety (li 禮). The *Quli* Chapter of the Confucian classic the *Book of Rites* states, "Without li, there can be no morals or rightness. Without li, there can be no education or correct custom. Without li, there can be no solution to disputes and litigation."[41] The Confucian notion of ritual propriety implies justice in the broad sense, even though it is by no means equivalent to our contemporary concept of justice. Certain forms of li definitely intersect with justice. Such matters in society as determining morals and rightness, and settling disputes and litigation, are matters of justice. For instance, the "Quli" chapter of the *Book of Rites* stipulates that old people in their eighties and nineties are not "to be subjected to corporal punishment even if they have committed crimes."[42] Chapter "Xianggong 19" of the *Zuo Commentary* stipulates the rule against "severe corporal punishment of women."[43]

Xunzi's theory of the establishment of li is relevant to our discussion. Xunzi said,

> From what did rules of ritual propriety arise? I say: Humans are born having desires. When they have desires but do not get the objects of their desire, then they cannot but seek some means of satisfaction. If there is no measure or limit to their seeking, then they cannot help but struggle with each other. If they struggle with each other then there will be chaos, and if there is chaos then they will be impoverished. The former kings hated such chaos, and so they established rules of ritual propriety and yi in order to divide things among people, to nurture their desires, and to satisfy their seeking. They made sure that the pursuit will not be confined to existing material things and material goods will never be depleted by desires, so that the two support each other and grow together. This is how ritual propriety arose.[44]

For Xunzi, without rules of right and wrong, people will contend with one another and society will be in chaos. Establishing social rules is for the purpose of preventing disharmony. Rules of ritual propriety guide society toward harmony. Without rules of ritual propriety, things cannot be done right (*yi* 義). *Yi*, as in the Chinese expression of *zhengyi* 正義 (justice), stands for what is right. It has been translated as "righteousness" in English, even though "rightness" or "appropriateness" may be more apt translations due the religious connotations associated with "righteousness."[45]

Similarly, the "Liqi" 禮器 chapter of the *Book of Rites* 禮記 states that rules of ritual propriety are "the rules for the multitudes; when the rules are loose, the multitudes fall into chaos."[46] Confucius's disciple Youruo 有若 is recorded as saying that "of the functions of the rules of ritual propriety (*li*), harmonization is the [most] precious."[47] In such an understanding, rules of ritual propriety are indeed for the purpose of harmony.

For these ancient Chinese thinkers, rules of justice are justified only if they serve the purpose of achieving social harmony and harmony between humanity and nature in a holistic way and in the long run. For example, criminal law punishes perpetrators for their offenses. Punishment in itself is not harmony. But it gives perpetrators what they deserve and helps to reduce similar offenses in society. In these ways, it contributes to harmony in society. Without criminal law, society will be disharmonious. Seen this way, rules of justice are needed for harmony.

Finally, it may be useful to draw on our own experience to make the point here. This paper was presented at a commemorative conference on Li Zehou organized by the University of Ljubljana on 2 November 2022. At the conference, participants with different academic/cultural backgrounds and different views came together to contribute our ideas and learn from one another. We engaged one another in the discussion and improved our understanding of various issues. Together, we created an important and productive event that could not have been achieved by each participant separately. The conference participants' efforts then led to a book, which recorded their new ideas on the work of Li Zehou and related philosophical issues. This event was one of harmony, and there was an element of justice in the process. We had rules, such as the rule of fifteen minutes for each speaker. We respected one another even when we disagreed. We did not cut others off when they spoke. All of these can be properly characterized in terms of the Confucian *li*. These explicitly and implicitly enforced rules served the purpose of generating a harmonious conference as it happened. Even though we usually do not think of these things in terms of justice, they definitely reflect our sense of justice: to be fair, to maintain equality, to be respectful to one another, and so on. At any rate, the philosophical point is the same: We stuck to these rules even when violating a certain rule at a certain time could yield more benefit, such as, for instance, if we had allowed a particularly interesting speaker to use more time than others in his or her presentation on an important point. We upheld these rules because as a whole they were most conducive to generating a harmonious conference. These rules, however, were not the ultimate purpose of our conference; the conference had a higher goal, to create a productive academic event that can be characterized as harmony. In other words, the participants were not there to enforce these rules for the sake of enforcing them. The rules served a higher purpose of fostering a harmonious academic event.

In discussing his view that harmony is higher than justice, Li Zehou claimed that "harmony 'regulates' and guides justice" (*hexie "fandao" zhengyi* 和谐 "范导" 正义).[48] *Fandao* (范导) literally means "to regulate" (规范) and "to guide" (引导). Li Zehou's claim should be understood at a philosophical or ontological level, rather than on a practical one. It does not mean that each instantiation of justice must contribute to social harmony directly and immediately. Instead, it is that the rules of justice must be established in such a way that they ultimately contribute to harmony. For Li Zehou, this means interpersonal harmony, harmony between the mind and body, and harmony between humanity and nature. Understood as such, my view of the relation between justice and harmony is consistent with that of Li Zehou.

To summarize. On the connections between harmony and justice, I have argued for three points. First, I agree with Li Zehou that harmony is higher than justice because harmony is a higher goal for human society and it takes justice as a precondition for its realization. Second, I hold that harmony is also higher than justice on a conceptual level. Philosophically, harmony is more fundamental than justice because deep harmony provides the ontological grounds for social justice. In this regard, ultimately, rules of justice have to be justified on the grounds of harmony, on how they contribute to social harmony on a larger scale and in the long run. Third and finally, on the level of social practice, even though actions in compliance with justice may not contribute immediately to "local" harmony or harmony in the short run, from a metaethical perspective these actions nevertheless contribute to maintaining rules of justice, which ultimately contribute to harmony in the long run and on a large scale. The last point also serves as a justification for Li Zehou's claim that harmony cannot replace justice and has to be achieved on the basis of justice. In the Confucian view of deep harmony, justice serves the ultimate purpose of harmony.[49]

# Notes

1. Freedom is another concept often perceived as in tension with harmony. For a recent discussion of how freedom can be congruent with harmony, see Philip Pettit, "Freedom and Harmony," in *The Virtue of Harmony*, ed. Chenyang Li and Dascha Düring (New York: Oxford University Press, 2022), 300–25.

2. John Rawls, *A Theory of Justice* (Cambridge, MA: Harvard University Press, 1971), 3.

3. Chenyang Li, *The Confucian Philosophy of Harmony* (London: Routledge, 2014), 120.

4. For a systematic study of Li Zehou's philosophy, see Jana S. Rošker, *Becoming Human: Li Zehou's Ethics* (Leiden: Brill, 2020).

5. "'和谐'属于'以德(教)化民,' '正义'属于'依法治国'。" Li, A Response to Sandel, 46.

6. "我提出'和谐高于正义'是认为：人际和谐、身心和谐、天人和谐（人与自然生态的和谐），它们作为'情理结构'、'关系主义'对现代社会性道德的'范导和适当构建,' 才是维系人类生存延续的最高层也是最根本的'共同善'和'好生活,' 才是'目的'所在。" Li Zehou, *A Response to Sandel*, 46. Translations of Li Zehou are mine unless otherwise indicated. Jana Rošker has translated "范导和适当构建" as "guide by example and appropriately construct" (Rošker, *Becoming Human*, 45).

7. Paul J. D'Ambrosio, "Li Zehou's 'Harmony is Higher than Justice': Context and a Collaborative Future," *Asian Studies* 8, no. 1 (2020): 129.

8. Rošker, *Becoming Human*, 140.

9. Rošker, 81. Here Rošker makes a reference to Li Zehou 李澤厚 and Liu Yuedi 劉悅笛, "Cong 'qing benti' fansi zhengzhi zhexue" 從「情本體」反思政治哲學 (Reflecting on Political Philosophy from "Emotion as Substance"), *Kaifang shidai* 4 (2014): 195.

10. "它高于是非明确、公平合理的'正义,' 但又不能替代正义，而是在'正义'基础上的和谐。所以它只能'范导和适当构建'而不能决定、管辖'正义'。" Li, *A Response to Sandel*, 46.

11. Wang Keping, "Behind Harmony and Justice," *Asian Studies* 8, no. 1 (2020): 103.

12. "有了'正义'才好讲'和谐'。" Li, *A Response to Sandel*, 57.

13. Li, *A Response to Sandel*, 12.

14. Li, *A Response to Sandel*, 59.
15. *Analects*, 15.28.
16. Erin Cline, *Confucius, Rawls, and the Sense of Justice* (New York: Fordham University Press, 2013), 144.
17. Cline, 144.
18. Cline, 144.
19. Dascha Düring, "Connecting Harmony and Justice: Lessons from Feminist Philosophy," *Journal of East-West Thought* 10, no. 2 (2020): 55–56.
20. Düring, "Connecting Harmony and Justice."
21. Joshua Mason, *Justice and Harmony: Cross-Cultural Ideals in Conflict and Cooperation* (Lexington Books, 2022), 255–6.
22. For a comprehensive discussion of these levels of harmony, readers can see Chenyang Li, *The Confucian Philosophy of Harmony* (London: Routledge, 2014).
23. Chenyang Li, *The Confucian Philosophy of Harmony*, 120.
24. Chenyang Li, *The Confucian Philosophy of Harmony*, 9.
25. Chenyang Li, *The Confucian Philosophy of Harmony*, 9.
26. Roger Ames, *Confucian Role Ethics: A Vocabulary* (Honolulu: University of Hawai'i Press, 2011), 84.
27. For a comprehensive account of various meanings of "harmony" in contemporary usages, readers can see Rebecca L. Oxford, "Seeking Linguistic Harmony: Three Perspectives," in *Harmony*, ed. Chenyang Li and Dascha Düring (New York: Oxford University Press, 2022), 279–301.
28. For more discussion of the active characteristic of deep harmony, readers can see Chenyang Li, "Active Harmony and Passive Harmony," in *Harmony in Chinese Thought: A Philosophical Introduction*, ed. Chenyang Li, Sai Hang Kwok, and Dascha Düring (Lanham, MD: Rowman and Littlefield, 2021), 41–56.
29. Chenyang Li, *The Confucian Philosophy of Harmony*, 28–29, 167–68.
30. "無晦無明，未有陰陽。陰陽未定，吾未有以名。今始判為兩，分為陰陽，離為四時。" Chen Guying, Huangdi Si jing *jin zhu jinyi* 黃帝四經今註今譯 (*A Contemporary Annotation, Interpretation and Commentary on the Four Classics of the Yellow Emperor*) (Beijing: Shangwu chuban she, 2007), 210.
31. "恆先之初，迥同太虛。虛同為一，恆一而止. . . . 一者其号也。虛其舍也，无为其素也，和其用也。" Quoted from Chen's annotations of the original text, Chen, 399, 402.
32. Ding Sixin 丁四新, "Benti zhi dao de lunshuo—lun boshu *Dao yuan* de zhexue sixiang" 本體之道的論說—論帛書《道原》的哲學思想 (*A Theory of the Dao of Reality: Philosophy in the Silk Text Dao-Yuan*), in *Xianqin zhexue tan* 先秦哲学探索 (*Explorations in Pre-Qin Philosophy*) (Beijing: Shangwu Chubanshe, 2015), 330–55.
33. Michael J. Sandel, *Liberalism and the Limits of Justice* (Cambridge: Cambridge University Press, 1998), 31.

34. Similarly, Aristotle famously held that there is no need for justice between friends (*Nicomachean Ethics*, Book VIII, Chapter 1).

35. "'正义'不是来自个体之间的约定,而是来自群体生存的历史情境。" Li, *A Response to Sandel*, 20. Here Li Zehou uses *zhengyi* (正义) to translate the English word "justice" as used by Sandel (Li, *A Response to Sandel*, 19). He also holds, however, that *gongzheng* (公正) may be a more appropriate translation (Li, *A Response to Sandel*, 19).

36. Rošker, *Becoming Human*, 7.

37. Cline, *Confucius, Rawls, and the Sense of Justice*, 144.

38. Cline, 144.

39. *Analects*, 13.23.

40. "建九紀以立純德,合十數以訓百體 . . . 夫如是,和之至也。" Lai Kehong, *Guoyu zhi jie* 國語直解 (*The Guoyu Explicated*) (Shanghai: Fudan University Press, 2000), 746–47. People often follow the annotator Wei Zhao 韋昭 (201–273 CE) and interpret *ji* 紀 as physical "organs." However, saying that ancient kings "established nine physical organs" hardly makes sense, unless the term is used as a metaphor. I translate *ji* as rules. For other uses of *ji* as rules in ancient texts, see my next reference to the *Book of Rites*.

41. *Shisan jing zhushu* 十三經注疏 (*Thirteen Classics with Commentaries*) (Beijing: Zhonghua shuju, 1985), 1231.

42. *Thirteen Classics*, 1232.

43. *Thirteen Classics*, 1968.

44. Xunzi, Chapter 19; *Xunzi: The Complete Text*, trans. Eric L. Hutton (Princeton: Princeton University Press, 2014), 201, modified.

45. Another ancient discussion of rules that gets close to the sense of justice is found in the "Lunwei" 論威 chapter of *Lüshi chunqiu* (吕氏春秋): "*Yi* is the principle for the myriad affairs" (義也者,萬事之紀也).

46. "眾之紀也,紀散而眾亂。" *Thirteen Classics*, 1434.

47. *Analects*, 1.12. Youruo's statement can also be interpreted as meaning that, when practicing *li*, we must not violate harmony. For additional discussion of *li* in relation to harmony, readers can see Chenyang Li, *The Confucian Philosophy of Harmony*, chapter 4.

48. Li, *A Response to Sandel*, 115.

49. This paper was presented at the conference "Remembering Li Zehou," organized by the University of Ljubljana on 2 November 2022. I am grateful to the participants, especially Karl-Heinz Pohl, Gregor Paul, Michael Nylan, and Roger Ames, for their comments and constructive criticisms. I am particularly grateful to Jana Rošker, who organized the conference and provided not only constructive comments at the conference but also detailed and insightful suggestions for the revision of this paper. The research of this paper was supported by a grant from the Singapore Ministry of Education (#RG114/20).

# Bibliography

Ames, Roger T. *Confucian Role Ethics: A Vocabulary*. Hong Kong: Chinese University Press, 2011.

Chen Guying 陳鼓應. *Huangdi Si jing jin zhu jinyi* 黃帝四經今註今譯 (*A Contemporary Annotation, Interpretation and Commentary on the Four Classics of the Yellow Emperor*). Beijing: Shangwu Chubanshe 商務出版社, 2007.

Cline, Erin. *Confucius, Rawls, and the Sense of Justice*. New York: Fordham University Press, 2013.

D'Ambrosio, Paul J. "Li Zehou's 'Harmony is Higher than Justice': Context and a Collaborative Future." *Asian Studies* 8, no. 1 (2020): 127–46.

Ding, Sixin 丁四新. "Benti zhi dao de lunshuo—lun boshu *Dao yuan* de zhexue sixiang" 本體之道的論說—論帛書《道原》的哲學思想 (A Theory of the Dao of Reality: Philosophy in the Silk Text *Dao-Yuan*). In *Xianqin zhexue tan* 先秦哲學探索 (*Explorations in Pre-Qin Philosophy*), 330–55. Beijing: Shangwu chuban she, 2015.

Düring, Dascha. "Connecting Harmony and Justice: Lessons from Feminist Philosophy." *Journal of East-West Thought* 10, no. 2 (2020): 45–64.

Lai Kehong 來可弘. *Guoyu zhi jie* 國語直解 (*The Guoyu Explicated*). Shanghai: Fudan University Press, 2000.

Li, Chenyang. "Active Harmony and Passive Harmony." In *Harmony in Chinese Thought: A Philosophical Introduction*, edited by Chenyang Li, Sai Hang Kwok, and Dascha Düring, 41–56. Lanham, MD: Rowman and Littlefield, 2021.

Li, Chenyang. *The Confucian Philosophy of Harmony*. London: Routledge, 2014.

Li Zehou 李澤厚. *Huiying Sangde'er ji qita* 回應桑德爾及其他 (*A Response to Sandel and Other Matters*). Beijing: Sanlian Bookstore, 2014.

Li Zehou 李澤厚 and Liu Yuedi 劉悅笛. "Cong 'qing benti' fansi zhengzhi zhexue" 從「情本體」反思政治哲學 (Reflecting on Political Philosophy from "Emotion as Substance"). *Kaifang shidai* 4 (2014): 194–215.

Mason, Joshua. *Justice and Harmony: Cross-Cultural Ideals in Conflict and Cooperation*. Blue Ridge Summit: Lexington Books, 2022.

Oxford, Rebecca L. "Seeking Linguistic Harmony: Three Perspectives." In *The Virtue of Harmony*, edited by Chenyang Li and Dascha Düring, 279–301. New York: Oxford University Press, 2022.

Pettit, Philip. "Freedom and Harmony." In *The Virtue of Harmony*, edited by Chenyang Li and Dascha Düring, 300–25. New York: Oxford University Press, 2022.

Rawls, John. *A Theory of Justice*. Cambridge, MA: Harvard University Press, 1971.

Rošker, Jana S. *Becoming Human: Li Zehou's Ethics*. Leiden: Brill, 2020.

Sandel, Michael J. *Liberalism and the Limits of Justice*, 2nd ed. Cambridge: Cambridge University Press, 1998.

*Shisan jing zhushu* 十三經注疏 (*Thirteen Classics with Commentaries*). Beijing: Zhonghua shuju, 1985.

Wang Keping. "Behind Harmony and Justice." *Asian Studies* 8, no. 1 (2020): 101–25.

Xunzi. *Xunzi: The Complete Text*. Translated by Eric L. Hutton. Princeton: Princeton University Press, 2014.

# Part 4

# Humanist Harmony and Limitless Equilibrium

# 9

# Emotion as Substance
## A Concrete Humanist Moral Framework

Robert A. Carleo III

Li Zehou's theory of "emotion as substance" is often misunderstood—partly due to its peculiar conceptions of both emotion and substance. The principal meaning of the theory is that concrete, lived and felt relations constitute the source and grounds of human reason, values, and ways of life. Within Confucian tradition, this presents a distinguished version of concrete humanism, as opposed to the more common (but philosophically problematic) versions of Confucian cosmic idealism. Below I explain this and attempt to show that the insights and theoretical framework of "emotion as substance" offer a valuable foundation for moral thinking today.

## "Emotion" Is Not Just Emotion

What is "emotion"? This is not a straightforward question in Anglophone philosophy. The Anglo-American "philosophy of emotions" struggled, from its founding, with the "notorious" proposal of distinguishing a class of phenomena called "emotions" from other affective states such as "motives, moods, and attitudes."[1] The question becomes even more complex—but also more fruitful—when investigated in terms of the

Chinese term *qing* 情. This is the term for "emotion" in Li Zehou's theory of "emotion as substance."

The richness and manifold nature of the term *qing* is well documented, although what exactly to make of it is a matter of (productive, and sometimes creative) philosophical dispute. In simple and general terms, we can see *qing* as possessing three basic connotations: emotion, environment, and essence. Liu Yuedi writes that *qing* "has the meanings of genuineness (情實), feeling or emotion (情感), and temperament (情性)."[2] Angus C. Graham authored a pivotal study explicating the term's early meaning of "the facts," "genuine," and "genuinely."[3] Cai Zongqi traces the development of the concept of *qing* in early China from the essential substance, reality, and constitutive nature of concrete phenomena to people's emotions and feelings, with the latter eventually mostly eclipsing the former.[4] Chenyang Li points out that in just the *Xunzi* the term *qing* possesses multiple connotations: "factual truth," "sincerity," and "emotions."[5]

Explaining these manifold connotations of *qing* has become something of a sport among Anglophone scholars. Regarding the dual definitions of the character as "affections-feelings" and "circumstance-facts," Chad Hansen notes, "On its face, this admixture is puzzling."[6] The two concepts are separate and often opposite in modern Western thought, the subjective quality of felt experience being typically contrasted to the objective nature of facts and environment. As Roger T. Ames and David L. Hall put it, "How can the same term mean both the facts of a situation and the feelings or emotions that attend it—both fact and value?"[7] The seemingly unrelated nature of these dual connotations suggests independent semantic meanings, similar to how "bat" can refer to a piece of sports equipment or a flying nocturnal mammal—that is, as homonyms. Hansen, however, is troubled by the implied presumption that the term thus "changes meaning" across the different uses it developed over time, which he sees as unlikely to have been the case.[8] Instead, we should recognize a "soft curve" connecting the two meanings: essence denotes what is truly the case and emotions respond to that same reality, and thereby the two meanings are connected as input and response. Brian Bruya instead connects the various meanings of *qing*—more multifarious in his account—through the cosmological dimensions attributed to emotions in the classical period[9] (an essential feature of early Chinese thought Li Zehou describes as its "emotional cosmology"). Michael Puett proposes that the term was just continuously (re-)appropriated by diverse thinkers of the pre-Qin period who each deployed it in ways that suit their particular philosophical needs, thus bestowing diverse semantic content on the single term.[10] These robust analyses, textual and conceptual, seek to answer how concepts entirely separate in English came to share residence in a single classical Chinese word.

On reflection, however, even those of us steeped in Anglophone semantics recognize that our (empirical) experience of and connection to circumstance, including the observable "facts" of our environment, occurs sensibly. These sensations are felt. They are also the medium of connection to our environment and others. Moreover, we judge what is true, authentic, and real via what we sense (e.g., in empirical observation) and what we feel (e.g., how I feel reveals my authentic self). Sensory perception, as our access to reality, is in vital dimensions always affective.[11] These senses differ from abstract "reason"—although they may plausibly be considered both the basis of that reason and shaped by it—and integrate with emotion: they are lived and felt, embodied and enacted, constituted by and constitutive of our relations to others. The concrete, situated, and sensible quality of human life connects environment, feelings, and facts.

From this we see that our connections to the world, to what is real, and especially to other people are inherently and essentially situated and sensible. *Qing* denotes the felt experience through which we relate to others and engage with the world.

## "Emotion" and "Substance" in Li Zehou's Theory of Emotion as Substance

Unsurprisingly, then, *qing* in Li Zehou's theory of *qing benti* 情本體 is not merely a matter of feelings. Li states clearly, "This 'emotion' (*qing*) is feelings (*qinggan* 情感) as well as circumstance (*qingjing* 情境),"[12] and elsewhere, explaining the relations between *qing*, morals, and reason in this theory, he makes sure to gloss *qing* with these same dual meanings.[13]

In addition to "emotion" (*qing*) not referring simply to feelings, "substance" is not the typical philosopher's notion of "substance." The term for substance, *benti* 本體, is common philosophical parlance in modern Chinese denoting noumenon and ultimate reality. These uses of the term are firmly rooted in traditional use of the terms *ben* and *ti* to denote metaphysical and ontologically fundamental concepts. Li, however, declares an explicit break with that orthodox dimension of tradition, proclaiming that the theory of emotion as substance "is equivalent to there being no *benti*" in the metaphysical sense. *Benti* in the theory of *qing benti* "is no longer the traditional sense of '*benti*.'" It "is not noumenon, but rather the root"; it is not a metaphysical concept but simply declares what is of "fundamental value."[14]

Thus, *qing benti* does not refer to a metaphysics of feelings, or even to feelings being ontologically fundamental, despite common misconceptions. These misconceptions persist notwithstanding Prof. Li's repeated, explicit corrections: positing *qing* as *benti* affirms that situated, lived and felt human experience is foundational to his ethical theory.

Perhaps the most direct way of explaining this is through Li's diagram of "Four Arrows" (fig. 9.1).

This simplistic schema of Li's ethics places *qing* at either extreme, here translated differentially as "emotion" on the right and "emotionality" on the left. In proposing that we see *qing* as *benti*, Li is primarily referring to *qing* as he uses the term here on the extreme left ("emotionality"), where it refers to "the circumstance (*qingjing*) of the living existence of the entire community."[15] The model of "Four Arrows" depicts the development of morality and reason from these basic communal conditions of lived and felt human interaction through social norms, which come to shape individual psychology. As Li summarily puts it, "social norms ('ritual') are rooted in concrete and emotional situatedness (*qing* 情) and go on to produce reason (*li* 理). Yet it is this reason, and not emotion, that governs individual moral action. In terms of the community, ritual (ethics) come from emotionality (as situated and felt circumstance), whereas in terms of the individual, reason governs emotions."[16] The ultimate foundation of ethics, then, is this *qing*—not as mere feelings

Figure 9.1. General schema of Li Zehou's ethics. *Source*: Jana S. Rošker, *Following His Own Path: Li Zehou and Contemporary Chinese Thought*. Used with permission.

| Ethics (external, cultural activities, the content of social historical period) | → | Morals (internal, human psychology or nature, individual psychological forms) |   |   |
|---|---|---|---|---|
| History |  | Education |  | Governance |
| Emotionality (the circumstances of communal existence) | → Ritual Regulations (customs, norms, institutions, social order, laws) | → ←---- | Reason (the will and conceptual thought) | → Emotion (individual emotions and desires, conduct) |
| Political Philosophy |  |  |  | Moral Psychology |

but rather as the medium of human experience and activity. This is mediated by the "reason" that develops therein. This reason is not metaphysical but rather psychological internalization of concrete patterns of communicative thinking that develop in communal life and structure individual cognition. Reason reigns supreme within the individual, but it is ultimately based in concrete communal life.

Qing benti, "emotion as substance," is, then, a theory that roots morality (and much more) in situated, lived and felt human experience. "Emotion," as qing, ties us to the world of things, of our communities and traditions, of science and technology, of politics, and of family, friends, colleagues, and homes. These connections denoted by qing are not purely of feeling, but also, as Li is ever at pains to point out, rationally, discursively structured. Thus, the following set of brief clarificatory remarks.

*"Emotion" as "substance" is a version of moral rationalism.* Li's theory of "emotion as substance" is a form of rationalism,[17] just one rooted in and affirming the essential roles of emotion and situated, sensible experience—both as the experiential basis of morals and as the affective components of human psychology. While communal qing gives rise to reason, the exercise of that reason is a necessary and perhaps sufficient condition of morality (being moral), which is in turn a necessary and perhaps sufficient condition of humanity (being human). Qing as individual feelings remain an ever present although ancillary and non-essential component of human morality; they are shaped and governed by moral reason. In this schema, qing in its two forms, communal and individual, flanks the interrelationship between external social norms and reason in personal psychology. This affirms that reason is ultimately rooted in and always interrelated with sensible social life—even as it plays a unique, prioritized role therein.

*It is also Confucian relationism.* Recognition of the fundamentality of actual, lived and felt human interrelations is, in Li's view, a crucial ethical insight that lies at the core of Confucian tradition. This "relationist" (guanxizhuyi 關係主義) view, for Li, offers a philosophically superior framework for understanding the nature of morality, one that provides a more cogent account of what constitutes good and bad. That is, it offers a workable second-order moral theory with immense explanatory and practical power.

*This Confucian relationism endorses liberal individualism.* Relationism is, of course, the counterpoint of individualism. "Relationism and individualism, representative of China and the West, respectively . . . set them on two separate paths: one integrating emotion with reason and the other focused on reason alone."[18] Yet Li affirms that, as a substantive, first-order (that is, action-guiding) ethic, individualism is nothing to sneeze at. The second-order relational framework, in fact, endorses individualism as a superior first-order ethic today: modern liberal individualism, with its emphases on fairness, human rights, and individual freedoms, is a set of ethical principles—including social norms and political morality—developed for and suited to modern life. They serve human well-being today, given modern societal and technological conditions. Unfortunately, most moral individualism, and indeed most philosophical debate over it, takes it as a second-order theory. This is, in Li's view, problematic. It is a mistake to take individualism as foundational, as it provides first principles from which we can and often do arrive at moral commitments that fail to serve human welfare and even blind us to it. This is the same charge that concrete humanists lodge at cosmic idealists within Confucian tradition more broadly (see below). (Note: It also parallels a charge that critics of natural rights lodge at rights theorists within liberal tradition,[19] and that some "communitarians" have lodged at "liberals" within what Li sees as the broader tradition of Western individualism.)

*"History enters metaphysics."* The model of "Four Arrows" links Li's proposal of "emotion as substance" to his "anthropo-historical ontology," in which humans themselves are the source and grounding of their being. Herein, the beliefs about reality that fundamentally constitute and shape that human experience and practice are culturally sedimented. This sedimentation gives us individually and culturally affirmed metaphysical beliefs, and these beliefs themselves are what constitute metaphysics. In this embodied (concrete, practical) psychologism and anthropocentrism, "history enters metaphysics." In other words, ideas generated through human culture are taken to be a priori in people's minds. The sedimented beliefs of human cultures do not perceive or reflect independent metaphysical reality but rather create it. Any set of beliefs, moreover, is never fully determined or determinative, but rather always open to alteration and influence.

## Concrete Humanism

This theory, I believe, offers a comprehensive, cohesive, robust, and unique form of concrete humanism. Concrete humanist outlooks have been a crucial although not orthodox tradition of Chinese Confucian thinking throughout history, a sometimes complementary and sometimes critical alternative to the more common cosmic idealist versions of Confucian thought. For the concrete humanist, right and wrong are products of empirical and sensible human life. There are no cosmic, absolute, universal, unchanging, or transcendent forms of reason and moral truth. The moral and epistemic projects are thus not matters of discovering, understanding, embodying, or carrying out a priori, cosmic moral principles, patterns, imperatives, and prescriptions. Rather, morals and reason are themselves products of sedimentation, historically formed through human cultures.

Let me briefly outline the two camps in broad strokes, along with Li's charges against the former set of theorists.

## Cosmic Idealism

Li rejects the traditionally orthodox formulations of Confucianism as cosmic idealism, that is, as affirming ontological and metaphysical truths and ideals that transcend concrete human experience and practice. The most celebrated and influential modern spokesperson for this camp of Confucian theory is also Li's main ideological target: New Confucian theorist Mou Zongsan, whose "moral metaphysics" has deep roots in the earlier idealism of Song and Ming Neo-Confucian theorists. The earlier Neo-Confucians asserted various conceptions of "humaneness" (*ren* 仁) as a metaphysical entity consisting in heavenly "principle" (*li* 理) and/or a cosmic heart-mind (*xin* 心) further identified with the distinctive humanness or "nature" (*xing* 性) of every person. The Neo-Confucians thus posited the pure "*Dao* heart-mind" (*dao xin* 道心) to contrast to the corrupt and corporeal (that is, lived and felt) "human heart-mind" (*ren xin* 人心). They likewise conceived of a heavenly, cosmic component of human "nature" (*tiandi zhi xing* 天地之性) consisting in pure "principle" to contrast to our impure (*zhuo* 濁) embodied humanness (*qizhi zhi xing* 氣質之性). The adulation of abstracts and denigration of concrete humanity is stark.

## Li's Rejection of Cosmic Idealism

Li voiced serious reservations about the cosmic idealist versions of Confucianism that have largely claimed orthodoxy for themselves. Their metaphysical and ontological commitments are unsuccessful attempts at exploratory speculation: "Song-Ming Neo-Confucianism's striving toward transcendent or transcendental rational *benti* as 'heavenly principle' and '*Dao* heart-mind,' despite its impassioned efforts, ultimately failed."[20] The main problem is incoherence. "The fundamental Neo-Confucian concept of '*ren*' (humaneness) . . . is both beyond the natural and itself natural, both *a priori* reason and actual experience," and both sides of these dualisms cannot hold at once.[21] The dualistic conception of *benti* at the heart of Song Confucianism founds it on a "contradiction," which "harbored the potentiality for the breakdown of the entirety of Neo-Confucianism."[22] As Li puts it, "Neo-Confucianism . . . emphasizes that *dao* heart-mind and human heart-mind are nevertheless one and the same heart-mind. There are a great many other examples like these, where transcendent ontological substance (*benti*) is unable to be fully separated from empirical reality. Neo-Confucian speculative theory is therefore unable to ultimately succeed. . . . However, in terms of social practice, Song-Ming Neo-Confucianism has actually proven successful due to its long-term inheritance of the shamanistic-historical tradition."[23] The internal inconsistency of Neo-Confucian *theory* was counteracted—and the Confucian tradition persisted—only through the situated, emotional, and communal nature of that tradition's shamanistic and historicist foundations.

The nature of Li's theory of emotion as substance and the substance of his criticism and rejection of cosmic idealist versions of Confucianism have been overlooked by many of the responses to his proposal, including creative and fruitful ones.[24]

## Concrete Humanism

Li Zehou's rejection of these moral metaphysical constructs is situated within a long-standing and influential, albeit non-orthodox, sub-tradition of Confucian philosophy. This tradition forgoes, and often explicitly rejects, the prioritization of metaphysical concepts in favor of focus on the well-being and, indeed, emotional lives of actual human persons.[25]

A short list of influential figures in the concrete humanist strand of later Confucian philosophy includes, in chronological order, Dai Zhen, Liang Shuming, Xu Fuguan, and Yang Guorong. Each emphasizes the fundamentality of concrete human life and rejects the idealization of abstractions in his own way. Perhaps the most explicit in this regard is Xu Fuguan. Xu rejects the transcendent New Confucian moral metaphysic originated by Xiong Shili and developed by Xiong's students Tang Junyi and especially Mou Zongsan.[26] At the heart of his objections is the observation that idealized abstractions and general principles can direct, motivate, and falsely justify harmful practices. Like Li, he believes the classical thinkers had it right and the later Neo-Confucian reinterpretations of them are where things went wrong. For example, Mencius "took the 'ritual and rightness,' which Ruists had emphasized, and subordinated them to the needs of people's actual lives, making ritual and rightness exist for human life instead of making human life exist for ritual and rightness."[27] Why is this important? Abstractions lead us away from moral truth, which is always concretely embedded in people's actual well-being. "Any high-sounding ism or doctrine can feign utility; only the needs of people's actual lives cannot be faked."[28] The hard check on right or wrong is human welfare. (As I point out below, the same Confucian principle can be applied to rights and freedoms.)

Xu's contemporary Liang Shuming and, long before them, Dai Zhen gave similar accounts of Confucian morality that embrace the primacy of epistemic and normative appeal to concrete persons. Liang draws on a similar conception of *qing* and the integration *qing* and *li* (as reason) in proposing this interpretation of Confucian morality.[29] Dai Zhen focuses instead on reconceptualizing *li* (moral principle, pattern, coherence)[30] to be constituted by concrete patterns of lived and felt human relations.[31] Moral "principle" does not exist in the mind but rather just is the balance of emotions in human community.[32] More recently, Yang Guorong has formulated a "concrete metaphysics" and "philosophy of affairs" that emphasize situated human discourse as the dynamic foundation of meaning generally and the good specifically.[33]

Li occasionally identifies with this tradition by drawing on or referencing Dai, Liang, and Xu. Mostly, though, he develops this outlook from classical Confucianism, to which he attributes the second-order framework of "emotion as substance." Herein, he prioritizes Xunzi (whereas Dai and Xu emphasize Mencius[34]):

> My own theory of sedimentation (*jidianlun* 積澱論) explains the *a priori* as the accumulation and consolidation of human experience (what I refer to as "experience becoming a priori" [*jingyan bian xianyan* 經驗變先驗]). This of course sides with Xunzi. Mencius discusses "emotions" (*qing*) in terms of an innate and *a priori* "heart-mind of compassion," and

contemporary scholars such as Donald Munro interpret this as the feelings (*qing*) of natural biology. However, the type of "emotion" that Xunzi and I talk about are different from these conceptions. We understand emotion to be infused with reason.[35]

But Li also appreciates Mencius. He does so in a non-orthodox way that prioritizes a classical rather than Neo-Confucian reading:

> I . . . understand Mencius's elevation of the feeling of compassion to become the foundation or starting point of "humaneness" as the "comprehensive virtue," which directs people to pursue, establish, and realize the meaningfulness of the "Way of heaven" in human life, and to do so in a deeply emotional manner and within the historical processes of tragedy and happiness of human life lived within its concrete limits. Precisely for this reason, history enters metaphysics to form an aesthetic metaphysics. This is Mencius's tremendous contribution to the emotional worldview of China's shamanistic-historical tradition, in which no personal god arises. We can top off my construction of an anthropological historical ontology with this. This is an extraordinarily high appraisal of Mencius.[36]

This appreciation of Mencius stands in contrast to the Neo-Confucian "elevation" of humaneness as a metaphysical principle and even entity—the precise object of other concrete humanists' criticisms of Neo-Confucian teachings. Li here breaks from orthodoxy to assert that the primary virtue of humane compassion resides within the concrete "historical processes" of lived and felt human life.

SEDIMENTATION—CULTURE AS CONFLUENCE

Li describes these historical processes as culturally accumulative—a component of his thinking that he describes as the "theory of sedimentation." This sedimentation is best understood in terms of a river. Cultures are like water, the flowing of which constitutes history. What is sedimented shapes the river: It *is* the bedrock and banks—the river's present (as well as past and future) contours. A river is thus defined by and through its sedimentation. At the same time, that sedimentation is always actively reshaped by the river. The thing defined (river) itself actively shapes its own definition (sedimented bedrock and banks).

This presents also the framework of classical Confucian teachings, wherein the "Way," *dao*, is a matter of cultural inheritance that is at every point shaped by and shaping the lives that constitute it. As Roger T. Ames and Henry Rosemont Jr. put it, for the early Confucians, "to realize the *dao* is to experience, to interpret, and to influence the world in such a way as to reinforce and extend the way of life inherited from one's cultural predecessors."[37] This Way is collectively determined. It is also a confluence of smaller components—diverse currents within a single river. At its most expansive, the river ("Way") may be thought of as the confluence of all currents of human culture. In a sense, this has already happened. Once-independent tributaries have now largely converged into a single stream shaped by their interaction, each still partly independent and exerting influence on the others while itself influenced by them.

The distinctive sedimentation of Chinese tradition is founded in the early shamanistic politics that precede "Confucian" tradition and laid its foundation. As David N. Keightley describes,

> It was the Shang . . . that literati of the Zhou and Han . . . came to regard as one of the dynastic models upon which later versions of the Chinese polity were founded. Modern research generally confirms that judgment. The oracle-bone inscriptions indicate the degree to which the Late Shang kings and their diviners articulate many of the concerns that were to be central to the classical Chinese tradition. In many cases they appear to have provided solutions that proved seminal.[38]

The artisan-divinatory leadership of the Shang shaman-kings, functioning through the emotional and relational practices of ritual and music, produced a system of societal relations that "were among the *great emotional resources* of the evolving state, in which religion and kin were inseparable from secular and political activities."[39] Prof. Li elaborates on how these components of classical thinking affirm a concrete humanist rather than cosmic idealist framework:

> The reason that certain qualities of "shamanism" are important is that the history of humans, as participants alongside heaven and earth in co-creation, possesses a sacred quality. In this way, it is only the "Way of humans" that can possibly be the "Way of heaven." And it is in this that we see history enter metaphysics. Seeking the "Way of heaven" from within history is a matter of significant difficulty. Yet historical ontology, which takes "humans living" as its first premise, still aims to reiterate this fundamental point of view.[40]

This, Li's affirmation of China's "shamanistic-historical tradition" and theory of sedimentation are part and parcel of his concrete humanism, wherein "metaphysics" is no more than particular sets of ideological commitments held by actual, historical persons and cultures.

Metaphysics is part and parcel of humans living, a sort of transcendental illusion that arises within human life to help structure and guide it.[41] This involves beliefs and forms of reason that empirically *occur* among people—inherited and debated among us, shaping our thought and life—but that have no empirically verifiable basis. "Reason arose from" and "history was established from" the inventive practices of human life.[42] In this view, moreover, reason and history will continue to develop through the innovative technologies, institutions, and ideas of "humans living." How we guide these developments is the ultimate—and ultimately meaningful—role of reason and morals.

Thus, Li Zehou's historicism and theory of sedimentation integrate with his theory of "emotion as substance" in establishing a comprehensive framework that places situated human agency at the source of value and meaning. This is what I call Li's concrete humanism, and what seems to be the main intention of promoting "emotion as substance."

## The Highest Good

As with other Confucian concrete humanists, this prioritizes actual human well-being over abstract moral principles and values. That is, it subordinates the validity of any substantive morality to its contribution to human flourishing, wherein the ever-developing conditions of lived and felt human life gradually shift what principles and values, as well as what norms and institutions, are valid (or good). This posits the highest or supreme good to lie in "the continuation of the living existence of the totality of humankind."[43] This gives an absolute (meta-)criterion for evaluating disparate particular moralities across time and place: we look to the concrete conditions of actual circumstance. Objective validation of good and bad, right and wrong, is provided not by metaphysical truths, principles, or powers, but rather by concrete humanity itself. "There is absoluteness in the notion of 'supreme goodness' as the preservation of human existence. As it serves as original fundamental value (or ontological value, *benti jiazhi* 本體價值), it does not require connection to divine intention, the will of Heaven, or God. This is basically my 'metaphysics.' I fill the blank space left by 'the death of God' with 'the continuous extension of human existence.'"[44] Historical and moral progress must therefore be not only recognized and accounted for, but also worked toward. This is what Li's ethics, based in "emotion as substance," tasks us with today: we must evaluate not only particular policies and actions, but also the principles and values we use to evaluate policies and actions, to ensure these promote well-being today and tomorrow.

## Emotion as Substance Today and Tomorrow

In times of extraordinary societal, cultural, and technological change, we must critically assess what worked in the past so as to judiciously apply it today, and we must remain vigilant as to whether what works today will serve well tomorrow. This situation is further complicated in many societies where, as in China, adapting to "modern" conditions means not only developing new technological and social institutions but also endorsing a new set of values, principles, and metaphysical commitments at stark odds with known values and beliefs. Li writes,

> At present China faces unprecedented social change. The rural population is urbanizing on a tremendous scale, and the free exchange of labor and contractual principles are "liberating" the individual both materially and spiritually from one's family, clan, and village. Daily life is being comprehensively modernized, the traditional family undermined, and familial clanship ceasing to exist entirely. The traditional institutions and spiritual guidance of the "three cardinal relations and six major virtues" (*sangang liuji* 三綱六紀) cannot be revitalized or reemerge. Individual equality, freedom, independence, and

rights have replaced traditional relationism (*guanxi zhuyi* 關係主義) and role ethics. Where do we look, then, in search of a foundation for Chinese virtue ethics?

This has already become a major issue. It seems to me the only solutions lie in promoting the outlook of "emotion as substance" (*qing benti* 情本體) and appreciating the emotions of human psychology, and in transformative creation of how we shape emotions and psychology based in the constitutive principles of ethical roles and relations.[45]

The subtext here is that modern values and principles—"individual equality, freedom, independence, and rights"—rightly come to predominate under modern societal conditions. But as a Confucian culture experiences them, it is clear that though they are good, they are not exclusively or supremely good. Many values and goods are left in the dust, lost to the empty spaces between atomic individuals.

For Li, "the Confucian tradition of emotion as substance" is integrated with its "one-world" outlook, which "sees the interpersonal human relations of daily life as the true substance (*benti*) that human existence cannot do without."[46] The "interpersonal emotions of caring in relationships between parent and child, spouses, siblings, and friends within this 'one-world' view" involve affective connections that "themselves constitute substance."[47] In Li's hands, the concrete humanism of Confucian tradition's taking situated emotional relations (*qing*) as what is most fundamental (*benti*) turns toward prioritizing human welfare. This reaffirms the tradition and its emphasis on felt human experience and situated relationality, and it endorses individual rights and freedoms in service of these.

In this view, we need "emotion as substance" not only to affirm but also to regulate rights and freedoms. One role of this second-order framework is practical:

> We might ask whether freedom of religious belief means that someone should be free to believe in malevolent and harmful doctrines. How do we differentiate between good or acceptable religious teachings and evil or harmful ones? In terms of welfare, what level of material assistance is appropriate, or should we oppose it altogether? Should military service be voluntary or compulsory? If we have freedom of the press, should this include pornography? In these and many other cases, we face

the challenge of measuring and balancing benefit and harm as well as questions of how to coordinate or harmonize formal and substantial justice when they conflict. In such cases, even small errors of judgment can have severe consequences.[48]

On the many questions of which rights, freedoms, and considerations of equality have priority when they conflict with each other and with other obvious goods, we have to look beyond those values for guidance. "Emotion as substance" can provide that guidance.

An additional role of this theory is justificatory. How can we affirm the priority of human rights and freedoms to the increasingly powerful and vocal proponents of traditional "Asian values," for instance, who have no reason to adopt the foundational metaphysical commitments of liberal individualism? By pointing out that reasonable implications of their own comprehensive commitments also endorse these rights and freedoms. Confucians are committed to the promotion of moral and social norms and institutions that foster human welfare, and under modern conditions certain individual rights and freedoms most effectively do so.

So we can affirm modern liberal morality on a Confucian basis. The "deep structures" of Confucianism—and traditional Confucian philosophy—support modern liberal principles, rights, and freedoms insofar as these morals and institutions support and promote human well-being and flourishing. This offers a new (and old) fundamentally Confucian basis for endorsing rights and freedoms. It embraces and affirms Western "modernity"—at least what is good about it, insofar as it *is* good. While the "modern social morals" of liberal individualism, rights, and freedoms are overriding for Li Zehou, they are not overriding eternally. This is his fundamental, radical Confucianism: for this time and place, liberal individualism is good—and that can and will change. We cannot blindly adhere to individualist rights-based thinking in the face of emerging global challenges. Consider: world hunger, climate change, global health, artificial intelligence, genetic screening and editing, animal rights, robot rights, social media—we must endorse rights and freedoms *humanely*, shaped by concrete human welfare and flourishing.

## Notes

1. Amélie Oksenberg Rorty, ed., *Explaining Emotions* (Berkeley: University of California Press, 1980), 1; Amélie Oksenberg Rorty, "Enough Already with

'Theories of the Emotions,'" in *Thinking about Feeling: Contemporary Philosophers on Emotions*, ed. Robert C. Solomon (Oxford: Oxford University Press, 2004), 269.

2. Liu Yuedi, "Integrating and Inheriting Mencius and Xunzi through 'The Mind Unifying and Governing *Qing* and Human Nature': On the Integration of Mencius's 'Heaven–Human Nature–*Qing*–Mind' with Xunzi's 'Heaven–*Qing*–Human Nature–Mind.'" *Confucian Academy: Chinese Thought and Culture Review* 7, no. 2 (2020): 21; see also Liu Yuedi 劉悅笛, "'Qingxing' 'qingshi' he 'qinggan': Zhongguo Rujia 'qing ben zhexue' de jiben mianxiang" "情性" "情實" 和 "情感"—中國儒家 "情本哲學" 的基本面向 (Genuineness, Emotion, and Temperament: Basic Facets of Chinese Confucian Ontology of *Qing*)," *Shehuikexuejia* (*Social Scientist*) no. 2 (2018): 12–21.

3. A. C. Graham, "The Background of the Mencian Theory of Human Nature," in *Essays on the Moral Philosophy of Mengzi*, eds. Xiusheng Liu, and Philip J. Ivanhoe (Indianapolis: Hackett, 2002 [1990]), 49–55.

4. Cai Zongqi 蔡宗齐, "'Qing' de gainian heyi tuozhan: Cong xian-Qin 'qing' 'xing' lunbiandao Liang Han Liu Chao wenlun zhong de qingwenshuo" "情" 的概念何以拓展——从先秦 "情" "性" 论辩到两汉六朝文论中的情文说 (How the Concept of *Qing* Developed: From Pre-Qin Debates Over *Qing* and *Xing* to Discourse on *Qing* in the Han and Six Dynasties)," *Tansuo yu zhengming* (February 2020): 39–48; Cai Zongqi (as Cai, Zong-qi), "A Study of Early Chinese Concepts of Qing 情 and a Dialogue with Western Emotion Studies," *Prism: Theory and Modern Chinese Literature* 17, no. 2 (2020): 399–429.

5. Li Chenyang, "Can Xun Zi's Proposition on 'Establishing Ritual Practices in Accord with *Qing*' Be Validated?" *Social Sciences in China* 35, no. 1 (2014): 147.

6. Chad Hansen, "*Qing* (Emotions) in Pre-Buddhist Chinese Thought," in *Emotions in East Asian Thought: A Dialogue in Comparative Philosophy*, eds. Joel Marks and Roger T. Ames (Albany: State University of New York Press, 1995), 182.

7. Roger T. Ames and David L. Hall, *Focusing the Familiar: A Translation and Philosophical Interpretation of the* Zhongyong (Honolulu: University of Hawai'i Press, 2001), 36.

8. Hansen, "*Qing* in Pre-Buddhist Chinese Thought," 183.

9. Brian Bruya, "Qing (情) and Emotion in Early Chinese Thought," *Late Imperial China* (Ch'ing shih wen t'i) no. 1 (2001): 151–76.

10. Michael Puett, "The Ethics of Responding Properly: The Notion of *Qíng* 情 in Early Chinese Thought," in *Love and Emotions in Traditional Chinese Literature*, ed. Halvor Eifring (Leiden: Brill, 2004), 37–68.

11. Ames and Hall, *Focusing the Familiar*, 36–37, 73–74; Roger T. Ames, *Confucian Role Ethics: A Vocabulary* (Hong Kong: The Chinese University Press, 2011), 73–74. Roger Ames notes that various binomials composed of

*qing*—"*qingkuang* 情況 or *shiqing* 事情 and *ganqing* 感情"—collapse a "perceived fact/value distinction" and further connects this to the Confucian view grounding individual psychology in communal communication. Herein we establish individuality through communal relations—"because we associate effectively in community we become distinguished as individuals"—and through these discursive relations we create not only ourselves but all meaning, thereby "defining and realizing a world through associated living"; Roger T. Ames, "'Human Becomings': Confucianism's Contribution to a Changing World Cultural Order," *Confucian Academy: Chinese Thought and Culture Review* 7, no. 2 (2020): 13.

12. Li Zehou 李澤厚, *Zhexue gangyao* 哲學綱要 (*Outline of a Philosophy*) (Beijing: Peking University Press, 2011), 40; translation of this work throughout the present chapter is my own.

13. Li Zehou 李澤厚, *Huiying Sangde'er ji qita* 回應桑德爾及其他 (*A Response to Sandel and Other Matters*) (Hong Kong: Oxford University Press, 2014), 15.

14. Li Zehou, *The Humanist Ethics of Li Zehou* (Albany: State University of New York Press, 2023), 126.

15. Li, *Humanist Ethics*, 173.

16. Li, *Humanist Ethics*, 129.

17. That it has been—and can understandably, though superficially, be—mistakenly taken otherwise is perhaps what motivates Li to title a section of one of his final dialogues "'Emotion as Substance' Is in Fact still Rational" ("情本體" 其實仍是理性的), in Li Zehou 李澤厚, *Lunlixue xinshuo shuyao* 倫理學新說述要 (*A New Sketch of Ethics*) (Beijing: Shijie tushu, 2019), 138–41.

18. Li, *Humanist Ethics*, 133.

19. E.g., Jeremy Bentham, "Anarchical Fallacies," in *Nonsense upon Stilts: Bentham, Burke and Marx on the Rights of Man*, ed. Jeremy Waldron (New York: Methuen, 1987), 46–69.

20. Li, *Outline of a Philosophy*, 45.

21. Li, *Outline of a Philosophy*, 46.

22. Li, *Outline of a Philosophy*, 46–47.

23. Li Zehou, *The Origins of Chinese Thought: From Shamanism to Ritual Regulations and Humaneness* (Leiden: Brill, 2018), 137.

24. E.g., Chen Lai 陳來, *Renxue bentilun* 仁學本體論 (*The Ontology of Humaneness*) (Beijing: SDX Joint Publishing, 2014).

25. See also Robert A. Carleo III, "Li Zehou's Concrete Humanism: His Legacy in Confucian Tradition," *Chinese Literature and Thought Today* 54, no. 1–2 (2023): 140–44; for an expanded account of Confucian concrete humanism, see Robert A. Carleo III, *Humane Liberality: A Confucian Proposal* (Lanham, MD: Rowman & Littlefield, 2024), especially chapter 5.

26. See, e.g., Yong Huang, "New Confucianism," in *A Concise Companion to Confucius*, ed. Paul R. Goldin (Hoboken: Wiley), 363; David Elstein, *Democracy in Contemporary Confucian Philosophy* (London: Routledge, 2015), 75.

27. Xu Fuguan, *The Chinese Liberal Spirit: Selected Writings of Xu Fuguan*, ed. and trans. David Elstein (Albany: State University of New York Press, 2022), 222.

28. Xu, *The Chinese Liberal Spirit*, 222.

29. Liang Shuming 梁漱溟, *Zhongguo wenhua yaoyi* 中國文化要義 (*The Essence of Chinese Culture*) (Taipei: Taiwan Commercial Press, 2013 [1949]); see also Fang Yong 方用, *20 shiji zhong Zhongguo zhexue jiangou zhong de "qing" wenti yanjiu* 20 世紀中中國哲學建構中的 "情" 問題研究 (*Research on Matters of "Qing" in the Constitution of Twentieth-Century Chinese Philosophy*) (Shanghai: Shanghai renmin chubanshe, 2011), 36–47.

30. For a nuanced explication of Neo-Confucian conception of *li* as patterned "coherence," see Stephen C. Angle, "Li 理/Coherence," in *Sagehood: The Contemporary Significance of Neo-Confucian Philosophy*, 31–50 (Oxford: Oxford University Press, 2010).

31. Such conceptions of *qing* and *li* as an interconnected and even mutually constitutive duality, moreover, seem to begin a couple millennia before Dai Zhen. Many thanks to Jana Rošker for pointing this out to me.

32. Dai Zhen 戴震, *Mengzi ziyi shuzheng* 孟子字義疏證 (*Evidential Commentary on the Meanings of Terms in the Mengzi*) (Beijing: Zhonghua shuju, 1961); Robert A. Carleo III, "Dai Zhen's Critique of Song Confucian Ideology," in *Critique, Subversion, and Chinese Philosophy: Sociopolitical, Conceptual, and Methodological Challenges*, ed. Andrew K. Whitehead and Hans-Georg Moeller (London: Bloomsbury Academic. 2021), 167–79.

33. See, for example, Liangjian Liu, "Yang Guorong and His Concrete Metaphysics," *Contemporary Chinese Thought* 43, no. 4 (2012): 3–4; Yang Guorong, "An Outline of Concrete Metaphysics," *Contemporary Chinese Thought* 43, no. 1 (2011): 43–59; Robert A. Carleo III and Liu Liangjian, "The Philosophy of Affairs," *Contemporary Chinese Thought* 52, no. 3 (2021): 125–36; Yang Guorong, "'Affairs' and the Actual World," *Contemporary Chinese Thought* 52, no. 3 (2021): 137–65.

34. That said, Dai has been charged often over the centuries with promoting a substantively Xunzian outlook in the guise of Mencian teachings, specifically regarding his culminating work, *Evidential Commentary on the Meanings of Terms in Mencius*. One recent instance in this line of critical interpretation is Kwong-loi Shun, "Mencius, Xunzi and Dai Zhen: A Study of the *Mengzi ziyi shuzheng*," in *Mencius: Contexts and Interpretations*, ed. Alan K. L. Chan (Honolulu: University of Hawai'i Press, 2002), 216–41.

35. Li, *Humanist Ethics*, 153.

36. Li, *Humanist Ethics*, 104.

37. Roger T. Ames and Henry Rosemont Jr., *The Analects of Confucius: A Philosophical Translation* (New York: Ballantine, 1998), 45.

38. David N. Keightley, "The Oracle-Bone Inscriptions of the Late Shang Dynasty," in *Sources of Chinese Tradition, Volume One: From Earliest times to 1600*, ed. Wm. Theodore de Bary and Irene Bloom (New York: Columbia University Press, 1999), 3–4.
39. Keightley, "Oracle-Bone Inscriptions," 4, emphasis added.
40. Li, *Humanist Ethics*, 110.
41. Jana S. Rošker, "Li Zehou's Critique of Marx through the Lens of Kantian Philosophy, or the Transcendental Illusion of Class Struggle," in *Critique, Subversion, and Chinese Philosophy: Sociopolitical, Conceptual, and Methodological Challenges*, ed. Andrew K. Whitehead, and Hans-Georg Moeller (London: Bloomsbury Academic, 2021), 119.
42. Li, *Humanist Ethics*, 111.
43. Li, *Humanist Ethics*, 108.
44. Li, *Humanist Ethics*, 192.
45. Li, *Humanist Ethics*, 42.
46. Li, *Humanist Ethics*, 51.
47. Li, *Humanist Ethics*, 51.
48. Li, *Humanist Ethics*, 206.

# Bibliography

Ames, Roger T. *Confucian Role Ethics: A Vocabulary*. Hong Kong: The Chinese University Press, 2011.
Ames, Roger T. " 'Human Becomings': Confucianism's Contribution to a Changing World Cultural Order." *Confucian Academy: Chinese Thought and Culture Review* 7, no. 2 (2020): 4–16.
Ames, Roger T., and David L. Hall. *Focusing the Familiar: A Translation and Philosophical Interpretation of the Zhongyong*. Honolulu: University of Hawai'i Press, 2001.
Ames, Roger T., and Henry Rosemont Jr. *The Analects of Confucius: A Philosophical Translation*. New York: Ballantine, 1998.
Angle, Stephen C. "Li 理/Coherence." In *Sagehood: The Contemporary Significance of Neo-Confucian Philosophy*, 31–50. Oxford: Oxford University Press, 2010.
Bentham, Jeremy. "Anarchical Fallacies." In *Nonsense upon Stilts: Bentham, Burke and Marx on the Rights of Man*, edited by Jeremy Waldron, 46–69. London: Routledge, 1987.
Bruya, Brian. "Qing (情) and Emotion in Early Chinese Thought." *Late Imperial China (Ch'ing-shih wen-t'i)* 10, no. 1 (2001): 151–76.
Cai Zongqi 蔡宗齐. " 'Qing' de gainian heyi tuozhan: Cong xian-Qin 'qing' 'xing' lunbiandao Liang Han Liu Chao wenlun zhong de qingwenshuo"

"情" 的概念何以拓展—从先秦 "情" "性" 论辩到两汉六朝文论中的情文说 (How the Concept of *Qing* Developed: From pre-Qin Debates Over *Qing* and *Xing* to Discourse on *Qing* in the Han and Six Dynasties). *Tansuo yu zhengming* (February 2020): 39–48.

Cai Zongqi (as Cai, Zong-qi). "A Study of Early Chinese Concepts of Qing 情 and a Dialogue with Western Emotion Studies." *Prism: Theory and Modern Chinese Literature* 17, no. 2 (2020): 399–429.

Carleo, Robert A., III. "Dai Zhen's Critique of Song Confucian Ideology." In *Critique, Subversion, and Chinese Philosophy: Sociopolitical, Conceptual, and Methodological Challenges*, edited by Andrew K. Whitehead and Hans-Georg Moeller, 167–79. London: Bloomsbury Academic, 2021.

Carleo, Robert A., III. *Humane Liberality: A Confucian Proposal*. Lanham, MD: Rowman and Littlefield, 2024.

Carleo, Robert A., III. "Li Zehou's Concrete Humanism: His Legacy in Confucian Tradition." *Chinese Literature and Thought Today* 54, no. 1–2 (2023): 140–44.

Carleo, Robert A., III, and Liu Liangjian. "The Philosophy of Affairs." *Contemporary Chinese Thought* 52, no. 3 (2021): 125–36.

Chen Lai 陳來. *Renxue bentilun* 仁學本體論 (*The Ontology of Humaneness*). Beijing: SDX Joint Publishing, 2014.

Dai Zhen 戴震. *Mengzi ziyi shuzheng* 孟子字義疏證 (*Evidential Commentary on the Meanings of Terms in the Mengzi*). Beijing: Zhonghua shuju, 1961.

Elstein, David. *Democracy in Contemporary Confucian Philosophy*. London: Routledge, 2015.

Fang Yong 方用. *20 shiji zhong Zhongguo zhexue jiangou zhong de "qing" wenti yanjiu* 20 世紀中國哲學建構中的 "情" 問題研究 (*Research on Matters of "Qing" in the Constitution of Twentieth-Century Chinese Philosophy*). Shanghai: Shanghai renmin chubanshe, 2011.

Graham, A. "The Background of the Mencian Theory of Human Nature." In *Essays on the Moral Philosophy of Mengzi*, edited by Xiusheng Liu and Philip J. Ivanhoe, 1–63. Indianapolis: Hackett, 2002 [1990].

Hansen, Chad. "*Qing* (Emotions) in Pre-Buddhist Chinese Thought." In *Emotions in East Asian Thought: A Dialogue in Comparative Philosophy*, edited by Joel Marks and Roger T. Ames, 181–211. Albany: State University of New York Press, 1995.

Huang, Yong. "New Confucianism." In *A Concise Companion to Confucius*, edited by Paul R. Goldin, 352–74. Hoboken: Wiley, 2017.

Keightley, David N. "The Oracle-Bone Inscriptions of the Late Shang Dynasty." In *Sources of Chinese Tradition, Volume One: From Earliest times to 1600*, edited by Wm. Theodore De Bary and Irene Bloom, 3–23, second edition. New York: Columbia University Press, 1999.

Li Chenyang. "Can Xun Zi's Proposition on 'Establishing Ritual Practices in Accord with *Qing*' Be Validated?" *Social Sciences in China* 35, no. 1 (2014): 146–62.

Li Zehou 李澤厚. *Huiying Sangde'er ji qita* 回應桑德爾及其他 (*A Response to Sandel and Other Matters*). Hong Kong: Oxford University Press, 2014.

Li Zehou. *The Humanist Ethics of Li Zehou*. Edited and translated by Robert A. Carleo III. Albany: State University of New York Press, 2023.

Li Zehou 李澤厚. *Lunlixue xinshuo shuyao* 倫理學新說述要 (*A New Sketch of Ethics*). Beijing: Shijie tushu, 2019.

Li Zehou. *The Origins of Chinese Thought: From Shamanism to Ritual Regulations and Humaneness*. Translated by Robert A. Carleo III. Leiden: Brill, 2018.

Li Zehou 李澤厚. *Zhexue gangyao* 哲學綱要 (*Outline of a Philosophy*). Beijing: Peking University Press, 2011.

Liang Shuming 梁漱溟. *Zhongguo wenhua yaoyi* 中國文化要義 (*The Essence of Chinese Culture*). Taipei: Taiwan Commercial Press, 2013 [1949].

Liu, Liangjian. "Yang Guorong and His Concrete Metaphysics." *Contemporary Chinese Thought* 43, no. 4 (2012): 3–4.

Liu Yuedi. "Integrating and Inheriting Mencius and Xunzi Through 'The Mind Unifying and Governing *Qing* and Human Nature': On the Integration of Mencius's 'Heaven–Human Nature–*Qing*–Mind' with Xunzi's 'Heaven–*Qing*–Human Nature–Mind.'" *Confucian Academy: Chinese Thought and Culture Review* 7, no. 2 (2020): 17–28.

Liu Yuedi 劉悅笛. "'Qingxing' 'qingshi' he 'qinggan': Zhongguo Rujia 'qing ben zhexue' de jiben mianxiang" "情性" "情實" 和 "情感"—中國儒家 "情本哲學" 的基本面向 (*Genuineness, Emotion, and Temperament: Basic Facets of Chinese Confucian Ontology of Qing*). *Shehuikexuejia* (*Social Scientist*) no. 2 (2018): 12–21.

Puett, Michael. "The Ethics of Responding Properly: The Notion of *Qíng* 情 in Early Chinese Thought." In *Love and Emotions in Traditional Chinese Literature*, edited by Halvor Eifring, 37–68. Leiden: Brill, 2004.

Rorty, Amélie Oksenberg. "Enough Already with 'Theories of the Emotions.'" In *Thinking about Feeling: Contemporary Philosophers on Emotions*, edited by Robert C. Solomon, 269–78. Oxford: Oxford University Press, 2004.

Rorty, Amélie Oksenberg, ed. *Explaining Emotions*. Berkeley: University of California Press, 1980.

Rošker, Jana S. "Li Zehou's Critique of Marx through the Lens of Kantian Philosophy, or the Transcendental Illusion of Class Struggle." In *Critique, Subversion, and Chinese Philosophy: Sociopolitical, Conceptual, and Methodological Challenges*, edited by Andrew K. Whitehead and Hans-Georg Moeller, 113–24. London: Bloomsbury Academic, 2021.

Shun, Kwong-loi. "Mencius, Xunzi and Dai Zhen: A Study of the *Mengzi ziyi shuzheng*." In *Mencius: Contexts and Interpretations*, edited by Alan K. L. Chan, 216–41. Honolulu: University of Hawai'i Press, 2002.

Xu Fuguan. *The Chinese Liberal Spirit: Selected Writings of Xu Fuguan*. Edited and translated by David Elstein. Albany: State University of New York Press, 2022.

Yang Guorong. "'Affairs' and the Actual World." *Contemporary Chinese Thought* 52, no. 3 (2021): 137–65.
Yang Guorong. "An Outline of Concrete Metaphysics." *Contemporary Chinese Thought* 43, no. 1 (2011): 43–59.

## 10

# Measure Without and Beyond Measure
## Brief Notes on the Primary Category of Li Zehou's *Anthropologico-Historical Ontology*[1]

### Wu Xiaoming

> Confucius had gone along until he was fifty-one and had still not heard the Way (*dao* 道). Finally he went south to Pei and called on Lao Dan. "Ah, you have come," said Lao Dan. "I've heard that you are a worthy man of the northern region. Have you found the Way?" "Not yet," said Confucius. "Where did you look for it?" asked Lao Dan. "I looked for it in rules (*du* 度) and regulations (*shu* 數), but five years went by and I hadn't found it."[2]
>
> —"The Turning of Heaven," *Zhuangzi*

This story in *Zhuangzi*, in which Confucius interrogates Laozi on *dao*, is probably fictional, but this is not the concern of the present study. I chose to begin the paper with this epigraph simply to draw attention to the term *du* 度. Nevertheless, Confucius' concern for *du* as rules or measures in this fictional story distantly and reciprocally echoes Li Zehou's real concern for *du* as a philosophical concept. This echo may not be purely coincidental, whereby the historical resonates with the contemporary, and the traditional resonates with the innovative. These distant echoes may not have been felt and recognized in our times' thought, nor were they anticipated in the traditional narrative; thus they remain at most as disguised potentialities and possibilities. Unraveling these potential dialogues in the history of ideas and rousing their potential meaning, thus shedding new light on these ideas, or at least creating space for the generation of new ideas, is one of the tasks for the study of intellectual history. Although the present study will focus only on the *du* as elaborated by Li in *Historical Ontology*, the two-thousand-year-old fictional tale of the conversation on the pursuit of *dao* between Confucius and Laozi could be an imagined background or the potential horizon of our discussion.

### Is *Du* the "Onto-" or "*Benti*" of Li Zehou's Ontology?

To this question Li's answer is clear: "'*du*' is not *benti* 本體." Then the expression "the *benti* of '*du*'" (*du de benti* 度的本體), which frequently occurs in *Historical Ontology*, can indeed be very confusing. In the following I will try to propose a solution to this problem.

Li wants the Chinese term *du* to remain as a transliteration in Western languages: "I hope in the coming decades the two Chinese terms '*qing*' 情 and '*du*' 度, which are central to my philosophy, should be transliterated like the Chinese terms '*dao*' 道 and '*yin-yang*' 陰陽 in Western languages, as none have appropriately corresponding translations in Western languages."[3] He explains, "It is not suitable to translate '*du*' as 'measure' or 'degree' in Western languages, as '*du*' refers to the grasping of the 'just right' by human beings in their actions. It is '*du*' that maintains the existence of human beings (including individuals, groups and mankind). Thus '*du*' is not *benti*, but it possesses an ontological nature (*bentixing* 本體性)."[4] If *du* is not *benti*, then how should we understand and translate the expression "the *benti* of '*du*'"? Does *du* itself have a *benti*? Then what can be *du*'s *benti*? Provided that we should let the term *du* remain untranslated, the question becomes how we should understand the term *benti* in order to understand "the *benti* of '*du*.'"

The Chinese term *benti* used as a translated Western philosophical term refers to the *onto-* in *ontology*, which is usually translated as *bentilun* 本體論. *Bentilun* means literally the theory (*lun*) of *benti*. *Benti* means literally body itself, body as such, or one's own body. Li asks for *benti* to be translated as "substance," "root," "body," or "final reality" in his philosophy. Given this, we could have the following possible translations for *du de benti*: the substance of *du*, the root of *du*, the body of *du*, or the final reality of *du*. Can *du* be said to have a substance, a root, or a body? And what could be the final reality of *du*? Or is *du* just what it is, i.e., *du*, *du* itself, *du* as such, or *du* proper in Li's philosophy? These will be our preliminary questions guiding the following analysis in this section.

Li is well aware of the unsuitability of the term *bentilun* for Chinese philosophy. He admits that "borrowing the term '*bentilun*' (ontology) and using it in the Chinese context may not be appropriate. This is reflected in its different translations, such as '*cunzailun*' 存在論 (theory of existence) and '*shilun*' 是論 (theory of to-be/being)."[5] Li thinks that ontology in Western philosophy is an investigation concerning "the ultimate essence or nature or 'the final reality' (the Being of beings) of all things," whereas "in the Chinese tradition of 'separation without separating and connection without connecting (*bujibuli* 不即不離),' which means the phenomenon (*xianxiang* 現象) and the noumenon (*benti*) are neither equated nor are separated," we "find it fundamentally difficult to propose an 'ontological question' concerning 'the final reality' (*zuizhong shizai* 最終實在)."[6] However, he continues to employ this allegedly Western term *ontology*:

> What I call "ontology" is to put emphasis on the total historical procession of humanity and nature (external nature and internal nature) as "the final reality" of all phenomena, including the very phenomenon of "I am alive." It definitely does not imply a departure from each and every instance of "I am alive." If we were to depart from each and every instance of "I am alive," then how could we speak of any sort of anthropologico-historical "*benti*." Therefore, the so-called "historical *benti*" or "anthropologico-historical *benti*" is not some sort of abstract object, nor an intellectual pattern or an idea. It is not the absolute spirit or an ideology and so forth; it is just the daily life itself of each living person (individual).[7]

If the *benti* in Li's anthropologico-historical ontology is determined as "the daily life itself of each living person (individual)," then *du*, determined by Li as the *primary category* of this ontology, should only concern the "how and what" of such a *benti*, as categories are just *different ways* in which *benti* as *benti* expresses what it is and how it is. If in Li's ontology *du* is not *benti* but a category, then how should the expression "the *benti* of '*du*'" be understood? As already mentioned above, the Chinese term *benti* also carries the literal meaning of "body itself," "body as such," or "one's own body." Understood in this way, the meaning of *benti* is very close to that of *benshen* 本身, a Chinese term meaning "one's self," "oneself," or "itself," which is commonly used to give emphasis to the person or the thing mentioned. Linguistically, the word *ti* in *ben-ti* and the word *shen* in *ben-shen* together form the compound word *shenti* 身體 meaning "body." If "the *benti* of '*du*'" could be translated simply as "the body itself of *du*" or "*du*'s body as such" or "*du*'s own body," then it would mean almost the same as saying *du benshen* 度本身, that is, "the very self of *du*" or simply "*du* itself." Given that Li says clearly that *du* is not *benti*, and given that *du* itself cannot have a *benti* as defined by Li in his ontology, the only possible interpretation of "the *benti* of '*du*'" for us would be that when Li uses this expression he simply wants to say *du* in an emphatic way: *du*, *du benshen*, i.e., *du* itself, or *du* as such.

To illustrate my point, let us take the following passage from *Historical Ontology* as an example: "The historical *benti* is established on the realization of '*du*' which is a dynamic and never-ceasing forward progression. [*Du*] is . . . the life force of anthropology and is also the profound mystery of the new interpretation for 'the unity of Heaven (*tian*) and humanity (*ren*).' The *benti* of '*du*' renovates itself day by day, day after day, pushing humanity's survival, continuation, and development."[8] To say that historical *benti* is established on the dynamic realization of *du* logically makes sense, but to then say that "the *benti* of '*du*'" renovates itself day by day, day after day, makes matters confusing. Actually, the expression "the *benti* of '*du*'" in the final sentence serves only as a qualifying emphasis of the previous sentences: the *du* that is dynamic and that constantly makes forward progression would certainly renovate *itself* day by day and day after day. Thus what renovates itself incessantly should be the "*du*" that occurs in previous sentences. It would be easy for us to think *du itself* is the anthropological life force that renovates itself constantly, but it would be difficult for us to imagine that "the *benti* of '*du*'" does the same thing, unless we know definitely what *du*'s *benti* can look like. This example can show concretely that when Li says "the *benti* of '*du*'" he simply means to emphasize the *itself* of the *du*—*du benshen*—rather than the "*benti*" of '*du*.'" Thus, any literal translations of this expression, such as "the substance of *du*," "the root of *du*," "the body of *du*," or "the final reality of *du*," would do no more than cause confusion.

Measure Without and Beyond Measure | 267

If the above analysis is acceptable, then almost all of the expressions "the *benti* of '*du*'" in *Historical Ontology* can simply be read as "*du* itself,*" "*du* as such," or simply "*du*": "The subject and object in the *benti* of '*du*' is initially mixed without distinction,"[9] "within the *benti* of '*du*,' subject and object completely merge into one,"[10] "the measurements, stipulations, consolidations, and declarations on the *benti* of '*du*' of the human subjectivity,"[11] "the *benti* of '*du*' . . . is greater than human rationality, precisely because it possesses some sort of indefinability and unpredictability,"[12] and so on.

## A Questionable Survival Teleology

*Du* possesses an essentially important position in Li's anthropologico-historical ontology. His basic propositions concerning *du* are as follows:

1. *Du* concerns the ontological nature of human existence. It is the "primary category of anthropologico-historical ontology."[13]

2. *Du* is "taking the right measures, doing things just right."[14]

3. *Du* is technique or art.[15]

4. *Du* does not exist within objects, but appears in the process of human production and living activities. *Du* is a human creation.[16]

5. Humanity relies on mastering *du* in the artistry in production to survive and thrive. *Du* constantly adjusts, changes, expands, and corrects itself in accordance with the survival and existence of humanity.[17]

6. "*Du* as the concretization of material practice (operational activities and others) represents itself in the establishment of various structures and forms":[18] throughout material practice and productive activities, humans "discover" the mutual adaptation between operation, tools (means) and objects. The specific formalization of any specific mutual adaptation is embodied as the *du* that could be used to guide some specific practical activity.[19] "All the rational forms,

outcomes, and achievements (knowledge and science) in later generations are simply the measurement, stipulation, consolidation and declaration of '*du*' itself ('*du*' *de benti*) by the human subjectivity."[20]

7. "*Du*" itself ("*du*" *de benti*) is greater than human rationality because it possesses some sort of indefinability and unpredictability.[21]

8. Historical *benti* is established on the realization of *du*, which is a dynamic and never-ceasing forward progression.[22]

9. In *Zhouyi* (*Yi-Jing*), the center curve that divides the *yin-yang* pictogram is the pictorial representation of *du*.[23]

We will follow the particular arguments in the text to commence our analysis of these propositions. Li starts his discourse on *du* with the age-old question "What is?" in philosophy. "What is '*du*'? '*Du*' is 'taking the right measures and doing things just right.'"[24] This answer is an abstract and formal determination of the meaning of *du*. Having made his first and foremost definition clear, Li then asks, "Why?" This abrupt "why" could be asking "why is *du* 'taking the right measures and doing things just right'?" It could also be questioning: "Why '*du*'? Why should '*du*' be a concern? Why does '*du*' come the forefront in the elaboration of historical ontology? Or rather, why do we grant *du* this privileged ontological position in the first paragraph of the first chapter of *Historical Ontology*?" Concerning this "why," Li gives a simple and straightforward answer: "Because this is the way to achieve the goal": "Humanity (and individuals) primarily regards survival (of kin and individual) as the goal. To achieve the goal of survival, it is necessary for humans to take the right measures and do things just right when going about their businesses."[25] Thereupon, the importance of *du* in Li's anthropologico-historical ontology begins to emerge: *du* concerns the very survival of humanity. *Du* directly serves the goal of humanity's survival, and survival is affirmed as the very goal of humanity without hesitation.

With regard to this teleology of survival, we may need to note two things. First, by using parentheses Li reveals some hesitation in his thought: on the one hand, he affirms that, as a collection of individuals or as a whole composed of many individuals, humanity seeks survival as the goal. On the other hand, if only as an appendix, he adds "and individuals" (*geren* 個人) in parentheses next to "humanity" (*renlei* 人類). The use of "and" may confuse the careful reader. Is "humanity" not already the collective noun for all the human individuals in the world? Is it necessary to add "and individuals" next to "humanity"? Perhaps, the "individual" was added by Li for the sake of accuracy or completeness, although it might be superfluous? However, this line of speculation is cut off by the second appearance of the word in parentheses. Almost as if Li were afraid of the reader misinterpreting his meaning, the phrase "of kin and individual" in parentheses is added in his affirmation of humanity "and" individuals "regarding survival as the goal." Clearly, in these instances Li repeatedly calls on the reader to understand his articulation as humanity *and* individuals both regard survival as the goal. The "and" in this instance is not raised incidentally but deliberately emphasized. However, its emphatic force is diluted by appearing as a piece of inconsequential supplementary information within parentheses. This might reveal that Li feels a problem that he also intends to understate: there is a tension or "incompatibility" between humanity and individuals. Second, Li uses the qualifier "primarily" in the articulation of his teleology. The use of "primarily" engenders further thinking and questioning: if humanity (let us not forget to add "and individuals") "primarily" regard survival as the goal, then what comes "next"? What would be the "ultimate" goal? If humanity as a species, or as a whole, "primarily" regards survival as the goal, then, what about individuals? For individuals, could they and ought they primarily regard survival as the goal? Li's usage of "primarily" without the "next" or "ultimately" leaves these questions open. But it could be that for Li the question (which may not even be a question) could not be simpler and more straightforward: certainly, humans "primarily" (and "ultimately"?) have to live. Therefore, the "philosophy of the food on the table" is the first philosophy. Further, if people were to live a life, they have to do things well (here it should be added, at least do the things related to being alive well). To do things well, then it is necessary to take the right measures and do things just right. Taking the right measures and doing things just right is *du*. This is the fundamental importance of *du*, which is not at all complicated.

This may be the straightforwardness, plainness, and simplicity that is requested by Li's "philosophy of the food on the table." However, this sort of simplicity creates unclarity, which leaves the reader with a sense of regret. This is because people could also say that to achieve the goal one must continue to break those established measurements and exceed the existing *du*. To achieve the goal one must be adventurous, break boundaries, and go to extremes. However, the lack of rigor in Li's philosophy is not the main concern of the present study. What needs to be pointed out is that from the very beginning a questionable teleology of survival dominates Li's entire discourse on *du*. But whether survival is the primary or ultimate goal is far from being certain. Of course, humans indeed live their lives. This is a tangible fact. Or, more rigorously speaking, *humans have always already found themselves surviving. It is a factuality that humans must have always already accepted concerning themselves.* It is only through this factuality that humans (or those as philosophers) can tell whether or not survival is the goal.

Thus, in order to assert that survival is the goal, Li needs to circumvent or overcome many obstacles. Within the Chinese tradition, he may need to first contend with Mencius's eloquent argument:

> I desire fish, and I also desire bear's paws. If I cannot have both of them, I will give up fish and take bear's paws. I desire life, and I also desire righteousness. If I cannot have both of them, I will give up life and take righteousness. It is true that I desire life, but there is something I desire more than life, and therefore I will not do something dishonorable in order to hold on to it. I detest death, but there is something I detest more than death, and therefore there are some dangers I may not avoid. If, among a person's desires, there were none greater than life, then why should he not do anything necessary in order to cling to life? If, among the things he detested, there were none greater than death, why should he not do whatever he had to in order to avoid danger? There is a means by which one may preserve life, and yet one does not employ it; there is a means by which one may avoid danger, and yet one does not adopt it. Thus there are things that we desire more than life and things that we detest more than death. *It is not exemplary persons alone who have this mind; all human beings have it.* It is only that the exemplary ones are able to avoid losing it; that is all. Suppose there are a basketful of rice and a bowlful of soup. If I get them, I may remain alive; if I do not get them, I may well die. If they are offered contemptuously, a wayfarer will decline to accept them; if they are offered after having been trampled upon, a beggar will not demean himself by taking them.[26]

Measure Without and Beyond Measure | 271

For those who choose to devote themselves to some sort of different or higher goal (for example, followers of certain religions or teachings), whether survival is their primary and ultimate goal is also far from obvious.

## Where Is the *Du* that Distinguishes Humans from Animals?[27]

Let us continue in our reading of the text. If survival is the goal for human beings and survival necessitates production, then "the '*du*' as 'doing things just right' would first be generated and appear in the artistry in production."[28] However, Li concedes immediately that "animals also have to survive" (although he does not tell us whether animals also "regard survival as the goal" in the same way as or to a greater extent than humans if only "unconsciously"), "and can also master 'doing things just right,'" even if this is just "the result of constant training on their species' instinct as living creatures after their birth."[29] He uses this qualification to limit the potentially subversive power of his concession. The question here is precisely whether if the "doing things just right" mastered by animals is the result of "training," then how would we distinguish this sort of "doing things just right" from the "doing things just right" that humans have come to master through constant training (through learning skills and artistry)? In other words, if *du* means "doing things just right," or "one extra inch is too long, one fewer inch is too short,"[30] and if, moreover, without mastering *du* "just right," it would lead to the danger of "a millimeter deviance, a thousand-mile error,"[31] then how would we (as humans that are different from animals) master the *du* (in the sense of measure or degree) that determines what makes humans a human and animals an animal? What could we use to measure (*du-liang*) the difference between humans and animals? Is this difference a difference in quantity, quality, or *du* (degree)? If the mastery of the *du* as "doing things just right" of humans and other animals is only a difference in *du* (in the sense of *cheng-du* 程度, degree or extent), then what could it otherwise mean by "doing things just right"? Could there be different kinds of "doing things just right"? Are there "doing things just right that is just right" and "doing things just right that is not quite right"? Is it possible to "excessively do things just right" and "insufficiently do things just right?"

These questions are not just nit-picking, as they concern the nature of *du* that Li regards as being ontological. According to Li's argument, we could say that even if humanity's "*du*, mastered through their ever-expanding technical ability of production, compared to the other species . . . is infinitely much more," and even if *du* "concerns the ontological nature of human existence,"[32] the *du* (in the sense as conceived by Li) that humanity and other species must master, throughout various activities that deal with external objects "for survival," refers to the same sort of "doing things just right," if "doing things just right" can fully define Li's *du* as *du*. But if that were the case, the difference in the mastery of *du* between humans and other animals would not be "ontological." Rather, it is only a difference of quantity or *du* in the sense of *cheng-du*, degree or extent.[33] The difference between humans and other animals is not that humans are able to do things more just right than other animals. Instead, it is that humans are able to do *more things* just right. As such, the *du* that humanity have mastered and are capable of mastering is more than that of other animals in its many varieties. But the so-called "many" is also a kind of *du*. It means that the degree to which "many" is "many" also has to be determined by a *du* that had been stipulated, in a sense whereby *du* is *chi-du* 尺度 or measurement. Without such a *du* as measurement, it would not be possible to speak of the multitude, since there would not be a set standard to *du-liang* or measure how many is many and how few is few.

As such, how should we *du-liang* or measure how many is many? How should we *du-liang* or measure that humanity's mastery of *du* (in either *du*'s type or quantity) is more than other animals? How much and to what *cheng-du* or extent should be regarded as "just right"? Or is it that there is no "just right" left here, and that we could no longer speak of "just right"? Is it, instead, that *du* is a matter of "the more the merrier" and infinitely much more? We have already seen that Li praises the latter approach: humanity's "*du*, mastered through their ever-expanding technical ability of production, compared to the other species . . . is infinitely much more."[34] But this "infinitude" (*wubi* 無比, incomparable) implies precisely *the inability to "du-liang" or measure, or the impossibility to "du-liang" or measure*. This "infinitude" would mean that there would be no more *du* or that *du* becomes unlimited (*wudu* 無度). It would mean that *du* is exceeding itself or has been exceeded, and thus *du* is no longer what it should be: "being just right," measure, degree, extent, and so on. It would also mean that people, who need to master *du* in various activities, would admit their powerlessness when they ultimately need to master *du* (or when they need to master the ultimate *du*). But Li might not have realized these serious consequences. Let us consider the following arguments.

First, according to Li, survival is the goal. In order to survive, humans and other animals need to master various skills and artistry. The technical ability (*ji-neng* 技能) and artistry (*ji-yi* 技藝), or the skill (*ji* 技) that ancients regard as being correlative of *dao*, are the capacity required to conduct specific activities. The core of this capacity is the mastery and application of a series of means or methods in order to achieve a specific goal. For instance, in the *Zhuangzi* the butcher Ding 庖丁 possessed the skill of dismembering oxen and the wheelwright Bian 輪扁 possessed the skill of making wheels, while the cobbler in Plato's *The Republic* possessed the skill of making shoes and so forth. However, on the matter of dismembering oxen, or making wheels or shoes, there are those who are able to perform well, while the others would perform poorly. The good performers would satisfy the need for survival, while for the poor performers the satisfaction of this need would be adversely affected. In this instance, the difference between matters done well or not done well is whether the matter is done "just right" or not. Learning to "do things just right" and thus being "just right" is proof of having mastered *du*. This means that the mastery of *du* is the essence of skill-artistry-technique, which is also to say that *du* is at the foundation of skills and artistry, or that the essence of skills and artistry is the *very* mastery of *du*.[35]

Second, Li thinks that humans are not the only ones capable of learning to "do things just right." Other species are also capable of doing so in their activities with survival as the goal. Therefore, there is nothing that can be used for us to essentially or "ontologically" differentiate the nature of *du* mastered by humans from the nature of *du* mastered by other animals for the activities conducted in order to survive.

Third, it is nevertheless said that there still exists some difference between humans and other animals regarding their mastery of *du*. But the difference is merely that it is not in the essence, but only in *cheng-du* (degree) or the quantity that the *du* that humans can master "infinitely" exceeds the *du* that other animals can master.

Fourth, the term "infinitude" implies that there would be no more *du*. The contradiction is thus: while humanity's mastery of *du*, in terms of quantity, exceeds the other species' "infinitely much more," humans would no longer master their ("infinitely much more") mastery of *du* in a manner that is "just right." But isn't this kind of "no longer just right" exactly the diagnosis of the fundamental problem of human society, made by philosophers such as Heidegger, claiming that modern technology has been developed in a way in which *du* (in the sense of proper measure) has been exceeded (*guo-du* 過度) or lost? In modern society, humans allow themselves to master various kinds of *du* infinitely or without limits—which overshoot *du* by either doing too much or being not limited by *du* altogether. Humanity's infinite and limitless mastery of *du*, or its unlimited pursuit of the development of modern technology, leaves no room for *du* as "being just right" or proper measure. When Li intends to elevate *du* as the primary category of anthropologico-historical ontology, he is also obviously thinking about the various problems that the development of modern technology has made humanity face, believing that his theory of *du* could be one possible solution to these. If we leave aside the background of philosophers such as Heidegger thinking on and criticizing the essence of modern technology, we could not fully comprehend the meaning of Li's philosophical undertaking. For instance, Li writes:

> Since technology (mainly those from modern industrialization), machines, numbers, and mass production . . . adopt an extremely rationalized form and type, they conversely strangle, congest, and obstruct the authentic display of humanity's ontological "*du*." Therefore, on the one hand, technology displays the ontological existence of the entire humanity's *du*. On the other hand, technology strangles the ontological existence of the individual. As a consequence, a rallying cry for anti-technology is sounded loud and clear. Going back to foundations, back to the origin to re-discover and to re-explain has become an important mission for philosophy in our times. Affirming the ontological nature of "*du*" is exactly this kind of effort.[36]

Li's point is that against the problems that modern technology has brought to modern humanity, people should do their best to recover their affirming and grasping of *du* in the sense of "being just right" or proper measure. However, he does not seem to have raised the question of how humans should grasp the *du* as the proper measure that can *measure* various kinds of *du* (as measures or degrees) in relation to one another. How should human beings be taking the right measures while also having a capacity to infinitely or boundlessly master various kinds of *du*? How should they maintain the balance among the different kinds of *du*? How should they uphold fairness and justice for the different kinds of *du* which might be in confliction to one another? These questions can be reduced to the questions "what is the *du* of *du*," what is the measure of/for measures, or what is the degree of/for degrees? One of the fundamental problems in modern society lies precisely in that humans may appear to be able to master different kinds of *du* infinitely or boundlessly, or they are able to infinitely and boundlessly expand their mastery of various kinds of *du*. Despite this, however, they are unable to master their infinite and boundless mastery of *du*. Human beings may even be regarded as not necessary or even "ought not" to do so, because the "infinitely much more" mastery of *du* is regarded as concerning the "ontological nature" of human existence. But if the mastery of *du* concerns the ontological nature of human existence, then the moment when humans allow themselves to endlessly pursue their mastery of various kinds of *du* (which is infinite in terms of quantity and in principle) would be the moment they begin to lose their humanity. Humanity would be lost because humans have lost their "ultimate" ability to master *du* or their "ultimate" mastery of *du*. According to the logic that is implied in Li's argument, this would mean that *humans are actually unable to master the du that defines their humanity*. It would mean that humans are unable to let themselves become human "just right." Consequently, the relationship between humans and animals could have become a difficult problem for modern man. When humans are wishing and endeavoring to "infinitely" or "boundlessly" master various kinds of *du*, what they actually begin to lose is precisely their *ultimate* mastery of *du*. In such unlimited pursuit of *du*, human beings would no longer know what is "just right" nor be able to do things "just right."

It is impossible to extract here everything that is implied in the above analysis. However, we can at least identify one point: if the mastery of *du* defines "ontologically" the humanity of the human being, then the moment when human beings fail to "properly" master their infinite mastery of the various kind of *du* would indicate a sort of self-deconstruction of the human-centered assumption implied in Li's theory.

## How Could *Du* Become a Human Creation?

The above reading of the beginning pages of *Historical Ontology* does not intend to suggest or provide a theory that would be different from the anthropologico-historical ontology that Li outlines. This "ontology," which is itself based on the wisdom of the Chinese tradition, deserves serious consideration and in-depth research, although we might not necessarily call it "ontology" in the rigorously Western sense of the term. My initial intention was to read this text closely from the beginning. However, I find myself having difficulty moving further than the first few pages and being entangled by these and other questions.

The question raised in the previous section concerning the difference between the *du* mastered by humans and the *du* mastered by other animals has forced us to think about the boundary drawn by Li between humans and other animals, as well as the complicated question implied in *du* as the primary category of anthropologico-historical ontology. In addition to these questions, Li's description of *du* "itself" being "a human creation, a human manufacture" could also prompt further questioning.

Li writes, "'*du*' does not exist in any objects, nor within consciousness. It first appears in human production and living activities, which means it is in the practice and the function. It is a human creation, a human manufacture. Therefore, rather than 'quality' or 'quantity,' 'being' (*you* 有) or 'nothingness,' it is '*du*' that is the primary category of anthropological ontology."[37] That this argument prompts further questions is first and foremost because Li affirms that animals can also master "*du*" as "doing things just right" (at least to some extent or *cheng-du*). If this were true, it is hard to claim that *du* is specifically a human creation and manufacture. However, if we concede that Li concerns himself mainly or exclusively with the "*du* of human beings," and that he does regard *du* as a human creation, then we need to ask, in what way can *du* be a human creation? In other words, how do human beings create their *du*? Let us roughly propose the following: if *du* means doing things just right, then *du* is merely or at least at first an *adaptation*. Li argues for *du* with the aid of the conceptions of *qiao* 巧 (skillfulness), *tiao* 調 (suit well, fit in perfectly), *zhong* 中 (central, not leaning to any side), and *he* 和 (harmony), which are all found in the Chinese tradition, implying that Li in fact also regards *du* as the mutual adaptation between active and passive actors, or between interacting actors. It is not that the one (a human as the active actor) imposes their own *du*, i.e., their own measures and standards (*chi-du*), onto the other.[38] In the example of horticulture, "doing things just right" means that humans first have to "suit" the "*du*" of the plant. Humans have to provide a "*shi-du*" 適度 or "suitable" living environment for the plant and "*shi-du*" or "suitably" water and fertilize the plant; they have to let the plant receive "suitable" or "*shi-du*" amounts of air circulation and exposure of light and so forth.[39] This conception of suitability (*shi-du*) contains a sort of *passivity* on the part of the active agency of the human. As cultivators and farmers, the first thing for humans is not to *create* a *du* that could be imposed on the plant. Instead, humans need to suit themselves to the *du* of the plant. Thus in the human activities of cultivating the plant, it is not that I *manufacture* the *du* for the plant, but rather it is the plant that *determines* the *du* for me. The *du* comes from the plant as the other. The reason why the plant is able to provide the *du* for me and thus determines my cultivating activities is that the plant (the plant which I am to cultivate and the plant that needs my cultivation) itself is the *du* of my cultivating activities. Therefore, here, it is the other that requires me to treat it in the most suitable (*shi-du*) way, or in the way that is most suitable for letting the other be what it is and how it is.

Accordingly, in the cultivating activities, although I seem to be the active actor, the imposer, it is always the other that first requires me to suit it (*shi-du*). The Chinese term "*shi-du*," literally "suit a certain measure," means here that I have to "suitably adapt" myself to the other's "*du*" or to the other as the very *du* in the sense of the proper measure for me, and that I do my best to let the other "most suitably" be as the other. Such an original suiting-to would be my original and unconditioned respect required by the other for the other to be the other. And such an original suiting-to should be exactly the ethics that we urgently need given the nature of today's modern technology (for instance, especially when we begin to not only welcome the revolutionary changes in human society brought by artificial intelligence, but also worry that artificial intelligence might have a devastating impact on humanity itself or on the very nature of being a human). Modern technology represents humanity's pursuit of the ever-strengthening control of the things and objects of the entire world. This is the ever-expanding power of dominance that humans pursue. Such an unlimited pursuit of human power and dominance over things has to be balanced and regulated by an ethics of "humans suitably adapting themselves to the other's *du*." In Heidegger's words, this sort of ethics would be the very requirement of Being (*Sein*) itself to the human being (*Dasein*).

As a matter of fact, in *Historical Ontology*, while Li makes the argument that "*du* is a human creation, a human manufacture," he also says things that are not in accordance with this argument or even contradict it outright. For instance, Li quotes his early works and says that *du* means "the unanimous amalgamation of the subjective purposefulness and the objective regularity in successful practical activities,"[40] whereas "the subjectivity and consciousness precisely could lack '*du*,' since it is lacking the direct limitation and regulation by the objective material existence."[41] In addition, he says that "the ontological nature of '*du*' as the origin (*benyuan* 本源) is not solely a (subjective) human invention (*faming* 發明), but also a discovery of nature (objects)."[42] Here, in the so-called "amalgamation" of "purposefulness" and "regularity," in the so-called subject's consciousness lacking "limitation and regulation by the objective material existence," and in the so-called "discovery of nature (objects)," he is actually admitting to or even emphasizing that it is impossible for *du* in the sense of "*shi-du*" or "doing things just right" to be a human "creation" and "manufacture" unless we redefine the meaning of "*du*" or the meaning of "creation" and "manufacture." Furthermore, the following descriptions that frequently appear in *Historical Ontology* seem also to run in the opposite direction from *du* being a human creation or manufacture. For instance, Li says that *du* contains "some sort of indefinability and unpredictability" or that it contains "unpredictable possibilities and contingencies."[43] He also says that *du* "is not the track, rules or consistency that can be framed by rationality (*lixing* 理性). It is filled with uncertainties, un-conventions, multi-centers, and contingencies. It is open, vacillating, ambiguous, and full of sensibility (*ganshou* 感受)."[44] These descriptions run in the opposite direction from Li's main argument, since human creation or manufacture requires definability, predictability, and consistency.[45] If the wheel I made is not round nor a square, or it seems round and a square at the same time, by lacking consistency, it would become impossible for it to exist and function as a wheel. If the shoes I made have no difference from hats, and if the straw sandals I made have no difference from straw baskets, then there could not be such a thing as the manufacturing of shoes and straw sandals.[46]

Surely, when Li proposes *du* as human creation or manufacture he is not discussing creation or manufacture in the sense of making wheels or shoes. Instead, if I may say so, Li is discussing the creation or manufacture of *du* itself that arises from the very activity of creating or manufacturing concrete or material things for satisfying the need of human survival. Such a creation or manufacture means that during the activity of wheelmaking or shoemaking the *du* itself as the "doing things just right" for the practical activities of wheelmaking and shoemaking will gradually emerge. In other words, this means that the very artistry of wheelmaking or shoemaking is formed through a process of trying constantly to do things "just right" and continually adapting (*shi-du*) the worker to the work. As the formation of *du*, the process of doing things just right and adapting oneself to the work is a process that is dynamic rather than static, changing rather than being fixed. But the creation or manufacture that produces specific material outcomes should still have to be definable, predictable, and consistent. If it were true that *du* cannot be framed by rationality, if *du* is filled with uncertainties, un-conventions, multi-centers, and contingencies, and if *du* is open, vacillating, ambiguous, and full of sensibility, then how could humans "create" or "manufacture" it as "some sort of thing" (a sort of thing that has identity and that could be differentiated from other things)?

But let us temporally parenthesize these difficult questions on whether *du* is a human creation or manufacture and how it could be so. Instead, let us stop for a moment and take a close look at the ambiguous expression of "*du* is . . . full of sensibility" cited above. Obviously, it is not possible that *du* itself is full of sensibility. Therefore, to make sense of the sentence, it seems that this expression has to be filled out as "humans are full of sensibility in the mastery of *du*." But why should humans have to be full of sensibility in the mastery of *du*? Because, according to Li, *du* is doing things and interacting with other people "just right." However, to be "just right," it is hard to have a singular and fixed rule. It is difficult to have a singular and fixed rule, because in the final analysis the other that I interact with is always individualized, different, and unique. For this reason, as the one who deals with different things and people, I need to be sensible and sensitive to the *du*, which is always different in each different occasion, since, in the sense of "doing things just right," *du* always means that "I suitably adapt myself to the other's *du* or to the other as my *du*." To take the example of cultivating a plant again: for me, the plant that I cultivate is the other. During the cultivating activity, I have to suit and adapt to the needs of the plant, which means that I have to suit (*shi*) the *du* of the plant I am cultivating. However, there is not any *du* directly inscribed on the surface of the plant, and thus I need to "sense" it out. In watering and fertilizing the plant, there is no single and certain *du* (in the sense of degree or extent) for me to suit and adapt to. Even with the same kind of plant planted in the same place, the cultivator still needs to constantly sense and adjust the *du* of watering and fertilizing according to the change of weather and soil. It is precisely because in the cultivating activities it is the plant itself as the *du* that measures the result of my planting activities, rather than that I "make the law" for the plant, that I need to be sensible and sensitive to the *du* of the plant.

In order to explain further the above proposition that "the other that I interact with is always individualized, different and unique," let me illustrate it with the example of the wheelwright Bian in "The Way of Heaven" in the *Zhuangzi*, which I mentioned earlier. When the wheelwright Bian described his experience of wheelmaking, or, to be precise, his sensibility of wheelmaking,[47] he said,

> When I chisel a wheel, if the blows of the mallet are too gentle, the chisel will slide and won't take hold. But if they're too hard, it will bite and won't budge. Not too gentle, not too hard—you can get it in your hand and feel it in your mind. You can't put it into words, and yet there's a knack to it somehow. I can't teach it to my son, and he can't learn it from me. So I've gone along for seventy years, and at my age I'm still chiseling wheels.[48]

Making wheels is an activity of creating and manufacturing. This activity will generate a consistent outcome—a wheel. The skill of wheelmaking in itself is indescribable since the subject of this activity needs to constantly and meticulously sense the appropriate strength and speed required by the object (in this case, the wooden materials that need to be made into a wheel) during his activity of wheelmaking. The wheelwright Bian has to apply his strength just right and control the speed just right, in order to make the wheel just right or to make a wheel that is just right. That is to say, in making wheels, the wheelwright Bian has to handle and control the "just right" in the mutual interactions of three things throughout the entire process: the activity, the instruments, and the materials. "Humans, in the practical operation of applying and producing instruments, discovered the relationship of geometric and physical adaptation, confrontation and isomorphism in the triad of their own activities, instruments and objects."[49] To put it differently, in this task, the wheelwright Bian needs to handle and control various kinds of *du*, which include the strength and speed in the application of instruments, the degree of sharpness of the instrument itself, the degree of hardness and humidity of the material itself, and so on. Thereby, all of these factors need to cooperate just right to generate the expected outcome. This kind of handle and control (the mastery of *du*) requires sensing out and is full of sensibility, since the activity of wheelmaking is a dynamic process in which every element and factor needs to be mutually coordinated just right. Therefore, this kind of human sensibility has to be maintained without remiss throughout the entire process of the activity. This means that the actor will have to constantly sense and then adjust for every single activity of wheelmaking, or every movement throughout the entire process of the activity of wheelmaking. In this kind of continuous mutual adaptation, or in this kind of activity of letting oneself constantly suit the others' *du*, every single activity of wheelmaking and even every single movement in the activity of wheelmaking is "full of sensibility" and unique, and it possesses the nature of un-repeatability and particularity. This is why the wheelwright Bian could not transmit this sort of sensibility—which is a sensibility that could not be formalized rather than a kind of "experience" that could be formalized—directly to his son. In order to learn the skill of wheelmaking well, his son must sense it for himself.

Alternatively, we can take traditional Chinese medicine as a further example. Every single diagnosis and treatment given by the doctor to the patient is first of all a unique activity of "I suit the other's *du*" (the patient's *du*), since each and every single patient is individualized, special, and unique. Therefore, despite the various kinds of proper names given to specific syndromes, and the fact that doctors are able to categorize such syndromes accordingly, patients presenting the same syndrome are always somewhat different. Each patient is always unique in being "this particular one." Hence, although the syndrome of "this particular patient" and that of others are in theory or abstractly the "same," the treatment needs to be adjusted from person to person and cannot be carried out according to a fixed pattern. The doctor needs to be constantly "full of unique sensibility for the specific patient." It is precisely from this perspective that we may understand that a good traditional Chinese medicine practitioner may give different treatments to different patients who appear to present "the same syndrome" while all of the treatments are the cures being just right—and this is what may be called "treatment based on syndrome differentiation" in traditional Chinese medicine.

## From *Shi-Du* 適度 (Suitability) to *Zhi-Du* 制度 (Institution), and to *Du* as "In-Between"

Yet, if the diagnosis of medical cases could not be finalized or generalized, thus always remaining unique, and if the diagnosis solely depends on the sensibility of individual doctors, then we could not speak of any sort of medical expertise and medical science. Likewise, if the skill of wheelmaking could not at all be taught and passed down as a sort of "craftsmanship," then we could not speak of any sort of expertise in wheelmaking. If the activity of practicing medicine and wheelmaking could not at all be "normalized, regulated" or formalized, and if each and every traditional Chinese medicine practitioner and wheelwright always had to start from scratch each and every time, it would then become impossible for humanity to master any sort of artistry or skill that is necessary for survival. Thus, it would become impossible for human beings themselves to have the so-called accumulation of progress. For this reason, it is necessary to normalize, regulate, and formalize. Li says rightly, "The subjective requirement of humans in their own subjectivity, which takes *du* as their basis (*benti*), is firstly the normalization and organization of operational activities."[50] On the one hand, *du* certainly has "some sort of indefinability and unpredictability" or contains "unpredictable possibilities and contingencies." *Du* is certainly "not the track, rules or consistency that can be framed by rationality. It is filled with uncertainties, un-conventions, multi-centers, and contingencies. It is open, vacillating, ambiguous, and full of sentiments."[51] In this sense, it is indeed difficult to normalize and regulate *du*. On the other hand, however, for the activities of production and operation to be done "just right," there is indeed a need for them to be normalized and regulated, which requires representing and establishing various kinds of structures and forms. To accomplish this, the subtle and unique sensibility of an operator, or the indescribable "experiences of an individual," need to be transformed into universal discourses that could then be conveyed. It has to become the expertise that could be taught and passed down, the artistry that could be learned, operational rules that could be mastered, and so forth. This would be the kind of transformation wherein lies the origin of Li's three-line teaching: "experience (a posteriori) transforms to a priori; history establishes rationality; psychology becomes ontology."[52]

As the primary category in Li's anthropologico-historical ontology, the concept of *du* within his discursive framework possesses a sort of duality or an internal tension, because although the necessity of being "just right" for the success of practical activities requires humans first to suit the other's *du* or the other as *du*, there is always a tendency for humans to transform the *passive* "suiting and adapting *du*" (*shi-du*) to the *active* "systematizing *du*" (*zhi-du*) (literally, "to making various kinds of *du* to form a system or an institution"; this would be close to what Li has in mind when he says *du* is human creation or manufacture). In fact, humans are *always in the process of transforming from passively suiting and adapting du to actively systematizing du*. Notably, the character *du* 度 in the Chinese language already contains this kind of transformation within itself. *Du* is not inherent to humans themselves, since *du* first comes from the other that humans encounter. *Du* is from the requirement or demand that the other addresses to humans and hence requires or demands human's sensibility of the other. As such, there is no pre-existing or a priori *du* for me to dominate or to impose on the other as an object that I believe I can grasp and control "properly."[53] I first need to suit myself to the *du* of the thing I have to deal with. This kind of suiting and adapting *du* as an activity that is paradoxically passive but also active (it is both at the same time), and requires differentiation based on its time, place, situation, and content. This makes it difficult for it to have fixed rules, thus it would be required each time for it to be sensed by people themselves corresponding to the particular time, place, situation, and content of the thing they have to deal with. Nevertheless, if every single interaction between humans and things ends up being in this manner, and people always need to learn from scratch, then the skills and artistry that could be passed on will not be formed. It would thus be impossible for any progress to be built through a "constant accumulation of experience." Therefore, the "suiting and adapting *du*" that is sensitively "sensed" or *subjectively* felt in humans' practical activities needs to be fixed *objectively*. That is to say, it needs to become an "object" that can be expressed and transmitted.

For this reason, humans require certain means or measures to objectively pinpoint and specifically fix the various kinds of *du*, which are the various kind of "doing things just right" that has been sensed in the ever-changing activities of "suiting the *du* of the object." If wheelwright Bian the craftsman needed to teach his son the skill of wheelmaking as the means to "put food on the table," then he would have to be able to transmit to his son the senses of the ever-changing speed, strength, force, hardness, and humidity that he had sensed in the activity of wheelmaking. He would have to transmit them in a way that his son could "handle" (*ba-wo* 把握) them.[54] In this instance, as I use the term "handle," I am referring to the word's most basic definition, which is to see, catch, and hold the thing in hand. To that end, certain means to measure and point out speed, strength, force, hardness, and humidity are needed. That is to say, something like a ruler that can let one measure the length of an object or a scale that can measures the weight of an object. These things may indeed be said to be "a human creation," and they relate closely to the human body.[55] At first, the human body performed the task of *du*, which was used to decide the objects' *du*: stretching fingers and arms or the steps taken by foot became the *du* of length; lifting objects either with two hands or by embracing the object with both arms became the *du* of weight and volume, and so on. In this specific sense, humans truly became the "measure" (*chi-du*) of everything. A time later, the *du* which originated from the human body was imprinted on the object. This means that humans started to manufacture specific tools and instruments for this *du* to be "normalized, regulated" and formalized. The produced tools and instruments such as rulers and scales are the *du* for me to decide on the various *du* of objects. The ruler would allow one to "objectively" measure the length of objects, and the scale would allow one to "objectively" measure the weight of object. Now in possession of "objective" and "objectified" *du*, humans can subsequently normalize, organize, and formalize various kinds of being "just right" in their activities of production and operation, which makes the various kinds of being "just right" expressible and conveyable. In this sense, in the dual meaning of *du* as both the standard for various kinds of measurement and the method for production or the procedure for operation, *du* could certainly be said to be a human creation or manufacture, i.e., "human-made."

In *Historical Ontology* Li mentions the method of smelting iron described in the *Kaogongji* 考工記, which could well be used to illustrate the process of human "systematizing *du*" (*zhi-du*), or the objectification of *du*. The iron ore will melt at a certain temperature within a certain timeframe. Before the days of precise instruments for measuring time and temperature, smelters had to rely on their experience, which was gained and accumulated from the practice of iron-smelting, to control this specific process. This includes, for instance, the performance of the different fuels used in smelting, the relationship between the specific color of the flame and its temperature, and the different timing required for the different kinds of iron ore, and so on. As Li puts it, "'*du*' is originally generated according to various concrete conditions, including favorable timing of heaven (*tianshi* 天時), geographic advantages of the earth (*dili* 地利), and the harmony of humans (*renhe* 人和) (group collaboration). Thereby, the handling of performance, scenarios, and conditions of various kinds of things, including favorable timing of heaven, geographic advantages of earth, and the harmony of humans, becomes '*du*' and the concrete content of mastering, understanding, and recognizing '*du*.'"[56] This kind of handling is itself *du* in the sense of "doing things just right," yet this "doing things just right" itself is still indescribable. That is to say, the objective measurement to measure *du* as "doing things just right" has not yet formed. What Li intends to emphasize is the *formalization* of these experiences themselves. This means, for instance, representing the *du* required for iron-smelting either through the traditional way of observing the specific color of the flame, or through the modern way of utilizing a thermograph. This is the exact reason why there is the term *wen-du* 溫-度 (the measurement of heat, temperature) in the Chinese language. In this regard, "doing things just right" in the smelting of iron has been formalized into concrete measurements (*chi-du*), which could then be "handled."

However, while *du* is inseparable from formalization, formalization might conversely set limits on the original adaptation of humans to the things that they have to deal with for survival. That is to say, formalization could be the limitation of "doing things just right" in humanity's practice and activities. For instance, I may still follow the regulated *du* in my operations when the specific situation has changed; then my operation will result in *ke zhou qiu jian* 刻舟求劍 (making a notch on the side of a moving boat to show where to look for the sword which was dropped overboard, i.e., taking measures without attention to changes in circumstances). The question raised here may be expressed as follows: without formalization, it is impossible to have *du* with any sense of objectivity. However, once it is formalized, the *du* understood as "doing things just right" will become affected. And exactly because *du* is human-made in this sense, different groups of people who lived in different times and places have come to possess different forms of *du*. Different forms of *du* may obstruct mutual communication or even become sources of conflicts. Therefore, in order to communicate and to ensure peace, it is necessary for different forms of *du* to be capable of being convertible. Here one can take the conversion between the British imperial system of weights and measures and the metric system for example. Furthermore, for the sake of modern technology, it becomes necessary to conduct "standardization" globally, which is to create and formalize unified and universal *du* for all different kinds of practice, operation, and production.

However, once humans possess various kinds of *du*, and once "the structure and formation of *du* could be universally applied on objective objects,"[57] the "doing things just right," as Li says of it, begins to dissolve. The wheels manufactured on the assembly lines are produced on an industrial scale. Each one of these thoroughly and indistinguishably conforms to the predetermined design, a design that is made according to the *du* that had already been mastered. Oxen in the slaughterhouse are slaughtered *en masse*. Each ox is dismembered perfectly (albeit bluntly) by machines (robotic arms or robots), while the dismemberment is executed according to the anatomical structure of the cattle that has been schematized and formalized. When all wheels are produced "just right" according to the *du* (design, craftsmanship, and operation) settled by humans, and when all oxen are slaughtered according to the anatomical schema that has been formalized, "doing things just right" in traditional artistry like the wheelwright Bian's skill of wheelmaking and the butcher Ding's skill of ox-dismembering appear to have lost their usefulness and the link that connects the skills (*ji*) and "*dao*" will be cut.[58] The artistry and skill in the traditional productive activities have been transformed into the technology and technical skill in the modern productive activities. The producer is no longer an artist, and the product no longer bears the personal mark. With all kinds of *du* becoming a set of procedures, therein lies the beginning of mechanization and automation, and productive activities need not depend on the individual's sense any longer. Consequently, the traditional way of "letting humans suit the objects' *du*" gave way to the modern way of "making objects suit the humans' *du*," or at least, the former became insignificant. Humans began to impose their *du* with increasing proactiveness (or violence) on objects. Now humans appear to have really become the measure (*chi-du*) of everything. If nowadays people are no longer required to "do things just right" in the way done by the wheelwright Bian making the wheel and the butcher Ding dismembering the ox, this might only be because it now seems that all products are automatically produced to the degree of "being just right." Throughout the process of normalization, regulation, and formalization, "*du*" has already lost its very meaning of being *du*.

Li's *du* first "appears in the process of human production and living activities."[59] *Du* means "being just right" in the satisfaction of an outcome that is generated through the process of human activities of production and subsistence. For survival, humans need to produce, and the activities of production rely on external things as materials. However, although humans are capable of learning to produce things that need to be done "just right," humans are not yet able to create the thing itself (natural thing) *ex nihilo* like the Creator or God. Before a thing can be used, and before becoming "a useful thing," the thing as thing needs to be fundamentally respected by humans. Things, as things that humans themselves have to first "suit" in a fundamental way, are still silently resisting the *du* imposed by humans. Put in a different way, things are still silently resisting, even in vain, the human violence in the form of systematized *du*. This resistance marks the finitude of the human being. Man is not God. Nowadays we are faced with problems with the Earth's atmosphere, the environment, global warming, the ecological system, and the extinction of species. The solution to all these problems fundamentally requires humans to first respect the *du* of the thing. This is a requirement for people first to passively, submissively, and considerately "do things just right" in dealing with things that constitute the world in which they exist and survive. Human beings would have to behave just like butcher Ding, who would become "frightened and very cautious" (*churanweijie* 怵然爲戒) every time he had to dismember an ox, or like the carpenter Zhi-Qing 梓慶, who would even let himself "forget that I have four limbs and a body" every time he had to carve wood to make a bell stand.[60] This kind of sincerity and respect of a person in front of a thing they have to utilize for survival shows that the relationship between the human being and the thing is ultimately *ethical*. As Li says: "from ancient times, Chinese philosophy always emphasizes '*zhong*' (the middle or mean) and '*he*' (harmony). '*Zhong*' and '*he*' is the very realization and objectification of '*du*.'"[61] "*Zhong-he* 中和" is a notion concerning the ethical relationship between humans themselves and between human beings and things. If Li's *du* realizes or objectifies itself as *zhong-he*, then *du* in the final analysis is essentially an ethical notion. Therefore, the important emphasis that Li puts on *du* as the "primary category" of his anthropologico-historical ontology can be understood as the very emphasis on the ethical.

The concept of *du* certainly deserves our attention and consideration. Li says,

> The existence of "*du*" contains enormous uncertainty. Therefore, it is different from "Being" or "quality" (*zhi* 質) in Hegel's science of logic. *Du* is provided by "the rationality of experience," relying on the basis of trial-and-error procedure in practical operations. It is the ever-changing and accumulated comprehension (*bawo*) of the world. "*Du*" goes from the "operational level" to the "existential level," playing the role of the mutual interchanger of the two levels.[62]

This is to admit that *du* is the "in-between" of the two. We could say that *du* is, actually, the in-between of all things. *Du* is simply "being in-between," a "being in-between" in a subtle and ungeneralizable, universal way. This might exactly be the "essence" of *du* as envisioned by Li. The reason why *du* has "some sort of indefinability and unpredictability," containing "unpredictable possibilities and contingency,"[63] the reason why *du* is "not the track, rules or consistency that can be framed by rationality," and why it is "filled with uncertainties, un-conventions, multi-centers, and contingencies. It is open, vacillating, ambiguous, and full of sentiments"[64] and so on, precisely because *du* is simply "being in-between": in between humans and things, and in between humans themselves. Within this "being in-between," the outcome of every single "doing things just right" as an activity (or as the passivity of the activity) would be a forthcoming or yet-to-come ideal, and thus an endless pursuit. However, once, as Li says, *du* begins to take on the concrete structures in the different kinds of shapes and colors, and once "the structure and formation of *du* could be universally applied on objective objects,"[65] *du* begins to lose itself from being *du*.

Li's thesis on *du* actually already points to a new direction. It points to the subtle state of "being in-between" as described above, and it points to a profound mystery in Chinese thought. In fact, his thesis on *du* has broken through his ontology, although he constantly draws it back into this ontology. Moreover, the present study is only a preliminary attempt at "explaining and liberating" (*jie-shi* 解釋, i.e., to untie, to analyze, to explain, and to release or liberate) the potential power of the omnipresent and elusive *du* in Li's thesis.

## Notes

1. The English title is a rather impossible translation of the untranslatable Chinese title 度之無度与無度之度. As Li emphasizes the untranslatability of the concept of "*du*" 度, which he makes central to his late philosophical discourse, I will keep this concept untranslated throughout my discussion unless situation dictates otherwise. This study was originally written in Chinese. A rough draft of the English translation was completed by Huang Yijia, to whom the work was commissioned. The present text is a substantially revised version by myself.

2. Zhuangzi, *The Complete Works of Zhuangzi*, trans. Burton Watson (New York: Columbia University Press, 2013), 113. Watson translates the term *du* 度 as "rules" and *shu* 數 as "regulations," whereas they are generally translated as "measure" and "number."

3. Li Zehou 李澤厚, "Guanyu 'Lunlixue zonglanbiao' de shuoming" 關於 "倫理學總覽表" 的說明 (An Explanation on the "General Scheme of Ethics")," *Zhongguo wenhua* vol. 47, no. 1 (2018): 1. The Chinese term *du* 度 may mean "measure," "degree," "limit," "extent," and "linear measure." Interestingly, it may also mean "tolerance," "magnanimity," and "consideration." Furthermore, with other Chinese characters it may form compounds, among which I will only mention two, *shidu* 適度 and *zhidu* 制度, normally translated as "adaptation/suitability" and "institution." These two compounds will be of particular interest in my discussion of Li's *du*.

4. Li, "An Explanation," 2.

5. Li Zehou 李澤厚, *Lishi bentilun* 歷史本體論 (*Historical Ontology*) (Beijing: SDX Joint Publishing Company 三聯書店, 2002), 13. The English "ontology" in the parentheses is Li's.

6. Li, *Historical Ontology*, 13. The English "Being of beings" in the parentheses is Li's. This indicates that Li seems to think what he calls "the final reality" can be thought as the "Being of beings," which sounds quite Heideggerian. But for Heidegger the Being of beings is not the final reality.

7. Li, *Historical Ontology*, 13. Li uses "historical ontology" and "anthropologico-historical ontology" interchangeably. I will adopt the expression "anthropologico-historical ontology" in my discussion. All the translations are mine unless otherwise specified.

8. Li, *Historical Ontology*, 7–8.

9. Li, *Historical Ontology*, 5.

10. Li, *Historical Ontology*, 6.

11. Li, *Historical Ontology*, 6.
12. Li, *Historical Ontology*, 7.
13. Li, *Historical Ontology*, 3.
14. Li, *Historical Ontology*, 1.
15. Li, *Historical Ontology*, 2. "度就是技術或藝術。" However, Li seems not very clear on *du* as technique or art. The fifth proposition states that "mankind relies on mastering the *du* in the artistry of production." According to this statement, *du* cannot be equated to technique or artistry. *Du* is always the *du* within technique, skills and artistry.
16. Li, *Historical Ontology*, 2.
17. Li, *Historical Ontology*, 3.
18. Li, *Historical Ontology*, 4.
19. Li, *Historical Ontology*, 4–5.
20. Li, *Historical Ontology*, 6.
21. Li, *Historical Ontology*, 7.
22. Li, *Historical Ontology*, 7.
23. Li, *Historical Ontology*, 8.
24. "什麼是'度'? '度' 就是'掌握分寸 [*fencun*, i.e., measure], 恰到好處'。"
25. Li, *Historical Ontology*, 1.
26. Mencius, *Mencius*, trans. Irene Bloom, ed. and an intro. Philip J. Ivanhoe (New York: Columbia University Press, 2009), 127–28.
27. This section title could also be "where is the 'measure' (*du*) that measures (*du-liang* 度量) the difference between humans and animals," if I can play with the term *du*.
28. Li, *Historical Ontology*, 1.
29. Li, *Historical Ontology*, 2.
30. Li, *Historical Ontology*, 2.
31. Li, *Historical Ontology*, 2.
32. Li, *Historical Ontology*, 2.
33. Although Li says that animals can also master "doing things just right," he does not say that *du* also concerns the "ontological nature" of the existence of other species. If animals also "regard survival as the goal" and thus need to master "doing things just right" when doing things for survival, which means they also need to master *du*, would *du* then also concern the "ontological nature" of the existence of other species? Would the survival of bees be affected if they could not build their honeycomb "just right"?
34. Li, *Historical Ontology*, 2.
35. Cf. note 15 above.
36. Li, *Historical Ontology*, 9.
37. "'度'并不存在於任何對象中,也不存在於意識中,而首先是出現在人類的生產—生活活動中,即實踐—實用中。它本身是人的一種創造 (creation),一種製作。從而,不是'質'或'量'或'存在'(有)或'無,'而是'度,'才是人類學本體論的第一範疇。" Li, *Historical Ontology*, 2–3.

38. "From ancient times, Chinese philosophy always emphasizes '*zhong*' (the middle or mean) and '*he*' (harmony). '*Zhong*' and '*he*' is the realization and objectification of *du*. It can extend across all field, form music to books on the art of war, and to politics. The origin . . . is the '*he*,' '*zhong*,' '*qiao*,' and '*tiao*' in the artistry of production." (從上古以來，中國思想一直強調'中'、'和'。'中'、'和' 就是 '度' 的實現和對象化 (客觀化)。它們遍及從音樂到兵書到政治等各個領域。其根源 . . . . . . 即生產技藝中的 '和'、'中'、'巧'、'調.') Li, *Historical Ontology*, 3. The expression of "the realization and objectification of *du*" seems to mean *du* is pre-existing and waiting to be realized, but Li's argument makes us feel that *du* does not exist prior to its realization.

39. That the Chinese term *du* lends itself to the formation of the Chinese compound *shi-du* 適度 shows that the term *du* itself already connotes a sense of "being suitable." This meaning is rendered clear by *shi-du*, which is normally used as adjective or adverb to mean "within the proper measure," "suitable" or "suitably." In Chinese, however, with a play of words, *shi-du* may be turned into a verb-object structure to mean "to suit (*shi*) the other's measure (*du*)." Such a play of words is not meant to be just a play, as it importantly shows the cluster of multiple meanings that the term *du* 度 denotes or connotes. This is why Li emphasizes the untranslatability of the term *du* in his antropologico-historical ontology.

40. "在成功的實踐活動中主觀合目的性與客觀合規律性的一致融合。" Li, *Historical Ontology*, 3.

41. "主觀性—意識性恰恰可以缺乏 '度,' 這是由於沒有客觀物質生存的直接制約。" Li, *Historical Ontology*, 4.

42. "'度' 的本體性, 作為本源, 不僅是人為 (主體的) 發明 (invention), 而且又是對自然 (客體的) 的發現 (discovery)。" Li, *Historical Ontology*, 6.

43. Li, *Historical Ontology*, 7.

44. 度有 "某種不可規定性, 不可預見性," 或 "難以預測的可能性和偶然性," 度 "不是理性所能框定的軌道、規則或同一性, 它充滿不確定、非約定、多中心、偶然性, 它是開放、波動、含混而充滿感受的。" Li, *Historical Ontology*, 9.

45. This might make us think of the two causes in Aristotle's "Four Causes," which are the final cause and the formal cause. Both are, in some way, concerning regularity, predictability, and consistency.

46. Mencius says that "If someone makes shoes without knowing the size of a person's feet, I know that he will not make baskets." Mencius, *Mencius*, 125.

47. Strictly speaking, experience can be formalized and become theory, while floating sensibility or sentiments cannot.

48. Zhuangzi, *The Complete Works of Zhuangzi*, 107.

49. "人類在使用—製造工具的實踐操作中, 發現了自身活動、工具和對象三者之間的幾何的、物理的性能的適應、對抗和同構。" Li, *Historical Ontology*, 4.

50. "以 '度' 作為本體的人類主體性對自己主觀性的要求, 首先是操作活動的規範化、秩序化。" Li Zehou 李澤厚, *Renleixue lishi bentilun* 人類學歷史本體論 (*Anthropologico-Historical Ontology*) (Tianjin: Tianjin Academy of Social Sciences

Press, 2008), 64. This sentence is cited from the *Historical Ontology*, which was incorporated into the 2008 edition of *Anthropologico-Historical Ontology*. It was not found in the 2002 edition of *Historical Ontology*. I read *benti* in this sentence as "basis."

51. Li, *Historical Ontology*, 9.
52. "經驗變先驗, 歷史建理性, 心理成本體."
53. This might be precisely opposite to the ancient Greek philosopher Protagoras's idea that "man is the measure of all things." However, affirming humans themselves are not the pre-existing *du*, or humans do not possess pre-existing *du*, does not mean that the object itself possesses *du* not relative to humans. *Du* is always a relative and relational concept. When saying the plant itself is the *du* for cultivators, it means that the plant, as "the other," provides measurement (*chi-du*) for planting activities and thus humans can measure whether their activities are "suitable" (*shi-du*).
54. The Chinese term *ba-wo* 把握 consists of two Chinese characters, *ba* 把, "a handle," and *wo* 握 "to hold, to grasp." It can be used as a noun to mean that one has a "handle" on a matter, or as a verb in sentences such as "one is proficient in 'handling' a matter." By extension, it can mean certainty or comprehension.
55. In Duan Yucai's 段玉裁 commentaries (*zhu* 注) in *Shuowen Jiezi* 説文解字, he analyses the character *du* 度 as follows: "There were five '*du*' (measurement) in ancient times, '*fen*' 分, '*cun*' 寸, '*chi*' 尺, '*zhang*' 丈, '*yin*' 引 . . . (they were) all based on human hands, and '度' is thus written with the radical '*you*' 又, which represents the hand 手." Xu Shen 許慎 and Duan Yucai 段玉裁, *Shuowen Jiezi zhu* 説文解字注 (Commentary on the Shuowen Jiezi) (Shanghai: Shanghai guji chuban she, 1981), 228. Confucius says, "Stretching fingers then one can know the length of '*cun*' 寸, stretching hands then one can know the length of '*chi*' 尺; stretching elbows then one can know the length of '*xun*' 尋." Therefore, the character is written with the 手 radical. Chen Shike 陳士珂, *Kongzi jiayu shuzheng* 孔子家語疏証 (Annotation on Family Sayings of Confucius) (Shanghai: Shanghai Bookstore, 1987), 14. In its etymological meaning, *du* as a noun means the standard (*chi-du*) that is accorded to when one measures an object. When *du* is used as a verb, it means to measure an object according to specific *chi-du*.
56. Li, *Historical Ontology*, 5.
57. Li, *Historical Ontology*, 6.
58. "The butcher Ding laid down his knife and replied, 'What I care about is the Way (*dao*), which goes beyond skill (*ji* 技).'" Zhuangzi, *The Complete Works of Zhuangzi*, 19. Wei Yuan also says, "Going beyond skill (*ji* 技) would be the Way (*dao*); going through art would lead to the Spirit (*shen* 神)." Wei Yuan 魏源, *Wei Yuan ji* 魏源集 (*The Collected Works of Wei Yuan*), ed. editorial department of Zhonghua Book Company (Beijing: Zhonghua Book Company, 2018), 96.
59. Li, *Historical Ontology*, 2.

60. Zhuangzi, *The Complete Works of Zhuangzi*, 152.
61. Li, *Historical Ontology*, 3.
62. "這個 '度' 的存在具有巨大的不確定性, 從而不同於 Hegel 邏輯學的'存在' 或 '質'。它由 '經驗合理性' 所提供, 依存於嘗試錯誤的操作實踐基礎之上, 是不斷變遷和積累出來的對世界的把握。'度' 是由 '操作層' 向 '存在層' 過渡並擔負著兩個層面相轉換的角色。" Li Zehou 李澤厚, "Lun shiyong lixing he legan wenhua" 論實用理性與樂感文化 (On Practical Rationality and the Culture of Optimism), in *Anthropologico-Historical Ontology*, author Li Zehou (Tianjin: Tianjin Academy of Social Sciences Press, 2008), 177.
63. Li, *Historical Ontology*, 7.
64. Li, *Historical Ontology*, 9.
65. Li, *Historical Ontology*, 6.

# Bibliography

Chen Shike 陳士珂. *Kongzi jiayu shuzheng* 孔子家語疏證 (*Annotation on Family Sayings of Confucius*). Shanghai: Shanghai Bookstore 上海書店, 1987.
Li Zehou 李澤厚. "Guanyu 'Lunlixue zonglan biao' de shuoming" 關於 "倫理學總覽表" 的說明 (An Explanation of the "General Scheme of Ethics"). *Zhongguo wenhua* 47, no. 1 (2018): 1–15.
Li Zehou 李澤厚. *Lishi bentilun* 歷史本體論 (*Historical Ontology*). Beijing: SDX Joint Publishing, 2002.
Li Zehou 李澤厚. "Lun shiyong lixing he legan wenhua" 論實用理性與樂感文化 (On Practical Rationality and the Culture of Optimism). In *Renleixue lishi bentilun* 人類學歷史本體論 (*Anthropologico-Historical Ontology*), 159–252. Tianjin: Tianjin Academy of Social Sciences Press, 2008.
Li Zehou 李澤厚. *Renleixue lishi bentilun* 人類學歷史本體論 (*Anthropologico-Historical Ontology*). Tianjin: Tianjin Academy of Social Sciences Press, 2008.
Mencius. *Mencius*. Translated by Irene Bloom. Edited and with an introduction by Philip J. Ivanhoe. New York: Columbia University Press, 2009.
Wei Yuan 魏源. *Wei Yuan ji* 魏源集 (*The Collected Works of Wei Yuan*). Edited by the editorial department of Zhonghua Book Company. Beijing: Zhonghua Book Company, 2018.
Xu Shen 許慎 and Duan Yucai 段玉裁. *Shuowen Jiezi zhu* 説文解字注 (*Commentary on the Shuowen Jiezi*). Shanghai: Shanghai guji chuban she 上海古籍出版社, 1981.
Zhuangzi. *The Complete Works of Zhuangzi*. Translated by Burton Watson. New York: Columbia University Press, 2013.

## 11

# A Post-Marxian Dialogue on the Subject–Object Relation

## Li Zehou and Adorno on the Dialectics of Aesthetic Subjectivity

JANA S. ROŠKER

### Prologue: The Marxist Framework

In premodern and modern Western epistemology and aesthetics, the subject–object dichotomy was mainly understood, following the Cartesian tradition, as meaning that the cognitive subject (the knower) is a thinking being that is not extended, and the object is an extended thing that does not think. This view or characterization of the concept of the cognitive subject has also prevailed in discussions of the nature of the Self, in both continental and analytic philosophy. Kant and the German idealists aimed to explain the human subject as something constituted in the process of perception and cognition, as the result of streams of sensory impressions.[1] This basic position was not changed by the fact that objects in this process had to adapt to the perceiving and cognizing subject. In such theories of knowledge there is an indissoluble difference between the object of knowledge and the knower. This is also true when the subject reflects on itself—that is, when it is a matter of objective self-awareness.

A basic characteristic of the Marxist approach to the analysis of cognition, then, can be found in a new approach to the exploration of cognitive activities: here, the cognition, meaning the grasping of knowledge about the object by the subject, is in the context of the practical transformation of natural and social reality. In such a framework, subjects are conditioned by their practice, by their activity in the function of social human beings. Thus, Marxism views the foundation of people's relationship with external reality in their practice, that is, in their acting upon it. These activities enable human beings to perceive the world, but at the same time, in the process of perception, they necessarily change both reality and themselves. In this view, such reflective practice constitutes humans as beings qualitatively different from other animals, because in confronting the outside world they are not passive receivers, but rather deal with the objects of cognition as something "that should be changed in accordance with some aim of their own."[2] Hence, in such an "actual practice" the perception of the object as it is, and the subject's intentions of the goal of changing the object, are directly united.[3]

From a Marxist perspective, then, practice is that which actually unites the subject and object of perception and comprehension. In such an understanding, grasping realty was intrinsically connected with changing reality.[4] However, in this context we must also be aware of the fact that in Marxist theory, the relationship between subject and object cannot be equated with the relationship between consciousness and being—it is not a relation between res cogitans and res extensa. The former is not confined to the limits of consciousness, for it is a real and acting person, while the latter is not merely part of the "objective reality," but "that part of it which has become the target of the practical or cognitive activity of the subject."[5] It is also important to understand that in this view the subject is not merely a physical and bodily individual, separated from his or her material and social environment. A human being can become a subject only under the condition of his or her mastery of the modes of existence and practices developed by society. Human language, the laws and categories of logic, the methodological systems of science, and other forms of complex cognition can only evolve on such a onto-epistemological basis. This practice is a material practice, it pertains to the material world, it changes this world and elaborates upon it.[6]

## The "Practical Philosophy of Subjectality" and the Underlying Theory of Perception

Li Zehou, who followed Marxist (especially the early Marxist) theory, labeled his philosophical system "anthropo-historical ontology"[7] (or in abbreviated form, "historical ontology"[8]), although he emphasizes that this new way of thinking is essentially a "practical philosophy of *subjectality*."[9] *Subjectality* is his own neologism denoting the practical and active aspects of the human subject, expressed in Chinese by the term *zhutixing* 主體性.[10] Although he agreed that the latter term might better capture the meaning of his philosophy, he felt that the name philosophy of *zhutixing* (or subjectality) would be more difficult for Western readers to understand. In Chinese, there are two different terms that refer to the nature of the human subject. In contrast to *zhuguanxing* 主觀性, which belongs to epistemology and refers to the properties of the cognitive subject, *zhutixing* means the acting person in practice who has the property of objectivity.[11] Traditionally, however, both terms have been translated into English with a single word, *subjectivity*. In order to maintain this important distinction between the epistemological and ontological aspects of the human subject, Li coined the term *subjectality*. In his view, however, the concept of subjectality was difficult to grasp for Western philosophers, who usually automatically assume an ontology based on the static notion of being. Li therefore feared that such a deep-seated, fixed view of the problem of existence would make it too difficult to understand his specific, dynamically changing concept of the human subject, which (along with their entire psychology) is a product of socio-historical development. For this reason, he preferred to call his "practical philosophy of subjectality" by the term "anthropo-historical ontology."[12] But the idea of subjectality was doubtless in the center of this theoretical system, and it represented a synthesis of a Kantian autonomous subject and the Marxist notion of practice as a vital element of human existence. While Li agrees with Marx's emphasis on the primary importance of objective conditions, productive forces, and the material base, he diverges from orthodox Marxism in his conviction that the objective content of human practice cannot be separated from all those factors that are constitutive of autonomy in human life, especially in their creativity, innovativeness, and the willingness to act. Li Zehou tried to fix this inconsistency with the help of Kantian philosophy, in order to provide a link between Marx's idea of a "humanized nature" on the one hand and Kant's understanding of the subject on the other. As he explained, "The work that I now needed to do was to provide a link between Marx's idea of a 'humanized nature' and the philosophy of Kant. That is the reason I associated 'subjectality' with subjectivity, giving 'a priori' subjectivity a materialistic 'subjectality' foundation."[13] In Li Zehou's philosophical system, the concept of subjectality had several different layers, and Li distinguishes between two different kinds of subjectality. The first refers to the personal identity of an individual, and the second to communities and to humanity as a whole:

> The so-called "subjectality" has precisely this meaning. The subject of humanity appears through the social realization of material reality (based upon material production). This is the objective level of subjectality. This level is elementary and manifests itself in the structural connection between technology and society, as well as in social existence. Simultaneously, it also embraces the subjective level of social consciousness, which manifests itself in culturally conditioned mental structures. Therefore, the mental structure of subjectality is not primarily the subjective awareness of an individual in the sense of his or her sensations, desires, etc. This notion refers primarily to the results of human history that manifest themselves in structures of spiritual and intellectual culture, as well as in structures of ethical and aesthetic consciousness.[14]

But the question of the subject and its connection to the concept of subjectality is not the only problem that needs to be clarified when speaking about Li Zehou's view of the subject–object relation, because in Chinese the semantic connotations of this relation do not entirely overlap with the English (or Western) ones.

As we have seen, there are different expressions for the Western concepts of subjectivity (e.g., *zhutixing* 主體性 versus *zhuguanxing* 主觀性). However, the semantic scope of the field involving Chinese notions of object or objectivity is also different from the Western one, though not in the same way. In the epistemological sense, that is, in the function of individual perception expressed in English by the word *objective* or *objectivity*, the Chinese use the term *keguan* 客觀 or *keguanxing* 客觀性, in contrast to the term *zhuguan* 主觀 or *zhuguanxing* 主觀性, which means "subjective" or "subjectivity."However, when expressing the general idea of an object as opposed to a subject (*zhuti* 主體), the Chinese language uses two different terms, *keti* 客體 or *duixiang* 對象:[15] "In the Chinese context, strictly speaking, the object (in the sense of *keti*) belongs to the category of epistemology, while the scope of the object (in the sense of *duixiang*) is much broader. . . . The aesthetic object (*shenmei keti*[16]) mainly belongs to the category of epistemological philosophy, and together with aesthetic subject, it forms an epistemological model in the field of aesthetics."[17] Since, at the level of terminology, these two different connotations of the object in the sense of *keti* and *duixiang* are expressed in English by a single term, we must be careful to maintain the distinction made by Li (and in Chinese in general) between the object in the sense of a thing existing in the external world, which is in general opposition to human beings, and the object in the sense of the epistemological opposition to the cognitive subject.

> The object (in the sense of *keti*) is relative to the subject and refers to the object (in the sense of *duixiang*) of the subject's understanding or practice, which can be either material or mental. But the correspondence of object (as *duixiang*) and subject refers to the material or mental phenomenon that is determined as the purpose of understanding and practice. Whether a particular thing or thought can become the object (as *keti*) of cognition and practice depends on the subject. In the context of cognition, object (as *duixiang*) and object (as *keti*) are synonyms. But the two are also different. In the strict sense, object (as *keti*) belongs to the field of epistemology, while the meaning of object (as *duixiang*) is different because of the different scope of application. For example, it is consistent that the object (in the sense of *keti*) is that which is in corresponding opposition to the subject. But the object (in the sense of *duixiang*) that stands in corresponding opposition to consciousness is matter, which is not limited to the category of cognition, and here the object (in the sense of *duixiang*) is not an object (in the sense of *keti*) but matter. Similarly, the object (*duixiang*) corresponding to social consciousness is social existence, not the object (in the sense of *keti*). The extension of the object (as *duixiang*) is larger. As mentioned above, it can refer to both the material and the

mental, which means that it can refer to both the object and the subject. The objective (*keguan*[18]) refers only to material objects. Its extension is therefore narrower. The object (as *keti*) is more limited to the part of the material or spiritual world that pertains to knowledge and practice, therefore its extension is even narrower.[19]

Thus, the two terms commonly translated as object, i.e., *duixiang* and the *keti*, both refer to entities that are opposite to the subject. In other words, they are both what the subject is directly confronted with. However, while *duixiang* includes all objects of the external world, *keti* refers only to the phenomena that are to be grasped (or understood) by the cognitive subject. This difference also has certain implications for understanding the idea of objectivity.

While *duixiangxing* 對象性 refers to objective reality in its entirety (including the subjects and objects of cognition), the counterpart to the subject (*keti*), which refers to objectivity, is only *keguanxing* 客觀性 and not *ketixing* 客體性. Here it is important to see the difference between the characters *guan* 觀 and *ti* 體. While the former expresses a particular point of view (thus, in the compound *keguan*, this is an objective, i.e., external, point of view), the latter implies the connotation of incorporation and thus, the compound *keti* can only be used in reference to discrete objects as such and not to the perception or understanding of those objects.

Li already defined this view of objectivity (in the former, epistemological sense) in his first important essay, titled "Lun meigan, mei he yishu" 美感, 美與藝術 (On Aesthetic Feeling, Beauty and Art). In this work, which was published in 1956, Li raised his famed idea of the "synthesis of objectivity and sociality" (客觀性與社會性統一), arguing that we could establish a seemingly intuitive and direct connection with a specific object not because an unmediated relation exists between the subject and the object, but because that object has always already been contextualized and conceptualized within a sociality of many other things and relations.[20]

In this early work, one can already sense the importance of subjectality, for he argued—in accordance with Marx's early work *The Economic and Philosophical Manuscripts of 1844*—that for us, there is no inert nature as such, but only the nature that is transformed by humans.[21] In this regard, Li upgraded and expanded the Marxist concept of the "humanization of nature" (*zirande renhua* 自然的人化). Indeed, in his early work Li often referred to this process as the "socialization of nature" (*zirande shehuihua* 自然的社會化) precisely because he wanted to emphasize its social and collective component. In such a view, perception is our activity of constituting humanized objects. Therefore, the object of perception should not be treated "as if in a 'disconnected' cognitive situation of the subject and object. It is constituted in the interaction between them."[22]

But the young Li Zehou also believes that these basic or essential characteristics of humanity, including their relations as subjects to the objects of their practice, have been seriously alienated in class society. Such estrangement is a state in which human beings are related to the *products of their labor* as to alien objects. Here, Li's theory was in complete accordance with early Marx, according to whom the estrangement of the workers from their products means not only that their labor becomes an object, an external existence, but that it exists outside them, independently, as something alien to them, and that it becomes a power that confronts them on its own. It means that the life that they have conferred upon the object confronts them as something hostile and alien. The workers put their lives into the object and, consequently, their life no longer belongs to them but to the object.[23] In this context, Li emphasizes that it is exactly this estrangement that tends to make humanness (or human nature) appear similar to animal nature.[24] Hence, for Li Zehou, the essence of "being human" lies precisely in the free activity of production—especially in the production of art. In this process humans become capable of achieving the free unification of their cognitive powers, as described by Kant, and find their way to the unity with the objects of their nature-humanizing practice. The highest stage of subjectality is therefore to be found in the realm of aesthetics, which, however, can not be reduced to the spiritual sphere. Instead, Li Zehou considers aesthetics to be the ultimate fruit of human subjects, and the most striking and prominent manifestation of humanity.[25] In this sense, beauty, as an aesthetic category, obtains an ontological dimension.[26] It is necessarily objective because it neither depends on individual consciousness nor is rooted in a metaphysical, supernatural order. But beauty is not objective because it would be an intrinsic property of the observed objects. Rather, it is a quality of humankind: "Nature as such is certainly not beautiful. Beautiful nature is a result of socialization; it is a result of the objectification (or alienation) of the essence of the human being. The sociality of nature is the origin of beauty."[27] Therefore, Li believes that beauty can only emerge through the interdependence of the subjective practice and objective reality.[28] Li Zehou's concept of subjectality was thus firmly rooted in his aesthetic theory, which was based on a critique or expansion of Kant's theory of perception. In this context, the vital and inseparable connection between subject and object is constituted by the fact that human essence, our subjectality, can be identified with the objectivity of our social nature. The aesthetic experience that stems from such a perception theory is necessarily different from that of the Western mainstream, which presupposes a simple dichotomy between subject and object.[29]

This elimination of a fixed borderline between the subject and the object of comprehension and practice was thoroughly maintained in Li's later writings on the theory of perception and its intrinsic axiological value, which manifests in the aesthetic feeling: "A human being, then, is no longer a subject facing the objective world (cognition) and interacting with it (actions), but an aesthetic noumenon that has abolished the distinction between subject and object or the 'realm of Heaven and Earth.'"[30] With regard to the subject–object relationship and the issue of their dialectical interaction, Li also emphasizes the instrumental role of the principle of "seizing the proper measure (du 度)" because it triggers both the separation and the union of the two antipodes that constitute this relationship. For Li Zehou, the original distinction between subject and object appears in this dynamic method, which humans need in order to deal productively with objects and process them in a way that is appropriate to the internal order of those objects and at the same time consistent with their own intentions. Since du is always relative and relational, there is, of course, no fixed, preexistent, or a priori du that could be grasped and imposed on objects in this process. Rather, as Wu Xiaoming explains in another chapter of this volume, different kinds of du represent different ways of being "just right" in the ever-changing activities of matching the du of the object. "The 'du' not only enables the establishment of the cognitive forms of the subject. The distinction between subject and object itself can also be realized only on the ontological basis of 'du.' On this existential basis of 'du,' they were originally merged together, but in the consciousness of subjectivity, the need for a distinction between them gradually arose."[31] In this view, the separation between subject and object is not something of ontological primacy, but rather a product of human cognition and practice. "It can be seen that the dichotomy of subject and object is secondary and second-order. It has its origin in human practice and was established by the grasping of the right and proper measure that can be of use to human beings."[32] This separation of subject and object is something that distinguishes humans from other animals that do not differentiate between them.[33] But, on the other hand, practice also "refers to the activities of the subject to purposefully and consciously transform the objective material world. It is the unity of subject and object."[34] In the natural, non-alienated process of productive practice, such a union of opposites is a result of the internalization of the intrinsic structures of the objects worked on and thus of their "humanization."

Practice, then, is a trigger for both the separation and the unification of subject and object. It constitutes humanness (ren xing 人性) and subjectality. In such a view, subject and object interact with each other in a mutually complementary and interdependent way. It is a dialectics guided by the laws of *du*, which always tends toward equilibrium and is the first epistemological category. It is precisely this category that establishes the separation and unity of cognition in the dialectical process of human practical activities.[35]

According to Li's understanding, human knowledge is thus able to grasp the internal structure of natural objects. In this way, the human understanding of the nature of things on the one hand, and the things in their objective states on the other, can be brought together.[36] In Li Zehou's system, it is tools that enable people to transform their social and natural worlds, which in turn shape them.[37] Thus, this process is a dialectical and reciprocal one.

## Negative Dialectics and the Critique of Identitarian Philosophy

Having already presented Li Zehou's understanding of the subject–object relationship and their mutually complementary interaction in the previous section, let us now take a brief look at Adorno's conception of the dialectics of the relationship between subject and object.

Adorno describes his understanding of knowledge about social reality as "negative dialectics" in the book of the same name. For him, a method based on the concept of dialectics is the prerequisite for a theory that remains open to what has not yet been conceptualized by the cognitive subjects. He points out, on the other hand, that thought itself is something that leads us to the identification of our subjective conceptualizations and observed objects. However, we rarely think about the fact that this identity is an illusion. Traditional Western dialectics is based on this illusion, which leads to the problem that whenever we are confronted with other concepts (i.e., different understanding) of the same reality, we inevitably see them as contradicting our original conception. Adorno formulates this problem in the following way:

> Yet the appearance of identity is inherent in thought itself, in its pure form. To think is to identify. Conceptual order is content to screen what thinking seeks to comprehend. The semblance and the truth of thought entwine. The semblance cannot be decreed away, as by avowal of a being-in-itself outside the totality of cogitative definitions. It is a thesis secretly implied by Kant—and mobilized against him by Hegel—that the transconceptual "in itself" is void, being wholly indefinite. Aware that the conceptual totality is mere appearance, I have no way but to break immanently, in its own measure, through the appearance of total identity. Since that totality is structured to accord with logic, however, whose core is the principle of the excluded middle, whatever will not fit this principle, whatever differs in quality, comes to be designated as a contradiction. Contradiction is non-identity under the aspect of identity; the dialectical primary of the principle of contradiction makes the thought of unity the measure of heterogeneity. As the heterogeneous collides with its limit it exceeds itself.[38]

In Adorno's view, Hegel's dialectic, based on such a problematic relationship between subjective concepts and external objects, can hardly lead to new insights. The shift in thinking proposed by Adorno, based on a critique of such forms of cognition, is of utmost importance not only for contemporary Western philosophy, but also for global philosophy, especially if we compare it to other theories developed in other cultures. In this sense, a contrastive analysis of Li and Adorno could prove itself to be quite fruitful. (Or not—let's see.)

Adorno is a mischievous child of the European Enlightenment. He recognizes the importance of its values, but on the other hand is very critical regarding the inner structure of its basic epistemology. Already Plato insisted on a fundamental separation of soul and body, and centuries later the Platonic separation of body and soul found its final manifestation in the Cartesian split between subject and object. But it is only after Kant that the subject of cognition no longer remains a passive moment in the process of perception, dependent only on the objects. Rather, the objects now proceed from the cognitive structure of the subject. Thought is thus conceived here as in itself concrete and self-determining. Adorno admires Kant's emphasis on the acting subject, but at the same time criticizes this epistemological model because it inevitably leads to an aporia. Here, the human being no longer has the possibility to conceive of herself as a sensuous subject; she can no longer define herself as a physical, material being in a material world. The Kantian conception is also not able to determine how problems in thinking can arise and (even less) how they can be solved. The objectivity that is attained in the process of cognition can therefore only be understood as constituted by the subject, and thus knowledge means nothing more than the subjectively produced objectivity of the world appearing to us. That which is perceived and objectified by the categories of the understanding is considered reality, but at the same time, it remains imprisoned within the limits of human reason. Since thought is a closed domain, cognition becomes tautology, since thinking and what is to be thought apparently lie in the same instance. But actually the act of cognition should refer to something that is outside the mind. Despite these problems, the Kantian "revolution of thought" was of enormous importance for the progress of European philosophy and culture, since it meant a shift from theological to human creation.

Adorno's critique, which is based on his concept of the "priority of the object," aims at overcoming such an aporetic ontological dualism of subject and object without falling behind Kant's progress in recapitulating human freedom. With his critique of Kant, Adorno tries to escape the aporia in which thought can only refer to itself, and to point out a possibility according to which subject and object are definable not only as opposites but also as a reciprocal relationship.[39] To this end, he opposes the strict separation between the empirical and the transcendental subject as carried out by Kant. According to Adorno, the concept of the subject refers not only to a general definition, to "consciousness in general," but always also to a single individual as well. "The element of individual humanity is indispensable in any concept of the subject; without any memory of it, the subject would lose all meaning. Conversely, the single human individual is already universalized as soon as it is reflected on in a general conceptual form as the individual, not only as some particular person."[40] By defining the subject not only as something general, but also as something particular and empirically concrete, Adorno highlights the importance of the experience and practice upon which the individual subject relies in acquiring knowledge.[41] As he emphasizes: "The key position of the subject in knowledge is experience, not form."[42]

Adorno here defines a "faculty of sensuousness,"[43] characterized by the fact that the subject is always in a sensuous relation to the object. In this way, Adorno abolishes the dichotomous separation of subject and object and the supremacy of the Kantian subject, but without revoking Kant's central insight that the givenness of the objects to which a subject refers cannot be uncritically presupposed. With Kant, Adorno emphasizes the view that the subject has of the world, but unlike Kant, he emphasizes the independence of the object of cognition from the subject of cognition.[44] For it is precisely the absence of this independence that makes cognition a tautology or pure identity. On the other hand, he emphasizes the non-identical—that part of the object that is included in the cognizing subject—because it is precisely this part that triggers thought by making it go beyond itself. Adorno's "priority of the object," then, by no means implies a return to a naïve rationalism. Instead, he establishes a different subject perspective, and one that seeks to reclaim the position of the object in the process of cognition in order to achieve a dialectical mediation between them.

The "priority of the object" implies that, in contrast to Kant's epistemology, the process of perception and understanding is directed not asymmetrically from the side of the cognitive subject to the side of the object of understanding, but from the center equally in both directions, namely to the subject and the object.[45] This also means that everything that is perceived is filtered through subjectivity and everything that exists is inconceivable without human practice.

The role of the object in the cognitive process must not be neglected. According to this view, the cognitive process consists of a coexistence of sensory and conceptual faculties. Thus, the origin of thinking and sensory abilities comes from the same source. The sensory experiences that give rise to sensory cognitions and the judgments that are sensory cognitions are thus to be understood as actualizations of one and the same faculty.

The concept and the conceived, the judgment and its sensuous basis, whose logical unity was still disputed according to Kant, can now be brought together by the idea of a sensuous faculty of understanding. Perception is here the basis of all cognition, which, however, does not only extend to conceptual rationality, but also includes feelings. This synthesis, however, is already present in the process of perception and is not first made possible by a transcendental consciousness. Things, then, can be known as they have been constructed through the concepts. However, this is not to be understood as absolute: Here it applies that a subject with conceptual faculties must also have a critical relationship to them and reflect on them. For like any ability, a sensory-cognitive ability is fundamentally fallible.[46] And therefore it is important to question the process of perception again and again and not to accept it as given and infallible.[47]

Adorno defines the subject–object relation as a relationship in which the two antipodes influence each other. But by no means does he want to level the dichotomy completely. Rather, he is concerned with presenting the two categories as interpenetrated by mediation. For the deformed perspective that Adorno sees in rational subject-centeredness stems not from a general separation of subject and object, of mind and nature, of reason and sensuality, but from the lack of reflexive mediation that can only be achieved through a "mindfulness of nature in the subject."[48]

Objectivity, according to Adorno, is solidified social practice expressed in terms of material and immaterial production as well as social structure and spheres of life. In this respect, the subject–object dichotomy is on the one hand pure thought abstraction and on the other hand social reality at the same time.[49] The separation of subject and object is thus reality and illusion at the same time: "True, because in the cognitive realm it serves to express the real separation, the dichotomy of the human condition, a coercive development. False, because the resulting separation must not be hypostasized, not magically transformed into an invariant."[50] Adorno sees in this dichotomy a contradiction, which is conveyed into epistemology. On the other hand, however, this contradiction has a pseudo-character, for while they can only be thought of separately, this separation is manifested in their being mutually mediated.

## Let's Imagine a Dialogue

Since we want to establish a theoretical relationship between the works of these two scholars, it would be good to start with their opinions of each other. However, this will only be a one-sided introduction since, as mentioned earlier, Adorno did not even know of Li Zehou's existence, let alone his work. But before we compare their epistemologies and turn to their respective conceptions of the subject and object of understanding, let us therefore at least briefly present Li Zehou's critique of the Frankfurt School and negative dialectics.

Li Zehou was not very fond of the European post-Marxist streams of thought. In his view, Marx (especially the early Marx) was still interested in sociality, whereas the post-Marxist theories—including the critical theory of the Frankfurt School—focused more and more on the individually conditioned type of subjectality. In fact, in his eyes this was the main common flaw of most "fashionable" contemporary streams of thought emerging in the West region throughout the twentieth century: "Analytical philosophy, structuralism, and many other streams of the contemporary capitalist world (like for instance philosophical methodology or epistemology) are cold philosophies, which overlook the substance of subjectality. In addition, Sartre's existentialism, the philosophies of the Frankfurt School and other fashionable currents (like for instance the philosophy of rebellion or the philosophy of emotion), on the other hand, are blindly propagating the individual subjectality. They have nothing to do with the practical philosophy of subjectality."[51]

To the best of my knowledge, Li never explicitly mentioned Adorno, although he was very critical of the idea and implications of negative dialectics, which is one of the most important concepts of Adorno's theory: "In my view, this 'negative dialectics' is an antidote or a decoration of contemporary capitalism. Capitalist society has locked them up within the academic walls where they can deal with the angry voices of the public, freedom, and democracy without seriously affecting or having any real impact on the economic foundation of capitalism. And they have not even seriously studied that foundation."[52] Li thus accuses critical theory of a privileged distance or separation from the facts and practical realities of the real world. According to him, the theory production of the members of the Frankfurt School originated in an academic ivory tower of "splendid isolation."

This criticism is probably somewhat exaggerated. Although Li Zehou himself had a truly remarkable influence on Chinese youth in the 1980s, several members of the Frankfurt School, notably Herbert Marcuse and Adorno himself, were similarly influential and the intellectual idols of critical leftist students and their movements in Europe in the 1960s and 1970s. As for Li's accusation regarding the lack of knowledge of the "economic foundations of capitalism" allegedly visible in Adorno's theories, it is only fair to add that we cannot find any profound development or elaboration of Marxist economic theory in Li's own philosophy, either.

Li also criticized members of the Frankfurt School (including Adorno) for focusing on the individual and neglecting the importance of the social, collective nature of being human. Such criticism is relatively weak if we consider the neo-Marxist theoretical framework of the Frankfurt School. As we have seen, for example, in Adorno the concept of individual humanity was introduced not as a negation of the indisputable importance of the universal and collective character of humanity, but as a necessary complement to arrive at a comprehensive conceptualization of the human subject. This complementary aspect was crucial for Adorno's emphasis on the importance of experience and practice, a view that is basically very much in line with Li Zehou's theory of subjectality, which, as we have seen, has several levels.

Be that as it may, it is worth comparing the works of Adorno and Li Zehou in some important respects. On a general level, the two theorists resemble each other in their shared concern to establish a productive connection among aesthetics, epistemology, and sociology. In the comparative reflections that follow, I will focus on one particular aspect of their philosophical interests that constitutes the central problem of this essay, namely their respective conceptions of the subject–object relationship. I believe that a contrastive analysis of their individual views of this relation may suggest some alternative ways of resolving the problems inherent in the prevailing Western model of dialectical thought.

Although they shared two decades of their adult lives, Li and Adorno did not know much, if anything, about each other's work. As we have seen above, Li Zehou's critique of the Frankfurt School and its critical theory (including his critique of the concept of "negative dialectics") was very general and vague, and Li never made any specific references to Adorno's theories. Therefore, it is probably safe to say that he never really engaged with his work. And Adorno, in turn, had no opportunity to read Li Zehou, since the first translation of his work into Western languages was published long after the German's death.

It is all the more surprising, then, that for all the differences in the theoretical structures of Li Zehou and Adorno that are apparent at first glance, a closer look reveals a remarkable number of similarities. And not all of these similarities can simply be attributed to the same zeitgeist and largely the same discursive foundation. What is certainly more interesting in this context are the differences that arise from this common ground. Since most of these differences can be traced to the different cultural and socio-political backgrounds on which the theories of these two great scholars were developed, they could be related to different paradigms of their respective traditions. Thus, a contrastive analysis of these differences might shed light on some aspects of the relationship between Chinese and European intellectual traditions. Through the lens of their particular views on the subject–object relationship, we will therefore start from their commonalities in order to place their differences in a framework that will allow us to construct a fruitful dialogue between the two philosophers.

Li and Adorno were both active in the field of modern philosophy, they were both supporters of Marxist (especially early Marxist) thought, and both were interested in aesthetics, especially in its social and political functions. Besides, the general epistemological basis of their respective theoretical models is a thoroughgoing questioning of the ontological dualism that both scholars also regard as the foundation of modern Western thought. They both see this dualism as the result of the hypostatization of rationality that emerged from the European Enlightenment and became a supposition with increasingly visible shortcomings.[53]

Both scholars assume a social nature or basis of human perception and understanding. In their view, objectivity is a social category, a coalesced social practice that manifests itself in the material and cultural production of human beings. Knowledge is therefore always socially constructed and cannot be simply and directly drawn from the external world. For both, then, there is no possibility of pure a priori knowledge. Any insight into reality is socially mediated, even if this mediation seems to be more directly conveyed in Adorno and transmitted via evolution in Li Zehou. Notwithstanding this difference (which manifests itself on the quantitative rather than the qualitative level), both Adorno and Li can be considered constructivists. However, both see social reality not as something constituted by purely discursive elements, but rather as something resulting from the mutual interaction between the social and the material. Since they consequently reject both natural and social determinism, their approach could be called "realist constructivism."

As we have seen, both assume—in a very general sense of the underlying ontology—a materialist worldview, even if Adorno's "primacy of the object" seems to offer a more complex and sophisticated problematization of the concepts of matter and form. The idea of human practice as an indispensable element not only for grasping the objects of the external world, but also for being (and becoming) human, is shared by both philosophers. With regard to epistemology, both aim at developing a dialectical relation between the subject and object of perception and knowledge. In this context, however, I think Li Zehou can offer an alternative solution to the problem highlighted by Adorno, namely the problem of the impasse inherent in the dialectical scheme of identitarian thought.

## The Dialectics of Subject and Object

As for the subject and object of cognition, both Li and Adorno are primarily interested in the nature of their mutual relationship. In his *Negative Dialectics*, Adorno warned that "it is not the purpose of critical thought to place the object on the orphaned royal throne once occupied by the subject. On that throne the object would be nothing but an idol. The purpose of critical thought is to abolish the hierarchy."[54] Li Zehou followed a similar view of a non-hierarchical relation between the subject and the object of comprehension. Even though he was always a zealous advocate of objectivity, he did not see it in an essentialist way, as most of his contemporaries did. Since for him objectivity was a manifestation of the objective nature of social existence, he was able to include the notion of subjectivity into this framework as an "indispensable social agency."[55] Like Gramsci, who argued that objectivity always means "humanly objective," or "universally subjective," Li's change in positions on subjectivity is grounded in historical considerations.[56] In this regard, the concept of practice was of utmost importance. Similar to most followers of early Marxism, Li Zehou considered practice a key link that mediated the subject and object.[57]

For Adorno, the reconciliation of subject and object was also of utmost importance. In spite of his persistent rejection of formulating a visionary alternative to the problems of society, he offered his readers a glance of something similar in his "moment of peace," which was necessarily defined by an egalitarian and mutually complementary relation between subject and object: "In its proper place, even epistemologically, the relationship of subject and object would lie in the realization of peace among men as well as between men and their Other. Peace is the state of distinctness without domination with the distinct participating in each other."[58] Such an idea of "peace" or reconciliation, however, was by no means feasible in the traditional dualistic model of dialectical opposites. Adorno therefore strongly criticizes the Hegelian schema, which strives for the identity of subjects and objects in a framework in which the antagonistic dichotomy of being and conceptuality is always reconciled in the identity of thought and reality. For Adorno, such an "identitarian philosophy" leaves no room for new insights, nor for a critique of reality. The impasse arises from Hegel's adherence to the theoretical framework determined by the elementary laws of formal logic, namely the law of identity, the law of non-contradiction, and the law of the excluded middle.[59] Such a dialectics strives for the identity (and thus unity) of contradictions, a unity that is seen as the only way to know reality. These laws are products of a static framework of unchanging meanings that provides an instrumental basis for their validity. With his negative dialectics, in which identity does not disappear but is qualitatively transformed, Adorno aims to overcome this model. In this new framework, the affinity of the object to the subject (or to the thought of the object) is reborn through mediation in a new identity.

In this way, Adorno attempts to overcome the static foundations of identitarian ontology with a dialectic that "turns against itself"[60] because it simultaneously implies the impression and critique of the illusory universal realm of being. The ultimate goal of the negative dialectic, however, is not to escape the identitarian context of delusion. On the contrary, it aims to break out of this context from within.[61] It is a dialectics that negates thought by thinking. This negation is precisely the ultimate realm (and starting point) that enables freedom of human thought. Because his "priority of the object" denies the constitutive role of the epistemic subject, it surpasses traditional methods of achieving identity and unity for thought, since it allows for the diversity of objects and does not impose on them the forms of the cognitive subject. But in the end, Adorno's critique still proceeds from the same scheme of identifying thought because it is still embedded in a static view of reality. His negation of identity merely offers us a turn to a new concept, that of non-identity.[62] More importantly for him, however, non-identity, as the central concept of negative dialectics, offers the possibility of "reflection on its own meaning," which for Adorno is "the way out of the concept's seeming being-in-itself as a unit of meaning."[63]

Since such reflection is a continuous process, it is quite capable of eliminating the illusion of a constitutive subjectivity and can be extended to objects belonging to the non-conceptual realm that can only be expressed in art. Hence, it enables aesthetic subjects to experience a unity of sensation and thought. Ultimately, however, Adorno's thesis still works with notions of identity and non-identity as separate and fixed stages. Although for him, "reflection on its own meaning is the way out of the concept's seeming being-in-itself as a unit of meaning,"[64] such a reflection is still insufficient, because the problem of identitarian thinking cannot be solved on the basis of the negation of identity, for a non-identity between identity and non-identity is ultimately still a conceptualization of a certain mode of objectivity.

Here, it seems that Li Zehou's aesthetics and epistemology can offer a better alternative to achieve a genuine mediation between the subject and object of understanding, which is based not on identity but on correlative complementarity. As mentioned earlier, his early aesthetic works were nevertheless still based on dualisms of Marxist materialist dialectics, which proceeded from a negation of the thesis to the negation of negation, a synthesis, which is the ultimate phase of a certain dialectical stage and simultaneously, the basis of the following one. In Li's early aesthetic thought, this highest realm of negating the negation was art: "Beauty is the negation of the aesthetic feeling, and art is the negation of negation."[65] Approximately at the same time, the much older Adorno criticized such naïve positivisms that could be found in modern Western art in the following way: "What is qualitatively new in recent art may be that in an allergic reaction it wants to eliminate harmonizations even in their negated form, truly the negation of negation with its own fatality: the self-satisfied transition to a new positivity, to the absence of tension in so many paintings and compositions of the postwar decades."[66] In this context, Adorno highlights[67] that the nonidentical is not to be obtained directly, as something positive on its part, nor is it obtainable by a negation of the negative. In his view, the claim of identity is a "magic circle that stamps critique with the appearance of absolute knowledge. It is up to the self-reflection of critique to extinguish that claim, to extinguish it in the very negation of negation that will not become a positing."[68] In this view, the negation of negation produces new negations, without reference to "that traditional logic which, more *arithmetico*, takes minus times minus for a plus."[69] Negation thus becomes the continuous non-identity, and the only reason for its failure to accomplish a genuine breakthrough out from the confines of the identitarian thinking is the fact that even the non-identity is a concept that refers to an object, and thus it is still identitarian in itself.

Later on, Li Zehou abandoned Western-style dialectics, along with all its negations and negations of negations. For the mature Li, not only the human conception of reality, but even the emergence and constitution of beauty itself, is closely related to this principle of complementarity,[70] which has its origin in the oldest Confucian classic, the *Book of Changes*. In a sense, the epistemology of this traditional cosmological scheme can be compared to the dialectical model that prevailed in Western philosophy, for both systems represent a particular mode of interaction between two mutually opposing ideas. Due to its embeddedness into the framework of formal logic, however, the latter can only function as a system in which every pair of oppositions is a contradiction, because in the identitarian schema different ideas are necessarily mutually exclusive. In contrast to such structures, in the traditional Chinese correlative model based on the principle of complementarity, pairs of opposites are not mutually exclusive and are often referred to as binary categories (*duili fanchou* 對立範疇). Quite the contrary, in fact: since the system is based on processual paradigms, these categories complement each other. They are interactive and interdependent.

In such a view, there can be no subject without an object, and vice versa. Therefore, neither can assume a purely constitutive role. Li Zehou considers this model of correlative complementarity as a basic framework in which human subjectality can actively seize the tool of dynamic proper measure *du* to act, adapt to, and make reality "just right." This model is clearly different from Adorno's idea, with which he wanted to replace the traditional model of contradictions and identities triggered by the constitutive role of the subject with a linear scheme in which "they constitute one another as much as—by virtue of such constitution—they depart from each other."[71]

In this dynamic scheme, *du* generates the ceaseless movement in which the subject and object of understanding are repeatedly separated and united, in a continuous and uninterrupted process of interdependent interaction. In this respect, the difference between Adorno and Li is that the latter was equipped with different methodological paradigms than the former, and thus for Li it was clear that subject and object cannot interact directly and quasi-automatically. The dialectical synthesis eliminated from Adorno's negative dialectics is also absent from the traditional Chinese principle of complementarity that guides the "Chinese type" of dialectical interactions. But in this complementary dialectics, synthesis is not a separate, isolated, and qualitatively new stage of dialectical development, but arises (and is hidden) in the very process of interaction between pairs of opposites Indeed, in this model, subject and object (or any other binary category) are not linearly juxtaposed and cannot enter into a direct and immediate or proximate relationship with each other. The system of correlative dialectics of complementarity is guided by the dynamic grasp of the proper measure—that is, by the principles of *du*, which mediate the relation between the subject's Self and the object's Otherness.

As we have seen, *du* is a kind of experience-based reasonableness, which is not determined by a priori reason. It is a dynamic criterion, which seeks to achieve the "middle way" in the mastering of every situation requiring choices or decisions. Li describes *du* as a dynamic structure of proportions, as something that changes according to the discrete conditions of a certain time and space. He highlights that it is by no means an eternal mediator and it does not always remains neutral. From an overall perspective, *du* can sometimes be extreme.

Therefore, *du* can be understood not as a simple and stagnant mathematical middle between two different possibilities, but rather as a vibrant situational principle.[72] It must be found and appropriately applied because in Li's view concrete problems require concrete analyses. The inner logic of *du* is operational rather than transcendental. Hence, it is not identical to any form of dialectical logic, which is based upon oppositions, but can rather be expressed by the form A ≠ A±, which is different from A = A, but also from A ≠ Ā.[73] This means that it is based upon and functions in accordance with the premise that A is not identical to any form of A, which refers to a kind of general contingency.

## Epilogue: The Discreet Charm of the Unthinkable

In Chinese tradition, *du* is closely associated with the concepts of harmony and the middle way or the way of equilibrium (*zhong yong* 中庸). In the West, such terms are usually seen as expressing an extremely conservative attitude based on conflict avoidance and obedient conformity. For reasons of space, I cannot elaborate on the misrepresentation inherent in such prejudices and can only emphasize that, with regard to the concept of harmony, we must distinguish between the official ideologies of the contemporary Chinese state, on the one hand, and the classical philosophical, especially Confucian, understanding of the concept, on the other. While the former is based on the decree of unification, the latter is rooted in diversity. The way of equilibrium is also often misunderstood. *Zhong yong* is often translated in Western languages as the "doctrine of the mean," which can be seen as an almost reactionary and surely completely uncreative method of always choosing the middle way in order to reach a static compromise between two opposing alternatives. In reality, however, it does not refer to a formal, statically unchanging "middle," but to a state of equilibrium that changes from moment to moment.

Notwithstanding such misconceptions, the dynamic concepts of harmony and equilibrium to which *du* is always oriented are possibly comparable to Adorno's concept of peace, which he seeks "in an unpeaceful whole,"[74] knowing well that "all images of reconciliation, peace, and tranquility resemble the image of death . . . as long as the world 'is as it is.'"[75] The world is still "as it is," and it may even evolve to the point where we find it much worse. But much like the idea of perpetual peace, the two great scholars I have tried to bring into conversation in this essay will always remain alive through their work and their ideas. For them there is no death. In their aesthetic writings, both find their final refuge in art, which, in the face of our last breath, represents a completion of artistic subjectivity[76] and a semblance of what lies beyond the reach of death.[77] For Adorno,[78] this is the realm of non-conceptual void, which is the direct expression of the inexpressible, and for Li Zehou,[79] it is the possibility of exploring the unlimited space within the limited time of our existence. And if one day we can reconcile all these different yet similar ideas, we can still hope to find a way out of the suffocating totality of identitarian thought and establish a real dialogue between this text and its readers, between me and you, between the subject and the object of what is inexpressible and hence unthinkable. Only in this way can thought be truly resolved through thinking.

## Notes

1. Even though the active subject has been highly valued for their autonomy and independent decisions guided by free will since Kant established the basic Enlightenment values, these decisions and the subsequent actions take place on the foundation of the subject already laid in the process of perceiving and grasping external reality. In this sense, Kant's epistemology presupposes his practical philosophy, and we must distinguish between epistemology and ethics in the context of premodern and modern European philosophy.

2. Vladislav Aleksandrovich Lektorskij, "The Dialectic of Subject and Object and some Problems of the Methodology of Science," *Marxists' Internet Archive* (2022), www.marxists.org/subject/psychology/works/lektorsky/essay_77.htm.

3. The destruction of this "natural" unity of subject and object lies at the core of Marx's notion of alienation, in which the worker (the subject of production) is (violently and system-immanently) separated from the products of his or her labour. See Karl Marx, *Ökonomisch-philosophische Manuskripte*, in *Werke, Ergänzungsband*, by Karl Marx and Friederich Engels, part 1 (Berlin: Dietz, 1972), 546.

4. Similar views can be found in late medieval Chinese philosophy and are especially visible in Wang Fuzhi's 王夫之 (1619–1692) philosophy. On the one hand, he acknowledged Wang Yangming's 王陽明 (1472–1529) hypothesis of the unity of knowledge and action (*zhixing heyi* 知行合一): "Knowledge and action complete each other; only together can they be efficient." Wang Fuzhi 王夫之, *Du si shu da quan shuo* 讀四書大全說 (*The Entire Recapitulation of the Teachings from the "Four Books"*) (Taipei: Heluo tushu chuban she, 1974), IV: 383. But in contrast to Wang Yangming, Wang Fuzhi's epistemology highlights that the relation between them is strictly hierarchical, for knowledge can only be gained through action: "If we wish to acquire reliable (substantiated, reasonable) knowledge, we must deal with concrete reality, which means that we have to act." Wang, *The Entire Recapitulation*, III: 316. For example, we are able to recognize the taste of food and drink only if we actually, actively, taste it: "First we have to eat or drink it, and then we can know its taste." Wang Fuzhi 王夫之, "Si shu xun yi" 四書訓義 (*A Standard Explanation of the "Four Books"*) in *Chuanshan yishu* (Shanghai: Taiping shudian, 1933), vol. 32, II: 8b. This premise was also used by Mao Zedong, who took it one step further in his epistemology of revolution with his famous maxim that we must change reality in order to recognize it. Using the example of a pear that had to be eaten in order to know what it tasted like, he noted that in the very act of eating it, we have already changed it. Mao Zedong 毛澤東, "Shijian lun—lun renshi he shijiande guanxi—he zhixingde guanxi" 實踐論—論認識和實踐的關係—和知行的關係 (On Practise—On the Relation Between Knowledge and Practice, Between Knowing and Doing), in *Mao Zedong xuanji*, I, ed. Zhonggong zhongyang Mao Zedong xuanji chuban weiyuan hui (Beijing: Renmin chuban she, 1966), 264.

5. Lektorskij, "The Dialectic of Subject," 3.

6. In this aspect of Marxist epistemology, however, we encounter a problem that is not very visible but has important implications for the general questions that are in the center of the present paper. As Klaus Gössler reveals ("Methodenprobleme der marxistisch-leninistischen Erkenntnistheorie," *Deutsche Zeitschrift für Philosophie* 26, no. 6 (1978): 771), there is probably no major account of Marxist epistemology in which essential methods of materialist dialectics are not described. In general, its basic principles are conscientiously recapitulated in

all their essential premises and working steps, and often meticulously explained with examples (mostly from the economic writings of the classics), but unfortunately without being applied to Marxist epistemology itself.

7. *Renleixue lishi bentilun* 人類學歷史本體論.

8. *Lishi bentilun* 歷史本體論.

9. *Zhutixingde shijian zhexue* 主體性的實踐哲學.

10. Actually, the term *zhutixing* could be translated into English with a word that already exists, namely *subjectness*, which refers to the quality of being a subject. However, in a personal conversation in which I suggested to Professor Li that the term *subjectality* could be changed to *subjectness* (because this would be easier for Western readers to understand), he claimed that the term referred only to the individual, which I believe is not necessarily true. However, at the time of this discussion the concept of subjectality was already an integral part of his philosophy, so it would be too complicated to change it anyway.

11. As we shall see, Li viewed the concept of objectivity not only as something that stands in opposition to subjectivity, but also as that which is common to both humanity and its sociality.

12. Li Zehou and Jane Cauvel, *Four Essays on Aesthetics: Toward a Global View* (Lanham, MD: Lexington Books, 2006), 171.

13. Li Zehou, "Subjectivity and 'Subjectality': A Response," *Philosophy East and West* 49, no. 2 (1999): 179.

14. All translations of original Chinese texts in this chapter are my own. The corresponding Chinese originals are provided in the footnotes following each translation. 所謂『主體性』也是這個意思。人類主體即展現為物質現實的社會實現活動 (物質生產活動是核心)，這是主體性的客觀方面即工藝-社會結構亦即社會存在方面，基礎的面向。史成果的精神文化，智力結構，理論意識，美感享受。 Li Zehou 李澤厚, *Meixue si jiang* 美學四講 (*Four Lectures on Aesthetics*) (Nanning: Guangxi shifan daxue chuban she, 2001), 43.

15. A similar differentiation can be found in German, which distinguishes between *Objekt* und *Gegenstand*. While the former relates to the Chinese *keti*, the latter is a rather literal translation of *duixiang*. Both nouns, derived from the two core notions, i.e., *Gegenständlichkeit* as well as *duixiangxing*, refer to the external phenomena.

16. 美感客體.

17. 在漢語語境中，嚴格講，客體屬於認識論範疇，對象的使用範圍則要廣泛得多 . . . 審美客體主要屬於認識論哲學範疇，它與審美主體一道構成美學領域中的認識論模式。 Zhang Yongqing 張永清, "Hanyu yujing zhongde shenmei duixiang yu shenmei keti" 漢語語境中的美感對象與美感客體 (Two Kinds of the Aesthetic Objects in the Context of Chinese Language), *Meixue* 12 (2002): 1.

18. The word *keguan* derives from *keti*.

19. 「客體是相對於主體而言的，指的是主體認識或實踐的對象，這種對象既可以是物質的，也可以是精神的。對象與主體相對應，指的是被確定為認識和實踐活動目的的物質現像或精神現象。 客體的對象則是物質, 這就不限於認識範疇了, 而且對象就不是客體而是物質了。前所述, 既可指物質, 也可指精神, 既可指客體, 也可指主體。精神世界, 外延更小。 Zhang, "Two Kinds of the Aesthetic Objects," 2–3.

20. Li Zehou 李澤厚, "Lun meigan, mei he yishu (Yanjiu tigang)—Jainlun Zhu Guangqiande weixinzhuyi meixue sixiang" 論美感, 美與藝術 (研究提綱)—兼論朱光潛的唯心主義美學思想 (On the Aesthetic Feeling, Beauty and Art (A Research Proposal)—Also on Zhu Guangqian's Idealist Aesthetic Thought), *Zhexue yanjiu* 5 (1956): 55.

21. Pang Laikwan, "Can Dialectic Materialism Produce Beauty? The 'Great Aesthetic Debates' (1956–1962) in the People's Republic of China," *International Journal of Asian Studies* (2022): 9.

22. Rafael Banka, *Cognition and Practice: Li Zehou's Philosophical Aesthetic* (Albany: State University of New York Press, 2022), 30.

23. Karl Marx, *Economic and Philosophic Manuscripts of 1844* (Mineola, NY: Dover, 2007), 29.

24. Li Zehou 李泽厚, *Zhexue tanxun lu* 哲学探寻录 (*Philosophical Inquiry*) (Tianjin: Tinajin shehui kexue chuban she, 1994), 320.

25. Gu Xin, "Subjectivity, Modernity, and Chinese Hegelian Marxism: A Study of Li Zehou's Philosophical Ideas from a Comparative Perspective," *Philosophy East and West* 46, no. 2 (1996): 216.

26. Lin Min, "The Search for Modernity: Chinese Intellectual Discourse and Society, 1978–88: The Case of Li Zehou," *China Quarterly* 132 (1992): 990.

27. 自然本身並不是美, 美的自然是社會化的結果, 也就是人的本質的對象化 (異化) 的結果。自然地社會性是美的根源。 Li, "On the Aesthetic Feeling," 57. The somehow strange claim that beauty was the product of the alienation of human essence is probably a mistake; what Li really meant in this context was probably externalization (*waihua* 外化). This confusion was a result of the fact that Marx frequently uses two similar German terms, "Entäußerung" and "Entfremdung," to express the notion of alienation or estrangement. In Chinese translations of the Manuscripts, the term "Entäußerung" (i.e., externalization) is usually translated with the term *waihua* 外化 and "Entfremdung" with the term *yihua* 异化.

28. Banka, *Cognition and Practice*, 362.

29. Eva Kit Wah Man, *Issues of Contemporary Art and Aesthetics in Chinese Context* (Berlin: Springer, 2015), 2.

30. 人從而不再是與客觀世界相對對峙 (認識) 相作用 (行動) 的主體, 而是泯滅了主客體之分的審美本體, 或 '天地境界'。 Li, *Philosophical Inquiry*, 24.

31. '度' 不僅使主體認識形式得以建立, 而且主客體之分也是在 '度' 的本體性基礎之上才能實現的。主客體在 '度' 的本體中本來混而不分, 但在主觀性的意識中, 卻逐漸需要區別。 Li, *Philosophical Inquiry*, 64.

32. 可見, 主客體的二分是第二位的、次要的, 它來自於人在實踐活動中恰到好處的 '度' 的建立。 Li, *Philosophical Inquiry*, 65.

33. Li Zehou 李澤厚, "Kangde zhexue yu jianli zhutixing lungang" 康德哲學與建立主體性論綱 (An Outline of Kant's Philosophy and the Construction of Subjectality), in *Lun Kangde Heigeer zhexue* 論康德黑格爾哲學 (Shanghai: Shanghai renmin chuban she, 2006), 15.

34. 實踐是指主體有目的、有意識地改造客觀物質世界的活動, 是主體與客體的統一。Ma Long 馬龍潛, "'Kangde zhexue yu jianli zhutixing lungang' pingxi" '康德哲學與建立主體性論綱』評析 (A Critical Analysis of 'An Outline of Kant's Philosophy and the Construction of Subjectality')," *Gaoxiao lilun zhanxian* 高校理論戰線 no. 6 (1991): 51.

35. Li, *Philosophical Inquiry*, 181.

36. Man, *Issues of Contemporary Art*, 24.

37. Jane Cauvel, "The Transformative Power of Art: Li Zehou's Aesthetic Theory," *Philosophy East and West* 49, no. 2 (1999): 156.

38. Theodor W. Adorno, *Negative Dialectics*, trans. E. B. Ashton (London and New York: Routledge, 2004), 5.

39. "Asymmetrische Dialektik? Bemerkungen zum Umgang mit der Subjekt-Objekt Dichotomie bei Theodor W. Adorno und Bruno Latour," *Tabula Rasa: Zeitschrift für Gesellschaft und Kultur*, May 30, 2010, www.tabularasamagazin.de/asymmetrische-dialektikbemerkungen-zum-umgang-mit-der-subjekt-objekt-dichotomie-bei-theodor-w-adorno-und-bruno-latour/.

40. Theodor W. Adorno, "Zu Subjekt und Objekt," in *Gesammelte Schriften*, vol. 10.2 (Frankfurt am Main: Suhrkamp, 2003), 741.

41. "Asymmetrische Dialektik?" 4.

42. Adorno, "Zu Subjekt und Objekt," 752.

43. "Asymmetrische Dialektik?" 5.

44. Theodor W. Adorno, *Negative Dialektik* (Frankfurt am Main: Suhrkamp, 1966), 70.

45. "Asymmetrische Dialektik?" 5.

46. Adorno, *Negative Dialektik*, 229.

47. Adorno, *Negative Dialektik*, 148.

48. "Asymmetrische Dialektik?" 6.

49. "Asymmetrische Dialektik?" 6.

50. Theodor W. Adorno, "Subject and Object," in *The Essential Frankfurt School Reader*, eds. Andrew Arato and Eike Gebhardt (New York: Urizen Books, 1978), 498–9.

51. 分析哲學、結構主義等等, 可說是無視主體性本體的冷哲學 (方法哲學、知性哲學), 而沙特的存在主義, 法蘭克福學派等, 則可說是盲目誇張個體主體性的熱哲學 (造反哲學、情緒哲學), 它們都應為主體性實踐哲學所揚棄掉。Li Zehou 李澤厚, "Guanyu zhutixingde buchong shuoming" 關於主體性的補充說明 (A Supplementary Explanation of Subjectality), *Zhongguo shehui kexue yuan yuanjiushengyuan xuebao* 1 (1985): 21.

52. 這種'否定辯證論,'我曾稱之為今日資本主義的解毒劑和裝飾品。資本社會把它放在學院院牆之內, 以示眾聲喧嘩、自由民主,而並不嚴重影響或真正觸動資本主義的經濟基礎。它們也沒有認真去研究這個基礎。Li, *Philosophical Inquiry*, 74.

53. In his earliest aesthetic work, for example in his aforementioned first academic paper "On Aesthetic Feeling, Beauty, and Art," Li still followed the dualistic dialectical principles of Marxist historical materialism, which was based upon Hegel's model, but transferred from the idealistic to a materialistic foundation via Feuerbach. Less than a decade later, however, he began to question the dualistic nature of such a dialectical approach, and to criticize the underlying "two-worlds-view."

54. Adorno, *Negative Dialectics*, 181.

55. Liu Kang, *Aesthetics and Marxism: Chinese Aesthetic Marxists and Their Western Contemporaries* (Durham, NC: Duke University Press, 2000), 134.

56. Liu, *Aesthetics and Marxism*, 134.

57. According to Liu Kang (*Aesthetics and Marxism*, 134), this notion helped him to shift from his earlier insistence on objectivity to his later passionate plea for a construction of aesthetic subjectivity. This shift, however, was not really an abrupt break with Li's earlier stance. The foundational position of practice featured prominently in his work from the beginning.

58. Adorno, "Subject and Object," 499–500.

59. Adorno, *Negative Dialectics*, 142.

60. Adorno, *Negative Dialectics*, 406.

61. Adorno, *Negative Dialectics*, 406.

62. Adorno, *Negative Dialectics*, 12.

63. Adorno, *Negative Dialectics*, 12.

64. Adorno, *Negative Dialectics*, 12.

65. 美是美感的否定, 藝術是否定之否定。Li, "On the Aesthetic Feeling," 62.

66. Theodor W. Adorno, *Aesthetic Theory* (New York: Continuum, 1997), 159.

67. Adorno, *Negative Dialectics*, 158.

68. Adorno, *Negative Dialectics*, 406.

69. Adorno, *Negative Dialectics*, 158.

70. 儒家 . . . 以自然的陰陽五行來說明自然美的產生。Li Zehou 李澤厚, *Meixue lunji* 美學論集 (*A Collection of Essays on Aesthetics*) (Shanghai: Shanghai wenyi chuban she, 1980), 27.

71. Li, *A Collection of Essays*, 174.

72. Li Zehou 李澤厚, "Renshilun dawen" 認識論答問 (Q & A about Epistemology), *Zhongguo wenhua* 1 (2012): 2.

73. Li, "Q & A about Epistemology," 2.

74. Adorno, *Negative Dialectics*, 153.

75. Adorno, *Negative Dialectics*, 153.

76. Li Zehou 李澤厚, *The Chinese Aesthetic Tradition*, trans. Maija Bell Samei (Honolulu: University of Hawai'i Press, 2009), 159.
77. Adorno, *Aesthetic Theory*, 27.
78. Adorno, *Negative Dialectics*, 110.
79. Li, Zehou 李澤厚, *Zhongguo gudai sixiang shilun* 中國古代思想史論 (*On Classical Chinese Intellectual History*) (Beijing: Renmin chuban she, 1985), 298.

# Bibliography

Adorno, Theodor W. *Aesthetic Theory*. New York: Continuum, 1997.
Adorno, Theodor W. *Negative Dialectics*. Translated by E. B. Ashton. London: Routledge, 2004.
Adorno, Theodor W. *Negative Dialektik*. Frankfurt am Main: Suhrkamp, 1966.
Adorno, Theodor W. "Subject and Object." In *The Essential Frankfurt School Reader*, edited by Andrew Arato and Eike Gebhardt, 497–512. New York: Urizen Books, 1978.
Adorno, Theodor W. "Zu Subjekt und Objekt." In *Gesammelte Schriften*, vol. 10.2, 741–58. Frankfurt am Main: Suhrkamp, 2003.
"Asymmetrische Dialektik? Bemerkungen zum Umgang mit der Subjekt-Objekt-Dichotomie bei Theodor W. Adorno und Bruno Latour." *Tabula Rasa: Zeitschrift für Gesellschaft und Kultur*, May 30, 2010. www.tabularasamagazin.de/asymmetrische-dialektikbemerkungen-zum-umgang-mit-der-subjekt-objekt-dichotomie-bei-theodor-w-adorno-und-bruno-latour/.
Banka, Rafal. *Cognition and Practice: Li Zehou's Philosophical Aesthetics*. Albany: State University of New York Press, 2022.
Cauvel, Jane. "The Transformative Power of Art: Li Zehou's Aesthetic Theory." *Philosophy East and West* 49, no. 2 (1999): 150–73.
Gössler, Klaus. "Methodenprobleme der marxistisch-leninistischen Erkenntnistheorie." *Deutsche Zeitschrift für Philosophie* 26, no. 6 (1978): 771–79.
Gu, Xin. "Subjectivity, Modernity, and Chinese Hegelian Marxism: A Study of Li Zehou's Philosophical Ideas from a Comparative Perspective." *Philosophy East and West* 46, no. 2 (1996): 205–45.
Lektorskij, Vladislav Aleksandrovich. "The Dialectic of Subject and Object and some Problems of the Methodology of Science." In *Marxists' Internet Archive*, 2022: 1–22. www.marxists.org/subject/psychology/works/lektorsky/essay_77.htm.
Li Zehou. *The Chinese Aesthetic Tradition*. Translated by Maija Bell Samei. Honolulu: University of Hawai'i Press, 2009.
Li Zehou 李澤厚. "Guanyu zhutixing de buchong shuoming" 關於主體性的補充說明 (A Supplementary Explanation of Subjectality). *Zhongguo shehui kexue yuan yuanjiushengyuan xuebao* 中國社會科學院研究生院學報 1 (1985): 14–21.

Li Zehou 李澤厚. "Kangde zhexue yu jianli zhutixing lungang" 康德哲學與建立主體性論綱 (An Outline of Kant's Philosophy and the Construction of Subjectality). In *Lun Kangde Heigeer zhexue* 論康德黑格爾哲學, 14–22. Shanghai: Shanghai renmin chuban she, 2006.

Li Zehou 李澤厚. "Lun meigan, mei he yishu (Yanjiu tigang)—Jainlun Zhu Guangqiande weixinzhuyi meixue sixiang" 論美感、美和藝術（研究提綱）—兼論朱光潛的唯心主義美學思想 (On Aesthetic Feeling, Beauty, and Art (A Research Proposal)—Also on Zhu Guangqian's Idealist Aesthetic Thought). *Zhexue yanjiu* 5 (1956): 43–73.

Li Zehou 李澤厚. *Meixue lunji* 美學論集 (*A Collection of Essays on Aesthetics*). Shanghai: Shanghai wenyi chuban she, 1980.

Li Zehou 李澤厚. *Meixue si jiang* 美學四講 (*Four Lectures on Aesthetics*). Guilin: Guangxi Normal University Press, 2001 [1988].

Li Zehou 李澤厚. "Renshilun dawen" 認識論答問 (Q&A about Epistemology). *Zhongguo wenhua* 1 (2012): 1–11.

Li Zehou. "Subjectivity and 'Subjectality': A Response." *Philosophy East and West* 49, no. 2 (1999): 174–83.

Li Zehou 李澤厚. *Zhexue tanxun lu* 哲學探究 (*Philosophical Inquiry*). Tianjin: Tinajin shehui kexue chuban she, 1994.

Li Zehou 李澤厚. *Zhongguo gudai sixiang shilun* 中國古代思想史論 (*On Classical Chinese Intellectual History*). Beijing: Renmin chuban she, 1985.

Li Zehou and Jane Cauvel. *Four Essays on Aesthetics: Toward a Global View*. Lanham, MD: Lexington Books, 2006.

Lin Min. "The Search for Modernity: Chinese Intellectual Discourse and Society, 1978–1988: The Case of Li Zehou." *China Quarterly* 132 (1992): 969–98.

Liu, Kang. *Aesthetics and Marxism: Chinese Aesthetic Marxists and Their Western Contemporaries*. Durham, NC: Duke University Press, 2000.

Ma Long 馬龍潛. "'Kangde zhexue yu jianli zhutixing lungang' pingxi" '康德哲學與建立主體性論綱』評析 (A Critical Analysis of "An Outline of Kant's Philosophy and the Construction of Subjectality"). *Gaoxiao lilun zhanxian* 6 (1991): 48–51.

Man, Eva Kit Wah. *Issues of Contemporary Art and Aesthetics in Chinese Context*. Berlin: Springer, 2015.

Mao Zedong 毛澤東. "Shijian lun—lun renshi he shijiande guanxi—he zhixingde guanxi" 實踐論—論認識和實踐的關係—和知行的關係 (On Practise—On the Relation Between Knowledge and Practice, Between Knowing and Doing). In *Mao Zedong xuanji*, vol. 1, edited by Zhonggong zhongyang Mao Zedong xuanji chuban weiyuan hui, 259–73. Beijing: Renmin chuban she, 1966 [1952].

Marx, Karl. *Economic and Philosophic Manuscripts of 1844*. Translated and edited by Martin Milligan. Mineola, NY: Dover, 2007.

Marx, Karl. *Ökonomisch-philosophische Manuskripte*. In *Werke, Ergänzungsband*, by Karl Marx and Friedrich Engels, part 1, 465–588. Berlin: Dietz, 1972.
Pang, Laikwan. "Can Dialectic Materialism Produce Beauty? The 'Great Aesthetic Debates' (1956–1962) in the People's Republic of China." *International Journal of Asian Studies* (2022): 1–14.
Wang Fuzhi 王夫之. *Du si shu da quan shuo* 讀四書大全說 (*The Entire Recapitulation of the Teachings from the "Four Books"*). Taipei: Heluo tushu chuban she, 1974.
Wang Fuzhi 王夫之. "Si shu xun yi" 四書訓義 (A Standard Explanation of the "Four Books"). In *Chuanshan yishu*, vol. 32–44. Shanghai: Taiping shudian, 1933.
Zhang Yongqing 张永清. "Hanyu yujing zhongde shenmei duixiang yu shenmei keti" 漢語語境中的美感對象與美感客體 (Two Kinds of the Aesthetic Objects in the Context of Chinese Language). *Meixue* 12 (2002): 1–6.

# Part 5

# From Aesthetics to Ethics

## 12

# Li Zehou on the Distinction and Interaction between Ethics and Morality

JINHUA JIA

Li Zehou claims that the most important notions of his ethical theory rest on three major distinctions—those between ethics and morality; between human emotions, concepts, and the will that constitute morality; and between traditional religious morals and modern social morals.[1] This paper focuses on the first distinction, especially on Li's innovative notion of the historical, evolutionary interrelation and interaction between ethics and morality.

As scholars have noted, there is no obvious semantic difference between the two English terms of *ethics* and *morals* in their etymological roots,[2] and thus in the common or broad sense the two have long been used synonymously and interchangeably. In the philosophical or narrow sense, however, the two terms have often been distinguished by philosophers with different or even opposite definitions of each term and of what distinguishes the two.[3] In the Chinese tradition, after the term *lunli* 倫理 was selected for translating *ethics* and the term *daode* 道德 for *morality*, first by Japanese scholars in the late nineteenth century,[4] the two terms have also been used interchangeably in common practice, just like their English counterparts. Etymologically and traditionally, however, the two Chinese terms have different implications. Basically, *lunli* refers to social customs and norms regulating interpersonal relationships,[5] while *daode* refers to moral virtues and behaviors.[6]

Li Zehou's distinction and definition of ethics and morality mainly develop from the traditional implications of *lunli* and *daode*. He defines *lunli* or ethics as social customs and norms, and *daode* or morality as individual conduct and psychology. This distinction and definition, however, are not utterly novel but roughly in accordance with those of some philosophers such as Schelling and Hegel.

What clearly distinguishes Li's notion from others is his exposition of the interrelation and interaction between the two categories. Applying his theory of anthropo-historical ontology, Li describes the historical, evolutional interaction of the two categories as external, social-ethical norms that constructs internal, psychological moral maxims, and morality in turn feeds back to ethics. This notion differs from relevant opinions of other philosophers, and better accords with the historical actuality of human experience. An examination of the interactional process between the ethical norms of early Chinese ritual culture and the ethical-moral conceptions of classical Confucianism provides a convincing and good example to support Li's theory.

## Ethics and Morality: Theory and Comparison

Li Zehou's *A New Sketch of Ethics*, published in 2019, is one of his final works, and in it he clearly defines the distinction and interaction of ethics and morality. Li argues, "In my opinion, humans' moral conduct and psychology come from social, ethical norms. Therefore, I strictly distinguish ethics (external institutions, customs, regulations, conventions . . .) from morality (internal psychology, i.e., the will, concepts, and emotions). I contend that the former constructs the latter and the latter feeds back to the former. This is the dialectical relationship between human culture (civilization) and human disposition (psychology)."[7] Li Zehou emphasizes the importance of distinguishing ethics and morality and offers his definition of the two categories. Ethics refers to external social norms such as institutions, regulations, and customs, representing human civilization. Moreover, ethical norms here are broadly inclusive, extending from primeval communities to the public regulations of contemporary societies, and ranging from early totems, taboos, shamanistic ceremonies, and superstitious norms to later legal laws, political institutions, and religious doctrines, as well as customs and conventions of all times. As Li concludes, "Ethical norms are demands, commands, restrictions, controls, jurisdiction, and formal promotion of the community over individual behavior, which are various, myriad, and complex."[8] Li defines morality as part of one's internal individual psychology, which comprises three major elements: emotions, concepts, and the will. Morality involves the integration of emotion and reason, and is characterized by reason's governance of emotion, desire, and instinct. Furthermore, reason is divided into its conceptual content and form of the will, and the most decisive force of moral psychology is the free will of moral autonomy. Meanwhile, morality is not just psychological concepts, but rather must also be good conducts that practice and implement good concepts.[9]

After distinguishing ethics and morality, Li Zehou goes on to describe the historical-evolutionary interrelation and interaction between the two. He argues that ethics constructs morality and morality in turn feeds back to ethics, thus evolving in an interactional, reciprocal process from external to internal and then back to external. In other words, the moral psychology of the human mind originates from the evolutionary internalization of social-ethical norms imposed from outside, going through a process of emotional-rational formation (*qingli jiegou* 情理結構) and gradually becoming the individual's psychological constitution of moral sentiments, conscience, and principles. Then the moral agent's rational principles and motivated moral conducts in turn influence the external community and society and bring changes to public values and ethical standards.[10]

Li Zehou's exposition on the distinction and interaction of ethics and morality is based on his theory of anthropo-historical ontology, especially his notion of historical sedimentation through lived human culture. He assumes that the movement from external to internal or from ethics to morality "can also be understood in terms of the movement from history to education, which is an important part of my philosophy of the historical sedimentation of human psychology."[11]

Li Zehou's distinction and definition of ethics and morality are not utterly novel, as a considerable number of philosophers have held similar opinions. What clearly distinguishes his theory from others is his exposition of the interrelation and interaction between the two categories, which differs from the related opinions of other philosophers. The ethical theories of three representative figures of German idealism, Kant, Schelling, and Hegel, are good examples for making a comparison here.

Kant does not make a direct distinction between ethics and morality. Interestingly, Li Zehou proposes viewing the second formulation of Kant's categorical imperative, "humans as ends," as part of external ethical norms, and the other two formulations, "universal legislation" and "free will," as constructs of individuals' internal moral psychology. Li argues that "humans as ends" proclaims a demand specific to modern society and therefore is not a universally valid categorical imperative.[12] In my opinion, we can use another Kantian notion for comparison. Kant's distinction between juridical duty and virtuous duty from a deontological perspective,[13] among the series of sharp conceptual distinctions that he draws throughout his *Groundwork for the Metaphysics of Morals*, seems to bear more similarities to Li Zehou's distinction between ethics and morality. Kant describes the juridical duty as external, resulting from social legislation and applying to actions a person is compelled to do by appropriate legal authorities, and thus "acting in conformity with duty." In contrast, the virtuous duty is internal, resulting from inner legislation and applying to actions originating from a person's awareness of the moral law, and thus "acting from duty."[14] The juridical duty enforced by external, authoritative laws and prescriptions is similar to Li Zehou's definition of ethics as external, social norms and regulations, while the virtuous duty originated from the internal moral autonomy of agents is similar to his definition of morality as internal psychological autonomy. Nevertheless, there are also certain differences between Kant's distinction between the two kinds of duty and Li's distinction between ethics and morality. For example, Kant's virtuous duty implies his two formulations of categorical imperative, "universal legislation" and "free will," and therefore is also viewed as ahistorical, metaphysical, transcendental a priori. As Li indicates, Kant emphasizes the individual psychological characteristics of free will and practical reason, but does not talk about their external, communal origin.[15] In contrast, Li Zehou stresses the historical, cultural, experiential development of moral psychology, which is gradually internalized, sedimented, and transformed from external social norms.

In his early work titled "New Deduction of Natural Right" (Neue Deduction des Naturrechts), first published in 1796,[16] Schelling clearly distinguishes ethics from morality. He defines ethics as a domain that "sets up a commandment which presupposes a realm of moral beings and which safeguards the selfhood of *all* individuals by means of the demand addressed to the individual," and morality as a domain that "lays down a law addressed only to the individual, a law that demands nothing but the absolute selfhood of the individual."[17] Ethics provides a commandment set up by external social authorities and demands that all individuals observe it, thus representing the "general will." In contrast, morality is an inner commandment of absolute selfhood and autonomous conscience, thus expressing the free "individual will."[18] These assertions are similar to Li's distinction and definition of ethics and morality. Concerning the relationship between the two, however, their notions are different. While Li describes a historical evolution from external social ethical norms to internal individual moral autonomy, Schelling proposes an opposite direction of a breakthrough from the moral domain of the individual will to the ethical domain of the general will. The purpose of this breakthrough is to maintain and safeguard the freedom of the individual will by the empirical general will and to harmonize the two to become equivalent concepts. As Schelling puts it, "This commandment of ethics depends on the higher commandment of morality," and "consequently, the problem of all ethics is to maintain the freedom of the individual by means of the general freedom, to safeguard the individual will by means of the general, or to harmonize the empirical will of all with the empirical will of the individual."[19] The highest commandment of ethics, Schelling believes, is that the entire moral world could will the individual's action in its matter and form, and the individual's action treats any rational being never as a mere object but always as a cooperating subject.[20] Schelling attempts to transcend Kant's abstract world of categorical imperative by introducing the empirical existential world of the social, general ethical domain, but his notion of a breakthrough from morality to ethics remains an ideal, metaphysical deduction.

In works such as the *Elements of the Philosophy of Right*, first published in 1820,[21] Hegel follows Schelling to make a distinction between the sphere of morality and the sphere of ethical life/order. He defines the former as the Kantian individual autonomy, subjectivity, and free will, and the latter as "ethical behaviour grounded in custom and tradition and developed through habit and imitation in accordance with the objective laws of the community."[22] These definitions are also about the same as those of Li Zehou. Like Schelling, however, Hegel's view regarding the relationship between ethics and morality is different from that of Li Zehou. Hegel proposes bridging individual subjective sentiments and the concept of general rights with a progressive transition from morality to ethics through the ethical orders of the family, civil society, and state.[23] As he contends, "The right of individuals to be subjectively destined to freedom is fulfilled when they belong to an actual ethical order, because their conviction of their freedom finds its truth in such an objective order, and it is in an ethical order that they are actually in possession of their own essence or their own inner universality."[24] Hegel adds a historical, progressive perspective to Schelling's breakthrough from morality to ethics, but his scheme is still an ideal, logical reasoning, not a conclusion drawn from the historical actuality of human experience.

The above discussions show that Li Zehou's distinction and definition of ethics and morality are roughly the same as that of some philosophers such as Kant, Schelling, and Hegel, especially the latter two. Li's notions of the interrelation and interaction between the two domains, however, are different from those of these and other philosophers. The schemes designed by Kant, Schelling, and Hegel for opposing, harmonizing, or bridging ethics and morality are significant contributions to the development of ethical-moral philosophy, but these are fundamentally abstract, idealistic, and logical deductions. These schemes are different from Li's unique notion that is grounded on the actual historical process of lived human experience, which I attempt to illustrate by examples of classical Confucian ethical-moral conceptions in the next section.

## Externality and Internality: Classical Confucian Ethical-Moral Conceptions

As discussed above, Li Zehou argues that, historically and progressively, ethics constructs morality and morality in turn feeds back to ethics, thus evolving in an interactional, reciprocal process from external to internal and then back to external. Li cites Christopher Boehm's research to support his argument. Boehm studies the activity and morality of primates and primeval human communities from the perspective of evolutionary sociobiology. He finds that morality originates in the demands of the community on the individual to be self-regulating in the context of the competition and continuous existence of the species, and therefore morality is the individual's biological mechanism of self-regulating. As Boehm repeatedly emphasizes, "the conscience of self-regulating was the first milepost in humankind's moral origin," and "norms imposed on individuals by some communities appeared as early as the age of the Common Ancestors and even more obvious with their successors."[25] Li Zehou claims that Boehm's finding provides evidence to support his description of the movement from ethics to morals and of external communal norms constructing internal moral psychology of individuals.[26]

The development of classical Confucian ethical-moral conceptions also supports Li Zehou's notion of the evolutionary interaction between ethics and morality, not only from external to internal, but also from internal back to external. As is well known, Li's theory of ethics is mainly grounded in a revival, modification, and reinterpretation of classical Confucian ethics. In his "General Schema of Ethics" (Lunlixue zonglan biao 倫理學總覽表), Li uses *li* 禮 (ritual) in the general sense of representing external social-ethical norms, but explains it with the example of traditional Chinese ritual culture and institutions that encompass ethical, religious, and political domains.[27] Li argues that Confucius explicates ritual-ethical norms as grounded on *ren* 仁 (humaneness) and hence internalizes external norms to become individual moral feelings and virtues: "Confucius transfers the practice of the external ritual institution into the internal drive and intention, and integrates reason and drive to become the specific process of emotion (humanity, i.e., *ren*)."[28] In particular, Li Zehou illustrates Confucius's stress on genuine affection (loving feelings toward one's parents) and reason (repaying parents' love and rearing) for caring for one's parents and observing the three-year mourning ritual, instead of merely performing the ritual norms of filiality superficially.[29]

During the Warring States period, Confucius's followers further elaborated the interrelation and interaction between external ethical norms and internal moral sentiments, thus providing more evidence supporting Li Zehou's theory. The distinction and debate between the internality and externality of ethical-moral virtues during this period is the best example for our discussion. Before the famous debate between Gaozi 告子 and Mencius on whether *ren*-humaneness and *yi* 義 (duty/rightness) are internal or external,[30] several excavated Guodian 郭店 bamboo manuscripts had already discussed this issue. For example, both the *Yucong yi* 語叢一 (Miscellaneous Discourses I; strips 21–23) and *Liu de* 六德 (Six Virtues; strip 26) identify *ren* as internal and *yi* as external, an opinion similar with Gaozi's argument.[31] The identification of *ren* as internal follows Confucius's identification, while the identification of *yi* as external still pertains to the ethical-role duty of the ritual tradition.[32] On the other hand, the most important Guodian text related to our discussion is *Wuxing* 五行 (*Five Conducts*), which holds a unique opinion that the cardinal virtues of *ren*, *yi*, *li*, and *zhi* 智 (wisdom/knowledge) can be both external and internal. This opinion is similar to Mencius's argument.[33]

Let us look at the beginning passages of the *Wuxing*:

> If *ren*-humaneness takes shape from within, it is called "conduct of virtue"; if it does not take shape from within, it is called "conduct." If *yi*-duty/rightness takes shape from within, it is called "conduct of virtue"; if it does not take shape from within, it is called "conduct." If *li*-ritual takes shape from within, it is called "conduct of virtue"; if it does not take shape from within, it is called "conduct." If *zhi*-wisdom/knowledge takes shape from within, it is called "conduct of virtue"; if it does not take shape from within, it is called "conduct." If *sheng*-sagacity takes shape from within, it is called "conduct of virtue"; if it does not take shape from within, it is called "conduct of virtue."[34]
>
> The conducts of virtue number five, and when all five in harmony it is called "virtue"; when four conducts in harmony it is called "goodness." Goodness is human's way, and virtue is heaven's way.[35]

The five types of conducts and their corresponding categories of virtue are *ren*-humaneness, *yi*-duty/rightness, *li*-ritual, *zhi*-wisdom/knowledge, and *sheng* 聖 (sagacity). *Nei* 內 (internal) refers to people's heart/mind, and *wai* 外 (external) refers to their social context. The text uses the boundaries of internality and externality to describe the first four conducts and virtues from two levels. On the first level, when these four conducts take shape within a person's heart/mind, they are identified as "conducts of virtue." In other words, "conducts of virtue" are motivated by a person's autonomous will and moral conscience.[36] On the second level, when these same four conducts are formed externally and imposed by social force, they are identified simply as "conducts." The external social force here refers to ritual norms, not only because *li* and *yi*, two of the four virtues, are originally the core content and concepts of the ritual tradition, but also because the *Wuxing* further states that when the four "conducts" are in harmony they are of the moral quality of "goodness" that belongs to humans' way (*rendao* 人道), which is often used identical with *li*, the ritual tradition, during this period.[37] Meanwhile, *sheng*-sagacity, the fifth conduct and virtue, is always "virtuous" no matter whether formed and motivated from within or without; when it and the four "conducts of virtue" motivated internally are in harmony, they are of the moral quality of *de* 德 (virtue), which originally belongs to heaven and represents heaven's way (*tiandao* 天道). What is heaven's *de*-virtue? As is well known, *de* is an extremely complicated concept with multiple implications and has been the focus of many studies and debates. Here I present only one possible interpretation. The commentary to the *Classic of Changes* (*Yijing* 易經) states, "The great *de*-virtue of heaven-earth is to generate [the myriad things]" (天地之大德曰生) ("Xici xia" 繫辭下); "The great man unifies with heaven-earth in their *de*-virtue" (大人者與天地合其德) ("Qian Wenyan" 乾文言). Heaven-earth (*tiandi* 天地) represents the cosmos, which is often simply referred to as "heaven" (*tian* 天), and the movement or operation of the cosmic order is called "heaven's way," whose *de*-virtue is the ceaseless generation of the myriad things including human beings. Heaven bestows its *de* to humans, especially to sage kings such as King Wen of Zhou and sages "without a crown," such as Confucius.[38] *Sheng*-sagacity pertains to heaven's *de*, and therefore always brings out "conduct of virtue" whether formed within or without.

Like many of their contemporary thinkers, the author(s) of the *Wuxing* are curious in searching for the origin and formation of ethical-moral virtues and conducts. However, unlike others who identify *ren* as internal and *yi* as external, they hold a unique view that all the conducts of *ren*, *yi*, *li*, and *zhi* can be motivated both externally and internally, and they obviously favor the internal source of moral motivation and affirm it as authentic virtue. This view represents an effort in following Confucius to further internalize the heteronomous ritual-ethical norms to become people's autonomous moral virtues. The Zhou ritual-ethical norms had regulated what were proper and good conducts for people to perform. Originally, *li* contained a set of normative social-ethical customs and rules guiding and regulating people's conducts and interpersonal relationships. *Yi* was the core and substance of *li*, referring to ethical-role duties and corresponding proper conducts, fitting each person's role and status in the hierarchical kinship group and society defined by ritual norms.[39] In the late Western Zhou to Spring and Autumn periods, *ren* mainly had two meanings, the first "virtuous government" and the second "to love one's family members."[40] Then, the second meaning is further explicated by Confucius, the author(s) of the *Wuxing*, and Mencius as an extension from *xiao* 孝 (filiality), the earliest ritual-ethical norm.[41] The original character for *zhi* 智 was *zhi* 知 that connotes both meanings of wisdom and knowledge,[42] which mainly refer to handling political affairs properly and wisely during the late Western Zhou and Spring and Autumn periods,[43] and are embodied in the classics of *Poetry, Documents, Ritual,* and *Music*, the heritage of the ritual cultural tradition. The author(s) of the *Wuxing* acknowledge the external ritual origin of these four virtues, but at the same time reidentify them as the internal conscience of moral agents, who are capable of motivating authentic virtuous conducts. In order to legitimize their efforts of internalizing the ritual norms to become the autonomous moral virtues, the author(s) trace the origin of those authentic virtues to the cosmic authority of heaven's way.

The *Wuxing*'s distinction of two levels of internal and external virtues is further developed by Mencius.[44] On the one hand, Mencius insists on the importance of continual observation of established external ritual norms; on the other, he places more emphasis on the internalization of those ethical norms for the purpose of fostering inner moral awareness and autonomy.[45] In addition to his argument of both *ren* and *yi* being internal in the debate with Gaozi, Mencius further elaborates the *Wuxing*'s four virtues as "four beginnings" inside a person's *xin* 心 (heart/mind):

> Whoever does not possess the heart/mind of compassion is not human; whoever does not possess the heart/mind of shame and dislike is not human; whoever does not possess the heart/mind of courtesy is not human; whoever does not possess the heart/mind of right and wrong is not human. The heart/mind of compassion is the beginning of *ren*-humaneness; the heart/mind of shame and dislike is the beginning of *yi*-rightness; the heart/mind of courtesy and modest is the beginning of *li*-ritual; the heart/mind of right and wrong is the beginning of *zhi*-wisdom/knowledge.[46]

Mencius's "four beginnings" along with his other relevant discourses have long been interpreted as presenting a theory of human nature that expounds inborn, universal, or transcendental morals.[47] Although there are solid reasons for supporting this interpretation, reading the *Mencius* as a whole and together with excavated Warring States manuscripts, however, we see that Mencius's project is not to shape a theory of human nature,[48] but rather to construct a theory of moral psychology, with a central focus on the moral autonomy of agents rather than the inborn goodness of human nature.[49] This theory is constructed mainly in two ways. The first way is to integrate the functions of the psychological properties of *xing* 性 (predisposition), *qing* 情 (emotion, circumstance), and *xin* 心 (heart, mind); the second way is to internalize the heteronomous ritual-ethical norms. With regard to the first way, there have been a considerable number of studies.[50] However, although there is still plentiful space for further investigation in this issue, because it is not closely related to this essay's central theme as well as the limited space, I focus only on the second way in my discussion here.

Just like the second level of the four conducts and virtues formed externally described in the *Wuxing*, Mencius's four beginnings are originated or derived from external ritual-ethical norms. Throughout the *Mencius*, Mencius stresses the importance of maintaining the function of the normative *li*-ritual and discusses frequently how a person observes ritual norms when interacting with others in various social contexts.[51] Mencius firmly defends *yi*'s social function as ethical-role duties fitting each person's role and status. For example, he praises a gamekeeper's refusal to transgress the rites of his role as following the path of *yi*.[52] Mencius is famous for advocating humane government (*renzheng* 仁政) by rulers and affirms that *ren*-humaneness is extended from the ritual norm of *xiao*-filiality,[53] just as Confucius and the author(s) of the *Wuxing* do. In the *Mencius*, among the thirty-three cases discussing the exercise of *zhi*-wisdom/knowledge, about half are on the ability and knowledge of kings and ministers to make proper judgments and strategies in accordance with circumstances of political contexts.[54] Clearly, like Confucius and the authors of the *Wuxing*, Mencius fully acknowledges the importance of the external ritual-ethical origin and function of *ren*, *yi*, *li*, and *zhi*.

Then, in 2A6, 6A6, and other places, Mencius redefines the implications of these four virtues. Now, *ren* begins with the moral emotion of compassion to all human beings, *yi* begins with the moral conscience of shame and disapproval of bad things,[55] *li* begins with the moral attitude of courtesy and modesty, and *zhi* begins with the moral judgment of right and wrong. The four external ethical virtues enforced by ritual norms now become inner moral virtues motivated by autonomous emotion and reason (ideas and the will), including *li*-ritual itself. This is a further development of the *Wuxing*'s first level of virtuous conducts motivated within a person's heart/mind.[56] Mencius uses humans' predispositional tendency of goodness as a starting point, but his main purpose is not to establish a theory of human nature, but rather to find a ground for internalizing the heteronomous demand of "acting in conformity with *ren* and *yi*" (*xing renyi* 行仁義) to become the autonomous moral practice of "acting from *ren* and *yi*" (*you renyi xing* 由仁義行).[57] This conceptual difference is similar to the *Wuxing*'s differentiation between "conducts" and "conducts of virtue," as well as to Kant's distinction between "acting in conformity with duty" and "acting from duty."[58]

We may explore further into the causes and process behind this tendency of internalization. From the Shang to the Zhou, the ritual ceremonies, norms, and customs have gradually formed codified or uncodified regulations and institutions encompassing religious, ethical, and political domains, whose content is recorded and embodied in the early classics. Then, through ritual education and practice over centuries imposed by states and communities, the ritual-ethical norms are gradually sedimented and internalized into people's heart/mind. The springing up of numerous inventories of virtue and virtuous conduct during the Spring and Autumn period is the result of such a development, sedimentation, and internalization.[59] On the other hand, the collapse of ritual institutions from the late Spring and Autumn to Warring States periods forced philosophers to reflect on the urgent issue of how to preserve or recover the ethical order previously maintained and enforced by ritual norms. Accordingly, Confucius and his followers reflect and elevate the importance of internal moral autonomy. Confucius's explanation of *li*-ritual as grounded on *ren*-humaneness and the distinction and debate of the internality and externality of virtues and virtuous conducts from the *Wuxing*, *Liude*, and *Yucong* to Gaozi and Mencius mark this process of moral internalization. As a result, the "conducts" stemmed from external ritual-ethical norms are transformed to become the "conducts of virtue" motivated by internal moral conscience, the heteronomous demand of "acting in conformity with *ren* and *yi*" becomes the autonomous moral practice of "acting from *ren* and *yi*," and the rites of reverence and submission to the superior and older become what Zhu Xi 朱熹 (1130–1200) explicates as "my heart/mind of respecting them" (我長之之心).[60] This process of internalization supports Li Zehou's description of how external, social ethics constructs internal, psychological morality, as well as his notion of the "cultural-psychological formation" (*wenhua-xinli jiegou* 文化心理結構) of humanity sedimented and constructed through historical process.[61]

By the late Warring States period, the Confucian theory of moral psychology is so well developed that the notion of internal moral conscience and virtues start to feed back to social-ethical standards and formulate new public values. This tendency is represented by the emergence of new concepts such as *gongyi* 公義 (public rightness), *gongdao* 公道 (the way of public rightness), *zhengyi* 正義 (righteousness, justice), and so forth, which transcend the ritual-ethical norms of the hierarchical society to a general context and often appear with the contrast and conflict between the two spheres of gong 公 (public) and si 私 (private). These new concepts appear simultaneously in many Warring States texts, including the *Xunzi* 荀子, *Mozi* 墨子, *Hanfeizi* 韓非子, *Lüshi chunqiu* 呂氏春秋, *Guanzi* 管子, and excavated manuscripts, indicating a common attitude regarding general, public values during this period. Among these texts, the *Xunzi*'s discussion of those new concepts is the clearest and most profound.[62]

The *Xunzi* states,

> As for being in charge of the post of prime minister, that is to prevail over people by means of one's position of authority. Treating what is right as right, treating what is wrong as wrong, treating the capable as capable, treating the incapable as incapable, shutting out private desires, all these must follow the way. The way of public *yi*-rightness and the current *yi*-duty can be compatible mutually—this is the way that prevails over people. . . . If things were like this, then who in the state would dare not to practice *yi*-duty? If the lords and the ministers, superiors and subordinates, noble and humble, senior and junior, right down to the common people, all practiced *yi*-duty, then who in the world would not want to conform to *yi*-duty/rightness?[63]

A good prime minister makes correct judgments on right and wrong and gives fair treatment with regard to the capable and incapable. In order to do so he must shut out his private desires to hold *gongdao* 公道 (the way of *gong*). In early Chinese texts, the character *gong* 公 connotes various meanings such as *gonggong* 公共 (public, common), *gongzheng* 公正 or *gongping* 公平 (fairness, rightness, or justice), and *gongmen* 公門 (the state or court).[64] Since here the "way of *gong*" involves the fair judgment of right and wrong and the fair treatment of people while rejecting private desires, it refers to the way of rightness, fairness, and public interest, and can be translated as the "way of public rightness." As the *Liji* says, "In the eras when the great way prevailed, the world was shared by *gong*-public. The worthy was selected and the capable was appointed. People stressed trustfulness and promoted harmony. Therefore, they did not regard parents as only their own parents, or sons as only their own sons"[65] In the *Xunzi*, *gongdao* is used synonymously with *gongyi*, which also rejects private desires or family interests, and holds unbiased, non-hierarchical fairness and rightness for the general public. For example,

> When the way of public rightness (*gongdao*) succeeds, the private gate is blocked; when public rightness (*gongyi*) shines bright, private things disappear.[66]

> Through public rightness (*gongyi*) the superior person can overcome private desires.[67]

On the other hand, in the term *tongyi* 通義, *tong* 通 means *tongxing* 通行 (current) or *changgu* 常規 (common norms or routines); together *tongyi* refers to the current role-duty hierarchically grounded on the traditional ritual norms, just as Xunzi uses this term in another place to explain the ritual-role duty of respecting the older and submitting to the noble: "For the young to serve their elders, for the humble to serve the noble, for the unworthy to serve the worthy—these are the current *yi*-duties of all people."[68] Xunzi believes that "the way of public *yi*-rightness and the current *yi*-duty can be mutually compatible,"[69] and if a minister holds to this, "who in the state would dare not to perform *yi*-duty/rightness?"[70] Here the fair minister represents the ideal moral character who both conforms with and goes beyond the prescriptive ritual-ethical norms regulating a person's duties and interests, thereby aligning with *yi*-rightness oriented by the interests of the public and state. In this way, Xunzi bridges internal moral autonomy with external public values. The moral virtue of *yi*, which first evolves from the external ritual-ethical norm of role duty to the internal individual moral conscience of rightness, now in turn goes back to influence social-public values and forms the general concepts of righteousness, fairness, and justice. This developing stage of classical Confucian ethical-moral theory provides an example supporting Li Zehou's description of the reciprocal process that morality also feeds back to ethics.

## Conclusion

Li Zehou emphasizes the distinction between ethics and morality, and defines ethics as social customs and norms, and morality as individual conduct and psychology. Li's distinction and definition are not utterly novel, but roughly in accordance with that of some philosophers such as Schelling and Hegel. What clearly distinguishes his notion from others is his description of the interrelation and interaction between the two categories. Applying his theory of anthropo-historical ontology, Li describes the historical, reciprocal interaction of the two categories as external social ethics constructs internal psychological morality and morality in turn feeds back to ethics. This innovative notion, differing from the related opinions of other philosophers, better accords with the historical actuality of lived human experience.

The formational process of classical Confucian ethical-moral conceptions provides a good example in support of Li Zehou's theory. While inheriting and developing the ritual tradition, Confucius and his followers also gradually internalize heteronomous ritual-ethical norms to become autonomous moral virtues, which in turn influence social-public values and ethical standards in a general way. During this process, classical Confucianism constructs an ethical-moral theory that integrates and harmonizes external ethical norms and internal moral virtues.

## Notes

1. Li Zehou 李澤厚, *Lunlixue xinshuo shuyao* 倫理學新說述要 (*A New Sketch of Ethics*) (Beijing: Shijie tushu chuban gongsi, 2019), 136.
2. Damian Grace and Stephen Cohen, *Business Ethics: Australian Problems and Cases* (Melbourne: Oxford University Press, 1998), 5.
3. For general reviews of discussions on various definitions of the two terms, see mainly Josie Fisher, "Social Responsibility and Ethics: Clarifying the Concepts," *Journal of Business Ethics* 52, no. 4 (2004): 397; Jana S. Rošker, *Becoming Human: Li Zehou's Ethics* (Leiden: Brill, 2020), 53–63.
4. Wei-fen Chen, "The Formation of Modern Ethics in China and Japan—The Contributions of Inoue Tetsujirō and Cai Yuan-pei," in *Facing the Twenty-First Century*, ed. Wing Keung Lam and Ching Yuen Cheung (Nagoya: Nanzan Institute for Religion & Culture, 2009), 195–210.
5. Rošker has made a good etymological analysis of the term *lunli*; see her *Becoming Human*, 58–62.
6. The compound *daode* comprises two characters: *dao* 道 and *de* 德. Originally, *dao* refers to *tiandao* 天道 (heaven's way), and *de* refers to heaven's virtue. In early cosmology, heaven generates humans and bestows its virtues on them, and *rendao* 人道 (humans' way) imitates heaven's way, and therefore *daode* gradually extends to refer to humans' virtues as well. See Jinhua Jia, "Religious

Origin of Dao and De and Their Signification in the *Laozi*," *Journal of the Royal Asiatic Society*, series 3, 19, no. 4 (2009): 459–88, and the discussions below.

7. "我以爲人的道德行爲和心理，都從社會倫理規範而來。從而，我嚴格區分倫理 (ethics, 外在制度，風俗，規約，習慣 . . .) 與道德 (morality, 內在心理，即意志，觀念，情感)，幷認爲由前者構建後者，後者反饋于前者。這也就是人文 (文明) 與人性 (心理) 的辯證關係。" Li, *A New Sketch of Ethics*, 24. Translations of all citations from Li's works are adapted from Li Zehou, *The Humanist Ethics of Li Zehou*, ed. and trans. Robert A. Carleo III (Albany: State University of New York Press, 2023).

8. "倫理規範是群體對個體行爲的要求，命令，約束，控制和管轄以及正面提倡，多種多樣，繁多複雜。" Li, *A New Sketch of Ethics*, 25.

9. Li, *A New Sketch of Ethics*, 26–28. For a detailed discussion of Li's particular explication on the rationality of moral psychology, see Robert A. Carleo III, "A Particular Sort of Rationalist Humanism," in *The Humanist Ethics of Li Zehou*, 1–20.

10. Li, *A New Sketch of Ethics*, 24–36.

11. "這也可以稱為歷史——教育路線。這是我的歷史主義人性積澱說哲學的重要部分。" Li, *A New Sketch of Ethics*, 25.

12. Li, *A New Sketch of Ethics*, 13–16.

13. This kind of duty is also called ethical duty by Kant. Here "ethical" refers to what Li Zehou means as "moral."

14. Immanuel Kant, *Groundwork for the Metaphysics of Morals*, ed. and trans. Allen W. Wood, with essays by J. B. Schneewind et al. (New Haven, CT: Yale University Press, 2002), 13–21.

15. Li, *A New Sketch of Ethics*, 38.

16. F. W. J. Schelling, "New Deduction of Natural Right," in *The Unconditional in Human Knowledge: Four Early Essays (1794–1796)*, trans. Fritz Marti (London: Associated University Presses, 1980), 221–52.

17. Schelling, §31.

18. Schelling, §32–33.

19. Schelling, §33, 36.

20. Schelling, §45.

21. Georg W. F. Hegel, *Elements of the Philosophy of Right* (Cambridge: Cambridge University Press, 1991).

22. Hegel, §106, 145, 150, 153.

23. Hegel, §142–340.

24. Hegel, §147, 153.

25. Christopher Boehm, *Moral Origins: The Evolution of Virtue, Altruism, and Shame* (New York: Basic Books, 2012), 176, 108.

26. Li, *A New Sketch of Ethics*, 29–31.

27. Li Zehou 李澤厚, *Lunlixue gangyao* 倫理學綱要 (*An Outline of Ethics*) (Beijing: Renmin wenxue chubanshe, 2019), 252–68; Li Zehou 李澤厚, *Huiying*

*Sangde'er ji qita* 回應桑德爾及其他 (*A Response to Sandel and Other Matters*) (Beijing: Joint Publishing, 2014), 73–76.

28. "孔子將實踐外在禮制化爲內心欲求, 融理欲于一體而成爲情 (人性, 即仁) 的具體過程。" Li Zehou 李澤厚, *Zhongguo gudai sixiangshi lun* 中國古代思想史論 (*On Ancient Chinese Intellectual History*) (Beijing: Renmin chubanshe, 1986), 15–33; Li Zehou 李澤厚, *Lunyu jindu* 論語今讀 (*Reading the Analects Today*) (Hefei: Anhui wenyi chubanshe, 1998), 270. Xu Fuguan and Benjamin Schwartz already held a similar view that Confucius internalizes *li*-ritual norms and places a new focus on the inner moral ideal of *ren*-humaneness, but Li offers more nuanced and comprehensive analysis on this view. See Xu Fuguan 徐復觀, *Zhongguo renxinglun shi: Xianqin pian* 中國人性論史: 先秦篇 (*A History of the Chinese Human Nature Theory: Pre-Qin Volume*) (Wuhan: Hubei renmin chubanshe, 2002 [1963]), 73–75; Benjamin Schwartz, "Transcendence in Ancient China," *Daedalus* 104, no. 2 (1975): 57–68, esp. 63–64.

29. Li, *On Ancient Chinese Intellectual History*, 15–33.

30. *Mencius*, 6A4–5. Scholars' discussions and debates on the issue of Mencius's internalism, though from different perspectives, are of interest in this context. See mainly Kwong-loi Shun, *Mencius and Early Chinese Thought* (Stanford, CA: Stanford University Press, 1997), 102–4; Xiusheng Liu, "Mengzian Internalism," in *Essays on the Moral Philosophy of Mengzi*, ed. Xiusheng Liu and Philip J. Ivanhoe (Indianapolis: Hackett, 2002), 101–31.

31. All citations of the Guodian manuscripts are from Chen Wei 陳偉, ed., *Chudi chutu zhanguo jiance [shisi zhong]* 楚地出土戰國簡冊 [十四種] (*Fourteen Bamboo Manuscripts of the Warring States Period Excavated from the Chu State*) (Beijing: Jingji kexue chubanshe, 2009). In the *Yucong yi*, inner *ren*-humaneness is identified with treating family members with affection (*qin qin* 親親), and outer *yi*-duty is identified as treating the noble reverently (*zun zun* 尊尊). The *Liude* uses "inside the gate" (*mennei* 門內) to define internal *ren*-humaneness, and "outside the gate" (*menwai* 門外) to define external *yi*-duty, the former referring to the emotional connection of father, son, and husband, and the latter to the differentiated status of lord, subject, and wife. Similar opinions or distinctions are also seen in the "Sangfu sizhi" 喪服四制 chapter of the *Liji* 禮記 (Record of Ritual), the "Benming" 本命 chapter of the *Dadai liji* 大戴禮記 (Elder Dai's Record of Ritual), and the "Wenyan" 文言 commentary on Haxagram #2 "Kun" 坤 in the *Yijing* 易經 (*Classic of Changes*). These opinions vary in expression, but they are essentially close to Gaozi's view. The "Jie" 戒 chapter in the *Guanzi* 管子 also expresses a similar view: "*Ren*-humaneness is from interior and *yi*-duty behaves in exterior" (仁從中出, 義從外作). See Li Xiangfeng 黎翔鳳 and Liang Yunhua 梁運華, eds., *Guanzi jiaozhu* 管子校注 (*Collation and Annotation of the Guanzi*) (Beijing: Zhonghua shuju, 2004), 10.509–10. Some scholars contend that those arguments and differentiations between *ren* and *yi*, including those of Gaozi and Mencius, present two divisive boundaries of family and heart. See

Qingjuan Sun, "Revisiting the Internal-External Issue of Ren and Yi in and beyond *Mengzi* 6A:4," *Philosophy East and West* 70, no. 2 (2020): 506–21. This distinction, however, does not seem to be meaningful because both concepts of *ren* and *yi* are embodied or derived from the ritual norms which are built on the ethical relationship of familial system, and therefore encompass both familial and psychological dimensions. For example, Confucius, Mencius, and others define *ren* as an extension from *xiao* 孝 (filiality) and implying biased, loving feelings toward one's family members (see further below). For more different interpretations of these Warring States debates and arguments, see mainly Wang Bo 王博, "Zaoqi rujia renyi shuo de yanjiu" 早期儒家仁義說的研究 (Study on Early Confucian Concepts of Ren and Yi), *Zhexuemen* 哲學門 11 (2005): 71–97; Liang Tao 梁濤, *Guodian zhujian yu Si-Meng xuepai* 郭店竹簡與思孟學派 (*Guodian Bamboo Manuscripts and the Zisi-Mencius School*) (Beijing: Zhongguo renmin daxue chubanshe, 2008), 308–309; Tang Wenming 唐文明, "Renyi yu neiwai" 仁義與內外 (Renyi and Internality/Externality), in *Rujia Si-Meng xuepai lunji* 儒家思孟學派論集 (*Collection of Studies on the Confucian Zisi-Mencius School*), ed. Shandong shifan daxue Qi Lu wenhua yanjiu zhongxin 山東師範大學齊魯文化研究中心 (Center for the Study of Qi-Lu Culture in Shandong Normal University) (Jinan: Qi Lu shushe, 2008), 388–403.

32. *Yi* presents dual categories in classical Confucian conception. The first category is ethical-role duty originated from the Zhou ritual culture, which is a set of social norms defining ethical duties that fit each person's role and status in the kinship group and society and regulating what was appropriate for a person's behavior. The second category is moral conscience and rightness resulted from the internalization of social norms and ethical duties. For a detailed discussion of this dual definition, see Jinhua Jia, "From Ritual Culture to the Classical Confucian Conception of *Yi*," *Dao: A Journal of Comparative Philosophy* 20 (2021): 531–47; see also further discussion below.

33. A silk manuscript of the same title and content along with an appended commentary is included in the excavated Mawandui silk manuscripts. Li Xueqin 李學勤 proposes that the *Wuxing* was written by Confucius' grandson Zisi 子思 (483–402 BCE) or his disciples; see his "Jingmen Guodian Chujian zhong de 'Zisizi'" 荊門郭店楚簡中的子思子 (The Zisizi as Seen in the Chu Bamboo Manuscripts of Jingmen Guodian), *Wenwu tiandi* 文物天地 2 (1998): 28–30. Although this proposal has been supported by many scholars, others have disagreed.

34. "仁形於內謂之德之行，不形於內謂之行。義形於內謂之德之行，不形於內謂之行。禮形於內謂之德之行，不形於內謂之行。智形於內謂之德之行，不形於內謂之行。聖形於內謂之德之行，不形於內謂之德之行。" (Strips 1–4) All translations of citations from Guodian manuscripts are adapted from Scott Cook, *The Bamboo Texts of Guodian: A Study and Complete Translation* (Ithaca, NY: East Asia Program, Cornell University, 2012).

35. "德之行五，和謂之德，四行和謂之善。善，人道也。德，天道也。" (Strips 4–5).

36. Mark Csikszentmihalyi argues that the *Wuxing* emphasizes the innate origin of virtue and genuine moral motivation. Chen-Feng Tsai views "conducts of virtue" as "based on an internal, independent will" and "stemming from an autonomous principle." See Mark Csikszentmihalyi, *Material Virtue: Ethics and the Body in Early China* (Leiden: Brill, 2004), 70–71; Chen-Feng Tsai, "Zisi and the Thought of Zisi and Mencius School," in *Dao Companion to Classical Confucian Philosophy*, ed. Vincent Shen (Dordrecht Heidelberg: Springer, 2014), 119–38, esp. 124.

37. Liu Xinlan 劉昕嵐 and Li Tianhong 李天虹 have offered plentiful evidence for this identification; see Liu Xinlan 劉昕嵐, "Guodian Chujian *Xing zi ming chu* pian jianshi" 郭店楚簡性自命出篇箋釋 (Commentary on the Chu Bamboo Manuscript Xing zi ming chu from Guodian), in *Guodian Chujian guoji xueshu yantaohui lunwenji* 郭店楚簡國際學術研討會論文集 (*Proceedings of the International Conference on Guodian Bamboo Manuscripts*) (Wuhan: Hubei renmin chubanshe, 2000), 330; Li Tianhong 李天虹, *Guodian zhujian Xing zi ming chu yanjiu* 郭店竹簡性自命出研究 (*Study on the Guodian Bamboo Manuscript Xing zi ming chu*) (Wuhan: Hubei jiaoyu chubanshe, 2003), 136–37.

38. E.g., *Shi Qiang pan* 史牆盤; *Analects* 7/23.

39. Jia, "From Ritual Culture to the Classical Confucian Conception of *Yi*," 531–47.

40. For example, the *Guoyu* 國語 records such a saying, "For those practice *ren*, to love their family members is called *ren*; for those rule the state, to benefit the state is called *ren*" (為仁者，愛親之謂仁；為國者，利國之謂仁) ("Jinyu yi" 晉語一). For more examples and discussions, see Chen Lai 陳來, *Gudai sixiang wenhua de shijie: Chunqiu shidai de zongjiao, lunli yu shehui sixiang* (古代思想文化的世界：春秋時代的宗教、倫理與社會思想) (*The Ancient World of Thought and Culture: Religion, Ethics, and Social Thought in the Spring and Autumn Era*) (Beijing: The Joint Publishing, 2009), 312–41.

41. *Analects* 1/6, 1/2; *Wuxing*, strip 33; *Mencius* 1A7. Jinhua Jia, "*Shu*-Considerateness and *Ren*-Humaneness: The Confucian Silver Rule and Golden Rule," *Journal of Value Inquiry* 58 (2024): 257–73.

42. Zong Fubang 宗福邦, Chen Shinao 陳世鐃, and Xiao Haibo 蕭海波, eds., *Guxun huizuan* 故訓匯纂 (*A Compilation of Old Commentaries*) (Beijing: Shangwu yinshuguan, 2003), 1032, 1573–74.

43. Chen Lai, *The Ancient World of Thought and Culture*, 312–41.

44. Scholars have discussed the influence of the *Wuxing* on Mencius from various perspectives; see mainly Csikszentmihalyi, *Material Virtue*, 103–113; Chen Lai 陳來, *Zhubo Wuxing yu jianbo yanjiu* 竹帛五行與簡帛研究 (*The Bamboo-Silk Manuscript Wuxing and the Study on Bamboo and Silk Manuscripts*) (Beijing: Sanlian shudian, 2009), 158–200.

45. David S. Nivison has noted that there are two sources of morality in the *Mencius*, one formal and public, and the other internal and motivational, and argued that to Mencius the ideal is the internal moral source. See David Nivison, "Motivation and Moral Action in Mencius," in *The Ways of Confucianism: Investigation in Chinese Philosophy*, ed. Bryan W. Van Norden (Chicago: Open Court, 1996), 101–104.

46. "無惻隱之心，非人也；無羞惡之心，非人也；無辭讓之心，非人也；無是非之心，非人也。惻隱之心，仁之端也；羞惡之心，義之端也；辭讓之心，禮之端也；是非之心，智之端也。" *Mencius*, 2A6; see also 6A6. Translations of all citations from the *Mencius* are adapted from D. C. Lau, *Mencius: A Bilingual Edition* (Hong Kong: Chinese University of Hong Kong Press, 2003).

47. For reviews of scholarly works on this theory, see mainly Shun, *Mencius and Early Chinese Thought*, 180–234; Junjie Huang, "Contemporary Chinese Studies of Mencius in Taiwan," *Dao: A Journal of Comparative Philosophy* 4, no. 1 (2004): 151–66, esp. 151–59; Winnie Sung, "Mencius and Xunzi on Xing (Human Nature)," *Philosophy Compass* 11, no. 11 (2016): 632–41; Xiaogan Liu, "Straightforward Reading, Injective Interpretation, and Scientific Implication: On the Mencian Theory of Human Nature," *Dao: A Journal of Comparative Philosophy* (2020) 19: 175–92.

48. A. C. Graham indicates that Mencius usually talks about *xing* or ethical inclinations only when dealing with his debating opponents; see A. C. Graham, "The Background of the Mencian Theory of Human Nature," in *Studies in Chinese Philosophy and Philosophical Literature* (Albany: State University of New York, 1990), 57–59. Hektor K. T. Yan argues that *xing* or "human nature" does not occupy a central role in the Mencian moral philosophy; see Hektor K. T Yan, "Beyond a Theory of Human Nature: Towards an Alternative Interpretation of Mencius' Ethics," *Frontiers of Philosophy in China* 9, no. 3 (2014): 396–416.

49. Some scholars have already explored the possibility of a Mencian moral psychology or a classical Confucian moral psychology from various perspectives. See mainly I. A. Richards, *Mencius on the Mind: Experiments in Multiple Definition* (Richmond, Surrey: Curzon, 1997); Antonio S. Cua, "Xin and Moral Failure: Notes on an Aspect of Mencius' Moral Psychology," in *Mencius: Contexts and Interpretations*, ed. Alan K. L. Chan (Honolulu: University of Hawai'i Press, 2002), 126–50; Csikszentmilhalyi, *Material Virtue*, 59–160; Kwong-loi Shun, "Early Confucian Moral Psychology," in *Dao Companion to Classical Confucian Philosophy*, ed. Vincent Shen (Dordrecht: Springer, 2014), 263–90.

50. For example, Xu Fuguan claims that Mencius is in fact "talking about the goodness of *xing* from the goodness of *xin*" (由心善以言性善), and *xin*'s independent activities are the ground of people's moral agency; see Xu, *A History of the Chinese Human Nature Theory: Pre-Qin Volume*, 160–62. Mou Zongsan 牟宗三 holds a similar opinion that Mencius's view of the goodness of *xing* cannot be separated from his conception of *xin*; see Mou Zongsan 牟

宗三, *Cong Lu Xiangshan dao Liu Jishan* 從陸象山到劉蕺山 (*From Lu Jiuyuan to Liu Zongzhou*) (Taipei: Xuesheng shuju, 1979), 216–17. Kwong-loi Shun argues that to say human nature is good is to make the claim that the heart/mind has predispositions towards the ethical attributes of *ren*, *yi*, *li*, and *zhi*; see Shun, *Mencius and Early Chinese Thought*, 180–234. Roger T. Ames challenges the use of "human nature" for translating *xing* and emphasizes the close relationship between *xing*, *qing*, and *xin*, describing *xing* as "a process of cultivation that includes *xin* as the ground for the habitual dispositions" and "fully informed by both feelings and circumstances (*qing* 情)"; see Roger T. Ames, "The Mencian Conception of Ren xing 人性: Does It Mean 'Human Nature'?" in *Chinese Texts and Philosophical Contexts: Essays Dedicated to Angus C. Graham*, ed. Henry Rosemont, Jr. (La Salle, IL: Open Court, 1991), 143–75; "Mencius and a Process Notion of Human Nature," in *Mencius: Contexts and Interpretations* ed. Alan K. L. Chan (Honolulu: University of Hawai'i Press, 2002), 72–90; "Reconstructing A.C. Graham's Reading of *Mencius* on *xing* 性: A Coda to 'The Background of the Mencian Theory of Human Nature' (1967)," in *Having a Word with Angus Graham: At Twenty-Five Years into His Immortality*, ed. Carine Defoort and Roger T. Ames (Albany: State University of New York Press, 2018), 185–213. In his review of scholarly works on the "Mencian theory of human nature," Xiaogan Liu criticizes Ames's studies as "injective interpretation" that is "not acceptable for discovering possible true meanings of Mencius' theory"; see Liu, "Straightforward Reading, Injective Interpretation, and Scientific Implication," 181–86. However, it seems that Ames's interpretation is more insightful and sophisticated than the straightforward and simplified reading advocated by Liu. As a matter of fact, the complicated integration of *xing*, *qing*, and *xin* already appears in Guodian manuscripts such as the *Xing zi ming chu* 性自命出 (*Xing*-predisposition Comes from Heaven's Mandate), *Wuxing*, *Yucong*, and so on. See mainly Csikszentmihalyi, *Material Virtue*, 67–82; Chen Lai, *The Bamboo-Silk Manuscript Wuxing and the Study on Bamboo and Silk Manuscripts*, 13; Franklin Perkins, "Motivation and the Heart in the *Xing Zi Ming Chu*," *Dao: A Journal of Comparative Philosophy* 8 (2009): 117–31; Shirley Chan, "Xing 性 and Qing 情: Human Nature and Moral Cultivation in the Guodian Text *Xing zi ming chu* 性自命出 (Nature Derives from Endowment)," in *Dao Companion to the Excavated Guodian Bamboo Manuscripts*, ed. Shirley Chan (Dordrecht: Springer, 2019), 213–38.

51. Shun, *Mencius and Early Chinese Thought*, 52–56.
52. *Mencius*, 5B7. For more examples and discussions on this issue, see Jinhua Jia, "From Ritual Culture to the Classical Confucian Conception of *Yi*," 531–47.
53. *Mencius*, 1A7.
54. Shun, *Mencius and Early Chinese Thought*, 66–71.
55. The feelings and attitudes of "shame and dislike" suggest many meanings (Shun, *Mencius and Early Chinese Thought*, 58–63), but they basically are

evaluations and determinations against conducts that are inappropriate, disgraceful, wrong, or unreasonable. As Mencius states, "All persons have things they are unwilling to do. To extend this to what they are willing to do is *yi*" (人皆有所不為, 達之於其所為, 義也). (7B31)

56. Pang Pu 龐樸 has argued that the views of Confucius's followers on the question of why human nature is *ren* can be divided into two camps of seeking internally and externally, and he identifies the authors of Guodian manuscripts and Mencius as the former; see Pang Pu 龐樸, "Kong Meng zhijian: Guodian Chujian de sixiangshi diwei" 孔孟之間: 郭店楚簡的思想史地位 (Between Confucius and Mencius: The Position of Guodian Chu Manuscripts in Intellectual History)," *Zhongguo shehui kexue* 中國社會科學 5 (1998): 88–95. Csikszentmihalyi has defined Mencius's view of the origin of virtuous conduct as an internalist account shared with the *Wuxing*; see Csikszentmihalyi, *Material Virtue*, 109.

57. *Mencius*, 4B19.

58. Mou Zongsan 牟宗三 identifies Mencian moral thought as "the same as the autonomy of will and self-legislation presented by Kant"; see Mou Zongsan 牟宗三, *Yuanshan lun* 圓善論 (*On the Summum Bonum*) (Taipei: Xuesheng shuju, 1985), 12–27. Although it is questionable whether Mencius's idea is completely the same as Kant's, Mou is acute and insightful in detecting Mencius's emphasis on the autonomy of moral agents. Xiaogan Liu again criticizes Mou Zongsan's opinion as "injective interpretation" that is "not acceptable for discovering possible true meanings of Mencius' theory." See Liu, "Straightforward Reading, Injective Interpretation, and Scientific Implication," 181–83. However, Mou's philosophical analysis of the Mencian thought seems to be more profound and nuanced than the straightforward and simplified approach advocated by Liu.

59. For examples of the inventories, see Chen Lai, *The Ancient World of Thought and Culture*, 306–56.

60. Zhu Xi, *Sishu zhangju jizhu* 四書章句集注 (*Collected Commentaries on the Four Books*) (Jinan: Qilu shushe 1992), 157.

61. Li, *On Ancient Chinese Intellectual History*, 31–33; Li, *Lishi bentilun* 歷史本體論 (*Historical Ontology*) (Beijing: Joint Publishing, 2002), 124–32. For discussions of Li Zehou's theory of "cultural-psychological formation" and historical sedimentation, see mainly Paul J. D'Ambrosio, Robert A. Carleo III, and Andrew Lambert, "On Li Zehou's Philosophy: An Introduction by Three Translators," *Philosophy East and West* 66, no. 4 (2016): 1057–67, esp. 1060, 1064–65; Marthe Chandler, "Li Zehou, Kant, and Darwin: The Theory of Sedimentation," in *Li Zehou and Confucian Philosophy*, ed. Roger T. Ames and Jinhua Jia (Honolulu: University of Hawai'i Press, 2018), 278–312; Jana S. Rošker, *Following His Own Path: Li Zehou and Contemporary Chinese Thought* (Albany: State University of New York Press, 2019), 47–102.

62. Scholars have identified the different ethical-moral tendencies between Mencius and Xunzi as the different emphases between *renyi* 仁義 (humaneness

and rightness) and *liyi* 禮義 (ritual and duty) or internalism and externalism. See mainly Cua, "*Xin* and Moral Failure," 126–27. However, as discussed above, Mencius still attaches importance to *li* or *liyi*. Although Xunzi places much stress on *li* or *liyi*, he also expounds the importance of *ren* or *renyi* to a large extent. For a detailed discussion of this issue, see Jinhua Jia, "From Ritual Culture to the Classical Confucian Conception of *Yi*," 531–47.

63. "夫主相者, 勝人以埶也, 是為是, 非為非, 能為能, 不能為不能, 併己之私欲, 必以道。夫公道通義之可以相兼容者, 是勝人之道也 . . . .如是, 則國孰敢不為義矣。君臣上下, 貴賤長少, 至於庶人, 莫不為義, 則天下孰不欲合義矣。" Wang Xianqian 王先謙, ed., *Xunzi jijie* 荀子集解 (*Collected Commentaries on the Xunzi*) (Beijing: Zhonghua Book Company, 1988), "Qiangguo" 彊國, 11.295. All translations of citations from the *Xunzi* in this essay are adapted from *Xunzi: The Complete Text*, trans. Eric Hutton (Princeton: Princeton University Press, 2014).

64. Mizoguchi Yūzō 溝口雄三, *Zhongguo de gong yu si* • *Gong si* 中國的公與私 • 公私 (*China's Gong and Si: Gongsi*), trans. Zheng Jing 鄭靜 (Beijing: Joint Publishing, 2011), 230–59.

65. "大道之行也, 天下為公。選賢與能, 講信修睦。故人不獨親其親, 不獨子其子。" Zheng Xuan 鄭玄 and Kong Yingda 孔穎達, eds., *Liji zhushu* 禮記注疏 (*Commentaries on the Record of Ritual*) (Beijing: Peking University Press, 2000), "Liyun" 禮運, 21.769a.

66. "公道達而私門塞矣, 公義明而私事息矣。" *Xunzi jijie*, "Jundao" 君道, 8.239.

67. "君子之能以公義勝私欲也。" *Xunzi jijie*, "Xiushen" 脩身, 1.36.

68. "少事長, 賤事貴, 不肖事賢, 是天下之通義也。" *Collected Commentaries on the Xunzi*, "Zhongni" 仲尼, 3.113.

69. "公道通義之可以相兼容."

70. "則國孰敢不為義."

# Bibliography

Ames, Roger T. "The Mencian Conception of Ren xing 人性: Does It Mean 'Human Nature'?" In *Chinese Texts and Philosophical Contexts: Essays Dedicated to Angus C. Graham*, edited by Henry Rosemont Jr., 143–75. La Salle, IL: Open Court, 1991.

Ames, Roger T. "Mencius and a Process Notion of Human Nature." In *Mencius: Contexts and Interpretations*, edited by Alan K. L. Chan, 72–90. Honolulu: University of Hawai'i Press, 2002.

Ames, Roger T. "Reconstructing A.C. Graham's Reading of *Mencius* on *xing* 性: A Coda to 'The Background of the Mencian Theory of Human Nature' (1967)." In *Having a Word with Angus Graham: At Twenty-Five Years into His Immortality*, edited by Carine Defoort and Roger T. Ames, 185–213. Albany: State University of New York Press, 2018.

Boehm, Christopher. *Moral Origins: The Evolution of Virtue, Altruism, and Shame*. New York: Basic Books, 2012.
Carleo, Robert A. III. "A Particular Sort of Rationalist Humanism." In *The Humanist Ethics of Li Zehou*, translated and edited by Robert A. Carleo III, 1–20. Albany: State University of New York Press, 2023.
Carleo, Robert A. III, and Andrew Lambert. "On Li Zehou's Philosophy: An Introduction by Three Translators." Philosophy East and West 66, no. 4 (2016): 1057–67.
Chan, Shirley. "Xing 性 and Qing 情: Human Nature and Moral Cultivation in the Guodian Text *Xing zi ming chu* 性自命出 (Nature Derives from Endowment)." In *Dao Companion to the Excavated Guodian Bamboo Manuscripts*, edited by Shirley Chan, 213–38. Dordrecht: Springer, 2019.
Chandler, Marthe. "Li Zehou, Kant, and Darwin: The Theory of Sedimentation." In *Li Zehou and Confucian Philosophy*, edited by Roger T. Ames and Jinhua Jia, 278–312. Honolulu: University of Hawai'i Press, 2018.
Chen Lai 陳來. *Gudai sixiang wenhua de shijie: Chunqiu shidai de zongjiao, lunli yu shehui sixiang* 古代思想文化的世界: 春秋時代的宗教, 倫理與社會思想 (*The Ancient World of Thought and Culture: Religion, Ethics, and Social Thought in the Spring and Autumn Era*). Beijing: The Joint Publishing, 2009.
Chen Lai. *Zhubo Wuxing yu jianbo yanjiu* 竹帛五行與簡帛研究 (*The Bamboo-Silk Manuscript Wuxing and the Study on Bamboo and Silk Manuscripts*). Beijing: Sanlian Bookstore, 2009.
Chen Wei 陳偉, ed., *Chudi chutu zhanguo jiance [shisi zhong]* 楚地出土戰國簡冊 [十四種] (*Fourteen Bamboo Manuscripts of the Warring States Period Excavated from the Chu State*). Beijing: Jingji kexue chuban she, 2009.
Chen, Wei-fen. "The Formation of Modern Ethics in China and Japan—The Contributions of Inoue Tetsujirō and Cai Yuan-pei." In *Facing the Twenty-First Century*, edited by Wing Keung Lam and Ching Yuen Cheung, 195–210. Nagoya: Nanzan Institute for Religion and Culture, 2009.
Cook, Scott. *The Bamboo Texts of Guodian: A Study and Complete Translation*, 2 vols. Ithaca, NY: East Asia Program, Cornell University, 2012.
Csikszentmihalyi, Mark. *Material Virtue: Ethics and the Body in Early China*. Leiden: Brill, 2004.
Cua, Antonio S. "Xin and Moral Failure: Notes on an Aspect of Mencius' Moral Psychology." In *Mencius: Contexts and Interpretations*, edited by Alan K. L. Chan, 126–50. Honolulu: University of Hawai'i Press, 2002.
Fisher, Josie. "Social Responsibility and Ethics: Clarifying the Concepts." *Journal of Business Ethics* 52, no. 4 (2004): 391–400.
Grace, Damian, and Stephen Cohen. *Business Ethics: Australian Problems and Cases*. Melbourne: Oxford University Press, 1998.
Graham, A. C. "The Background of the Mencian Theory of Human Nature." In *Studies in Chinese Philosophy and Philosophical Literature*. Albany: State University of New York Press, 1990.

Hegel, Georg W. F. Elements of the Philosophy of Right. Edited by Allen W. Wood. Cambridge: Cambridge University Press, 1991.
Huang, Junjie. "Contemporary Chinese Studies of Mencius in Taiwan." *Dao: A Journal of Comparative Philosophy* 4, no. 1 (2004): 151–66.
Jia, Jinhua. "From Ritual Culture to the Classical Confucian Conception of *Yi*." *Dao: A Journal of Comparative Philosophy* 20 (2021): 531–47.
Jia, Jinhua. "Religious Origin of Dao and De and Their Signification in the *Laozi*." *Journal of the Royal Asiatic Society*, series 3, 19, no. 4 (2009): 459–88.
Jia, Jinhua. "*Shu*-Considerateness and *Ren*-Humaneness: The Confucian Silver Rule and Golden Rule." *Journal of Value Inquiry* 58 (2024): 257–73.
Kant, Immanuel. *Groundwork for the Metaphysics of Morals*. Edited and translated by Allen W. Wood, with essays by J. B. Schneewind et al. New Haven, CT: Yale University Press, 2002.
Li Tianhong 李天虹. *Guodian zhujian Xing zi ming chu yanjiu* 郭店竹簡性自命出研究 (*Study on the Guodian Bamboo Manuscript Xing zi ming chu*). Wuhan: Hubei jiaoyu chuban she, 2003.
Li Xiangfeng 黎翔鳳 and Liang Yunhua 梁運華, eds. *Guanzi jiaozhu* 管子校注 (*Collation and Annotation of the Guanzi*). Beijing: Zhonghua shuju, 2004.
Li Xueqin 李學勤. "Jingmen Guodian Chujian zhong de 'Zisizi'" 荊門郭店楚簡中的子思子 (*The Zisizi as Seen in the Chu Bamboo Manuscripts of Jingmen Guodian*). *Wenwu tiandi* 文物天地 2 (1998): 28–30.
Li Zehou 李澤厚. *Huiying Sangde'er ji qita* 回應桑德爾及其他 (*A Response to Sandel and Other Matters*). Beijing: Joint Publishing, 2014.
Li Zehou. *The Humanist Ethics of Li Zehou*. Edited and translated by Robert A. Carleo III. Albany: State University of New York Press, 2023.
Li Zehou 李澤厚. *Lishi bentilun* 歷史本體論 (*Historical Ontology*). Beijing: SDX Joint Publishing, 2002.
Li Zehou 李澤厚. *Lunlixue gangyao* 倫理學綱要 (*An Outline of Ethics*). Beijing: Renmin ribao chubanshe, 2010.
Li Zehou 李澤厚. *Lunlixue xinshuo shuyao* 倫理學新說述要 (*A New Sketch of Ethics*). Beijing: Shijie tushu, 2019.
Li Zehou 李澤厚. *Lunyu jindu* 論語今讀 (*Reading the Analects Today*). Hefei: Anhui wenyi chubanshe, 1998.
Li Zehou 李澤厚. *Zhongguo gudai sixiang shilun* 中國古代思想史論 (*A History of Classical Chinese Thought*). Beijing: Renmin chuban she, 1985.
Liang Tao 梁濤. *Guodian zhujian yu Si-Meng xuepai* 郭店竹簡與思孟學派 (*Guodian Bamboo Manuscripts and the Zisi-Mencius School*). Beijing: Zhongguo renmin daxue chubanshe, 2008.
Liu, Xiaogan. "Straightforward Reading, Injective Interpretation, and Scientific Implication: On the Mencian Theory of Human Nature." *Dao: A Journal of Comparative Philosophy* (2020) 19: 175–92.
Liu Xinlan 劉昕嵐. "Guodian Chujian *Xing zi ming chu* pian jianshi" 郭店楚簡性自命出篇箋釋 (*Commentary on the Chu Bamboo Manuscript Xing zi ming*

chu from Guodian). In *Guodian Chujian guoji xueshu yantaohui lunwenji* 郭店楚簡國際學術研討會論文集 (*Proceedings of the International Conference on Guodian Bamboo Manuscripts*). Wuhan: Hubei renmin chubanshe, 2000.

Liu, Xiusheng. "Mengzian Internalism." In *Essays on the Moral Philosophy of Mengzi*, edited by Xiusheng Liu and Philip J. Ivanhoe, 101–31. Indianapolis: Hackett, 2002.

Mencius. *Mencius: A Bilingual Edition*, rev. ed. Translated by D. C. Lau. Hong Kong: Chinese University of Hong Kong Press, 2003.

Mizoguchi Yūzō 溝口雄三. *Zhongguo de gong yu si • Gong si* 中國的公與私 • 公私 (*China's Gong and Si: Gongsi*). Translated by Zheng Jing 鄭靜. Beijing: Joint Publishing, 2011.

Mou Zongsan 牟宗三. *Cong Lu Xiangshan dao Liu Jishan* 從陸象山到劉蕺山 (From Lu Jiuyuan to Liu Zongzhou). Taipei: Xuesheng shuju, 1979.

Mou Zongsan 牟宗三. *Yuanshan lun* 圓善論 (*On the Summum Bonum*). Taipei: Xuesheng shuju, 1985.

Nivison, David. "Motivation and Moral Action in Mencius." In *The Ways of Confucianism: Investigation in Chinese Philosophy*, edited by Bryan W. Van Norden. Chicago: Open Court, 1996.

Pang Pu 龐樸. "Kong Meng zhijian: Guodian Chujian de sixiangshi diwei" 孔孟之間: 郭店楚簡的思想史地位 (Between Confucius and Mencius: The Position of Guodian Chu Manuscripts in Intellectual History). Zhongguo shehui kexue 5 (1998): 88–95.

Perkins, Franklin. "Motivation and the Heart in the *Xing Zi Ming Chu*." *Dao: A Journal of Comparative Philosophy* 8 (2009): 117–31.

Richards, I. A. Mencius on the Mind: Experiments in Multiple Definition. Richmond, Surrey: Curzon, 1997.

Rošker, Jana S. *Becoming Human: Li Zehou's Ethics*. Leiden: Brill, 2020.

Rošker, Jana S. *Following His Own Path: Li Zehou and Contemporary Chinese Philosophy*. Albany: State University of New York Press, 2019.

Schelling, F. W. J. "New Deduction of Natural Right." In *The Unconditional in Human Knowledge: Four Early Essays (1794–1796)*, translated by Fritz Marti, 221–52. London: Associated University Presses, 1980.

Schwartz, Benjamin. "Transcendence in Ancient China." *Daedalus* 104, no. 2 (1975): 57–68.

Shun, Kwong-loi. "Early Confucian Moral Psychology." In *Dao Companion to Classical Confucian Philosophy*, edited by Vincent Shen, 263–90. Dordrecht: Springer, 2014.

Shun, Kwong-loi. *Mencius and Early Chinese Thought*. Stanford, CA: Stanford University Press, 1997.

Sun, Qingjuan. "Revisiting the Internal-External Issue of Ren and Yi in and beyond *Mengzi* 6A:4." *Philosophy East and West* 70, no. 2 (2020): 506–21.

Sung, Winnie. "Mencius and Xunzi on Xing (Human Nature)." *Philosophy Compass* 11, no. 11 (2016): 632–41.
Tang Wenming 唐文明. "Renyi yu neiwai" 仁義與內外 (Renyi and Internality/Externality). In *Rujia Si-Meng xuepai lunji* 儒家思孟學派論集 (Collection of Studies on the Confucian Zisi-Mencius School), edited by Shandong shifan daxue Qi Lu wenhua yanjiu zhongxin 山東師範大學齊魯文化研究中心 (Center for the Study of Qi-Lu Culture in Shandong Normal University), 388–403. Jinan: Qi Lu shushe, 2008.
Tsai, Chen-Feng. "Zisi and the Thought of Zisi and Mencius School." In *Dao Companion to Classical Confucian Philosophy*, edited by Vincent Shen, 119–38. Dordrecht Heidelberg: Springer, 2014.
Wang Bo 王博. "Zaoqi rujia renyi shuo de yanjiu" 早期儒家仁義說的研究 (Study on Early Confucian Concepts of Ren and Yi). *Zhexuemen* 哲學門 11 (2005): 71–97.
Wang Xianqian 王先謙, ed. *Xunzi jijie* 荀子集解 (Collected Commentaries on the Xunzi). Beijing: Zhonghua Book Company, 1988.
Xu Fuguan 徐復觀. *Zhongguo renxinglun shi: Xianqin pian* 中國人性論史：先秦篇 (A History of the Chinese Human Nature Theory: Pre-Qin Volume). Wuhan: Hubei renmin chubanshe, 2002 [1963].
*Xunzi: The Complete Text.* Translated by Eric Hutton. Princeton: Princeton University Press, 2014.
Yan, Hektor K. T. "Beyond a Theory of Human Nature: Towards an Alternative Interpretation of Mencius' Ethics." *Frontiers of Philosophy in China* 9, no. 3 (2014): 396–416.
Zheng Xuan 鄭玄 and Kong Yingda 孔穎達, eds. *Liji zhushu* 禮記注疏 (Commentaries on the Record of Ritual). Beijing: Peking University Press, 2000.
Zhu Xi 朱熹. *Sishu zhangju jizhu* 四書章句集注 (Collected Commentaries on the Four Books). Jinan: Qilu shushe, 1992.
Zong Fubang 宗福邦, Chen Shinao 陳世鐃, and Xiao Haibo 蕭海波, eds. *Guxun huizuan* 故訓匯纂 (A Compilation of Old Commentaries). Beijing: Shangwu yinshuguan, 2003.

# 13

# The Philosophy of Beauty as an Ethics of Freedom

## From Kant to Li Zehou; Perspectives of an Attractive Line of Thought

GREGOR PAUL[1]

### Experience of Beauty as Harmonious Freedom[2]

It seems to be a dream or an ideal of humankind: that what you like to do is just what you ought to do, and what you ought to do is what you like to do. This would entail that to act voluntarily is to act morally, and to act morally is to act voluntarily. It is an idea of freedom in which self-determination and moral or social demands accord with each other. As self-determination (and thus an act of positive freedom), it is a kind of self-assertion and self-realization, something enjoyable, free of oppression, fear, abasement, and humiliation. One does not feel forced by moral obligations to do something one actually does not like to do. As such, it is also an instance of negative freedom. For example, one cares for one's elderly parents because one wants to care for them, and not because one feels obliged to follow a juridical law or moral principle, perhaps even grudgingly. As an act in accord with moral and social demands, it is also socially agreeable and thus a further source of positive emotion. Such an idea of freedom differs from both willfulness, which means to just follow one's inclinations and desires, perhaps even recklessly, and moral action in the Kantian sense, according to which an action should be called "moral" only if it is exclusively determined by (respect for) the moral law ("Achtung für das moralische Gesetz"). Kant admits that an action motivated by individual wishes and desires could be *in accord* with moral rules. However, since he is convinced that the aesthetic and the moral are different, and that one ought to follow the moral law even if one does not like to abide by it, he insists on clear terminological distinctions.

Of course, since ancient times it has been known that individual desires often contradict moral or social requirements. As a matter of consequence, the question arose how to reconcile them with each other. In China, the *Book of Xunzi* advanced the theory that abiding by *li* 禮, i.e., beautiful and becoming socially accepted conventions, can achieve such reconciliation.[3] For instance, to bury one's parents in a beautifully ordered way, accompanied by beautiful music, may prevent one from being overwhelmed by one's grief, as well as from completely neglecting one's parents' burial. Xunzi[4] was aware that certain desires, such as sexual desire, cannot be completely suppressed, while certain other emotions one actually lacks, such as grief about the death of one's parents, ought to be felt and displayed, and that, in both cases, *li*, because of its beautifying force, would enable a satisfying behavior, harmonizing individual inclinations with moral demands.[5]

In Germany, Friedrich Schiller (1759–1805) put forward the notion of aesthetic education. He conceived of beauty as freedom in appearance—that is, in what one sees—and accordingly asked for behaving in a beautiful way. He also maintained that full, or perfect, humaneness requires that humans, in thinking and behavior, bring into play in a harmonious way all their faculties. In his approach, Schiller was strongly influenced by Kant's notions of the free and harmonious play of the faculties of mind (as the "experience" of beauty) and beauty as a symbol of morality ("Sittlichkeit")—in other words, moral freedom. Schiller's idea of aesthetic education in turn influenced Herbert Marcuse's (1898–1979) theory of political freedom. Marcuse emphasized the importance of, and right to, positive emotion as a means against what he regarded as anti-sensual and capitalist oppression, and as an instrument to ultimately create a society whose people enjoy their lives in a harmonious way.

In short, freedom in Schiller's sense, similar to conceiving of beauty as a symbol of morality, is a kind of pleasant self-determination (autonomy) that is free of heteronomy and automatically meets social and moral requirements. The pleasure one finds in autonomy and morality is both motive (cause) and result (effect) of freedom. It is a continuous incentive for maintaining and cultivating one's freedom. In the following, I call this kind of freedom "harmonious freedom," in contrast to willfulness and moral freedom such as mere subjugation under the categorical imperative.

## The Notion of Harmonious Freedom in Li Zehou

Kant's notion of beauty as a symbol of morality and Schiller's notion of beauty as freedom in appearance refer to what Kant called "dependent beauty." Whereas pure beauty (in the Kantian sense) is an object of uninterested pleasure, namely, not determined by anything else than the pleasure felt in contemplating the beautiful object, the pleasure in dependent beauty is not confined to mere contemplation, but is also characterized by an awareness that this pleasure complies with one's moral interest (namely respect for the moral law). Also important in this context is the fact that Kant sharply distinguishes the emotion determined by such factors as sexual attraction, prestige, possession (e.g., of an artwork), economic advantages, and power, from the pleasure(s) felt in the experience of morally dependent beauty. He conceives of the former kind of emotion as pleasure connected with and manifesting "inclinations" and "leanings" ("Neigungen") that, in contrast and perhaps even in contradiction to intersubjective moral interest, may differ from individual to individual. As may become clear from the following, Kant's and Schiller's notion of beauty is narrower than the one that Li Zehou employs in his theory of beauty as an ethics of freedom. Because of his understanding of the sense of beauty as a function of historical development,[6] Li offers a wide range of "definitions" of beauty. He even then conceives of an experience of beauty as an experience of freedom if this experience is determined by individual inclinations that do not violate moral and social norms, whereas Kant would have classified such an experience as a lack of moral autonomy. In other words, Li includes in his notion of beauty what Kant, in §3 of his *Critique of Judgment*, excluded as "merely" sensually "agreeable," such as for instance the "graceful, lovely, delightful, gladdening, etc."[7] Thus, Li's concept of harmonious freedom is less speculative, more "realistic," and less "rigorous" than Kant's, much in keeping with Li's general criticism of Kant's apriorism and abstractness.[8]

The concept of freedom as an aesthetic and ethical notion is one of the central themes in Li Zehou's philosophy. In what follows, I try to show that, according to Li, following perceptions of beauty in one's thought and behavior ultimately enables one to realize harmonious freedom. Li characterizes beauty variously as grounded in "nature's humanization,"[9] as "unity of truth and good manifest as free sensible form in objective nature,"[10] as expression of "the ideal pursued in the humanization of nature,"[11] and, most significantly, as "practice of freedom,"[12] or (as Li says in several works) "a form of freedom" (ziyou de xingshi 自由的形式),[13] stating that "aesthetic experience or sense of beauty . . . is, in essence, a pleasant sense of freedom."[14] For instance, humanization of nature by way of beautification turns eating into dining and sexual desire into love.[15] Li arrives at these characteristics by interpreting Kant and Schiller, and accepting, or implying in his characterizations, their basic notions. However, in my opinion these notions are easier to understand than Li's characterizations. Kant points out that perceptions of beauty consist of a harmony, and an oscillation, between concepts and sensual intuitions that do not lead, or enable, objective or conceptual knowledge. Kant also speaks of the free play between imagination and understanding. Schiller then introduced his notion of "play impulse," and, as Li quotes approvingly,[16] maintained that humans are "really free . . . only . . . when [they] are playing." Now, since according to Kant concepts comprise both theoretical and practical notions, the latter being related to the idea of morality or moral freedom, it follows that Kant's notion of beauty is in harmony with notions of truth and moral freedom without, however, being such notions.

Li's repeated characterization of beauty as "unity of truth and good" could thus be misleading. It seems to contradict Li's agreement with Kant's notion of perception of beauty as a state and process of reflection that, as a free play of the faculties of mind, is in harmony with the respective knowledge without constituting, or being, conceptual knowledge. If "truth" is understood as (a function of) conceptual knowledge and "good" as something moral or useful, then it is difficult to see how their "unification" could constitute "beauty." Though Li, in the given context, probably does not intend to refer to "truth" as *conceptual* truth, the meaning of the expression "unity of truth and good" does not become much clearer, if one takes into account his definitions of truth as "the law of nature" and goodness as "the fundamental character of human beings."[17] Applying these definitions, he maintains that it is the merging of "the purposiveness of the subjective goodness and the regularity of objective truth" that constitutes beauty.[18] Perhaps "purposiveness of the subjective goodness" could be interpreted as what meets one's individual aims and longings, and "*regularity* of objective truth" as concurrence with the *general* conditions of theoretical and practical knowledge, namely harmony between concepts and (sensual) imaginations, without constituting or being "fixed" in the form of conceptual knowledge. Rafal Banka,[19] in sections entitled "Beauty as Practice of Freedom" and "Beauty's Persistence through Time and Extension over Technology," explains Li's notion of "beauty as a form of freedom" by understanding the unification of truth and goodness as a kind of human practice that accords (harmonizes) with the laws of nature by man's spontaneously realizing his individual (or subjective) intentions or goals.[20]

In my opinion, however, it would be more precise and clearly consistent with Li's reception of Kant's notion of "free play"—and thus also more convincing than the explanations related above—to understand "unity of truth and good" in the sense indicated by Li's notions of "beauty as revelation of truth" (*yi mei qi zhen* 以美啟真) and "beauty as a store of good" (*yi mei chu shan* 以美储善).[21] As in the case of the notion of free play, the source of both notions is *Kant's Critique of Judgment*, as is especially clear from Li's explaining "truth" in "beauty as revelation of truth" as "a type of feeling or understanding prior to or accompanying logical thought."[22] This is to say, as a non-conceptual experience of truth that, however, would be compatible with conceptual knowledge—an interpretation that also enables a better understanding of the explanation of "truth" in "beauty as unity of truth and good" as "*regularity* of objective truth." In everyday language, one for instance often speaks of "poetic truth," thus referring to the indicated phenomenon. Because of his uncompromising interest in conceptual and terminological clarity, Kant would never have called perception of beauty "knowledge." (One could perhaps more adequately say that the "truth" conveyed by beauty is in harmony with conceptual knowledge.) As to the notion of "beauty as a store of good," this notion is evidently indebted to Kant's notion of "beauty as a symbol of morality."

Nevertheless, in comparison to Li's notion of the "unity of truth and good," Li's characterizations of beauty as "practice of freedom" and "a form of freedom" as (experience of) free play of the faculties of mind are easier to understand. As pointed out, they are adaptations of Kant's and Schiller's definitions and they are also empirically sound. The first one looks like a rephrasing of Schiller's "beauty is freedom in appearance," invoking all of Schiller's arguments in favor of this definition.

However, though Li Zehou, in his own conceptions of beauty, relies on Kant's and Schiller's notion(s) of "free play," he rejects Kant's apriorism and what he calls both thinkers' idealism.[23] Instead, he argues in favor of an empirical and historical approach of a Marxist kind.[24] In his criticism of Kant and Schiller as idealists, however, Li does not refer to ontological idealism: theories according to which immaterial ideas (or, more generally, entities) are the basis of everything existing. Li was probably aware that neither Kant nor Schiller held such position. This may also have been one reason why he maintained that instead of speaking of the "sequence—Kant—[the idealist] Hegel—Marx," "the sequence should be: Kant—Schiller—Marx."[25] Li even basically approved of Kant's concept of regulative ideas,[26] very much in keeping with his appreciatively quoting[27] *Lunyu* 14.38 that Confucius works "toward a goal the realization of which he knows to be hopeless."[28] What Li, by his criticism of "idealism" and "abstractness," wanted to point out was that Kant and Schiller put forward ideas of an aesthetic and/or moral behavior that are difficult to realize because they did not imply adequate notions of human emotions as functions of man's physicalness—though Kant and Schiller were by no means so naïve as not to have been well aware of the difficulties of realizing their ideas. Schiller even explicitly emphasized that fulfillment of basic needs is a condition for realizing morality.[29] In my opinion, what Li means in his criticism of Kant is best illustrated and exemplified by his down-to-earth statements that "proscriptions against suicide and lying cannot serve as unchanging universal ethical principles and standards of conduct for all places and times," and that Kant's assertion of these proscriptions "creates myriad difficulties that cannot be adequately explained."[30] Of course, Li rightly criticizes Kant's mystical speculations about something supernatural and even divine as sources of beauty.[31] Such conceptions are no bases for a theory of how to realize harmonious freedom. Kant only vaguely touched on this issue. For Kant, morality was simply more important than anything aesthetic—or, more precisely, for him moral freedom and fulfillment of moral duty was more important than harmonious freedom, though he did *not reject* harmonious freedom, as is clear from his comments on Schiller's essay "Gracefulness and Dignity" in his *Religion in the Boundaries of Mere Reason*.[32]

In sum, though Li is well aware that Kant and Schiller put forward a theory of a "unity" of moral, aesthetic, and cognitive experience, he is convinced that their theory cannot explain how to *actually realize* harmonious freedom. Since he attributes this deficiency to a lack of empiricalness, concreteness, and, so to speak, down-to-earthness, he argues for a Marxist solution to the problem.[33] Inspired by Marx, Li sees the most important solution in turning estranging and boring labor that serves as a means of mere subsistence, into pleasant and pleasing creativity, meaning—according to Li—something beautiful.[34] In this way, Li's philosophy of beauty becomes an ethics of freedom.

### Li's Philosophy of Humanization as Historical Development toward Harmonious Freedom by Transforming Labor into Work that Accords with the Laws of Beauty

By calling Li's philosophy of beauty an ethics of freedom, I conceive of it, as I said at the beginning, as a philosophy that tries to solve the question of how to realize a practice in which what one likes to do is also what one ought to do, and what one ought to do is also what one likes to do. Li does not express his notion of beautiful practice as harmonious freedom in such words. In my opinion, however, his own characterizations of beauty and beautiful practice imply this, and can even be summed up in such a way.[35] Otherwise Li would have fallen back even behind the abstract notions of free play of the faculties of mind advanced by Kant and Schiller, which would be rarely compatible with his explicitly high estimation of Kant's "idea of the interplay or free play of the imagination and understanding"[36] and Schiller's notion of the "play impulse."[37] Li's agreement with Kant may go further than he himself believes. But what is at issue is of course not an adequate Kant interpretation, but an adequate account of our experience of beauty.

As indicated above, Li maintains that the experience of "beauty as a form of freedom" is a feature of the humanization of nature, which, as process of civilization and refinement, amounts to a humanization of humankind (in the sense of realizing an ideal of humankind). To repeat, Li illustrates his notion of beautiful practice as humanization of nature with the example of turning merely satisfying one's sexual desire into courting and love[38]—turning something one likes and even needs to do into something a cultivated or moral person ought to do. Following Marx in criticizing torturous and exploitative labor, he demands that labor should be turned into work acceptable and even pleasing for those who do it. Taking into account Marx's respective explanations quoted and agreed with by Li—and also quoted by Bruya[39]—this implies, first, that laborers should be able to freely choose their labor, and, second, that they could do this in following ideas of beauty. Li conceives of Marx's observation that "man produces in accordance with the laws of beauty"[40] not merely as a simply descriptive statement, but also as a norm, namely that man, as a free and autonomous individual, should be able to produce in such a way, thus avoiding estrangement. In short, this would indeed mean that labor should be a kind of pleasant and pleasing creativity, doing or producing something beautiful.[41] Li seems to believe that such goal can indeed be realized. In his view human history, and especially the continuous invention and use of new "tools," could make possible such an achievement.[42] Of course, in such contexts "beauty" should be understood in a broad sense, including what is simply pleasant or enjoyable, in other words sensually "agreeable" (*angenehm* as Kant put it in §3 of *Critique of Judgment*), without, however, violating social or moral norms. This applies not only to Marx's but, as indicated, also to Li's notion of beauty.

## Human Interest in Beauty, and Labor as a Production According to Laws of Beauty, Furthered by the Development and Use of Tools

### Pleasing Paleolithic Creations and the Problem of Beautifying Labor

If work that in a significant way involves aesthetic design counts as "labor," such as for instance architectural planning and the production of beautiful cloth, embroidery, animal sculptures, and instruments employed in social or religious practice, then we have examples of pleasing and/or pleasant creativity for more than 40,000 years. However, there may always exist labor that simply cannot be beautified or turned into a kind of aesthetic creativity. Think for instance of waste disposal, though one could perhaps imagine that even waste disposal could be turned into completely computerized and remotely controlled labor that, as such, enables satisfying creativity on part of those who carry it out. Li also mentions the possibility of replacing "dehumanizing labor" by using robots.[43] Actually, the development of what Nick Bostrom calls "superintelligent" systems,[44] and progress in the construction of artificial intelligence, may open up promising (though also sometimes questionable) possibilities in this regard, which could indeed be tools in Li's sense. However, there may be problems in enabling everybody to use technologically highly developed tools. Instead, or in addition, incentives such as high wages and public respect for waste disposal as socially valuable work could turn it into a job people would like to do, though, because of their interest in profit (additional expenses), employers may oppose turning every kind of labor into something attractive. Moreover, employing more and more new tools—for example, utilizing sophisticated technology—could lead to a shortage of labor, which would ultimately demand shortening labor time, again making labor more costly for employers. Finally, shareholder value ideology, with shareholders actually earning the fruits of employees' labor, and the continuous widening of the gap between the rich and poor, indicate "modern" problems of "bondage" and estrangement (hire and fire practices, wage dumping, burn out, etc.) that are not easily solved. All this is to say that even if, *in principle*, every kind of labor could be turned into a creative or at least attractive practice, certain ethical, social, and political problems would remain. In other words, in spite of the force and efficiency of ideas of beauty (in a wide sense of the term), realization of harmonious freedom would have to overcome many hindrances, and this even applies to the task of making labor attractive. Li seems to be aware of all such problems, however, and perhaps his insistence on Marxist solutions also results from this awareness.

## Intentions, Functions, and Symbolism of Early Beautiful Creations

If I understand Marx and Li correctly, the goal of harmonious freedom is, among others, based on three presuppositions: (1) that humans, in a significant way, indeed want, try, and achieve, to act following laws of beauty; (2) that this means striving for harmonious freedom; and (3) that humans ultimately can (almost) completely carry through this pursuit. Of course, historically and systematically, it was above all others Kant and Schiller who paved the way for conceiving that harmonious freedom ought to be an ideal of humanity.

As to the first and second points, it is bewildering that even in such societies as ancient Egypt and the (Chinese) Liangzhu jade culture, humans already produced extremely beautiful objects. One wonders why people spent so much time with such production while conditions of living often were rather precarious. Of course, these were strictly stratified societies, and beautiful objects were signs of power and prestige. But was there any need to display power and prestige by *beautiful* symbols? Everybody could know about the power of the mighty by experiencing their political control. The logical implication is that *beauty was understood as a symbol of power and prestige* that furthered its awareness and recognizability. The crucial point I have in mind can be addressed by the following questions: Why did the ancient Egyptians—and many other people—attribute beauty to their revered gods? And to their evil gods and demons ugliness? Think of various Egypt sculptures, and Akhenaton's "Hymns to Aton." *They must indeed have regarded beauty as a symbol of goodness,* as much as did the ancient Chinese in their understanding of pine trees or chrysanthemums,[45] or as most Germans do in their notion of the dove of peace. Apparently, humans have always been interested in what may be called optimizing or perfecting what they regard as valuable, thus connecting the good with the beautiful (or even truth), or the other way round, connecting the beautiful with the good. Kant and Schiller captured this universal everyday phenomenon in their philosophical notions of beauty as a symbol of morality. Note, however, that in ancient societies beauty as a sign of power and/or goodness referred only to supernatural beings and mighty or otherwise privileged people. Importantly in our context, these people could already also conceive of beauty as a *symbol of (their) individual freedom*, though this may have been a kind of freedom that often amounted to willfulness.[46] In contrast, the ancient worlds lacked the conditions that would have enabled ordinary people to conceive of beauty not only as a symbol of the good or goodness (such as of their gods) or (though probably rarely) of the mighty, but also of freedom. This is to say (much in keeping with Li's "historicization of the transcendental") that certain political and social processes were necessary preconditions for developing a sense of beauty that became an experience of harmonious freedom.

## Hannah Arendt's Theory of Labor, Work, Beauty, and Freedom

In the given context, it may be helpful to also consider Hannah Arendt's theory of labor, work, beauty, and freedom,[47] which from quite different points of view supports the notion of beauty as an independent incentive of human thinking and behavior, and which, by its notion of *art as durable work* that contributes to creating stable environments in which people can feel at home, could even significantly supplement Marx's and Li's aesthetics and ethics of freedom.

Arendt sharply distinguishes between "labor" and "work." Labor, as she understands it, produces something nondurable, whereas work produces something durable. Arendt regards this as the main difference between the two kinds of "activities." She then maintains that "whatever has a shape and is seen cannot help being either beautiful or ugly or something in-between," and she also says that, if such "things" exist for a certain time-span, humans cannot but judge them not only by their functionality and/or utility but also by their "beauty" and "ugliness," or "something in-between," when perceiving them. Since, according to Arendt, works of art are the most durable results of work, they especially contribute to creating a "stable" environment, and since they are, moreover, significantly independent from utilitarian functions, they at the same time most clearly exhibit "beauty." Durable objects, and especially works of art, thus create an environment in which humans can feel "at home." Following Arendt, one could supplement Marx's and Li Zehou's theories by pointing out that the creation of durable beauty as such could sustain and improve human existence.[48]

As far as the problem of how to realize freedom is concerned, the question can of course not be how to transform labor into work, which in cases such as cooking would be impossible. Moreover, like labor, work could be forced production, as the work of a slave is. One could, however, perhaps argue that as far as art works contribute to creating an aesthetically appreciative and stable world, they also serve to establish conditions of living favorable to developing a sense of freedom. But this would require a separate study.

In her discussions of the relationships among labor, work, beauty, and freedom, Arendt states that free "activities" were already regarded as beautiful by Aristotle, with the property of beauty referring to (the enjoyment) of physical beauty, active participation in the politics of the *polis*, and what may be called contemplation (theoretical reflection) about ultimate being. In Catholicism only the last "action" remained as an instance of beautiful "acting."[49] Implicit in such distinctions is the conviction that, in clear contrast to (hard) bodily (or manual) labor, "mental work" by which one does not wear out or dirty oneself can be emotionally attractive and an action of freedom. Perhaps more than 4,000 years ago Egyptian texts already expressed this conviction in their eulogies to the work of the scribe, associating it with ideas of beauty and the sureness of not being bullied.[50] For instance, translations of these texts say that the scribe occupies a "beautiful office" and that his work "beautifies" the hands and body—in my view really amazing assertions. A famous example for distinguishing elegant work from hard and dirty work is Leonardo's distinction between painting and sculpting.[51] One could perhaps speculate that such distinctions testify to an age-old human dream to only perform work that (at least unconsciously) allows for experiencing beauty and personal freedom—which would again provide empirical evidence for Marx's and Li's theories of labor, beauty, and freedom.

## Progress in the Beautification of Labor

Returning to point (1), one may thus safely conclude that examples from the history of humankind abound, proving that humans in their practice, in a significant way and as far as political and social conditions permitted, followed rules of beauty. Regarding this point, I need not go further.[52] This brings me back to point (3): the question of progress in the beautification of labor and the realization of harmonious freedom, implicitly already also touched on. Already about 600,000 years ago the production of certain tools such as bifaces or stone axes developed into aesthetic creation. Actually, the independent creation of similarly beautiful bifaces for more than hundreds of thousands of years in different cultures at different places[53] is one of the strongest proofs for the assertion that humans (as humans) "produce according to the laws of beauty," and also one of the most convincing examples that manufacturing and using tools serve to improve human life.[54] Perhaps from about 25,000 BCE, symmetric stone tools were further worked on. They were polished to create ground stones, some of which are extremely beautiful.[55]

In the twenty-first century, industrial design is often seen as an example of aesthetic creativity, and thus documents progress in such endeavors. Moreover, in highly industrialized and digitalized democracies such as the Scandinavian states, there are many individuals who—of course aware of their privileges—call their labor a hobby, usually implying by this that they like, and enjoy, doing the work they are obliged to do, though this may not reflect any beautification (in a Kantian or otherwise narrow sense of the term) but just that it may be called ("merely") pleasant and pleasurable work.[56] In this context I must also confess, when asked about my profession, or about what work I have to do, I often reply that I am in the privileged position of being able to just pursue a hobby, namely my philosophical interests. In medieval German, *arebeit* (modern *Arbeit*), "labor," meant "hardship." Though this is no longer the case in modern German, I am used to saying that I am lucky not to be obliged to do any "*Arbeit*," but permitted to pursue my hobbies—as I have done and keep doing, nevertheless taking what I do "seriously."

In sum, in spite of the hindrances mentioned above, and even if, in many cases, beautification of labor and harmonious freedom cannot be realized, there are many possibilities to make labor sufficiently attractive—to aestheticize the obligatory—that people like to do it without acting willfully or violating social or moral norms. The Confucian ideal of "following the desires of the heart without overstepping the bounds of right," formulated in *Analects* 2.4, and several times quoted approvingly by Li,[57] expresses the same goal.[58] (It provokes, however, the unwanted association that this is not so difficult when you are old, for the saying is attributed to seventy-year-old Confucius.) The invention and improvement of tools, especially robots and artificial intelligence systems, a welcome job environment, including a pleasant social climate, high wages, a reduction in working hours, public recognition, et cetera,[59] may indeed aestheticize labor so far that laborers enjoy at least a feeling of subjective freedom.

By almost limiting my discussions about Li Zehou's ideas of realizing freedom to reflecting on his deliberations on the development and usage of "tools," I do not want to disregard the role that everyday behavior, especially the way humans communicate with each other, and the aesthetic appreciation of the arts and natural beauty, can and should play in this context. Li leaves no doubt that he basically agrees with the *Lunyu*'s high estimation of what could be called a pleasant and pleasing (and as such ordered) way of social intercourse, as well as of the impact music and poetry especially could have in causing a subjective pleasure that harmonizes with social requirements. In other words, showing individual liking for poetry and music could be accompanied by a conscious awareness (or justified expectation) of common appreciation. An interesting question here would be how labor, everyday behavior (especially social intercourse), and appreciation of literature, poetry, the visual arts, and music could be integrated in a way that they mutually reenforce each other in enabling feelings of freedom. The notion of "life-work-balance" indicates certain aspects of such a goal. Moreover, the previously mentioned attempts to not only create useful but thereby also beautiful tools points to a kind of integration in this regard.

## The Independence of Human Sense of, and Interest in, Beauty from Non-Aesthetic Interests, Especially Religious Ones

Differing from Li, who somehow distances himself from calling Paleolithic cave paintings "beautiful"[60] and who thinks "the primitive paintings of the Stone Age in Spain and France are the relics of shamanistic rituals,"[61] I hold that the Paleolithic painters, *in executing their works*, were guided by rules of beauty rather than by non-aesthetic interests or demands (though Li would perhaps have argued that shamanistic dances have *also* been a kind of *aesthetic* occurrences or events). First of all, in their paintings they followed and we can say interpreted the structures of the cave walls, thus striving for a kind of pleasing harmony, though perhaps only unconsciously. More important, there is simply no need to believe that it was mainly non-aesthetic factors that determined the aesthetic qualities of their creations. The painters could have drawn identifiable pictures of animals that would have been sufficient for performing, say, related hunting rites. There is an anecdote in the *Zhuangzi* emphasizing that, in sculpting, following the form and inherent patterns of the raw material creates beauty.[62] The method of interpreting natural pre-formation as a means to create something beautiful has been used in different cultures for tens of thousands of years, and has been employed even in Surrealism. It is still common in, for example, Chinese and European folk arts.[63] It is important to recognize that the category of beauty is logically independent from such categories as truth, goodness, power, or prestige, and so on, for it is this independence that gives significance to the thesis that humans produce according to the laws of beauty.[64] To radically illustrate this independence, even truth could be displeasing, and a humane person could be ugly.

To repeat, Li seems to hold that beauty first originated in connection with, or dependence on, shamanist or religious beliefs. As I argue above, beauty may have been used *as an additional factor* to enhance the value of something religious, as has been the case in ancient Egypt. One may also ask the question why the aesthetic reason for creating something beautiful, namely pleasure, could not have been a sufficient one for the early production of *beauty*. All over Africa, drilled or pierced shells 135,000 to 150,000 years old have been found that probably served early humans as parts of pendants (for example).[65] I find it difficult to understand them as signs of something like a religious or shamanistic belief. Also, as became known in 2018, the Neanderthals already produced cave paintings and other art objects 60,000 years ago.[66] Could it not be possible that these facts attest to a universal human interest in beauty, or the pleasure caused by beauty, as such?

In sum, if I understand Li correctly, he (like many anthropologists) holds that *beautiful* creation was originally (i.e., in primeval communities) motivated by *non-aesthetic factors* such as religious interests (but somehow then became part of religious practices). Since such interests, however, were motived by humans' interest in survival, this could imply that to create according to rules of *beauty* also resulted from this interest. Did the *beauty* of beautiful creation indeed presuppose *religious* interest? In other words, could it not be possible that, from the very beginning, the "production according to the laws of beauty" was an independent means besides political and social organization and religious belief—logically on par with these factors—for sustaining, and even improving, conditions of living favorable to survival? This would be very much in keeping with Marx's related statement, and it would *strengthen* Li's argument that the beautification of life contributes to improving human life, since it has (ultimately and in general successfully) functioned this way since the earliest days of humankind.

My assertion that our "sense for beauty" is an interest, and faculty, independent from such principally non-aesthetic interests as religious ones can be supported by the historical evidence provided below, by neurological evidence, and by Denis Dutton's comprehensive study *The Art Instinct* (2009), in which he convincingly argues that "the pleasure-seeking at the art of artistic experience . . . is . . . a discrete instinct in itself that has clear survival value."[67] As to the neurological evidence, already in 1988 I tried to show that the Kantian notion of free play of the faculties of mind could be "translated" into a neurological theory. Referring to my article, the neurologist Christoph Redies proposed a model that "is universal and predicts that all human beings share the same general concept of esthetic judgment." According to this model, "esthetic perception reflects fundamental functional properties of the nervous system."[68] In her discussions of ancient Mediterranean art, Lagogianni-Georgakarakos[69] approvingly refers to my article and Redies's and Dutton's findings, and also to the respective ethological theories. To emphasize: if I am right, this would be more consistent with and more convincingly support Li's conceptions of beautification than his own theory about the origins of art does.

The assertion that human interest in beauty is basically independent from non-aesthetic interests (such as religious interests) but often contributes to realizing such interests can even be explained further. As pointed out above, an interest in beauty, from early times on, often led to clearly demonstrating power, high status, and/or goodness. Time, wealth, and natural and human resources were "wasted" to produce beautiful things (while the production of more useful things would have seemed more reasonable). One reason for succeeding with such demonstrations was that thereby the signal effects connected with power and/or benevolence, as such already inherent in divineness, hierarchical position, and generous acts, could be significantly strengthened. This, in turn, was not only due to the fact that such combinations of values are strived for optimizations. The very possibility that a person is in a position to waste resources testifies to his power. Such an action signals *surplus* (or *excess*) power. Now, as has been shown, the signal effect of beauty *ultimately* derives from an *innate* tendency to display extraordinary survival capabilities,[70] and the *innate* ability to understand the signal as a reliable sign of such capability. This, again, renders explanations of the origin of beauty as a function of, for example, religious interests superfluous.

## A Categorization of Li Zehou's Aesthetics

Pointing out the general features of Li Zehou's aesthetics may contribute to an understanding of both Li's indebtedness to Kant, Marx, and Confucius and his deviations from their ideas, thus finally arriving at his notion of beautification as a means to realize harmonious freedom.

First, Li's philosophy of beauty is mainly reception aesthetics. Li focuses on the way(s) humans experience beauty. The most important experience is of course that of the free play of the faculties of mind. (If a human being's faculties of mind are in a state or process of free play, then they experience this as a perception of beauty.) Also, as pointed out above, a notion such as "beauty as revelation of truth," which can serve as an explanation of the notion of free play, is a concept of reception aesthetics that has its sources in Kant. Second, Li's philosophy of beauty is a significant contribution to production aesthetics—which is no surprise given Li's reliance on Marx and his emphasis on the importance of beautifying human life (thereby including beautification of nature) as the most important means to realizing harmonious freedom. As for object aesthetics, Li states that, in contrast to Western history, Chinese history—Confucius included—was not so much concerned with saying what beauty *is*,[71] which is to say with defining or describing the properties of the beauty of beautiful objects, and he himself also seems not to have been very much interested in this question. Apparently Li believes that he thus follows traditional "Chinese discussions [which, as he asserts], rather focus on what to do and how to do it."[72] From a logical point of view, this implies favoring production aesthetics over object aesthetics.

Actually, since Li wants to argue for a global aesthetics,[73] reception aesthetics, especially if of a transcendental kind, is probably the best choice, for it is more promising to reflect on what all humans have in common and which faculties all must develop to survive (such as the biological disposition to think logically and the capability of manufacturing and using certain tools, like bifaces) than to try to identify and list the properties of aesthetic objects acknowledged by all humans. Significantly, Karen Gloy,[74] a German professor of philosophy who argues against what she calls "universalism," also rejects transcendental philosophy.

This leads me to Li's "derivations." First, Li replaced Kantian apriorism and moral rigorism with (what may be called) a historical transcendentalism, and he "broadened" (and thereby strengthened) Marx's materialism by supplementing it with the Chinese, and especially Confucian, notion of emotion as a basic source of human perception and practice that must not be blocked. (At least, he made explicit various indications already found in Marx.) This led Li to develop a wider and more common and commonplace notion of beauty than Kant. Second, Li departed from Marx by giving up the idea of a class struggle, and, third, he differs from the "Chinese tradition" by not "making light of the vital importance of abstract speculation"[75] (which can again be understood as also due to Kantian influence, and which of course motivated Li's extensive and detailed theorizations). All this enabled Li to argue in favor of a human freedom that, in principle, should and (at least to a considerable degree) could be realized by all people without asking too much of them, and without the use of force, and ultimately even by autonomously following their individual feelings.

## Conclusion

If my analyses and explanations are correct, then Li Zehou uses a wider notion of beauty than Kant and even Schiller did. Li's various definitions of beauty show that his notion includes not just pure beauty and dependent beauty as a symbol of morality, but also what Kant called "the agreeable" (*das Angenehme*): to quote again, "what the senses like in sensation," namely what is "graceful, lovely, delightful, gladdening, etc." However, Li argues that what he describes as the experience of beauty nevertheless is, in principle, not only a pleasure reflecting individual preference, but also the fulfillment of social demands. Taken in this sense, the beautification of labor means making labor so aesthetically attractive that people like doing their work. Since they like doing it, they abide by social or moral norms without feeling forced to do so, and experience their labor as an act of freedom. Harmonious freedom would thus consist in what the saying attributed to Confucius describes as "following the desires of the heart without overstepping the bounds of right." As explained above, the beautification of labor, understood in Li's sense, though in many cases difficult, is—as Li argues—at least realizable to a significant degree by further development of certain "tools." Labor that cannot be beautified, or otherwise made attractive for laborers, could be taken over completely by such tools as robots and superintelligent and artificial intelligence systems.

The persuasiveness of Li's philosophy of beauty as an ethics of freedom results from his careful and comprehensive analyses and explanations of the history of human emotionality and rationality (including morality). Because of its empiricalness, concreteness, and—we could say—"down-to-earthness," informed by insights provided by Marxism and Confucianism (*Lunyu* and *Xunzi*), Li's philosophy is more convincing and "realistic" than (especially) Kant's apriorism and "rigorism." However, the Kantian influence is nevertheless significant. Like Kant, Li is convinced that there exist subjective conditions of the possibility of intersubjective aesthetic experience of beauty (though they are historically developed), and his reconstructions of the Kantian notion of the experience of beauty as a free play of the faculties of the mind and as a symbol of morality are based on this. Most important: the notion of such free play remains applicable even if beauty is, in certain respects, understood in a wider sense than in Kant.

There remains the sobering fact that even in the twenty-first century there exist states in no condition to offer many of their people the prospect of realizing such a thing as harmonious freedom. Even worse, there are ongoing wars. The solutions to such problems must not be left to politics alone. Marx was right in demanding that philosophy ought to be concerned with the issue of how to make the world a better place, and

Li Zehou shares this conviction. Bruya[76] adequately calls Li's aesthetics a political one. In this respect, Li's philosophy is similar to Marcuse's, though less radical. Indeed, the philosophy of beauty must not remain an isolated field of lofty illusions. In spite of all the difficulties existing, to reflect on beautification as a possible means of freedom remains an important endeavor.

## Notes

1. I thank Jana Rošker for having commented on a draft of my paper. Her remarks helped me to correct certain mistakes and to clarify certain points.

2. In my contribution I presuppose that (1) one can deal with questions of beauty without using words such as *beauty* or *mei* 美, and that traditional European and Chinese texts often did this; that (2) there is no one-to-one translation from words such as *beauty* to words such as *mei*, or vice versa; that (3) English and Chinese words (and words in other languages too) that refer to beauty can have many meanings and connotations; and that (4) there are significant overlaps between English and Chinese notions of beauty that permit the use of a general term that refers to both. I have elaborated on these premises in Gregor Paul, *Philosophy in the History of China* (Bochum: Projekt-Verlag, 2022), 165–284.

3. Gregor Paul, *Aspects of Confucianism* (Frankfurt/Main: Lang, 1990).

4. When I use the name "Xunzi" I always refer to the *Book of Xunzi*.

5. On pages 17–19 in his *Chinese Aesthetic Tradition*, trans. Maija Bell Samei (Honolulu: University of Hawai'i Press, 2009), Li emphasizes the obligatory character of *li* as ritual rules of individual and social behavior. This differs from Xunzi's notion of *li* as beautiful and beautifying conventions, though it may do justice to earlier notions of *li*. When explicitly dealing with the *Xunzi*, Li seems to agree with my interpretation (in Paul, *Aspects of Confucianism*). For instance, on p. 65 Li states that Xunzi demanded "that internal desire be satisfied within the constraints of external ritual, or conversely, that external ritual be implemented through the satisfaction of internal desire." On p. 66, Li quotes from the "Li lun" chapter of *Xunzi* that "artifice" "beautifies" "nature." In his *The Path of Beauty* (*Der Weg des Schönen*, trans. project-group of Tübingen University, ed. Karl-Heinz Pohl and Gudrun Wecker (Freiburg: Herder, 1992), 92), he even maintains that the *Xunzi* emphasizes that art effectuates and molds everyday emotions in an ideal way. That is to say that, if people lack the feelings they should have, such as grieving the death of one's parents, music and ceremonies can and should bring about such feelings, and if people are in danger of injuring themselves because of their grief, music and ceremony can, and should,

alleviate their pain. In *A History of Classical Chinese Thought* (trans. Andrew Lambert (New York: Routledge 2020), 123), Li approvingly quotes from the *Xunzi* the following statement: "Through them [i.e., the rites], love and hatred are tempered, and joy and anger made to fit the occasion."

Contrary to Li (*The Chinese Aesthetic Tradition*, 17–19), I do not sharply distinguish between the goals and workings of *li* on the one hand and those of music on the other. In the *Xunzi*, *li* is not merely (or simply) an "external, coercive institution," while music is an "internal[ly]" founded "guide." Again, Li's distinction probably refers to earlier versions of *li*. In his reconstructions of the *Lunyu* and the *Xunzi* (*Der Weg des Schönen*, 90–94) Li points out that these earlier versions were refined by (re-)constructing and justifying them as rooted in (or based on) universal human feelings (such as the parent-child-relationship) and (somewhat different from the earlier versions) requirements of social harmony (instead of mere order and peace).

Admittedly, one could argue that the *Lunyu* and the *Xunzi* explicitly distinguish between *li* and music. The *Xunzi* even has separate essays on *li* ("Li lun") and music ("Yue lun"). However, this does not change the fact that, on a general level, music is part or kind of *li*, since rituals usually comprised musical performances.

6. In his "Preface to the English Edition" of his book on Kant (*A New Approach to Kant: A Confucian-Marxist's Viewpoint*, trans. Jeanne Haizhen Allen and Christopher Ahn (Springer Nature Singapore, 2018), viii), Li emphasizes that he "begin[s] where Darwin ends." That is to say that he deals with the evolutionary developed biological species *Homo sapiens* without, however, devoting much space to discussing man's biological evolution. Like Marx (in *Economic and Philosophical Manuscripts* of 1848, www.marxists.org/archive/marx/works/1844/epm/index.htm), Li in his approach sharply distinguishes between human beings and other animals, and like Marx he bases this distinction mainly on what he regards as the most significant (qualitative) difference between humans and other animals: the difference in the kind and degree of freedom (brought about by different ways of practice and especially by man's manufacture and use of "tools"). Li Zehou, *The Origins of Chinese Thought: From Shamanism to Ritual Regulations and Humaneness*, trans. Robert A. Carleo III (Leiden: Brill, 2018), 265. One could perhaps rightly state that according to Li and Marx humans are not "true" or "real" humans if they are not free. And as I argue below, both are convinced that the experience of beauty (as they understand beauty) is a necessary property of human freedom.

In his "differentiation of humans from animals," Li (*The Origins of Chinese Thought*, 219) also agrees with Mencius and Xunzi, who, according to Li, regarded the "transformation of people's animalistic emotions and desires into 'human' emotions"—that is, "humanization of nature"—as a way to transform instinctive and uncontrolled "physical" desires into cultivated attitudes and behavior.

However, beyond what Li believed, his deliberations may overlap with Darwin's account in *The Descent of Men*. Denis Dutton (*The Art Instinct. Beauty Pleasure, and Human Evolution* (New York, Berlin London: Bloomsbury Press, 2009), 135–65), who did not know Li's work, conceives of this account as a theory of "human self-domestication" that is strongly reminiscent of Li's theory of "humanization of nature." Interestingly, Darwin regarded as the main reason for self-domestication the evolution of sexual and erotic habits, in that they are no mere outcome of natural selection, but also determined by teleological causes such as purposes and intentions.

7. Immanuel Kant, *Critique of Judgment*, trans. with an Introduction Werner S. Pluhar (Indianapolis/Cambridge: Hacket Publishing Company, 1987), 206.

8. I differ from Sernelj's otherwise (as I see it) adequate and instructive account of Li's notion of (as Sernelj calls it) "aesthetic experience as a pleasant sense of freedom" (Téa Sernelj, "Different Approaches to Modern Art and Society: Li Zehou *versus* Xu Fuguan," *Asian Studies* 8, no. 1 (2020): 83–84) in that I do not think that, for Li, "[all] aesthetic experience is 'disinterested.'" Li's various definitions of aesthetic experience and beauty may be somewhat confusing, but either Li uses "disinterested" in quite a different way than Kant did or he contradicts himself when maintaining that aesthetic experience as a sense of freedom could be "disinterested"—not only according to Kant's rather specific (technical and narrow) notion of being "uninterested," but also according to common usage of the term "to be interested," as humans are certainly interested in freedom. A "pleasant sense of freedom" (in Li's sense) includes awareness of satisfied interests.

9. Li, *A New Approach to Kant*, 329.

10. Li, *A New Approach to Kant*, 324, 331.

11. Li, *A New Approach to Kant*, 333.

12. Li Zehou and Jane Cauvel, *Four Essays on Aesthetics: Toward a Global View* (Lanham: Lexington Books, 2006), 57.

13. See for instance Jana S. Rošker, *Following His Own Path: Li Zehou and Contemporary Chinese Thought* (Albany: State University of New York Press, 2018), 65, 99.

14. Li and Cauvel, *Four Essays on Aesthetics*, 93.

15. Li, *A New Approach to Kant*, 329; cf. also Li, *The Chinese Aesthetic Tradition*, 41; most clearly, however, in Li and Cauvel, *Four Essays on Aesthetics*, 90–94. Brian Bruya ("Li Zehou's Aesthetics as a Marxist Philosophy of Freedom," *Dialogue and Universalism*, no. 11–12 (2003): 138) emphasizes this feature of Li's characterization of beauty.

16. Li and Cauvel, *Four Essays on Aesthetics*, 94.

17. Li and Cauvel, *Four Essays on Aesthetics*, 63.

18. Li and Cauvel, *Four Essays on Aesthetics*, 63.

19. Rafal Banka, *Cognition and Practice: Li Zehou's Philosophical Aesthetics* (Albany: State University of New York Press, 2022), 119–123.

20. I confess that I find Li's terminology a bit confusing here. Usually, natural laws are understood as principles that simply cannot be violated. If taken in this sense, human practice *cannot but* follow natural laws. (In Li and Cauvel, *Four Essays on Aesthetics*, 57, Li defines "freedom" as a power that enables "overcoming [!] natural necessity," something simply impossible, if taken literally.) Are the individual intentions and goals (the "purposiveness") referred to above "good" ones, *because* they *are, as such,* in harmony with the "natural," or because they *lead* to harmony? Could it not be possible that one can commit a crime in accordance with natural laws, perhaps even spontaneously? Is Li ontologizing ethics, thus committing a natural fallacy?

21. Li, *The Origins of Chinese Thought*, 267–68.

22. Li, *The Origins of Chinese Thought*, 267.

23. Li and Cauvel, *Four Essays on Aesthetics*, 39; Li, *A New Approach to Kant*, 306, 324, 325.

24. As indicated above, Li argues that Kant's apriorism is no basis for creating a better world. Moreover, Li rightly holds that Kant's "transcendentalism" is untenable. Li criticizes Kant mainly from epistemological, materialist, and historical points of view. I agree with Wilhelm K. Essler (*Wissenschaftstheorie II*. (Freiburg/München: Alber, 1971)) that Kant's transcendental deductions are logically invalid since they beg the question(s).

Li calls his philosophy of how humans gained (and gain) the faculties that are necessary conditions for enabling intersubjective epistemological, moral, and even aesthetic judgments a theory of sedimentation and subjectality. Roughly speaking, he holds that the history of humanity should be conceived of as a development that consisted of certain steps ("sediments"), with each step resulting in and constituting a stage of humankind that becomes the basis for developing a further stage. Thereby, each stage remains "efficient." (This approach reminds of the Hegelian concept of *aufgehoben*.) As I would like to put it: the whole development has the character of a (possibly endless) "piling" of layers. Of course, according to Li's approach, the development of each stage needs thousands or even hundreds of thousands of years. As to Li's notion of subjectality, it refers to humans as biological, material, historical, and social beings (humans as socially interconnected rather than isolated individual beings). What is important to understand is that this subjectality results from *social* sedimentation; in other words, because of its being *collectively* constituted, it is found (and efficient) in every human being. *It does not, however, exclude individual autonomy*. Aside from Li's own publications, see Jana Rošker's and Rafal Banka's explanations (Jana S. Rošker, *Becoming Human: Li Zehou's Ethics* (Leiden: Brill, 2020), and Banka, *Cognition and Practice*, respectively). Banka's book led me to add this note though—regarding the aims of my article—Li's theory of sedimentation and subjectality is important only insofar as it replaces Kant's apriorism—which (to repeat) Li views as untenable. In my opinion, what is relevant remains, namely the concept (or approach) of a kind of "transcendental epistemology" (*Transzendentalphilosophie*, though, to repeat, not as apriorism). Ady Van den Stock ("Imprints of the Thing in Itself: Li Zehou's *Critique of Critical Philosophy* and the Historicization of the Transcendental," *Asian Studies* 8, no. 1 (2020): 15–35) adequately speaks of a "historicization of the transcendental." Li himself states (*The Origins of Chinese Thought*, 231): "the forms of *a priori* knowledge are formed through historical sedimentation of human experience." See also Li, *A New Approach to Kant*, v.

25. Li and Cauvel, *Four Essays on Aesthetics*, 39; Li, *A New Approach to Kant*, 330.

26. Li, *The Origins of Chinese Thought*, 255.

27. Li, 55.

28. Confucius, *Confucius: The Analects*, trans. D. C. Lau (Hong Kong: The Chinese University Press, 1992), 145.

29. See Friedrich Schiller, "Würde des Menschen," de.wikisource.org/wiki/W%C3%BCrde_des_Menschen, from *Musen-Almanach für das Jahr 1797* (Tübingen: J. G. Cottaischen, 1797).

30. Li, *The Origins of Chinese Thought*, 233 and 236.

31. Li, *A New Approach to Kant*, 320.

32. Immanuel Kant, *Religion in the Boundaries of Mere Reason*, ed. Allen Wood and George di Giovanni (Cambridge: Cambridge University Press, 1998), 48–49.

33. Li, *A New Approach to Kant*, 332–35, especially 333.

34. Li, *A New Approach to Kant*, 332.

35. My interpretation can also be supported by such quotes as "unification [harmonization] . . . of the sensuous [emotional, pleasing and pleasant] and the rational [moral]" (Li, *The Chinese Aesthetic Tradition*, 6), unification "of the senses and reason" [faculties of desire and morality] (ibid., 10), and similar passages (ibid., 34; Li, *A New Approach to Kant*, 332–35). The following statement from Li (*The Origins of Chinese Thought*, 237) comes close to at least implying a notion of harmonious freedom: "support of moral action by emotion of love and hate make people 'want to' do something they recognize that they 'ought to' do." Also, in "A Response to Michael Sandel and Other Matters" (*Philosophy East and West* 66, no. 4 (2016): 1068–1147), Li repeatedly uses the expression "emotio-rational structure" (see for instance p. 1071) in the sense of "integration of emotion and reason," which implies a kind of optimal (holistic) synthesis of feelings, knowledge, and moral and social consciousness. Of course, Li does not maintain that this structure, as such, is a harmonious one, but characterizes it as a "structure in which natural feelings and desires variously conflict and integrate with reason" (*The Origins of Chinese Thought*, 269). He regards the indicated integration as a goal rather than a fact—as something to be achieved by the (further) humanization of nature than actually already realized to a satisfactory

degree. (By the way, here Li's conception is close to Kant's conception of regulative ideas. See Li, *Origins*, 237, 255.) Other passages that can be read as advocating harmonious freedom are Li Zehou's praise of (as he sees it) Confucius's aim of "harmoniously coordinating the community, maintaining satisfaction along with balance of emotions and desires within daily affairs, and the avoidance of anti-rational passions and mania or blind and ignorant obedience" (ibid., 215), and Li's emphasis on what he regards as a feature of "the deep structures of Confucianism," namely the interest to avoid "emotional and rational conflict and distress in the relationships between the individual and family or rights and obligations" (ibid., 223).

In his history of *The Chinese Aesthetic Tradition* (31, cf. also 23, and 37), Li also maintains that even Chinese governments "perennially" [!] strived for the "unity or identity of the beautiful and the good": something both beautiful and good, apparently welcoming this pursuit. In taking over Kant's and Schiller's general notions of perception and manifestation of beauty as a free play of the faculties of mind that harmonizes emotions and moral obligations, Li does not only simply argue for a "unity" of the beautiful and the good, but rather for individual harmonious freedom.

According to Li (ibid., 20), "harmony is by necessity . . . unification" and the resultant "unity" no identity but "mutual complementarity" "of opposing elements" and "intermingling of plural elements" and thus harmony. In other words, Li, in the quoted passages, uses the term "unification" in the sense of "harmonization."

36. Li and Cauvel, *Four Essays on Aesthetics*, 174.
37. Li and Cauvel, *Four Essays on Aesthetics*, 94.
38. Li, *A New Approach to Kant*, 329.
39. Bruya, "Li Zehou's Aesthetics as a Marxist Philosophy of Freedom."
40. Marx, "Die ökonomisch-philosophischen Manuskripte"; cf. Li, *A New Approach to Kant*, 326–35, especially 333; see also Li and Cauvel, *Four Essays on Aesthetics*, 179.
41. The German original reads "der Mensch formiert daher auch nach den Gesetzen der Schönheit." An English translation runs "hence [!], man also produces in accordance with the laws of beauty."

As the context shows, this proposition is an explanation of Marx's statement that humans beings can "truly produce" only if they are "free from physical needs." Since, according to Marx, "truth" in production is a necessary condition for unestranged labor, and since labor must not involve estrangement, one of its requirements is that it ought to be carried out following the laws of beauty. Or, closer to Marx's own wording, since man, different from other animals, only truly produces if free from basic needs, and free from estrangement, man "therefore also formats according to laws of beauty." This implies, if he would not format according to these laws, he would not "truly" act as a free person.

The Philosophy of Beauty as an Ethics of Freedom | 379

In my opinion, an adequate paraphrase of the relevant passages in Marx could be that humans only realize themselves as human beings if they act as free beings. Since this entails that their practice follows rules of beauty, their ways of production, and especially labor, which are the main means of self-realization as free beings, should accord with these rules. Clearly, Li's philosophy that humanization as a realization of freedom in the form of beauty is (mainly) achieved by "the making and use of tools," is indebted to such a position.

42. Li, *A New Approach to Kant*, 323–24.
43. Li and Cauvel, *Four Essays on Aesthetics*, 179.
44. See nickbostrom.com.
45. E.g., Li, *A New Approach to Kant*, 300, 308–9, 311–12.
46. But rarely to harmonious freedom. However, the mighty could have taken into account certain social requirements when deciding not only to pursue their own interests but also to fulfill the interests and desires of the people close to them, such as family members, friends, and political advisors. In such way privileged persons could probably experience harmonious freedom.
47. I thank Jana S. Rošker for suggesting that I take into account Hannah Arendt's distinctions between labor and work.
48. See Hannah Arendt, *Vita activa oder Vom tätigen Leben* (München: Piper, 2002), 201–12, especially 209–12; and Hannah Arendt, *The Human Condition* (Chicago: University of Chicago Press, 2018), 167–74, particularly 172–74.
49. Arendt, *The Human Condition*, 12–14.
50. For example, *The Instruction of Dua-Kheti* (also referred to as *The Satire of the Trades*), about 2000 BCE, and *Papyrus Lansing*, nineteenth century BCE. See Miriam Lichtheim, ed., *Ancient Egyptian Literature* (Oakland: University of California Press, 2019 [1973]), 230–9, and 495–509. A German translation of the *Papyrus* even more clearly expresses the beauty of the work of a scribe than the English version. See Otto Kaiser et al., eds., *Texte aus der Umwelt des Alten Testaments* (Darmstadt: WBG, 2019), vol. III/2: 132, 139–41. In this connection it may be helpful to come back to my note 2, above. If one wants to express oneself precisely one could perhaps say that, in a language L (e.g., German), a person P (e.g., Kant) characterizes something S (e.g., an artwork or object of nature) as B by using *a word "W"* (e.g., "schön") that *in English is (usually) translated "T"* (e.g., "beautiful"). It should thus actually go without saying that almost nobody believes that, for example, Akhenaton, Aristotle, Hume, Kant, Confucius, Zhuangzi, or Li Zehou held *identical* notions of beauty. For instance, Akhenaton emphasized shining brightness, Zhuangzi (seeming) naturalness, Kant valued form higher than content. However, to characterize the way in which humans perceive or "experience" what they refer to by words such as *beautiful* or words that are translated by "beautiful," a wide notion of a free play of the faculties of mind may be generally applicable.

51. Leonardo da Vinci, *Das Buch von der Malerei* [*Treatise on Painting*], trans. Heinrich Ludwig (Wien: Wilhelm Braumüller, 2016 [1882]); Kenneth Clark, *Leonardo da Vinci* (Stuttgart: Reclam, 1969), 81; Kenneth Clark, *Leonardo da Vinci* (Harmondsworth: Penguin, 1989), 136.

52. For a more comprehensive and detailed discussion of the history and systematic significance of conceptions of beauty, and especially beautiful art (with particular reference to China), see Paul, *Philosophy in the History of China*, 165–235.

53. Lutz Fiedler, *Faustkeile: Vom Ursprung der Kultur* (Darmstadt WBG Academic, 2022). Of course, even most of the bifaces and hand axes produced after about 600,000 years ago lacked aesthetic features such as symmetry or smoothness, but this does not lessen the significance of the huge number of beautiful pieces created since then.

54. Fiedler (*Faustkeile: Vom Ursprung der Kultur*) comprehensively and in detail explains how (especially during the Acheulean, i.e., 1.76–0.13 Mya) bifaces and hand axes were created (and designed) as tools for sustaining and improving human life, and that their production originated in social contexts and was a social endeavor. Fiedler's study in an impressive way confirms Li's view that (mainly) the manufacture and use of tools (as social achievements) enabled/enables the humanization of man. The study even supports Li's concepts of sedimentation and subjectability.

55. Fiedler, *Faustkeile: Vom Ursprung der Kultur*, 2022.

56. To explain again: According to Kant, pure beauty is an object of uninterested pleasure, whereas beauty as a symbol of morality is an object of dependent pleasure. As Li emphasizes, Kant attributed higher value to such dependent pleasure than to uninterested pleasure. Since pursuing a hobby involves interest, namely the idea of bringing something into existence, and is not mere imagination or contemplation of something, a hobby could at best be realization of dependent beauty. Hobbies such as playing cards, mountain climbing, or car racing that nobody is obliged to pursue, however, are simply motivated by individual inclinations, and not even examples of dependent beauty (in the Kantian sense). Even teachers who make their living by teaching, and are at the same time obliged to teach, and who like and enjoy teaching, may thereby follow not laws of beauty but simply individual inclinations. Thus, what in many cases could be achieved at best would be something pleasant and pleasurable that does not violate social and moral obligations.

57. See especially Li, *The Chinese Aesthetic Tradition*, 48.

58. Though one should not read too much into *Lunyu* 2.4 (ctext.org/analects/wei-zheng), it is probably safe to say that the passage emphasizes the importance of finding pleasure in one's actions. This would be in keeping with Li's characterization of Chinese culture as a culture of joy (*legan wenhua* 樂感

文化) (a culture based on emotion) or, as Andrew Lambert (in Li, *A History of Classical Chinese Thought*, 322) translates it, "a culture characterized by sensitivity to delight."

59. Cf. again Li and Cauvel, *Four Essays on Aesthetics*, 179.
60. Li, *The Chinese Aesthetic Tradition*, 3.
61. Li and Cauvel, *Four Essays on Aesthetics*, 177.
62. Zhuangzi, "達生 [Da sheng]—The Full Understanding of Life," trans. James Legge, *Chinese Text Project*, ctext.org/zhuangzi/full-understanding-of-life; Chuang-Tzŭ [Zhuangzi], *Chuang-Tzŭ: The Inner Chapters*, trans. and commentary Angus Graham (London: Allen & Unwin, 1981), 135. Another anecdote in the *Zhuangzi* tells of the cook Ding who effortlessly, and even elegantly, dissects an ox. He explains his admirable method by pointing out that his "knife unerringly . . . follows the natural markings, slips into the natural cleaverages, finds its way into natural cavities . . . [thus] conforming [his] work to the structure with which [he] is dealing" (*Yang sheng zhu* 養生主, trans. Waley, as quoted by William R. B. Acker, trans. and annot., *Some T'ang and Pre-T'ang Texts of Chinese Painting* (Leiden: Brill, 1954), 181. For other translations, see James Legge, ctext.org/zhuangzi/nourishing-the-lord-of-life, and Graham, *Chuang-Tzŭ*, 63–64.) The anecdote in *Da sheng* can be, and has been, understood as indicating that, in visual art, one should "follow" the structure of the material, i.e., apply the principle of preformation.
63. Cf. Paul, *Philosophy in the History of China*, 216–35.
64. Regarding the beauty of ancient objects of utility, Li (*Der Weg des Schönen*, 46) seems to be of a different opinion.

In my opinion, the distinctions between truth, goodness, and beauty, or—more generally—the cognitive, moral, and aesthetic, strongly indicate a conviction that these are logically independent values or categories. On the other hand, the equally/similarly significant attempts to somehow combine or "unify" them testify to an *interest to construct an optimum of what is existentially relevant for human beings*. In different ways, the philosophies of Plato, Confucius, Kant, and even Marx (to mention only a few) are examples of both intentions. As to Confucius, he spoke of "the bounds of [what is morally or socially] right," and "the desires of the heart" [something aesthetic], though "right" in "bounds of right" seems to also include a kind of "truth." The *Lunyu* also explicitly referred to correctness in the usage of names (implying a kind of truth), humaneness (*ren* 仁 in mourning the death of one's parents) (Yang Huo 陽貨, ctext.org/analects/yang-huo, 24), and pleasure (in greeting friends and enjoying poetry), though Confucius certainly advocated a behavior that, at the same time, accorded with truth and morality and was, moreover, a pleasure. In short, though Confucius did not sharply distinguish between beauty, goodness, and truth, and left no doubt that *acceptable* beauty ought to be also something good or true, this does not change the—indicated—fact that he did also use words to distinguish between the three categories. As to Marx, he spoke of "true," "unestranged," and beautiful production, and asked for a "production according to the laws of beauty" that, *as such production*, would also be "true" and "unestranged."

65. "Mit 150.000 Jahren ältester Schmuck der Welt entdeckt," *Trtdeutsch*, November 19, 2021, www.trtdeutsch.com/kultur/marokko-mit-150000-jahren-altester-schmuck-der-welt-entdeckt-7177871.

66. "Neandertaler dachten wie wir," *Max Planck Gesellschaft*, February 18, 2018, www.mpg.de/11947682/neandertaler-hoehlenmalerei.

67. Dutton, *The Art Instinct*, 4–5; see also 100.

68. Christoph Redies, "A Universal Model of Esthetic Perception Based on the Sensory Coding of Natural Stimuli," in *Art and Perception: Towards a Visual Science of Art*, ed. Baingio Pinna, part 1 (Leiden: Brill, 2008), 181.

69. Maria Lagogianni-Georgakarakos, ed., *The Countless Aspects of Beauty in Ancient Art* (Athens: Archaeological Receipts Fund, 2018), 40–41.

70. Dutton, *The Art Instinct*, 155–58.

71. Li, *The Origins of Chinese Thought*, 98.

72. Li, 98.

73. Li and Cauvel, *Four Essays on Aesthetics*.

74. Karen Gloy, *Das Projekt interkultureller Philosophie aus interkulturreller Sicht* (Würzburg: Königshausen und Neumann, 2022), 58.

75. Quoted from Wang Keping's translation in this volume.

76. Bruya, "Li Zehou's Aesthetics as a Marxist Philosophy of Freedom," 140.

# Bibliography

Acker, William Reynolds Beal. *Some T'ang and Pre-T'ang Texts of Chinese Painting*. Translated and annotated by W. R. B. Acker. Chinese and English. Leiden: Brill, 1954.

Arendt, Hannah. *The Human Condition*. 2nd ed. Chicago: University of Chicago Press, 2018.

Arendt, Hannah. *Vita activa oder Vom tätigen Leben*. München: Piper, 2002.

Asian Studies. "Ethics and Beauty of Human Becoming: Special Issue Dedicated to Li Zehou on His 90th Birthday." *Asian Studies* 8, no. 1 (2020).

Banka, Rafal. *Cognition and Practice: Li Zehou's Philosophical Aesthetics*. Albany: State University of New York Press, 2022.

Blackman, Aylward M., and T. Eric Peet. "Papyrus Lansing: A Translation with Notes." *Journal of Egyptian Archaeology* 11, no. 3/4 (1925): 284–298. www.academia.edu/5200741/Egypt_Exploration_Society_Papyrus_Lansing_A_Translation_with_Notes_Author_s_.

Bruya, Brian. "Li Zehou's Aesthetics as a Marxist Philosophy of Freedom." *Dialogue and Universalism*, no. 11–12 (2003): 133–40.
*Chinese Text Project*. 2006–2024. ctext.org.
Chuang-Tzŭ [Zhuangzi]. *Chuang-Tzŭ: The Inner Chapters*. Translated with commentary by A. C. Graham. London: Allen & Unwin, 1981.
Clark, Kenneth. *Leonardo da Vinci*. Stuttgart: Reclam, 1969.
Clark, Kenneth. *Leonardo da Vinci*. Harmondsworth: Penguin, 1989.
Confucius. *Confucius: The Analects*. Chinese and English. Translated by D. C. Lau. 2nd ed. Hong Kong: The Chinese University Press, 1992.
Dutton, Denis. *The Art Instinct: Beauty Pleasure, and Human Evolution*. New York: Bloomsbury Press, 2009.
Erman, Adolf, trans. and ed. "The Instruction of Dua-Kheti." In *The Literature of the Ancient Egyptians: Poems, Narratives, and Manuals of Instruction, from the Third and Second Millennia B.C.*, 67f. London: Methuen, 1927. web. archive.org/web/20190308063715/http://www.reshafim.org.il/ad/egypt/texts/instructions_of_kheti.htm.
Essler, Wilhelm K. *Wissenschaftstheorie II*. Freiburg: Alber, 1971.
Fiedler, Lutz. *Faustkeile: Vom Ursprung der Kultur*. Darmstadt: WBG Academic, 2022.
Gloy, Karen. *Das Projekt interkultureller Philosophie aus interkulturreller Sicht*. Würzburg: Königshausen und Neumann, 2022.
Kaiser, Otto, Rykle Borger, Wilhelmus C. Delsman, Manfred Dietrich, Ursula Kaplony-Heckel, Hans Martin Kümmel, Oswald Loretz, Walter W. Müller, and Willem H. Ph. Römer, eds. *Texte aus der Umwelt des Alten Testaments*. 4 vols. Darmstadt: WBG, 2019.
Kant, Immanuel. *Critique of Judgment*. Translated by Werner S. Pluhar. Indianapolis: Hackett, 1987.
Kant, Immanuel. *Kritik der Urteilskraft und Schriften zur Naturphilosophie*. Vols. 9 and 10 of *Immanuel Kant, Werke in zwölf Bänden*. Edited by Wilhelm Weischedel. Frankfurt am Main: Suhrkamp, 1968.
Kant, Immanuel. *Religion in the Boundaries of Mere Reason*. Edited by Allen Wood and George di Giovanni. Cambridge: Cambridge University Press, 1998.
Lagogianni-Georgakarakos, Maria, ed. *The Countless Aspects of Beauty in Ancient Art*. Athens: Archaeological Receipts Fund, 2018.
Leonardo da Vinci. *Das Buch von der Malerei [Treatise on Painting]*. Translated by Heinrich Ludwig. Wien: Wilhelm Braumüller, 2016 [1882].
Li Zehou. *The Chinese Aesthetic Tradition*. Translated by Maija Bell Samei. Honolulu: University of Hawai'i Press, 2009.
Li Zehou. *A History of Classical Chinese Thought*. Translated by Andrew Lambert. New York: Routledge, 2020.
Li Zehou. *A New Approach to Kant: A Confucian-Marxist's Viewpoint*. Translated by Jeanne Haizhen Allen and Christopher Ahn. Singapore: Springer, 2018.

Li Zehou. *The Origins of Chinese Thought: From Shamanism to Ritual Regulations and Humaneness*. Translated by Robert A. Carleo III. Leiden: Brill, 2018.

Li Zehou. *Der Weg des Schönen: Wesen und Geschichte der chinesischen Kultur und Aesthetik*. Translated by Karl-Heinz Pohl and Gudrun Wecker. Freiburg: Herder, 1992.

Li Zehou and Jane Cauvel. *Four Essays on Aesthetics: Toward a Global View*. Lanham, MD: Lexington Books, 2006.

Lichtheim, Miriam, ed. *Ancient Egyptian Literature*. Oakland: University of California Press, 2019 [1973].

Marx, Karl. *Ökonomisch-philosophische Manuskripte aus dem Jahre 1844*. www.zeno.org/nid/20009214658/. English translation: www.marxists.org/archive/marx/works/1844/epm/index.htm.

"Mit 150.000 Jahren ältester Schmuck der Welt entdeckt." *Trtdeutsch*, November 19, 2021. www.trtdeutsch.com/kultur/marokko-mit-150000-jahren-altester-schmuck-der-welt-entdeckt-7177871.

"Neandertaler dachten wie wir." *Max-Planck-Gesellschaft*, February 18, 2018. www.mpg.de/11947682/neandertaler-hoehlenmalerei.

Paul, Gregor. *Aspects of Confucianism*. Frankfurt/Main: Lang, 1990.

Paul, Gregor. *Philosophy in the History of China*. Bochum: Projekt-Verlag, 2022.

Redies, Christoph. "A Universal Model of Esthetic Perception Based on the Sensory Coding of Natural Stimuli." In *Art and Perception: Towards a Visual Science of Art*, edited by Baingio Pinna, part 1. Leiden: Brill, 2008.

Rošker, Jana S. *Becoming Human: Li Zehou's Ethics*. Leiden: Brill, 2020.

Rošker, Jana S. *Following His Own Path: Li Zehou and Contemporary Chinese Philosophy*. Albany: State University of New York Press, 2019.

Sernelj, Téa. "Different Approaches to Modern Art and Society: Li Zehou versus Xu Fuguan." *Asian Studies* 8, no. 1 (2020): 77–98.

Van den Stock, Ady. "Imprints of the Thing in Itself: Li Zehou's *Critique of Critical Philosophy* and the Historicization of the Transcendental." *Asian Studies* 8, no. 1 (2020): 15–35.

14

# Li Zehou's Major Works on Chinese Aesthetics
*The Path of Beauty* and *The Chinese Aesthetic Tradition*[1]

KARL-HEINZ POHL

Li Zehou's *The Path of Beauty* (*Mei de lichen* 美的歷程) was first published in 1981. An English translation by Gong Lizeng appeared 1988 (richly illustrated) and 1994 (with only a few illustrations).[2] The book had a tremendous impact in China, leading to an "aesthetics craze" (*meixue re* 美學熱). In the following text, the main characteristics of the book will be introduced and compared with *The Chinese Aesthetic Tradition* (*Huaxia meixue* 華夏美學), which appeared in 1988.

## The Path of Beauty

In a 1983 lecture "On Some Problems of a Chinese History of Aesthetics," Li Zehou described *The Path of Beauty* as a "broad" history of aesthetics.[3] First, he points out some fundamental problems of a Chinese history of aesthetics: compared to the West, aesthetics in China has no tradition as a systematic discipline. The word for "aesthetics" (literally "study of beauty": *meixue*) is a neologism that is often still misunderstood. (Li begins his article "What is Aesthetics?" with the anecdote that, when asked

385

the question in the title of the article, someone replied helplessly that it was probably an abbreviation for "American studies."[4]) The category of "beauty" was not discussed by the literati and artists in traditional China. The "beautiful" had no special value in art; they valued the "balanced" (*he* 和) or the "natural-spontaneous" (*ziran* 自然).[5] In this respect, we find "aesthetically" relevant expressions mostly in literary or art-critical writings, which are often also characterized by an unsystematic and un-theoretical character, as well as in isolated statements of philosophers related to artistic activity.

What, then, asks Li Zehou, should belong to a Chinese historiography of aesthetics? The aphorisms of Chinese thinkers of Confucian, Daoist, and other provenance that apply to music, art, or literature? Or the well-known literature and art tracts? All of this undoubtedly belongs to a historiography of aesthetics, but to a "narrow" one.[6] Such a history, however, runs the risk of distorting or contradicting the historical development of aesthetic consciousness. Thus, for example, Confucian comments on the odes of the *Book of Songs* do not necessarily reflect the aesthetic consciousness that produced these early testimonies of Chinese literature. In contrast to such a limited view, it is necessary to include the most important works of literature and art in a "broadly" conceived history of aesthetics. Moreover, in order to document the development of Chinese aesthetic consciousness, one must also take into account other forms of artistic design, such as architecture, arts and crafts, and ceramics, especially from prehistoric and early historic times, as well as the social, material conditions that produced them. In this respect, the "Path of Beauty" that Li traces logically begins with the production of jewelry and the magical rituals of prehistoric people—with "totem cults from the earliest times."

In view of the inclusiveness of Li Zehou's approach, his work can also be understood as cultural anthropology in the broadest sense, because his actual goal, as Heinrich Geiger formulates it, is "to work out the context of an organic, meaningful development process of the Chinese civilization oriented to the idea of beauty."[7] Although, as mentioned, the idea of the beautiful did not play a role in the traditional consideration of art and literature, Chinese intellectuals of the modern era were all influenced by Western thought—by the appreciation of the "Good, True and Beautiful"—and therefore Li Zehou's pursuit of "the path of beauty" is no exception.

As his work can be understood as cultural anthropology, anthropological questions dominate the beginning of the book. By understanding humans primarily as producers and their products as a reflection of their social conditions and social consciousness, it starts from basic Marxist anthropological premises.

Hence, important for understanding this work are leading Marxist ideas regarding anthropology and history. As such, we find repeated reference to Marx's scheme of five social stages in historical development: primitive communism, slave society, feudalism, mercantilism, and capitalism. There is also repeated mention of "class struggle" as well as Marx's concepts of "basis and superstructure." Apart from this, there are significant references to Marx's "Economic and Philosophic Manuscripts of 1844," in particular to his concept of human nature—*Humanismus der Natur* (humanism of nature). The following quote from Marx's "Manuscripts" is crucial: "Thus *society* is the complete unity of man with nature—the true resurrection of nature—the consistent naturalism of man and the consistent humanism of nature."[8]

It is interesting and significant, though, that Marx's terms "humanism of nature" and "naturalism of man" were interpreted by Li with a certain twist: "humanism of nature" is understood as "humanization of nature" (*ziran de renhua* 自然的人化) and "naturalism of man" as "naturalization of man" (*ren de ziranhua* 人的自然化).[9] Interestingly, the sections referring to Marx's anthropology (in the first chapter of the book) are not included in the English translation (not so in the German translation . . .).

While Marx still applied his terms to anthropological and sociological considerations, Li Zehou transfers the "humanization/humanism of nature" (*ziran de renhua*) into an aesthetic dimension. Regarding the "humanization/humanism of nature," Li Zehou makes a distinction between outer or external and inner humanization. The external one is the shaping of the objects of nature by man's labor, whereby nature becomes man's nature, and "beauty" can be realized in the external world. More important, however, is an inner "humanization of nature," which Li himself considers the pivotal point of his theory of aesthetic sensibility.[10] Inner "humanization of nature" means humanization of humans themselves, their sensory perceptions and their emotions, through which only aesthetic feeling can be realized in the human psyche.

Li also distinguishes two kinds of aesthetic feelings in people, a sensual, intuitive, disinterested kind, and a rational, social-beneficial kind.

In order to explain how both are interlocked with each other—"how the sensible is expressed in the sensual, the social in the individual, and the historical in the psychic"[11]—Li coined a word that, as the cultural debate of the 1980s in China showed, has since become widely used: "sedimentation" (*jidian* 積澱). What is the meaning of this metaphor borrowed from geology, which evokes processes that take place over a long period of time? Li thus attempts to grasp the emergence of aesthetic sensation and artistic form in the process of the "humanization of nature," namely how ideas and concepts—that is, the mental—are deposited in aesthetic-sensual sensations, as well as social content in individual forms. In *The Path of Beauty*, he develops this idea using the example of prehistoric and early historical art, in which he not only demonstrates the first beginnings of aesthetic consciousness and artistic creativity, but also shows how there was a development in Chinese prehistory from rough images of animals with still concrete content—such as figures of totems—to abstract, linear symbols on Neolithic (*Yangshao* 楊紹) ceramics or *Taotie* (饕餮) bronze masks, in which original social content was deposited and dissolved. As Li explains:

> What is the key to understanding the mystery of the eternal nature of art? . . . Why is it that the aesthetic value and artistic style of works of long ago still accord with the sentiments and interests of people of our time? Why do they still evoke such intimate feelings in us? Is it that the sentiments accumulated and condensed in them are related to and act upon the psychological structure of people today? Is the human psychological structure a product of the accumulation and condensation of historical experience? If so, the secret of the eternal nature of art may reside therein. Or, it may be the other way round—that is, the universal human psychology resides in and is promoted by the eternal nature of art. . . . Psychological structure is a product of the sedimentation of human history and civilization; art is the psychology that reveals the soul of the times. Maybe this can explain human nature as related to art.[12]

In this respect, the beautiful is not ordinary beauty of form, but, in that meaningful social content has been sedimented into form, "significant form" (*you yiwei de xingshi* 有意味的形式), a term Li has borrowed from the writings of Clive Bell (1881–1964) and Susanne Langer (1895–1985):[13]

> The social consciousness—the passions, concepts, and psychology of primitive humans—crystallized and concentrated in these pictorial symbols, invested them with a meaning and significance that was beyond pure graphic representation. Primitive humans perceived in them properties and values that transcended pure psychological responses. In other words, these natural forms were sedimented with social values and content, and man's perceptual power and sensibility had acquired a rational quality. This unquestionably was the beginning of an aesthetic awareness and artistic creation.[14]

In an even more comprehensive way, Li understands "sedimentation" as the culture-specific shaping of social and historical content, which he calls "cultural-psychological structure" (*wenhua xinli jiegou* 文化心理結構)—another key concept in Li's thought. This cultural-psychological structure is that which has been deposited throughout history in a culture-specific way in psychic conditions: human behavior patterns, ways of thinking, emotional attitudes, and also art.

As a structure of cultural and social sedimentations over a long period of history, it also implies the question of cultural identity. On the one hand, the formation is inherited through a process of education; hence it is important for the people of today to become conscious of the forces of history that have shaped their present. On the other hand, the formation is constantly formed anew, as it is not determined by the sedimentations.

In the Chinese cultural-psychological structure Li locates—as coordinates, as it were—three basic elements to which not only general cultural phenomena but also "aesthetics" can be related: Confucianism, Zhuangzi's Daoism with its transitions into Chan (Zen 禪) Buddhism and, as a third, the poetry of the "Elegies of Chu" (*Chu ci* 楚辭) associated with the name Qu Yuan 屈原 (ca. 340–278 BCE). Confucian beauty is characterized by humanistic contents; here the Marxian idea of "humanism of nature"—in the form of humanization and harmonization of the inner nature of humans—finds its most perfect Chinese expression. The beautiful in Zhuangzi 庄子, on the other hand, is the free, spontaneous, natural beauty, which Li sees as the Chinese equivalent of the ideal of a "naturalism of man" that also appears in Marx's "Manuscripts." Finally, the beautiful in Qu Yuan is symbol of moral integrity.[15]

In his book, Li shows how the development process of Chinese culture—"the path of beauty"—after its beginnings in prehistoric times, unfolds in constant relation to these coordinates: apart from its humanistic contents, the ideal of an artistically balanced design, a "harmonious beauty" (*zhonghe zhi mei* 中和之美), which is a harmony of content (*zhi* 質) and form (*wen* 文), of reason (*li* 理) and emotion (*qing* 情), originates from Confucian thinking. The ideas of Daoism and Chan Buddhism, on the other hand, play an important role in capturing the unfathomable (*shen* 神) essence of artistic creativity, of intuition and inspiration, in images and words. Finally, with Qu Yuan begins the tradition of lyrical expression, that is, the creation and interpretation of poetry (the most important art form in Chinese cultural history) as an expression of an individual and morally cultivated personality. Within these basic directions, Li Zehou relates literature, art, and philosophy to each other in many ways and shows a wealth of structural correspondences and classification possibilities: for example, three types of Buddhist sculptures, three "worlds" of poetry, and three conceptions of landscape painting, whereby the typifications correspond to each other to a certain degree.

In his lecture mentioned at the beginning, Li Zehou also points out four characteristics of Chinese aesthetics, partly formal and partly substantive, which are also reflected in *The Path of Beauty*: (1) the central importance of music; (2) the art of line; (3) the fusion of reason (*li*) and emotion (*qing*); and (4) the unity of Heaven/nature and humans (*tian ren he yi* 天人合一).[16] Music is, as it were, the art form of Confucianism. Confucius says of it that humans are "perfected in music" (*cheng yu yue* 成於樂).[17] The harmonizing effect of music on humans and its socially unifying function—in contrast to the ordering and dividing effect of the rites, with which it is always mentioned in the same breath—is also in the foreground of the "Chapter on Music" in the *Book of Rites* (*Liji* 禮記). Its educational significance, so important for early Confucian thought, lies in its ability to temper humans' primal feelings, thereby socializing them and guiding their emotional worlds in a "reasonable" direction.[18] In this respect, the third characteristic is already implied in this first one: the fusion of emotion and reason, which also implies a harmonious unity of the individual and society.

The second characteristic is the "art of the line." Compared to the more sensual color, the line possesses something spiritually abstract. It is, as it were, the visible form of music, its melodic slurs and rhythms. The "art of the line" finds its most perfect artistic realization in Chinese calligraphy—an art form that in China is ranked far higher than painting. Remarkable again is the development from rough, line-like illustration in the form of simple pictographic characters to spontaneous, rhythmic lines and abstract structures, in which not only the original pictorial quality, but also the feeling, thinking, and power of the writer have been "sedimented," and which have thus become "significant form" in the truest sense.

Finally, the last trait, the "unity of Heaven/nature and man," occupies a central position in Li's thinking: he regards it as a core idea of traditional Chinese philosophy, which is reflected in art in manifold ways. We encounter it in analogies between nature or Heaven (*tian* 天) and human virtues, as in the *Book of Changes* ("The action of Heaven is strong and dynamic. In the same manner, the noble man never ceases to strengthen himself")[19] or in the sayings of Confucius ("The wise man delights in the water, the kind man in the mountains"),[20] but also in the demand for fusion of emotion (*qing* 情) and landscape/nature (*jing* 景) in poetry and landscape painting.

This idea of the "unity of Heaven/nature and man," which can be traced in different interpretations from the *Book of Changes* to Daoist philosophy, the Han Confucianism of Dong Zhongshu (董仲舒, 179–104 BC), and the Neo-Confucians throughout the history of Chinese philosophy, has also given Li, albeit in a different context, a new, current significance, namely as a Chinese alternative with universal relevance to the Judeo-Christian opposition of human and nature, which has begun to show threatening consequences for the whole of humanity.[21]

When Li Zehou, finally, offers "unity of Heaven/nature and man" as a Chinese elaboration of Marx's "humanization/humanism of nature" and the "naturalization/naturalism of man," this is more than a simple correspondence, because Li starts from Marx, but he returns to traditional Chinese philosophical themes. One could speak of a dissolution of Marxian thought in Chinese structures: Marx's speculative anthropology is adapted and sinicized in a "practical-rational" way—for Li a trait of Confucian thought.

Summing up, the characteristics of *The Path of Beauty* are, first, its design as a "broad" explication of the Chinese aesthetic tradition and, second, its Marxist approach by referring to the latter's anthropology and history. Hence, we find for each historical period that he discusses, first, an explication of the socioeconomic situation and class affiliation of actors (the "base") before he turns to literature and art (the "superstructure"). This also accords with Li's position of "unity of objectivity and sociality," which he took in the great "Aesthetics Debate" of 1956: There arose a discussion between Zhu Guangqian 朱光潛 (1897–1986), for whom beauty was a "synthesis of the subjective and the objective" (*zhuguan he keguan de tongyi* 主觀與客觀的統一), and Li Zehou, whose counter argument was "unity of objectivity and sociality" (*keguanxing yu shehuixing xiang tongyi* 客觀性與社會性統一). With this he referred to the possibility of establishing a connection with a specific object because that object has always already been contextualized and conceptualized within a sociality of many other things and relations.[22]

Apart from that, we also find in Li's book Marx's optimism regarding human progress, as well as his critical attitude toward religion, in this case Buddhism (chapter 6: "A Miserable World" and "Illusionary Praise"). Criticism of religion may have been part of mainstream Western thought in Europe since the Enlightenment; for China, however, it could be alienating when it applies to Buddhism, which is so popular in the West and often perceived as an alternative religion. Yet it is important to know that Chinese Marxists, on the one hand, are only continuing the tradition of Confucian criticism of Buddhism, while, on the other, the Confucians, especially the Neo-Confucians (from around the eleventh century), were significantly influenced by Buddhism. In this respect, Li Zehou's treatment of Buddhism also has this ambivalent attitude. Worth mentioning, lastly, not as a homage to Marx but as an inheritance of thought patterns of the early twentieth century, is the way Li transfers classifications of the European intellectual history to China, in this case "Romanticism" (chapters 4 and 10)—both to the time of the Chu and Han culture and, after a jump of about 1,500 years, to the Ming and Qing Dynasties. This—from today's point of view uncritical—handling of Western thought patterns goes back to the time of the May 4th movement (around 1919), during which European Romanticism was the favored style of Chinese intellectuals.

## The Chinese Aesthetic Tradition

Li Zehou published *The Chinese Aesthetic Tradition* (*Huaxia meixue* 華夏美學) in 1988. An English translation by Maija Bell Samei appeared in 2009.[23] Li considered it to be one of his major works, and more important—i.e., more philosophical—than *The Path of Beauty*. What are the major differences between the two works? *The Chinese Aesthetic Tradition* is also a history of Chinese aesthetics, but in a "narrow" sense, as it traces more the philosophical tradition, based on the written documents.

Li focuses on themes that are—in his view—constitutive for a Chinese aesthetics, such as:

- "Rites and Music"—according to Li Zehou, China is a "culture of rites and music" (*li yue zhi wenhua* 禮樂之文化);
- "Confucian Humanism"—with a focus on the harmony between emotion and reason, society and individual;
- Daoist "Free and Easy Wandering" (*xiaoyao you* 逍遙遊)—with an emphasis on the concept of freedom;
- Qu Yuan and the *Elegies of Chu*—its themes are human emotionality and mortality;
- "Metaphysics"—such as in Chan Buddhism and Neo-Confucianism; here Su Shi 蘇軾 (1037–1101) comes in as a main figure in Chinese aesthetics;
- Encounter with Western thought—from Ming Dynasty thinkers such as Wang Yangming 王陽明 (1472–1529) and Yuan Hongdao 袁宏道 (1568–1610) to the introduction of Western thought by Wang Guowei 王國維 (1877–1927) and Cai Yuanpei 蔡元培 (1868–1940).

The book is, most of all, oriented toward Confucianism. In the preface Li says, "What I mean by 'Chinese Aesthetics' in this volume is Confucian-based traditional Chinese aesthetics."[24] However, as in *The Path of Beauty*, the basis of his approach is an "anthropological ontology," in Li's words: "To talk about and to seek the root of human existence."[25] Hence we find also in this work reference to Marx's "Economic and Philosophic Manuscripts of 1844," that is, to the already mentioned concepts of "humanism/humanization of nature" (chapter 2) as well as "naturalism/naturalization of man" (chapter 3). When Marx writes, as already quoted at the beginning in the context of *The Path of Beauty*, that "*society* is the complete unity of man with nature—the true resurrection of nature—the consistent naturalism of man and the consistent humanism of nature,"[26] we see that for Li this idea corresponds to the Chinese tradition of the "unity of Heaven/nature and man" (*tian ren he yi*): "The unity of Heaven and humans (天人合一) . . . is a very widespread and long-lasting notion in Chinese aesthetics and artistic creation. . . . From today's perspective, however, this principle can be seen to be simply a roughhewn and roundabout expression of the 'humanization of nature' in Chinese philosophy and aesthetics."[27]

Li Zehou considers aesthetic experiences to be the most meaningful experiences in life. In this context he elaborates on concepts of aesthetics which were introduced by Wang Guowei, a thinker who represents the early encounter of Chinese with European ideas. He coined some basic aesthetic concepts for the twentieth century such as *jingjie* 境界 ("aesthetic state," often also understood as "aesthetic realm" or "consciousness") and *yijing* 意境 ("aesthetic idea")[28] to denote a perfect aesthetic fusion of an artistic idea (or feeling) with a concrete scene (*qing/yi jing ronghe* 情/意景融合). Wang first used the term *jingjie* only with regards to poetry and without any theoretical explanation, but this term soon gained a general aesthetic meaning, signifying both an aesthetic idea as well as a most sublime state of mind. Wang Guowei derived his concepts from Chinese tradition, using Buddhist vocabulary. The term *yijing* was first used in Yogacara Buddhism (*Faxiangi zong/Weishi zong* 法相宗/唯識宗) of the Tang Dynasty. The character *jing* 境 (Sanskrit: *viṣaya*), as Wing-tsit Chan explained, has the meaning "realm, conception, domain of perception, external world" (the "sphere or realm in which the mind gropes for an object which is its own imagination").[29] There we find the distinction between the following three realms or conceptions: *wujing* 物境 (realm of things), *qingjing* 情境 (realm of feelings), and *yijing* 意境 (realm of ideas).[30] Today, the Buddhist origin of these ideas is hardly a subject of discussion anymore, and the influence of Western thought appears to be more interesting, as in Wang Guowei's thought the terms *yijing* and *jingjie* are imbued with meaning that he found in Kant and Schopenhauer (Kant's "aesthetic idea"), and thus represent early intercultural exchanges of thought between China and the West.

In *The Chinese Aesthetic Tradition*, Li Zehou defined Wang Guowei's concept *jingjie* in the following way: "The aesthetic realm [*jingjie*] is the revelation of life through the relationship between feeling and scene, and the objectified realm of the artistic subject—in other words, it is a manifestation of the realm of human life."[31] Hence, in their monumental (though not completed) *History of Chinese Aesthetics* (*Zhongguo meixue shi* 中國美學史), Li Zehou and Liu Gangji 劉綱紀 (1933–2019) marked as the last and most important characteristic of traditional Chinese aesthetics the idea that an "aesthetic consciousness" (*shenmei jingjie* 審美境界) was regarded as the "highest and noblest consciousness to be attained in life" (*yi shenmei jingjie wei rensheng de zui gao jingjie* 以審美境界為人生的最高境界).[32]

The more philosophical bent of *The Chinese Aesthetic Tradition* reveals itself predominantly in its reference to Kantian thought and terminology, such as *noumenon* (*benti* 本體). It has to be added, though, that the usage of the term *benti* in Chinese does not quite correspond to the term *noumenon* in Western philosophy—nor the term *bentilun* (本體論; literally "theory of original substance") to "ontology," which is the usual translation for it.[33] Both terms—*benti* and *bentilun*—have experienced an inflationary usage in China, which cannot be said of the corresponding terms *noumenon* and *ontology* in Western writings. The reasons for the popularity of these terms with modern Chinese intellectuals might be manifold, and one is certainly due to their uncritical adoption of, if not infatuation with, Western terminology. However, because of their literal meanings in Chinese they have a broader range, and not such a narrow philosophical focus as the corresponding Western terms.

As to the *noumenon*, Li Zehou explains:

> The Confucian dominated Chinese tradition of philosophy, aesthetics, art, and literature, as well as ethics and government [with Daoism and Chan-Buddhism incorporated] are all founded on a certain "psychologism." . . . This psychologism . . . is a philosophical proposition that takes emotion as the *noumenon*. From its ethical origins to the "realm of life," the entire stream of the history of Chinese thought has taken this type of sensuous psychology as the *noumenon*. The thing-in-itself is not, then, the spirit, nor is it a deity, nor morality or reason. Instead it is the psychology of human nature in which emotion and rationality are blended.[34]

What, then, is the *noumenon*—not only in an aesthetic, but in a most comprehensive sense?

It is ultimate reality, the origin of everything. According to the Confucian-based Chinese tradition, the *noumenon* is not nature, for a universe without humanity is meaningless. Nor is the *noumenon* a deity, for to ask humans to prostrate themselves before a god would not fit with the notions of "partnering in the transformation and nurturing of all things" or "establishing the heart of Heaven and earth" (*Doctrine of the Mean, Zhongyong* 中庸). It must follow, then, that the *noumenon* is humankind itself.[35]

Li's emphasis that the *noumenon* is the "psychology of human nature in which emotion and rationality are blended" reveals the way he understands his work as a contribution to an "anthropological ontology."

Lastly, it is interesting to note some analogies between past and present, specifically between the adaption of Buddhist thought and vocabulary, particularly by the Neo-Confucians of the Song period, and the present transferal of Western thought and terminology. Regarding the former, Li himself remarked, "In Returning to Confucianism by way of Chan-Buddhism, [the Neo-Confucians] greatly enriched their own thought by establishing this metaphysical *noumenal* realm in which aesthetics supersedes religion."[36] One is reminded here of Cai Yuanpei's assessment of the role of aesthetics for China: as is well known, Cai regarded Westerners to be largely shaped by religion, whereas for China he held aesthetics (a combination of ritual, art, and ethics) to be the functional "spiritual" equivalent to religion in the West. For this reason, he demanded for modern China "aesthetic education in the place of religion" (*yi meiyu dai zongjiao* 以美育代宗教).[37]

Returning to the analogy between China's intellectuals of today and the Song Dynasty Neo-Confucians, the present-day equivalent of Buddhism is Marxism. Just as the Neo-Confucians of the Song and Ming Dynasties were attracted by the "Western," foreign religion, Buddhism, but returned to Confucianism, incorporating much Buddhist thought in their new interpretation of Confucianism, so Li Zehou is greatly influenced by the new "Western" (civil) religion: the ideas of Karl Marx; but he also returned to Confucianism, incorporating much Marxian thought into his new interpretation of the Chinese aesthetic—and ethical—tradition. Li writes: "We have to pass through Marxist thought and go beyond it," and he sees Marxism as "a theory of the construction of material and spiritual life."[38]

Hence Marxism, in a sinicized form, has entered the Chinese "cultural-psychological formation." As the translator of Li's *The Chinese Aesthetic Tradition*, Maija Bell Samei, writes in her introduction, the Western scientific worldview and post-Enlightenment theories like Marxism "are being 'sedimented' into the latest incarnation of the Chinese people's 'cultural-psychological formation'"[39]—just like Buddhism before.

Seen from this perspective, Li Zehou's own development regarding aesthetics corresponds to his thesis in "Western learning as substance, Chinese learning for application" (*xi ti zhong yong* 西體中用), summarized as "one material civilization, multiple spiritual cultures."[40] Marxist thought refers to the universal conditions of our common (i.e., universal) material civilization, that is, to the "outer/external humanization of nature," whereas Confucian/Daoist thought refers to the particular Chinese spiritual culture: its ethics and aesthetics—the "inner humanization of nature."

## Final Remarks

Modern Chinese aesthetics must be seen in the context of the identity crisis triggered by the break with tradition at the beginning of the twenty-first century. China's self-perception since it was forced (in the late nineteenth and early twentieth centuries) by the violent actions of the colonial powers to come to terms with Western thought was that of a Chinese culture supported by aesthetics—in contrast to European culture, which Chinese intellectuals saw as dominated by religion (Christianity). Hence, the first approaches of this discipline, which was taken over from the West, were based on the endeavor to "discover one's own buried essence" by means of beauty and art—in other words, to rediscover a cultural identity and make it usable for gaining a new national integrity.[41] Today, aesthetics may have become, in the West, a barely noticed sub-discipline of philosophy, but not so in China: There, it occupies an eminent position in intellectual life. If one wants to better understand modern China, it would be necessary—through a change of perspective—to take a closer look at China's self-image, which is shaped by its own cultural and aesthetic tradition.

Li Zehou's historiography of aesthetics at the end of the 1970s, which "emerged in the immediate aftermath of the equally radical rupture of the Cultural Revolution,"[42] as well as his second book written at the end of the 1980s, follow this new line by also viewing Chinese culture predominantly as an "aesthetic" one, namely as a "culture of rites and music" (*liyue zhi wenhua*). But there are clear differences. Now it is also important to help the tradition, which was taboo during the Cultural Revolution, to regain its value. As the trauma of the encounter with the

West was a hundred years ago, the focus is, therefore, no longer on the sometimes rather constrained efforts resulting from national humiliation, such as those of the first generation of aestheticians, to point out the superiority of their own intellectual and artistic traditions. Much better, in Li Zehou's assessment of his own cultural tradition, that Chinese intellectuals find a new self-understanding, or a new stage of development, occasionally mixed with pride and pathos. The "aesthetic fever" triggered by Li's works, however, shows how much he hit the nerve of the time with his histories of aesthetics in China. It was the prelude to the "cultural fever"—the hot debate about one's own tradition and identity—that characterized the second half of the 1980s in China until it was ended by the events of the summer of 1989. The fact that Western theoretical approaches, such as those of Marx, still serve as a starting point but in the further course are transferred into Chinese thinking, is only a further sign of the now more unbiased attitude toward one's own tradition as well as for China's well-known strength, already demonstrated in the reception of Buddhism, of turning foreign thought into something unmistakably Chinese.

# Notes

1. This article is based on my introduction to the German translation of Li's *The Path of Beauty* as *Der Weg des Schönen: Wesen und Geschichte der chinesischen Kultur und Ästhetik*, ed. Karl-Heinz Pohl and Gudrun Wacker (Freiburg: Herder, 1992), 10–19; (Bochum: Europäischer Universitätsverlag, 2022), 18–27.

2. Li Zehou, *The Path of Beauty: A Study of Chinese Aesthetics*, trans. Gong Lizeng (Beijing: Morning Glory Publishers, 1988; Oxford: Oxford University Press, 1994). The page references in the following are to the 1994 edition.

3. Li Zehou 李澤厚, "Guanyu Zhongguo meixueshi de jige wenti" 關於中國美學史的幾個問題 (A Few Questions Concerning a History of Chinese Aesthetics), in 李澤厚哲學美學文選 (*A Collection of Li Zehou's Works on Philosophy and Aesthetics*) (Changsha: Hunan renmin chubanshe, 1985), 413–16. See also Heinrich Geiger, "Die Pragmatik der großen Systeme: Überlegungen zu einer eng- und einer weitgefaßten Geschichtsschreibung der chinesischen Ästhetik, ausgehend von einem Text Li Zehous," *Chinablätter* 18 (November 1991): 166–77. Geiger, however, characterizes *The Path of Beauty* there as a "narrowly conceived" history of aesthetics.

4. America is called in Chinese *meiguo* 美國—literally "beautiful land," thus *mei* (beautiful) often stands for "America" or "American"; the word for

"studies" in Chinese is *xuewen* 學問. Hence, the combination *meixue* can also be understood as "American studies." Li Zehou 李澤厚, "Shenme shi meixue" 什么是美学 (What is Aesthetics?)," in *Zou wo ziji de lu* 走我自己的路 (*Going My Own Way*) (Taipei: Fengyun shidai chubangongsi, 1990), 73.

5. As to the development of aesthetics in the modern period, see my article: Karl-Heinz Pohl, "'Western Learning as Substance, Chinese Learning for Application': Li Zehou's Thought on Tradition and Modernity," in *Li Zehou and Confucian Philosophy*, eds. Roger T. Ames and Jinhua Jia (Honolulu: University of Hawai'i Press, 2018), 57–73.

6. Li Zehou began a "narrow" history in 1984 in collaboration with Liu Gangji: his multi-volume (though unfinished) *History of Chinese Aesthetics* (*Zhongguo meixue shi* 中國美學史) (Beijing: Zhongguo shehui kexue chubanshe, vol. 1, 1984).

7. Heinrich Geiger, *Philosophische Ästhetik im China des 20. Jahrhunderts: Ihre Stellung zwischen Tradition und Moderne* (Frankfurt: Peter Lang, 1987), 36.

8. Karl Marx, "Private Property and Communism," in *Economic and Philosophic Manuscripts of 1844*, trans. Martin Milligan, www.marxists.org/archive/marx/works/1844/manuscripts/comm.htm, 44. ("Also die *Gesellschaft* ist die vollendete Wesenseinheit des Menschen mit der Natur, die wahre Resurrektion der Natur, der durchgeführte Naturalismus des Menschen und der durchgeführte Humanismus der Natur.")

9. In the original German, the phrases "consistent humanism of nature" and "consistent naturalism of man" are translations of "durchgeführter Humanismus der Natur" and "durchgeführter Naturalismus des Menschen." I am thankful to Gregor Paul, who remarked that, unlike the English "consistent," the German word "durchgeführt" (carried through) implies completed processes; hence, the "certain twist" with which Li Zehou interprets these phrases—as humanization and naturalization—appears justified on the basis of the original German wording. Today, the official Chinese translation of the passage is as follows: 因此, 社會是人同自然界的完成了的本質的統一, 是自然界的真正復活, 是人的實現了的自然主義和自然界的實現了的人道主義. www.marxists.org/chinese/marx/marxist.org-chinese-marx-1844.htm. The Chinese wording, *shixianliao de ziranzhuyi/rendaozhuyi* (實現了的自然主義/人道主義: realized naturalism/humanism) appears closer to the original German (*durchgeführt*) than the Englisch "consistent." Paul also pointed out that, a page earlier, Marx has the phrases "vollendeter Humanismus/Naturalismus" (completed humanism/naturalism), which is translated into English as "fully developed humanism/naturalism": "This communism, as fully developed naturalism, equals humanism, and as fully developed humanism equals naturalism; it is the *genuine* resolution of the conflict between man and nature and between man and man" ("Dieser Kommunismus ist als vollendeter Naturalismus Humanismus, als vollendeter Humanismus Naturalismus, er ist die *wahrhafte* Auflösung des Widerstreites zwischen dem Menschen mit der Natur und mit dem Menschen").

10. Li Zehou 李澤厚, "Meigan tan" 美感談 (On Aesthetic Perception), in *Li Zehou zhexue meixue wenxuan* 李澤厚哲學美學文選 (*A Collection of Li Zehou's Works on Philosophy and Aesthetics*) (Changsha: Hunan renmin chubanshe, 1985), 384.

11. Li, "On Aesthetic Perception," 386.

12. Li, *The Path of Beauty*, 235f.

13. Clive Bell, *Art* (New York: Frederick Stokes Co.,1914); Susanne Langer, *Feeling and Form: A Theory of Art Developed from Philosophy in a New Key* (New York: Macmillan, 1953).

14. Li, *The Path of Beauty*, 9.

15. Li, "A Few Questions Concerning a History of Chinese Aesthetics," 432f.

16. Li, "A Few Questions," 419–30; see also Geiger, "Die Pragmatik," 168–71.

17. *Analects*, 8.8. Cf. James Legge, *Confucian Analects, The Great Learning and The Doctrine of the Mean* (New York: Dover, 1971), 211. See also Li, *The Chinese Aesthetic Tradition*, 49.

18. Li, "A Few Questions Concerning a History of Chinese Aesthetics," 429f.

19. Picture-Commentary to the first Hexagram *Qian* (乾) in the *Book of Changes* (*Yijing* 易經). Richard John Lynn, *The Classic of Changes: A New Translation of the I Ching as Interpreted* (New York: Columbia University Press, 1994), 130.

20. *Analects*, 6.21. Cf. Legge, *Confucian Analects*, 192.

21. Li Zehou 李澤厚, "Shitan Zhongguo de zhihui" 試談中國的智慧 (Some Remarks on Chinese Wisdom), in *Lun Zhongguo chuantong wenhua* 論中國傳統文化 (*On Traditional Chinese Culture*) (Beijing: Academic Lecture Series on Chinese Culture, vol. 1, 1988), 37f.

22. Li Zehou 李澤厚, "Lun meigan, mei he yishu (janjiu tigang)—jianlun Zhu Guangqian de weixinzhuyi meixue sixiang" 論美感、美與藝術 (研究提綱)—兼論朱光潛的理想主義美學思想 (On Aesthetic Perception, Beauty, and Art (A Research Proposal)—Also on Zhu Guangqian's Idealist Aesthetic Thought), *Zhexue yanjiu* 哲學研究 (*Studies of Philosophy*) 5 (1956). See also Qi Zhixiang 祁志祥, *Li Zehou shijian meixue sixiang ji chengjiu de xitong pingxi* 李澤厚實踐美學思想及成就的系統性評析 (*A Systematic Review of Li Zehou's Practical Aesthetic Thought and Achievements*) (Shanghai: Jiaotong University, 2021).

23. Li Zehou, *The Chinese Aesthetic Tradition*, trans. Maija Bell Samei (Honolulu: University of Hawai'i Press, 2009).

24. Li, *The Chinese Aesthetic Tradition*, vii.

25. Li, *The Chinese Aesthetic Tradition*, x, 225; Li Zehou and Jane Cauvel, *Four Essays on Aesthetics: Toward a Global View* (Lanham, MD: Lexington Books, 2006), 170–71.

26. See note 8 above.

27. Li, *The Chinese Aesthetic Tradition*, 72.

28. Adele Rickett, *Wang Kuo-wei's Jen-chien Tz'u-hua—A Study in Chinese Literary Criticism* (Hong Kong: Hong Kong University Press, 1977), 23ff;

Karl-Heinz Pohl, *Ästhetik und Literaturtheorie in China: Von der Tradition bis zur Moderne* (München: Saur, 2007), 409ff.

29. Wing-tsit Chan, *A Source Book in Chinese Philosophy* (Princeton, NJ: Princeton University Press, 1963), 372. The term entered the realm of poetics through Wang Changling's 王昌齡 (Tang Dynasty) "Poetical Patterns" (*Shige* 詩格, transmitted in Japanese by the Japanese monk Kûkai 空海, 774–835: *Bunkyô hifuron* 文鏡秘府論).

30. Pohl, *Ästhetik und Literaturtheorie in China*, 165f.

31. Li, *The Chinese Aesthetic Tradition*, xvi, 210.

32. Li and Liu, *History of Chinese Aesthetics*, 33f.

33. Jana Rošker informed me some more about the usage of these terms and made the following helpful comment: "There are two 'usual translations' for ontology in Chinese; namely *bentilun* and *cunyoulun* 存有論. Although the latter is more commonly used in Taiwan than in PRC, it might be more appropriate, especially because it avoids the problematic rendering of the Western philosophical term substance, which actually has no equivalent in the Chinese intellectual history."

34. Li, *The Chinese Aesthetic Tradition*, xvii, 219.

35. Li, *The Chinese Aesthetic Tradition*, 223.

36. Li, *The Chinese Aesthetic Tradition*, xv, 191.

37. Li, *The Chinese Aesthetic Tradition*, 212; Liu Gangji, "Verbreitung und Einfluß der deutschen Ästhetik in China," *Trierer Beiträge: Aus Forschung und Lehre an der Universität Trier* Sonderheft 10 (July 1996): 8–13. And the famous writer of this époque, Lin Yutang 林語堂 (1895–1976), remarked that "poetry may well be called the Chinaman's religion." Lin Yutang, *My Country and My People* (London: William Heine Mann, 1936), 230.

38. Li and Cauvel, *Four Essays on Aesthetics*, 170, cited by Maija Bell Samei in her translation of *The Chinese Aesthetic Tradition* (Honolulu: University of Hawai'i Press, 2010), 225. Bell Samei adds that Marxism is not seen here with its narrative of class struggle.

39. Li, *The Chinese Aesthetic Tradition*, xviii.

40. Li Zehou, "Human Nature and Human Future: A Combination of Marx and Confucius," in *Chinese Thought in a Global Context. A Dialogue Between Chinese and Western Philosophical Approaches*, ed. Karl-Heinz Pohl (Leiden: Brill, 1999), 129–44. Cf. also Pohl, "'Western Learning as Substance, Chinese Learning for Application.'"

41. Geiger, *Philosophische Ästhetik*, 19.

42. By his own admission, Li completed *The Path of Beauty* in a few months in 1979, drawing on older preparatory work. Li Zehou 李澤厚, "Yu Taiwan xuezhe Jiang Dongguan yu *Mei de licheng* de duitan lu" 與台灣學者蔣勳關於"美的歷程"的對談錄 (Record of a Conversation on the *Path of Beauty* with the Taiwanese Scholar Jiang Dongguan), in *Zou wo ziji de lu* 走我自己的路 (*Going My Own Way*) (Taipei, Fengyun shidai chubangongsi, 1990), 438ff.

# Bibliography

Bell, Clive. *Art*. New York: Frederick Stokes Co., 1914.
Chan, Wing-tsit. *A Source Book in Chinese Philosophy*. Princeton, NJ: Princeton University Press, 1963.
Geiger, Heinrich. *Philosophische Ästhetik im China des 20. Jahrhunderts: Ihre Stellung zwischen Tradition und Moderne*. Frankfurt: Peter Lang, 1987.
Geiger, Heinrich. "Die Pragmatik der großen Systeme: Überlegungen zu einer eng- und einer weitgefaßten Geschichtsschreibung der chinesischen Ästhetik, ausgehend von einem Text Li Zehous." *Chinablätter* 18 (Nov. 1991): 166–77.
Langer, Susanne. *Feeling and Form: A Theory of Art Developed from Philosophy in a New Key*. New York: Macmillan, 1953.
Legge, James. *Confucian Analects, The Great Learning and The Doctrine of the Mean*. 1893. Reprint, New York: Dover, 1971.
Li Zehou. *The Chinese Aesthetic Tradition*. Translated by Maija Bell Samei. Honolulu: University of Hawai'i Press, 2009.
Li Zehou 李澤厚. "Guanyu Zhongguo meixueshi de jige wenti" 關於中國美學史的幾個問題 (A Few Questions Concerning a History of Chinese Aesthetics). In *Li Zehou zhexue meixue wenxuan* 李澤厚哲學美學文選(*A Collection of Li Zehou's Works on Philosophy and Aesthetics*), 413–33. Changsha: Hunan renmin chubanshe, 1985.
Li Zehou 李澤厚. *Huaxia meixue* 華夏美學 (*The Chinese Aesthetic Tradition*). Beijing: Xinhua Shudian, 1989.
Li Zehou. "Human Nature and Human Future: A Combination of Marx and Confucius." In *Chinese Thought in a Global Context. A Dialogue Between Chinese and Western Philosophical Approaches*, edited by Karl-Heinz Pohl, 129–44. Leiden: Brill, 1999.
Li Zehou 李澤厚. "Lun meigan, mei he yishu (janjiu tigang)—Jianlun Zhu Guangqian de weixinzhuyi meixue sixiang" 論美感、美和藝術（研究提綱）—兼論朱光潛的唯心主義美學思想 (On Aesthetic Feeling, Beauty, and Art (A Research Proposal)—Also on Zhu Guangqian's Idealist Aesthetic Thought). *Zhexue yanjiu* 哲学研究 (*Studies of Philosophy*) 5 (1956): 43–73.
Li Zehou 李澤厚. *Mei de licheng* 美的歷程 (*The Path of Beauty*). Beijing: Wenwu chubanshe, 1981.
Li Zehou 李澤厚. "Meigan tan" 美感談 (On Aesthetic Perception). In *Li Zehou zhexue meixue wenxuan* 李澤厚哲學美學文選 (*A Collection of Li Zehou's Works on Philosophy and Aesthetics*), 377–412. Changsha: Hunan renmin chubanshe, 1985.
Li Zehou. *The Path of Beauty: A Study of Chinese Aesthetics*. Translated by Gong Lizeng. Beijing: Morning Glory Publishers, 1988; Hong Kong: Oxford University Press, 1994.

Li Zehou 李澤厚. "Shenme shi meixue" 什麼是美學 (What is Aesthetics). In *Zou wo ziji de lu* 走我自己的路 (*Going My Own Way*), 73–79. Taipei: Fengyun shidai chubangongsi (revised edition), 1990.

Li Zehou 李澤厚. "Shitan Zhongguo de zhihui" 試談中國的智慧 (Some Remarks on Chinese Wisdom). In *Lun Zhongguo chuantong wenhua* 論中國傳統文化 (*On Traditional Chinese Culture*). Beijing: Academic Lecture Series on Chinese Culture, vol. 1, 1988.

Li Zehou 李澤厚. "Shitan Zhongguo de zhihui" 試談中國的智慧 (Exploring Chinese Wisdom). In *Zhongguo sixiangshi lun* 中國思想史論 (*On China's Intellectual History*), part 3, 299–325. Hefei: Anhui wenyi chubanshe, 1999.

Li Zehou 李澤厚. "Yu Taiwan xuezhe Jiang Dongguan yu *Mei de licheng* de duitan lu" 與台灣學者蔣動關於 "美的歷程" 的對談錄 (Record of a Conversation on the *Path of Beauty* with the Taiwanese Scholar Jiang Dongguan). In *Zou wo ziji de lu* 走我自己的路 (*Going My Own Way*), 438–47. Taipei, Fengyun shidai chubangongsi (revised edition), 1990.

Li Zehou and Jane Cauvel. *Four Essays on Aesthetics: Toward a Global View*. Lanham, MD: Lexington Books, 2006.

Li Zehou 李澤厚 and Liu Gangji 劉綱紀. *Zhongguo meixue shi* 中國美學史 (*History of Chinese Aesthetics*), vol. 1. Beijing: Zhongguo shehui kexue chubanshe, 1984.

Lin Yutang. *My Country and My People*. London: William Heine Mann, 1936.

Liu Gangji. "Verbreitung und Einfluß der deutschen Ästhetik in China." *Trierer Beiträge: Aus Forschung und Lehre an der Universität Trier* Sonderheft 10 (July 1996): 8–13.

Lynn, Richard John. *The Classic of Changes: A New Translation of the I Ching as Interpreted*. New York: Columbia University Press, 1994.

Marx, Karl. *Economic and Philosophic Manuscripts of 1844*. Translated by Martin Milligan. www.marxists.org/archive/marx/works/1844/manuscripts/comm.htm.

Pohl, Karl-Heinz. *Ästhetik und Literaturtheorie in China: Von der Tradition bis zur Moderne*. München: Saur, 2007.

Pohl, Karl-Heinz. "Einführung." In *Der Weg des Schönen. Wesen und Geschichte der chinesischen Kultur und Ästhetik*, edited by Karl-Heinz Pohl and Gudrun Wacker, 10–19. Freiburg: Herder, 1992. (New edition: Bochum: Europäischer Universitätsverlag, 2022, 18–27).

Pohl, Karl-Heinz. "'Western Learning as Substance, Chinese Learning for Application': Li Zehou's Thought on Tradition and Modernity." In *Li Zehou and Confucian Philosophy*, edited by Roger T. Ames and Jinhua Jia, 57–73. Honolulu: University of Hawai'i Press, 2018.

Rickett, Adele. *Wang Kuo-wei's Jen-chien Tz'u-hua—A Study in Chinese Literary Criticism*. Hong Kong: Hong Kong University Press, 1977.

Qi Zhixiang 祁志祥. *Li Zehou shijian meixue sixiang ji chengjiu de xitong pingxi* 李澤厚實踐美學思想及成就的系統性評析 (A Systematic Review of Li Zehou's Practical Aesthetic Thought and Achievements). Shanghai: Jiaotong University, 2021.

# Part 6
# Discursive Dialogues

15

# The Origins of Chinese Culture and the Question of Shamanism

## Li Zehou and Xu Fuguan

Maja Maria Kosec

### Writing the History of Thought: Philosophically vs. Historically

Li Zehou was one of the leading theorists of the modern Confucian renewal, world theory of humanism, ethics, aesthetics, and philosophical anthropology. He was also the author of one of the most influential and scholarly innovative studies analyzing the beginnings of Chinese culture.[1] As Paul D'Ambrosio notes in his chapter in this volume, contemporary philosophy professors usually write in clear, logical, and tightly argued structures, with very little variation from what is "acceptable" to academic standards.[2] In terms of this type of style Li is, as we will see, often lacking. "But when we contextualize him in a master and commentator tradition," argues D'Ambrosio, "we can better appreciate the breadth and consequence of his manner of philosophizing *with* texts, rather than merely *on* them."[3] In order to evaluate Li Zehou's theory of the shamanistic-historical tradition in the context of his time, the present article offers a critical comparison of his and Xu Fuguan's (徐復觀, 1903–1982)[4] understandings of the origin of Chinese culture.

Xu Fuguan is known as one of the representatives of the second generation of Modern New Confucians (*xin ruxue* 新儒學),[5] the stream of thought that, to some extent, also influenced Li Zehou's work. And although Li disagreed in many ways with Modern New Confucians, their common point was a strong emphasis on Chinese history and traditions, with which they were all well familiar. This helped them interpret where China was at the time and where it might be headed in the future.[6] A small part of this analysis that both Li and Xu dealt with was the role of the ruler during the period of transition between the Shang (商, 1600–1046 BCE) and Zhou (周, 1046–221 BCE) dynasties.

The present article thus aims to compare Li and Xu's respective understandings of the roles and positions of King Wen (文王, 1112–050 BCE) and the Duke of Zhou (周公, reigned 1042–1035 BCE) in Chinese history. King Wen and the Duke of Zhou—the legendary founders of the Zhou dynasty—were those who the two authors believed embodied the roles of both religious and political rulers during this period. The social changes and the transformation of beliefs during this time, when China slowly moved away from religion and into the realm of humanism and ethics, provide an important exception to Jaspers's proposed Axial Age. However, based on textual analysis, Li Zehou and Xu Fuguan develop their own views on the origins of the roles of religious and political authority, the reasons for the merging of these two authorities, and the impact of these early rulers on the further development of Chinese culture. The many similarities in Li's and Xu's understanding of these merged roles are accompanied by their differing views on whether or not these rulers were also shamans (*wu* 巫). This paper will focus on the key elements of their theories that explain the similarities and differences between their interpretations of the roles of King Wen and the Duke of Zhou, and the implications of these differences for their understanding of Chinese culture. These differences that manifest themselves through the present contrastive analysis of the ideas of both authors and their ideational backgrounds can simultaneously serve as an exposition of certain discursive or paradigmatic differences between the work of a philosopher and a historian. Their methodological starting point, as we will read in the following quotations, is just the opposite. In his book on Xu, Huang Chun-Chieh notes that Xu believes that researchers into intellectual history should start with the tangible (the written text) and move toward the abstract (thought).[7] Then, from the abstraction of thought, these researchers should turn to the concrete reality of human life. This approach is exactly the opposite of Li's own description of his work.

In 1978 I claimed that one can write the history of thought in two ways, historically and philosophically, and that these correspond to the respective methods of "my thought commentating on the classics" and "the classics commentating on my thought." My statements roused a bit of criticism. Regrettably, to this day I remain able to write only through the method of "the classics commentating on my thought": fabricating concepts and providing perspectives with which to examine the phenomena of our world.[8]

In the following we will examine how these conflicting methodological clues are reflected in Li's philosophical and Xu's historical interpretation of the origin of Chinese culture.

## Early Chinese Shamanism and Religion

To put the discussion in a broader theoretical context, we can begin with the so-called Axial Age. Many Chinese scholars believe that during the time that Karl Jaspers[9] refers to as the Axial Age, China transitioned from a period of natural religion to a period where the ethics of humanism were prominent.[10] While the Shang religion emphasized fertility worship based on its agricultural system, the nomadic Zhou culture focused primarily on the sun and star worship typical of nomads and their mostly shamanistic religiosity. In the merging of these two cultures, the cults of the victorious Zhou culture naturally prevailed, but at the same time some of the elements from the heritage of the overthrown Shang were also adopted. The result of this fusion was the rise in importance of the ancestor cult, which retained its significance throughout China's history.[11] It is also worth noting that although the Shang people believed in the supreme ruler *Shangdi* (上帝) or Heaven (*Tian* 天), the latter originally contained no ethical or anthropomorphic elements. It was only in the beginning of the Zhou dynasty that *Tian* became perceived almost as an anthropomorphic entity. However, this belief in *Tian* as creator and supreme moral authority began to wane rapidly in the following decades, leading to a transition from religion to humanism in the period between the Western Zhou (西周, 1046–771 BCE) and Eastern Zhou periods (東周, 770–221 BCE).[12] According to numerous Chinese scholars, China is a major exception to Jaspers's theory of the Axial Age, which states that in the period between the eighth and fourth centuries BCE, all developed cultures began to doubt the systems of natural religions and developed higher forms of mostly monotheistic religious systems.[13] As Chen Lai points out,[14] this change occurred because people recognized the limitations of deities and therefore shifted their focus to the real world of human relations and social regulations. Thus, the breakthrough that Jaspers understands as a "breakthrough towards transcendence" was, according to the Modern New Confucians and especially Xu Fuguan, actually a "breakthrough towards humanities" in China.

## Interconnection of Religion and Politics in the Early Zhou Dynasty

Researching the interconnection between religion and politics in the early Zhou dynasty, some of the key questions are as follows: What were the reasons for the breakthrough toward humanities that occurred in this time? And what consequences did this have for the further shaping of Chinese culture and history? Here, of course, the ideational and philosophical explanations differ greatly between different streams of thought and authors. Xu and Li worked roughly in the same historical period, but, as already mentioned, belonged to different currents and methodologies. Before elaborating on their theories we will take a look at their backgrounds.

Despite the many similarities and points of agreement between Li Zehou and the Modern New Confucians, there are also many significant differences between them. One of the major points of divergence comes from their different views on the history of Confucian philosophy, on ontology (especially on the question of transcendence and immanence), on the question of the human self, and on the question of relation between the individual and society.[15] The Modern New Confucians saw the humans as immanent and transcendent, a view developed in China at the same period, when religion was abolished and transformed into morality and a part of the human mind. Through this historical process of social transformation, the Modern New Confucians believed, the idea of *Tian* was transformed from an almost anthropomorphic higher force into the criteria for an inner human morality and ethics.[16] Li Zehou does not rely on the same hypothesis as the second generation of Modern

New Confucians. Instead, he describes the worldview that he believes prevailed in the Chinese tradition as a "one-world view" (*yige shijie* 一個世界觀). This view, which he believes developed from rationalized shamanism, means that there is only one world, the world in which we live. There is neither the need nor the possibility to transcend to any higher realm. Based on this belief, Li sharply criticizes the Modern New Confucians' concept of immanent transcendence and their notion of double ontology.[17]

## Xu Fuguan and the Awakening of the Humanistic Spirit

Xu's historically based theory about the position and importance of political and religious leaders in early Chinese history, while not directly touching on Jaspers's theory of the Axial Age, deals with the same period and its developments. Xu begins his explanation, which he sets forth most clearly in *The History of Humanness in China* (*Zhongguo renxinglun shi* 中國性論史), with a discussion of early Chinese religion and its transition to the spirit of humanism in the early Zhou dynasty. At the same time, he also assesses the role that King Wen and his son, the Duke of Zhou, played in this process. He draws his conclusions from an in-depth hermeneutical analysis of Zhou dynasty texts,[18] highlighting in particular the concept of *concerned consciousness* (*youhuan yishi* 憂患意識) of the new rulers at the time of coming to power. This concept of *concerned consciousness* forms the main concept of Xu Fuguan's philosophy.

Xu emphasizes the importance of ancestor worship in ancient China, saying that the religious lives of the people during the Shang dynasty were mainly determined by their ancestral gods. Their relationship with Heaven functioned through their ancestors as intermediaries, and the same form of worship was later adopted by the Zhou. Although the rise of the Zhou has often been interpreted as "the barbarian state taking power over the civilized one," Xu believes that the Zhou's victory over the Shang was due to the fact that a more spiritually conscious group defeated a less conscious group.[19]

> All human cultures begin with religion. China is no exception. But cultures also form a set of clear and rational ideas that influence the development of human behavior—they must develop a certain level of self-awareness in people. The original religions, however, are usually characterized by

a primitive belief in supernatural miracle powers, rooted in a sense of dread of extinction and catastrophes that can be caused by Heaven/nature. In such religions there is absolutely no consciousness of self-awareness. Highly developed religions differ from each other depending on the society and epoch in which they originated. Therefore, they can either accelerate or inhibit human self-consciousness.[20]

Xu believes, on the basis of the bronze vessels from the Shang period, that Chinese culture appears relatively highly developed. However, looking at the inscriptions on bones and tortoise shells from that period, we can see that the spiritual lives and the religion of the Shang people were still primitive. Their lives were completely dependent on various deities, especially of the ancestral spirits, the nature deities, and the supreme ruler Shang Di.[21] "The contribution of the people of the Zhou period was to bring into this traditional religious life the spirit of self-awareness. In doing so, they brought a culture that had until then been based on material achievements into the realm of ideas, helping to establish a humanistic spirit of Chinese morality."[22]

Traditional Chinese culture and philosophy developed from a sense of *anxiety* or *concerned consciousness*, which arose from awakening to one's own responsibility.[23] As Xu explains it,

> Anxiety (*youhuan*) is the psychological state of a person when his feeling of responsibility urges him to overcome certain difficulties, and he has not got through them yet. . . . In a religious atmosphere centered around faith, a person relies on faith for salvation. He hands all the responsibilities to God and will therefore have no anxiety. His confidence is his trust in God. Only when one takes over the responsibility oneself will he have a sense of anxiety. This sense of anxiety entails a strong will and a spirit of self-reliance.[24]

Xu Fuguan particularly highlights the emergence and development of the concept of *concerned consciousness* in the period between the Shang and Zhou Dynasties. He points out that the new Zhou kings were afraid of losing the Mandate of Heaven (*Tian ming* 天命) after the Shang were overthrown. "The Zhou people did change the mandate of the Yin [Shang]; in other words, they became the new winners. However, what one understands from reading the texts and documents from the beginning of the Zhou dynasty does not give the impression of a high-and-mighty atmosphere that characterizes most nations after winning a war. The feeling reflected in those texts appears more like what the classic Yizhuan called a 'concerned' consciousness."[25] Through this constant deep fear (*kongbu* 恐怖), they became aware of the connection between their own actions and "fortune or misfortune," which led to a shift from the "the divine" to the "the human" and gave rise to specific Chinese humanism.[26] Xu believes that as people began to doubt the Mandate of Heaven, they slowly shifted the focus of their concern from external deities to their own inwardness, which gradually freed them from dependence on religion. However, in the early Zhou era, according to Xu, it was still too early to completely break away from religion, so another transformation of religious thought had to take place first. People began to understand the Mandate of Heaven through their political leader.[27] Since there was no independent monastic class, political activities and religious activities were mostly inseparable. Consequently, people tended to view the will of the gods in the actions of political leaders, so that the immorality of political leaders simultaneously became a failure of the gods' credibility. With the lack of self-awareness of the humanistic spirit at the end of Shang rule, the loss of divine power only contributed to spiritual chaos, but did not seem to cause a fundamental rethinking of religion. However, in the Western Zhou dynasty this failure of the ruler led to the fall of the idea of the Mandate of Heaven, which led to the further development of humanism in China.[28]

## Li Zehou and the Shamanistic-Historical Tradition

Let us now compare this historically based theory with another approach presented by Li Zehou. Li, the author of one of the most influential and scholarly innovative studies analyzing the beginnings of Chinese culture, approaches his interpretation from the standpoint of philosophical anthropology based on anthropo-historical ontology and his own elaboration of Marxist theory. Building on this, Li develops the idea of a shamanistic-historical tradition as the basic foundation of Chinese culture, which he details in his work *The Origins of Chinese Thought: From Shamanism to Ritual Regulations and Humanness* (2018).[29]

As mentioned earlier, Li sharply criticized the Modern New Confucian concept of immanent transcendence and their notion of double ontology. He therefore introduced his own concept, called the "one-world view," emphasizing that there is only one world: the concrete, historical, social world of human beings. This idea is closely related to another concept of Li Zehou's, namely the idea of "culture of joy" (*legan wenhua* 樂感文化). Li uses this concept, also translated as the "culture of optimism," to distinguish the Chinese cultural tradition from the Japanese "culture of shame" (*chigan wenhua* 耻感文化) or the Western "culture of guilt" (*zuigan wenhua* 罪感文化).[30] Since the "one-world view" rejects the possibility of the existence of any higher transcendental world that affects human life, Li believes that the Chinese tradition did not focus on the search for a higher meaning to reach a higher transcendent world. Therefore, their way of searching for ethical and social rules was more joyful, Li argues.[31] As he explains, the term *culture of joy* thus has a threefold semantic connotation, as it refers simultaneously to the "culture of worldly happiness" that characterizes Chinese tradition, to an optimism about one's ability to improve one's living conditions, and to the "culture of music and aesthetics."[32] "In Chinese heritage, such joy (*le*) is a symbol of the essence and function of music (*yue*), both of which are considered to be integral to human nature in the light of the teleological pursuit of ultimate joy or happiness."[33] The feeling of joy (*legan*) here refers to a set of emotions that were a necessary precondition for the formation of a sense of humaneness that developed in people from the union of their material and spiritual lives.[34] As Li explains, early shamanistic ceremonies played an extremely important role in this process. It was only during the transition from the Shang to the Zhou that the worship of totems in shamanistic dances and songs was gradually replaced by the humanized and rationalized worship of heroes and ancestors,[35] which became one of the most important primordial phenomena of Chinese culture. In his explanation, Li relies on a Chinese archaeologist, Chen Mengjia 陳夢家 (d. 1966), who tells us that ancestor worship and the worship of celestial gods gradually converged and intermingled, giving rise to the paradigm of post-Shang Chinese religion, specifically the predominance of ancestor worship over the worship of celestial gods. With this gradual integration of gods and ancestor worship, the integration of religious and political authority also took place. According to Li, this fusion and subsequent continuation of the rationalized form of shamanism became key to understanding Chinese thought and culture.[36] As Byung-seok Jung explains, Li believes that shamanic culture ensured that religion and politics could not develop independently in China. Since ethics, religion, and politics were based on the system of rites rooted in shamanism, they became unified and formed a ruling structure and ideology—Confucianism.[37] The line between the dead and the living, between people and their spirits, had always been blurred in Chinese tradition, and the practice of serving the dead was tantamount to serving the living, and this continued for centuries. Jana Rošker[38] explains that Li believes that, because of the relics passed down from shamanistic culture that closely linked the spiritual and human worlds, the latter's position was elevated to the point that people generally could not fully comprehend their human limitations and began to search for meaning themselves, without the help of external forces. However, this connection between the realms of the dead and the living had very particular means of realization that fell within the domain of the shamans.[39] Here Li relies again on Chen Mengjia, who asserts "The king himself, although a political leader, was also the community's head shaman."[40] Without further discussion Li concludes, "That is to say, although various aspects of shamanistic practice were taken on by the various specialist positions of shaman, supplicant, diviner, and historian, the ultimate and most important shaman was the political leader. This 'king' was the principal communicator between the spiritual and human realm, as well as the final authority in decision and direction of activity. This means that the political leader fundamentally possessed the highest religious authority for communicating with heaven."[41] Li's assumptions are, however, problematic on several levels. Since Chen Mengjia bases his statement entirely on Mircea Eliade's work *Shamanism: Archaic Techniques of Ecstasy*,[42] which has been widely and severely criticized for making romantic overgeneralizations based on little or no archaeological evidence, one might doubt the basis of Li's theory as at least a little shaky. Marthe Chandler points out:[43] "Of course there is no requirement that a philosopher do anthropological fieldwork, but it is important that philosophical theories at least be consistent with the scientific evidence, particularly perhaps a theory calling itself 'anthropological ontology.'"

However, as we have already noted, Li was never methodically looking for precise or thorough arguments, but to "lead people toward new ideas."[44] With this idea, then, Li points to further evidence that supports his notion of the unity of shaman and king. Li cites several examples of the close connection between divination practices and the duties of the political ruler. From the oracles, for example, it appears that both divination and dancing belonged to the king's domain. The divination, for example, said "Divination: the king will dance"[45] and

"Divination: The king will not dance."[46] That being said, Li also claims that shamans, who were first the ones in charge of the divination, evolved into historians over time. To support this claim he notes the character for divination itself (shi 筮), which shows that divination was definitely the domain of the shaman in the beginning, as it is composed of the radicals for bamboo (zhu 竹) and for shaman (wu 巫). Li therefore argues that ancient divination practices evolved from the dynamic activity of shamans (shamanic ecstasy and dance ceremonies) to static numerical calculations, which he explains as a process of slow rationalization of shamanistic practices.[47]

> Divination, even more so than "shamanism," was pronounced in its connection to the activity of the king, especially political activity. Because of this, divinations recorded and preserved various important political and military experiences. . . . This is precisely the concrete expression of the process of rationalization "from shamanism to historicism." The world of shamanistic practice transformed into a world of symbolism, numbers, and historical events. Clearly, the emergence of divination, numerology, the Book of Changes, and the system of ritual regulations . . . forms a crucial link in the movement from shamanism to historicism.[48]

Another interesting point in Li's theory is his alternative interpretation of a passage from the Record of Rites, which states, "Before the king were shamans and behind him historians."[49] Li interprets this line, normally read as referring to the physical space, as referring to time "seeing the historian as a general office of following and inheriting the shaman's role in carrying out rituals of divination and sacrifice in service of the king."[50]

Li's explanation of the role of the shamans and rulers is based on the works of two previous scholars. In Li's chapter Reevaluating Confucius,[51] he explains that the Confucians emerged from the organizers and leaders of primitive ritual and shamanic practices—the shamans, officials, and scribes—and became preservers of what we know today as Confucian ritual and ceremony.[52] In this part Li quotes a late Qing scholar Zhang Binglin 章炳麟 (d. 1936), who wrote that Confucians, originally in charge of ritual and helping the ruler to accord with yin and yang forces,[53] were "shaman-officials" (shushi 術士)[54]—important figures both religiously and politically.[55] Based on this, Li argues, "The great Confucian figures of antiquity, such as Emperor Shun's minister Gao Yao 皋陶, Shang minister Yi Yin 伊尹 and the Duke of Zhou 周公 were all such shaman-officials, serving as both overseers of ritual and auxiliary rulers. The later Confucian idealization of a 'prime minister' (*zaixiang* 宰相) who helped the emperor rule the empire originated from this earlier role."[56] His other source on this matter is Chen Mengjia, based on whom in his essay *Preliminary Remarks on the Deep Structures of Confucianism*[57] Li argues that the ancient sage-kings of the Chinese tradition were shaman leaders, including those celebrated in Confucianism. "From the earliest shaman leaders to Yao 尧, Shun 舜, Yu 禹, Tang 汤, Wen 文, Wu 武, and the Duke of Zhou 周公, and even including Yi Yin 伊尹, Wu Xian 巫咸, and Bo Yi 伯益, all of these revered ancient legendary or historical political figure can be seen as great shamans who had consolidated both political power (kingly authority) and spiritual power (religious authority) into single person."[58]

So, should we understand the Duke of Zhou to be a ruler or an auxiliary ruler? If the latter, this explanation is much closer to that described by Xu Fuguan. While Li equates the role of the shaman with that of "king" or an "auxiliary ruler" or, later in Zhou, with that of "historian," Xu Fuguan notes that the status of the shaman was very high in the Shang dynasty, but that even in this period the main responsibility for worship lay with the king, not the shaman.[59] Thus, his opinion coincides with Li's regarding shaman-officials who later became historians in the Zhou dynasty, but not at all with that regarding shaman-kings.

After this outline of Xu and Li's respective interpretations of the development of the intertwining of politics and religion in the early periods of Chinese history, we can now analyze their theories about the role of the first rulers of the Zhou dynasty.

## King Wen and the Duke of Zhou

Before we begin discussing what role the first rulers of Zhou play in the theories of Li Zehou and Xu Fuguan, let us briefly look at King Wen and the Duke of Zhou from a historical perspective. King Wen was the ruler of Zhou, one of the semi-barbarian states on the western border of the Shang Empire. He began annexing part of the territory on the Shang border, but died before he could threaten the Shang capital. After his death, his son and successor, King Wu 武王 (d. 1043 BCE), destroyed the Shang and founded the Zhou dynasty. King Wen was posthumously honored as the founder of the Zhou dynasty and titled King. He was also the father of the Duke of Zhou, who later became one of the most important figures of reference in Confucian thought. King Wen died in 1050 BCE and was succeeded by his son and the actual founder of the Zhou dynasty, King Wu. Since Wu died at a young age, the throne was left to his son, thirteen-year-old King Cheng 成王 (reigned ca. 1042–1021 BCE). Since Cheng was too young to ascend the throne, his uncle, Wu's younger brother, the Duke of Zhou, took over the regency over the young king. He successfully suppressed the Rebellion of the Three Guards (1042–1039 BC),[60] but more importantly contributed much to the formation of Chinese culture.[61]

Let us now take a look at Xu Fuguan's understanding of their roles. As we have already seen, Xu emphasizes the inseparable connection between political and religious activities throughout Chinese history. This tight connection between both consequently led to the will of the gods being interpreted through the actions of political leaders, which meant that the immorality of political leaders simultaneously became a failure of the credibility of the gods, which was later followed by doubts about the Mandate of Heaven. Thus, in the early Zhou period people began to understand the Mandate of Heaven through King Wen.[62] They no longer revered him only as their ancestor or as a great political leader, but also associated him with the Mandate of Heaven for religious reasons. Xu points out that the *Book of Poetry* states,

> The appointment is not easily [preserved],
> Do not cause your own extinction.
> Display and make bright your righteousness and name,
> And look at [the fate of] Yin in the light of Heaven.
> The doings of High Heaven,
> Have neither sound nor smell.
> Take your pattern from King Wen,
> And the myriad regions will repose confidence in you.[63]

Xu Fuguan thus says that King Wen became the concrete manifestation of the Heavenly command, and "the virtue of King Wen" became the true substance of Shangdi. Therefore, the relationship between King Wen and the Divine went beyond the role of an intermediary and Wen actually became a representation of the gods. Xu says this has given some modern scholars the impression that King Wen was a shaman. However, Xu emphasizes that according to Shang period materials, the person responsible for worshipping the gods was already a political leader, not a shaman.[64] Unlike a religious leader, King Wen did not focus his mind on Heaven, but was primarily concerned with the problems of the present world. This position of King Wen in the eyes of the Zhou people is actually an expression of the awakening of the humanistic spirit in religion. The focus in that time started to slowly move away from Heaven and turn toward the role and responsibility of the people. This humanistic spirit became one of the characteristics of religion in the early Zhou dynasty and represents a crucial difference from Shang religion, Xu concludes.[65] King Wen's preoccupation with the present world was already part of the process of the awakening spirit of self-awareness and taking over of the responsibility for oneself, which led to a growing sense of anxiety.[66]

When Xu speaks of this sense of anxiety, or *concerned consciousness*, he emphasizes the role of the Duke of Zhou even more than that of King Wen. Although Xu does not claim that *concerned consciousness* was created by King Wen or the Duke of Zhou personally, as it is a concept that developed gradually during a long-term historical process, he closely associates its emergence with the early Zhou period. He points out that the new Zhou kings were afraid of losing the Mandate of Heaven after the Shang had been overthrown. By constantly keeping this deep fear in mind and becoming aware of the connection between their own actions and the consequences they had, a shift from religion to a specific Chinese humanism took place. As we have seen, King Wen gave great power to the country of Zhou, but he was not honored as the founder of the new dynasty until after his death. Thus, Xu believes that this concept of *concerned consciousness* emerged with King Wen, but developed mainly under the Duke of Zhou and was eventually manifested as ritual, and integrated into classical Confucianism under Confucius.[67]

But what about Li's interpretation? He believes that Confucian ethics goes back to a demand from the rulers that grew out of the ancient shamanistic tradition. It was the "magical" charisma or virtue (*de* 德) of the shamanic ruler that later gave rise to the idea of the sage-king and the integrated religious, ethical, and political requirements of ritual education.[68] Regarding King Wen, Li quotes *The Record of the Rites*—"When King Wen made sacrifice, his serving the dead was equivalent to serving the living"[69]—and interprets this as evidence that King

Wen was a shaman, who in this case was responsible for the practical and particular means of connecting with the ancestors. Li backs this up with a quote from the *Great Announcement*: "The Tranquillizing king [King Wen] left to me the great precious tortoise-shell, to bring into connection with me the intelligence of Heaven."[70] Li also emphasizes that it was believed that both King Wen and later the Duke of Zhou would receive the Mandate of Heaven and then ascend to Heaven, which he supports with the quotes from the Book of Poetry: "King Wen is on high, how bright is he in Heaven,"[71] and "The mandate of Heaven, oh how boundless in its profundity, how grandly illustrious, the purity of King Wen of Zhou's virtue."[72] Finally, in his opinion, the most important role of King Wen was that he was one of the pioneers of the process of rationalizing shamanism.

As we have seen from the above quotes, he also attributes the role of one of the last shaman-kings/shaman-officials to the Duke of Zhou. But more importantly, Li believes that the Duke of Zhou was the one who actually completed the process of rationalization of shamanism and historicism, and thus laid the foundation for China's predominant cultural tradition.[73] Historically, the first Chinese dynasties up to the Western Zhou are often referred to as cultures of "ritual and music" (*liyue* 禮樂), because the cultivation of human emotions was equated with an understanding of music during this period. Through ritual and music, the Duke of Zhou comprehensively rationalized and institutionalized the shamanistic ritual ceremonies of sacrificial ancestral worship and communication with the spirits that guided human affairs. This unification of government and religion then served as the normative criterion for the social order that characterized Zhou culture. In this way, the rituality of the Zhou dynasty began to represent a system of rules that maintained social order by orienting people to social norms.[74] In this regard, the establishment of the patrilineal, feudal, and sacrificial system, which was also realized by the Duke of Zhou, was also of epochal importance for Chinese history. Thus, the real reason Confucius praised him so highly is precisely his systematization of rites and music.[75] "It was not Confucius but the Duke of Zhou who comprehensively sorted, remolded, and standardized the primitive rituals of high antiquity up to the Shang dynasty," states Li.[76] And we can see that Confucius repeatedly emphasized that he was a "transmitter and not a maker, believing in and loving the ancients,"[77] "followed the Zhou,"[78] and "dreamed of the Duke of Zhou."[79] This indicates that he intended to preserve the inheritance of the Duke of Zhou in toto, Li argues. In the context of the Duke of Zhou's contribution, virtue (*de*) took on a very high status, gradually evolving "from a requirement to 'follow' norms and rules to an aspect of personal character." Simultaneously, *Tian* replaced Shang Di, displacing the previously important ruling anthropomorphic deity and marking a significant shift in thought between the Shang and Zhou periods.[80] "In the early Zhou period, 'virtue' was then raised to a new height, and became connected to the Duke of Zhou's comprehensive establishment of the clan-tribe-state's institutional norms of ritual and music, which centered on the political activity of the king. The 'virtuous governance' (*dezheng* 德政) of the institutionalization of ritual and music can be divided into two aspects, 'reverence *jing* 敬' and 'ritual *li* 禮,' which are respectively internal and external."[81] It was Confucius who, later, when music and ritual had already lost their social significance, rooted ritual in humaneness, this way ultimately completing the process of rationalization of internal shamanistic or magical emotion.[82]

## Conclusion

The differences in Xu's and Li's interpretation of the roles of political and religious rulers in the early Zhou period originate in their different interpretations of the developments that took place during the Axial Age. In his historically based theory, Xu claims that the Zhou people brought the culture based on material achievements into the realm of ideas and, through awakening to one's own responsibility, developed a sense of *concerned consciousness*. He believes that doubt about the Mandate of Heaven gradually freed people from dependence on religion and led the Chinese toward the formation of a humanistic spirit of Chinese morality. Since it was still too early in the early Zhou era to completely break away from religion, people began to understand the Mandate of Heaven through King Wen. Therefore, his relationship with the divine went beyond the role of a mediator, and Wen actually became a representation of the gods. Since King Wen did not focus on Heaven, but was primarily concerned with the problems of the present world, Xu believes that the concept of *concerned consciousness* as an expression of the awakening humanistic spirit in China originated with King Wen, developed further under the Duke of Zhou, and was finally integrated into classical Confucianism under Confucius. Somewhat the opposite of Xu's *concerned consciousness* is Li's concept of the *culture of joy*. Li bases his theory on the "one-world view," which rejects the possibility of the existence of a higher transcendental world. He believes that as Chinese tradition did not focus on the search for a higher meaning in order to reach a higher transcendental world, its way of searching for ethical and social rules was more joyful. This feeling of joy, a *culture of joy*, refers to a range of emotions that were a necessary precondition for the emergence of humaneness (ren 仁), which developed from the union of material and spiritual life. As Li explains, early shamanistic ceremonies played an extremely important role in this process, and it is precisely the understanding of this continuation of the rationalized form of shamanism that became key to understanding Chinese thought and cultures. Li here connects the role of the shaman-king with the power of the ruler over divination, thus interpreting King Wen as one of the last shaman-kings and, more importantly, as one of the pioneers of this rationalization of shamanistic practices. Since the cultivation of human emotions was equated with the understanding of music during this period, which can also be referred to with the same notion of a *culture of music and aesthetics* (*legan wenhua*), Zhou dynasty rituality began to represent a system of regulations, which through guiding people with social norms was able to sustain the social order. Through ritual and music, the Duke of Zhou then comprehensively rationalized and institutionalized the shamanistic ritual ceremonies of sacrificial ancestral worship and communication with the spirits that guided human affairs. This unification of government and religion then served as the normative criterion of the social order that characterized Zhou culture. It was Confucius who later, rooting ritual in humaneness, finally completed the process of the rationalization of shamanism.

Xu and Li both believe that the close connection between religion and politics in China originated in the practice of ancestor worship, and that in the Shang and early Zhou periods the highest religious role, that of the person responsible for serving the ancestors, was given to the political leader, the king. They also agree that during the Zhou dynasty shamans evolved into historians. However, Li's interpretation of how this occurred differs greatly from Xu Fuguan's. While Xu firmly rejects the idea that the kings of the Zhou period may also have been shamans, Li posits two different theories. In the first, he identifies the early auxiliary rulers with shaman-officials, as proposed by Zhang Binglin, while in the second, he asserts that the early kings were also the supreme shamans, as first proposed by Chen Mengjia. Although Li's two theories are not incompatible, they never appear together, as Li classifies the Duke of Zhou first as a shaman-official and then as a shaman-king. Here we need to keep in mind that the political role of the Duke of Zhou was also ambiguous: on the one hand, he was a ruler (ruling as a regent), while on the other hand, he was officially only one of the officials (advisers). So he could in some sense (and in parallel) be regarded as a shaman-official and as a supreme shaman.

In sum, the content of Xu's and Li's views on the position of King Wen and the Duke of Zhou are relatively similar. Their prominent role as political and religious leaders is undeniable, while whether or not they should also be understood as shamans is debatable. The role they attribute to these two kings, however, is somewhat less similar. The role Li attributes to King Wen is much more active (pioneer of the rationalization of shamanic practices) than that of Xu (symbol of the awakening of the humanistic spirit). In interpreting the role of the Duke of Zhou, however, we can note that Xu associates him primarily with the development of the concept of *concerned consciousness*, while Li presents him as the ruler who comprehensively established the institutional norms of ritual and music, which then served as the normative criteria of the social order of Chinese culture.

By comparing Li Zehou and Xu Fuguan, this article aimed to place Li's philosophical interpretation of the origins of Chinese culture in dialogue with Xu's historically grounded interpretation. Detached from the key elements of their theories that explain the similarities and differences between their interpretations of the roles of King Wen and the Duke of Zhou, and the implications of these differences for their understanding of Chinese culture, the significance of this contrastive analysis of the ideas and ideational backgrounds of both authors also manifests itself as an exposition of numerous differences between the work of a philosopher and a historian—something that readers of Li Zehou should definitely keep in mind when approaching his work.

## Notes

1. Jana S. Rošker, *The Rebirth of the Moral Self: The Second Generation of Modern Confucians and their Modernization Discourses* (Hong Kong: The Chinese University Press, 2016), 229.

2. See D'Ambrosio's contribution to this volume, "Li Zehou in the Tradition of Masters and Commentators."

3. See D'Ambrosio's contribution to this volume.

4. Xu was born in China in 1903, studied under Xiong Shili (熊十力, 1885–1968), and later devoted himself to philosophy, the sociology of culture, and literary and art criticism, becoming most famous as one of the first theorists of a specifically Chinese aesthetics in contemporary China. See Tea Sernelj, "Xu Fuguan's Concept of Anxiety and Its Connection to Religious Studies," *Asian Studies* 1, no. 2 (2013): 72.

5. Sernelj, "Xu Fuguan's Concept of Anxiety," 72.

6. Jana S. Rošker, "Li Zehou and the Modern Confucianism," lecture at Summer School on Li Zehou and Contemporary Chinese Thought, University of Ljubljana, June 17, 2022, *Klara Sofija Sanja*, July 23, 2022, video, 58:54, www.youtube.com/watch?v=g6o4I3RCPHE.

7. Chun-Chieh Huang, *Xu Fuguan in the Context of East Asian Confucianisms*, trans. Diana Arghirescu (Honolulu: University of Hawai'i Press, 2019), 21.

8. Li Zehou, *The Origins of Chinese Thought: From Shamanism to Ritual Regulations and Humanness*, trans. Robert A. Carleo III (Leiden: Brill, 2018), 11.

9. Karl Jaspers, *The Origin and Goal of History* (New Haven, CT: Yale University Press, 1965).

10. Zebo Yang 澤波楊, "Mou Zongsan chaoyue cunyou lun boyi—cong xian Qin tianlunde fazhan guiji kan Mou Zongsan chaoyue cunyou lunde quexian" 牟宗三超越存有論駁義—從先秦天論的發展軌跡看牟宗三超越存有論的缺陷 (Refutation of Mou Zong-san's Theory of Beyond Existence—Viewing the Defects of the Theory in Terms of the Evolution of Heaven Theory of Pre-Qin Period), *Journal of Literature, History and Philosophy* 284, no. 5 (2004): 111.

11. Jana S. Rošker, *Subjektova nova oblačila—idejne osnove modernizacije v delih druge generacije modernega konfucijanstva* (The Subject's New Clothes—the Ideational Foundations of Modernization in the Works of the Second Generation of Modern Confucians) (Ljubljana: Ljubljana University Press, 2021), 170–71.

12. Xu Fuguan 復觀徐, *Zhongguo renxinglun shi* 中國人性論史 (*The History of Humanness in China*) (Beijing: Huong shifandaxue chuban she, 2014), 152; Rošker, *The Subject's New Clothes*, 174–75. See also Benjamin I. Schwartz, *The World of Thought in Ancient China* (Cambridge, MA: The Belknap Press of Harvard University, 1985), 122.

13. Jaspers, *The Origin*, 2–6.

14. Chen Lai 陳來, *Gudai zongjiao yu lunli: Rujia sixiang de genyuan* 古代宗教與倫理: 儒家思想的根源 (*Ancient Religion and Ethics: The Source of Confucian Thought*) (Beijing: Beijing Daxue Chuban She, 2017), 4.

15. Rošker, "Li Zehou and the Modern Confucianism."

16. Rošker, *The Rebirth of the Moral Self*, 186–88.

# The Origins of Chinese Culture and the Question of Shamanism | 425

17. Rošker, *The Rebirth of the Moral Self*, 186–88.
18. Most of these texts would no longer be dated to the Zhou period by historians.
19. Xu, *The History of Humanness*, 15–16.
20. Xu, 15–16.
21. Xu, 15–16.
22. Xu, 15–16.
23. Sernelj, "Xu Fuguan's Concept of Anxiety," 78.
24. Xu, *The History of Humanness*, 20; trans. Sernelj, "Xu Fuguan's Concept of Anxiety," 79.
25. Xu, *The History of Humanness*, 19; trans. Huang, *Xu Fuguan in the Context of East Asian Confucianisms*, 24.
26. Xu, *The History of Humanness*, 20.
27. Xu, 25–26.
28. Xu, 37.
29. Published in Chinese as Li Zehou 李泽厚, *You wu dao li, shi li gui ren* 由巫到禮, 釋禮歸仁 (*From Shamanism to Ritual Regulations and Humaneness*) (Beijing: Sanlian shudian, 2015).
30. Jana S. Rošker, *Following His Own Path: Li Zehou and Modern Chinese Philosophy* (Albany: State University of New York Press, 2019), 119.
31. Paul J. D'Ambrosio, Robert A. Carleo III, and Andrew Lambert, "On Li Zehou's Philosophy: An Introduction by Three Translators," *Philosophy East and West* 66, no. 4 (2016): 1059.
32. Wang Keping, "Li Zehou's View of Pragmatic Reason," in *Li Zehou and Confucian philosophy*, ed. Roger T. Ames and Jinhua Jia (Honolulu: University of Hawai'i Press, 2018), 235.
33. Wang, "Li Zehou's View of Pragmatic Reason," 235.
34. Rošker, *Following His Own Path*, 120.
35. Tea Sernelj, "Modern Chinese Aesthetics and Its Traditional Backgrounds: A Critical Comparison of Li Zehou's Sedimentation and Jung's Archetypes," in *Li Zehou and Confucian Philosophy*, ed. Roger T. Ames and Jinhua Jia (Honolulu: University of Hawai'i Press, 2018), 339.
36. Li, *The Origins of Chinese Thought*, 12–14.
37. Byung-seok Jung, "Li Zehou's Doctrine of Emotion as Substance and Confucian Philosophy," in *Li Zehou and Confucian Philosophy*, ed. Roger T. Ames and Jinhua Jia (Honolulu: University of Hawai'i Press, 2018), 204.
38. Rošker, *Following His Own Path*, 122–23.
39. Li, *The Origins of Chinese Thought*, 14.
40. Chen Mengjia 陳夢家 in Li, *The Origins of Chinese Thought*, 15.
41. Li, *The Origins of Chinese Thought*, 15.
42. Mircea Eliade, *Shamanism: Archaic Techniques of Ecstasy*, trans. Willard R. Trask (Princeton, NJ: Princeton University Press, 1964).

43. Marthe Chandler, "Li Zehou, Kant, and Darwin: The Theory of Sedimentation," in *Li Zehou and Confucian Philosophy*, eds. Roger T. Ames and Jinhua Jia (Honolulu: University of Hawaiʻi Press, 2018), 279.

44. Li, *The Origins of Chinese Thought*, 11.

45. "貞，王其舞。" See Moruo Guo 沫若郭, ed., 甲骨文合集 (*Oracle Script Collection*) (Beijing: Zhonghua shuju, 1978–1983), No. 11006a.

46. "貞，王勿舞。" See Moruo Guo, No. 11006a.

47. Li, *The Origins of Chinese Thought*, 26.

48. Li, *The Origins of Chinese Thought*, 27.

49. "王，前巫而後史。" See James Legge, trans., *Liji* 禮記 (*The Book of Rites*), "Lu Yun, 25," *Chinese Text Project*, ctext.org/liji.

50. Li, *The Origins of Chinese Thought*, 27–28.

51. Originally published in the *Journal of the Chinese Academy of Social Sciences* 2 (1980): 77–96.

52. Li Zehou, *A History of Classical Chinese Thought*, trans. Andrew Lambert (New York: Routledge, 2020), 1–2.

53. Here we encounter an analysis that is ahistorical, for we know that the terms *yin* and *yang* first appear together only in the *Book of Odes*, and even there only as a designation for the results of the sun's reflection on the hill, and not yet as part of the *yin-yang* theory. See Robin R. Wang, *Yinyang: The Way of Heaven and Earth in Chinese Thought and Culture* (New York: Cambridge University Press, 2012), 24.

54. The English translation of the term is based on Andrew Lambert, translation of Li, *A History of Classical Chinese Thought*, 4.

55. Li, *A History of Classical Chinese Thought*, 4.

56. Li, *A History of Classical Chinese Thought*, 4.

57. Originally published as 初擬儒學深層結構說 (*Preliminary Remarks on the Deep Structures of Confucianism*) in 1996. For whole text see Appendix 3 in Li, *The Origins of Chinese Thought*, 211–28.

58. Li, *The Origins of Chinese Thought*, 16.

59. Xu, *The History of Humanness*, 36.

60. The rebellion of the Three Guards was a rebellion of the other three brothers of King Wu, who ruled the eastern part of the territory, against the self-appointed regency of the Duke of Zhou over the young King Cheng. See Mitja Saje, *Zgodovina Kitajske* (*History of China*) (Ljubljana: Slovenska matica, 2015), 72.

61. Saje, 71–72.

62. Xu, *The History of Humanness*, 25–26.

63. "命之不易、無爾卑。宣昭義問、有虞殷自天。上天之載、無聲無臭。儀刑文王、萬邦作孚。" See James Legge, trans., *Book of Rites* 礼记, "Ai Gong Wen" 哀公问, *Chinese Text Project*, ctext.org/liji/ens.

64. Xu, *The History of Humanness*, 27.

65. Xu, *The History of Humanness*, 26.
66. Xu, *The History of Humanness*, 20.
67. Xu, *The History of Humanness*, 30, and Huang, *Xu Fuguan in the Context of East Asian Confucianisms*, 149.
68. Li Zehou, "A Response to Michael Sandel and Other Matters," trans. Paul J. D'Ambrosio and Robert A. Carleo III, *Philosophy East and West* 66, no. 4 (2016): 1137.
69. "文王之祭也：事死者如事生。" See *Liji*, "Ji Yi 6," trans. Robert A. Carleo III in Li, *The Origins of Chinese Thought*, 14.
70. "天降威，龜用寧王遺我大寶，紹天明。" See James Legge, trans., *Shang shu* 尚書 (*The Book of History*), "Zhou Shu, Da gao, 3," *Chinese Text Project*, ctext.org/shang-shu/great-announcement.
71. James Legge, trans., *Shi jing* 詩經 (*The Book of Poetry*), "Da ya, Wen Wang zhi shi, Wen Wang 1," *Chinese Text Project*, ctext.org/book-of-poetry.
72. James Legge, trans., *Shi jing*, "Song, Zhou Song, Qing Miao zhi shi, Wei Tian Zhi Ming 1."
73. Li, *The Origins of Chinese Thought*, 32.
74. Li, *The Origins of Chinese Thought*, 32, and Jana S. Rošker, *Humanizem v medkulturni perspektivi: primer Kitajske* (*Humanism in Intercultural Perspective: The Case of China*) (Ljubljana: Ljubljana University Press, 2022), 61–62.
75. Li Zehou, *The Chinese Aesthetic Tradition*, trans. Majia Bell Samei (Honolulu: University of Hawai'i Press, 2009), 11.
76. Li, *A History of Classical Chinese Thought*, 4.
77. "述而不作，信而好古。" See James Legge, trans., *Lunyu* 論語 (*Analects*), "Shu Er, 1," *Chinese Text Project*, ctext.org/analects.
78. "吾從周。" See *Lunyu*, "Bayi, 14," trans. Andrew Lambert in Li, *A History of Classical Chinese Thought*, 4.
79. "與周公。" See *Lunyu*, "Shu Er, 5," trans. Andrew Lambert in Li, *A History of Classical Chinese Thought*, 4.
80. Li, *A History of Classical Chinese Thought*, 86.
81. Li, *The Origins of Chinese Thought*, 32.
82. Li, *The Origins of Chinese Thought*, 42.

# Bibliography

Chandler, Marthe. "Li Zehou, Kant, and Darwin: The Theory of Sedimentation." In *Li Zehou and Confucian Philosophy*, edited by Roger T. Ames, and Jinhua Jia, 278–312. Honolulu: University of Hawai'i Press, 2018.

Chen Lai 陳來. *Gudai zongjiao yu lunli: Rujia sixiang de genyuan* 古代宗教與倫理：儒家思想的根源 (*Ancient Religion and Ethics: The Source of Confucian Thought*). Beijing: Beijing Daxue chuban she, 2017.

D'Ambrosio, Paul J., Robert A. Carleo III, and Andrew Lambert. "On Li Zehou's Philosophy: An Introduction by Three Translators." *Philosophy East and West* 66, no. 4 (2016): 1057–67.
Eliade, Mircea. *Shamanism: Archaic Techniques of Ecstasy*. Translated by Willard R. Trask. Princeton, NJ: Princeton University Press, 1964.
Guo Moruo 郭沫若, ed. *Jiaguwen heji* 甲骨文合集 (*Oracle Script Collection*). Beijing: Zhonghua shuju, 1978–1983.
Huang, Chun-Chieh. *Xu Fuguan in the Context of East Asian Confucianisms*. Translated by Diana Arghirescu. Honolulu: University of Hawai'i Press, 2019.
Jaspers, Karl. *The Origin and Goal of History*. New Haven, CT: Yale University Press, 1965.
Jung, Byung-seok. "Li Zehou's Doctrine of Emotion as Substance and Confucian Philosophy." In *Li Zehou and Confucian Philosophy*, edited by Roger T. Ames and Jinhua Jia, 187–207. Honolulu: University of Hawai'i Press, 2018.
*Li ji* 禮記 (*The Book of Rites*). With translation by James Legge. *Chinese Text Project*. ctext.org/liji.
Li Zehou. *The Chinese Aesthetic Tradition*. Translated by Majia Bell Samei. Honolulu: University of Hawai'i Press, 2009.
Li Zehou. *A History of Classical Chinese Thought*. Translated by Andrew Lambert. New York: Routledge, 2020.
Li Zehou. *The Origins of Chinese Thought: From Shamanism to Ritual Regulations and Humaneness*. Translated by Robert A. Carleo III. Leiden: Brill, 2018.
Li Zehou. "A Response to Michael Sandel and Other Matters." Translated by Paul J. D'Ambrosio and Robert A. Carleo III. *Philosophy East and West* 66, no. 4 (2016): 1068–1147.
Li Zehou 李泽厚. *You wu dao li, shi li gui ren* 由巫到禮、釋禮歸仁 (*From Shamanism to Ritual Regulations and Humaneness*). Beijing: Sanlian Bookstore, 2015.
*Lun yu* 論語 (*Analects*). With translation by James Legge. *Chinese Text Project*. ctext.org/analects.
Rošker, Jana S. *Following His Own Path: Li Zehou and Contemporary Chinese Philosophy*. Albany: State University of New York Press, 2019.
Rošker, Jana S. *Humanizem v medkulturni perspektivi: primer Kitajske* (*Humanism in Intercultural Perspective: The Case of China*). Ljubljana: Ljubljana University Press, 2022.
Rošker, Jana S. "Li Zehou and the Modern Confucianism." Lecture at Summer School on "Li Zehou and Contemporary Chinese Thought." University of Ljubljana, June 17, 2022. *Klara Sofija Sanja*, July 23, 2022, video, 58:54, www.youtube.com/watch?v=g6o4I3RCPHE.
Rošker, Jana S. *The Rebirth of the Moral Self: The Second Generation of Modern Confucians and Their Modernization Discourses*. Hong Kong: The Chinese University Press, 2016.

Rošker, Jana S. *Subjektova nova oblačila—idejne osnove modernizacije v delih druge generacije modernega konfucijanstva* (*The Subject's new Clothes—the Ideational Foundations of Modernization in the Works of the Second Generation of modern Confucians*) (Razprave FF). Ljubljana: Ljubljana University Press, 2021.

Saje, Mitja. *Zgodovina Kitajske* (*History of China*). Ljubljana: Slovenska matica, 2015.

Schwartz, Benjamin I. *The World of Thought in Ancient China*. Cambridge, MA: The Belknap Press of Harvard University, 1985.

Sernelj, Tea. "Modern Chinese Aesthetics and Its Traditional Backgrounds: A Critical Comparison of Li Zehou's Sedimentation and Jung's Archetypes." In *Li Zehou and Confucian Philosophy*, edited by Roger T. Ames, and Jinhua Jia, 335–55. Honolulu: University of Hawai'i Press, 2018.

Sernelj, Tea. "Xu Fuguan's Concept of Anxiety and Its Connection to Religious Studies." *Asian Studies* 1, no. 2 (2013): 71–87.

*Shang shu* 尚書 (*The Book of History*). With translation by James Legge. *Chinese Text Project*. ctext.org/shang-shu/great-announcement.

*Shi jing* 詩經 (*The Book of Poetry*). With translation by James Legge. *Chinese Text Project*. ctext.org/book-of-poetry.

Wang Keping. "Li Zehou's View of Pragmatic Reason." In *Li Zehou and Confucian Philosophy*, edited by Roger T. Ames and Jinhua Jia, 225–52. Honolulu: University of Hawai'i Press, 2018.

Wang, Robin R. *Yinyang: The Way of Heaven and Earth in Chinese Thought and Culture*. New York: Cambridge University Press, 2012.

Xu Fuguan 徐復觀. *Zhongguo renxinglun shi* 中國人性論史 (*The History of Humanness in China*). Beijing: Huong shifandaxue chuban she, 2014.

Yang, Zebo 楊澤波. "Mou Zongsan chaoyue cunyou lun boyi—cong xian Qin tianlunde fazhan guiji kan Mou Zongsan chaoyue cunyou lunde quexian" 牟宗三超越存有論駁義—從先秦天論的發展軌跡看牟宗三超越存有論的缺陷 (Refutation of Mou Zong-san's Theory of Beyond Existence—Viewing the Defects of the Theory in Terms of the Evolution of Heaven Theory of Pre-Qin Period). *Journal of Literature, History and Philosophy* 284, no. 5 (2004): 109–17.

# 16

# Fruits of Practice

## A Comparative Analysis of Li Zehou's Concept of Sedimentation and the Buddhist Idea of the Transformations of Storehouse Consciousness (Ālaya)

### Dawid Rogacz

The concept of sedimentation (*jidian* 积淀) plays a pivotal role in the philosophy of Li Zehou. While the term *jidian* was coined by Li himself as a metaphor of the geological settling of layers of sand and dust, its connotations cross-refer to a family of more or less similar ideas. Among them, Li explicitly mentions the Piagetian theory of cognitive development;[1] there are also significant links between Li Zehou's notion of sedimentation and recent discoveries in evolutionary psychology and paleoarcheology.[2] Most importantly, Li's idea of sedimentation is deeply rooted in the processual nature of classical Chinese (and particularly Confucian) philosophy, giving a dialectical and also transcendental twist to its approach to subjectivity.

This essay explores the alternative "family resemblance" by means of examining the parallels between Li Zehou's concept of sedimentation (particularly with reference to mental structures) and the idea of the transformations of storehouse consciousness (*ālaya vijñāna*) in Yogācāra Buddhism. Notably, it is not claimed that Li Zehou "took" from Yogācāra, as there are no traces of such borrowing.[3] Both ideas are rather expressions of a more fundamental paradigm that manifests itself in a dynamic way of thinking that sees reality as perpetually changing. However, the affinity between Li's theory of sedimentation, on the one hand, and some views on the transformations of the storehouse consciousness, on the other, is striking and intriguing, and given the influential position of the Yogācāra in the landscape of twentieth-century Chinese philosophy,[4] its actual impact cannot be fully ruled out.

This is all the more surprising as Li Zehou's account of Buddhist thought is not particularly charitable. Li often treats Buddhism as the epitome of fanaticism, an apology for suffering, or a religious narcotic conducive to the maintenance of feudal society,[5] a perspective clearly indebted to the Marxist critique of religion. As Sandra Wawrytko points out, Li Zehou interprets Buddhism (at best) "as a catalyst for rather than a major component of Chinese philosophy," whose main philosophical contributions are not far from the assumptions of Confucian thought.[6] Intrigued by this, Wawrytko traces the tacit influence of the Buddhist-Confucian compound on Li's aesthetics, specifically the aesthetical version of his view on the "humanization of nature."[7] I would like to argue that the parallels between the thought of Li Zehou and Buddhist philosophy may go even further and concern the very understanding of the "mechanism" of sedimentation, which bears significant similarities with the Yogācārist idea of the transformations of storehouse consciousness, mostly as elaborated in *Mahāyāna Saṃgraha* and *Laṅkāvatāra Sūtra*. And while this particular comparison might be controversial, it is noteworthy that attempts to demonstrate the complementarity of some Marxist and Buddhist categories are not new, since they date back to the writings of Bhimrao Ramji Ambedkar (1891–1956) and have recently taken a deserved place in academic debates due to, among others, Graham Priest.[8]

## Coagulated Seeds: Yogācāra on the Generation and Transformation of Individual Consciousness

The concept of storehouse consciousness (*ālaya vijñāna*) has a long history that predates the emergence of the Yogācāra school.[9] Early Buddhist philosophy already contained an idea of the underlying latent dispositions (*anusaya*), which are psycho-ontologically instrumental in perpetuating samsaric existence. As *Saṃyutta Nikāya* (S II 66) reads, "If, monks, one does not intend, and one does not plan, but one still has a tendency towards (*anuseti*) something, this becomes a basis for the maintenance of consciousness."[10] It is because all these tendencies give rise to an unending series of conceptual proliferation (*prapañca*).[11] Questions about the exact mechanism of such proliferation, and regarding its "place" and ways to overcome it, led to the emergence of the concept of *ālaya*.

Essentially, the concept of *ālaya vijñāna* was introduced to denote both the storer of impressions (the "backup" for consciousness) and that which is stored. Since conscious life is an end product of its fluctuations, ultimately we have no (conscious) control over the transformation of the impressions of our past experiences into the objects of cognition.[12] According to *Mahāyāna Saṃgraha* (MSg I.3), "It is called *ālaya vijñāna* because all afflicted dharmas which have an origin dwell (*ālīyante*) in this [vijñāna] as a fruit (*phalabhāva*), and because this [vijñāna] also dwells in them as cause (*hetubhāva*)."[13] "Fruit" serves here as more than a metaphor, as the first phase of dependent arising (MSg I.26–28) refers to the emergence of the manifest forms of cognitive awareness (*pravṛtti vijñāna*) out of that which had been experienced (*aupabhogika*) in all the past existences. *Ālaya* is, therefore, understood both in transcendental ("the storer") and psycho-genetic ("the stored") terms. On the one hand, in principle, "without that [*ālāya vijñāna*], existence (*bhāva*) conditioned by appropriation (*upādāna*) would also be impossible" (MSg I.33). Yet, on the other, from the viewpoint of the result of such conditioning, "vijñāna coagulates (*saṃ mūrcchati*) as an embryo in the mother's womb" (MSg I.34).[14] In this sense, the process of the coagulation of the seeds (*bīja*) of past actions guarantees the psycho-physical (that is, empirical) continuum of an individual.

From such a viewpoint it is clear that each individual has her or his own *ālaya*. However, as an ever-changing process, a simultaneously "perfumed" and "perfuming" entity, *ālaya* is not to be confused with the idea of permanent self, although in the opinion of Paul Williams it does "give a degree of personal identity."[15] In fact, the illusion of a permanent self is a product of the transformation of *ālaya*, resulting from the emergence of reflexive consciousness (*manas vijñāna*). But if it is *manas vijñāna* that creates the mental image of one's ego and erroneously regards its cognitive processes as belonging to some self, so that the self/I is not to be found in the *ālaya* itself, then why suppose that *ālaya* is individually differentiated? Such questions led to the interfusion of the Yogācāra school with the Tathāgatagarbha tradition, as best exemplified by the *Laṅkāvatāra Sūtra*.

For the authors of the *Laṅkāvatāra Sūtra*, *ālaya* is basically and perfectly one. It is an unconditional absolute, comparable to a vast ocean unmoved by the churning of waves. For this reason, *ālaya* is seen as the noetic aspect of Suchness (*Tathatā*), "the conscious modality of *Tathatā* [that] grounds and animates the individual human psyche whose form s are the immanent transformations of (the Alaya) itself."[16] It also means that the totality of phenomenal beings is nothing other than self-manifesting Mind. In this way, however, as Brian E. Brown points out, the *Laṅkāvatāra Sūtra* confuses ontology with epistemology, which in his eyes also jeopardizes the value of human subjectivity.[17] This opinion may be accurate due to the link that the *Laṅkāvatāra Sūtra* makes between the way-things-truly-are (Suchness) and our cognitive objects. On the other hand, such a connection is to some extent unavoidable, given that our conceptualizations are karmically determined, while these karmic seeds come from our actions, which change the world itself. *Mahāyāna Saṃgraha*, too, quite literally states that dharmas dwell in *ālaya* and that the causal chain of dependence arising due to their accumulation is, par excellence, real. In other words, the transformation of *ālaya* may be justifiably interpreted as a psycho-ontological process. As such, it bears some affinity with the way the Chinese philosopher Li Zehou understands the process of "sedimentation."

## Subject in the Making: Li Zehou's Concept of Sedimentation

Li Zehou's notion of sedimentation grows out of his innovative and controversial reading of Kantian philosophy, specifically from the historization of his transcendentalism. What Kant took to be a priori—the universal and necessary structures of subjective cognition—are in Li's eyes nothing but the result/fruit (*chengguo* 成果) of the historical, and are therefore also the contingent experience of humanity, the experience that is carried on now and in future generations.[18] Li's provocative take on Kantianism is justified by the fact that while Kant elaborated on the transcendental character of categories, he did not explain their source.[19] Strictly speaking, Kant could not provide such an explanation, as the categories are transcendental in the sense that they are the condition of all possible experience, but they themselves cannot derive from any (possible) experience; otherwise they would not be a priori. In all fairness, Li admits that his interpretation requires a clearly non-Kantian assumption, namely that enduring forms of experience can be and are transformed into the transcendental (*jingyan bian xianyan* 经验变先验).[20] The exact shape of such transformation is explained by the concept of sedimentation: "In short, that which seems to be 'transcendental' to an individual is actually sedimentation, which has been historically acquired through the collective experience of humankind."[21]

By stating this, Li fully endorses the historicization of the transcendental, if not interpreting transcendentalism itself as essentially a genealogical enterprise. This, however, as pointed out by Ady Van den Stock, entails precluding any bifurcation between the conditioned and unconditioned, namely that which is supposedly independent of all experience.[22] Consequently, Li Zehou undermines another crucial distinction of modern Western philosophy, namely that between humans and nature. In Li's own words, sedimentation refers to "the accumulations and deposits of the social, rational, and historical in the individual through the process of humanizing nature."[23] The humanization of nature—a concept taken from Marxian philosophy—relates to the specifically human process of transforming both external and inner nature. While the humanization of external nature results in the creation of material civilization, and thus technical-social structures (*gongyi shehui jiegou* 工艺社会结构), the transformation of inner human nature(s) generates cultural-mental formations (*wenhua xinli jiegou* 文化心理结构).[24] As Sylvia Chan points out, the latter "refers to the mental powers individuals have: cognition, emotion, and volition."[25] In this way, the collective "subjectality" (*zhutixing* 主體性) shapes individual subjectivity (*zhuguanxing* 主觀性). On the other hand, since sedimentation "stores human experiences and shapes collective memory,"[26] human subjectivities are being molded from practical transformations of the objective world, which leads to the complementary process of the "naturalization of humans" (*ren de ziranhua* 人的自然化) and enables Li Zehou to engage in a dialogue with evolutionary psychology.

Importantly, the concept of the naturalization of humans involves not all experiences, but one particular experience that according to Li genuinely shapes our cognitive faculties: the manufacturing and use of tools (*shiyong-zhizao gongju* 使用－制造工具). For this reason, Li Zehou eagerly puts forward a number of concrete hypotheses regarding the origin of language or motor thinking.[27] This aspect of his theory of sedimentation, however, is not evolutionistic (Darwinian), but essentially Lamarckian. The accumulation of experiences, or rather features acquired during the practical taming of reality and under the influence of current needs, is gradually "transcendentalized," thus extending human cognitive abilities.

It is not merely about "the survival of the fittest" when it comes to those preestablished and arbitrarily found faculties that happen to adapt to reality in the way that makes their survival possible. No matter how these faculties are shaped, at a certain stage of technological development the production and use of tools actively and continuously transforms and expands them, and there seems to be no room for pure contingency in this process. On the other hand, Jane Cauvel argues that there are two more meanings of sedimentation present in Li Zehou's theory: cultural, referring to the accumulation of the customs of thinking and feeling, and individual, pertaining to the accretion of personal experiences during one's own life.[28] The latter two are clearly "Lamarckian" in the sense discussed above, which means that even if Li's transformativist approach to human subjectivity remains controversial from the scientific viewpoint, it is definitely consistent with the actual development of human culture and the way we live our own lives.

At the end of the day, however, Li Zehou's concept of sedimentation should be read not as a scientific hypothesis, but as a philosophical theory of human subjectivity and culture that quite effectively interprets it on the scale of the *longue durée*. In his interpretation of the course of Chinese culture, which given its universal claims can possibly be related to other cultures as well, Li Zehou argues that the humanization of inner nature took place due to shamanistic activities, so that "all kinds of uniquely human psychological functions, like imagination, cognition, comprehension, and other intellectual activities, sprouted and developed while preserving their connection to elementary animalistic mental functions."[29] These activities themselves are described by Li as "based upon a unity of body and mind and by no means separated soul and flesh. They attached importance to the very process of activity and not to its objects."[30] This means that human subjectivity has been historically shaped through the collective practice of shamanistic transformation, or, using Li Zehou's terminology, that individual "small self" (*xiaowo* 小我) has been created, or sedimented, out of the collective "greater self" (*dawo* 大我)—a communal form of consciousness. The collective consciousness is logically and historically prior to the individual self.[31] For this reason, Li Zehou understands this process in transcendental terms: "just as in the case of material production, I insist that without the activities of the collective social consciousness, i.e., without primitive shamanist ritual activities and without linguistic and symbolic activities, the formation of a human psyche that is different from that of the animals would not have been possible."[32] At the stage of this initial and elementary sedimentation, as Marthe Chandler reminds us, humans had much less sense of themselves as individuals than in the modern era; losing themselves in these collective activities, they "were in a sense 'one being' with one set of intentions, desires, and goals."[33] Treating shamanistic activities on a par with material technological practice may be surprising, but, as a matter of fact, magic and rituals were the first efforts to tame and manipulate nature, even phenomena seemingly beyond human control.

It has to be observed, however, that Li's focus on the long-range sedimentation of external nature and collective inner nature (and generally his almost post-structuralist understanding of subjectivity) could raise some questions about the extent to which the processes in question may be described as autonomous and free. Li Zehou himself was well aware of this theoretical problem and addressed it mostly in his *Historical Ontology* (*Lishi bentilun* 历史本体论). First of all, the manufacturing and use of tools is a variant form of the process of measuring (*du* 度), which is practiced everyday by all human beings in all spheres of their *Lebenswelt*; in this sense, the substance/body (*wuti* 物体) of history is tantamount to social life.[34] All such acts are free within the limits of the current level of technological and economic development. They are necessary only in the long term and post factum: it is from the viewpoint of time that we see that some things could not have happened otherwise, but it is impossible to predict in advance which single practice should necessarily lead to what sort of structures. All these stipulations notwithstanding, Li argues, the necessity arising from long-term practices of manipulating and transforming nature, resulting in sedimented mental formations (*xinli xingshi* 心理形式), is no less fundamental than economic relations, although its pivotal role was long omitted by Marxists.[35] People are both the products and creators of history. And since "people actively create their own history, they take moral responsibility for their choices."[36] Sedimentation does not overrule this responsibility, but in fact it strengthens it, showing that the results of human practices are, in the strict sense, historical, and that what emerges from this process is ultimately nothing but the human subject itself.

## A Comparison

This often neglected ethical dimension of sedimentation provides further opportunities for an effective comparison between the Yogācāra concept of the subject (specifically the version from the *Laṅkāvatāra Sūtra*) and

Li Zehou's approach to subjectivity. In terms of the theoretical structure of these two conceptions, there are some intriguing and deep similarities and differences that need to be pointed out.

First, similarly to the transformation of storehouse consciousness, sedimentation can be described as a process, to use Rošker's formulation once again, that "stores human experiences and shapes collective memory." Second, all these experiences come from free actions or practices, for which their agents bear moral responsibility. Third, both systems use similar imagery: whereas for Yogācāra this process is portrayed as a coagulation of the seeds of actions, Li Zehou depicts it as a sedimentation of the fruits (*chengguo*) of practices. Fourth, the result of this process—the "coagulated seeds" or "sedimented fruits"—are nothing but the manifest forms of cognitive awareness or consciousness in the language of Yogācāra, or mental or cultural-psychological formations/structures (or simply categories of cognition) in the vocabulary of Li Zehou. Fifth, both approaches go further and state that what is transformed or sedimented is actually the individual subject itself (the individual self). For this reason, they introduce a communal form of consciousness—*ālaya* or *dawo*, which as an entity that logically precedes the creation of strictly cognitive faculties is also described in a more ontological way: as noetic Suchness or subjectality (*zhutixing*, literally "body-nature of the subject"). This is connected with the sixth affinity between these two conceptions. Both Li Zehou and the Yogācārins understand the generation of subject(-ivity) in both transcendental and psycho-ontological ways. It is, on the one hand, something without which individual consciousness would not be possible; on the other hand, the sedimentation or transformation of *ālaya* both refer to the actual, "psycho-genetic" process that is extended throughout the generations. From a bird's eye view, Li's struggles to present Kantian categories as the "sediments" of the practice of manufacturing and using tools are akin to Vasubandhu's efforts to root reason qua reflexive consciousness (*mānas vijñāna*), understanding/apperception qua mental consciousness (*manovijñāna*), and six sensory consciousnesses, into a deeper repository of the results of human actions. Finally, both Li Zehou and the Yogācārins operate on the scale of the *longue durée* and do not assume that every individual and every generation writes history anew: just as the way one's world is seen in the current life is a result of the actions from all previous lives, so contemporary subjectivity should be seen as an effect of the long-term transformations of subjectality starting, at the very latest, from the shamanistic humanization of nature.

Despite all these resemblances, none were spotted by either Li Zehou or the scholars of his thought. Of course, in order to make such a comparison feasible we need to make an assumption enabling us to read Yogācāra (also) as a philosophy of history. Such a reading, however, was not alien to modern Chinese philosophers due to the contribution of Zhang Taiyan (also known as Zhang Binglin, 1869–1936). As Viren Murthy observes, "Zhang explains the objectivity of history and time using the concepts of Yogācāra Buddhism" based on the idea that "karmic seeds produce phenomena and are stored in ālaya consciousness."[37] As Murthy continues, in Zhang's view the collective karma stored in *ālaya* drives history and is responsible for the biological evolution of species from "the earliest amoeba" up to the emergence of human beings out of the realm of animals.[38] These ideas could certainly be viewed as an attempt to modernize Yogācāra in dialogue with both Hegelianism and evolutionism, and eventually even as the missing link between classical Yogācāra and Li's concept of sedimentation. This is not, however, the way Li Zehou interpreted Zhang Taiyan. In his eyes, the evolution Zhang Taiyan speaks about is a spiritual rather than a biological process. As such, it is a mere "reactionary speculation" that mirrors the capitalist mode of production that Zhang (allegedly) stood behind. And as if this typically Marxist criticism was not enough, Zhang's philosophy is also described as "relativist," "cabalistic," and "nihilist," falling back from transcendentalism to the "subjective idealism" of Buddhist epistemology, which does not go beyond the phenomena of sensual experience.[39]

However, as uncharitable as such a reading may be, it certainly follows crucial discrepancies between the Yogācārist and Li's approaches to subjectivity. First of all, Yogācāra Buddhism is still a form of idealist philosophy, be it subjective or even transcendental. The quoted sutras clearly state that the perceived and cognized reality is the manifestation of reflexive consciousness and *ālaya*, and not vice versa. That the "material" for these manifestations may come from external stimuli (a view held explicitly by, for example, Xuanzang) does not change the fact that it is various forms of consciousness that determine how these entities are synthesized into meaningful phenomena. Li Zehou, on the other hand, openly advocates the dependence of the cultural and mental "superstructure" upon the economic and technological base, although he insists that Marxism has to be purged of all elements that do not belong to the core of historical materialism (*weiwu shiguan de hexin* 唯物史观的核心), namely the idea of the constitutive role of the manufacturing and use of tools.⁴⁰ Second, consequently, the practice Li Zehou has in mind refers mostly to the use of tools, and more generally to all forms of manipulative and harmonizing measuring (*du*). In Yogācāra the seeds are brought about by all kinds of acts, and those of a non-instrumental nature are probably even more saturated with karmic significance.

Third, Yogācāra does presuppose the existence of two or—counting the world of dreams—three realms of being (*trisvabhāva*). Specifically, the unconditioned, non-dual and perfect reality, Suchness or *ālaya* is distinct from, if not opposed to, impermanent and imperfect phenomena. Such dualism is openly rejected by Li Zehou, and his "one-world view" is strengthened by a radical endorsement of historicism. The fourth significant difference regards the mechanism of subject-making in both approaches. In Yogācāra, *ālaya* stores the seeds from a person's own actions and transmits them to the next lives of that individual: the subject, its consciousness—and the world of experience such consciousness presents is the result of her or his own actions "saved" within *ālaya*. For Li Zehou, in turn, modern subjectivity, and therefore the cognitive faculties of contemporary human subjects, result from the collective long-term practice of all humanity. This entails another difference between the two views. Although the Yogācārist account clearly guarantees the continuity and accumulation of the fruits of one's deeds, it does not necessarily imply any progression or improvement in this process. Due to the transmission of bad karma, things can actually go from bad to worse. Li Zehou believes, on the other hand, that since the manufacturing and use of tools serves as an instrument in adapting to external reality, with proper effort sedimentation and the accompanying "peaceful evolution" (*heping jinhua* 和平進化) will lead to the increasing amelioration (*gailiang* 改良) of social life.⁴¹ Needless to say, Li Zehou lacks the soteriological perspective of Yogācāra Buddhism. But even assuming that the notion of revolution constitutes, to some extent, the Marxist counterpart of the idea of liberation (salvation), the views of the Yogācārins and Li Zehou could not be more different. While for the former the only way to liberation lies in the disruption of the stream of karmic seeds, Li Zehou condemns revolutions and all other disruptive forms of social liberation as utopian, counter-effective and simply dangerous.⁴²

All these differences, however, do not overrule the affinities in their understanding of the genesis of the subject: for both Yogācārins and Li Zehou, individual subjectivity and its cognitive faculties are the long-term result of the sedimentation (coagulation) of the results of human action (practice), which are collectively stored and transmitted through generations. The view of Li Zehou may be interpreted as a materialist, historicist, collectivist, and antiutopian "philosophical nephew" of Yogācāra thought, with both belonging to a larger, transformativist and processual philosophical family of the conceptions of subjectivity.

## Notes

1. Cf. Jana S. Rošker, "Human Memory as a Dynamic Accumulation of Experiences: Li Zehou's Concept of Sedimentation," *Ars and Humanitas* 12, no. 2 (2018): 135–37.

2. Marthe Chandler, "Li Zehou, Kant, and Darwin: The Theory of Sedimentation," in *Li Zehou and Confucian Philosophy*, ed. Roger T. Ames and Jinhua Jia (Honolulu: University of Hawai'i Press, 2018), 279–312.

3. Quite tellingly, Yogācāra is entirely omitted in Li's overview of Chinese philosophy; see *Zhongguo gudai sixiang shilun* 中國古代思想史論 (*A History of Classical Chinese Thought*) (Beijing: Xinhua Shudian, 2008), 208–30.

4. John Makeham, ed., *On Transforming Consciousness: Yogacara Thought in Modern China* (Oxford: Oxford University Press, 2014).

5. Li Zehou, *The Path of Beauty: A Study of Chinese Aesthetics*, trans. Song Lizeng (Hong Kong: Oxford University Press, 1994), 107–13, 126.

6. Sandra A. Wawrytko, "Sedimentation in Chinese Aesthetics and Epistemology: A Buddhist Expansion of Confucian Philosophy," *Journal of Chinese Philosophy* 40, no. 3–4 (2013): 477–79.

7. Wawrytko, 485–89.

8. Graham Priest, *Capitalism—its Nature and its Replacement: Buddhist and Marxist Insights* (New York: Routledge, 2021). For a synoptic view on Priest's approach to the complementarity of Buddhism and Marxism, see Graham Priest, "Marxism and Buddhism: Not Such Strange Bedfellows," *Journal of the American Philosophical Association* 4, no. 1 (2018): 2–13. Cf. also Karsten J. Stuhl, "Buddhism and Marxism: Points of Intersection," *International Communication of Chinese Culture* 4 (2017): 103–16.

9. For the classical philological and historical study of that concept, see Lambert Schmithausen, *Ālāyavijñāna. On the Origin and the Early Development of a Central Concept of Yogacara Philosophy* (Tokyo: International Institute for Buddhist Studies, 1987).

10. Translated by William S. Waldron, *The Buddhist Unconscious: The alaya-vijñāna in the Context of Indian Buddhist Thought* (London: Routledge, 2003), 35.

11. See Waldron, *The Buddhist Unconscious*, 33–37.

12. Shun'ei Tagawa, *Living Yogacara: An Introduction to Consciousness-only Buddhism* (Somerville: Wisdom Publications, 2009), 29–37.

13. Cited from Waldron, *The Buddhist Unconscious*, 130.

14. Waldron, *The Buddhist unconscious*, 140–41.

15. Paul Williams, *Mahayana Buddhism: The Doctrinal Foundations* (New York: Routledge, 2008), 97–99.

16. Brian E. Brown, *The Buddha Nature: A Study of the Tathāgatagarbha and Ālayavijñāna* (Delhi: Motilal Banarsidass Publishers, 1991), 183–84.

17. Brown, *The Buddha Nature*, 188, 192.

18. Li Zehou 李澤厚, *Pipan zhexue de pipan: Kangde shuping* 批判哲學的批判: 康德述評 (*Critique of Critical Philosophy: A Commentary on Kant*), 6th ed. (Beijing: Sanlian Shudian, 2007), 70–72.

19. Cf. passages A 95–96 of Immanuel Kant's *Critique of Pure Reason*, trans. P. Guyer and A. W. Wood (Cambridge: Cambridge University Press, 1999), 226–27.

20. See Jana S. Rošker, *Following His Own Path: Li Zehou and Contemporary Chinese Philosophy* (Albany: State University of New York Press, 2019), 28.

21. Li Zehou, *A New Approach to Kant. A Confucian-Marxist's Viewpoint*, trans. J. H. Allen (Singapore: Springer, 2008), viii.

22. Ady Van den Stock, "Imprints of the Thing in Itself: Li Zehou's *Critique of Critical Philosophy* and the Historicization of the Transcendental," *Asian Studies* 8, no. 1 (2020): 17.

23. Li Zehou, *Four Essays on Aesthetics: Toward a Global View*, trans. Jane Cauvel (Lanham, MD: Lexington Books, 2006), 94.

24. Li, *Four Essays*, 37.

25. Sylvia Chan, "Li Zehou and New Confucianism," in *New Confucianism: A Critical Examination*, ed. John Makeham (New York: Palgrave Macmillan, 2003), 109.

26. Rošker, "Human Memory," 135.

27. Li Zehou, "An Outline of the Origin of Humankind," *Contemporary Chinese Thought* 31, no. 2 (1999): 20–25.

28. Jane Cauvel, "The Transformative Power of Art: Li Zehou's Aesthetic Theory," *Philosophy East and West* 49, no. 2 (1999): 158.

29. Jana S. Rošker, "Li Zehou's Ethics and the Importance of Confucian Kinship Relations: The Power of Shamanistic Rituality and the Consolidation of Relationalism (關係主義)," *Asian Philosophy* 30, no. 3 (2020): 232.

30. Li Zehou 李澤厚, *You wu dao li, shi li gui ren* 由巫到禮, 釋禮歸仁 (*From Shamanism to Rituals: Explaining the Roots of Rituals in Humaneness*) (Taibei: Sanlian shudian, 2015), 13.

31. Cf. Rošker, "Human Memory," 143.

32. Li Zehou 李澤厚, *Meixue yu weilai meixue* 美學和未來美學 (*Aesthetics and Future Aesthetics*) (Beijing: Zhongguo Shehui Kexue Chubanshe, 1990), 191–92.

33. Chandler, "Li Zehou, Kant, and Darwin," 300.
34. Li Zehou, *Lishi bentilun* 歷史本體論 (*Historical Ontology*) (Beijing: Sanlian Shudian, 2008), 18–22.
35. Li, *Historical Ontology*, 39, 42–43.
36. Li Zehou, *Critique of Critical Philosophy*, 380–81.
37. Viren Murthy, *The Political Philosophy of Zhang Taiyan* (Leiden: Brill, 2011), 151, 156.
38. Murthy, *The Political Philosophy of Zhang Taiyan*, 157–58.
39. Li Zehou 李澤厚, *Zhongguo jindai sixiang shilun* 中國近代思想史論 (*A History of Modern Chinese Thought*) (Beijing: Sanlian Shudian, 2008), 411–27.
40. Li Zehou 李澤厚, *Makesizhuyi zai Zhongguo* 馬克思主義在中國 (*Marxism in China*) (Hongkong: Minbao Chubanshe, 2006), 141–48.
41. Li Zehou 李澤厚 and Liu Zaifu 劉再復, *Gaobie geming: huiwang ershishiji Zhongguo* 告別革命: 回望二十世紀中國 (*Farewell to Revolution: Looking Back at the Twentieth-Century China*) (Hongkong: Tiandi Tushu, 2004), 302–4.
42. Li and Liu, *Farewell to Revolution*, 65.

## Bibliography

Brown, Brian E. *The Buddha Nature: A Study of the Tathāgatagarbha and Ālayavijñāna*. Delhi: Motilal Banarsidass Publishers, 1991.
Cauvel, Jane. "The Transformative Power of Art: Li Zehou's Aesthetic Theory." *Philosophy East and West* 49, no. 2 (1999): 150–73.
Chan, Sylvia. "Li Zehou and New Confucianism." In *New Confucianism: A Critical Examination*, edited by John Makeham, 105–25. New York: Palgrave Macmillan, 2003.
Chandler, Marthe. "Li Zehou, Kant, and Darwin: The Theory of Sedimentation." In *Li Zehou and Confucian Philosophy*, edited by Roger T. Ames and Jinhua Jia, 279–312. Honolulu: University of Hawai'i Press, 2018.
Kant, Immanuel. *Critique of Pure Reason*. Translated by P. Guyer and A. W. Wood. Cambridge: Cambridge University Press, 1999.
Li Zehou 李澤厚. *Lishi bentilun* 歷史本體論 (*Historical Ontology*). Beijing: Sanlian Bookstore, 2008.
Li Zehou 李澤厚. *Makesizhuyi zai Zhongguo* 馬克思主義在中國 (*Marxism in China*). Hongkong: Minbao chuban she, 2006.
Li Zehou 李澤厚. *Meixue he weilai meixue* 美學和未來美學 (*Aesthetics and Future Aesthetics*). Beijing: Zhongguo shehui kexue chuban she, 1990.
Li Zehou. *A New Approach to Kant: A Confucian-Marxist's Viewpoint*. Translated by Jeanne Haizhen Allen and Christopher Ahn. Singapore: Springer, 2018.
Li Zehou. "An Outline of the Origin of Humankind." *Contemporary Chinese Thought* 31, no. 2 (1999): 20–25.

Li Zehou. *The Path of Beauty: A Study of Chinese Aesthetics*. Translated by Gong Lizeng. Hong Kong: Oxford University Press, 1994.
Li Zehou 李澤厚. *Pipan zhexue de pipan: Kangde shuping* 批判哲學的批判: 康德述評 (*Critique of Critical Philosophy: A New Approach to Kant*), 6th ed. Beijing: SDX Joint Publishing, 2007.
Li Zehou 李澤厚. *You wu dao li, shi li gui ren* 由巫到禮、釋禮歸仁 (*From Shamanism to Ritual Regulations and Humaneness*). Beijing: Sanlian Bookstore, 2015.
Li Zehou 李澤厚. *Zhongguo gudai sixiang shilun* 中國古代思想史論 (*A History of Classical Chinese Thought*). Beijing: Xinhua shudian, 2008.
Li Zehou 李澤厚. *Zhongguo jindai sixiang shilun* 中國近代思想史論 (*A History of Modern Chinese Thought*). Beijing: Sanlian Bookstore, 2008.
Li Zehou and Jane Cauvel. *Four Essays on Aesthetics: Toward a Global View*. Lanham, MD: Lexington Books, 2006.
Li Zehou 李澤厚 and Liu Zaifu 劉再復. *Gaobie geming: huiwang ershishiji Zhongguo* 告別革命: 回望二十世紀中國 (*Farewell to Revolution: Looking Back at the Twentieth-Century China*). Hongkong: Tiandi tushu, 2004.
Makeham, John, ed. *On Transforming Consciousness: Yogacara Thought in Modern China*. Oxford: Oxford University Press, 2014.
Murthy, Viren. *The Political Philosophy of Zhang Taiyan*. Leiden: Brill, 2011.
Priest, Graham. *Capitalism—Its Nature and Its Replacement: Buddhist and Marxist Insights*. New York: Routledge, 2021.
Priest, Graham. "Marxism and Buddhism: Not Such Strange Bedfellows." *Journal of the American Philosophical Association* 4, no. 1 (2018): 2–13.
Rošker, Jana S. *Following His Own Path: Li Zehou and Contemporary Chinese Philosophy*. Albany: State University of New York Press, 2019.
Rošker, Jana S. "Human Memory as a Dynamic Accumulation of Experiences: Li Zehou's Concept of Sedimentation." *Ars and Humanitas* 12, no. 2 (2018): 135–48.
Rošker, Jana S. "Li Zehou's Ethics and the Importance of Confucian Kinship Relations: The Power of Shamanistic Rituality and the Consolidation of Relationalism (關係主義)." *Asian Philosophy* 30, no. 3 (2020): 230–41.
Schmithausen, Lambert. *Ālāyavijñāna. On the Origin and the Early Development of a Central Concept of Yogacara Philosophy. Part I: Text, Part II: Notes, Bibliography and Indices*. Tokyo: International Institute for Buddhist Studies, 1987.
Stuhl, Karsten J. "Buddhism and Marxism: Points of Intersection." *International Communication of Chinese Culture* 4 (2017): 103–16.
Tagawa, Shun'ei. *Living Yogacara: An Introduction to Consciousness-Only Buddhism*. Somerville, MA: Wisdom Publications, 2009.
Van den Stock, Ady. "Imprints of the Thing in Itself: Li Zehou's *Critique of Critical Philosophy* and the Historicization of the Transcendental." *Asian Studies* 8, no. 1 (2020): 15–35.
Waldron, William S. *The Buddhist Unconscious: The* alaya-vijñana *in the Context of Indian Buddhist Thought*. London: Routledge, 2003.

Wawrytko, Sandra A. "Sedimentation in Chinese Aesthetics and Epistemology: A Buddhist Expansion of Confucian Philosophy." *Journal of Chinese Philosophy* 40, no. 3–4 (2013): 473–92.

Williams, Paul. *Mahayana Buddhism: The Doctrinal Foundations*. New York: Routledge, 2008.

17

# Number and Mathematics in Li Zehou's *Critique of Critical Philosophy*

SYDNEY MORROW

Li Zehou's interpretation of Kant's metaphysics meets what he sees as the both the Chinese reader's and the historical materialist's requirement of providing an explanation of the origin and root of the a priori. His interpretation creates a curious puzzle. Those familiar with Kant would say that the a priori is not accessible to sensibility and so it is beyond the bounds of understanding. In other words, understanding cannot understand itself. A priori concepts such as the thing-in-itself, the moral law, the sublime, and God (as an ultimate being) provide the "therefore for every wherefore" and have no further explanation or foundation.[1] These ideas are indicative of the unconditioned and necessary foundation of all conditions of experience. Kant writes, "Although the unconditioned is not in itself and according to its mere concept given as real, yet it alone can complete the series of conditions traced to their grounds. This is the natural course, taken by the reason of every, even the most ordinary, human being, although not everyone can hold onto it. It does not begin with concepts, but with common experience, and thus lays at the foundation something really existing."[2] Unconditioned ideas have no counterpart in sensible experience. They are a function of the rational mind's desire to understand the world absolutely, in its totality, and to overcome the limits of the sensible and the piece-meal understanding that our experience affords. The existence of a priori ideas is revealed as their necessity for the cessation of the regress of conditioned ideas.

Imagine the Western reader's shock at Li Zehou's breezy pronouncement that Chinese readers and Marxists will not be satisfied with this transcendental coda that has held the West transfixed for so long.[3] What, for Kant, elevated the rational mind into the realm of the infinite and the perfection of its completeness Li mires in the slog of our development as a human species. These ideas are things that we once needed, in Li's view, so we created them. Our creations so fit our continuing needs that we kept them. And now we have had them for so long that they are ensconced in our way of knowing and understanding the world *to the point that we cannot imagine ourselves without them*. Thus, the creation of a priori concepts via a process that Li calls "sedimentation." While finding a path to a materialist ground for the a priori is not unique to Li Zehou's thought, the analogizing of geological accretion and human cultural development is taken as his original contribution.

## Li's Theory of Sedimentation

Li Zehou's concept of sedimentation describes the gradual accretion of knowledge and principles over the course of material human evolution, namely as a result of "making and using tools over millions of years."[4] According to Li, the structures of knowledge that we take to be absolute, a priori, and at the very least unquestionably true or correct, are not something present in the human mind since the beginning of the species. Rather, psychological concepts gradually extracted from social practices over millennia have been moored in the human mind for so long we take them for granted as a part of the landscape. In other words, the "conditions of the possibility of knowledge are . . . themselves also a product of human activity throughout history, and thus equally conditioned and contingent."[5] Li Zehou is resolute that nothing cognitive precedes, or ever has preceded, experience. Rather, humans, the particular societies to which they belong, and the inclusive, global society to which all belong are sites of continual cognitive construction. An individual's exposure to the external and social "cultural-psychological formation" consists in education, broadly construed as the experience of living in these two, dialectical senses of society. This formation is composed of ideals and norms that have been given rise by human social and material development.[6] "Thus, an individual's development of reason, and indeed of one's general psychology, occurs through the 'education' of concrete experiences that include continuous exposure to (and generally internalization of) ideas and practices 'sedimented' in one's culture."[7]

Li interprets Kant's a priori concepts as sedimented ideas. In a beguiling twist, Li writes, "Kant deserves praise for an *a priori* cultural-psychological form of the sedimentation of reason that is universal, sublime, and absolute. His moral theory is rooted in actual history, and shows his awareness of history's largest vistas."[8] Why beguiling? This is certainly not what Kant intended! Put simply, Li takes to heart Kant's pronouncement in the *Critique of Pure Reason* that "all our knowledge begins with experience there can be no doubt"—but not his claim a few sentences later: "But, though all our knowledge begins with experience, it by no means follows that all arises out of experience."[9] There are some ideas (concepts) that are pure and unconditioned, according to Kant. And these constitute pure a priori knowledge.

Li's interpretation could be dismissed out of hand as deliberately infelicitous. But Li admits that he is not concerned with utter felicity when he writes, "One should devote attention to the living Kant, namely, his influence on the history of philosophy, and in particular, his influence on modern times; rather than losing oneself in digging up the dead Kant, as in the all-too-many massive scholarly works on Kant's philosophy."[10] So, the challenge greater than simple dismissal is to see whether, if Li's theory of the condition of a priori knowledge is accepted, the rest of Kant's system still functions. That is, can the faculties of understanding, sensibility, and reason still play their respective parts to perform the synthesis of experience and concepts? Where the Chinese reader, by Li's estimation, may find the demystified explanation of a priori concepts edifying, this Western reader, rug pulled out, now asks what difference does it make whence the a priori arises? Perhaps Li puts his finger precisely on it when he writes that "the task of appeasing the restless wandering ghost of Kant's philosophy has fallen to the Marxists."[11] Kant's descriptions of metaphysics as a "bottomless abyss" and "a dark and shoreless ocean, marked by no beacons" have lost sway over contemporary philosophers.[12] Li bottoms the abyss with a provocative idea: "empirical turns into the transcendental, history constructs reason, and psychology becomes ontology."[13]

## Kant's Theory of Mathematics

Kant's theory of mathematics differs from the theories circulating during his time because of the uniqueness of his theory of space and time. For Kant, space and time are forms of inner sense; that is, they do not exist outside of the faculties of the rational mind. No apperception, that is, no cognition of sensible experience, is possible without the passage of time. Time marks each synthetic unity that is accomplished between the sensible, the world exterior to us as presented by our senses, and the a priori content of understanding, the categories or concepts that allow us to form judgments about the sensible. Comprehension, the formation of a unity of apperception, takes place in the ordered sequence of time. According to Kant, this activity could go on forever, ad infinitum. Thus, time is infinite. It is a potentially unending sequence that structures and orders a priori synthetic unities.

The structure of Kant's system of perception and cognition makes an interesting setting for mathematics. For Kant, no part of mathematics is analytic, that is, given to understanding without a counterpart in experience, or a priori. Mathematical truths, the unassailable rules that govern arithmetic and geometry, were held by Kant to be synthetic a priori judgments. Understanding them is not possible without the sensible. Kant wrote that not only are there no analytic a priori concepts associated with numbers, for example 7 and 5, but also, there is nothing about these numbers that gives 12. Understanding these numbers is the accomplishment of the judgment of their unity in experience: counting. So, counting is the result of two types of unity. First, something is presented to the senses that forms a unity with a category of understanding, a judgment. Second, that something is presented in homogeneous, discrete, *countable* units. Thus, only in time can things be numbered and counted and all things are countable, that is, they comprise a magnitude, in time.

For Kant, number is inseparable from the act of counting because numbers are generated in the *sequential* apperception of homogeneous unities. You know, counting. Remember, numbers are not given in advance. Number is the schematism, the set of rules, for the application of the concept of magnitude to the experience of extended (countable) things. In theory, there is no end to the counting that we can do because the application of the rule of counting does not change regardless of how high we count. And, for Kant, it seems that if the units counted are homogeneous, then unities of their sums are never too large to comprehend. Again, this is not because we have the capacity to truly comprehend enormous sums, for example, the number of grains of sand on a beach, but that there is nothing limiting our counting of the grains. Kant believes that we can easily get a sense of such a large magnitude by comparisons of relation. This countable amount of sand grains is in my shoe, a number of comparable shoefulls will fill a bucket, a number of buckets will fill a dump truck. . . . And again, we could imagine if, given endless time, every grain could be counted. Whether the total number of grains is too large to apprehend all at once is not what is at stake for Kant because whatever number that is must have a counterpart in experience (that is, in time) the judgment of which generated that number.

Of course, the immediately salient response to this is that making number a rule the application of which yields the judgment of magnitude must limit the availability of exceptionally large numbers! In most cases, our attention span limits the application of the rule, but theoretically death would, too. Our corporeality must be considered in these erstwhile longings for the mathematically infinite. This is where Kant turns the idea of the infinite around. We can indeed have an idea of the infinite! We simply cannot count to it! Things that are absolutely large, large beyond comparison, cannot be known mathematically or objectively. Rather, they can be known *aesthetically and subjectively*.[14] Things that are infinitely large occur in nature, and their magnitudes are not calculated in the same mathematical way.

Things in nature such as lofty mountains and frothy seas may be judged absolutely large, that is, large beyond comparison. This judgment is not accomplished by the synthetic unity of apperception. Instead, the idea of the infinitely large originates in the faculty of reason. Once the understanding reaches the limit of apperception, and still no countable single unity is made, only the ideas of reason, *which are given as infinite*, can be used to cognize the sensible. This is the judgment of the sublime. For Kant, the origin of the ideas of reason is simply that they are called forth when we reach the limits of understanding.

Kant characterizes the sublime as the feeling that arises when sensibility and understanding are surpassed by reason. To judge nature, aesthetically, as sublime, one must experience the awful tempest of an ocean squall while at a suitably far, safe distance. What we are judging, crucially, is not the storm itself but our feelings that arise from our attempts to understand its "magnitude and might."[15] The infinitute of the ideas of reason are defined by the lack of a suitably conceivable unity, that is, a *countable* unity. In other words, in attempting to apprehend the magnitude of, say, a hurricane, there is no homogeneous pairing of sensibility and understanding, so there is no 1, no first unity, to begin with. The idea overwhelms our mathematical capabilities. Our ability to cognize these natural occurrences that overwhelm our sensibility is likened to our ability to conceive the possibility of our moral perfection, that is, to recognize the moral law. Kant writes: "The vast ocean heaved up by storms cannot be called sublime. The sight of it is horrible; and one must already have filled one's mind with all sorts of ideas if such an intuition is to attune it to a feeling that is itself sublime, inasmuch as the mind is induced to abandon sensibility and occupy itself with ideas containing a higher purposiveness."[16] Kant explains this reference to "all sorts of ideas" a little later in the *Critique of Judgment*. Without the ideas of reason, a person is limited to sensibility, which cannot conceive of the infinite. Reason expands sensibility, "letting it look outward toward the infinite, which for sensibility is an abyss."[17] Unlike the categories of understanding, ideas of reason are not present in every rational mind as a mode of cognition. Although the *predisposition* to understand and call forth ideas of reason is present in every mind, they are cultivated. Kant writes, "It is a fact that what is called sublime by us, having been prepared through culture, comes across as merely repellent to a person who is uncultured and lacking in the development of moral ideas."[18]

This rounds out my brief and selective introduction to Kant's theory of mathematics. For Kant, the infinite is present at every turn. The continued progress of a priori synthesis may continue as long as homogeneous unities can be formed between sensibility and understanding. And when sensibility is stymied by heterogeneity, the ideas of reason, which are given as infinite (and impossible to fully represent by sensibility), subsume sensibility and lend a higher aesthetic purpose to human life. But one must cultivate moral feeling in order to properly call forth other infinite ideas.

This discussion puts into context the few remarks that Li Zehou makes in his *A New Approach to Kant*, which I will turn to now.

## Li Zehou's Interpretation of Kant's Theory of Mathematics

In his section "On the Nature of Mathematics," Li contextualizes the place of Kant's theory of mathematics in the broader field of pre-Cantorian theory. He emphasizes the fact that Kant's theory of number is not analytic or formal. The reason, of course, is the relationship of mathematics to the forms of intuition, space, and time, as discussed above. Li writes that Kant is wrong about the formulation of mathematics as transcendental intuition.[19] After observing his agreement with Kant that mathematics is not comparable to the analytic forms of logic, he departs from Kant to say that "[mathematics] is related to aesthetic intuition. However, it is not related to Kant's a priori forms of intuition but rather to human sensible experience."[20] Aesthetic intuition, for Kant, is what allows for the judgment of the sublime, or in other words, judgments of absolute quantities as opposed to quantities that can be derived via comparison, such as in the example of counting sand above. Li seems to be making the point that judgments, that is, the formation of synthetic a priori unities, cannot be mathematical because there are no a priori ideas to form mathematical judgments. Half of the equation is missing. All that is left is the sensible.

The problem with this lopsided equation is that, in Kantian terms, no judgment can be made with sensible content alone. This is the context of the well-known quote "Thoughts without content are empty, intuitions without concepts are blind."[21] Li rejects the application of this pithy chiasmus to mathematics directly: "It is evident that mathematics is [not] . . . a priori synthesis (Kant), but the unity of the analytic and synthetic, with practice as its basis and synthesis as its nature."[22] The crux of this statement is Li's theorizing about the analytic. He likens the analytic to the mathematical work that can be done by a computer, "such as demonstration," as opposed to "the synthetic nature of mathematics in discovery and invention."[23] But the origin of the analytic is primitive, practical human activity. Li writes,

> I believe that the rigorous demand for conformity in primitive society, manifested first in religious ritual, then in morality, expressed this quality. Through these powerful ideological activities, primitive people transcended their chaotic and confusing minds and their dream-like pre-logical thinking about right and wrong, and shifted to a logical-thinking stage that was characterized by the law of identity. It was a long historical process, the consequence of which eventually constituted the analytic aspect of mathematics. In short, structural features of primitive practical labor were abstracted, extracted, internalized, and composed into the elements of language, thought, logic, and mathematics. Thus was universal necessity established.[24]

Li goes on to emphasize that the stability of sedimented analytic ideas is derived from consistently reproduced practices in human history. This is his adaptation and application of historical materialism, which rejects the transcendental origins of rational thought in order to "discover its ground in reality."[25] In his essay titled "The Proof of Necessity Lies in Human Activity, in Experiment, and in Labor," Li brings the focus specifically to the historical materialist critique of Kant's schemata, which is useful for theorizing about Li's interpretation of Kant's theory of number. Recall that Kant believed number to be the schema, the rule, of number for the application of the concepts associated with the category of quantity to sensible content. For Kant, the schemata are a priori functions of imagination that are inseparable from time, the a priori form of inner sense. Li holds that this is in error on both counts. The schemata are neither a priori nor temporal (inasmuch as they conform with the manifold of inner sense). Li writes, "Transcendental doctrine believes that schemata are the work of a priori imagination employed to combine the material of sensibility and organize experience, while the theory of practice regards these schemata as an abstraction from sensibility, although still a creative, objective abstraction. So, should the spontaneity of cognition be explained in a mystical manner, or traced to the spontaneity of practice?"[26]

Beyond the call to root the a priori in reality, Li takes another issue with Kant's exposition of the role of the schemata. On Li's account, Kant is not constructing a theory of mathematics that stands on its own as much as he is constructing a theory of mathematics *to serve as an example of a transcendental deduction*.[27] The formulation of number as the schema for the category of quantity becomes the explanation for a priori synthesis, in general. This is so because, as lain out above, Kant believes that the temporal synthesis of understanding and sensibility is *countable*. It is composed of homogeneous units that conform to time. Li criticizes Kant for placing so much importance on the schema that unites understanding and sensibility but providing no sufficient explanation of its provenance.[28] In his theory, Li overcomes Kant's inability to fully explain the origin of the schema by pairing it with the category of quantity and effectively tracing their origin to the same source. He writes, "In my view, it is the homogeneity of time and the identity of quantity that caused the primitive ideology of human beings to gradually grow from an illusory mythology to scientific and historical knowledge."[29] Here Li unites the a priori aspects of the category of quantity and the schema of number in a way that undermines their differences, in terms of form and content, in Kant's theory. In order to explain this further, we will turn to Li's discussion of number.

## Li Zehou's Brief Mention of Number

In *A New Approach to Kant*, Li mentions number only a few times. As mentioned in the previous section, Li believed that Kant's theory of mathematics was tied too tightly to his formulation of time. He writes, "Sensible intuitions sediment social reason; and therefore, to individuals, time and space seem to be a priori forms of intuition without origin. However, from the perspective of humankind as a totality, they are nonetheless the fruits of social practice. Such fruits, unlike formal logic, are not merely internalized operations or external practical activities transformed into internal structures of reason; rather, they are a sedimentation by which social reason becomes sedimented in sensible perceptions."[30] It is true, for Kant there is no mathematical cogitation, and indeed no thoughts at all, that are not rooted in time. Number is central to Kant's exposition of cognition as the schema that allows for the homogeneity of the category and sensibility necessary to form a synthetic judgment about magnitude. For Kant, it is important to note, magnitude is not simply about size in the sense of the size of a sandcastle. Remember, Kant is not theorizing about the qualities of whatever it is that spurs sensibility but only about the presentations of sensibility and how they are combined with a priori concepts and ideas. In a manner of speaking, these presentations *are* magnitudes.

For Kant, the schema of number is given a priori to the imagination. So, for Li's theory to map onto Kant's, he must present a grounding for it. He writes,

> I believe that the origin of number lies in primitive practical activities, that is, in primitive labor characterized by using and making tools. The origin of mathematics, first of all, is not in external things, but in the abstraction of subjective activities of sensibility. The basic forms of mathematics, such as pure quantity, are not deduced from external objects but abstracted from the practical activities of the subject. Yet what they reflect are aspects of objective reality, instead of

the perceptional relations we have with the external world in our observation of it.[31]

Here Li describes number as arising due to its usefulness. As in Kant's theory, Li affirms that number does not exist "out there" with the object, but rather with the subject who does the counting. But that is where fidelity begins to fade. While it is true that there is a sense in which number is objective for Kant, inasmuch as any rational mind has access to the same set of schema, Li's understanding of objectivity, as well as universality and necessity, relies on his theories of sedimentation and cultural-psychological formation. In brief, the objective, universal, and necessary aspects of things are a result of their accumulated stability throughout human history rather than their givenness, in any sense, prior to experience.

Perhaps the Western mind is always eager for a regress, but the question remains as to what would initially spur the idea of number *in order for it to become sedimented*. Li writes that, "originally, natural numbers emerged from the abstract quantities (pure quantity) that appeared and were apprehended in practical activities."[32] Granted that Li also writes that "the universal necessity of mathematics, from its origin, is a universal necessity of abstract practical activities (labor and operation),"[33] it would seem as though number was abstracted from practical activities and that it also emerged along with practical activities. Li is likely not bothered by this distinction because his theory of gradual accretion does not depend on the discrete existence of a first historical instance of numbering. Its ontological existence is attributed to its continued presence in the human psyche.

The same can be said for Li's interpretation of infinity. He is not at pains to prove that the infinite exists or that the rule of numbering can be applied indefinitely in time. The proof that the infinite exists need only go as far as the belief that it exists. Li writes, "'Infinity' does not refer to things in the actual world, the infinity of objects, but rather to the idea that human beings can continue indefinitely or endlessly. This idea eventually becomes an indispensable concept in mathematics. It is because people believe in the infinity of the universe that human beings can carry on infinitely. Therefore, this mathematical concept of infinity is also applicable to the objective world."[34] For Li, the usefulness of a concept or idea heralds the ontological necessity of a concept or idea. It is no different with mathematics. Li writes that "such forms of knowledge as logic, mathematics, and the concept of causality are unique to human beings as representations of the spontaneity of knowledge, and they fundamentally originate from the operational practice of human beings."[35] Mathematics has been abstracted from human activity over the millennia of their mutual development. Mathematical truths have become sedimented, and so, universal, necessary, and objective, over this time. Li implores us then to say that the truths of mathematics and indeed number itself have become a priori.

Li's main critique seems to be that Kant's description of the role of number does more to gird Kant's system than contribute to a theory of mathematics. It may well turn out that the same conditions apply to the metaphysical speculation of the infinite ideas of reason. To this we now turn.

## Li's Exposition of the Origin of the Idea of the Sublime

There is one more loose thread to tie up. Kant's theory of magnitude, hence his theory of number, reaches its limit in the explication of the idea of the mathematically sublime. Here, the unit is heterogeneous rather than homogeneous and so cannot be understood via the typical synthesis of the concepts and the sensible manifold. That intuitions cannot be the sole condition of an idea is true *unless* there is a suitable idea of reason to form an aesthetic judgment, such as the idea of the sublime.[36] Aesthetic judgments of the sublime, crucially for Kant, are not judgments about objects; instead, they are judgments about the interaction between ideas of reason and the content of sensibility. Specifically, aesthetic judgments of the sublime are the triumph of reason over that which overwhelms sensibility, as discussed previously.

Li does not spend much time discussing the sublime, and he gives a felicitous synopsis of Kant's theory, which is explained in detail above. Li emphasizes the connection between the idea of the sublime and moral ideas, even as far as to call them "incomparably sublime moral ideas."[37] Just as Kant did, Li emphasizes that objects themselves are not sublime, but rather, that the feeling of pleasure that "comes from the subject's rejoicing over his own rational power and dignity" produces the "aesthetic feeling of the sublime."[38]

Li quotes Kant, just as I did above, to show that moral ideas are formed prior to sublime ideas and that moral ideas are rooted in culture.

Now, given what I have explained above about Li's theories of sedimentation and cultural-psychological formation, this would seem to give Li's interpretation of Kant, at least regarding the origin of the idea of the sublime, a solid foundation. Throughout A New Approach to Kant, Li consistently points out the instances when Kant gives precedence to the empirical and, as here, refers to culture as a font for rational ideas.

However, Li's readers will not find this quote from Kant: "But the fact that a judgment about the sublime in nature requires culture still in no way implies that it was initially produced by culture and then introduced to society by way of (say) mere convention."[39] For Kant, the ideas of reason and the infinite that they encompass (but cannot pierce through) are forever veiled, forever noumenal. The inability to fully cognize these ideas is precisely what lends them their potential universality and objectivity. This is where Li's interpretation of Kant, just as Li alluded to in the preface of A New Approach to Kant, steps away from congruence. The effect of this incongruity, though, is drastic. Li has systematically undone the mathematical underpinning of Kant's system. Li's theory of number, if it can be called a theory, is not intended to fill the void left by Li's dismissal of Kant's theory of mathematics as a mere rehearsal of synthetic a priori judgment. For Kant, without number there is no magnitude; without magnitude there are no judgments. For Li, number plays not an abstract role, but, of course, a material one.

## Conclusion: Interpretation, Critique, or Neither?

Here at the end, the question of whether Li retains enough of Kant's theory to suitably be called an interpretation arises. If one reads Li's A New Approach to Kant, it is, more than anything, a summary of Kant's work with interspersed references to other philosophers to form a historically broad context of Kant's impact. Yet there are topics, like mathematics, where Li diverges far from Kant. Li does not seem particularly concerned with fealty or felicity when he discusses, especially, Kant's theory of mathematics and the importance of the schemata, of which number is the most important for Kant.

Li maintains that the idea of the potentially infinite progression is necessary for the experience of the sublime. His exposition of the mathematical sublime is very brief and does not significantly deviate from Kant's theory. This is strange because of how heavily the idea of the mathematical sublime rests on judgments of magnitude rendered by or, more accurately, failing to be rendered by the schema of number! Still, Li holds that the idea of the sublime is given as infinite. On my reading, Li provides a simple explanation for why the sublime is given as infinite without reference to number: the mathematical and the dynamical sublime are one and the same. Li writes, "These two kinds of sublime are essentially the same and their division is due to Kant's fondness for architectonic dichotomies."[40] Li is more interested in the dynamical sublime because it more clearly demonstrates *aesthetic feelings*, which Li takes to also be *moral feelings*. His concern, once again, is not to rehearse Kant's synthetic a priori route to experience, but to undermine it while still holding to subjective experience.

Truly the thrill of reading Li's work on Kant is that he can arrive at the same conclusion by such a different route. *A New Approach to Kant* is a screed against Kant just as much as it is a celebration of Kant. Even though Li cores Kant's system, he replaces that core with something very intriguing.

## Notes

1. Immanuel Kant, *Critique of Pure Reason*, trans. Max Müller (New York: Penguin Books, 2007), A586/B614.

2. Kant, *Critique of Pure Reason*, A584/B612, A585/B613.

3. Of course, Li is not the first to proceed to dismantle the idea of the a priori. The academic assault on all things termed "idealist" was undertaken by Chinese Marxist academics as early as the 1920s. See Jan Vrhovski, *Patterns of Thought and Numbers: A History of Mathematical Logic in Late Republican and Early Socialist China (1930–1960)* (Prague: Univerzita Karlova v Praze, 2021).

4. Li Zehou, *A New Approach to Kant: A Confucian-Marxist Viewpoint*, trans. Jeanne Haizhen Allen, and Christopher Ahn (Singapore: Springer Nature, 2018), v.

5. Ady Van Den Stock, "Imprints of the Thing in Itself: Li Zehou's *Critique of Critical Philosophy* and the Historicization of the Transcendental," *Asian Studies* 8, no. 1 (2020): 16.

6. Paul J. D'Ambrosio, Robert A. Carleo III, and Andrew Lambert, "On Li Zehou's Philosophy: An Introduction by Three Translators," *Philosophy East and West* 66, no. 4 (2016): 1059.

7. D'Ambrosio, Carleo, and Lambert, 1063–64.
8. Li, *A New Approach to Kant*, 287.
9. Kant, *Critique of Pure Reason*, B1.
10. Li, 32.
11. Li, 37.
12. Immanuel Kant, "The Only Possible Argument in Support of a Demonstration of the Existence of God," in *Theoretical Philosophy, 1755–1770*, trans. and ed. David Walford with Ralf Meerbote (Cambridge: Cambridge University Press, 1992), 111.
13. Li, *A New Approach to Kant*, 237.
14. Immanuel Kant, *Critique of Judgment*, trans. Werner S. Pluhar (Indianapolis: Hackett, 1987), 251.
15. Kant, *Critique of Judgment*, 245.
16. Kant, *Critique of Judgment*, 246.
17. Kant, *Critique of Judgment*, 265.
18. Kant, *Critique of Judgment*, 265.
19. Li, 64.
20. Li, 65.
21. Kant, *Critique of Pure Reason*, A52/B76.
22. Li, 67.
23. Li, 67.
24. Li, 67.
25. Li, 130.
26. Li, 131.
27. Li, 106.
28. Li, 103.
29. Li, 106.
30. Li, 91.
31. Li, 65.
32. Li, 66.
33. Li, 65.
34. Li, 65.
35. Li, 160.
36. One will of course note that I'm leaving out entirely the aesthetic judgment of the beautiful. My reason for doing this is that my focus on Kant's theory of mathematics, especially quantity and unity, must include the discussion of the *mathematically sublime*.
37. Li, 305.
38. Li, 304.
39. Kant, *Critique of Judgment*, 265.
40. Li, 304.

## Bibliography

D'Ambrosio, Paul J., Robert A. Carleo III, and Andrew Lambert. "On Li Zehou's Philosophy: An Introduction by Three Translators." *Philosophy East and West* 66, no. 4 (2016): 1057–67.

Kant, Immanuel. *Critique of Judgment*. Translated by Werner S. Pluhar. Indianapolis: Hackett, 1987.

Kant, Immanuel. *Critique of Pure Reason*. Translated by Max Müller. New York: Penguin Books, 2007.

Kant, Immanuel. "The Only Possible Argument in Support of a Demonstration of the Existence of God." In *Theoretical Philosophy, 1755–1770*, translated and edited by David Walford with Ralf Meerbote, 107–10. Cambridge: Cambridge University Press, 1992.

Li Zehou. *A New Approach to Kant: A Confucian-Marxist Viewpoint*. Translated by Jeanne Haizhen Allen and Christopher Ahn. Singapore: Springer, 2018.

Van Den Stock, Ady. "Imprints of the Thing in Itself: Li Zehou's *Critique of Critical Philosophy* and the Historicization of the Transcendental." *Asian Studies* 8, no. 1 (2020): 15–35.

Vrhovski, Jan. *Patterns of Thought and Numbers: A History of Mathematical Logic in Late Republican and Early Socialist China (1930–1960)*. Prague: Univerzita Karlova v Praze, 2021.

# Li Zehou's Key Works

## A Comprehensive Chronological Bibliography of His Most Significant Publications

### Li Zehou's Works in Chinese

Li Zehou 李澤厚. "Lun meigan, mei he yishu (Yanjiu tigang)—Jianlun Zhu Guangqian de weixinzhuyi meixue sixiang" 論美感、美和藝術（研究提綱）—兼論朱光潛的唯心主義美學思想 (On Aesthetic Feeling, Beauty, and Art (A Research Proposal)—Also on Zhu Guangqian's Idealist Aesthetic Thought). *Zhexue yanjiu* 哲學研究 5 (1956): 43–73.

Li Zehou 李澤厚. "Meide keguanxing he shehuixing" 美的客觀性和社會性 (The Objectivity and the Social Nature of Beauty). *Renmin ribao*, January 9, 1957.

Li Zehou 李澤厚. "Guanyu dangqian meixue wentide zhenglun" 關於當前美學問題的爭論 (About the Current Controversies on Aesthetics). *Xueshu yuekan* 10 (1957): 25–42.

Li Zehou 李澤厚. *Kang Youwei Tan Sitong sixiang yanjiu* 康有為譚嗣同思想研究 (*Studies on the Thoughts of Kang Youwei and Tan Sitong*). Shanghai: Shanghai renmin chuban she, 1958.

Li Zehou 李澤厚. "Shilun xingxiang siwei" 試論形象思維 (On Image-Thinking). *Wenxue pinglun* 2 (1959): 101–17.

Li Zehou 李澤厚. "Xingxiang siwei xutan" 形象思維續談 (Continuing the Debate on Image-Thinking). *Xueshu yanjiu* 1 (1978): 94–102.

Li Zehou 李澤厚. "Guanyu Kangdede 'wu ziti' xueshuo" 關於康德的「物自體」學說 (On Kant's Theory of the "Thing in Itself"). *Zhexue yanjiu* 6 (1978): 43–52.

Li Zehou 李澤厚. *Meixue lunji* 美學論集 (*A Collection of Essays on Aesthetics*). Shanghai: Shanghai wenyi chuban she, 1980.

Li Zehou 李澤厚. "Kongzi zai pingjia" 孔子再評價 (A Re-evaluation of Confucius). *Zhongguo shehui kexue* 2 (1980): 77–96.

Li Zehou 李澤厚. "Xingxiang siwei zai xutan" 形象思維再續談 (A New Continuation of the Debate on Image-Thinking). *Wenxue pinglun* 3 (1980): 29–40.

Li Zehou 李澤厚. *Zhexue meixue wenxuan* 哲學美學文選 (*Philosophic and Aesthetic Writings*). Changsha: Hunan renmin chuban she, 1984.

Li Zehou 李泽厚. *Pipan zhexue de pipan: Kangde Shuping* 批判哲學的批判：康德述評(*Critique of the Critical Philosophy: A Commentary on Kant*). Beijing: Renmin Press, 1984.

Li Zehou 李澤厚. "Pipan zhexuede pipan (Kangde shuping): Xiuding zaiban houji" 批判哲學的批判(康德述評)：修訂再版後記 (Critique of the Critical Philosophy [A New Key to Approach to Kant]: Afterword to the Second, Revised Edition). *Du shu* 4 (1984): 114–18.

Li Zehou 李澤厚. *Zhongguo gudai sixiang shilun* 中國古代思想史論 (*A History of Classical Chinese Thought*). Beijing: Renmin chuban she, 1985.

Li Zehou 李澤厚. "Guanyu zhutixing de buchong shuoming" 關於主體性的補充說明 (A Supplementary Explanation of Subjectality). *Zhongguo shehui kexue yuan yuanjiushengyuan xuebao* 中國社會科學院研究生院學報 1 (1985): 14–21.

Li Zehou 李澤厚. "Zhongguo sixiang shi zatan" 中國思想史雜談 (Various Conversations on the History of Chinese Thought). *Fudan xuebao (Shehui kexue ben)* 5 (1985): 31–39.

Li Zehou 李澤厚. "Xin chun hua zhishi—zhi qingnian pengyoumen" 新春話知識—致青年朋友們 (Knowledge in the New Spring: For My Young Friends). *Wenshi zhishi* 1 (1985): 3–7.

Li Zehou 李澤厚. *Shilun renlei qiyuan* 試論人類起源/提綱 (*On the Origin of Mankind [An Outline]*). Changsha: Hunan renmin chuban she, 1985.

Li Zehou 李澤厚. *Zhongguo xiandai sixiang shilun* 中國現代思想史論 (*A History of Contemporary Chinese Thought*). Beijing: Dongfang chuban she, 1987.

Li Zehou 李澤厚. "Manshuo Xiti Zhongyong" 漫說西體中用 (A Simple Lecture on Western Substance and Chinese Function). *Kongzi Yanjiu* 4 (1987): 15–28.

Li Zehou 李澤厚. "Guanyu zhutixing de di san tigang" 關於主體性的第三個提綱 (The Third Outline on Subjectivity). *Zouxiang weilai* 3 (1987): 10–21.

Li Zehou 李澤厚. *Dangdai sichao yu Zhongguo zhihui* 當代思潮與中國智慧 (*Contemporary Currents of Thought and Chinese Wisdom*). Taibei: Fengyun shidai chuban she, 1989.

Li Zehou 李澤厚. *Huaxia meixue* 華夏美學 (*The Chinese Aesthetic Tradition*). Beijing: Xinhua Shudian, 1989.

Li Zehou 李澤厚. *Meixue he weilai meixue* 美學和未來美學 (*Aesthetics and Future Aesthetics*). Beijing: Zhongguo shehui kexue chuban she, 1990.

Li Zehou 李澤厚. *Pipan zhexuede pipan (Kangde shuping)* 批判哲學的批判 (康德述評) (*Critique of the Critical Philosophy [A New Approach to Kant]*). Taibei: Fengyun sichao, 1990.

Li Zehou 李澤厚. "Ruxue zuowei Zhongguo wenhua zhuliude yiyi" 儒學作為中國文化主流的意義 (The Significance of Confucianism as the Mainstream of Chinese Culture). *Kongzi yanjiu* 1 (1992): 9–10.

Li Zehou 李澤厚. "Kangde zhexue yu jianli zhutixing lungang" 康德哲學與建立主體性論綱 (An Outline of Kant's Philosophy and the Construction of Subjectality). In *Li Zehou shi nian ji* 李澤厚十年集 (*Li Zehou's Decadal Collection*), vol. 2, 459–75. Hefei: Anhui wenyi chuban she, 1994.

Li, Zehou 李澤厚. *Zhexue Tanxun lu* 哲學探究 (*Philosophical Inquiry*). Tianjin: Tinajin shehui kexue chuban she, 1994.

Li Zehou 李澤厚. "Di si tigang" 第四提綱 (The Fourth Outline). *Xueshu yuekan* 10 (1994): 18–40.

Li Zehou 李澤厚. "'Lunyu jindu' qinyan" 《論語今讀》前言 (Foreword to the "Reading the Analects Today"). *Zhongguo wenhua* 1 (1995): 26–34.

Li Zehou 李澤厚. *Zou wo ziji de lu* 走我自己的路 (*Going My Own Way*). Taipei: Sanmin shudiuan, 1996.

Li Zehou 李澤厚. *Wode zhexue tigang* 我的哲學提綱 (*The Outline of My Philosophy*). Taibei: Sanmin shuju, 1996.

Li Zehou 李澤厚. *Pipan zhexuede pipan (Kangde shuping)* 批判哲學的批判 (康德述評) (*Critique of the Critical Philosophy [A New Approach to Kant]*). Taibei: San min, 1996.

Li Zehou 李澤厚. *Lunyu jindu* 論語今讀 (*Reading the Analects Today*). Hefei: Anhui wenyi chubanshe, 1998.

Li Zehou 李澤厚. *Shiji xin meng* 世紀新夢 (*The New Dream of the Century*). Hefei: Anhui wenyi chuban she, 1998.

Li Zehou 李澤厚. *Li Zehou xueshu wenhua suibi* 李澤厚學術文化隨筆 (*Essays on Li Zehou's Academic Culture*). Beijing: Zhongguo qingnian chuban she, 1998.

Li Zehou 李澤厚. *Zhongguo sixiang shilun* 中國思想史論 (*A History of Chinese Thought*). Hefei: Anhui wenyi chuban she, 1999.

Li Zehou 李澤厚. *Li Zehou zhexue wencun* 李澤厚哲學文存 (*A Deposit of Li Zehou's Philosophy*). Hefei: Anhui wenyi chuban she, 1999.

Li Zehou 李澤厚. *Jimao wushuo* 己卯五說 (*Five Essays from 1999*). Beijing: Zhongguo dianying chuban she, 1999.

Li Zehou 李澤厚. "Man shuo 'Xiti Zhongyong'" 漫說「西體中用」 (A Simple Lecture on "Western Substance and Chinese Function"). In *Zhongguo sixiang shilun*, part 3, 1139–69. Hefei: Anhui wenyi chuban she, 1999.

Li Zehou 李澤厚. "Shitan Zhongguo de zhihui" 試探中國的智慧 (Exploring Chinese Wisdom). In *Zhongguo sixiang shilun* 中國思想史論 (*On China's Intellectual History*), part 3, 299–326. Hefei: Anhui wenyi chuban she, 1999.

Li Zehou 李澤厚. "Lishi yanjie yu lilunde 'Du'" 歷史眼界與理論的 "度" (The Historical Perspective and the Theoretical "Proper measure"). *Tianya* 2 (1999): 128–135.

Li Zehou 李澤厚. *Tanxun yusui* 探尋語碎 (*Exploring Fragments*). Shanghai: Shanghai wenyi chuban she, 2000.

Li Zehou 李澤厚. *Meixue si jiang* 美學四講 (*Four Essays on Aesthetics*). Guilin: Guangxi Normal University Press, 2001 [1988].

Li Zehou 李澤厚. *Meixue san shu* 美學三書 (*Three Books on Aesthetics*). Hefei: Anhui wenyi chuban she, 2002.

Li Zehou 李澤厚. *Meixue jiu zuo ji* 美學舊作集 (*Earlier Writings on Aesthetics*). Tianjin: Tinajin shehui kexue yuan chuban she, 2002.

Li Zehou 李澤厚. *Zou wo zijide lu* 走我自己的路 (*Going My Own Way*). Beijing: SDX Joint Publishing, 2002.

Li Zehou 李澤厚. *Lishi bentilun* 歷史本體論 (*Historical Ontology*). Beijing: Sanlian Bookstore, 2002.

Li Zehou 李澤厚. *Mei de licheng* 美的歷程 (*The Path of Beauty*). In *Meixue sanshu* 美學三書 (*Three Books on Aesthetics*), edited by Yi Jing, 3–193. Tianjin: Tianjin Academy of Social Sciences Press, 2003.

Li Zehou 李澤厚. "Wo zoude lu" 我走的路 (*My Own Way*). *Yuwen shijie* Z1 (2003): 19–20.

Li Zehou 李澤厚. "2004 Chuantong wenhua fuxing sichao" 2004 傳統文化復興思潮 (The Revival of Traditional Culture in 2004). *Asixiang*. www.aisixiang.com/data/12137.html.

Li Zehou 李澤厚. "Ruxue siqi yu zhuanhuanxingde chuangzao" 儒學四期與轉換性創造 (The Four Phases of Confucianism and the Transformative Creation). *Henan ribao* 5, no. 12 (2005): 1–2.

Li Zehou 李澤厚. *Makesizhuyi zai Zhongguo* 馬克思主義在中國 (*Marxism in China*). Hong Kong: Minbao chuban she, 2006.

Li Zehou 李澤厚. "Qing benti he liangzhong daode" 請本體和兩種道德 (Emotion-Based Substance and Two Kinds of Morality). *Ai sixiang* (2006). www.aisixiang.com/data/12125.html.

Li Zehou 李澤厚. *Pipan zhexue de pipan: Kangde shuping* 批判哲學的批判: 康德述評 (*Critique of Critical Philosophy: A New Approach to Kant*). Beijing: SDX Joint Publishing, 2007.

Li Zehou 李澤厚. "Qing benti zai jinri" 情本體在今日 (Emotion-Based Substance in Present Time). *Zhongguo meixue yanjiu* 1 (2007): 1–9.

Li Zehou 李澤厚. *Shiyong lixing yu legan wenhua* 實用理性與樂感文化 (*Pragmatic Reason and a Culture of Optimism*). Beijing: Sanlian Bookstore, 2005.

Li Zehou 李澤厚. *Lishi bentilun: Jimao wu shuo* 歷史本體論: 己卯五說 (*Historical Ontology: Five Essays from 1999*). Beijing: SDX Joint Publishing, 2008.

Li Zehou 李澤厚. *Za zhu ji* 雜著集 (*A Collection of Various Essays*). Beijing: SDX Joint Publishing, 2008.

Li Zehou 李澤厚. "Wo he bashi niandai 'meixue re'" 我和八十年代「美學熱」 (The "Aesthetic Fever" from the 1980s and Me). *Jingji guancha wang*, August 6, 2008. www.eeo.com.cn/2008/0609/102665.shtml.

Li Zehou 李澤厚. *Renleixue lishi bentilun* 人類學歷史本體論 (*Anthropological Historical Ontology*). Tianjin: Tianjin Academy of Social Sciences Press, 2008.

Li Zehou 李澤厚. *Li Zehou ji* 李澤厚集 (*A Collection of Li Zehou's Works*), 10 vols. Beijing: Sanlian Bookstore, 2008.

Li Zehou 李澤厚. "Guanyu xingxiang siwei" 關於形象思維 (On Image-Thinking). *Zhonghua huoye webxuan* 9 (2008): 23–25.

Li Zehou 李澤厚. *Zhongguo gudai sixiang shilun—Zhongguo jindai sixiang shilun—Zhongguo xiandai sixiang shilun (quan san ce)* 中國古代思想史論—中國近代思想史論—中國現代思想史論(全三冊) (*A History of Classical Chinese Thought; A History of Modern Chinese Thought; A History of Contemporary Chinese Thought, 3 vols.*). Beijing: Sanlian Bookstore, 2009.

Li, Zehou 李泽厚. "Guanyu 'mei yu dai zong jiao' de za tan da wen" 關於"美育代宗教"的雜談答問 (An Interview: A Rambling Talk about "Aesthetic Education Replacing Religion"). In *Li Zehou mei xue gai lun* (*An Introduction to Li Zehou's Aesthetics*), edited by Liu Zaifu. Beijing: Sanlian Bookstore, 2009.

Li Zehou 李澤厚. *Mei de lichen* 美的歷程 (*The Path of Beauty*). Beijing: SDX Joint Publishing, 2009 [1981].

Li Zehou 李澤厚. *Li Zehou meixue gailun* 李澤厚美學概論 (*An Introduction to Li Zehou's Aesthetics*). Beijing: Sanlian Bookstore, 2009.

Li Zehou 李澤厚. "Guanyu 'Youguan lunlixue de dawen' de buchong shuoming" 關於《有關倫理學的答問》的補充說明 (Additional Explanation to "Some Questions and Answers Regarding Ethics"). *Zhexue dongtai* 哲學動態 11 (2009): 26–33.

Li Zehou 李澤厚. *Lunlixue gangyao* 倫理學綱要 (*An Outline of Ethics*). Beijing: Renmin ribao chuban she, 2010.

Li Zehou 李澤厚. "Zhong Ri wenhua xinli bijiao shi shuo lue gao" 中日文化心理比較試說略稿 (A Small Experimental Draft on the Comparison of Chinese and Japanese Cultural Psychology). *Huawen wenxue* 100, no. 5 (2010 [1997]): 15–36.

Li Zehou 李澤厚. "Chu ni ruxue shenceng jiegou shuo" (1996) 初擬儒學深層結構說 (1996) (A Draft Proposal of a Theory of Confucian Deep Structures). *Huawen wenxue* 5 (2010): 7–14.

Li Zehou 李澤厚. *Zhexue gangyao* 哲學綱要 (*Outline of a Philosophy*). Beijing: Peking University Press, 2011.

Li Zehou 李澤厚. "Cong 'Liangde lun' tan pushi jiazhi yu Zhongguo moshi" 從「兩德論」談普世價值與中國模式 (On Universal Values and the Chinese Model from the Perspective of the 'Theory of two Moralities'). *Dongwu xueshu* 4 (2011): 5–10.

Li Zehou 李澤厚. *Shuo wenhua xinli* 說文化心理 (*On Cultural Psychology*). Shanghai: Shanghai wenyi chuban she, 2012.

Li Zehou 李澤厚. *Shuo Xiti Zhongyong* 說西體中用 (*On Western Substance and Chinese Application*). Shanghai: Shanghai wenyi chuban she, 2012.

Li Zehou 李澤厚. "Renshilun dawen" 認識論答問 (Q&A about Epistemology). *Zhongguo wenhua* 1 (2012): 1–11.

Li Zehou 李澤厚. "Lunlixue dawen bu" 倫理學答問補 (A Supplement to the Dialogue on Ethics). *Du shu* 11 (2012): 47–60.

Li Zehou 李澤厚. "Shengmingde tongxingyuan" 生命的同心圓 (The Concentric Circles of Life). *Shehui kexue luntan* 12 (2012): 70–83.

Li Zehou 李澤厚. "'Qing benti' de wai tui yu neitui" 「情本體」的外推與內退 (The Extension and Intention of 'Emotion-Based Substance'). *Xueshu yuekan* 44, no. 1 (2012): 14–21.

Li Zehou 李澤厚. "Goujian zhengyi jichushangde hexie—cong Sangde'erde 'Gongzheng' shuoqi" 構建正義基礎上的和諧—從桑德爾的「公正 」說起 (Constructing Righteousness on the Basis of Harmony—On Sandel's Concept of Justice). *Shanghai Shehui kexue bao*, December 31, 2013. blog.sina.com.cn/s/blog_63959b6d0101d444.html.

Li Zehou 李澤厚. "Zai tan shiyong lixing" 再談實用理性 (Another Talk about Practical Rationality). *Wucu qinghuade boke*, April 25, 2014. blog.sina.com.cn/s/blog_a404f6dd0101ra3j.html.

Li Zehou 李澤厚. "Xingshi ceng yu yuanshi jidian" 形式層與原始積澱 (Formal Layers and Elementary Sedimentation). *Meixue* 1 (2014): 5–8.

Li Zehou 李澤厚. *Li Zehou duihua ji: Bashi niandai* 李澤厚對話集：八十年代 (A Collection of Dialogues with Li Zehou from the 1980s). Beijing: Zhonghua shuju, 2014.

Li Zehou 李澤厚. *Li Zehou duihua ji: Jiushi niandai* 李澤厚對話集：九十年代 (A Collection of Dialogues with Li Zehou from the 1990s). Beijing: Zhonghua shuju, 2014.

Li Zehou 李澤厚. *Li Zehou duihua ji: Ershi yi shiji (yi)* 李澤厚對話集：廿一世紀（一） (A Collection of Dialogues with Li Zehou: The Twenty-First Century—Part 1). Beijing: Zhonghua shuju, 2014.

Li Zehou 李澤厚. *Li Zehou duihua ji: Ershi yi shiji (er)* 李澤厚對話集：廿一世紀（二） (A Collection of Dialogues with Li Zehou: Twenty-First Century—Part 2). Beijing: Zhonghua shuju, 2014.

Li Zehou 李澤厚. *Li Zehou duihua ji: Yu Liu Zaifu duitan* 李澤厚對話集：與劉再复對談 (A Collection of Dialogues with Li Zehou: Conversations with Liu Zaifu). Beijing: Zhonghua shuju, 2014.

Li Zehou 李澤厚. *Li Zehou duihua ji: Fushenglun xue* 李澤厚對話集：浮生論學 (A Collection of Dialogues with Li Zehou: On the Science of the Floating Life). Beijing: Zhonghua shuju, 2014.

Li Zehou 李澤厚. *Li Zehou duihua ji: Zhongguo zhexue dengchang* 李澤厚對話集：中國哲學登場 (A Collection of Dialogues with Li Zehou: Chinese Philosophy is Appearing on the Stage). Beijing: Zhonghua shuju, 2014.

Li Zehou 李澤厚. *Huiying Sangde'er ji qita* 回應桑德爾及其他 (A Response to Sandel and Other Matters). Beijing: Sanlian Bookstore, 2014.

Li Zehou 李澤厚. *Li Zehou huayu* 李澤厚話語 (Li Zehou's Discourse). Shanghai: Huadong shifan daxue chuban she, 2014.

Li Zehou 李澤厚. "Gao Ertaide zhiyi" 高爾泰的質疑 (Gao Ertai's Question). *Xinlan boke* (2014). blog.sina.com.cn/s/blog_676299bb0102wubg.html.

Li Zehou 李澤厚. *You wu dao li, shi li gui ren* 由巫到禮、釋禮歸仁 (*From Shamanism to Ritual Regulations and Humaneness*). Beijing: Sanlian Bookstore, 2015.

Li Zehou 李澤厚. "Da 'Gauguin san wen'" 答「高更 (Paul Gauguin) 三問」 (The Answer to "Three Questions Posed by Paul Gauguin"). *Zhonghua dushu bao*, April 11, 2015.

Li Zehou 李澤厚. *Shenme shi daode* 什麼是道德 (*What Is Morality?*). Shanghai: ECNU Press, 2015.

Li Zehou 李澤厚. "Li Zehou duitan lu" 李澤厚對談錄 (Recordings of Li Zehou's Conversations). *Dai yue ting yu zhu jilu* (2016). www.doc88.com/p-7030124841.html.

Li Zehou 李澤厚. "Guanyu Makeside lunli ji qita (xia)" 關於馬克思的倫理及其他 (下) (On Marxist Ethics and Other Issues, Part 2). *Tongsu wenda—zai tan makesizhuyu zai Zhongguo*, May 2, 2016. blog.sina.com.cn/s/blog_63959b6d010182uw.html.

Li Zehou 李澤厚. *Renleixue lishi bentilun* 人類學歷史本體論 (*Anthropo-Historical Ontology*). Qingdao: Qingdao chuban she, 2016.

Li Zehou 李澤厚. "Lunlixue buzhu" 倫理學補注 (Additional Remarks to Ethics). *Tansu yu zhengming* 9 (2016): 4–13.

Li Zehou 李澤厚. "Ruxue, Kangde, Makesi san heyi" 儒學、康德、馬克思三合一 (Confucianism, Kant and Marx—a Tripartite Synthesis). *Shehui kexue bao* 8 (2016): 1–8.

Li Zehou 李澤厚. *Zhongguo xiandai sixiang shilun* 中國現代思想史論 (*A History of Contemporary Chinese Thought*). Beijing: Sanlian Bookstore, 2016.

Li Zehou 李澤厚. *Lunlixue gangyao xupian* 倫理學綱要續篇 (*Outline of Ethics—Continuation*). Beijing: Sanlian Bookstore, 2017.

Li Zehou 李澤厚. "Ju Meng qi xing Xun xue—wei 'Lunlixue gangyao' yi bian" 舉孟旗 行荀學—為《倫理學綱要》一辯 (Raise the Mencian Banner, Practice Xunzian Philosophy: A Defense of the *Outline of Ethics*). *Tansuo yu zhengming* 探索與證明 4 (2017): 58–62.

Li Zehou 李澤厚. "Guanyu 'Lunlixue zonglan biao' de shuoming" 關於 "倫理學總覽表" 的說明 (An Explanation of the "General Scheme of Ethics"). *Zhongguo wenhua* 47, no. 1 (2018): 1–15.

Li Zehou 李澤厚. *Lunlixue xinshuo shuyao* 倫理學新說述要 (*A New Sketch of Ethics*). Beijing: Shijie tushu, 2019.

# Li Zehou's Works in Western Languages

Li Zehou. "The Philosophy of Kant and a Theory of Subjectivity." In *Analecta Husserliana—The Yearbook of Phenomenological Research 21, The Phenomenology of Man and of the Human Condition, II: The Meeting Point between*

Occidental and Oriental Philosophies, edited by Anna-Teresa Tymieniecka, 135–49. Dordrecht: D. Reidel, 1986.
Li Zehou. Der Weg des Schönen: Wesen und Geschichte der chinesischen Kultur und Aesthetik. Translated by Karl-Heinz Pohl and Gudrun Wacker. Freiburg: Herder, 1992.
Li Zehou. The Path of Beauty: A Study of Chinese Aesthetics. Translated by Gong Lizeng. Hong Kong: Oxford University Press, 1994.
Li Zehou. "A Supplementary Explanation of Subjectality." Contemporary Chinese Thought 31, no. 2 (1999): 26–31.
Li Zehou. "An Outline of the Origin of Humankind." Contemporary Chinese Thought 31, no. 2 (1999): 20–25.
Li Zehou. "Some Tentative Remarks on China's Wisdom (Excerpts)." Contemporary Chinese Thought 31, no. 2 (1999): 44–65.
Li Zehou. "The Dual Variation of Enlightenment and Nationalism: (Excerpt)." Contemporary Chinese Thought 31, no. 2 (1999): 40–43.
Li Zehou. "The Image Level and Artistic Sedimentation (Excerpts)." Contemporary Chinese Thought 31, no. 2 (1999): 77–88.
Li Zehou. "The Western is the Substance, and the Chinese is for Application (Excerpts)." Contemporary Chinese Thought 31, no. 2 (1999): 32–39.
Li Zehou. "Modernization and the Confucian World." Address given at the Colorado College's 125th Anniversary Symposium "Cultures in the Twenty-First Century: Conflicts and Convergences," in a discussion forum entitled "The Confucian World." Colorado Springs, February 5, 1999. www.topicdiscussion.org/article/9753920641/.
Li Zehou. "A Few Questions Concerning the History of Chinese Aesthetics (Excerpts)." Translated by Peter Wong Yih Jiun. Contemporary Chinese Thought 31, no. 2 (1999 [1985]): 66–78.
Li Zehou. "Human Nature and Human Future: A Combination of Marx and Confucius." In Chinese Thought in a Global Context: A Dialogue Between Chinese and Western Philosophical Approaches, edited by Karl-Heinz Pohl, 129–44. Leiden: Brill, 1999.
Li Zehou. "Subjectivity and 'Subjectality': A Response." Philosophy East and West 49, no. 2 (1999): 174–83.
Li Zehou. The Chinese Aesthetic Tradition. Translated by Maija Bell Samei. Honolulu: University of Hawai'i Press, 2009.
Li Zehou. 2010. "Human Nature and Aesthetic Metaphysics." In International Yearbook of Aesthetics: Diversity and Universality in Aesthetics, vol. 14, edited by Wang Keping, 4. Beijing: International Association for Aesthetics, 2010.
Li Zehou. "A Response to Michael Sandel and Other Matters." Translated by Paul J. D'Ambrosio and Robert A. Carleo III. Philosophy East and West 66, no. 4 (2016): 1068–1147.

Li Zehou. "Response to Paul Gaugin's Triple Question." In *Li Zehou and Confucian Philosophy*, edited by Roger T. Ames and Jia Jinhua, 18–30. Honolulu: University of Hawai'i Press, 2018.

Li Zehou. *A New Approach to Kant: A Confucian-Marxist Viewpoint*. Translated by Jeanne Haizhen Allen and Christopher Ahn. Singapore: Springer, 2018.

Li Zehou. *The Origins of Chinese Thought: From Shamanism to Ritual Regulations and Humaneness*. Translated by Robert A. Carleo III. Leiden: Brill, 2018.

Li Zehou. *A History of Classical Chinese Thought*. Translated by Andrew Lambert. New York: Routledge, 2020.

Li Zehou. *The Humanist Ethics of Li Zehou*. Edited and translated by Robert A. Carleo III. Albany: State University of New York Press, 2023.

## With Co-authors

Li Zehou 李澤厚 and Liu Gangji 劉鋼紀. *Zhongguo meixue shi* 中國美學史 (*A History of Chinese Aesthetics*). Hefei: Anhui wenyi chuban she, 1999.

Li Zehou 李澤厚 and Chen Ming 陳明. *Fusheng lun xue* 浮生論學 (*On the Science of Floating Life*). Beijing: Huaxia chuben she, 2002.

Li Zehou 李澤厚, Lü peng 呂澎, and Zhao Shilin 趙士林. *Ziran shuo hua* 自然說話 (*Nature Speaking*). Changsha: Hunan meishu chuban she, 2004.

Li, Zehou and Jane Cauvel. *Four Essays on Aesthetics: Toward a Global View*. Lanham, MD: Lexington Books, 2006.

Li Zehou 李澤厚 and Liu Xuyuan 劉緒源. "Li Zehou tan xueshu sixiang san jieduan" 李澤厚談學术思想三階段 (Li Zehou Discusses the Three Phases of His Academic Thought). *Shanghai wenxue* 1 (2011): 72–77.

Li Zehou 李澤厚 and Liu Xuyuan 劉緒源. *Gai Zhongguo zhexue dengchang le?* 該中國哲學登場了? (*Should Chinese Philosophy Appear on the Stage?*). Shanghai: Shanghai yiwen chuban she, 2011.

Li Zehou 李澤厚 and Liu Xuyuan 劉緒源. "'Qing benti' shi yizhong shijiexing shijiao" 「情本體」是一種世界性視角 ("Emotion-Based Substance" is a Global Perspective). *Juece yu xinxi* 3 (2011): 51–61.

Li Zehou 李澤厚 and Liu Xuyuan 劉緒源. "'Qing benti' shi yizhong shijiexing shijiao" 「情本體」是一種世界性視角 ("Emotion-based Substance" Is a Global Perspective). *Juece yu xinxi* 3 (2011): 9–13.

Li Zehou 李澤厚 and Liu Xuyuan 劉緒源. "Li Zehou tan xueshu sixiang san jieduan" 李澤厚談學术思想三階段 (Li Zehou Discusses the Three Phases of His Academic Thought). *Shanghai wenxue* 1 (2011): 72–77.

Li Zehou 李澤厚 and Liu Xuyuan 劉緒源. "'Qing benti' de wai tui yu neitui" 「情本體」的外推與內推 (The Extention and Intention of the "Emotion-based Substance"). *Xueshu yuekan* 44, no. 1 (2012): 14–21.

Li Zehou 李澤厚 and Liu Xuyuan 劉緒源. *Zhongguo zhexue ruhe dengchang?* 中國哲學如何登場? (*How can Chinese Philosophy Appear on the Stage?*). Shanghai: Shanghai yiwen chuban she, 2012.

Li Zehou 李澤厚 and Liu Yuedi 劉悅笛. "Cong 'qing benti' fansi zhengzhi zhexue" 從「情本體」反思政治哲學 (Reflecting on Political Philosophy from "Emotion as Substance"). *Kaifang shidai* 4 (2014): 194–215.

Li Zehou 李澤厚 and Liu Yuedi 劉悅笛. "'Qing benti' shi shijiede" 「情本體」是世界的 ("Emotion as Substance" Belongs to the World). *Tansuo yu zhengming* 4 (2014): 4–9.

Li Zehou 李澤厚, and Liu Yuedi 劉悅笛. "Guanyu 'qing benti' de Zhongguo zhexue duihualu" 關於"情本體"的中國哲學對話錄 (Records of Dialogues on the "Emotion-based Substance" of Chinese Philosophy). *Wen shi zhe* 3 (2014): 18–29.

Li Zehou 李澤厚, and Liu Yuedi 劉悅笛. "Li Zehou, Liu Yuedi 2017 nian zhexue duitan lu (xia): Ziyou yizhi, yinguo lü yu juedgin lun" 李澤厚、劉悅笛2017年哲學對談錄（下）自由意志、因果律與決定論 (The Philosophical Debate between Li Zehou and Liu Yuedi from 2017, Part II: Free Will, the Law of Causality and Determinism). In *Ziyou ruan zhide boke* (*Free Sina block*) (2017): 1–10. blog.sina.com.cn/s/blog_5fab50bf0102x7dq.html.

Li Zehou 李澤厚 and Liu Yuedi 劉悅笛. "Lunlixue zatan—Li Zehou, Li Yuedi 2018 nian duitan lu" 倫理學雜談—李澤厚、劉悅笛 2018 年對談錄 (Various Debates on Ethics—Li Zehou's Talks with Liu Yuedi in 2018). *Hunan shifan daxue shehui kexue xuebao* 5 (2018): 25.

Li Zehou 李澤厚 and Liu Zaifu 劉再復. *Gaobie geming—ershi shiji Zhongguo duitan lu* 告別革命—二十世紀中國對談錄 (*Farewell to Revolution—A Critical Dialogue on Twentieth-Century China*). Taibei: Maitan chuban, 1999.

Li Zehou 李泽厚 and Wang Desheng 王德胜. "Guanyu wenhua xianzhuang, daode chongjian de duihua" 關於文化現狀道德重建的對話 (Dialogue on the Current Cultural Situation and Moral Reconstruction). *Dongfang* 東方 5 (1974): 69–73; 6 (1974): 85–87.

Li Zehou 李澤厚 and Wang Shuren 王树人. "Wenhua de weiji, ronghe yu chongjian" 文化的危機, 融與與重建 (The Crisis of Culture, Reconciliation, and Reconstruction). *Yuandao* 原道 1 (1994): 95–114.

Li Zehou 李澤厚 and Tong Shijun 童世骏. "Guanyu 'tiyong,' 'chaoyue' he chongdie gongshi deng duihua" 關於'體用'、'超越' 和 '重疊共識' 等的對話 (Discussions on 'Essence and Function,' 'Transcendence,' the 'Overlapping Consensus' and Other Matters). *Zhexue fenxi* 3, no. 1 (2012): 167–78.

Li Zehou 李澤厚 and Yang Guorong 楊國榮. "Lunli wenti ji qita—guocheng fenxide shijiao" 倫理問題及其他—過程分析的視角 (About Ethics and Other Issues—From the Perspective of Processual Analysis). *Shehui kexue* 9 (2014): 117–28.

# Contributors

**Roger T. Ames** (安樂哲) is Humanities Chair Professor at Peking University, Senior Academic Advisor of the Peking University Berggruen Research Center, and Professor Emeritus of Philosophy at the University of Hawai'i. He is former editor of *Philosophy East and West* and founding editor of *China Review International*. Ames has authored several interpretative studies of Chinese philosophy and culture: *Thinking Through Confucius* (1987), *Anticipating China* (1995), *Thinking from the Han* (1998), and *Democracy of the Dead* (1999) (all with D. L. Hall), *Confucian Role Ethics: A Vocabulary* (2011), and most recently *Human Becomings: Theorizing Persons for Confucian Role Ethics* (2020). His publications also include translations of Chinese classics: *Sun-tzu: The Art of Warfare* (1993), *Sun Pin: The Art of Warfare* (1996) (with D. C. Lau), the *Confucian Analects* (1998) and the *Chinese Classic of Family Reverence: The Xiaojing* (2009) (both with H. Rosemont), *Focusing the Familiar: The Zhongyong* (2001), and *The Daodejing* (with D. L. Hall) (2003). Almost all of his publications are now available in Chinese translation, including his philosophical translations of Chinese canonical texts. He has most recently completed the new *Sourcebook in Classical Confucian Philosophy* (2023) with its companion *A Conceptual Lexicon for Classical Confucian Philosophy* (2021), and is writing articles promoting a conversation between American pragmatism and Confucianism.

**Rafal Banka** received his PhD in Philosophy from Jagiellonian University. He was PI of a European Research Council grant "Mereological Reconstruction of the Metaphysical System in the Daodejing" (hosted by Faculty of Philosophy, University of Oxford, 2020–2023). His areas of research include Chinese and Western comparative (metaphysics, aesthetics, methodology) philosophies. He has published in *Dao: A Journal of Comparative Philosophy*, *Journal of Chinese Philosophy*, and *Philosophy East and West*, among others. His book *Cognition and Practice: Li Zehou's Philosophical Aesthetics* was published by State University of New York Press in 2022.

**Robert A. Carleo III** received his MPhil in Chinese Philosophy from Fudan University and his PhD in Philosophy from The Chinese University of Hong Kong. He teaches in the international graduate program in Chinese Philosophy at East China Normal University and serves as a fellow of the digital Collaborative Learning project 四海為學. Inspired by Li Zehou, he researches ethical and political questions in comparative and Chinese philosophy, investigating especially questions of the ultimate foundations of right and wrong, how we come to know right and wrong, and freedom, equality, and moral personhood. His translation of Li's *The Origins of Chinese Thought* was named *Choice* Outstanding Academic Title of 2019. He is also co-editor, with Yong Huang, of *Confucian Political Philosophy: Dialogues in the State of the Field* (2021), editor and translator of *The Humanist Ethics of Li Zehou* (2023), and author of *Humane Liberality: A Confucian Proposal* (2024).

**Paul J. D'Ambrosio** is fellow of the Institute of Modern Chinese Thought and Culture, professor of Chinese philosophy, and Dean of the Center for Intercultural Research, all at East China Normal University in Shanghai, China. Additionally, he is founder of the 四海为学 "Collaborative Learning" academic forum. He holds a PhD in philosophy from the National University of Ireland, and specializes in Chinese philosophy and technology–human relations including AI and social media. Books by D'Ambrosio include *Zhen jia zhi jian* 真假之间 (*Between Genuineness and Pretense*) (2020); *You and Your Profile* (2021) and *Genuine Pretending* (2017), both with Hans-Georg Moeller; and *Encountering China* (2018) with Michael Sandel. His new co-edited volume *Four Exemplars of Ru* 儒 (*Confucianism): Beyond Comparisons: Philosophizing Beyond Comparisons* is scheduled to appear in 2025 from Springer Press. Additionally, he has authored over 100 articles, chapters, and reviews, and is translator of over a dozen books on Chinese philosophy.

**David Elstein** is Professor of Philosophy and Asian Studies at SUNY New Paltz. He received his PhD from University of Michigan and was a postdoctoral fellow at Academic Sinica in Taiwan. His research focuses on contemporary Confucian philosophy. He is author of *Democracy in Contemporary Confucian Philosophy* (2014), editor of *Dao Companion to Contemporary Confucian Philosophy* (2020), and translator of *The Chinese Liberal Spirit: Selected Writings of Xu Fuguan* (2022). In addition, he has published articles in *Philosophy East and West*, *Dao: A Journal of Comparative Philosophy*, *Contemporary Political Theory*, and *European Journal of Political Theory*.

**Jinhua Jia** (賈晉華) earned her MA from Xiamen University and her PhD from University of Colorado at Boulder. She is Research Professor at the Center of Traditional Chinese Cultural Studies in Wuhan University and Adjunct Professor at the Department of Philosophy and Religious Studies in University of Macau. She has held membership/fellowship at the Institute for Advanced Study (Princeton), National Humanities Center (USA), and Harvard Divinity School, and has taught at Hong Kong Polytechnic University, University of Macau, City University of Hong Kong, and Xiamen University. Her research interests include traditional Chinese thought, religion, literature, and women and gender studies. She is the author of many books and articles, including *From Ritual Culture to Classical Confucianism* 從禮樂文明到古典儒學 (2020); *Gender, Power, and Talent: The Journey of Daoist Priestesses in Tang China* (2018); *Study on Classical Chan Buddhism* 古典禪研究 (2010); *The Hongzhou School of Chan Buddhism in Eighth- through Tenth-Century China* (2006); and *Study on the Collections of Gathering and Groups of Poets in Tang Dynasty* 唐代集會總集與詩人群研究 (2001/2015).

**Wang Keping** (王柯平) is a senior fellow of Chinese Academy of Social Sciences (CASS), and emeritus professor of philosophy at CASS University and Beijing International Studies University, China. He received his PhD from Beijing Normal University. He was formerly a visiting fellow of St. Anne's College of Oxford University (2001), visiting professor to the School of Philosophical and Historical Inquiry of Sydney University (2010), Institute des Sciences Politiques Bordeaux (2017), and the School of Philosophy of Athens University (2019). His research areas include East-West aesthetics, classical studies, and cultural philosophy. His main publications in English include *Beauty and Human Existence in Chinese Philosophy* (2021), *Harmonism as an Alternative* (2019), *Chinese Culture of Intelligence* (2019), *Rediscovery of Sino-Hellenic Ideas* (2016),

*Reading the Dao: A Thematic Inquiry* (2011), and *Perceiving Plato's Concern* (forthcoming). He is the co-editor of *Reflections on Plato's Poetics* (2016), and the author of ten Chinese books on classical poetics, aesthetics and philosophy.

**Maja Maria Kosec** is a doctoral student and junior researcher at the Department of Asian Studies, Faculty of Arts, University of Ljubljana. She holds a master's degree in Sinology with a thesis on the preservation of Confucian traditions in the Chinese diaspora in Cuba. Her current research focuses on the history of ideas and theories about the origins of Chinese culture.

**Andrew Lambert** is an Associate Professor of Philosophy at City University of New York, College of Staten Island. He received his PhD from the University of Hawai'i, and has been a visiting scholar at Peking University and at the Chinese University of Hong Kong. His research focuses primarily on ethics and Chinese thought. His translation of Li Zehou's book *A History of Classical Chinese Thought* (中国古代思想史论) was published by Routledge in 2019. He has also published several articles on the work of Li Zehou.

**Chenyang Li** is Professor of Philosophy at Nanyang Technological University, Singapore, where he founded the philosophy program. His primary areas of research are Chinese philosophy and comparative philosophy. He is the author of *The Tao Encounters the West: Explorations in Comparative Philosophy*, *The Confucian Philosophy of Harmony*, *Reshaping Confucianism: A Progressive Inquiry*, and over 100 journal articles and book chapters. His edited volumes include *The Sage and the Second Sex*, *The East Asian Challenge for Democracy* (with Daniel Bell), *Moral Cultivation and Confucian Character* (with Peimin Ni), *Chinese Metaphysics and its Problems* (with Franklin Perkins), *Harmony in Chinese Thought: A Philosophical Introduction* (with Sai Hang Kwok and Dascha Düring), and *The Virtue of Harmony* (with Dascha Düring). He was president of the Association of Chinese Philosophers in North America (ACPA), president of the International Society for Chinese Philosophy (ISCP), Senior Visiting Fellow at the City University of Hong Kong, an American Council on Education ACE fellow, and an inaugural Berggruen Fellow at the Center for Advanced Study in the Behavioural Sciences in Stanford University.

Currently he serves on the editorial/academic boards of over two dozen scholarly publications and organizations.

**Jordan B. Martin** (馬兆仁) is an Australian postdoctoral researcher at Hunan University's Yuelu Academy, the same institution at which he received his master's and doctorate. His doctoral thesis, "An Evolutionary Perspective on Divergence and Concordance in Mencius and Xunzi," was authored in Chinese (Yanhua lun shi yu xia de Meng Xun yitong 演化論視域下的孟荀異同) and supervised by Zhu Hanmin 朱漢民. His research interests are broad, with a focus on pre-Qin Ruist thought and its evolutionary basis, and in addition to recently published articles in *Dao: A Journal of Comparative Philosophy* and *Chinese Literature and Thought Today*, he has published several articles in Chinese under his Chinese name, Ma Zhaoren 馬兆仁.

**Sydney Morrow** is an Assistant Professor at the University of Central Oklahoma. She received her PhD from the University of Hawai'i at Mānoa in Spring 2018. Her research interests include Pre-Qin and Han Chinese philosophy, twentieth-century Chinese philosophy, applied and place-based philosophy, and comparative and cross-cultural philosophy.

**Michael Nylan** (戴梅可), trained by Michael Loewe, Nathan Sivin, Robert Bagley, Qu Wanli, and Paul L-M Serruys, teaches in the History Department of the University of California, Berkeley, where she holds the Jane K. Sather Chair of History. Her current work focuses on the theory and practices of the early empires (323 BCE–316 CE), where she finds abundant evidence that the Ancients were "in better shape" than we in the modern world. She teaches courses at the graduate and undergraduate level on conceptions of the body and body politic, on the environment and environmental ethics, and on local communities, inside and beyond the capital, at the county level. All these topics she teaches from both received and excavated texts.

**Gregor Paul**, born 1947, studied at the universities of Tübingen, Heidelberg, and Mannheim, graduating in philosophy, mathematics, and German studies. In philosophy, he holds a PhD and habilitation degree. Currently, he is a Professor of Philosophy at Karlsruhe Institute of Technology and Honorary President of the German China Association, of which he has been president for twenty years. Dr. Paul spent about ten years in Japan, China, Hong Kong, and Taiwan, teaching as guest professor, docent, or lecturer. For twenty years, he was an academic advisor to a Japanese culture center in Germany. His main interests are in aesthetics, logic, and philosophy of human rights.

**Karl-Heinz Pohl** (卜松山), born 1945, received his PhD from the University of Toronto in 1982. From 1987 to 1992 he was Professor of Chinese Studies at Tübingen University, and from 1992 to 2010 was Chair of Chinese Studies at Trier University (Germany). He is now retired. His fields of research include Chinese History of Ideas; Ethics and Aesthetics of Modern and Pre-Modern China; Chinese Literary Theory; and Intercultural Communication and Dialogue between China and the West. His publications include *Cheng Pan-ch'iao* (郑板桥): *Poet, Painter and Calligrapher* (1990); *Aesthetics and Literary Theory in China—From Tradition to Modernity* (2006) (in German and Chinese translation: 卜松山: 中国的美学和文学理论); and *China for Beginners* (in German: *China für Anfänger*, 2008), in Chinese translation as 卜松山: 发现中国—传统与现代 (2016). Works he has edited include *Chinese Thought in a Global Context: A Dialogue Between Chinese and Western Philosophical Approaches* (1999) and *Chinese Ethics in a Global Context. Moral Bases of Contemporary Societies* (2002). Works he has translated into German include Tao Yuanming's (陶渊明) complete collection of poetry, *Der Pfirsichblütenquell* (*The Peach Blossom Spring*) (1985), and Li Zehou's *The Path of Beauty* (美的历程): *Der Weg des Schönen* (1992).

**Dawid Rogacz** is Assistant Professor at Adam Mickiewicz University in Poznan (Poland). He is the author of the monograph *Chinese Philosophy of History: From Ancient Confucianism to the End of the Eighteenth Century* (Bloomsbury, 2020) and over a dozen peer-reviewed papers. He is currently co-editing a three-volume set *Chinese Philosophy and Its Thinkers: From Ancient Times to the Present Days* to be published with Bloomsbury in 2024. His research interests include Chinese philosophy, philosophy of history, and Marxism.

**Jana S. Rošker** (羅亞娜) studied Sinology and obtained her PhD at the Vienna University in Austria. She is the first Slovene Sinologist, co-founder and long-standing Head of the Department of Asian Studies at the University of Ljubljana (Slovenia). She is head of the National

Research Program Asian Languages and Cultures and director of several national and international research projects. Her main academic interests include traditional and modern Chinese philosophy and theory of knowledge, methodology of transcultural research, classical Chinese logic, and Modern Confucianism. Jana S. Rošker is chief editor of the academic journal *Asian Studies*, current president of the International Society of Chinese Philosophy (ISCP), and the cofounder, first president, and honorary member of the European Association of Chinese Philosophy (EACP). Her recent books include *Chinese Philosophy in Transcultural Contexts: Comparative Approaches and the Method of Sublation* (2024), *Humanism in Trans-civilizational Perspectives: Relational Subjectivity and Social Ethics in Classical Chinese Philosophy* (2023), *Confucian Relationism and Global Ethics: Alternative Models of Ethics and Axiology in Times of Global Crises* (2023), and *Interpreting Chinese Philosophy: A New Methodology* (2022). She also wrote two books on Li Zehou: *Following His Own Path: Li Zehou and Contemporary Chinese Philosophy* (2019), and *Becoming Human: Li Zehou's Ethics* (2020).

**Wu Xiaoming** (伍曉明) received his BA in Chinese literature from Fudan University, his MA in comparative literature from Peking University, and his DPhil from the University of Sussex. He worked as a research fellow in the Tianjin Academy of Social Sciences, and has taught in Peking University, Westminster University and the University of Canterbury. He was chair professor of Chinese in Sichuan University from 2019 to 2022. He is the author of *Wudao yiyi guanzhi: chongdu Kongzi* 吾道一以贯之：重读孔子 (*Rereading Confucius*), *You (yu) cunzai: Tongguo "cunzai" er chongdu zhongguo chuantong zhi "xingershan" zhe* 有 (与) 存在：通过"存在"而重读中国传统之"形而上"者 (*The Concept of Being Compared with the Concept of You in the Chinese Tradition*), *Tianming zhiwei xing: Piandu zhongyong "天命：之谓性!"：片读中庸* (*Rereading the Doctrine of Mean*), *Wenben zhijian: Cong Kongzi dao Lu Xun* 文本之间：从孔子到鲁迅 (*Between Texts: From Confucius to Lu Xun*), and *Zhiqian, zhijian, zhihou, zhiwai: Zhexue, wenxue, wenhua de yixu zhisi* 之前、之间、之后、之外：哲学、文学、文化的异序之思 (*Before, Between, After, and Outside: Unconventional Thoughts on Philosophy, Literature, and Culture*). He is also the Chinese translator of several books, including Emmanuel Levinas's *Autrement qu'être ou au-delà de l'essence*.

# Index

a priori, 447–50, 453–55: experience 249, 283, 434, 450; knowledge 169, 174–75, 310, 449; morality, 164–67, 170–74, 179–81
abstractness, 360
abstract principles, 64, 67, 190
academia, 60
adaptive motivations, 151
Adorno, Theodor W., 7, 88, 303–16
aesthetic: awareness, 82, 94, 389; engagement 79, 87; experience, 90–93, 98, 144, 146, 150, 154, 199–200, 207, 394; feeling, 93, 302, 387, 459; goods, 200–11; judgment, 33, 86, 93, 457; metaphysics, 92, 96, 99, 250; realm, 394; sedimentation, 86; transcendence, 89–91, 99
aesthetics, 92–99, 143–46, 151–56, 355–73: Adorno's, 88; Confucian, 82, 147–49, 390, 395; Kantian, 150, 453, 457; Li Zehou's, 33, 60–61, 89–90, 109, 143, 146–56, 203, 313, 370–71, 385–98, 457; Marxist, 15, 149, 313; philosophical, 144–46
agency: human, 66, 147, 252, 277; social, 311
alienation, 29, 96, 301, 319

ālaya (storehouse consciousness), 431–34, 438
Analects, 71–73, 148, 191, 202–3, 209, 230, 367
anthropo-historical ontology, 79–80, 83, 94, 109, 228, 246, 265–67, 276, 297, 328, 413
anthropology, 79–80, 107, 110, 201–2, 266, 387
application of reason, 84
appraisal theory, 152
appropriateness, 232
apriorism: Kantian, 357, 360, 371–72, 376
awareness, 169, 298, 433: aesthetic, 82, 94, 389; moral, 169–70, 336
autonomy, 85, 125, 164–65, 330–31, 336, 357
axial age, 408–11, 421

balance of reason and emotion, 191, 195, 204, 210
beautiful, 86, 92, 364, 386: illuminating the true through the, 92–94; furnishing the good through the, 94–96; making life worthwhile through the, 96–98
beauty, 33–35, 153, 301–2, 356–73, 386

behavior, 29, 147–48, 329, 331, 360, 367, 411
Beijing Union of Intellectuals, 23
beliefs, 33, 246, 254, 368–69; metaphysical, 209, 246–48
benti 本體 (substance, noumenon), 65, 200, 243–44, 248, 254, 264–68, 395; of 'du', 264, 266–68
Book of Changes, 314, 335, 391
Buddhism, 392, 394, 396, 432; Chan, 389–90, 396; Yogācāra, 394, 431–34, 438–41

categorical imperative, 68, 125, 165, 170–71, 176, 181, 330–31
Chinese Aesthetic Tradition, 392–97
"Chinese characteristics," 15, 26, 30–31
choices, 315
Christianity, 100, 391, 397
cognition, 146, 151–52, 296, 299, 305–7; situated, 144, 151, 153
cognitive process, 144–46, 151, 155, 306, 433
cold philosophies, 87–88, 308
collective, 17, 149, 190, 202, 309, 436–37: existence, 228; memory, 25, 435, 438; social consciousness, 436
Communist Party (CCP), 16–28, 38
Confucianism, classical, 66, 80, 93, 209, 249, 328, 419
Confucius, 63, 72–73, 81, 148, 209, 222, 230, 263, 333, 338
contextualizing, 226
cosmic rhythm, 91
cosmology: emotional, 242
cosmos, 93–95, 335
creation, 276, 278–79, 284, 366, 369: of art, 33, 389; free, 84
creativity, 362, 390

critique: of free market capitalism, 198; of justice, 190–91, 195
Critique of Critical Philosophy, 447
Critique of Judgment, 357, 359, 452
cultivation, 67–68, 91, 420, 422; self-cultivation, 148, 203
cultural-psychological formation, 16, 83, 96, 115, 124, 166, 338, 389, 396, 448

Daoism, 390, 393
Darwin, Charles, 115, 123, 127–29
deep harmony, 219, 225–29
democracy, 15–16, 20, 34
dialectics, 303, 308, 311–15: negative, 303, 308–9, 312
doctrine, 71, 249
du 度 (proper measure), 67, 71, 93, 195, 263–89, 302, 314–16, 437
Duke of Zhou, 408, 417–23
dynamic process of change, 124–25

embodied humanness, 247
emotio-rational structure, 66–67, 168, 171, 191, 220–21
emotion, 191, 197, 199, 210, 241–45, 250, 390; as substance, 66, 241, 244–45, 249, 252–55
enactivism, 151–53
environment, 29, 87, 127–28, 144, 151–53, 228, 243; stable, 365
epistemology, 146, 297, 299, 308, 311; Western, 295, 305
equilibrium, 315–16
ethics, 61, 170, 244, 278, 327–33; Confucian, 147, 164, 419
evolution, 108, 112–17, 122–24, 126–30, 331–33, 439
evolutionary psychology, 126, 431, 435
existentialism, 87, 308

experiential, 203; practice, 109
externality, 332–34

feminist philosophy, 223
flourishing, 32, 195, 252, 255
formation; cultural-psychological, 16, 83, 96, 115, 124, 166, 338, 389, 396, 448
Frankfurt School, 87, 308–9
free will, 85–86, 125–27, 130, 164–65, 167, 329–30
freedom, 30, 85, 99, 254–55, 331, 355–67; spiritual, 91–92, 99
freedom of speech, 38

genealogical, 125–26, 435
Gene-Culture Coevolution (GCC), 108–30
good life, 189, 192, 199, 204, 211, 220, 225
guanxi 關係 (social bonds, relational attachment), 66, 189, 191–92, 199–200, 210
guanxi-ism (relationism), 65–66, 68, 191, 220–21, 245
guoxue 國學, 34

harmony, 68–69, 189, 191–96, 199–200, 210, 219–33, 287, 315; cosmic, 95; deep, 219, 225–29; higher than justice, 66, 68–69, 189, 192, 195, 200, 210, 219–21, 225, 233; interpersonal 220, 223, 225, 233
Heaven/nature, 91, 109, 266, 285, 335, 391, 394, 411–13, 418–21
Heaven-Earth realm, 79, 94–95, 99, 302, 335, 396
Hegel, Georg W. F., 304, 312, 331–32
hermeneutic, 223

historical: process, 250, 265, 332, 338; sedimentation, 89, 329
how-to-live concern, 79–80, 83
human: agency, 27, 147, 252; capacity, 79, 83–84, 89, 92, 98; practice, 149, 310; subjectality, 79, 86–89, 98, 314
humanism, 393, 409, 413; concrete, 246, 248, 252
humanistic spirit, 411–13, 419, 421
humanization, 149, 303, 358, 361, 358, 387, 436
humanized nature, 16, 29, 86, 91, 95, 298, 301, 358, 361, 387–88, 391, 397, 435
humankind, 85–86, 109, 113, 174, 190, 361
humanness, 147, 176, 248, 333–38
hundun 混沌 (primordial chaos), 226

idealism, 360; cosmic, 241, 247
ideational background, 408, 410, 423
identitarian philosophy, 303, 312–14
identity, 304, 312–13; politics, 39
imagination, 93, 454–55
individuality, 88, 246
inheritance, 111, 116
infinity, 415, 452, 456
infinitude, 272–73
innate, 173–75, 370; knowledge, liangzhi 良知, 125
intercultural, 190, 224, 394
interdependence, 302–3, 314
internality, 332–34
internalization, 303, 329, 336, 338, 449: psychological, 245; rational, 84–86, 96
interpersonal: relations, 66, 128, 191, 202, 208–10, 254, 335: harmony, 220, 223, 225, 233

interpretation, reinterpretation: of early Chinese culture; 421–23, 436; of Kant, 447, 454, 458; of Ruism, 32, 163–64, 167–68, 172, 179, 249, 333, 396, 416, 419; of *Yijing*: 335, 391
intuition, 84–86, 453, 455

*jingjie* 境界 (aesthetic realm), 394
joy, 82, 84, 86, 99–100, 148, 167–68, 172, 414, 422
justice, 68–69, 73, 189–93, 204, 219–25, 228–34

Kant, Immanuel, 38, 64, 83, 85, 124–26, 150, 164, 176, 179–81, 305–6, 330, 357–61, 372, 434, 447, 449–59
King Wen, 408, 417–23
kinship, 86, 191, 335

labor, 29, 149–50, 301, 361–67, 372
language, 74, 122–23; metaphorical, 63
*legan wenhua* 樂感文化 (culture of joy), 203, 414, 422
*li* 理 (reason, structure), 189, 244, 247, 390
liberals, 16, 28, 38, 246
liberal tradition, 198, 246
liberalism, 189–91, 197, 255
linguistic, 119, 123
logic, 74, 313, 315, 453: formal, 312, 314

Maoists, 15, 17
Marx, Karl, 16, 19–20, 29, 83, 149, 308, 362, 371, 387, 391–92
Marxism, 15–16, 19, 38, 149, 163, 295–98, 361, 396–97
Marxist theory, 16, 25, 163, 296–97, 308–10, 387, 392, 396–97, 413
masters texts, 70–71

material production, 19–20, 34–35, 298, 307, 436
mathematical: concept, 169, 450–51, 456; sublime, 457–59
mathematics, 94, 169, 450–59
May Fourth Movement, 26, 35
Mencius, 125, 168–72, 179, 249–50, 270, 336–37
medicine, 281–82
metaphorical language, 63
metaphysical beliefs, 209, 246–48
metaphysics, 92, 99, 171, 209, 244, 246–50, 252–53, 449
middle way, 287, 315–16
moral: autonomy, 85, 89, 125, 329–31, 336, 338; character, 81, 170, 340; feeling, 85, 170, 172, 181, 333, 459; metaphysics, 247–48; principles, 68, 83, 164–68, 174–80, 190–92, 194–95, 204–5, 249, 252, 355–58, 452, 457; psychology, 190, 204, 329–30, 332, 336, 338; rules, 229–30; values, virtues, 147–48, 245, 327, 335–37, 341
morality, 128, 164–68, 173–74, 177–81, 245, 327–32, 360, 372; Confucian (Ruist), 164, 170–71, 176, 249, 255
morals, 66–67, 175, 255, 327
motivations: adaptive, 151
Mou Zongsan, 163–73, 179–80, 247
music, 82, 148, 203, 209, 367, 390, 393, 414, 420–22
mystical experience, 90–91

nationalist agenda, 35
naturalization of humans, 387, 435
Neo-Confucianism, 82, 247–50, 391–92, 396
neoliberal, 16, 26, 28
New (Modern) Confucianism, 247–48, 408, 410–11

New Cultural Conservatism, 26
norms, 111, 190, 328, 333, 340
noumenon, 243–44, 265, 395–96
number, 450–51, 454–59

object, 93, 153, 165, 267, 283–86, 295–96, 299–307, 311–15, 456; primacy of the, 310
objectivity, 90, 153, 278, 297–300, 307, 310–11, 392, 456
one-world view, 67–68, 254, 411, 414, 422, 440
ontological moral feelings, 170, 172, 244
ontology, 79–80, 147, 265–66, 275, 395, 434; anthropo-historical ontology, 79–80, 83, 94, 109, 228, 246, 265–67, 276, 297, 328, 413; historical, 83–85, 99, 252, 264, 268, 437

*Path of Beauty*, 385–86, 390–93
pattern, 178, 249
philosophy, 60, 74, 79, 165–67: analytical, 87, 308; of art, 145; Chinese, 71–72, 203, 208, 391, 395, 412, 431–32; feminist, 223; of perception, 154; Western, 59, 65, 70, 173–74, 241, 304–5, 308, 435
pleasure, 90, 148, 153, 203, 209, 357
post-Marxist, 308
practical philosophy of subjectality, 80, 87, 297, 308
practical reason, 85
pragmatic reason, 84, 99
praxis, 88
prehistory, 111, 123, 386, 388
proper measure. See under *du* 度
psychological feelings, 72, 167–71, 175–76, 179–80
psychology, 16, 171–73, 177, 196–97, 245, 254, 328–29, 388, 395: cultural, 82, 86, 100; evolutionary, 126, 431, 435; gestalt, 153; moral, 190, 204, 329–30, 336, 338; social, 107

qi 氣 (energy-matter), 227
qing 情 (emotion). See under emotion

reason, 67, 73, 84–85, 96, 116, 174, 189–91, 244–45, 252, 329, 390, 449, 451–52; application of reason, 84; condensation of, 125–27; practical, 85; pragmatic, 84, 99
reasoning: analytical, 70; instrumental 204; practical, 206–7
reforms, 18, 24, 28, 89
relational attachment. See under *guanxi* 關係
relationality, 191, 198–200, 208, 211
relationism, 65–66, 68, 191, 220–21, 245
religion, 203, 392, 396, 409–14, 419
ren 仁 (humaneness, benevolence), 147, 176, 248, 333–38
ren xing 人性 (humanness), 303, 411
representations, 153, 389
revolution: Cultural, 17, 25, 88–89, 397; economic, 19–20; of thought, 305
ritual culture, 333
rituality (of Zhou), 420, 422
*River Elegy*, 18, 22, 32
rule, 229–30; by law, 38, 220
Russian literary critics, 36

Sandel, Michael, 63–64, 190, 228
Schiller, Friedrich, 356, 358, 360
sedimentation, 68–69, 107–8, 110, 116–19, 121, 124, 130, 173–75, 249–52, 388–89, 431–40, 448; cultural, 86, 117–19, 121, 130
self-awareness, 295, 411–13, 419

self-determination, 355–56
sensibility, 145, 150, 167, 169–72, 278–79, 281, 452–55: aesthetic, 82, 90, 97–100, 199, 387; musical, 82
shamanism, 409, 415–16; rationalized, 411, 414, 420, 422
shamanistic-historical tradition, 248, 252, 407, 413
shame, 198, 203: culture of, 414
social: enlightenment, 25; feelings, 176–77, 198–99; harmony, 192, 220, 222, 232–33; interaction, 205–11; justice, 225, 228, 233; morality, 67, 128, 220, 255, 355–56; norms, 166, 244–46, 328–31, 340, 420; order, 27, 193–95, 200–2, 221, 422; reality, 36, 303, 310; structure, 87, 192–93, 230–32, 296, 307, 367, 387–89
socialism, 34, 38
socialization, 83, 121, 149, 390: of nature, 301–2
spiritual freedom, 91–92, 99
subject, 267, 295–307, 311–16, 440
subjectality, 86–89, 114, 151–53, 297–98, 302, 308, 435, 438
subjectivity, 16, 89, 282, 297–99, 311, 435–41
substance. See under *benti* 本體
symbol: beauty as, 356–57, 364, 372
symbolism, 416
synthetic-analytic distinction, 453

techno-social: practice, 114–15, 123, 130; structure, 83
Tiananmen, 17–28, 38
*tian ren he yi* 天人合一 (unity of cosmos and human), 210, 220, 266, 390–91, 394
tradition, 59–60, 67, 310: Chinese, 21, 26–27, 31, 39, 70–73, 84, 91, 192–93, 251, 276, 371, 391, 394, 397, 412–14; Confucian, 66, 195–96, 203, 207–8, 219, 225, 245–48, 254, 395; liberal, 198, 246; ritual, 333–35; shamanistic, 248, 250, 252, 407, 413, 419
transcendence, 203, 410–11: aesthetic, 89–91, 99; moral, 95
transcendental, 109, 115–16, 173–74, 198, 371, 422, 434–35, 454
transcendentalism, 371, 434–35

ultimate reality, 243, 395
unity, 450–51: of cosmos and human. See under *tian ren he yi* 天人合一; of objectivity and sociality, 392; of subject and object, 303; of truth and good, 358–59
universal: human nature, 115–16; legislation, 330; morality, 166, 170, 174–80, 194–95; reasoning, 73
universality, 31, 72, 170, 177, 179, 456
unthinkable, 315–16

virtue ethics, 72, 147, 254
virtues, 333–38

Wang Guowei, 394
Western learning as substance, Chinese for application (*xiti zhongyong* 西體中用), 33, 397

Xiong Shili, 249
Xu Fuguan, 248–49, 408, 411–13, 417–23
Xunzi, 128, 168, 173–74, 231, 249, 339–40, 356

*yin* 陰 and *yang* 陽, 226–27, 264, 268, 416

Zhuangzi, 61, 95, 263, 280, 389

*zhuguanxing* 主觀性 (subjectivity). *See under* subjectivity

*zhutixing* 主體性 (subjectality). *See under* subjectality